Money and the Economy

SECOND EDITION

The Harbrace Series in Business and Economics

Second Edition

Money
and the Economy

JOHN J. KLEIN
Georgia State University

 HARCOURT, BRACE & WORLD, INC.
New York / Chicago / San Francisco / Atlanta

To Sylvia and Leslie

FU

Preface

This textbook is designed to fill the needs of a comprehensive one-semester course in money and banking. It was primarily written for two types of students: the liberal arts student who takes only one course in money and banking and the business student who studies money and banking in those economics and finance departments that stress money and the economy rather than bank management. For both it attempts to provide a basic but rigorous exposition of banking, theoretical analysis, and economic policy.

I have written this book in the belief that a textbook should be addressed primarily to the student rather than to the professional economist. It should be clear, self-contained, and self-explanatory, and at the same time it should be timely and challenging; this is a hard balance to strike. Furthermore, I think that the student should be able to understand the basic principles of a discipline from a close reading of a text with a minimum of assistance from the instructor. It does not seem to me that the function of the instructor is to teach a textbook. A textbook may serve as a helpful guide to him, but in the final analysis he should teach his own course.

The theme of this book is that money plays an important role in the economy. With historical perspective, the text discusses the operation of the banking system and presents a critical analysis of monetary theory and policy. It is divided into four parts. Part I, "Money and Private Financial Institutions," examines the private financial institutions that determine the volume and composition of our monetary resources. The commercial banking system is also studied in some detail. Emphasis is placed on financial institutions as potential sources of economic disturbance. Part II, "Money and Government," offers a concise history of central banking in the United States and evaluates the federal government's attempts over the years to regulate money in order to prevent the extremes of inflation and deflation. Part III, "Money and Aggregate Economic Activity," traces the historical development of monetary theory and posits a contemporary framework of analysis for studying the impact of money supply-and-demand forces upon economic activity. Part IV, "Money and Economic Policy," uses the analytical framework developed in the preceding section to evaluate various alternative monetary, fiscal, and international economic policies.

It is my hope that the student will emerge from his reading of this book neither with a banker's view of the system, nor with the Federal Reserve's view, nor with the bias of any school of economic theory, but rather with a well-integrated, overall perception of the monetary system and the theory on which it is based. Obviously, both my value judgments and professional judgments show throughout the text, but I trust I have given a balanced view of monetary economics.

I have tried in the second edition, as in the first, to provide the book with both a sense of historical perspective and a feel for contemporary monetary theory and policy. The overall outline of the text, of course, remains much the same. There was some reorganization of Part IV, on aggregate economic policy, and the formal theory of the money supply has been postponed from Chapter 15 to Chapter 20. The text is one chapter longer than the first edition. Each chapter has been gone over carefully; numerous changes and additions have been made, and in many instances completely new material has been incorporated. Particularly significant in the second edition is the treatment of Regulation Q throughout the text and the increased importance given to the "portfolio" approach to the theory of the demand for money. Chapters 5, 12, 13, 14, 19, 20, 21, 24, and 25 have probably undergone the most extensive revision.

My gratitude extends to many people. I owe an intellectual debt to my past teachers of monetary and fiscal economics, Milton Friedman, Earl J. Hamilton, Lloyd Mints, and Kenyon Poole. Detailed and extremely useful critiques of the first edition were provided by Joseph Perry, Edward Shapiro, and Richard Towey. Additional portions of the manuscript were read and commented upon by Richard Clemmer, Will Mason, Frank Steindl, and James Maynard. Miltiades Chacholiades provided a detailed and useful critique of the chapters on international economics. David Fand, David Meiselman, and Boris Pesak, by providing copies of some of their as yet unpublished manuscripts, challenged me to rethink parts of the analysis. George Manners, Assistant Vice President of Georgia State University, and James Crawford, Chairman of the Department of Economics, Georgia State University, have given me encouragement and assistance. My wife, Sylvia, served as editor at home and made the volume more readable.

I must also express appreciation to Bee Hutchins, Secretary of the Department of Economics, Georgia State University, and her staff for providing clerical assistance. Brenda Butler most diligently typed the entire manuscript. Among my graduate students who provided assistance from time to time are Forest Denman, Frank Egan, Gary Leff, Frank McGrath, Michael Rendich, Warren Shows, and Bruce Yandle. Neal McKenzie, my research assistant in 1968 and 1969, helped to prepare the tables.

JOHN J. KLEIN

Contents

x | *Contents*

CHAPTER 1

Introduction

The economist is concerned with how man makes his living. How the individual earns his income, how businesses use resources to produce goods and services, and how the economy as a whole functions are all important aspects of the study of economics. It is for many of us a fascinating and stimulating discipline, for separate individuals and separate businesses from thousands of political communities somehow manage to work together to produce the goods and services that satisfy people's basic wants.

How does the economy accomplish this? Part of the answer lies in the fact that our economy runs on money. Individuals use money to purchase goods and services. Businesses use it to expand production. National governments use it to satisfy social wants.

Money does not always function properly, of course. There are times when businesses, individuals, and governments all feel that there is a shortage of funds. This may happen during periods of either recession or inflation. In periods of recession people with insufficient incomes and monetary resources are forced to reduce their spending. This, in turn, results in a decreased demand for goods, lower production, and fewer jobs. On the other hand, during periods of inflation almost everyone may be employed and earning apparently adequate incomes but still feel that their incomes and monetary resources are inadequate in light of rapidly rising prices.

How do such paradoxical situations arise? *Money and the Economy* will concentrate on problems of this sort. The theme of the book is that money is important for the economy. Along with other forms of wealth holding, money influences interest rates and spending; it thereby has a significant impact on aggregate economic activity.

WHAT IS MONEY?

Definitions of money abound. It is sometimes defined in terms of the job it does. As we shall see shortly, it serves as a medium of exchange, a store of value, a standard of deferred payments, a unit of account, and a means of paying off debt. Money may also be defined according to its physical properties. Sometimes it is coin, paper currency, and checking deposits. It may exist in many other forms, however. In Europe, for example, after World War II, cigarettes were widely used as a medium of exchange, since the supply of currency was so abundant and prices were rising so rapidly that currency had little actual value. In addition, gold, silver, wampum, stone, and even leather have been considered money.

Money Defined

For our purposes, the most suitable definition of money is one that focuses on the primary use to which money is put in the American economy, as follows: *money is anything generally acceptable as a means of paying off debt.* The term "paying off debt" is emphasized in our definition because in most economic transactions a debt is created and subsequently extinguished. Businesses seldom make immediate payment for goods and services. Similarly, individuals often are not billed for goods and services they have purchased until the end of the month. Here too a debt arises and is subsequently extinguished through the use of either checking deposits or currency. Even when one purchases groceries at a grocery store a momentary debt is created, which is, of course, immediately extinguished by a cash payment to the clerk.

Before any item can function as money it must be "generally acceptable," and to retain this quality of acceptability, money must exhibit some degree of stability in value over time. History is full of examples of monies that lost their value and were consequently abandoned. Money must have stable purchasing power in order to retain the public's faith.

The Uses of Money

Money as a medium of exchange. Money is used principally in the payment of debts created when goods and services are purchased. Most of us use our productive resources to acquire money and, in turn, use money to purchase goods and services. In reality, then, goods and services are exchanged for goods and services. Money merely facilitates this exchange. For this reason it is often called a *medium of exchange.*

Why do we need a medium of exchange? Consider for a moment what the economy would be like without money. How would one exchange goods for goods? Some people might answer that there need be no exchange of goods. Let everyone produce what he needs for himself. But this would overlook the tremendous advantages of specialization. Obviously, some men can make shoes better than others; some can produce machines more efficiently; others are talented in the arts. The total production in an economy will usually be greater when everyone is doing that job for which his talents and training best suit him. Civilization depends upon specialization for its very existence. Men have long recognized its importance. Even Plato argued ". . . we must infer that all things are produced more plentifully and easily and of a better quality when one man does one thing that is natural to him and does it at the right time, and leaves other things." [1]

Imagine, then, a specialized economy with no money. How would goods be exchanged? The producer of shoes who wanted food would have to find a producer of food who wanted shoes. This is known as *double coincidence of wants.* If there were thousands of goods produced and desired, it would be almost impossible to arrange the necessary number of exchanges. One would also have to work out innumerable ratios of exchange of one good for another. How many shoes must one give up to acquire guns, stockings, bread, etc.—and vice versa? If there were just 1,000 commodities in the economy, there would have to be almost 500,000 rates of exchange between the goods. [2]

Money eliminates all these complexities. One need no longer seek out those who have the goods one needs and who also desire the goods one has produced. Instead, goods may be exchanged for money and the money may then be used to buy other goods and services. We ". . . give money in exchange for goods to those who desire to sell and . . . take money from those who desire to buy." [3] Much wasted effort in exchanging goods for goods is thus eliminated, and the total production of the economy can be substantially increased.

Money as a unit of account. In a money economy, all goods have a price, which is stated uniformly in terms of the amount of money that must be given to acquire them. Thus it may also be said that money acts as a *unit of account.* The dollar, the peso, the lira, the franc, the Deutsche mark, the hwan, the yen, the ruble, are all units of account. The things that function as money—in our economy, currency and demand deposits— are also counted in terms of the unit of account. Thus, the unit of account is simply an abstract measure of value, just as the pound and the ounce are abstract measures of weight.

Money as a store of value. People want money not only for the goods and services that they purchase today but also for the goods and services they will want to buy in the future. Of course, money is only one way of storing up the ability to buy goods and services. Stocks, bonds, and life insurance policies are also means of doing this. However, these must first be converted into money before goods can actually be purchased. Thus money is sometimes said to be the most *liquid* of the various types of claims over future goods and services because it is the one thing that can be used immediately to acquire them.

---

[1] Plato, *The Republic,* Book II. In Robert Hutchins, ed., *Great Books of the Western World,* Vol. 7, p. 317.
[2] The formula $n(n-1)/2$, where n refers to the number of goods, may be used to determine the number of different ratios of exchange. This formula is the standard expression for the number of possible combinations of n items taken two at a time.
[3] Plato, *op. cit.,* p. 317.

Money as a standard of deferred payments. Another function of money is to serve as a *standard of deferred payments.* This role is an outgrowth of the use of money as a means of paying debt and as a unit of account. Contracts are often written providing for future payments to be made in specific sums of money. A bond, for example, is the contractual promise of a corporation to make periodic interest payments to bondholders and to redeem the bond at full face value at some specified time in the future. It is agreed that interest on bonds, and the principal when due, is to be paid in the form of money. Thus money is both the standard by which deferred payments of bond interest are to be reckoned and the means by which these payments are to be made.

Types of Money

In our economy, hand-to-hand currency and checking deposits are considered money, since nearly everyone will accept them in payment of debt.

Hand-to-hand currency. Hand-to-hand currency consists of coins and paper currency. Coins may be either full bodied or token. In the United States our unit of account, the dollar, is defined by law as being equal to a specific amount of a commodity. This commodity is gold and the dollar is legally defined as being equal to 1/35 of an ounce of gold. If gold coins circulated in the United States, and if the amount of gold contained in the coins were equal in value to their legally stated face value, then our coins would be *full-bodied money*. However, gold does not circulate in the United States as money. Some of our coins do contain silver, but in such small amounts that the market value is less than the face value of the coins. Hence all our coins are *token coins*. The market value of the commodities of which the coins are made is much less than the value of the coins as money.

Paper currency may be either *representative full bodied paper money* or *fiat money*. Paper money is full bodied when it represents a claim to a specific amount of a commodity, such as gold or silver. Fiat money, on the other hand, is irredeemable. All paper currency in the United States is now fiat. It cannot be redeemed in either gold or silver. Until 1933, gold certificates could be redeemed in full-bodied gold coins. Until 1968, silver certificates could be redeemed in silver bullion at the U.S. Treasury.

Since none of our hand-to-hand currency is full bodied, why are people willing to accept it? As we shall see in subsequent chapters, hand-to-hand currency is accepted as a medium of exchange because it has a high degree of stability in value. It has this stability because our monetary authorities effectively limit its quantity.

Checking deposits. It is readily apparent why coin and paper currency are money; however, it is not so obvious why checking deposits are also considered money. Checking deposits are money because they function like currency. They serve as a medium of exchange and their quantity is limited by our monetary authority, the Federal Reserve. By far the greater volume of all monetary transactions in the economy involves the use of checks. The extensive utilization of checking deposits, or demand deposits, as they are more correctly called, is illustrated by the fact that the Federal Reserve banks handle more than $2.5 trillion worth of checks a year.[4]

Demand deposits are very nearly as liquid as currency. The average man, even when he questions the credit-worthiness of a check user, will still be willing to accept a cashier's check from him in lieu of a personal check. The checks themselves are not money. They are the means by which people transfer the ownership of demand deposits when making purchases and paying off debt. The creation of demand deposits and their use as money will be discussed extensively in subsequent chapters.

MONEY AND STABLE PURCHASING POWER

We have previously noted that in order to retain acceptability, money must exhibit stability in value. Its purchasing power must not diminish over time. For example, consider the effect on the pensioner who is receiving an annual pension of $1,500 when the price level suddenly doubles. The purchasing power of the income from his pension and whatever savings he has are cut in half. The human misery that this entails is not something hypothetical, but very real. Imagine what would have happened to you and your family if you had lived in the Deep South from January of 1861 to January of 1864, when prices rose 27.8 times,[5] or in Germany from August 1922 to November 1923, when prices rose 1.02×10^{10}, over ten billion times. After World War II in Hungary, from August 1945 to July 1946, prices rose by 3.81×10^{27}![6]

How do such tremendous price increases, and consequent reductions in the purchasing power of money, occur? Several possible answers to that question will be considered later in the text. For the moment, however, suffice it to say that these price-level increases were associated with a money stock that went "out of order." For example, in the Confederacy the money stock increased 11.6 times during the previously mentioned period.[7] In Germany after World War I it increased 7.32×10^9, and in Hungary after World War II 1.19×10^{25}.[8]

On the other hand, do periods of price deflation and accompanying in-

[4] Board of Governors of the Federal Reserve System, *Annual Report* (1968), p. 378.
[5] Eugene M. Lerner, "Money, Prices, and Wages in the Confederacy, 1861–65," *Journal of Political Economy* (1955), p. 29.
[6] Phillip Cagan, "The Monetary Dynamics of Hyperinflation," *Studies in the Quantity Theory of Money,* Milton Friedman, ed. (Chicago: Univ. of Chicago Press, 1956), p. 26.
[7] Lerner, *op. cit.,* p. 21.
[8] Cagan, *op. cit.,* p. 26.

creases in the value of money lead to any lessening of economic distress? Apparently not, since unemployment and a drop in production have usually accompanied price declines in the modern world. For example, in the United States from 1929 to 1933 the price level dropped some 25 percent.[9] Thus, a dollar spent in 1929 would have bought $1.33 worth of goods in 1933, yet unemployment rose from a yearly average of 1,550,000 to 12,830,000 in that period.[10] This was accompanied by a 27-percent drop in the money stock and a 30-percent drop in real output.[11]

Thus we can see that money does not always have stable purchasing power. The ability of money to command goods and services decreases with inflation and increases with deflation. This change in the value of money is accompanied by employment and output changes. In our everyday experience a dollar can buy tomorrow about as much as it can buy today, but over longer periods its value may change significantly. Consumer prices in the United States in 1929, 1933, 1945, and 1968 were 60, 45, 63, and 121 percent, respectively, of their 1957–59 average.[12] Thus, the United States, which has had relatively minor price fluctuations, has nevertheless experienced both inflation and deflation at various times. The behavior of prices in other countries has often been disastrous by comparison. In economies as complex as those of the modern world, society must regulate money and spending to ensure a relatively stable price level. Serious damage may be done to the economy if money is either issued to excess or not issued and spent in sufficient quantities.

---

[9] *Federal Reserve Bulletin,* June 1964, p. 776.
[10] U.S. Department of Commerce, *Statistical Abstract of the United States,* Washington, D.C.
[11] *Federal Reserve Bulletin,* June 1964, p. 778.
[12] *Federal Reserve Bulletin,* various issues.

PART I

Money and Private Financial Institutions

CHAPTER 2

Money and Liquid Wealth in the United States

Where does money fit within a general scheme of property holding? How does it differ from other forms of wealth, and how do other forms of wealth influence money? In this chapter we will first try to answer these questions. We will then describe the currency component of our money stock in greater detail. Subsequent chapters will deal intensively with the demand-deposit component of the money stock.

WEALTH AND CLAIMS TO WEALTH

Individual Wealth

The wealth of an individual consists of the total value of his physical goods (*real wealth*) and the total amount of his claims to real wealth (*liquid wealth*). When held in the form of money, wealth represents generalized purchasing power—the ability to buy goods and services today and in the future. Money is only one of the forms in which an individual may choose to hold his liquid wealth. Among the alternatives to money are such claims to wealth as certificates of deposit and savings accounts in commercial banks, savings deposits in mutual banks, savings and loan share accounts, the stocks and bonds of private businesses and governments, and the cash value of life insurance policies.

What determines the distribution of an individual's wealth-holding among the various forms of liquid wealth? The question is a difficult one. Which alternatives are chosen depend on individual tastes and preferences, the rate of interest, expectations concerning future prices of goods versus liquid assets, or simply the amount of these items that one already has. For example, a decline in interest rates may well induce people to hold more money and stocks relative to bonds, other things being equal. If prices are expected to rise, it should be advantageous to reduce one's money holdings and bonds in order to acquire goods that will shortly cost considerably more. If an individual's money holdings have increased relative to other forms of wealth, then he may feel able to purchase additional goods and services. Chapters 20 and 22 will provide a more detailed analysis of the fluctuations in the demand for various forms of wealth.

The Wealth of a Nation

The wealth of a nation is not computed in the same way as the wealth of an individual. On the national level, one cannot arrive at a total by adding up the amount of real and liquid wealth in the economy. To do so would be double counting, since *liquid wealth* represents only *a claim to physical goods*. Whereas the individual can add to his total real wealth by converting his liquid wealth into physical goods, this is impossible for the economy as a whole. Were everyone to convert his claims to wealth into real goods, there would still be no more real goods than existed before the conversion, since there is only one stock of physical goods. The ultimate amount of real wealth in an economy depends not upon claims to wealth but upon productive resources and technology.

Nor does the aggregate amount of liquid wealth in the country equal the aggregate amount of real wealth. Liquid and real wealth are not created in the same way. As already indicated, real wealth is created in the productive process. Liquid wealth, on the other hand, is created when individuals or institutions such as businesses and governments issue and sell obligations. The funds received from the sale of these obligations may be used to help in the creation of real wealth through production, to purchase existent real goods, to purchase other forms of liquid wealth, or they may simply be held idle.

THE LIQUID WEALTH SYSTEM OF THE UNITED STATES

The liquid wealth forms of a nation may be classified according to degrees of *liquidity,* by which we mean the relative ability of a liquid asset to be converted into money with rapidity and without loss.[1] Liquid assets that may be converted into money with great rapidity and with little or no loss are known as *near monies*. Assets other than those that are near monies are not as reliable a source of funds. For example, an asset such as common stock, whose price can fluctuate widely, cannot be expected to provide a fixed number of dollars in the future.

This does not mean that other forms of liquid wealth are unimportant. Actually there are many markets for financial instruments such as Treasury bills, commercial paper, bankers' acceptances, etc. These markets and their related financial institutions are important for understanding banks

---

[1] The term "liquidity" is used here instead of the term "moneyness," which was used in the first edition. Although there is no meaningful difference between the two terms, introducing the concept of "liquidity" here forms a basis for the discussion of the demand for money and liquidity in subsequent chapters.

and monetary policy. Some discussion of these markets will be found in subsequent chapters. First it is important to understand the relationship between money and near monies. As will be explained more fully in Chapters 8 and 22, many economists believe that the creation of close money substitutes significantly weakens the effectiveness of monetary policy.

Table 2–1 lists the forms of liquid wealth that possess a high degree of liquidity.

TABLE 2–1. MONEY AND NEAR-MONEY HOLDINGS
OF THE NONBANK PUBLIC
DECEMBER 31, 1968
(IN BILLIONS OF DOLLARS)

FORM OF LIQUID WEALTH	AMOUNT	
Currency	43.5	
Demand deposits*	162.5	
Total money stock		206.0
Time deposits in commercial banks	202.2	
Time deposits in mutual savings banks	64.6	
Total time deposits		266.8
Marketable and convertible U.S. government securities	111.6	
Savings bonds held by individuals	52.3	
Total U.S. government securities		163.9
Savings and loan shares		131.6
Cash value of life insurance†		149.6
Total money and near-money holdings of the nonbank public		917.9

* Excluding interbank deposits.
† Estimated at 80 percent of the book value of life insurance company assets.
SOURCE: *Federal Reserve Bulletin*, February 1969, pp. A-18, A-36, and A-40.

Money as a Form of Wealth

The most liquid asset is, of course, money itself, since it can be used immediately without loss to purchase goods and services. Our total *money stock* consists of all currency and commercial bank demand deposits not owned by the Treasury, the Federal Reserve banks, or commercial banks. It is owned and held by private individuals, businesses, state and local governments, and nonbank financial institutions such as savings and loan associations, mutual savings banks, foreign banks, and insurance companies. This listing of those who own money is sometimes called "the nonbank public," sometimes simply "the public."

Table 2–1 shows that the currency holdings of the nonbank public, as of December 31, 1968, were $43.5 billion, whereas the total holdings of demand deposits amounted to $162.5 billion. Demand-deposit money is thus clearly the more important component of our money stock. The phrase "commercial bank demand deposits" does not mean that the banking system owns these deposits; rather, it means that the deposits are "liabilities" of the banking system. This type of money is owned by the nonbank public and owed to them by the commercial banks. Furthermore, as we shall discuss in greater detail in later chapters, the deposits do not exist physically; they are bookkeeping claims of the nonbank public on the banking system.

Demand-deposit claims on the banking system may be transferred from one part of the nonbank public to another by the use of checks. This happens whenever debt is paid off or when goods and services are purchased with checks. In addition, people often demand currency from the banks in exchange for their "demand deposits." How can the banks meet these demands, when the amount of currency available in the economic system amounts to only a fraction of total demand-deposit liabilities? Fortunately, the number of demands for currency at any one time is generally offset by the number of deposits. If this were not the case, a cash drain from the banking system might occur, causing economic distress. However, it is very unlikely that people in our economy will ever again sustain significant losses on their demand-deposit holdings. The existence of deposit insurance almost precludes bank panics from occurring when too many people attempt to convert their deposits (either demand or time deposits) into currency at the same time. Deposits are insured up to a limit of $15,000 by the Federal Deposit Insurance Corporation. Only $1.37 billion of the demand-deposit liabilities of the commercial banks are not insured by the FDIC.[2]

Time Deposits as a Form of Wealth

Time deposits of various sorts are another part of the nonbank public's total wealth. Savings and loan share accounts and time deposits in commercial and mutual savings banks constitute some 43 percent of our total money and near-money holdings. Most of these forms of time deposits are also insured by some agency of the federal government. For example, some 87 percent of mutual savings bank time deposits are insured by the FDIC.[3] The Federal Savings and Loan Insurance Corporation insures the share accounts of most savings and loan associations.

How do time deposits differ from demand deposits? Why cannot the former be included in the money stock? There is usually no possibility of loss on time deposits, and they can be used quickly to make payments. There are, however, a number of important differences between time and checking deposits that should be noted.

First, time deposits need not be paid on demand. The debtor institutions

[2] *Federal Reserve Bulletin*, May 1969, p. A-21.
[3] *Ibid.*, p. A-22.

can legally require the holder of a time deposit to give 30 days notice of a withdrawal, provided that the time deposit is in the form of a savings account.[4] For all practical purposes, however, this is not an important distinguishing feature of savings accounts because most financial institutions do redeem these accounts on "demand." Competitive conditions are such that a required 30-day waiting period could be enforced only if all debtor institutions followed this practice.

Second, interest is paid on time deposits. The law does not permit the payment of interest on checking accounts.

Third, and most important, time-deposit accounts must first be converted into either currency or checking deposits before they can be used as money. They cannot be used directly to purchase goods or services.

There are also a number of differences in form between the various kinds of time deposits that will affect the volume of money and total liquid wealth differently when the deposits are converted to money. For example, when a savings and loan share account is converted into money there will be no change in the money holdings of the nonbank public, but there will be a reduction in the total volume of liquid wealth. Assume that you have a $1,000 savings account with a savings and loan association. Your ownership of the account means that you have a claim on the assets of the association. Hence your ownership claim is equal in value to a certain percentage of what the association owns. What will happen if you decide to convert that claim into money? The savings and loan association will either give you currency or write a check on its checking account at a commercial bank. There will thus be a transfer of money holdings from one part of the nonbank public, the savings and loan association, to another part, you. The total volume of money in the economy remains the same. On the other hand, your claim to the assets of the association will have been reduced. You no longer have a share account. As a result the total liquid wealth of the economy will have been reduced. This transaction may be formulated in terms of the entire economy as follows: money + savings and loan shares + other forms of liquid wealth = total liquid wealth.[5] When savings and loan shares are converted into money, the total amount of money remains the same, but total savings and loan shares decrease. Therefore, total liquid wealth decreases.

When holders of mutual savings bank time deposits decide to convert their deposits into money, the effects are exactly the same as when savings and loan shares are converted, since mutual savings banks are part of

[4] The 30-day requirement applies to time deposits that are savings and loan share accounts, mutual savings bank time deposit accounts, and commercial bank time deposits that are in the form of savings accounts. Most people maintain savings accounts at commercial banks, but some hold other forms of time deposits that have variable maturities. Corporations are prohibited by law from owning savings accounts, but they do own significant numbers of other types of time deposits at commercial banks. A more detailed discussion of the various forms of time deposits will be found in Chapters 5 and 8.

[5] See Table 2–1 for a list of near monies.

the nonbank public. The effects are entirely different, however, when the holder of a time deposit with a commercial bank demands money in place of his time deposit. For example, assume a depositor wishes to transfer his $1,000 account from an interest-earning savings account to a demand deposit. The commercial bank simply creates a new checking-deposit account for him in that amount. It switches his savings account to demand deposits. The amount of money in the economy has therefore increased by $1,000, since time deposits are not considered money. Total liquid wealth remains the same, however, and no member of the nonbank public has lost purchasing power. The results are the same if the depositor wants currency. The bank gives up an asset, vault cash, in return for a reduction in time-deposit liabilities. It should be noted that currency held by the commercial banking system as vault cash is neither money nor part of the liquid-wealth system of the nonbank public. Vault cash is not owned by the nonbank public and hence cannot be used to purchase goods and services until distributed to the public by banks.

The T-Account as a Tool of Analysis

The T-account can be effectively used to illustrate the examples discussed in the preceding section. The T-account shows the change in a balance sheet that occurs as a result of a transaction. Briefly, the balance sheet is a means of showing, at a moment of time, the balance between what one owns (*assets*) and what one owes (*liabilities plus capital accounts*). These are always equal. On the asset side of the balance sheet are such items as cash assets, security holdings, and furniture. Liabilities would include demand deposits, time deposits, borrowings, and securities issued, such as bonds. Examples of capital accounts are the book value of a common stock issued by a corporation to its owners and earned surplus. (A more complete discussion of the nature of the balance sheet will be found in Chapters 5 and 6.) The following simple rules will help you analyze correctly the elementary T-accounts and balance sheets in the text:

1. Assets must always equal liabilities plus capital accounts.
2. If assets increase or decrease in their total size, then there must be a corresponding increase or decrease in the sum of liabilities plus capital accounts.
3. If there is an increase or decrease in the total liabilities and capital accounts, there must be a corresponding increase or decrease in the total size of assets.
4. An increase in one type of asset item means a decrease in some other asset or an increase in a liability and capital-account item.
5. A decrease in an asset means an increase in the value of some other asset or a decrease in a liability and capital account.

6. An increase in a liability or capital account means a decrease in some other liability or capital account or an increase in an asset.

7. A decrease in a liability or capital account means an increase in some other liability or capital account or a decrease in an asset.

For example, take the case in which the depositor in a commercial bank wanted to convert his $1,000 time deposit into a demand deposit:

BALANCE-SHEET CHANGES FOR INDIVIDUAL 1

ASSETS		LIABILITIES + CAPITAL ACCOUNTS
Demand deposits	+$1,000	
Time deposits	−$1,000	

BALANCE-SHEET CHANGES FOR COMMERCIAL BANK A

ASSETS	LIABILITIES + CAPITAL ACCOUNTS	
	Demand deposits	+$1,000
	Time deposits	−$1,000

Here we see that the depositor has changed the nature of his assets—an increase in one type of asset has meant a decrease in another. The bank, on the other hand, has experienced a decrease in one type of its liability and an increase in another type.

The analysis becomes somewhat more complicated in the case of a depositor in a savings and loan association who wants to convert his savings and loan shares into a demand-deposit account:

BALANCE-SHEET CHANGES FOR INDIVIDUAL 1

ASSETS		LIABILITIES + CAPITAL ACCOUNTS
Savings capital	−$1,000	
Demand deposits	+$1,000	

BALANCE-SHEET CHANGES FOR THE COMMERCIAL BANKING SYSTEM

ASSETS	LIABILITIES + CAPITAL ACCOUNTS	
	Demand deposits (of savings and loan association)	−$1,000
	Demand deposits (of Individual 1)	+$1,000

BALANCE-SHEET CHANGES FOR THE SAVINGS AND LOAN ASSOCIATION

ASSETS		LIABILITIES + CAPITAL ACCOUNTS	
Demand deposits	−$1,000	Savings capital	−$1,000

Here we see that there has been no change in the stock of money, but that total liquid wealth has decreased by $1,000 due to the reduced amount of savings capital. The commercial banking system, which formerly owed money to the savings and loan association, now owes it to the private individual depositor.

U.S. Government Securities as a Form of Wealth

Quantitatively, United States government securities are almost as important a form of liquid wealth as money itself. In December of 1968, government securities held by the nonbank public totaled $163.9 billion, whereas the stock of money was $206.0 billion.

Government securities are basically of two types: marketable and nonmarketable.

Nonmarketable securities cannot be transferred from one owner to another. To get back one's financial investment, the securities must be returned to the original issuer. Savings bonds are the principal type of nonmarketable securities held by individuals. They presently yield 4.25 percent interest at maturity. Thus, if a $25 bond were purchased for $18.75, in seven years and nine months it could be redeemed for $25, or the purchase price plus the accumulated interest. There is no possibility of loss on these securities, except that which may occur in purchasing power if the price level in the economy increases sharply. These securities are redeemable upon demand only after they have been held by the purchaser for more than 60 days, however. Thus, during the initial period of ownership, they are not as liquid as other forms of near money.

Marketable securities, on the other hand, are transferable. The market for them is composed of the nonbank public, commercial banks, and various agencies of the federal government itself. For example, the Federal Reserve banks alone owned some $52.1 billion of these securities in January 1969.[6]

The market price for U.S. government securities is ultimately determined by the market forces of supply and demand. If the securities are held until maturity—that is, until the time when the United States Treasury is obligated to redeem them—there is no possibility of loss. Normally they are not redeemable before maturity, however. If one chooses to regain one's financial investment prior to the redemption date, they must be sold on the open market for what they will bring. Thus there may be a gain or a loss. Short-term securities that can be redeemed within one year are usually not subject to wide fluctuations in value. Longer-term securities, however, may appreciate or depreciate in value significantly, depending upon market conditions. United States government securities yielding 3 percent and due in 1995 were selling at 70.28 in October of 1969, for

[6] *Federal Reserve Bulletin, February* 1969, p. A-12.

example.[7] This means that a $1,000 security of this type, if purchased when first issued for about $1,000, could be sold on the open market for only $701, which is a substantial loss. For this reason, marketable public securities are not usually considered to be good near monies: one can be certain of not incurring a loss only if they are held till maturity. On the other hand, they are immediately marketable and thus highly liquid. The funds obtained from the sale of securities may be used immediately to pay off debt or to purchase goods and services.

When nonmarketable U.S. government securities are converted into money, the stock of money increases without changing the total of liquid wealth. The treasury redeems these securities by drawing on its own deposit balances (which are not part of the money stock). This leads to an increase in the deposit balances of the nonbank public. If the Treasury redeems marketable securities at maturity, the results are the same. Results will vary, however, when marketable securities are bought and sold on the open market. For example, assume that one individual sells a security to another for $900:

BALANCE-SHEET CHANGES FOR INDIVIDUAL 1

ASSETS		LIABILITIES + CAPITAL ACCOUNTS
Demand deposits	− $900	
U.S. securities	+ $900	

BALANCE-SHEET CHANGES FOR INDIVIDUAL 2

ASSETS		LIABILITIES + CAPITAL ACCOUNTS
U.S. securities	− $900	
Demand deposits	+ $900	

BALANCE-SHEET CHANGES FOR THE COMMERCIAL BANKING SYSTEM

ASSETS	LIABILITIES + CAPITAL ACCOUNTS
	Demand deposits (of Individual 1) − $900
	Demand deposits (of Individual 2) + $900

Individual 1, who purchases the security, does so by writing a $900 check on his checking account. Individual 2 receives the check, deposits it in his checking account, and turns the security over to the new owner, Individual 1. The whole transaction takes place within the nonbank public. Thus there is no change in total money holdings or in total liquid wealth of the nonbank public. There is merely a redistribution. Nor is there a change in the total liabilities of the commercial banking system.

[7] *Wall Street Journal,* October 20, 1969.

The results are different when the banking system purchases the security. Assume that the security is sold by Individual 1 to the banking system for $900:

BALANCE-SHEET CHANGES FOR INDIVIDUAL 1

ASSETS		LIABILITIES + CAPITAL ACCOUNTS
U.S. securities	−$900	
Demand deposits	+$900	

BALANCE-SHEET CHANGES FOR THE COMMERCIAL BANKING SYSTEM

ASSETS		LIABILITIES + CAPITAL ACCOUNTS
U.S. securities	+$900	Demand deposits (of Individual 1) +$900

The banking system creates a demand deposit for the seller of the security, thus increasing the total money holdings of the nonbank public. Total liquid wealth remains unchanged, however, since the U.S. security component of the nonbank public's assets decreases by the same amount.

We have included U.S. government securities among the principal forms of the nonbank public's liquid-wealth holdings. Why not include privately issued stocks and bonds also? For several reasons. First, privately issued securities exhibit considerable variation in price depending upon (1) the financial condition of the firm issuing the securities and (2) the business prospects for the economy and the industry in general. If the firm has had stable earnings, the chances are good that its securities will sell well. But a brief setback in earnings or a decline in the demand for the products of the firm and industry could initiate a wave of security sales that would drive bond and stock prices down. These sales would cause security holders to suffer extensive capital losses. Thus, the liquidity of these securities, their ability to be converted into money quickly and without loss, is seriously hampered. Marketability is uncertain. Similarly, even with adequate earnings and good prospects, a firm may have difficulty marketing its securities if it is small or if its success depends on a few key individuals. The securities of larger, better-established firms will frequently command a higher price than those of smaller, younger corporations.

The prevailing rate of interest is another factor that influences the price of both public and private securities. If prevailing interest rates are higher than rates in the past, then previously issued securities must be sold by their holders at a lower price. There is an inverse relationship between interest rates and bond prices.[8] This factor also tends to reduce the liquidity of private and public securities.

Finally, private securities have less secure backing than federal securities.

---

[8] This will be examined in more detail in Chapter 19.

The U.S. government stands behind its securities, but only the issuing corporation guarantees its stocks and bonds. No one doubts the permanence of the government or its ability to redeem securities. Few enterprises exhibit such permanence or inspire such confidence.

Life Insurance as a Form of Liquid Wealth

The cash value of life insurance is another type of near money. As long as the insurance company remains in business, the policy holder can, within a matter of days, either acquire the cash surrender value of his policy or borrow on the basis of that value. Since life insurance companies are classified as part of the nonbank public, there is no change in the stock of money when policy holders choose to convert their life insurance into money. There is, however, a decrease in total liquid wealth. The policy holder also suffers a small loss by converting to cash. He loses insurance protection and the excess of premium payments over the cash value of the policy.

Summary

So far in Chapter 2 we have (1) classified the liquid-wealth system of the United States by degrees of liquidity and (2) developed the T-account as a tool of analysis. Insured time deposits, savings and loan shares, and U.S. savings bonds are the safest and most liquid near monies available. There is virtually no possibility of loss and they may be quickly converted into cash. Life insurance policies and marketable U.S. government securities, while usually safe and quickly convertible, are less safe as near monies

TABLE 2–2. PROBABLE EFFECTS ON THE STOCK OF MONEY AND TOTAL LIQUID WEALTH FOLLOWING CONVERSION OF NEAR MONIES INTO MONEY

FORM OF NEAR MONEY CONVERTED	DIRECTION OF CHANGE OF STOCK OF MONEY	DIRECTION OF CHANGE OF TOTAL LIQUID WEALTH
Time deposits in commercial banks	+	0
Time deposits in mutual savings banks	0	—
Savings and loan shares	0	—
Savings bonds	+	0
Marketable U.S. government securities	+*	0*
	0†	0†
Cash value of life insurance	0	—

* If redeemed by the U.S. government or purchased by the banking system.
† If purchased by other members of the nonbank public.

because of possible losses. Table 2–2 summarizes the effects that the conversion of near monies has upon the stock of money and total liquid wealth.

In a later chapter we will consider the importance of these liquid-wealth holdings to aggregate economic activity.

CURRENCY IN THE UNITED STATES

The American unit of account is the dollar, which is divisible into 100 cents. Coins are made in convenient divisibles of 100: 1, 5, 10, 25, 50, and 100 cents. Similarly, paper comes in convenient 1, 5, 10, 20, 50, and 100 dollar denominations. (Beginning in July 1969, the Federal Reserve discontinued the issuance of 500, 1,000, 5,000, and 10,000 dollar denomination notes due to a decline in their use.) All this currency must, by law, be accepted by creditors in payment of debt. It is, in other words, *legal tender*. The other component of our money stock, demand deposits, is *not* legal tender; it is only a generally accepted substitute for it. Issuing currency and defining the unit of account are the prerogatives of the federal government.

The Federal Reserve Note

Table 2–3 shows the present composition of currency in the United States. Clearly the most important type of currency is the Federal Reserve note, which is issued in denominations of $1 and up. These notes make up 90 percent of the total currency in circulation. They are liabilities of the Federal Reserve banks that issue them.

The backing of Federal Reserve notes consists of U.S. government

TABLE 2–3. UNITED STATES CURRENCY IN CIRCULATION,
DECEMBER 31, 1968

(IN MILLIONS OF DOLLARS)

KIND OF CURRENCY*			AMOUNT
Coins			
Silver dollars	482		
Fractional coin	5,209		
Total amount of coins		5,691	
Paper currency—Treasury			
United States notes	310		
In process of retirement	308		
Total amount of Treasury paper currency		618	
Paper currency—Federal Reserve			
Federal Reserve notes		44,653	
Total currency in circulation			50,962
Currency in commercial bank vaults			−7,462†
Currency in circulation outside commercial bank vaults			43,500†

* Includes all currency outside the Treasury and Federal Reserve banks.
† Preliminary data.
SOURCE: *Federal Reserve Bulletin*, February 1969, pp. A-16 and A-18.

securities and commercial paper held by the Federal Reserve banks, almost all the collateral being in the form of U.S. government securities. This does not mean, however, that you can convert your Federal Reserve notes into government securities merely by presenting them at any Federal Reserve bank. If you as an individual want United States government securities, you will have to purchase them through a securities dealer. What is it, then, that makes Federal Reserve notes "good"? Three things: (1) they are legal tender, (2) the public has faith in them, and (3) the Federal Reserve banks issue and retire currency only in response to the demands of the public.

Assume, for example, that the public demand for currency in the form of Federal Reserve notes rises by $1 million. How may it get this additional amount? By writing checks out to "cash" at commercial banks. This causes the banks to lose both a liability, demand deposits, and an asset, vault cash:

BALANCE-SHEET CHANGES FOR THE COMMERCIAL BANKING SYSTEM

ASSETS		LIABILITIES + CAPITAL ACCOUNTS	
Vault cash	− $1,000,000	Demand deposits	− $1,000,000

BALANCE-SHEET CHANGES FOR THE NONBANK PUBLIC

ASSETS		LIABILITIES + CAPITAL ACCOUNTS
Demand deposits	− $1,000,000	
Currency	+ $1,000,000	

Commercial banks now need to replenish their depleted currency holdings. Where do they get the currency? From the Federal Reserve banks. Commercial banks exchange their reserve accounts (checking deposits at the Federal Reserve banks owned by commercial banks and owed to them by the Federal Reserve banks) at the Federal Reserve banks for currency. The Federal Reserve banks then issue and turn over to the commercial banks the desired type of currency (in this case, Federal Reserve notes of various denominations). This transaction appears as follows:

BALANCE-SHEET CHANGES FOR THE COMMERCIAL BANKING SYSTEM

ASSETS		LIABILITIES + CAPITAL ACCOUNTS
Reserves with Federal Reserve banks	− $1,000,000	
Vault cash	+ $1,000,000	

BALANCE-SHEET CHANGES FOR THE FEDERAL RESERVE BANKS

ASSETS		LIABILITIES + CAPITAL ACCOUNTS	
		Member bank reserves	− $1,000,000
		Federal Reserve notes	+ $1,000,000

When the public wants less currency than it has, this process is reversed. People exchange currency for increased deposits at the commercial banks. The commercial banks, with excess holdings of vault cash, return currency to the Federal Reserve banks, who increase their reserve accounts. The Federal Reserve banks then retire the currency that has been returned.

Treasury Currency

The Treasury, along with the Federal Reserve, has a monopoly of currency issue. There are two types of Treasury currency: coin and paper. Coin amounts to approximately 10 percent of the total amount of currency in circulation. Treasury paper currency is now less than 2 percent of all currency. Coins are issued by the Treasury Department in response to the needs of the public for "change."

United States notes are the other type of Treasury currency. They were first issued during the Civil War, and the quantity available is limited. Of the $323 million of these notes now in existence, only $310 million are presently in circulation. These notes now come only in $5 denominations. All other types of Treasury paper currency, including silver certificates, are being retired.

Treasury currency gets into circulation in much the same manner as Federal Reserve notes. When there is a need for currency, commercial banks may procure Treasury money from the Federal Reserve banks. There is this difference, however: since the Federal Reserve banks do not issue Treasury currency, they are giving up an asset, one that they previously purchased from the Treasury at face value.

The Nature of Our Currency System

This discussion points up an important characteristic of our currency system. In the United States, changes in the amount and composition of currency occur almost exclusively in response to the demands of the public. There are no accompanying changes in the money stock. When the amount of currency in the economy increases, there is a corresponding decrease in demand-deposit money. When the supply of currency decreases, demand-deposit money increases. This causes a constant redistribution of the components of the money stock but not a change in the total stock itself. This is true whether the redistribution involves Treasury currency or Federal Reserve notes. *The United States government does not issue currency to defray its own expenses or to finance its own operations.*

In other words, the United States has a self-regulatory paper currency system. It is a "paper" system because currency is the money of ultimate redemption. Coin and paper-currency holdings of United States citizens are redeemable in coin and paper currency. It is a self-regulatory system because the money stock does not change when the currency total changes.

Data Sources

Board of Governors of the Federal Reserve System. *Federal Reserve Bulletin* (monthly).

————. *Annual Reports.*

————. *Banking and Monetary Statistics.* Washington, D.C.: 1943.

————. *All Bank Statistics United States 1896–1955.* Washington, D.C.: 1959.

Comptroller of the Currency. *Annual Reports.*

Federal Deposit Insurance Corporation. *Annual Reports.*

U.S. Department of Commerce. *Survey of Current Business* (monthly).

CHAPTER 3

The Commercial Banking System and the Economy

Economists frequently use income and employment statistics to measure the economic importance of a given industry. These statistics are thought to reveal the extent to which economic activities contribute to the national economy in terms of jobs created and income generated. In this chapter we will first use these statistics to assess the overall importance of the financial sector. We will then discuss some special characteristics of the commercial banking system, our most important financial subsector.

FINANCE IN THE ECONOMY

Tables 3–1 and 3–2 show the contribution of various industries to the national income and employment for selected years since 1929. Ranking these various sectors of the economy in order of their contribution to national inome for 1929 and 1968, we have:

1929	1968
Manufacturing	Manufacturing
Wholesale and retail trade	Wholesale and retail trade
Finance	Government
Services	Services
Agriculture	Finance
Transportation	Contract construction
Government	Communications and public utilities
Contract construction	Transportation
Communications and public utilities	Agriculture
Mining	Mining

The most impressive changes in the relative contribution of the various industrial sectors to national income are the move to ninth place of the agricultural sector and the increased importance of the government sector. The other major economic sectors for the most part maintained their respective positions. Although there was some percentage gain by manufacturing, this has become stabilized. Mining has gradually declined. The finance sector, as one might expect, showed a sharp decline during the depression; since then it has been unable to increase its relative contribution, possibly because it is subject to restrictive barriers to entry. Transportation is also less important because of the continually expanding private use of the automobile.

The employment figures tell much the same story as the national-income figures. The greatest relative gain was made by the government, with the initial impetus provided by the expansion of federal civilian payrolls during the depression. The number of people employed by the government rose from 8.9 percent of all employees in 1929 to 20.4 percent in 1968. In contrast, agriculture dropped from 9.8 percent in 1929 to 2.0 percent in 1968 as a result of the technological revolution in farm equipment and the higher income possibilities in other sectors of the economy. Transportation and mining were the only other industries to experience any substantial relative decline. Manufacturing, wholesale and retail trade, and services continued to be large employers.

As a direct source of income and employment, the financial sector of the economy has not changed much in importance since the depression. In 1940, it contributed 10.1 percent of national income and 3.7 percent of employment. In 1968, it was the source of only 10.9 percent of income and 4.4 percent of employment.

Why, then, is the financial sector of the economy thought to be so important? The answer is simple: *it is our most important creator of liquid assets.* Hence, it is in a unique position to affect economic developments.

Although decisions regarding the direction and timing of future expenditures are initially dictated by business and consumer desires, financial institutions, acting as sources of funds, also help shape those decisions. Whether they make direct loans to business and consumers or extend real-estate credit, they help determine the uses to which much of our money will be put. By making one form of loan or security purchase and not another, they influence the nature of expenditures. As money on loan is spent by borrowers, the demand for certain goods and services is increased. This in turn may stimulate investment in plant and equipment in the industries most affected by the increased demand. The economy's overall level of prosperity, its rate of growth, the level of employment, the rate of inflation, and the composition of the nation's output are all heavily influenced by the financial sector and the rate at which it finances various activities. Unlike other industrial sectors, therefore, the financial sector cannot be accurately evaluated in terms of its contributions to income and employment; it must be judged in terms of its functions.

The financial institutions most influential in shaping expenditure decisions are the commercial banks, savings institutions, insurance companies, and various governmental agencies. These institutions give rise to 39.8, 21.4, 16.3, and 17.9 percent, respectively, of the principal liquid-

TABLE 3-1. UNITED STATES NATIONAL INCOME BY INDUSTRY, 1929, 1940, 1950, 1960, AND 1968

INDUSTRY	INCOME CONTRIBUTED BY EACH SECTOR (IN MILLIONS OF DOLLARS)					PERCENT OF INCOME CONTRIBUTED BY EACH SECTOR				
	1929	1940	1950	1960	1968	1929	1940	1950	1960	1968
Agriculture, forestry, and fisheries	8,278	6,247	17,923	17,295	21,891	9.4	7.7	7.4	4.2	3.1
Mining	2,048	1,868	5,010	5,510	6,548	2.3	2.3	2.1	1.3	0.9
Contract construction	3,808	2,569	11,833	21,786	36,367	4.3	3.1	4.9	5.3	5.1
Manufacturing	21,888	22,336	74,371	121,025	215,383	24.9	27.4	30.7	29.2	30.2
Wholesale and retail trade	13,358	14,337	42,707	67,698	105,200	15.2	17.6	17.7	16.3	14.7
Finance, insurance, and real estate	12,693	8,208	21,789	42,586	78,158	14.5	10.1	9.0	10.3	10.9
Transportation	6,636	5,040	13,278	17,909	27,156	7.6	6.2	5.5	4.3	3.8
Communications and public utilities	2,864	3,056	7,198	16,808	27,892	3.3	3.7	3.0	4.1	3.9
Services	10,338	8,854	23,089	49,065	86,077	11.8	10.8	9.5	11.8	12.0
Government and government enterprises	5,093	8,762	23,490	52,528	104,978	5.8	10.7	9.7	12.7	14.7
Other	810	357	1,188	2,287	4,745	0.9	0.4	0.5	0.6	0.7
All industries (total)	87,814	81,634	241,876	414,497	714,395	100.0	100.0	100.0	100.1*	100.0

* Does not equal 100.0 because of rounding.
SOURCE: Office of Business Economics, U.S. Department of Commerce, *National Income, A Supplement to the Survey of Current Business*, Washington, 1954; *U.S. Income and Output, A Supplement to the Survey of Current Business*, Washington, 1958; *Survey of Current Business*, 1963 (July), p. 17; 1969 (July), p. 21.

TABLE 3-2. UNITED STATES NUMBER OF FULL-TIME EQUIVALENT EMPLOYEES BY INDUSTRY, 1929, 1940, 1950, 1960, AND 1968

INDUSTRY	FULL-TIME EQUIVALENT EMPLOYEES* (IN THOUSANDS)					PERCENT OF TOTAL CONTRIBUTED BY EACH SECTOR				
	1929	1940	1950	1960	1968	1929	1940	1950	1960	1968
Agriculture, forestry, and fisheries	3,530	2,781	2,219	2,060	1,398	9.8	7.3	4.6	3.6	2.0
Mining	993	927	916	674	612	2.8	2.4	1.9	1.2	0.9
Contract construction	1,484	1,285	2,381	2,846	3,398	4.1	3.4	4.9	4.9	4.9
Manufacturing	10,428	10,882	14,969	16,364	19,855	29.1	28.4	30.8	28.4	28.4
Wholesale and retail trade	5,846	6,526	9,005	11,041	12,143	16.3	17.0	18.5	19.2	17.4
Finance, insurance, and real estate	1,415	1,422	1,805	2,593	3,081	3.9	3.7	3.7	4.5	4.4
Transportation	2,873	2,072	2,652	2,459	2,443	8.0	5.4	5.4	4.3	3.5
Communications and public utilities	1,031	898	1,270	1,445	1,629	2.9	2.3	2.6	2.5	2.3
Services	5,112	5,274	6,073	7,830	11,060	14.2	13.8	12.5	13.6	15.8
Government and government enterprises	3,184	6,267	7,380	10,323	14,246	8.9	16.3	15.2	17.9	20.4
Other	0	2	5	4	4	—	—	—	—	—
All industries (total)	35,896	38,336	48,675	57,639	69,869	100.0	100.0	100.1†	100.1†	100.0

* Full-time equivalent employment measures man-years of full-time employment of wage and salary earners and its equivalent in work performed by part-time workers. Full-time employment is defined in terms of the number of hours customary at a particular time and place.

† Does not equal 100.0 because of rounding.

SOURCE: Office of Business Economics, U.S. Department of Commerce, *National Income, A Supplement to the Survey of Current Business,* Washington, 1954; *U.S. Income and Output, A Supplement to the Survey of Current Business,* Washington, 1958; *Survey of Current Business,* 1963 (July), p. 33; 1969 (July), p. 40.

wealth holdings of the nonbank public.[1] We shall first study, here and in the next four chapters, the commercial banking system. Chapter 8 discusses the other financial subsectors.

THE COMMERCIAL BANKING SYSTEM

Distinguishing Characteristics

Like other financial institutions, commercial banks make loans and investments, take deposits, act as securities underwriters and brokers, provide safety-deposit facilities, and administer estates. Unlike other financial institutions, however, they also *create and destroy money* and *allow their creditors to transfer claims to money through the use of checks.* No other financial institution is able to do this.

When banks make a loan they give the borrower either a deposit or cash. Most people and businesses prefer deposits to cash because they are more convenient. A deposit is money created by the bank. For example, if someone borrows $500 from Bank A to finance emergency medical payments, the T-account entries will look like this:

BALANCE-SHEET CHANGES FOR COMMERCIAL BANK A

ASSETS		LIABILITIES + CAPITAL ACCOUNTS	
Loans to individuals	+$500	Demand deposits	+$500

Thus, in making a loan, the commercial bank has created money.

Similarly, when a borrower repays a loan, he does so with cash or by check. The majority of loan repayments are negotiated by check. Hence, on repayment, Bank A's balance sheet will show:

BALANCE-SHEET CHANGES FOR COMMERCIAL BANK A

ASSETS		LIABILITIES + CAPITAL ACCOUNTS	
Loans to individuals	−$500	Demand deposits	−$500

Here money has been destroyed.[2] Thus, *as long as the total loan volume is increased,* the stock of money *is increased.* Given stable prices, the ability of the public to purchase goods and services will thus be enhanced.

What is the difference when a borrower obtains a loan from a consumer

---

[1] See Table 2–1.
[2] We are assuming for the sake of simplicity that the bank collected interest on the loan in advance. Also, note that the effects of these transactions on the stock of money would be the same if people took cash instead of deposits. Vault cash is not part of the money stock; hence if it is given to a borrower by the bank, the money holdings of the nonbank public increase. Chapter 7 examines the mechanics of the creation and destruction of money in more detail.

finance company rather than from a bank? Assume that the finance company gives the borrower a check. This check is not money created by the finance company; it is simply a check written on its account at a commercial bank.[3] The balance-sheet changes that take place are:

BALANCE-SHEET CHANGES FOR CONSUMER FINANCE COMPANY

ASSETS		LIABILITIES + CAPITAL ACCOUNTS
Demand deposits	− $500	
Loans	+ $500	

BALANCE-SHEET CHANGES FOR THE COMMERCIAL BANKING SYSTEM

ASSETS		LIABILITIES + CAPITAL ACCOUNTS	
		Demand deposits (of consumer finance company)	− $500
		Demand deposits (of individual borrower)	+ $500

The individual borrower deposits the check in his own account at the bank with which he does business. Subsequently, he writes out checks on his increased demand deposit account. Thus, there has been only a transfer of deposits from one part of the nonbank public to another. Likewise, when the loan is repaid, there is no corresponding reduction of the money supply.

Other financial institutions are in a position similar to that of the consumer finance company. When they make loans and investments they are merely transferring their money holdings. Only commercial banks can create and destroy money because only they are permitted to allow creditors to transfer claims through the use of checks. In addition, only commercial banks among financial institutions have liabilities legally payable on demand.

Special Responsibility of the Commercial Banking System

The commercial banking system shares one very important characteristic with other members of the financial sector and the rest of the business community—the desire to maximize profits and to expand its share of the market. Commercial banks are profit-seeking enterprises. As such, they share with other businesses the same set of expectations concerning the "health" of the economy. When the consensus among businessmen is that the future will be prosperous, businesses generally expand their operations. When the economy is expected to take a turn for the worse, businesses usually limit their plans for expansion, hire fewer new workers, and may even contract their work force. Commercial banks follow suit. They tend to expand their loans during periods of economic upturn and

---

[3] It is assumed here that the finance company has adequate funds to engage in lending and therefore need not borrow from the banking system.

contract loans (or at least contract the rate of growth of loans) during an economic downturn. In the absence of compensating actions by government, this expansion and contraction of loans results in a parallel expansion and contraction of the deposit part of our money stock.

This in turn means that in periods of economic upturn, commercial banks add to the money stock and thereby help expand the demand for goods and services. However, once the economy arrives at full employment of men and resources, a continued expansion of loans and deposits simply adds to price level increases. Once full employment is reached, it is difficult to increase real production, except by increasing the utilization of men and equipment through a longer work week, adding a number of retired people, women, and students to the work force, or bringing obsolete machinery back into production.

On the other hand, if banks contract loans in periods of mild economic decline, experience shows that we are not likely to have a drop in the price level. Prices in the United States seem to have some downward "stickiness." As a consequence, the reduced amount of deposits accompanying the reduction in loans usually tends to aggravate the downturn in demand and output.

In short, banks share the general business outlook on economic conditions. *Commercial banks, in the absence of regulation, tend to intensify whatever phase of the business cycle is current. They do this through their unique ability to create and destroy money when making loans and investments.*

The real bills doctrine. An individual banker may counter the preceding analysis by arguing that all he really does is respond to the loan demands of the public, that he supplies credit and money according to the needs of trade. His standards with respect to granting loans do not change. Rather, when people want more funds, in periods of upturn, he supplies them. In periods of decline, fewer loans are made because fewer loans are requested. Furthermore, he contends, this is a safe loan policy. On business loans, for example, the borrower uses the funds to purchase productive resources. Shortly after the loan is made, the business borrower will have produced the goods which are to be sold. The proceeds from the sale of the goods can then be used to repay the loan. This line of reasoning is sometimes called the "commercial theory of banking" or the "real bills doctrine."

There are two loopholes in this line of reasoning. First, though it may be neither intentional nor conscious, such a procedure usually involves disproportionate stringency during periods of declining business activity. What may appear to be a sound loan on the upward side of the cycle may not appear safe on the downward side. In periods of economic decline, banks examine their loan applications more carefully, in addition to reducing the amount of loans in response to the increased reluctance of businesses and individuals to borrow. This places additional downward pressure on loans, when what is needed in a period of decline may well be added demand, further expansion of loans, and an increase in the money stock.

Also, although many loans are granted on the basis of future production, no increase in production may occur if the economy is in a period of full employment. During upswings demand may outrun production. The future production on which banks base their loans may never materialize because resources are already being used to the fullest extent possible. All that a business can do is use its borrowed funds to bid resources away from other enterprises. Thus, a shift in the type, but not the total amount, of production takes place. In addition, prices of resources, and hence of final goods and services, are bid up. If a business wants to renew its loan in the future to facilitate production, it will have to borrow an amount larger than the initial loan to meet increased costs. A vicious circle of increased borrowing and rising prices may easily ensue.

Bank responsibilities and federal regulation. This analysis suggests that normal commercial bank loan operations can perversely affect the economy at both ends of the cycle, either worsening recession or feeding inflation. Yet commercial banks are given the right to create demand deposits, which constitute the major part of our money supply. Almost 80 percent of our money is in this form and about 90 percent of all transactions in the economy are check transactions. For this reason, they have a responsibility that transcends that of other business enterprises. Banks are responsible for the creation, destruction, and administration of our money. As a consequence, they are also responsible to a great extent for the welfare of the economy.

This dual responsibility—to itself as a business enterprise and to the nation—puts a tremendous burden on the individual commercial bank. If it acts in the national interest, it may hurt its competitive position. If its lending policy is conservative during periods of prosperity and full employment, it reduces its potential profits since borrowers will seek funds from competing banks and savings institutions. If its lending policy is liberal during periods of recession, unpaid loans may weaken its financial soundness. On the other hand, if it acts purely on the basis of self-interest, it may worsen the national economic picture.

Because of the contradictory nature of this dual responsibility, the government exercises considerable control over the commercial banking system. As we shall see later, various governmental regulatory agencies, such as the Federal Reserve, the Federal Deposit Insurance Corporation, the Comptroller of the Currency, and comparable state agencies are all engaged in the business of regulating commercial banks. Some supervisory agencies are concerned solely with banks as businesses, seeing to it that they operate in the interest of their stockholders. Others, such as the

Federal Reserve, are concerned with maintaining employment levels, stimulating economic growth, and holding the price line. These latter agencies regulate commercial banks and their money-creating activities with an eye to the national interest.[4] This permits the banks to act in their own interest without too much concern for the national welfare. The ultimate responsibility for the safety of the money stock and aggregate economic activity rests with the federal government.

[4] As previously indicated, other financial institutions also affect the national economy. Because of this, some economists argue that these institutions should also be subject to extensive regulation. This point is discussed further in Chapter 8.

CHAPTER 4

The Structure of the Commercial Banking System

The commercial banking system of the United States is composed of more than 13,700 banks. Listed below are the types of banks and the types of banking with which we will be concerned in this chapter. Having defined our terms, we will then proceed to examine the structure of our banking system in some detail.

TYPES OF BANKS

Member bank. A bank that is a member of the Federal Reserve System. Member banks are classified by the system as Reserve city or country banks.

Nonmember bank. A bank that is not a member of the Federal Reserve System.

National bank. A bank that holds a charter from the federal government. National banks must be members of the Federal Reserve System.

State bank. A bank that has a state charter. State banks may or may not be members of the Federal Reserve System.

Insured bank. A bank whose deposits are insured by the Federal Deposit Insurance Corporation. All member banks must be so insured.

Noninsured bank. A bank whose deposits are not insured by the Federal Deposit Insurance Corporation.

TYPES OF BANKING

Unit banking. The operation of only one banking office by a commercial bank.

Branch banking. The operation of two or more banking offices by a commercial bank.

Chain banking. The association of a number of commercial banks through an interlocking directorate.

Group banking. The control of two or more banks by a holding company with a controlling interest in the stock of the banks.

Correspondent banking. Commercial bank maintenance of checking-deposit accounts with another bank in return for such services as bond and security purchases and check clearance.

MEMBER AND NONMEMBER BANKS

Table 4–1 summarizes changes in commercial bank membership in the Federal Reserve System between 1947 and December 1968. Of the 13,679

TABLE **4–1.** COMMERCIAL BANKS IN THE UNITED STATES
AND POSSESSIONS, DECEMBER 31, 1947 AND DECEMBER 31, 1968

TYPE OF BANK	NUMBER		DEMAND DEPOSITS (IN MILLIONS OF DOLLARS)*		TIME DEPOSITS (IN MILLIONS OF DOLLARS)*	
	1947	1968	1947	1968	1947	1968
Member banks						
National	5,005	4,716	53,541	116,422	19,278	122,597
State	1,918	1,262	27,068	47,498	9,062	40,945
Total member banks	6,923	5,978	80,609	163,920	28,340	163,542
Nonmember banks						
Insured state	6,478	7,504	12,366	34,615	6,558	40,060
Noninsured state	783	197	1,392	1,366	478	767
Total nonmember banks	7,261	7,701	13,758	35,981	7,036	40,827
Total commercial banks	14,184	13,679	94,367	199,901	35,376	204,369

* Excluding U.S. and interbank deposits. Totals may differ because of rounding.
SOURCE: *Federal Reserve Bulletin*, April 1969, pp. A–19 to A–22.

commercial banks in the United States and its possessions in 1968, only 5,978 or 44 percent, were member banks. These member banks accounted for 82 percent of demand deposits, however, and 80 percent of commercial bank time-deposit liabilities. Their average deposit liabilities at the end of 1968 amounted to $55 million, whereas those of nonmember banks came to only $10 million. Clearly, member banks figure more importantly in the economy than nonmember banks.

The trend in Federal Reserve membership has been slightly downward in recent years, largely because the number of consolidations and mergers among existing members has been greater than the number of new members created. In addition, there has been some tendency for small member banks to withdraw from the system and to operate as insured nonmember banks.

The total number of banks in the economy has also declined. The biggest drop, of course, came with the large-scale bank failures of the thirties, when the number of banks almost halved. Since then the total has declined only slightly, through absorptions, consolidations, and mergers, with some increase in the number of banks becoming apparent in the mid- and late-sixties.

Banks wishing to become members of the Federal Reserve System must meet certain standards. Primarily, they must (1) have sufficient capital relative to assets and deposit liabilities and (2) redeem at par all checks drawn by their depositors and presented by out-of-town banks for collection. In addition, the banks' past operations, their solvency, and their managerial talent must be satisfactory to the Federal Reserve. Many banks do not meet these requirements and must therefore remain outside the system. However, if a bank applies for and receives a national charter from the Comptroller of the Currency, membership in the Reserve System is automatic.

The Importance of the Capital Requirement

The ratio of deposits to capital accounts is thought to be an important measure of bank solvency by bankers. A low ratio indicates sound investment policies. The higher this ratio, the smaller is the presumable margin of safety for depositors, although, almost always, bank supervisors will step in prior to actual insolvency. In those few cases where banks are forced to liquidate, the average depositor need not fear for the safety of his funds, since deposit insurance is likely to cover any losses. Liquidation is particularly painful to bank directors and stockholders, who are not protected by deposit insurance. When a bank fails, creditors have first claim to the assets of the corporation; stockholders have only a residual claim to assets. They receive whatever funds are available after the claims of creditors have been met. Deposit claims constitute almost all the liabilities of a commercial bank. If capital accounts are low in relation to these claims nearly all the assets of the bank would have to be used to meet them in the event of liquidation. Furthermore, when corporate assets are sold in liquidation, they usually do not bring their full book value; if there is a high deposit/capital ratio, all creditor claims may not be met.

It is the responsibility of the Federal Reserve System and other examining groups to see that commercial banks do not engage in unsound practices that might lead to insolvency. A low deposit/capital ratio coupled with sound assets may serve to protect both depositors and stockholders. The examining authorities carefully study the qualitative composition of assets as well as the deposit/capital ratio. Cash, deposits with Federal Reserve banks, and short-term U.S. government securities are considered very good assets since there is almost no risk of loss.

In recent years, the deposit/capital ratio for all commercial banks has been a little less than 10/1.[1] There have been few bank failures. In addition, the number of annual absorptions and mergers of commercial banks is low relative to the total number of banks in the banking system. Neither the current ratio nor any other ratio is necessarily a safe one, however. Research shows that the deposit/capital ratio and other measures of bank solvency ". . . do a relatively poor job of measuring capital adequacy."[2] Additional research is necessary to establish more relevant measures.

The Par Collection Requirement

Any bank that is a member of the Federal Reserve System must remit checks drawn on it at par. Nonmember banks wishing to use Federal Reserve check-clearing facilities must also remit at par.[3] Banks that do not do so are called "nonpar" banks. They cannot be members of the Federal Reserve System, and the Federal Reserve banks will not accept their checks for collection.

Only a small and declining number of banks are nonpar. In 1954 there were 1,787 nonpar banks; by the end of 1968 there were only 932.[4] These banks represent about 7 percent of the total number of banks in the United States, and they control even a smaller percentage of total bank-deposit liabilities. Although nonpar banks are not particularly important in the national economy, they are quite important regionally, especially in the South and in the west north-central states where they are concentrated. States having more than 50 nonpar banks in 1968 were Alabama, Arkansas, Georgia, Louisiana, Mississippi, North Dakota, South Dakota, and Tennessee.[5]

Nonpar banks usually impose a minimum "exchange charge" of 0.1 percent on checks presented for collection by out-of-town banks. Thus, on a $1,000 check, a nonpar bank will remit only $999. Any checks drawn on a nonpar bank and presented at the teller's window, however, will be paid at par.

Why do some commercial banks choose to operate in this manner? Nonpar bankers argue that an exchange charge is required to cover the costs of making payment to out-of-town banks since expensive checking-deposit accounts must be maintained with the large out-of-town banks. This is hardly a valid argument, however, since local banks must maintain deposit balances with out-of-town banks anyway in order to collect on

---

[1] *Federal Reserve Bulletin,* April 1969, p. A-19.

[2] Richard V. Cotter, "Capital Ratios and Capital Adequacies," *The National Banking Review,* March 1966, p. 345.

[3] For a more complete account of the process of check clearing and collection, see Chapter 10.

[4] *Federal Reserve Bulletin,* February 1955, p. 209; February 1969, p. A-95.

[5] *Federal Reserve Bulletin,* February 1969, p. A-95.

the deposit of checks drawn on these banks. The real reason for staying nonpar is that the exchange charge is profitable. Since checks sent to the par banks for collection are paid at par, whereas checks drawn on non-par banks are paid at less than par, a profit margin exists. Nonpar banks are typically small, rural banks that are not as efficient as the city banks, nor as skilled in making profitable investments; hence, some have come to rely on the exchange charge as a source of earnings. Furthermore, they are often located in one-bank towns where there is little competitive pressure to force them to abandon their nonpar status.

Other Member Bank Obligations and Privileges

Banks that are members of the Federal Reserve System must also meet certain other requirements. First, they must be insured by the Federal Deposit Insurance Corporation. This comes automatically with system membership. Second, they are subject to periodic examination by the Reserve System. (Actually the Federal Reserve usually examines only state member banks, since national banks are examined by the Comptroller of the Currency.) Third, they must subscribe to the Federal Reserve bank stock. At present, a member bank must subscribe to an amount of stock equal in value to 3 percent of its own capital accounts. The Board of Governors of the Federal Reserve System may increase this requirement by as much as an additional 3 percent. Finally, member banks must maintain a certain level of reserves.

This *reserve requirement* is a *ratio* of *vault cash plus deposits at the Federal Reserve Bank* to the bank's *deposit liabilities*. The amount of reserves required to back demand-deposit liabilities at banks designated as Reserve city banks by the Federal Reserve System is now 17 percent for banks with demand-deposit liabilities less than $5 million and 17.5 percent for banks with demand-deposit liabilities in excess of $5 million. For banks designated as country banks, the reserve requirements for demand-deposit liabilities are now 12.5 percent for banks with demand-deposit liabilities less than $5 million and 13 percent for banks with demand deposits in excess of $5 million. The requirement is 3 percent for savings accounts in all member commercial banks. The reserve requirement for other time deposits is 3 percent for all banks having these deposits in amounts less than $5 million; the requirement is 6 percent where these deposits exceed $5 million.[6]

Reserve System membership carries with it certain privileges. Member banks (1) may have their checks cleared and collected free of cost by the Federal Reserve banks; (2) may obtain currency free of charge; (3) may obtain loans and advances from the Reserve banks; (4) receive a 6-percent dividend on their holdings of Reserve bank stock; and (5) participate in the selection of six of the nine directors of each district

[6] *Federal Reserve Bulletin*, July 1969, p. A-10.

Federal Reserve bank. In addition, a bank gains a certain amount of prestige merely by being a member bank.

Advantages of Nonmember Bank Status

Nonmember banks are typically small banks that either do not meet the membership requirements or do not care to become members. There are a number of reasons why a bank may not become a member. First, its capital accounts simply may be too small to meet the requirements set by the System. Second, some state banking authorities set lower reserve requirements for nonmember banks than the Federal Reserve sets for member banks. State bank reserve requirements are generally some ratio of *vault cash plus deposits at other commercial banks* (and, in some instances, plus certain types of U.S. government securities) to *deposit liabilities*. Member banks, on the other hand, are not permitted to count deposits at other commercial banks as part of their reserves. In short, nonmember banks in some states do not need to keep as large a percentage of their monetary resources idle as do member banks. This is not generally the case, however. During the 1950's and early 1960's the Board of Governors of the Federal Reserve System regularly lowered reserve requirements; state legislatures and banking authorities were somewhat dilatory in adjusting their reserve requirements to keep pace with these changes. The net effect is that in about half the states today, reserve requirements for nonmember banks are higher and more restrictive than those for member banks.

A third advantage of nonmembership is that a bank is subject to audit by one less supervisory agency than a member bank: it is not audited by the Federal Reserve.

Fourth, many nonmember banks, particularly those that remit at par, are able to obtain most of the advantages of membership, without any of its responsibilities, by maintaining checking-deposit balances with large "city correspondents" (in some instances, with a Federal Reserve bank). The correspondent banks are almost always member banks and can use the facilities of the Federal Reserve banks to clear checks, obtain currency, and arrange for loans on behalf of nonmember banks.

Finally, banks that are nonpar banks may not wish to relinquish their profitable exchange charge.

NATIONAL AND STATE BANKS

During 1968 there were 4,716 national banks, 1,262 state member banks, and 7,701 state nonmember banks. The average deposit liability of national banks at that time was $45 million, as against $17 million for state banks. As previously indicated, average deposit liabilities were $55 million for member banks and $10 million for nonmember banks.

Although one would expect deposit liabilities of state member banks to average less than those of the national banks, this is not the case. The average deposit liability of national banks in 1968 was $51 million, whereas for state member banks the figure came to $70 million.[7]

There appear to be two principal reasons for the larger size of state member banks. One concerns the prestige factor. Many small banks apparently feel that they need "national" status in order to maintain their competitive position. Small "storefront" national banks are not uncommon in small rural communities, for example. Many of these banks have held their charters since the early days of the national banking system and are now reluctant to relinquish their national status. The officers of these banks believe that a change to a state charter would cause their customers to transfer deposits to larger banks in the big city. Thus, many national banks are quite small. On the other hand, a number of very large banks feel that the advantages of a state charter outweigh the prestige factor. Some of these banks—principally the large downtown New York City banks, whose operations are international in scope—are so well known that a national charter would add little to their already high prestige.

The mid-1960's saw some increase in the number of national banks, as a result of the liberalization of rules concerning national bank operations under James Saxon as Comptroller of the Currency. The Chase Manhattan Bank, for example, became a national bank in 1965 when its directors felt that national bank rules had become more flexible than those of New York State banking authorities. National banks had the ability to sell unsecured promissory notes, to go into equipment leasing, and to act as factors (i.e., to purchase directly business accounts receivable), whereas New York State banking rules did not permit such operations.

National Bank Charter Requirements

The capital requirements for national banks vary with the size of the city in which the bank is located, as the table below shows:

POPULATION	CAPITAL REQUIREMENT
Under 6,000	$ 50,000
6,000–50,000	100,000
Over 50,000	200,000

The capital requirement for new state banks, on the other hand, is usually $25,000, although some states have larger requirements. Connecticut, for example, has a $100,000 requirement.

The four basic criteria upon which the Comptroller of the Currency and the various state banking departments rely when judging an application

[7] See Table 4–1.

for a charter are: (1) the access of the community to other banking facilities, (2) the need of the community for additional banking facilities, (3) the talent of the managers of the proposed bank, and (4) the adequacy of the proposed capital size of the bank. These considerations help the authorities determine whether or not to grant a charter.

INSURED AND NONINSURED BANKS

Almost all commercial banks in the United States are insured. In 1968 only 197 banks, just under 2 percent, were not insured by the FDIC. Their deposits totaled only 0.5 percent of all deposit liabilities.

Banks that are members of the Federal Reserve System are automatically covered by deposit insurance. Nonmember banks are insured only after examination by the FDIC, which bases its decision on (1) the financial condition of the bank, (2) its prospective earnings, (3) its managerial talent, and (4) the needs of the community. The standards for FDIC coverage are thus much the same as those for national and member bank status.

Insured banks are under certain obligations to the FDIC. They are subject to periodic FDIC examination,[8] they must secure FDIC permission before merging with another bank,[9] and they must pay an annual assessment fee.[10]

THE AMERICAN BANKING SYSTEM: TYPES OF OPERATION

Unit and Branch Banking

Most American banks operate only one office and are not controlled by any other bank or corporation. This is known as unit banking. At the end of 1968 the United States had 13,678 banks, of which 9,951 were

[8] In practice, the FDIC examines only state nonmember insured banks. The Comptroller of the Currency and the Federal Reserve bank authorities examine all member banks and the FDIC simply reviews these reports.

[9] If the resulting bank is to be national, permission for a merger must be obtained from the Comptroller of the Currency. If the new bank is to be a state member bank, the Board of Governors of the Federal Reserve must give its approval. If the bank is to be a nonmember insured bank, the FDIC must give its consent. Notice that the approving agency in the case of consolidation is the same as the examining agency for each class of bank.

[10] The assessment rate is $\frac{1}{12}$ of 1 percent. This rate is assessed against the average of deposits less $16\frac{2}{3}$ percent of demand deposits and 1 percent of time deposits. Actually, the amount paid by the banks does not equal this rate. After deducting its expenses and losses from the total amount due according to the assessment rate, the FDIC credits two-thirds of what is left to the insured banks. The total amount collected from deposit-insurance assessments from 1933, when the FDIC was created, through 1968 amounted to only $2.54 billion, while deposit-insurance losses were even less, $55.2 million. (Federal Deposit Insurance Corporation, *Annual Report*, [1968], p. 28.)

unit banks and 3,727 were banks operating a total of 19,013 branches.[11] In contrast, foreign banks have developed extensive systems of multiple banking offices.

Historically, the American tradition of free enterprise has tended to encourage the establishment of many small banks. In addition, underpopulation was for a long time a fact in the United States. The great distances between population centers, the difficulty of travel and communication, and the primarily agrarian nature of the economy all tended to foster the development of unit banks—locally owned, operated, and controlled. By 1921, for example, there were 31,076 banks operating only 1,455 branches.[12] The large-scale bank failures of the twenties and thirties demonstrated all too clearly, however, that there were too many small and inefficient banks. Because of this "overbanking," state and national authorities made it more difficult to set up a new bank. Today, banking is a "free" field for entrepreneurs only to the extent that the authorities believe we need additional banks. To receive a charter, a new bank should prove that need for its services exists and that it is able to meet that need. For this reason there has been relative stability in the total number of banks during the last 30 years. The small decline that has occurred is a result of the fact that recently there have been more mergers than newly chartered banks. Many of these mergers are the result of FDIC efforts to have small, inefficient bank operations taken over by larger banks.

With an expanding economy, a need arises for more banking facilities. This has been met, in recent years, not through the establishment of larger numbers of new banks, but through the establishment of an increasing number of branches by existing banks. Branch banks are thought to be able to meet the needs of the community better than unit banks because of the greater financial resources at their disposal. Our statutes, however, continue to encourage unit banking and discourage other forms of banking operations. In addition, the Supreme Court has ruled that bank mergers are subject to the antitrust laws.[13]

Table 4–2 summarizes the present status of unit and branch banking in the United States on a state-by-state basis. Here we see that in over one-third of the states, those having approximately 25 percent of all bank assets, unit banking is still dominant. In those states with extensive branch banking systems, we find that expansion is severely limited. Almost one-third of the states, for example, permit a bank to establish a branch only within its home-office county, or at best in a contiguous county.

These restrictions apply to national as well as to state banks. United States banks are "national" only in the sense that they have a charter from the Comptroller of the Currency. They are still allowed to operate only

[11] See Table 4–2.
[12] Federal Deposit Insurance Corporation, *Annual Report* (1960), p. 29.
[13] *United States* v. *The Philadelphia National Bank et al.,* 374 U.S. 321 (1963).

TABLE 4–2. UNIT AND BRANCH BANKING
IN THE UNITED STATES, DECEMBER 31, 1968*

STATE AND TYPE OF BANKING OPERATION	NUMBER OF BANKING OFFICES	NUMBER OF UNIT BANKS	NUMBER OF BANKS WITH BRANCHES	NUMBER OF BRANCHES
States permitting statewide branch banking				
Alaska	67	4	8	55
Arizona	291	6	7	278
California	2,955	32	130	2,793
Connecticut	441	21	45	375
Delaware	97	10	9	78
District of Columbia	114	1	13	100
Hawaii	134	3	8	123
Idaho	168	12	14	142
Maryland	591	50	72	469
Nevada	87	2	7	78
North Carolina	1,051	46	75	930
Oregon	357	22	28	307
Rhode Island	171	—	13	158
South Carolina	469	51	67	351
Utah	169	35	19	115
Vermont	116	22	23	71
Washington	581	46	48	487
States permitting branch banking within limited areas				
Countrywide				
Indiana	991	227	188	576
Kentucky	632	221	125	286
Louisiana	558	115	114	329
Massachusetts	841	38	120	633
Michigan	1,439	145	193	1,101
New Jersey	1,026	55	174	797
New Mexico	177	20	43	114
Ohio	1,655	264	261	1,130
Tennessee	720	172	131	417
Other				
Alabama	504	191	77	236
Georgia	676	340	88	248
Maine	243	10	33	200
Mississippi	481	83	102	296
New York	2,533	139	180	2,214
Pennsylvania	2,028	270	239	1,519
Virginia	946	88	149	709
States where unit banking is prevalent				
With limited branch banking				
Arkansas	389	176	72	141
Iowa	955	463	210	282
Kansas	662	542	59	61
North Dakota	238	119	50	69
Oklahoma	479	372	52	55
South Dakota	256	126	39	91
Wisconsin	826	463	140	223

TABLE 4-2 (*Continued*)

STATE AND TYPE OF BANKING OPERATION	NUMBER OF BANKING OFFICES	NUMBER OF UNIT BANKS	NUMBER OF BANKS WITH BRANCHES	NUMBER OF BRANCHES
Without branch banking†				
Colorado	257	248	9	10
Florida	486	438	23	25
Illinois	1,119	1,031	43	45
Minnesota	733	717	6	10
Missouri	752	582	85	85
Montana	140	130	5	5
Nebraska	478	405	36	37
New Hampshire	118	47	30	41
Texas	1,214	1,091	60	63
West Virginia	199	191	4	4
Wyoming	71	69	1	1
United States (total)	32,691	9,951	3,727	19,013

* These figures include commercial banks and nondeposit trust companies.
† The few branches in these states were established prior to existing prohibiting legislation or under unusual circumstances.
SOURCE: Federal Deposit Insurance Corporation, *Annual Report* (1968), pp. 170–77.

within the confines of a state. No bank is permitted to establish branches outside the state in which its home office is located,[14] and under present regulations, a national bank is allowed to establish branches only to the extent permitted by the statutes of the state where it is located.

Even when a state does permit extensive branch banking, a national bank is not authorized to establish an unlimited number of offices. It must file an application with the Comptroller of the Currency for permission to establish each branch. When an application is presented, it is studied with a view not only to the need for the branch, but also to the potential effects on bank competition and concentration. Not every branch application is approved. During 1967, for example, some 1,012 applications were filed with the Comptroller of the Currency. Of these, only 438 were approved; 254 were rejected and 61 were withdrawn. The remaining 16 were still in process at the end of the year.[15]

Why do we impose these restrictions on branch banking? Why does state law apparently favor unit banking? Tradition is part of the answer, but part of the answer also lies in the fact that many state legislatures are still dominated by the rural sectors of their states.[16] Legislatures of this type are concerned with "home rule" and fear a shift of political power to the urban centers. They are reluctant to permit an expansion of branch banking

[14] This restriction, however, does not apply to the setting up of branches in U.S. territories and foreign countries.
[15] Comptroller of the Currency, *Annual Report* (1967), p. 11.
[16] The recent Supreme Court decision concerning legislative reapportionment may well cause this situation to change.

because they fear that the big banks in the urban areas would set up branches. Thus the competitive position of the country bank would be lessened, and economic as well as political power would be transferred to the city.

Arguments for and against Branch Banking

A number of arguments may be advanced against branch banking. One has already been mentioned: branch banking leads to a concentration of economic power and lessens competition. The following arguments are also frequently cited: first, branch banks draw funds away from local areas and channel them to the big cities. Second, the unit bank can make loan decisions more quickly, since the branch manager must consult the home office before making a loan over a certain size. Third, the unit bank is best equipped to make correct loan and investment decisions because its managers are more aware of local conditions. Branch managers frequently come from out of town and do not have a "feel" for the community and its problems. Finally, the unit bank is able to meet almost any legitimate financial need of the local business community through its correspondent arrangements with large city banks.

Proponents of branch banking, on the other hand, counter with these arguments: first, the competitive position of large banks has, if anything, worsened in recent years. With the movement of the population to the suburbs, banks in outlying areas have grown more rapidly than large city banks, even those with branches. The city banks have often been prevented from expanding into suburban districts by the restrictive prohibitions against branch banking. As a result, banks in these areas are not faced with competition. This monopoly of banking power increases with the distance from competing financial centers and is particularly strong in "one-bank" communities. Banks in these areas frequently charge more for loans and pay less interest than banks in areas where alternative banking facilities are available.

Second, those in favor of branch banking argue that the unit bank is frequently too small to handle the large borrower. Nor can it provide skilled banking services such as investment counseling, which the branch bank can provide through its contact with the home office.

Third, a large branch bank is usually financially sounder and more efficiently managed than a unit bank. Most bank mergers in recent years have been between large banks and small, weak banks. Most of the smaller banks were unit banks. For example, in 1968, 130 banks having resources of $2.2 billion were absorbed by 119 banks having resources of $42.0 billion. Prior to the transaction, the number of offices operated by the absorbing banks was 2,890. The absorbed banks had operated a total of 284 offices. After absorption, 3,168 were in operation, some six offices having been discontinued.[17]

Finally, when a branch needs funds, it is able to acquire them through the home office from branches that have a surplus. Hence a branch may immediately draw upon the resources of the whole bank. Unit banks, on the other hand, may be embarrassed by a shortage of loan funds.

Certainly there are valid points on each side in this controversy. The unit bank probably does know the needs of the community best and through its correspondents is able to provide almost as many services as a large branch bank. On the other hand, it tends to be monopolistic where there is a lack of competing bank facilities. The large bank and its branches, in competition with other large banks and their branches, do provide a greater variety of services. In addition, they charge relatively low interest rates on loans and pay close to the maximum interest allowed on deposits. Recent economic research tends to support the view that branch banking enhances rather than lessens competition. For example, one study

. . . suggests that neither in terms of number of competitors, nor concentration (measures of actual competition), nor in terms of the condition of entry (potential competition) have the structures of local banking markets been adversely affected by branch banking in the United States. The weight of evidence suggests that, to the contrary, market structures are adversely affected by restrictions on branch banking.[18]

Chain Banking

Chain banking is a term used to describe the association of a number of commercial banks through an interlocking directorate. It is not an important feature of American banking. Each bank in a chain is counted as a separate bank; some may operate branches. Control over the chain is exercised by an individual or a group of individuals who own stock in or are directors of the separate banks in the chain. This type of banking originated in the 1880's in the South and central Northwest and it reached the peak of its popularity around 1920. Since then it has declined markedly, primarily because individual control has tended to give way to corporate control.

Group Banking

Group banking usually exists in one of two forms. In one, a nonbanking corporation, sometimes called a bancorporation, owns the stock of the constituent banks and acts as the controlling agency. In the other, one bank controls the stock of the other banks in the group. Both of these are hold-

[17] Federal Deposit Insurance Corporation, *Annual Report* (1968), p. 19.
[18] Bernard Shullin and Paul M. Horvitz, "Branch Banking and the Structure of Competition," *The National Banking Review*, March 1964, p. 341.

ing company arrangements. Each bank in a group is counted as a separate bank; some even operate branches.[19]

As a whole, bank holding company groups are not very important in American banking. As of December 31, 1968, there were 80 registered bank holding companies operating 629 banks and 2,262 branches. These groups accounted for 8.9 percent of all bank offices and held 13.2 percent of all deposits in the United States.[20] There has been no relative growth of bank holding companies since the 1920's; if anything, there has been a decline since 1936, when group banks operated 7 percent of the offices and controlled 14 percent of all deposits. This decline is surprising, since the holding company device has certain advantages over branch banking as a form of expansion. It can be used to establish systems that cross city, country, and even state lines. (This is the only way that banks are able to cross state lines.) Despite this advantage, holding companies have not increased in number for the following reasons: first, the liberalization of branch banking laws in some states has led some banking groups to convert into branch bank systems. Second, in 1938 President Roosevelt publicly advocated the abolition of bank holding companies. This proposal placed the status of group banking in a position of uncertainty, which did not end until the passage of the Bank Holding Company Act of 1956. During the intervening 18 years, unit-banking interests waged an extensive campaign against group banking.

The arguments for and against group banking are similar to those for and against branch banking. It has been contended on one side that group banking concentrates banking power, decreases competition, and is neither concerned nor able to cope with the problems of the small financial centers. On the other side, it is argued that the bank holding company can increase competition and is a sounder financial institution than the unit bank.

Group banking, like branch banking, has encountered some restrictive legislation. According to the provisions of the Bank Holding Company Act of 1956, all bank holding companies controlling two or more banks (1) must register with the Board of Governors of the Federal Reserve System, (2) must obtain the permission of the Board prior to the purchase of additional bank voting stock, and (3) can hold no stock in subsidiaries that are not engaged in banking.

The one-bank holding company. One frequently neglected aspect of bank holding company structure is the one-bank holding company which is unregistered and is not subject to the provisions of the Bank Holding Company Act of 1956. Many of these holding companies are small; others are large, but the bank whose stock is controlled by the holding company

[19] This means that single banks in a unit will be counted as unit banks, while those operating branches will be counted as branch banks. Our methods of counting banks, therefore, fail to distinguish clearly between unit, branch, and group banking.
[20] *Federal Reserve Bulletin*, August 1969, p. A–96.

is a minor part of its activity. A development of the late 1960's, however, is the holding company formed by the bank itself, with the bank being the principal affiliate of the organization. The other subsidiary companies are not banks, but frequently are financial in nature. Insurance companies and factors (companies that purchase the accounts receivable of other firms) are examples of firms that may be part of a one-bank holding company. The purpose of such a corporate structure is to permit commercial banks to diversify their operations.

While these holding companies are not subject to the provisions of the Holding Company Act of 1956, nevertheless, their constituent components are subject to the regulations of various regulatory agencies. For example, national bank affiliates are still subject to examination by the Comptroller of the Currency and the regulations of the FDIC and the Federal Reserve.

Correspondent Banking

A correspondent bank is one that maintains checking-deposit accounts for other, usually smaller, customer banks. These deposits are called interbank deposits. As of March 26, 1969, there was $20.9 billion in interbank deposits, $19.9 and $1.0 billion of this amount respectively in demand and time deposits.[21]

Maintaining these accounts benefits both the correspondent and customer banks. To the correspondent bank the deposit is a source of funds like any other new deposit; thus, when a small bank with excess funds makes a new interbank deposit of $1,000, the T-account entries would look as follows:

BALANCE-SHEET CHANGES FOR A LARGE MEMBER BANK

ASSETS		LIABILITIES + CAPITAL ACCOUNTS	
Cash assets	+$1,000	Interbank deposits	+$1,000

The large bank, on the basis of increased cash assets, is now in a position to extend its loans and deposits.[22] The total cash assets of the small bank, however, remain unchanged. To the small bank a deposit with a correspondent bank is as good as cash, since it is subject to call on demand.

Small banks maintain these deposit balances because of the variety of services provided by the larger banks. Among these are (1) the clearing and collection of checks for both member and nonmember banks, (2) security analysis, (3) the handling of bond and security purchases, (4) currency shipments, (5) participation in loans that the small banks cannot handle alone, (6) the making of loans to customer banks, and (7)

---

[21] *Federal Reserve Bulletin,* April 1969, p. A–19.
[22] See Chapter 7 for a more complete account of deposit creation.

the providing of foreign monies (exchange) so that the customers of small banks may buy and sell abroad.

Supplementary Readings

The Administrator of National Banks, United States Treasury, *Studies in Banking Competition and the Banking Structure.* Articles reprinted from the *National Banking Review,* Washington, D.C., 1966.

Alhadeff, David A. *Monopoly and Competition in Banking.* Berkeley, Calif.: Univ. of California Press, 1954.

Commission on Money and Credit. *Money and Credit: Their Influence on Jobs, Prices, and Growth.* Englewood Cliffs, N.J.: Prentice-Hall, 1961, Chapter 6.

Nadler, Marcus, and J. I. Bogen. *The Bank Holding Company.* New York: New York Univ. Graduate School of Business Administration, 1959.

Wallace, Richard. "Non-Par Banking in Georgia," *Southern Journal of Business* (1968), pp. 176–86.

CHAPTER 5

Commercial Bank Sources of Funds

Preceding chapters examined the structure of commercial banking and the relative importance of the financial community to the U.S. economy. We have seen that commercial banks differ from other members of the financial community in their unique ability to create and destroy money. In Chapter 7 we will examine this peculiar money-creating ability of the commercial banking system in some detail. In Chapters 5 and 6 we shall study commercial bank operations as they are summarized on a bank balance sheet. The focus is upon the sources and uses of commercial bank funds. What are the sources of funds? To what uses do banks put these funds? Are they invested in securities, loans, or real estate, or are they merely held idle in the form of cash? What do the differing sources and uses of funds mean for the national economy and for bank earnings and operations? These are some of the questions that will concern us in these chapters.

THE BALANCE SHEET FOR A
REPRESENTATIVE COMMERCIAL BANK

The balance sheet of a commercial bank shows its financial position at a moment of time. Table 5–1 gives a simplified, hypothetical balance sheet for a typical commercial bank.

TABLE **5–1.** BALANCE SHEET FOR A TYPICAL
COMMERCIAL BANK

ASSETS		LIABILITIES + CAPITAL ACCOUNTS	
Cash assets	$1,000,000	Demand deposits	$3,500,000
Securities	2,000,000	Time deposits	1,900,000
Loans and discounts	3,000,000	Miscellaneous liabilities	200,000
Miscellaneous assets	100,000	Capital accounts	500,000
Total	$6,100,000	Total	$6,100,000

The *asset* side of the balance sheet shows what the bank owns, that is, the uses to which it has put its funds. Here we see that the bank has $1 million in *cash assets,* which consist of cash in the bank's vaults and demand deposits maintained with other banks. They are idle assets, for they do not enhance the bank's earning powers and are kept on hand primarily to enable the bank to meet reserve requirements and the cash demands of depositors.

Almost one-third of our typical bank's assets are in the form of *security holdings,* primarily U.S. government securities. In addition, banks hold substantial quantities of state and local government securities. Relatively small quantities of privately issued stocks and bonds are held. Government securities are viewed by banks as secondary reserves, since they are easily marketable and can be converted to cash quickly to meet depositor demands.

The largest category of assets for our bank is *loans and discounts,* composed primarily of real estate loans, business loans, and loans to individuals. This is the most profitable and the most important use to which commercial banks can put their funds and is the principal source of their earnings.

Miscellaneous assets is a catchall category representing all non-income-yielding assets, such as the book value of the bank's premises, furniture, and fixtures.

Claims of creditors to the assets of a bank are termed *liabilities;* residual claims of stockholders, on the other hand, are termed *capital accounts.* Both liabilities and capital accounts are sources of funds. As they increase, banks are provided with the funds that enable them to acquire earning assets.

We have said that *demand deposits* are claims upon the commercial bank that may be transferred on demand by the use of checks. The owners of these checking-deposit accounts are the depositors. As our balance sheet shows, demand-deposit liabilities are almost always the largest category of liabilities. Because any amount of these liabilities may be demanded in cash, by depositors at any given time, commercial banks must maintain assets that can be quickly liquidated to meet the current demand. Cash assets and U.S. government securities usually perform this function.

The other form of deposits on our hypothetical balance sheet is *time deposits,* which amount to $1.9 million, or almost one-third of all liabilities and capital accounts. Time deposits, unlike demand deposits, are not legally subject to call upon demand. Banks may require up to 30 days' notice prior to withdrawal. Nevertheless, time deposits are used as a method of holding idle funds since they yield interest to the depositors. They are an important source of funds to commercial banks because they are not asked to redeem time deposits as often as demand deposits. Thus, to cover time deposits banks need not maintain idle cash reserves as large as those covering demand deposits.

Miscellaneous liabilities consist mainly of rediscounts and borrowings. A *rediscount* refers to money that a bank has raised by selling assets, such as loans to other banks. It is treated as a liability because the bank is liable for the note in the event of default by the borrower. *Borrowings* arise when banks borrow funds, principally from the Federal Reserve banks. Rediscounts and borrowings are discussed in more detail in Chapter 12.

Capital accounts, the last items on the bank's balance sheet, consist of cash surplus and the par value of the bank's common and preferred stock. Most of the surplus is created when the bank makes profits on its loans and investments.

LIABILITIES AND CAPITAL ACCOUNTS

We began our discussion of commercial-bank operations with the balance sheet because it serves as a convenient outline of the more detailed discussion that follows. We shall examine the right-hand side of the balance sheet in the remainder of this chapter. First, we shall see how liabilities and capital accounts provide funds for the commercial bank. Second, we shall examine the composition and size of the banking system's sources of funds. And third, we shall consider how certain changes in these sources of funds might affect the national economy. We shall reserve a more detailed discussion of assets for Chapter 6.

How Liabilities and Capital Accounts Provide Funds

When a commercial bank accepts deposits, sells stock, or borrows funds from other banking institutions, it is provided with funds that it can use to expand its holdings of earning assets. For example, when an individual deposits $1,000 in cash into either his checking- or savings-deposit account, the bank acquires an asset, $1,000 in cash, and also a liability, since it is liable to the depositor for the amount of his deposit. The T-account entries for this transaction are

BALANCE-SHEET CHANGES FOR COMMERCIAL BANK A

ASSETS		LIABILITIES + CAPITAL ACCOUNTS	
Reserves (vault cash)	+$1,000	Deposits	+$1,000

The asset entry is recorded as an increase in reserves rather than in vault cash because vault cash is usually part of a bank's reserves. If the depositor deposits a check drawn on some other bank, the T-account entries remain the same, because once the checks written on other banks are collected, the reserves of Bank A will increase, while the banks on which the checks were drawn will experience a decrease in reserves.

Very much the same thing occurs when a bank sells stock. If it sells stock for cash, reserves are increased as is common stock under capital accounts. The entries for such a transaction are

BALANCE-SHEET CHANGES FOR COMMERCIAL BANK A

ASSETS		LIABILITIES + CAPITAL ACCOUNTS	
Reserves	+$1,000	Common stock	+$1,000

Likewise, if the stock is paid for with checks drawn on other commercial banks, both reserves and common stock increase by $1,000.[1] Other banks, of course, are faced with a decrease in reserves. *The reserves that the acquiring bank receives provide it with the basis for an expansion of its earning assets.*

A bank, however, will sometimes not receive cash or deposits drawn on other banks when it sells stock. This occurs when a bank's own depositors purchase stock. A bank frequently attempts to induce its depositors to become stockholders. Although this does not provide the bank with additional funds, its lending ability is enhanced nevertheless! Assume that a depositor of Bank A purchases $1,000 in Bank A stock by drawing $1,000 from his checking-deposit account. The T-account entries are

BALANCE-SHEET CHANGES FOR COMMERCIAL BANK A

ASSETS	LIABILITIES + CAPITAL ACCOUNTS	
	Demand deposits	−$1,000
	Common stock	+$1,000

Note that no change has occurred in assets. The bank has not acquired funds through the sale of stock. Nevertheless, its lending ability has increased because its deposit liabilities have decreased. A commercial bank must maintain reserves, as we have seen, to cover its demand-deposit liabilities. If demand deposits decrease, the bank will have more reserves relative to demand-deposit liabilities than formerly and may, accordingly, grant new loans and create new deposits.

Commercial banks also obtain funds by borrowing from other banks. A common source of borrowings is the Federal Reserve System. Thus, if a bank wants to increase its lending operations or feels that it is short of funds, it may borrow from its district Federal Reserve bank. The T-account entries for such a transaction are

[1] If it happens that the stock is sold for more than its par value, common stock increases by $1,000, and surplus increases by the difference between the amount received by the bank and the par value of the stock; reserves will increase by the amount of the proceeds from the sale of the stock. On the other hand, if the stock sells for less than its par value, surplus will be reduced by the amount that the par value exceeds the receipts from the sale of the stock, and common stock will be increased by the par value of the stock; reserves will again increase by the amount received from the stock sale.

BALANCE-SHEET CHANGES FOR COMMERCIAL BANK A

ASSETS		LIABILITIES + CAPITAL ACCOUNTS	
Reserves	+$1,000	Borrowings	+$1,000

Commercial banks and other business institutions differ in their use of funds. When a nonbanking business enterprise receives additional money from operations, from sales of stock, or from outside lenders, it is likely to spend this money sooner or later to acquire income-producing assets. If the money is used to purchase a $50,000 machine, this increase in the company's income-producing assets is accompanied by an equal decrease in its cash holdings. The balance sheet changes are recorded in items (a) and (b):

BALANCE-SHEET CHANGES FOR COMPANY A

ASSETS		LIABILITIES + CAPITAL ACCOUNTS
Cash	−$50,000 (a)	
Plant and equipment	+$50,000 (b)	
Cash	−$50,000 (c)	
Loans	+$50,000 (d)	

If Company A were to extend a $50,000 loan to some other business, there would normally be an equal and offsetting increase and decrease in the corresponding asset items also. This is illustrated by the changes in (c) and (d) in the balance sheet above.

When a commercial bank receives additional funds from new deposits, borrowings, or sales of stock, however, it does not use its cash increase directly to make loans and investments. As mentioned previously, when a commercial bank grants a loan, it acquires an asset—an interest-earning loan—and it creates a demand-deposit liability for its customer. For Bank A, the entries would be

BALANCE-SHEET CHANGES FOR COMMERCIAL BANK A

ASSETS		LIABILITIES + CAPITAL ACCOUNTS	
Loans	+$50,000	Demand deposits	+$50,000

An increase in demand deposit liabilities necessitates an increase in bank reserves to back these additional liabilities. Consequently, banks add additional incoming funds to reserves, instead of lending them or investing them directly. When the bank has more reserves than it needs to meet its legal reserve requirement (see Chapters 4 and 7), it may then expand its loans by the amount permitted by its excess reserves.

Most borrowers find demand deposits more convenient than cash for all but very small amounts. When cash loans are made, however, the bank uses its vault cash reserves directly. Thus, in this case, reserves will decline by an amount equal to the loan.

Generally a bank should not expand its loans and create new deposits beyond an amount equal to its excess reserves. A fuller discussion of excess reserves is found in Chapter 7, but for the present we may define *excess reserves as the amount by which the reserves of a bank exceed what it legally must have to back its outstanding deposit liabilities.*

This general rule is important. When a commercial bank lends and creates deposits, it cannot expect its borrowers to do business only with those firms and individuals that maintain accounts with it. If Individual 1 borrows $1,000 from Bank A, he is quite likely to use the money to purchase goods or services from Individual 2, who maintains deposit balances with another bank, Bank B. Hence, when Individual 1 writes checks, those checks will find their way into the deposit accounts of Individual 2, increasing the reserves of Bank B, while Bank A loses reserves. The appropriate T-account entries are

BALANCE-SHEET CHANGES FOR COMMERCIAL BANK A

ASSETS		LIABILITIES + CAPITAL ACCOUNTS	
Loans	+$1,000 (a)	Demand deposits of Individual 1	+$1,000 (a)
Reserves	−$1,000 (b)	Demand deposits of Individual 1	−$1,000 (b)

BALANCE-SHEET CHANGES FOR COMMERCIAL BANK B

ASSETS		LIABILITIES + CAPITAL ACCOUNTS	
Reserves	+$1,000 (b)	Demand deposits of Individual 2	+$1,000 (b)

Entries labeled (a) show the results of Bank A's loan to Individual 1. Entries labeled (b) show the effects of Individual 1's purchase of $1,000 worth of goods and services from Individual 2, who deposits the check in his account with Bank B. Bank B in turn collects from Bank A, and the checking account of Individual 1 is decreased.

If Bank A had had only $500 in excess reserves, it would now be $500 short of its legal reserve requirement. It probably would be forced to reduce its loans or borrow additional reserves from a Federal Reserve bank. Either alternative is costly, however, since the Federal Reserve banks charge for borrowed reserves and since fewer loans mean less income.

We can see, therefore, that a commercial bank should expect to lose reserves to other banks when it makes a loan. Hence, it should expand loans and investments only by an amount equal to its excess reserves. Thus an increase in funds that increases excess reserves indirectly permits the bank to expand its loans and investments. A stable volume of funds means that the bank should maintain about the same volume of loans and investments, since continuous repayment of outstanding loans enables it to make new loans even though it is not receiving additional excess reserves.

There appears to be a paradox in this line of reasoning, however. Demand-deposit liabilities of a commercial bank have been described as *a source of funds.* While it is true that deposits of checks drawn on other banks or deposits of cash provide funds that enable a bank to make loans and create additional demand deposits, these additional deposits are *not* sources of funds. Only a *primary deposit,* a deposit that increases the bank's holding of reserves, provides a bank with additional funds. Deposits created when a bank makes loans are called *derivative deposits.* Derivative deposits can become sources of funds only when they are used and thus increase the reserves and deposits of some other bank. Such a case was described in the last T-account illustration under entry (b).

Composition and Size of Bank Sources of Funds

Table 5–2 shows that demand deposits are the chief source of bank funds. They comprise 45.9 percent of all liabilities and capital accounts. Time deposits are the second largest source of funds, accounting for

TABLE **5–2.** COMMERCIAL BANK LIABILITIES AND
CAPITAL ACCOUNTS, DECEMBER 31, 1968

TYPE OF LIABILITY OR CAPITAL ACCOUNT	AMOUNT (IN MILLIONS OF DOLLARS)	PERCENT OF TOTAL
Demand deposits		
Interbank		
Domestic	22,501	
Foreign	2,245	
U.S. government	5,010	
State and local government	16,876	
Certified and officers' checks, etc.	9,684	
Individuals, partnerships, and corporations	173,341	
Total	229,657	45.9
Time deposits		
Interbank	1,211	
U.S. government and Postal Savings	368	
State and local government	19,110	
Individuals, partnerships, and corporations	184,892	
Total	205,581	41.1
Borrowings	8,899	1.8
Other liabilities	19,514	3.9
Capital accounts	37,006	7.3
Total liabilities and capital accounts	500,657	100.0

SOURCE: *Federal Reserve Bulletin,* July 1969, pp. A–19 and A–25.

41.1 percent of liabilities and capital accounts. Only 7.3 percent of the total are in the form of capital accounts.

Individuals, partnerships, and corporations, the federal government, state and local governments, and American and foreign banks all own demand deposits in U.S. banks. More than 75 percent of these deposits are held by individuals, partnerships, and corporations. This group also owns over 90 percent of all time deposits. The federal government and domestic commercial banks keep almost all their funds in the form of demand deposits. State and local governments and foreign banks, on the other hand, maintain substantial amounts in time deposits, principally for the purpose of earning interest.

Demand deposits. The demand deposits owned by individuals, businesses, and state and local governments are usually held for transaction purposes, that is, in order to have money readily available for the purchase of goods and services. Deposits held at commercial banks by the federal government, on the other hand, are not used to purchase goods and services; the Treasury uses its balances with the Federal Reserve banks for this purpose.

The Treasury's deposit balances at commercial banks are called *Tax and Loan Accounts.* These balances normally increase as commercial banks sell U.S. government savings bonds, as they purchase new issues of government securities, and as employers make social security and income-withholding payments. The purpose of these accounts is to help banks avoid the reserve losses that would otherwise occur when the private sector of the economy makes payments to the government.

Tax and Loan Accounts decrease when the Treasury orders the commercial banks to transfer a portion of the accumulated deposits to the U.S. government balances with the Federal Reserve banks. This is reflected on the balance sheets as follows:

BALANCE-SHEET CHANGES FOR THE
COMMERCIAL BANKING SYSTEM

ASSETS		LIABILITIES + CAPITAL ACCOUNTS	
Reserves	−$1,000,000	U.S. government demand deposits	−$1,000,000

BALANCE-SHEET CHANGES FOR THE FEDERAL RESERVE BANKS

ASSETS	LIABILITIES + CAPITAL ACCOUNTS	
	Deposits	
	Member bank reserves	−$1,000,000
	U.S. government general account	+$1,000,000

The Treasury orders this type of decrease in its balances at commercial banks when the government needs money to meet its obligations. This is generally done at regular intervals. As the T-account entries show, banks lose reserves when the Treasury balances are transferred to the Federal Reserve banks. As the Treasury spends funds, however, bank reserves are built up again. In the meantime, to offset possible adverse economic repercussions of this decrease in reserves, the Federal Open Market Committee will usually see to it that banks are provided with additional reserves from other sources. (More will be said of this in Chapter 13.)

Interbank demand deposits, as indicated in Chapter 4, are maintained at large banks by small banks in return for a variety of services. The interbank deposits are important as a source of funds for the large banks—as these deposits increase, so do reserves.[2]

Time deposits. Time deposits, which constitute the second most important source of funds for commercial banks, have increased in significance in recent years. Adjusted demand deposits increased from $92.3 billion at the end of 1950 to $167.1 billion at the end of 1968, an increase of almost 80 percent. In that period, however, all commercial bank time deposits increased from $36.3 to $205.6 billion—over 400 percent.[3] The increased interest yield now allowed by the Federal Reserve is one significant reason for this growth of time deposits. The yield on these deposits has increased relative to yields on financial assets created by other financial institutions, thus making them more attractive as a savings form. As a consequence, more time deposits are demanded—more time deposits are purchased and fewer other liquid assets. The maximum interest rate payable on time deposits from 1936 to 1957 was 2.5 percent. This was raised to 3 percent in 1957 and to 4 percent in 1962. A $15 billion increase in time deposits occurred after the limit was raised in early 1962.[4] More recently, the Federal Reserve has used what is called "Regulation Q" to change the interest rates payable on time deposits.[5] These later changes, in 1963, 1964, 1965, 1966 (two changes), and 1968, have been closely connected with Federal Reserve implementation of monetary policy. (A full discussion of these changes will be found in Chapter 13.) Another reason for the increase in time deposits is that commercial banks are more actively

---

[2] It should be noted that interbank demand deposits are excluded from the data on the money stock in Table 2–1.

[3] *Federal Reserve Bulletin,* April 1969, p. A–25. Adjusted demand deposits include all demand deposits other than interbank and U.S. government, less cash items in process of collection. Commercial bank time deposits include all commercial bank time deposits other than interbank and Treasurer's open account deposits and those of the Postal Savings System.

[4] *Federal Reserve Bulletin,* June 1964, pp. 729 and 735.

[5] Under the provisions of Regulation Q, the Board of Governors sets the maximum interest rates payable on savings deposits and other time deposits.

working to acquire these sources of funds. Reserve requirements on time deposits are lower than those for demand deposits. Consequently, for every new deposit going into time deposits rather than checking deposits, the bank is able to create a substantially greater amount of loans and demand deposits.

What form do time deposits take? Principally three: savings deposits, certificates of deposit, and open-account time deposits. Of these, *savings deposits* are the most familiar. These accounts are held mainly by individuals. They are payable upon presentation of a passbook and are usually paid on demand. Few banks enforce the legal 30-day waiting period.

Businesses may not hold savings deposits, but they may invest idle funds in time certificates of deposit or in open-account time deposits. *Certificates of deposit* (CD's) are for a fixed amount and are issued in both single and multiple maturities. They may or may not be negotiable. CD's are offered by banks to both their corporate and noncorporate customers. They have become increasingly important since 1961, when large money-market banks in New York City began to offer them in readily marketable form. Until the mid-1960's, business enterprises were the principal purchasers of these certificates. Since that time the number of individual purchasers has grown appreciably because of the increased yield on these securities relative to liquid assets created by other financial institutions. It is interesting to note that the yield on certificates of deposit has even increased relative to the yield on savings accounts. As a result, commercial bank CD liabilities have increased relative to savings accounts.

Open-account time deposits are similar to time certificates of deposit in that payment will not be made by the bank until some specific date. On the other hand, open-account deposits are not for a fixed amount; they may be increased.

Borrowings. Borrowings, as previously indicated, are liabilities that a bank incurs when it borrows funds from the Federal Reserve district banks or other commercial banks. Borrowings usually take place when banks are temporarily deficient in reserves or wish to expand earning assets. Only 1.8 percent of bank liabilities and capital accounts are in this form.

Borrowing funds from other commercial banks is called trading in the *federal funds market.* "The federal funds market refers to the borrowing and lending of a special kind of money—deposit balances in the Federal Reserve Banks—at a specified rate of interest." [6]

Banks that are short of reserves will borrow funds—generally for very short periods such as a single day—from banks with excess reserves. Since excess reserves yield no income, banks are willing to lend them for a short time at a positive yield. The federal funds market has become increasingly important since the late 1950's. Aside from 1960–63, this has

---

[6] Board of Governors of the Federal Reserve System, *The Federal Funds Market— A Study by a Federal Reserve System Committee* (Washington, D.C.: 1959), p. 1.

been a period of generally high employment, calling for some credit restraint. The use of monetary controls to restrict the reserves available to the banking system forces a more efficient use of existing reserves and thus encourages borrowing in the federal funds market. Trading in federal funds was formerly limited to very large banks, with the amounts involved in excess of $1 million. Recently, however, small banks have become active in the market.

Capital accounts. Capital accounts consist of the sum of a bank's surplus and the par value of its stock. Surplus usually includes capital surplus, undistributed profits, and reserves. Capital stock increases when a bank issues new stock. Capital surplus changes when a bank receives more or less than par value from the proceeds of the sale of newly issued stock. Undistributed profits are profits remaining after dividend payments have been made. They increase when profits on bank operations are not entirely distributed to stockholders and decrease when there are operational losses. Banks frequently reduce the size of undistributed profits by setting up reserves. Actually, this involves no transfer of cash or setting aside of funds. The reserve account is merely a segregation of undistributed profits designed to reduce stockholder claims to these profits.

As mentioned earlier in the chapter, the total of capital accounts is simply a measure of the claims of stockholders to the assets of the bank. Thus, accounts such as capital surplus and undistributed profits are claims to bank assets. The bank does not segregate any of its cash assets for the purpose of distributing them to stockholders. If the bank has earnings, it is highly probable that it will reinvest the funds in income-producing assets such as loans or securities. Consequently there is no cash surplus that can be used to pay stockholders' dividends. Profitable banks generally do pay dividends, however, but the total of dividends does not equal the total of profits.

The relative importance of capital accounts as a source of funds has remained approximately the same in recent years. The ratio of capital accounts to assets increased only from 5.5 percent in 1945 to about 8 percent in the 1960's. While their relative importance remained at about the same level during the 1960's, the total value of capital accounts increased along with the total growth in commercial bank assets. Most of the absolute increase in commercial bank capital accounts is accounted for by a rise in retained profits rather than by any significant increase in common stock outstanding. Common stock today constitutes approximately 25 percent of total commercial bank capital accounts.[7]

There are numerous reasons for this limited volume of new bank common stock sales. First, there is the memory of the depression. The number of banks was cut almost in half between 1929 and 1933, and earnings were poor throughout the 1930's. Second, many small banks are either

[7] Federal Deposit Insurance Corporation, *Annual Report,* 1968.

family dominated or controlled by a small group of individuals who do not want to expand the bank ownership for fear of losing control. Third, *bank earnings are low in comparison with many other industries.* Member bank net income after taxes as a percentage of total assets ranged between 7 and 7.5 percent during the 1960's.[8] This third factor probably has been the source of most of the difficulty in expanding stock ownership.

A Banking Industry Dilemma—Earnings versus Safety

To raise earnings, banks must grant more loans and make more investments. In order to do so, however, they need more funds (reserves). Additional usable reserves for the commercial banking system are provided when the monetary authorities lower reserve requirements or purchase U.S. government securities on the open market. Thus the ability of the system to get additional reserves does not depend upon its own decisions, but on those of the regulatory agencies. True, individual banks can compete more aggressively with one another for deposits and thus acquire additional reserves, but this would only benefit some banks at the expense of others.

How can banks increase earnings when additional reserves are not available to them? One obvious solution is to reduce expenses. In a competitive industry like banking, however, most firms are already striving for reduced costs. The alternative is to make relatively more' high-income-producing loans and investments. Higher-yielding loans and investments, however, are likely to be risky. An increased proportion of risk assets would impair the quality of bank assets in the view of government supervisory agencies. The ratio of capital accounts to risk assets in the form of bank loans has declined from 26.4 percent in 1947 to 14.1 percent in 1969.[9] Nevertheless, increased supervision in recent decades has resulted in a very low rate of bank failure and deposit loss.

Ultimately, it appears that the solution to what many bankers view as a serious problem—the inadequacy of bank capital—lies in the creation of more usable reserves by the Federal Reserve System. With increased reserves banks would be able to make more loans and investments, increase earnings, and thereby induce greater stock sales. With increased earnings, increased surplus, and increased stock sales, the ratio of capital accounts to assets would rise, thereby providing a greater margin of protection for bank depositors.

THE NATIONAL ECONOMY AND SOURCES OF FUNDS

The contribution of the commercial banking system to economic growth and stability depends in large part upon the uses to which the banks put

[8] *Federal Reserve Bulletin,* May 1969, p. A–95.
[9] *Federal Reserve Bulletin,* April 1969, p. A–19.

their funds. To help promote growth, the banks need expanding sources of funds. Bank sources of funds have not always grown proportionately with the rest of the economy, however. From 1945 to 1968, commercial bank liabilities and capital accounts increased almost three times while gross national product rose almost five times. Other financial institutions also increased their lending activity relative to the commercial banking system. Mutual savings bank assets and life insurance company assets each increased by more than four times during this period, while savings and loan association assets increased more than fifteenfold.[10] This slower growth rate for commercial banks has, however, reversed itself markedly in the 1960's, particularly after 1963.

Competition Between Commercial Banks and Nonbank Financial Institutions for Funds

Periods of relative decline by commercial banks. Table 5–3 shows the rate of growth of the financial assets of various financial institutions for

TABLE 5–3. FINANCIAL INSTITUTION GROWTH OF ASSETS, PERCENT INCREASE FOR SELECTED PERIODS 1945–69

PERIOD	COMMERCIAL BANKS	MUTUAL SAVINGS BANKS	LIFE INSURANCE COMPANIES	SAVINGS AND LOAN ASSOCIATIONS
1945–60	60.7	139.2	166.9	717.1
1945–69*	198.9	325.3	321.8	1410.1
1960–69*	86.1	77.8	58.0	119.9
1960–61	8.2	5.6	6.1	14.9
1961–62	6.7	7.7	5.1	14.0
1962–63	5.3	7.8	5.9	14.9
1963–64	10.9	9.1	5.9	11.0
1964–65	8.7	7.4	6.3	8.6
1965–66	6.9	4.7	5.1	3.4
1966–67	11.8	8.8	6.1	7.2
1967–68	10.3	7.2	5.8	6.4

* Figures for 1969 are based on the month of February. All other computations are based on end-of-year figures.
SOURCE: Computed from *Federal Reserve Bulletin*, October 1961, p. 1197; February 1964, p. 190; March 1966, p. 368; January 1968, p. A–19; June 1968, pp. A–19, A–35, and A–36; and April 1969, pp. A–19, A–35, and A–36.

selected periods from 1945 through 1968. The period ending around 1960 was one of relative decline for commercial banks as direct contributors to the pecuniary assets of the economy. This decline was partly a consequence of the characteristic that sets commercial banks apart from other financial

[10] Computed from *Federal Bulletin*, June 1968, pp. A–19 and A–36.

institutions: their creation and administration of the principal part of our money stock, demand deposits. The level of economic activity is closely related to the stock of money. When the money supply is allowed to increase rapidly, inflation generally follows. Depressions, on the other hand, are usually accompanied by a fall in the stock of money. In our economy, the monetary authorities attempt to prevent inflation and recession by manipulating interest rates and the money supply. In an attempt to manipulate the money stock, the Federal Reserve regulates the reserve position of the commercial banking system. In periods of high employment, it limits the ability of commercial banks to create demand deposits. When these limitations are imposed upon the banking system, borrowers turn to other lending institutions. This worsens the competitive position of the commercial banks.

When one borrows from a lender other than a commercial bank, money is not created. These financial institutions lend funds directly, usually in the form of demand deposits at commercial banks. For example, the balance-sheet changes that occur when other financial institutions lend $10,000 are

BALANCE-SHEET CHANGES FOR NONBANK LENDING INSTITUTIONS

ASSETS	LIABILITIES + CAPITAL ACCOUNTS
Demand deposits at commercial banks −$10,000 Loans and investments +$10,000	

BALANCE-SHEET CHANGES FOR THE COMMERCIAL BANKING SYSTEM

ASSETS	LIABILITIES + CAPITAL ACCOUNTS
	Demand deposits of the nonbank lending institutions −$10,000 Demand deposits of the borrowers +$10,000

As a result, the dollar volume of loans and investments made by commercial banks decreases in relation to those of other institutions, although for the economy as a whole there is an increase in economic activity. The total of the money stock is unchanged but there has been an increase in its turnover. In other words, the *velocity* with which the money stock changes hands in the economy has increased.

Other lending institutions obtain funds for loans by successfully competing with commercial banks for the idle cash and deposits of individuals in the economy. For example, here is what happens to the balance sheet when a depositor in a commercial bank is induced to switch $1,000 from deposits (either time or demand) in a commercial bank to a savings and loan share account:

BALANCE-SHEET CHANGES FOR THE COMMERCIAL BANKING SYSTEM

ASSETS	LIABILITIES + CAPITAL ACCOUNTS
	Deposits of individual depositor $-\$1,000$
	Deposits of savings and loan association $+\$1,000$

BALANCE-SHEET CHANGES FOR THE SAVINGS AND LOAN ASSOCIATION

ASSETS	LIABILITIES + CAPITAL ACCOUNTS
Deposits at the commercial banking system $+\$1,000$	Savings and loan share accounts $+\$1,000$

The savings and loan association is now in a position to make a loan and will probably choose to make a mortgage loan.

In a period of full employment and rising prices when this situation prevails throughout the economy, there is an added incentive for the monetary authorities to impose tighter controls. The Federal Reserve System can be expected to restrict commercial bank lending activity in hopes of causing interest rate increases that will discourage borrowers. Thus, the main brunt of monetary restraints is borne by the commercial banking system. The effects of such action on other financial institutions will be only indirect—that is, their lending activities will be curtailed only to the extent that rising interest rates will also discourage borrowers from seeking funds at these institutions.

Periods of relative growth for commercial banks. Table 5–3 shows that mutual savings bank and life insurance company assets grew somewhat less rapidly than commercial bank assets during the period 1960–68. Only savings and loan association assets grew more rapidly, and their growth has slowed relative to commercial bank assets since 1964. The relative growth in commercial bank assets during the late 1960's is partly attributable to a change in Federal Reserve policy. The Federal Reserve has increasingly used Regulation Q to regulate the maximum rates payable by commercial banks on time deposits, raising these rates relative to those payable by nonbank financial institutions such as savings and loan associations. The result has been a marked increase in outstanding certificates of deposit issued by commercial banks. Many members of the nonbank public have increased their rate of purchase of CD's, decreased their investments in other near-money forms issued by nonbank financial institutions, and in some instances actually converted their near-money holdings into CD's. When this occurs, severe contractionary pressures are felt by the nonbank financial institutions that created the near-money forms. People with claims on these institutions will demand payment. To make payment the institutions must draw down their own checking-deposit accounts at commercial banks. When these funds are then used to purchase certificates of deposit issued by commercial banks, the net effect will be an increase in commercial bank time deposit liabilities. For example, the balance-sheet changes that take place when individuals switch $1,000 from savings and loan share accounts to time deposits at commercial banks are

BALANCE-SHEET CHANGES FOR THE COMMERCIAL BANKING SYSTEM

ASSETS	LIABILITIES + CAPITAL ACCOUNTS
	Demand deposits of savings and loan association −$1,000 Time deposits of individual depositor +$1,000

BALANCE-SHEET CHANGES FOR THE SAVINGS AND LOAN ASSOCIATION

ASSETS	LIABILITIES + CAPITAL ACCOUNTS
Demand deposits at the commercial banking system −$1,000	Savings and loan share accounts −$1,000

Commercial bank demand deposits decrease. Total wealth holdings of those members of the nonbank public who are not financial institutions remain the same, but the composition of their liquid-wealth holdings changes as a result of the decrease in liabilities of nonbank financial institutions and the increase in commercial bank time deposits. Since the demand deposits that are destroyed are those of the nonbank financial institutions, and since these deposits serve as their cash reserves, any reduction constitutes a decrease in reserves and thus in their lending ability. The Federal Reserve action in increasing maximum interest rates on time deposits thus may ultimately be deflationary, since the reduction in lending will serve to contract the demand for goods and services.

At the same time it should be noted that commercial bank reserve positions will have improved because of the lower reserve requirements for time deposits relative to demand deposits. To the extent that commercial banks previously were rationing credit because of reserve limitations, they may now expand loans and investments and accordingly demand deposits. These newly created demand deposits are most likely to be active deposits that add to the demand for goods and services. The final result will be a total of demand and time deposits at commercial banks greater than that which existed prior to the rise in interest rates, but a somewhat smaller volume of demand deposits. The Federal Reserve, of course, is well aware of the liberalizing effect of higher interest rates and has used other measures to restrict the scope of expansion by the commercial banking system. Overall, the effect of Federal Reserve action has been to increase the rate of growth of commercial banks relative to other financial institutions while slowing the growth of demand during a period of high employment and rising prices.

Conclusion. The fact that much of monetary policy works directly only upon commercial banks limits their ability to compete for funds. Ironically, the tighter the restraint placed by the Federal Reserve on commercial banks, the less direct control it may have over the economy. Increased lending activity by nonbank financial institutions increases the demand for goods and services just as do loans by the commercial banks, and the Federal Reserve has little direct control over these institutions. On the other hand, the activities of nonbank financial institutions can be indirectly controlled through the use of Regulation Q to raise the interest rates paid by commercial banks on CD's relative to the rates paid by nonbank financial institutions on their liabilities. However, since this technique was not brought into play until 1963, the monetary policy of the Federal Reserve for a long time hampered the ability of the commercial banks to compete for loans and sources of funds.

Supplementary Readings

American Bankers Association. *The Commercial Banking Industry.* Englewood Cliffs, N.J.: Prentice-Hall, 1962, Chapters 2 and 12.

Gramley, L. E., and S. B. Chase. "Time Deposits in Monetary Analysis," *Federal Reserve Bulletin* (1965), pp. 1093–1101.

Robinson, Roland I. *The Management of Bank Funds.* New York: McGraw-Hill, 1962, Chapter 23.

Willis, Parker B. "A Study of the Market for Federal Funds," a study prepared for the Steering Committee for *The Fundamental Reappraisal of the Discount Mechanism* appointed by the Board of Governors of the Federal Reserve System, 1967.

CHAPTER 6

Commercial Bank Uses of Funds

NATURE OF COMMERCIAL BANK USES OF FUNDS

The asset side of a commercial bank's balance sheet indicates the many ways in which the bank is able to make use of available funds. It may hold funds idle, it may extend credit to business firms, consumers, farmers, financial institutions, and buyers of real estate, and it may invest in corporate and government securities. As one study pointed out, a

characteristic of commercial banks is the multifunctional nature of their lending and investing. In contrast, savings banks and nonbank financial institutions are essentially specialized institutions, although a few lend to more than one category of borrower. Commercial banks, on the other hand, deal in a wide variety of debts and accommodate all types of borrowers.[1]

Table 6–1 shows the asset side of the combined balance sheets of all commercial banks in the United States. The liability and capital account data for these banks are given in Table 5–2.

CASH ASSETS

Cash assets consist of reserves with the Federal Reserve banks, vault cash (currency and coin), balances with domestic banks, and other cash assets (a very small amount of deposit balances held with foreign banks and a large volume of cash items in process of collection).

Cash assets, as indicated in Chapter 5, have several functions. First, they are used to meet legal reserve requirements. Member banks can meet their reserve requirements with vault cash and with deposits at the Federal Reserve banks. Nonmember banks can usually meet state requirements by vault cash and deposits with other domestic banks. Second, cash assets, in the form of vault cash, provide banks with funds to meet the demands of depositors for cash. And third, cash assets, in the form of deposit balances with the Federal Reserve and other banks, are used to redeem checks drawn on a bank by its customers and presented for collection by other banks.

Cash items in process of collection are the value of checks drawn on

---

[1] The American Bankers Association, *The Commercial Banking Industry* (Englewood Cliffs, N.J.: Prentice-Hall, 1962), p. 1.

TABLE **6–1.** COMMERCIAL BANK ASSETS, DECEMBER 31, 1968

ASSETS	AMOUNT (IN MILLIONS OF DOLLARS)	PERCENT OF TOTAL
Cash assets		
Reserves with Federal Reserve banks	21,230	
Currency and coin	7,195	
Balances with domestic banks	18,910	
Other	36,417	
Total cash assets	83,752	16.7
Loans		
Commercial and industrial	98,357	
Agricultural	9,718	
For purchasing or carrying securities		
To brokers and dealers	6,625	
To others	4,108	
To financial institutions		
To banks	2,206	
To others	13,729	
Real estate	65,137	
Other loans to individuals	58,337	
Other	6,724	
Total loans	264,941	52.9
Investments		
U.S. government securities	64,446	
Bills		
Certificates		
Notes		
Bonds		
State and local government securities	58,570	
Other securities	12,967	
Total investments	135,983	27.2
Other assets	15,981	3.2
Total assets	500,657	100.0

SOURCE: *Federal Reserve Bulletin*, May 1969, pp. A–19 and A–24.

other banks and not yet collected. These cash assets are not considered usable as a source of funds. Bankers realize that the items which they have for collection on other banks will probably be matched by the checks that other banks will present.

Finally, some banks use their cash assets to secure valuable services from larger city banks and from foreign banks. Smaller banks, for example, often leave substantial sums of money on deposit with large city banks in return for such services as security analysis, the handling of bond and security purchases, the clearing and collection of checks, and participation in loans that the small banks cannot handle alone. These deposits are termed *interbank deposits* and represent another function of cash assets.

BANK LOANS

Bank loans are distinguished from investments in that they are generally made directly to a bank's customers. Bank investments are usually made indirectly, through the various securities markets. Loans are the largest category of bank assets; more than 50 percent of all assets are in the form of loans. Table 6–1 shows the diversity of these loans.

Commercial and Industrial Loans

The greater part of commercial bank lending has traditionally taken the form of commercial and industrial loans. These loans are extended to manufacturing, mining, wholesale trade, retail trade, transportation, public utility, construction, and service concerns. In short, commercial and industrial loans include loans to all types of business enterprises except competing financial institutions and farms, which are covered by other types of loans.

Commercial loans may be *secured* or *unsecured* and of any duration. Most commercial and industrial loans are secured loans. The collateral may consist of plant and equipment, accounts receivable, merchandise inventory, or even the stock and bond holdings of the borrowing firm.[2]

The most important unsecured loan made by a commercial bank is that created when a firm draws on its *line of credit*. Only firms with excellent credit ratings are granted a line of credit. Under the terms of this arrangement, a business enterprise may borrow up to a predetermined limit, provided that it maintains a compensating balance—usually around 10 percent of the line of credit—and repays the loan annually. Assume, for example, that a firm has a $100,000 line of credit and a 10-percent compensating-balance requirement. To utilize the line of credit, it must maintain an average deposit account of $10,000 with the lending bank. Having a line of credit, however, does not necessarily mean that the firm has borrowed from the bank. Only when the line of credit is used is a debt created and interest collected by the bank. Many firms hardly ever use their line, maintaining it simply for purposes of prestige or to have funds available in cases of emergency.

Commercial loans are often designed to provide businesses with funds to take care of temporary discrepancies between receipts and expenditures. For example, a business may borrow to meet a monthly payroll and repay the loan through the month as receipts come in. A retailer may borrow substantial amounts in the fall of the year to build up inventories, in anticipation of heavy Christmas sales. When businesses borrow for *seasonal* reasons such as these, the maturity of the loan is usually short.

---

[2] An account receivable is created when a firm delivers merchandise to the purchaser with payment to be made at some future date.

On the other hand, when a firm borrows to expand plant and equipment, the loan is likely to be made for a longer period.

As previously indicated, the maturity of both secured and unsecured loans varies considerably, although unsecured loans generally have a shorter life than secured loans. Approximately two-thirds of all commercial and industrial loans mature within a year, however, and very few have a maturity of over five years.

Agricultural Credit

Another form of credit extended by commercial banks to borrowers is agricultural credit. Although agricultural loans make up less than 4 percent of all bank loans, they are, nevertheless, an important source of funds for the agricultural sector of the economy and a major source of earnings for a large number of U.S. commercial banks.

Agricultural loans are generally seasonal and are made principally to provide the farmer with money for current expenses. However, banks also provide farmers with funds to buy livestock and machinery; these loans usually have a longer maturity than those designed to meet current expenses. Still other loans are made to repay debts and to finance real-estate purchases.

Real-Estate Credit

Real-estate credit is the second most important type of credit extended by commercial banks. Some 25 percent of all bank loans are mortgage loans, most of these for residential construction. Since the real-estate assets purchased by the borrowers have a long life, the maturity of mortgage loans usually runs from ten to twenty-five years.

Many commercial banks compete aggressively for mortgage loans, which, because of their long maturities, provide a steady source of income. Mortgage loans have, in fact, acquired great importance for banks in the postwar period. In 1968, for example, commercial banks had $65.1 billion in mortgages, contrasted with only $4.8 billion in mortgages in 1945. Some $30.8 billion were uninsured conventional mortgage loans; an additional $10.6 billion were insured and guaranteed by the government.[3] The Federal Housing Administration and Veterans Administration underwrite many different types of mortgages for residential construction and insure remodeling and rehabilitation loans. FHA and VA mortgage insurance removes almost all risk for lenders, thus encouraging the expansion of mortgage credit. Bank holdings of conventional mortgage loans have grown more rapidly than VA and FHA guaranteed loans, principally because of higher interest yields.

[3] *Federal Reserve Bulletin*, May 1969, p. A–48.

Consumer Credit

Loans to consumers are another important use of commercial banks' funds. Most of the $58.3 billion listed under "Other loans to individuals" in Table 6-1 consists of consumer loans. These loans are quite varied and may be made on an installment or a noninstallment basis. Banks lend funds to finance the purchase of automobiles and make other "personal" loans, for repairs and modernization or for the purchase of various consumer durables. In addition to making direct loans to consumers, banks also purchase installment paper created by the sellers of consumer goods.

Table 6-2 shows the amount of consumer credit outstanding in the economy in 1968 and the relative importance of the commercial banks as sources of this type of credit. Out of a total $113.2 billion in consumer credit in 1968, $43.9 billion was furnished by commercial banks. Collectively, they are the largest supplier of consumer credit in the economy. Sales finance companies, credit unions, retail outlets, and consumer finance companies follow in that order as additional suppliers of consumer credit.[4]

TABLE **6-2.** CONSUMER CREDIT, DECEMBER 31, 1968

(IN MILLIONS OF DOLLARS)

TYPE OF CREDIT	TOTAL CREDIT		CREDIT HELD BY COMMERCIAL BANKS	
Installment				
Automobile paper	34,130		19,318	
Other consumer goods paper	24,899		6,060	
Repair and modernization loans	3,925		2,719	
Personal loans	26,936		8,855	
Total		89,890		36,952
Noninstallment				
Single payment loans	9,138		7,975	
Charge accounts	7,755		—	
Service credit	6,408		—	
Total		23,301		7,975
Total consumer credit		113,191		44,927

SOURCE: *Federal Reserve Bulletin*, May 1969, pp. A-52, A-53.

This strong position of commercial banks in consumer credit is a relatively recent phenomenon. For the most part it has developed since the 1930's. With the weak credit demands of traditional business borrowers during the depression, commercial banks increased the variety of their lending activities, particularly in the area of consumer credit. By 1939, commercial banks accounted for 24 percent of all consumer credit. This

---

[4] *Ibid.*, p. A-52.

figure has continued to grow. Banks presently extend almost 40 percent of total consumer credit.

Other Lending Activity

Banks lend to one another and to various financial intermediaries too. For example, finance companies, which make personal loans to individuals, may borrow from commercial banks. There are many other ways in which commercial banks lend to competing financial institutions. The amount of loans to financial intermediaries in 1968 was $13.7 billion.

Banks also lend to brokers, dealers, and individual purchasers of securities. The total volume of such loans in 1968 was $6.6 billion. When individuals wish to purchase stock but have insufficient funds to cover the full purchase price, they may borrow up to a certain percentage of the purchase price from the bank. The Federal Reserve determines how high this maximum percentage, or *margin,* may be.[5] Banks also lend directly to securities brokers, who put up their customers' securities as collateral.

INVESTMENTS

Commercial bank holdings of investments consist primarily of U.S. government securities. In 1968, commercial banks held $64.4 billion in U.S. government securities. These holdings represented approximately 13 percent of all bank assets. In addition, banks held $58.6 billion in state and local government securities and $13.0 billion in other securities.

U.S. Government Securities

Commercial banks purchase U.S. government securities for a variety of reasons. First, they are very safe; there is no risk that the U.S. government, like a private borrower, may default on its obligations. Second, they are highly liquid: there is a wide market for these securities; when banks need cash, they can quickly find purchasers for their security holdings. Third, banks are permitted to use U.S. government securities as collateral when borrowing reserves from the Federal Reserve banks. Finally, banks earn interest on their security holdings. *In short, commercial banks purchase and hold U.S. government securities because they are safe, highly liquid, interest-yielding assets.*

The "lock-in effect." This is not to say, of course, that banks never lose money on U.S. government securities. While there is no risk of default on the part of the government, the danger does exist that a commercial bank will lose on its security holdings if these are sold prior to

[5] See Chapter 13 for a discussion of margin requirements.

maturity. For the same reasons, a security sold prior to maturity may occasionally lead to a capital gain, and a bond purchased at less than par may yield a profit when redeemed. For example, when a bank purchases a $1,000, 3-percent U.S. government security at time of issue for $1,000 and interest rates on comparable U.S. government securities subsequently increase to 3.5 percent, the market price of the 3-percent security will decline. For a 3-percent, $1,000 security to be sold in the face of such competition, its price must be sufficiently low to give the purchaser the same return on his investment that he could get on the 3.5-percent securities. How much of a loss will the bank suffer? The $1,000, 3-percent security yields $30, and $30 is 3.5 percent of $857. Hence, figuring backward, the old security probably cannot be sold for more than $857. Therefore, if a bank that originally purchased the security for $1,000 decides to sell at this point, it will lose $143 on the transaction. On the other hand, if the security had been purchased when it was selling at less than par, the purchasing bank would have gained either by holding it until maturity or by selling it when interest rates on comparable securities had eased and their prices had consequently risen.

In short, when government bonds held by commercial banks have a lower nominal interest yield than is currently available on comparable new security issues, the older bonds can no longer be described as highly liquid. They can no longer be quickly converted into cash assets without substantial loss. To break even, the banks must hold the bonds until maturity or until such time as their prices again increase. This situation leads to what economists call the *lock-in effect*.[6] The hypothesis is that, rather than suffer a loss, commercial banks will hold on to their government securities. In effect, they are "locked in" to their investments in these securities.[7] Furthermore, with funds tied up in U.S. government securities, banks will be unable to expand loans. In a period of full employment and rising prices, this restraint on bank lending is thought to be a deterrent to inflation.

If it is true that holding U.S. government securities tends to restrain commercial bank lending operations in periods of rising interest rates and strong demand for loans, why do banks bother to hold them at all? For reasons already given: they are safe investments and may be used as collateral when borrowing reserves. Furthermore, almost a quarter of the U.S. government securities held by banks have a short maturity. Most government bills mature in 90 to 92 days, most certificates in less than a year, most notes in one to five years, and most bonds at the end of five years. Banks with a high proportion of short-term U.S. government securities in their investment portfolios can overcome frequently the lock-in effect in periods of inflation by gradually replacing some of these securities

[6] "The Influence of Monetary Policy on Lenders and Borrowers," *Federal Reserve Bulletin,* May 1953; and "The Lock-in Effect: Bank Reactions to Security Losses," *Monthly Review* (Federal Reserve Bank of Kansas City, June 1960).
[7] Actually, commercial banks are only occasionally locked in. See Table 6–4.

as they come due with high-yielding private investments and loans. Caution must be observed, however, since private securities and loans involve more risk and can be illiquid on the downward side of the business cycle. Banks must be careful not to sacrifice too much safety for higher yields.

State and Local Government Securities

Investment in state and local government securities represents the final major use of commercial banks' funds. Approximately 12 percent of all bank assets are in this form.

Since state and local government securities are tax exempt, they are a highly attractive investment for commercial banks and for persons in high income-tax brackets. The after-tax yield of these securities is generally higher than that of comparable non-tax-exempt securities. Thus, if a tax-exempt security yields 4 percent, the actual return to the security holder is substantially higher than that on a comparable but taxable investment. For example, if the bondholder is a bank in the 48-percent corporation-income-tax bracket, the 4-percent tax-exempt security is equivalent to a 7.7-percent taxable security.[8] For this reason, tax-exempt securities tend to carry a lower nominal yield than private securities with a comparable face value. This difference in nominal yields tends to diminish the difference in actual yields of taxable and tax-exempt securities with the same face value.

Nevertheless, the actual yields of most tax-exempt securities are higher than the after-tax yields of taxable securities of comparable face value, largely for competitive reasons. A large volume of municipal securities has been issued since World War II to pay for expansion in educational, sewage, water, electric, and gas facilities to meet the needs of our rapidly growing population. Local governments, in order to increase their ability to get funds, must offer higher yields. Thus, a favorable spread is maintained by state and local governments between the after-tax yields on taxable securities and the yields on tax-exempt securities.

Investment in state and local government securities by commercial banks does pose several problems, however. Banks are subject to community pressures to purchase securities that may be somewhat risky. Also, the market for tax-exempt securities is limited, with banks and individuals in high income-tax brackets the principal purchasers. This limited market means that the relative liquidity of these securities is reduced. Consequently, when banks purchase tax-exempt securities, they tend to hold them to maturity.

---

[8] A $1,000, 4-percent tax-exempt security yields $40 per year. What rate of interest would a $1,000 security subject to tax have to yield for the bondholder to be left with $40 after taxes? Let x be the rate of interest. Then $(1,000)(x) - (.48)($1,000$)(x) = 40; solving for x, we get 7.7 percent.

Other Securities

Commercial banks purchase a limited number of privately issued securities, primarily corporate bonds. Government agencies closely regulate bank purchases of privately issued securities, and banks are not permitted to buy stocks as investments.

BANK EARNINGS

Bank revenue comes almost exclusively from its earning assets, its loans and investments. Table 6–3 shows bank sources of income in 1967 and 1968 and how this income was accounted for. Here we see that almost 68 percent of all member bank revenue in 1968 came from loans. Bank ownership of securities provided another 20 percent. In comparison, all other sources of income were relatively insignificant.

It may seem peculiar that bank loans earned three times as much as investments despite the fact that their dollar volume was about 90 percent greater than that of investments. The differing characteristics of these assets are responsible for this striking difference in return. Loans are held primarily for return, whereas investments are held primarily for safety and liquidity. Since investments are less risky and more liquid than loans, their yield is lower. To put it another way, the higher interest returns on loans are a way of compensating commercial banks for the risks they assume.

How did commercial banks dispose of this income? A quarter went into wages and salaries. Interest paid on deposits took 34 percent, respectively, of income. Taxes took another 5 percent. The 34 percent of income used to pay interest on time deposits represents a marked increase over previous interest costs. For example, in 1963 interest paid on time deposits was only 25 percent of total income.[9] This change is attributable in part to increased interest rates on commercial bank time deposits and in part to a sharp rise in the total volume of time-deposit liabilities as a result of the higher yields.

Compared with other industries, banks have a low but steady level of earnings. Although an increase in loans, which are by far the most lucrative of bank assets, could be used to raise the level of earnings, two-thirds of bank revenue comes from loans already. A substantial increase in lending at the expense of investments would reduce the liquidity of the banking system and lower the ratio of capital accounts to risk assets. The solution, as we suggested in Chapter 5, would seem to be for the monetary authorities to provide banks with sufficient reserves to enable them to expand both loans and investments and thereby increase earnings. The soundness of such an approach, of course, depends on the national economic situation.

[9] Federal Deposit Insurance Corporation, *Annual Report* (1963), p. 153.

TABLE 6–3. MEMBER BANK INCOME, EXPENSES, AND DIVIDENDS, BY CLASS OF BANK, 1968 AND 1967

			RESERVE CITY BANKS							
	TOTAL		NEW YORK CITY		CITY OF CHICAGO		OTHER		COUNTRY BANKS	
ITEM	1968	1967	1968	1967	1968	1967	1968	1967	1968	1967
	IN MILLIONS OF DOLLARS									
Revenue	20,819	17,859	3,675	3,080	889	763	7,777	6,673	8,479	7,344
On U.S. Govt. securities	2,208	1,934	268	245	83	69	686	611	1,170	1,009
On other securities	1,929	1,561	280	232	72	60	701	578	875	691
On loans	14,143	12,128	2,599	2,159	612	527	5,389	4,598	5,543	4,843
All other	2,540	2,236	527	444	121	106	1,000	885	898	800
Expenses	15,758	13,507	2,640	2,189	642	558	5,950	5,092	6,525	5,667
Salaries and wages	4,730	4,211	780	666	164	150	1,769	1,572	2,018	1,823
Interest on deposits	7,108	6,091	1,175	1,037	327	274	2,708	2,331	2,899	2,449
All other	3,919	3,205	685	485	152	134	1,474	1,190	1,609	1,396
Net current earnings before income taxes	5,061	4,353	1,035	891	246	205	1,827	1,580	1,953	1,676
Recoveries and profits*	359	398	60	36	14	21	119	163	166	179
Losses and charge-offs†	1,185	807	253	109	66	25	424	315	442	358
Net increase (or decrease, +) in valuation reserves	377	327	107	98	15	11	124	96	130	123
Net income before related taxes	3,859	3,616	734	721	179	189	1,398	1,332	1,547	1,375
Taxes on net income	1,054	1,007	228	237	55	58	374	362	396	351
Net income	2,805	2,607	506	484	124	131	1,024	970	1,151	1,024
Cash dividends declared‡	1,385	1,248	320	284	56	52	546	493	463	420
	IN PERCENT									
Ratios										
Net current earnings before income taxes to—										
Average total capital accounts	17.4	16.0	17.3	16.1	17.8	16.3	17.6	16.2	17.2	15.7
Average total assets	1.30	1.24	1.34	1.31	1.40	1.33	1.29	1.22	1.28	1.21
Net income to—										
Average total capital accounts	9.6	9.6	8.5	8.7	9.0	10.4	9.9	9.9	10.1	9.6
Average total assets	.72	.74	.65	.71	.74	.85	.72	.75	.76	.74
Average return on—										
U.S. Govt. securities	4.78	4.48	4.71	4.60	4.79	4.41	4.81	4.56	4.77	4.41
Loans	6.82	6.39	6.41	5.81	6.38	5.88	6.90	6.45	7.01	6.69

* Includes recoveries credited to valuation reserves.
† Includes losses charged to valuation reserves.
‡ Includes interest on capital notes and debentures.
SOURCE: Board of Governors of the Federal Reserve System, *Annual Report* (1968), p. 387.

BANK USES OF FUNDS AND THE NATIONAL ECONOMY

In Chapter 5 we suggested that the monetary policy of the Federal Reserve System may hamper the ability of banks to compete for loans and sources of funds. During inflationary periods, for example, the actions of other financial institutions may cause the Federal Reserve to impose monetary restraints that work directly only on commercial banks.

This should not be taken to suggest that commercial banks always exert a stabilizing influence on economic fluctuations. On the contrary, as stated in Chapter 3, commercial banks, in the absence of regulation, tend to intensify whatever phase of the business cycle is current, through their unique ability to create and destroy money when making loans and investments. Put another way, the uses to which banks put their funds when lending and making investments may intensify the upward and downward swings of business fluctuations, necessitating action by the monetary authorities.

The Behavior of Bank Loans and Investments and Gross National Product

Table 6–4, which compares the growth of commercial bank loans, investments, and demand deposits with the growth of gross national product

TABLE 6–4. COMMERCIAL BANK LOANS, INVESTMENTS, U.S. GOVERNMENT SECURITIES, AND DEMAND DEPOSITS AT MID-YEAR, 1951–68; GROSS NATIONAL PRODUCT, 1951–68

(IN BILLIONS OF DOLLARS)

YEAR	LOANS	TOTAL INVESTMENTS	U.S. GOVERNMENT SECURITIES	DEMAND DEPOSITS*	GROSS NATIONAL PRODUCT
1951	54.8	71.2	58.5	96.3	328.4
1952	59.2	75.2	61.2	103.4	345.5
1953	65.0	73.0	58.6	105.7	364.6
1954	67.3	79.1	63.5	107.0	364.8
1955	75.2	80.1	63.3	113.0	398.0
1956	86.9	73.1	56.6	115.8	419.2
1957	93.3	72.3	55.5	115.7	441.1
1958	93.6	84.0	64.2	117.1	447.3
1959	104.5	81.4	60.9	121.6	483.6
1960	114.8	74.1	54.2	119.5	503.8
1961	118.0	83.8	61.8	125.2	520.1
1962	129.2	91.5	64.4	128.8	560.3
1963	145.0	97.0	63.5	133.6	590.5
1964	164.5	95.7	59.3	135.6	632.4
1965	188.6	99.1	56.9	145.3	683.9
1966	212.0	102.2	53.5	153.8	743.3
1967	224.0	110.9	54.2	161.0	785.0
1968	244.6	122.4	58.6	177.8	860.6

* Excluding interbank and U.S. government demand deposits.
SOURCE: Board of Governors of the Federal Reserve System, *Supplement to Banking and Monetary Statistics*, Section 1 (1962), pp. 26–28; *Federal Reserve Bulletin*, December 1962, p. 1650; June 1963, p. 808; June 1964, p. 736; December 1964, p. 1554; December 1965, p. 1742; January 1967, p. 102; December 1967, p. 2092; June 1968, May 1969, p. A–19. See Table 19–1 for gross national product sources.

from 1951 to 1968, shows the close relationship between bank loan and investment activity and the condition of the economy. The growth of bank loans slackened in the recession years, 1954, 1958, and 1961. Gross national product remained steady in 1954 and 1958, and increased by 3 percent in the very mild recession of 1961. Bank investments, on the other hand, rose substantially in each of these years. Conversely, during economic recovery and prosperity, bank loans increased rapidly, while investments usually declined or remained steady (1962 and 1967, as we shall discuss in a moment, were exceptions).

For the most part Federal Reserve monetary policy during this period was one of ease in the recession years and gradually increasing restraint through recovery and prosperity, on the theory that in recession we need an expansion of loans, and in prosperity some restraint on lending. Yet the actual situation was the reverse of that hoped for by monetary theorists. Why? Bankers argue that loan volume does not grow during recessions because demand is slack. As a result, banks place their funds in safe investments, primarily U.S. government securities. With prosperity, however, the demand for loans increases sharply. Banks are eager to expand their loan volume to increase their earnings, but restriction of bank reserve positions by the Federal Reserve may prevent this. Consequently, banks cut back on their investments in low-interest-yielding government securities so as to make more profitable use of their funds in loans. Thus, we find that in years of relative prosperity, bank investments usually remained comparatively steady or declined.

Exceptions to this rule occurred in 1962 and 1967. Although the economy was in some respects prosperous in 1962, the Federal Reserve retained an expansive monetary policy because of continued high unemployment levels. This permitted banks to expand both loans and investments. In addition, most of the growth in investments in that year was in state and local government securities. Banks showed a strong demand for tax-exempts because they needed high-interest long-term investments to provide funds to meet rising interest charges on an increasing volume of time deposits. The year 1967, unlike 1962, was very prosperous overall. Stimulated by the Viet Nam war, the economy was growing and prices and employment were rising, particularly in the latter half of the year. There was some slack in the economy early in the year. The result was a comparatively easy monetary policy, designed in part to stimulate the housing market, which had been hurt by the tight money policies of 1966. Banks, as in other periods of prosperity, expanded both loans and investments. Almost all the increase in investments was again in highly profitable state and local tax-exempt securities.

For the period 1951–68 as a whole, bank uses of funds were expansive. Loans increased from $54.8 to $244.6 billion, or 311 percent. Investments, however, rose only from $71.2 to $122.4 billion, or 73 percent. Thus, bank loans, which tend to stimulate demand in the economy more than bank investments, increased almost four times as much as investments. The government-securities component of investments varied contracyclically during these years, but the period as a whole showed almost no change in the total of these holdings. Demand deposits increased only 85 percent, yet gross national product rose 162 percent. This means that bank loan and investment activity, coupled with federal monetary restraint, has resulted more in an increased *use* than in an increased *volume* of demand deposits. The monetary restraints used by the federal authorities have caused banks to economize on the creation of demand deposits. This is what the Federal Reserve wants to accomplish. But such Federal Reserve action could be self-defeating since the velocity of money increases. The section below discusses this more fully.

The Commercial Banking System's Role in Economic Fluctuations

The manner in which commercial banks build up loans and decrease investments in periods of prosperity and hold down the level of loans and increase investments in recessions suggests the following conclusions concerning the role of the commercial banking system during economic fluctuations.

First, it shows that banking activities as a whole are not always effectively circumscribed by the "lock-in effect." Banks may readily decrease investments in periods of prosperity by failing to reinvest as bonds mature or by selling off some of their holdings. And they apparently have not been afraid to do so, even taking, in some cases, a capital loss in order to unload securities.

Second, commercial bank loan creation in periods of recovery helps to increase demand deposits and stimulates demand, output, and employment in the economy. Demand deposits have grown in the last two decades and—aside from the relatively prosperous Viet Nam war period—most of the growth has come in the year or two following each recession. These were periods of monetary ease, when commercial banks had adequate reserves.

Third, when banks put their funds in investments rather than in loans during recessions, it slows down the pace of recovery. The money balances held by borrowers are active and stimulate the economy, but the money balances used in the purchase and sale of securities are relatively inactive. This behavior by banks is justified; available funds go into securities in part because of the lack of qualified borrowers. The alternative would be for banks to hold excess reserves. Since putting funds into securities tends to push down interest rates, it contributes more to recovery than would a policy of holding excess reserves.

Finally, commercial bank activity may also have an adverse effect on the economy during periods of high employment, rapidly growing gross national product, and rising prices. In these periods, banks are able to avoid monetary restrictions by reducing investments and increasing loans. This transfers money balances from security purchasers (relatively inactive) to borrowers (active spenders). Thus, even with no change in the money supply, bank loan and investment policy may increase inflationary pressures by increasing the velocity of money and thus the demand for goods.

A balance-sheet transaction may be used to illustrate this last situation:

BALANCE-SHEET CHANGES FOR THE COMMERCIAL BANKING SYSTEM

ASSETS		LIABILITIES + CAPITAL ACCOUNTS	
Investments	−$1,000,000 (a)	Demand deposits of security purchasers	−$1,000,000 (a)
Loans	+$1,000,000 (b)	Demand deposits of borrowers	+$1,000,000 (b)
		Demand deposits of sellers of goods to borrowers	+$1,000,000 (c)
		Demand deposits of borrowers	−$1,000,000 (c)

Transaction (a) records a sale of securities by the commercial banks. Those who purchase the securities from the banks do so by drawing down their checking accounts. This reduces the demand-deposit liabilities of the commercial banking system, thus freeing reserves. The banks can then use these reserves to back new loans; the new deposits created by these loans are recorded in transaction (b). Bank loans and the demand-deposit accounts of borrowers are increased by $1 million. Subsequently, the borrowers purchase goods and services, and the $1 million in demand deposits is transferred to the sellers of goods and services. This is recorded in transaction (c).

Thus, despite Federal Reserve monetary controls, commercial banks tend to intensify, rather than dampen, the cyclical swings of the economy.

Supplementary Readings

American Bankers Association. *The Commercial Banking Industry.* Englewood Cliffs, N.J.: Prentice-Hall, 1962, Chapters 4–8, 10.
Beckhardt, Benjamin, ed. *Business Loans of American Commercial Banks.* New York: Ronald Press, 1959.

CHAPTER 7

Commercial Banks
and the Creation of Money

Preceding chapters have repeatedly emphasized the importance of the commercial banking system in the creation and destruction of the principal component of our nation's money supply, demand deposits. It has been explained that individual commercial banks create deposits when they accept new deposits, grant loans, or make investments. This chapter will demonstrate how this is done. Deposit creation will then be studied from the larger perspective of the entire banking system.

CREATION AND DESTRUCTION OF DEPOSITS
BY INDIVIDUAL BANKS

Creation of Deposits

Primary deposits. A commercial bank creates deposits when it accepts *deposits of cash.* Assume that Individual 1 deposits $1,000 in currency with Bank A. This results in a $1,000 increase in Bank A's reserves (since vault cash is part of a bank's reserves) and a $1,000 increase in its deposit liabilities:

BALANCE-SHEET CHANGES FOR COMMERCIAL BANK A

ASSETS		LIABILITIES + CAPITAL ACCOUNTS	
Reserves	+$1,000	Deposits of Individual 1	+$1,000

The deposits thus created are called *primary deposits* because they result from the deposit of cash.

Primary deposits may also result from the *deposit of checks drawn on other banks.* These checks will also increase the reserves of the receiving bank. Suppose that Individual 1 wishes to deposit a $1,000 bonus check from his employer. If the individual makes the deposit with Bank A, and if the employer writes the check out on the company account at Bank B, the appropriate balance-sheet changes, after the check has cleared,[1] are

[1] Check clearing is discussed in Chapter 10.

BALANCE-SHEET CHANGES FOR COMMERCIAL BANK A

ASSETS		LIABILITIES + CAPITAL ACCOUNTS	
Reserves	+$1,000	Deposits of Individual 1	+$1,000

BALANCE-SHEET CHANGES FOR COMMERCIAL BANK B

ASSETS		LIABILITIES + CAPITAL ACCOUNTS	
Reserves	−$1,000	Demand deposits of employer	−$1,000

Notice that no distinction is made between the time and demand deposits of Individual 1 since he may choose to increase either account.

What are the overall effects of the creation of these primary deposits upon the total money stock? If Individual 1 chooses to keep his funds in the form of demand deposits, the money stock is not affected. A cash deposit decreases the currency holdings of the nonbank public, but it increases demand deposits. Thus, there is no change in the total money stock. Similarly, when demand deposits are transferred from one part of the nonbank public (the employer) to another part (Individual 1), there is no effect on the total money stock. On the other hand, if Individual 1 puts his cash in a time deposit, there is a *decrease* in total money stock. Before time deposits become active money, before they may be used in the purchase of goods and services, they must be converted into either currency or demand deposits. Therefore, they are not considered part of the money stock. The total *liquid wealth* holdings of the nonbank public undergo no change, however, because both time and demand deposits are part of liquid wealth.

Derivative deposits. When commercial banks make *loans and investments,* deposits are also created. Assume that Individual 1 borrows $1,000 from Bank A. He will probably receive the proceeds of the loan in the form of a demand-deposit increase.[2] Thus, bank loans and demand deposits increase by $1,000:

BALANCE-SHEET CHANGES FOR COMMERCIAL BANK A

ASSETS		LIABILITIES + CAPITAL ACCOUNTS	
Loans	+$1,000	Demand deposits of Individual 1	+$1,000

These newly created deposits are called *derivative deposits.* They increase

---

[2] Of course, the borrower always has the option of increasing his time deposits. If he does, total bank deposit liabilities increase but there is no increase in the money stock. Total liquid wealth increases because of the increase in time deposits. This sequence of events, however, is unlikely to occur because people generally borrow either to make purchases or to repay debts.

the money stock and liquid-wealth holdings of the economy, and they contribute to economic expansion by increasing spending power. They do *not* increase the reserves of the lending bank, however.

Investment expansion also causes an increase in the money stock. Suppose that Bank A increases its holdings of securities by $10,000 and pays for them by writing a cashier's check on itself. If the seller of the securities deposits the check in his checking account at Bank B, this will increase Bank B's reserves and decrease Bank A's reserves:

BALANCE-SHEET CHANGES FOR COMMERCIAL BANK A

ASSETS		LIABILITIES + CAPITAL ACCOUNTS
Reserves	− $10,000	
Securities	+ $10,000	

BALANCE-SHEET CHANGES FOR COMMERCIAL BANK B

ASSETS		LIABILITIES + CAPITAL ACCOUNTS
Reserves	+ $10,000	Demand deposits of securities-seller + $10,000

For the banking system as a whole, both demand-deposit liabilities and security holdings have increased, but reserves remain unchanged. Thus, although the money holdings of the nonbank public have increased, Bank A's purchase of securities has brought about no change in the total liquid wealth of the nonbank public.

Are the deposits created in the second transaction primary or derivative? From the point of view of Bank B, they are primary deposits because they increased reserves by an amount equal to the increase in deposit liability. From the perspective of the whole banking system, however, they are derivative deposits because there has been no increase of the total volume of bank reserves.

Destruction of Deposits

Commercial bank demand deposits are destroyed when cash is withdrawn, when loans are repaid, when bank investments are sold, and when reserves decline.

Assume that Individual 1 needs additional cash for vacation expenses and draws $1,000 from his checking account:

BALANCE-SHEET CHANGES FOR COMMERCIAL BANK A

ASSETS		LIABILITIES + CAPITAL ACCOUNTS
Reserves	− $1,000	Demand deposits of Individual 1 − $1,000

As the balance-sheet changes show, the bank loses reserves and deposit liabilities. The nonbank public experiences no change either in the money stock or in liquid wealth; it merely has exchanged one form of money, demand deposits, for another, currency. This bank and the banking system as a whole have lost reserves, however. Hence, as we shall discuss shortly, commercial bank lending activity will be restricted.

A bank also loses reserves and deposits when its depositors write checks payable to persons maintaining accounts with other banks. This was the situation confronting Bank B in the illustration on page 81. When the employer paid Individual 1, a primary deposit was made at Bank A. As a consequence, Bank B's deposit liability and its reserves were diminished.

Loan repayments also cause deposits to be destroyed. Assume that Individual 1 repays a $1,000 loan with Bank A by drawing down his checking account. The T-account entries are

BALANCE-SHEET CHANGES FOR COMMERCIAL BANK A

ASSETS		LIABILITIES + CAPITAL ACCOUNTS	
Loans	−$1,000	Demand deposits of Individual 1	−$1,000

If the loan is repaid with checks drawn on other banks, $1,000 in demand deposits is still destroyed from the point of view of the entire banking system. Bank A does not experience this loss directly, however:

BALANCE-SHEET CHANGES FOR COMMERCIAL BANK A

ASSETS		LIABILITIES + CAPITAL ACCOUNTS
Reserves	+$1,000	
Loans	−$1,000	

BALANCE-SHEET CHANGES FOR THE REST OF THE COMMERCIAL BANKING SYSTEM

ASSETS		LIABILITIES + CAPITAL ACCOUNTS	
Reserves	−$1,000	Demand deposits	−$1,000

Finally, deposits are destroyed when banks reduce their investments. Suppose, for example, that Bank A sells $10,000 in U.S. government securities. If the purchasers are members of the nonbank public, payment usually is made with checks drawn on commercial banks. Assume that Bank A sells the securities and that depositors of Bank B are the ultimate purchasers. The balance-sheet changes for this transaction are

BALANCE-SHEET CHANGES FOR COMMERCIAL BANK A

ASSETS		LIABILITIES + CAPITAL ACCOUNTS
Reserves	+$10,000	
U.S. government securities	−$10,000	

BALANCE-SHEET CHANGES FOR COMMERCIAL BANK B

ASSETS		LIABILITIES + CAPITAL ACCOUNTS	
Reserves	−$10,000	Demand deposits	−$10,000

Here the money supply of the nonbank public has decreased, while total liquid wealth and the reserves of the banking system remain unchanged.

LIMITATIONS TO INDIVIDUAL BANK DEPOSIT CREATING AND DESTROYING ABILITIES

Deposit Creation and the Reserve Requirement

The ability of an individual commercial bank to create deposits is not unlimited. The reserve requirement and the volume of each bank's reserves restrict its power to create deposits.

The reserve requirement is the legally required ratio of those cash assets defined by law as reserves to deposit liabilities. Reserves are divided into two categories: required and excess. *Required reserves* are those which a bank must have to meet its reserve requirement. *Excess reserves* are the amount of reserves that a bank has in excess of its required amount. When required reserves exceed actual reserves, the bank has a *deficiency* (or *shortage*) *of reserves*.

Assume, for example, that a bank has $1 million in reserves, a 20 percent reserve requirement, and $4 million in deposit liabilities. The bank's required reserves are $800,000. Since its actual reserves are $1 million, the bank has $200,000 in excess reserves. On the basis of this volume of excess reserves, it may expand loans and investments by $200,000 and create up to $200,000 in demand deposits. Of course, the bank could expand beyond this amount, but it would consider this a very risky policy. On the basis of past experience, the bank expects to lose reserves in an amount equal to its loan and investment expansion, unless it has a favorable clearing balance—as we shall discuss in a moment.

What would happen if some of the givens in this illustration changed? If the volume of reserves increases by $50,000 because of loan repayments, the lending and money-creating ability of our bank increases by $50,000. Similarly, if the legal reserve requirement drops to 15 percent, then the excess reserves of our bank increase from $200,000 to $400,000. In general terms, the lower the reserve requirement, the greater the amount of excess reserves, and hence the lending and money-creating ability of the bank. Also, the greater the volume of reserves available to meet a fixed reserve requirement, the greater is the volume of excess reserves, and hence the greater the lending and money-creating abilities of the bank.

Deposit Destruction and the Reserve Requirement

If a bank becomes deficient in reserves, it will cease expanding loans and investments; it may even cut back on loans and investments outstanding. For example, if the bank discussed in the preceding section had had $600,000 instead of $1 million in reserves, it would have had a $200,000 shortage of reserves. In such a situation, the bank might refuse to renew $100,000 in loans and it might sell $100,000 in investments. If those who repay the loans and purchase the investments do so with checks drawn on other banks, the first bank will no longer be deficient in reserves, and other banks will have lost reserves:

BALANCE-SHEET CHANGES FOR COMMERCIAL BANK A

ASSETS		LIABILITIES + CAPITAL ACCOUNTS
Reserves	+$200,000	
Loans	−$100,000	
Investments	−$100,000	

However, these methods of meeting reserve requirements have several shortcomings. First, it is not good business practice to refuse to renew loans for customers—it may hurt future lending opportunities since in a subsequent period, when the bank has adequate excess reserves, borrowers may decide to go elsewhere for a loan. Second, too great a reduction of investments may jeopardize the safety and liquidity of the bank. Third, a reduction of loans lowers bank earnings. And, finally, if those who repay loans do so with checks drawn on the deficient bank itself, a contraction in an amount *greater* than the deficiency of reserves will be necessary:

BALANCE-SHEET CHANGES FOR COMMERCIAL BANK A

ASSETS		LIABILITIES + CAPITAL ACCOUNTS	
Loans	−$200,000	Demand deposits	−$200,000
Addenda: Original deficiency of reserves		$200,000	
New deficiency of reserves		$160,000	

When depositors repay $200,000 in loans, a corresponding amount of demand deposits is destroyed. With $200,000 less in deposit liabilities, the required reserves of the bank are reduced by 20 percent of $200,000, or $40,000. Thus, there is still a shortage of reserves amounting to $160,000. To make up a $200,000 deficiency in required reserves in this fashion, the bank would have to reduce its loans by $1 million:

BALANCE-SHEET CHANGES FOR COMMERCIAL BANK A

ASSETS		LIABILITIES + CAPITAL ACCOUNTS	
Loans	− $1,000,000	Demand deposits	− $1,000,000
Addenda: Original deficiency of reserves		$200,000	
Reduction in required reserves		$200,000	
New deficiency of reserves		0	

Thus, to improve Bank A's reserve position by not making new loans once the old loans have been repaid, the total dollar volume of loans must be reduced by an amount *five times as large* as the initial deficiency in reserves: *required reserves are reduced only by $1 for every $5 decrease in deposit liabilities when the reserve requirement is 20 percent.* The reason for this is quite simple: since $200,000 in reserves represents 20 percent, or one-fifth, of a given amount of demand deposits, it will take $200,000 in demand deposits multiplied by the reciprocal of one-fifth (5) to restore an equivalent amount in lost reserves.

How Banks Get Additional Reserves

For the reasons just discussed, banks try not to rely solely on contracting loans and investments to eliminate deficiencies in reserves. Instead, they use a variety of techniques. They may reduce investments slightly to bring in some reserves from other banks, and they may also reduce loans by granting fewer new loans than are currently running off. (This will bring in some reserves and lower deposit liabilities, since some loans will be repaid with checks drawn on other banks.) But there are other ways to increase reserves. If the shortage appears likely to be temporary, a bank may borrow reserves from other banks. As was pointed out earlier in discussing the federal funds market, banks with a surplus of excess reserves are generally willing to lend them to other banks for short periods. These excess reserves, maintained at Federal Reserve banks in the form of deposit balances, are usually loaned to deficient banks on an overnight basis. Banks may also borrow reserves from their district Federal Reserve banks, which almost always meet legitimate requests for borrowings.

When banks borrow reserves from other banks or from their district Federal Reserve bank, the balance-sheet entries are

BALANCE-SHEET CHANGES FOR COMMERCIAL BANK A

ASSETS		LIABILITIES + CAPITAL ACCOUNTS	
Reserves	+ $200,000	Borrowings	+ $200,000

Thus, Bank A's $200,000 deficiency in reserves is removed without reducing its earning assets. The borrowed funds will have to be repaid with interest, of course, but the bank hopes that future operations will provide the means of repayment. Borrowing reserves permits banks with temporary reserve deficiencies to provide credit continuity to customers.

The placement of *Euro-dollars* by overseas branches with their American head office is another source of additional reserves for some commercial banks. Euro-dollars are created when the ownership of demand-deposit liabilities at American banks is transferred to foreign banks. Assume, for example, that a holder of demand deposits in an American commercial bank makes a deposit in a foreign bank and wants to keep the claim denominated in dollars. The foreign bank gains an asset, deposits at an American bank, and creates a liability (usually time deposits denominated in dollars), which it owes to the depositor. If the foreign bank then sells its Euro-dollar holdings on an American bank to a foreign branch of another U.S. bank, the Euro-dollars are now owned by the foreign branch of an American bank. The dollars, of course, are still in the United States as liabilities of some American bank. The foreign branch that owns the Euro-dollars will now transfer the ownership to its home office in the United States. The home office will seek payment, and in so doing will acquire reserves from the American bank whose deposit liabilities had served as Euro-dollars.

American banks need not purchase Euro-dollars from foreign banks. They may also borrow them. Such transactions generally take place on an overnight basis with a resultant increase in reserve assets and borrowing liabilities of the borrowing banks.

The Euro-dollar market has become an important part of the international money market in the last decade. We shall mention it again in a later chapter. For our present purposes, we should recognize that American banks can acquire additional reserves by buying or borrowing Euro-dollars. Total commercial bank reserves are unchanged by such actions, however. The reserves acquired are those of American commercial banks whose demand deposit liabilities served as Euro-dollars.

Other Factors Affecting Commercial Bank Deposit Creation

Many other things affect the ability of a commercial bank to create and destroy demand-deposit money. Some of the more important factors are (1) the demands of the nonbank public for currency, (2) the relative preferences of the nonbank public for time and demand deposits, (3) the bank's clearing balances, (4) the willingness of the bank to lend and the borrower to borrow, (5) the unpredictability of business conditions, and (6) government economic policy.

The demand for currency. The reserve position of a commercial bank, and, for that matter, of the whole banking system, depends in part upon the willingness of the nonbank public to maintain its present distribution of currency and demand deposits. When people decide that they need more currency, they draw down their deposit balances. This reduces commercial bank reserves and deposits by an equal amount. The effect of a $1,000 cash withdrawal upon a bank that has extended as many loans as its reserves will permit and is faced with a 20-percent reserve requirement is shown by the following T-account entry:

BALANCE-SHEET CHANGES FOR COMMERCIAL BANK A

ASSETS		LIABILITIES + CAPITAL ACCOUNTS	
Reserves	− $1,000	Demand deposits	− $1,000

Addenda: Change in reserves − $1,000
Change in required reserves − $ 200
Overall change in excess reserves − $ 800

Since only 20 percent of $1,000, or $200, was required to back the $1,000 in demand-deposit liabilities, required reserves decrease by only $200. On balance, the bank is short $800 in reserves. To make up this deficiency, it must either contract loans, investments, and deposits or borrow additional reserves. This type of currency drain is usually seasonal; more currency is needed during vacation periods, for example, when people travel, and during the Christmas season, when people make more cash purchases than usual. Fortunately, the Federal Reserve System generally provides banks with the needed reserves in such periods.

During other periods, for example, following the holiday seasons, there are sizable influxes of currency into the banking system, and reserves, excess reserves, and deposits all increase. This would seem to be an ideal time for commercial banks to expand their loans. Unfortunately, the demand for loans typically falls off during these same periods. In addition, the Federal Reserve usually takes measures to mop up the excess reserves.

The demand for time deposits. Up to this point in the chapter we have not distinguished between the reserve requirements for demand and time deposits, in order to keep the numerical illustrations comparatively simple. As we know from earlier chapters, reserve requirements vary a great deal, depending on the location of the bank and the type of deposit. In 1969, for example, the reserve requirements for member banks were 3 and 6 percent for various types of time deposits at member banks, 12.5 and 13.0 percent for demand deposits at country banks, and 17.0 and 17.5 percent for demand deposits at reserve city banks. This difference in reserve requirements means that commercial bank reserve positions are weakened by a switch from time to demand deposits. Suppose, for example, that reserve requirements are 4 percent for time deposits and 15 percent for demand deposits and that Bank A is initially loaned up. If depositors should decide to increase their demand deposits by $100,000 and decrease their time deposits by an equal amount, the result would be a shortage in reserves:

BALANCE-SHEET CHANGES FOR COMMERCIAL BANK A

ASSETS	LIABILITIES + CAPITAL ACCOUNTS	
	Demand deposits	+$100,000
	Time deposits	−$100,000
Addenda: Change in existing amount of reserves	0	
Change in required reserves	+$11,000	

Bank A is now deficient in reserves by $11,000. The reduction in time deposits releases $4,000 in required reserves, but the demand-deposit increase calls for an additional $15,000 in reserves. The net effect is that Bank A needs $11,000 more in reserves.

On the other hand, when a bank's customers decide to shift funds from demand deposits to time deposits, the reserve position of the bank is improved. The amount of reserves released by the reduction in demand deposits is greater than the amount of reserves required to back the new time deposits. Thus, the bank receives additional excess reserves.

Favorable and adverse clearing balances. A bank continually receives checks drawn on other banks. Conversely, it is also continually redeeming checks presented for collection by other banks. If the total value of the checks a bank redeems is less than the value of the checks it presents for collection, then that bank is said to have a *favorable clearing balance.* If the reverse is true, then the bank has an *adverse clearing balance.*

A bank that continues to experience a favorable clearing balance over a period of time is in a position to expand loans and deposits beyond its excess reserves. On the other hand, if it regularly has an adverse clearing balance, it must limit its expansion of loans and deposits to an amount less than the volume of excess reserves.

Assume, for example, that Bank A has $10,000 in excess reserves, a 20 percent reserve requirement, and a consistently favorable clearing balance equal in value to 2 percent of its newly created demand deposits. What additional volume of loans and deposits can the bank create? Without a favorable or adverse clearing balance it could create $10,000 in loans and deposits, the amount of its excess reserves. With the favorable balance, a $10,000 deposit creation would lead to a $200 deposit return to the bank. Thus, the bank can create more than $10,000 in deposits. It can create additional deposits equal to 1/.984 times the volume of excess reserves,[3] or $163.

[3] The figure 1/.984 is based on the following formula:

$$p = \frac{1}{1 - q + (r)(q)}$$

where *r* is the reserve requirement, *q* is the percentage of new deposits that return to the bank, and *p* is that multiple of its excess reserves by which the bank may expand its loans and deposits. As study of the formula shows, *q* acts as an expansive force on

The following T-account entries show the effects of Bank A's expanding loans by 1/.984 times its excess reserves when the new loan is made:

BALANCE-SHEET CHANGES FOR COMMERCIAL BANK A

ASSETS		LIABILITIES + CAPITAL ACCOUNTS	
Loans	+$10,163	Demand deposits	+$10,163

and when all its checks have been cleared:

BALANCE-SHEET CHANGES FOR COMMERCIAL BANK A

ASSETS		LIABILITIES + CAPITAL ACCOUNTS	
Reserves	−$9,960	Demand deposits	−$9,960
Addenda: Net increase in demand deposits after all transactions			$ 203
Net increase in required reserves			$ 40
Net decrease in total reserves			$ 9,960
Former volume of excess reserves			$10,000
New volume of excess reserves			0

The checks presented by other banks for collection are 2 percent less than the volume of newly created deposits. Hence, total deposit liabilities are $203 greater than they were at the start of these transactions and required reserves have increased by $40. The bank lost $9,960 in reserves. Without the favorable clearing balance the bank would have lost $10,000 in reserves.[4] Thus, a favorable clearing balance of 2 percent enabled the bank to expand loans and deposits beyond its excess reserves.

Other banks are not so fortunate, however. If one bank has a favorable balance, another bank must have an adverse balance. Thus, for the entire banking system there can be neither a favorable nor an adverse clearing position.

To the individual bank, however, an adverse clearing balance means that it cannot create loans and deposits to the full extent of its excess reserves. Assume that Bank B has excess reserves of $10,000, a reserve requirement of 20 percent, and a consistently adverse clearing balance equal to 2 percent of its newly created deposits. This bank would experience difficulty if it expanded to the extent of its excess reserves. If it expanded loans and deposits by $10,000, for example, it would lose $10,200 in reserves. Therefore, using the formula in footnote 3, Bank B should expand demand

deposit creation, while r acts as a contractive force. As deposits return to the bank, the reserve requirement calls for an increase in excess reserves.

This same formula is used when a bank has an adverse clearing balance. In this case p and r have the same meaning, but q now refers to the percentage by which checks drawn on the bank exceed the volume of newly created deposits. Under these circumstances, q takes a negative value and tends to hold down deposit creation, while r, the reserve requirement, helps maintain it.

[4] All amounts less than $1 have been dropped.

deposits by only 1/1.016 times its excess reserves. When the new loan is made, loans and deposits will rise:

BALANCE-SHEET CHANGES FOR COMMERCIAL BANK B

ASSETS		LIABILITIES + CAPITAL ACCOUNTS	
Loans	+$9,843	Demand deposits	+$9,843

When all its checks have been cleared, the result will be

BALANCE-SHEET CHANGES FOR COMMERCIAL BANK B

ASSETS		LIABILITIES + CAPITAL ACCOUNTS	
Reserves	−$10,040	Demand deposits	−$10,040
Addenda: Net decrease in demand deposits after all transactions			$ 197
Net decrease in required reserves			$ 39
Net decrease in total reserves			$10,040
Former volume of excess reserves			$10,000
New volume of excess reserves			0

Various factors affect the clearing position of a bank. For instance, a bank located in an economically developing area may expect to gain reserves at the expense of banks in areas of declining economic activity. This shifting of reserves to a growing area is considered necessary by the banks whose resources are increased, of course. Growing areas generally experience a shortage of funds, since the demand for loans is strong relative to the supply. A bank with increasing loans and reserves is not necessarily one with a favorable clearing balance, however. Extensive lending activity may produce an adverse clearing balance: if a bank is rapidly expanding credit, it can usually expect sharp drains on its reserves. On the other hand, banks that make few loans may find their reserves rising. Thus, the movement of reserves to a district with a growing economy may simply offset losses attributable to the increased volume of bank lending.

Willingness to borrow and lend. Changes in the reserve requirement, in the demand for currency, in the demand for time deposits, and in clearing balances all tend to affect a commercial bank's reserve position and thus its ability to create money. In addition, the extent to which a bank creates new deposits through loans also depends on its own willingness to lend and upon the demand of borrowers. For example, banks are more willing to lend when there is prosperity in the community and the economy. In recession, they generally follow a more cautious lending policy, expanding investments instead.

Although most banks tend to vary the size of their loan and investment portfolios according to changes in the business cycle, there are, of course, many differences among individual banks. Some have a fundamentally conservative lending policy and keep a relatively large proportion of their assets in safe investments. Others follow a more liberal lending policy.

The attitude of borrowers is also important. When businesses expect a decline in sales, for example, they borrow less and repay loans. If economic conditions are expected to improve, however, businesses want to be prepared for the anticipated increase in demand. They borrow more from banks in order to build up inventories.

The unpredictability of business conditions. While a bank may expect transfers from time to demand deposits, cash drains, and adverse clearing balances to confront it regularly, it cannot always predict the size and timing of these occurrences. Random disturbances, such as unanticipated cash drains, occur frequently. Since these disturbances cannot always be precisely anticipated, a bank must set aside a certain proportion of its excess reserves to meet these contingencies.

Small banks lack the skilled personnel and the specialized knowledge of the money markets that large banks have. As a result, they are not as well able to economize on reserves; often they must maintain substantial amounts of excess reserves as precautionary balances. The large banks must maintain precautionary balances, too, but these balances can be smaller relative to deposit liabilities. Regularly maintained precautionary balances of excess reserves do help to cover the unexpected demands for cash and reserve losses, but they also cut down the lending ability of the bank because they do not permit it to expand to the full extent of its excess reserves.

Government economic policy. In many ways, government economic policy is the single most important determinant of the commercial bank's power to create money. When the federal government feels that the economy needs to expand, it attempts to stimulate the economy through various agencies. The Federal Reserve System, for example, may lower the reserve requirement for member banks. This action will directly increase the lending ability of each member bank. Their improved reserve position, of course, does not guarantee that the banks will actually increase their lending activities, but it is a step in the right direction.

The Federal Reserve may also aggressively expand its holdings of U.S. government securities. When this happens, commercial bank reserves increase: the sellers of the securities receive checks drawn on the Federal Reserve banks and deposit them in checking accounts at commercial banks.[5] Although this action is expansive, its effects are not felt directly by every bank. Only those banks whose depositors have sold securities to the Federal Reserve are affected initially. Other banks may be affected indirectly, depending on the lending actions of the banks that receive the additional reserves.

---

[5] This type of action by the Federal Reserve System is called an open-market operation. See Chapter 13 for a full discussion.

Other government agencies also help stimulate the economy. Their actions affect commercial banks only indirectly, however. For example, the federal government may increase its rate of spending. If the government demand for goods and services is increased in this fashion, businesses may be stimulated to borrow at commercial banks to meet this added demand. Hence, there may be increased willingness to borrow and more lending activity. Also, bank reserves may increase as businesses deposit checks received from the government in payment for its increased orders of goods and services. These checks are usually drawn on U.S. Treasury accounts at the Federal Reserve banks. The deposit of these checks with commercial banks increases both their deposit liabilities and their reserves. Suppose, for example, that the federal government increases its spending by $50 million in an effort to stimulate the economy:

BALANCE-SHEET CHANGES FOR THE FEDERAL RESERVE BANKS

ASSETS	LIABILITIES + CAPITAL ACCOUNTS
	Deposits Member bank reserves +$50,000,000 U.S. Treasurer—general account −$50,000,000

BALANCE-SHEET CHANGES FOR THE COMMERCIAL BANKING SYSTEM

ASSETS		LIABILITIES + CAPITAL ACCOUNTS	
Reserves	+$50,000,000	Demand deposits	+$50,000,000

The checks deposited by businesses were drawn on the government accounts at the Federal Reserve banks. When commercial banks present these checks for collection, the Federal Reserve banks pay them by increasing commercial bank reserve accounts and decreasing the Treasury deposit accounts. Not all banks participate in the initial increase in reserves. As the banks that receive these additional reserves expand loans and investments, however, other banks will receive increased reserves and deposits.

During prosperity and inflation, government economic policy may be contractionary rather than expansionary. The Federal Reserve may attempt to restrain inflationary pressures in the economy by restricting commercial bank lending. For example, it may sell U.S. government securities to the nonbank public. The purchasers of the securities will pay for them with checks drawn on their demand-deposit accounts at commercial banks. The Federal Reserve banks, when they receive these checks, will collect by lowering the reserve balances of member banks. The Federal Reserve could also raise reserve requirements to reduce inflationary pressure, but this is not the normal procedure.

Federal government spending may also be restricted in a period of inflation, since a decrease in the government's demand for goods and services can normally be expected to reduce spending and borrowing by the nonbank public. Also, as the rate of federal spending decreases, government receipts relative to expenditures tend to increase. Thus, Treasury balances with the Federal Reserve banks increase, while commercial bank reserves and deposit liabilities diminish.

Summary. So far Chapter 7 has dealt with some of the more important factors influencing the ability of a commercial bank to create money. Our analysis has concentrated on *potential* influences on bank money creation; the focus, for the most part, has been on the individual bank. The ability of a commercial bank to create demand-deposit money depends principally on its reserve position. In general, a bank may create demand deposits in an amount equal to its excess reserves. Whether the bank actually expands to this extent depends on its willingness to lend, the demand for loans, its clearing balances, and its precautionary margin of excess reserves. If the bank has a shortage of reserves, it must either contract its loans and investments or obtain additional reserves. Government economic policy and changes in the demand for time deposits and currency affect banks principally by altering their reserve position.

CREATION AND DESTRUCTION OF DEPOSITS
BY THE COMMERCIAL BANKING SYSTEM

The ability of the entire banking system to create and destroy money differs from that of the individual bank. It is true that the ability of the banking system to create and destroy money, like that of individual banks, depends upon reserve positions. The individual bank may safely create new deposits only to the extent of its excess reserves, whereas the banking system may create new deposits by *a multiple of* banking system *excess reserves.*

Banking System Creation of Deposits

To illustrate the money-creating ability of the commercial banking system, let us begin by making the following assumptions: (1) the reserve requirement is 20 percent; (2) the deposit liabilities of the banking system are $140 billion; (3) the reserves of the banking system are $28 billion; (4) there is normally no cash drain or influx; (5) unless otherwise specified, all transactions are by check; (6) there are no time deposits; (7) banks require no minimum precautionary reserve balances; and (8) monetary-fiscal policy is neutral in its effects on commercial bank lending and investing activities. Under these conditions, banks would be loaned up; required reserves would thus equal actual reserves.

Now, imagine that there is a $100 million influx of cash into the banking system. These cash deposits increase both commercial bank reserves and demand-deposit liabilities by $100 million. Required reserves increase by $20 million. Excess reserves are no longer zero; they now amount to $80 million. What will happen to the lending and money-creating ability of the commercial banking system?

Initially, the banks will increase deposits only by the amount of their excess reserves, $80 million. They expect to lose their excess reserves to other banks as borrowers pay off debts to depositors of other banks. This will not cause a loss in reserves for the entire banking system, however. Because the reserves stay in the system, deposit creation will continue to occur. As the newly created funds are spent, other banks receive these reserves and create new primary deposits to the extent of $80 million. These banks now have excess reserves. With $80 million more in deposits and reserves, they have $64 million in excess reserves and may create additional deposits to this amount.

Summarizing the discussion up to this point in T-account form, we have

1. A hypothetical initial balance sheet for the commercial banking system when loaned up:

BALANCE SHEET FOR THE COMMERCIAL BANKING SYSTEM
(IN BILLIONS OF DOLLARS)

ASSETS		LIABILITIES + CAPITAL ACCOUNTS	
Reserves	$ 28	Demand deposits	$140
Other assets	122	Other liabilities and capital accounts	10

2. Balance-sheet changes that occur when people make cash deposits of $100 million (banks receiving these deposits are called Group 1 banks):

BALANCE-SHEET CHANGES FOR GROUP 1 BANKS
(IN MILLIONS OF DOLLARS)

ASSETS		LIABILITIES + CAPITAL ACCOUNTS	
Reserves	+$100	Demand deposits	+$100

BALANCE-SHEET CHANGES FOR THE COMMERCIAL BANKING SYSTEM
(IN MILLIONS OF DOLLARS)

ASSETS		LIABILITIES + CAPITAL ACCOUNTS	
Reserves	+$100	Demand deposits	+$100

3. Balance-sheet changes that occur when the banks acquiring the $100 million in cash deposits create loans and derivative deposits:

BALANCE-SHEET CHANGES FOR GROUP 1 BANKS
(IN MILLIONS OF DOLLARS)

ASSETS		LIABILITIES + CAPITAL ACCOUNTS	
Loans	+$80	Demand deposits	+$80

BALANCE-SHEET CHANGES FOR THE COMMERCIAL BANKING SYSTEM
(IN MILLIONS OF DOLLARS)

ASSETS		LIABILITIES + CAPITAL ACCOUNTS	
Loans	+$80	Demand deposits	+$80

4. Balance-sheet changes that occur when the newly created deposits are spent and passed to other (Group 2) banks:

BALANCE-SHEET CHANGES FOR GROUP 1 BANKS
(IN MILLIONS OF DOLLARS)

ASSETS		LIABILITIES + CAPITAL ACCOUNTS	
Reserves	−$80	Demand deposits	−$80

BALANCE-SHEET CHANGES FOR GROUP 2 BANKS
(IN MILLIONS OF DOLLARS)

ASSETS		LIABILITIES + CAPITAL ACCOUNTS	
Reserves	+$80	Demand deposits	+$80

BALANCE-SHEET CHANGES FOR THE COMMERCIAL BANKING SYSTEM

ASSETS	LIABILITIES + CAPITAL ACCOUNTS
0	0

5. Balance-sheet changes that occur when Group 2 banks create loans and deposits:

BALANCE-SHEET CHANGES FOR GROUP 2 BANKS
(IN MILLIONS OF DOLLARS)

ASSETS		LIABILITIES + CAPITAL ACCOUNTS	
Loans	+$64	Demand deposits	+$64

BALANCE-SHEET CHANGES FOR THE COMMERCIAL BANKING SYSTEM
(IN MILLIONS OF DOLLARS)

ASSETS		LIABILITIES + CAPITAL ACCOUNTS	
Loans	+$64	Demand deposits	+$64

The above entries show that $100 million, $80 million, and $64 million in new demand deposits have successively been created. Theoretically, in the banking system as a whole, banks will continue to create deposits in this fashion until all the excess reserves in the system become required reserves. Under our assumptions, this point will be reached when the total of the newly created deposits is five times the initial increase in reserves of the commercial banking system. This means that *the banking system as a whole, with an initial increase in reserves of $100 million, can theoretically expand deposits by $500 million.* Since, in our illustration, the first $100 million created were primary deposits, the remaining $400 million were, in a general sense, *derivative deposits* created when banks made loans and investments in that amount. Thus, the total nonbank public holdings of money have increased by $400 million.

The essential difference between deposit creation by individual banks and by the banking system is this. When the individual bank makes investments, it expects to lose an equal amount of reserves; when it makes loans and creates deposit liabilities, it also expects to lose reserves equal to the amount of those deposit liabilities. When the banking system makes loans and investments and creates demand-deposit money, however, there is no change in reserves. They are merely redistributed among the various banks in the system.

Banking System Destruction of Deposits

The banking system, like individual banks, must contract deposits when it is short of reserves. Unlike an individual bank, however, it must contract deposits by *a multiple of the deficiency of reserves.* An individual bank may make up its shortage of reserves by getting reserves from other banks by reducing loans and investments, acquiring Euro-dollars, and borrowing reserves in the federal funds market. Such action by an individual bank, however, will not relieve a systemwide shortage of reserves. Instead, it only makes the problems of other banks more severe. This is particularly true when the Federal Reserve, for purposes of restraining inflation, does not undertake to provide commercial banks with additional reserves.

To explain the multiple destruction of deposits that occurs in the commercial banking system, let us start with the same initial set of assumptions we used in illustrating the multiple expansion of deposits. The banking system is initially loaned up. Now, let us imagine that there is an increase in the reserve requirement from 20 to 21 percent. Let us assume further that additional reserves are not available. What will happen in the banking system?

To begin with, the required amount of reserves increases from $28 to $29.4 billion. With only $28 billion in reserves, banks now have a $1.4 billion deficiency of reserves. The system must therefore contract its loans and investments. Assume that the banks try to get additional reserves by lowering their investment holdings. Since each bank will try to acquire enough additional reserves to remove its deficiency, each will contract its investments by that amount. Thus, all banks together sell off investments worth $1.4 billion. The purchasers of the investments probably will be members of the nonbank public, since it is unlikely that banks, being short of reserves, will be buying any securities. When the nonbank public pays for the securities with checks written on its demand-deposit accounts, the commercial banking system's deposit liabilities will contract by $1.4 billion, but the banks will have been unsuccessful in their attempt to get additional reserves:

BALANCE-SHEET CHANGES FOR THE COMMERCIAL BANKING SYSTEM
(IN BILLIONS OF DOLLARS)

ASSETS		LIABILITIES + CAPITAL ACCOUNTS	
Investments	−$1.4	Demand deposits	−$1.4
Addenda: Initial shortage of reserves			$1.4
Decrease in required reserves after decrease in demand deposits			0.294
New deficiency of reserves			1.106

The sale of securities results in no change in reserves for the banking system. The parallel decrease in demand-deposit liabilities, however, reduces required reserves by 21 percent of $1.4 billion, or $294 million. Thus, the banking system is still $1.106 billion short in its reserves.

Given our assumptions, the banking system will continue to contract. Another means of contraction open to banks is loan reduction. As loans come due, depositors usually repay with demand deposits. If, prior to loan repayment, depositors build up their accounts with creditor banks by depositing checks received from others who have accounts with other banks, the creditor banks acquire reserves. These banks also lose reserves, however, since other banks are in approximately the same position. With a $1.106 billion shortage of reserves, all banks together may reduce loans and deposits by $1.106 billion. Are banks still short of reserves? Yes, because a $1.106 billion deposit reduction reduces required reserves by only 21 percent of $1.106 billion, or $232.26 million. The deposit, investment, and loan contraction must continue.

At this point deposits have already dropped by $1.4 and $1.106 billion, a multiple of the initial $1.4 billion shortage in reserves. They must continue to fall, however, until the overall decrease in demand deposits equals 1/.21 times $1.4 billion, or $6.67 billion. Only when demand-deposit liabilities are reduced by a total of $6.67 billion will the original $1.4 billion shortage be made up:

BALANCE-SHEET CHANGES FOR THE COMMERCIAL BANKING SYSTEM
(IN BILLIONS OF DOLLARS)

ASSETS		LIABILITIES + CAPITAL ACCOUNTS	
Loans and investments	− $6.67	Demand deposits	− $6.67

Addenda: Decrease in required reserves (.21)($6.67) = $1.4
Initial deficiency of reserves $1.4
Present level of excess reserves   0

A Shorthand Formula
to Predict the Deposit Creation and Destruction Potential
of the Commercial Banking System

The results of the preceding analysis may be more readily obtained by means of the formula

$$D = \frac{R}{r} \qquad [7\text{--}1]$$

where r is the reserve requirement, R is the volume of reserves in the commercial banking system, and D is the amount of demand deposits that a given volume of reserves (R) can support. For example, if R is $28 billion and r is 20 percent, then D is $140 billion, the initial demand-deposit figure given on page 95.

So long as R and r are unchanged, the maximum volume of deposits the banking system may maintain will be $140 billion. But if r were to increase to 21 percent, for example, D would then equal $133.33 billion. A 1 percent increase in the reserve requirement would thus lead to a $6.67 billion drop in deposits. On the other hand, a 1-percent decrease in the reserve requirement would lead to a $7.368 billion increase in deposit liabilities:

$$D = \frac{\$28 \text{ billion}}{.19} = \$147.368 \text{ billion}$$

Given any value of r, the formula will indicate to what level deposits may expand. There is no requirement that the banking system must expand to this extent, of course, but the profit motive may encourage it to do so.

This formula may also be used to demonstrate the effects of a change in the volume of reserves. For example, if the level of reserves is increased by $100 million, the lending ability of the banking system is increased by $500 million:

$$D = \frac{\$28.1 \text{ billion}}{.20} = \$140.5 \text{ billion}$$

Similarly, a $100 million decrease in reserves would lead to a $500 million decrease in lending ability.

Banking System Deposit Creation and Destruction
Under Relaxed Assumptions

The assumptions used to illustrate bank deposit creation and destruction capabilities in the preceding discussion are quite unrealistic, of course. They simply show the theoretical extent to which a given level of reserves and a given reserve requirement can be used to support deposits. In the following section we will consider what happens when certain of these limiting assumptions are relaxed.

Cash drains and influxes. The nonbank public tends to maintain a relatively stable ratio of currency to deposits; an increase in nonbank public demand-deposit holdings is typically accompanied by an increased demand for currency. This tends to modify the potential increase in deposits and loans. When deposits contract, nonbank public holdings of currency also tend to decrease; currency flows into the banking system, building up commercial bank reserves.

Ironically, the very lending activities of banks that lead to deposit creation tend to restrain the money-creating abilities of the banking system. For example, when banks make loans, some people prefer to take cash, and others take both cash and deposits. These withdrawals of cash reduce the system's reserves, and hence its lending and money-creating abilities. If businesses that get loans for payroll purposes take deposits, cash withdrawals also take place. Employees generally have a higher ratio of cash to deposits than do employers. Paychecks are usually converted into both cash and deposits by employees.

On the other hand, when loans are repaid, they are not repaid solely with demand deposits. Instead, some portion of the repayments are in the form of cash. This means that loan repayment usually leads to reserve increases for the banking system. If banks reduce investments, some security purchasers will use cash. This also leads to reserve increases. Thus, if banks contract because of a reserve deficiency, the extent to which they must contract will be reduced by the resultant cash inflow.

The ability of the banking system to create and destroy money, with this change in assumptions, is now determined by R, the level of reserves; r, the reserve requirement; and c, the ratio of currency to deposits desired by the nonbank public. Changes in the volume of demand deposits that can be maintained by the banking system, *given changes in reserves,* are governed by the equation

$$\Delta D = \frac{\Delta A}{r + c} \qquad\qquad [7\text{--}2]$$

where ΔD is the change in demand-deposit liabilities and ΔA is some beginning change in the volume of reserves.

Assume that R originally equals \$28 billion, r is .20, c is .10, and that

r then increases by $1 billion (that is, $\Delta A = \$1$ billion). Using equation 7–1, we can determine that reserves of $28 billion can support $140 billion in deposits, and reserves of $29 billion can support $145 billion. However, this new higher level of $29 billion in reserves is unlikely to be maintained, since the cash drain created when banks grant loans holds down the money-creating ability of the banking system. From equation 7–2 we see that banks will create only an additional $3.33 billion in deposits. With c at .10, for every $1 billion increase in demand-deposit liabilities, the banking system must allow for a $100 million cash drain, which means, of course, a withdrawal of $100 million from commercial bank reserves. If banks were to attempt to expand deposits by $5 billion on the basis of the $1 billion in additional reserves, they would experience a $500 million loss in cash reserves. This would leave them, on balance, with $4.5 billion in additional demand-deposit liabilities and only $500 million in additional reserves, whereas legally $900 million in additional reserves would be required. Using equation 7–2, we can determine to what extent banks can safely expand demand deposits, given an initial $1 billion increase in reserves. Thus,

$$\Delta D = \frac{\$1 \text{ billion}}{.20 + .10} = \$3.33 \text{ billion}$$

Banks expand demand deposits by $3.33 billion. They will lose $333 million of the initial $1 billion increment in reserves and be left with $667 million in reserves to cover the .20 reserve requirement against the newly created demand deposits. Bank loan and investment expansion during this time will total $3.66 billion: $3.33 billion extended to those customers who took deposits and $.33 billion extended to those who took currency. Equation 7–1 now gives

$$D = \frac{\$28.66 \text{ billion}}{.20} = \$143.333 \text{ billion}$$

On the other hand, if R were initially reduced by $1 billion, the resultant cash inflow would hold down the potential deposit destruction to $3.333 billion.

Excess reserves. Many banks maintain precautionary and working balances of excess reserves, thus further reducing the extent to which the banking system can create and destroy demand deposits. Assume that $R = \$28$ billion, $r = .20$, $c = .10$, and that banks wish to have excess reserves equal to 5 percent of their demand-deposit liabilities. Let the symbol i' represent this percentage. The formula for the volume of demand deposits that the banking system can support now becomes

$$D = \frac{R}{r + i'} \qquad [7\text{–}3]$$

Thus, in terms of our hypothetical situation,

$$D = \frac{\$28 \text{ billion}}{.20 + .05} = \$112 \text{ billion}$$

Now, suppose that R increases by an initial $1 billion ($\Delta A = \$1$ billion). Banks must now maintain reserves sufficient to cover the reserve requirement, precautionary demands for excess reserves, and the cash drain. As a consequence, the formula for changes in the volume of demand deposits that can be supported by the banking system, given changes in reserves, is now

$$\Delta D = \frac{\Delta A}{r + c + i'} \tag{7-4}$$

Again, in terms of our hypothetical situation,

$$\Delta D = \frac{\$1 \text{ billion}}{.20 + .10 + .05} = \$2.857 \text{ billion}$$

For every $1 billion increase in demand-deposit liabilities, the banking system must allow for a $100 million cash drain and also build up excess reserves by $50 million. Consequently, banks will create a maximum of only $2.857 billion in new deposits.

On the other hand, a $1 billion decrease in reserves results in a $2.857 billion drop in deposits, rather than a $5 billion drop. Thus, the tendency of banks to maintain working balances of excess reserves dampens both the money-creating and the money-destroying capacities of the banking system.

Time deposits. Banks create both time and demand deposits. Equations 7–1 and 7–3, however, are applicable only for a banking system with no time deposits. Although we are primarily concerned with the ability of the banking system to create demand-deposit money, we need to know the volume of reserves required to cover time deposits in order to ascertain this.

Let r be the reserve requirement for demand deposits, r' the reserve requirement for time deposits, and TD the volume of time deposits. If $r' = .04$ and $TD = \$60$ billion, then $2.4 billion in reserves is needed to meet the reserve requirement for time deposits. If total reserves, R, are $28 billion, then $25.6 billion in reserves is available to support demand deposits. Thus, the formula for the demand deposit supporting ability of the commercial banking system is

$$D = \frac{R - r'(TD)}{r + i'} \tag{7-5}$$

If $R = \$28$ billion, $D = \$102.4$ billion:

$$D = \frac{\$28 \text{ billion} - (.04)(\$60 \text{ billion})}{.20 + .05} = \frac{\$25.6 \text{ billion}}{.25} = \$102.4 \text{ billion}$$

The greater the volume of time deposits and the larger the reserve requirement for time deposits, the lower is the ability of the banking system to create demand deposits. The reverse is also true. These statements should not be taken too literally, however, for, as previously indicated, if people can be persuaded to switch from demand to time deposits, the ability of the banking system to make loans and create deposits (both demand and time deposits) is increased. A switch from demand to time deposits allows some portion of R to become excess reserves, since the reserve requirement for time deposits is lower than that for demand deposits. Equation 7–5 simply tells us how much in demand deposits the banking system can maintain. Clearly, if there are more time deposits, fewer demand deposits can be maintained; but the total dollar volume of time and demand deposits is greater. This means, moreover, that all bank loans and investments can be increased.

SUMMARY AND PREVIEW

It has been demonstrated that the ability of the banking system to create and destroy demand-deposit money depends on (1) r, the reserve requirement for demand deposits, (2) r', the reserve requirement for time deposits, (3) R, the volume of reserves, (4) TD, the volume of time deposits, (5) c, the ratio of currency to demand deposits desired by the public, and (6) i', the ratio of excess reserves to demand deposits desired by commercial banks. These six variables are all direct determinants of D, the volume of demand deposits that the banking system may maintain. Changes in any of the variables will change D. Equations 7–4 and 7–5 incorporate all these determinants.

Three determinants of D, r, r', and R, are controlled by the monetary authorities. The current values of these variables are easy to ascertain.[6] Two determinants, TD and c, are determined by the nonbank public. One determinant, i', is controlled by the commercial banking system. To explain and predict movements in the stock of money successfully, we must understand how the banking system and the nonbank public react to changes in excess reserves and in our monetary base, R.

Chapter 20 is devoted in part to a study of contemporary money supply theory. It develops behavior relations showing how the banking system reacts to changes in economic conditions and the monetary base as a basis for determining the level of money in the economy. Before we turn to this

---

[6] There is, it is true, a spectrum of reserve requirements for demand deposits. They differ for member banks that are country and reserve city banks. They also differ for member and nonmember banks. Yet, by calculating the percentage of deposits subject to each of the differing requirements, it is possible to calculate an average reserve requirement for the commercial banking system. For example, if 75 percent of deposits are subject to a 10 percent requirement and the remaining 25 percent of deposits come under a 20 percent requirement, the average reserve requirement, r, would be 12.5 percent.

study, however, it is essential that we first understand the influence of other financial institutions and our monetary authorities on our monetary resources. This is discussed in Chapters 8 through 15.

Supplementary Readings

Board of Governors of the Federal Reserve System. *The Federal Reserve System: Purposes and Functions.* Washington, D.C.: 1963, Chapter 4.

Crick, W. F. "The Genesis of Bank Deposits," reprinted in American Economic Association, *Readings in Monetary Theory.* Homewood, Ill.: Irwin, 1951, pp. 41–53.

Orr, Daniel, and W. J. Mellon. "Stochastic Reserve Losses and Bank Credit," *American Economic Review* (1961), pp. 614–23.

Pritchard, Leland J. *Money and Banking.* Boston: Houghton Mifflin, 1964, Chapter 6.

CHAPTER 8

Nonbank Financial Institutions: Sources and Uses of Funds

As commercial banks, in the process of increasing and decreasing their loans and investments, create and destroy money, they measurably affect economic growth. Commercial banks are not the only private financial institutions that help determine the rate of progress of the economy, however. Other financial institutions create and destroy financial assets that compete with currency and bank deposits as forms of liquid wealth. The greater the success of these nonbank institutions in attracting funds, the greater is the total liquid wealth of the nonbank public and the weaker is the direct control of our monetary authorities over the economy.

Previous chapters examined some of the problems that are created for banks and for the economy in general because the principal regulatory devices used by the monetary authorities have their initial impact on commercial banks. This chapter discusses briefly various competing financial institutions—institutions that, it is sometimes claimed, escaped the brunt of monetary controls until the Federal Reserve began an aggressive use of Regulation Q. We shall first study institutions that create assets with a high degree of liquidity—mutual savings banks, savings and loan associations, and life insurance companies. Other financial institutions will then be considered. Finally, the relationship between these nonbank financial institutions and the national economy will be examined. (Government financial institutions will be treated in later chapters.)

PRINCIPAL NONBANK FINANCIAL INSTITUTIONS

Mutual Savings Banks

Mutual savings banks, like commercial banks, create deposits in large volume. However, this is where the similarity ends. Whereas commercial banks create both time and demand deposits, mutual savings banks today create only time deposits. These deposits arise when individuals deposit cash or checks drawn on commercial banks. Although all time deposits are legally subject to withdrawal only after notice, in practice, depositors at mutual savings banks, like those at commercial banks, need give no advance notice.

As Table 8–1 indicates, deposits are the principal source of funds for

TABLE 8–1. MUTUAL SAVINGS BANKS, SOURCES
AND USES OF FUNDS, MARCH 30, 1969

(IN BILLIONS OF DOLLARS)

Assets (uses of funds)		
Financial assets		
Mortgage loans	54.0	
Other loans	1.6	
U.S. government securities	4.0	
State and local securities	0.2	
Corporate and other securities	10.6	
Total		70.4
Cash assets		0.9
Other assets		1.3
Total		72.6
Liabilities and surplus accounts (sources of funds)		
Deposits		65.8
Other liabilities		1.5
General reserve accounts		5.3
Total		72.6

SOURCE: *Federal Reserve Bulletin*, May 1969, p. A–35.

mutual savings banks. They constituted 90 percent of total mutual savings bank liabilities and surplus accounts in 1969, with the remaining 10 percent of funds provided by other liabilities and surplus accounts.[1]

Mortgages and other investments represent the principal uses to which mutual savings banks put their funds. In 1969, more than 75 percent of their assets was in the form of mortgages, and an additional 20 percent was in federal, state, local, and corporate securities. Only 1 percent of assets was in the form of cash. This would appear to be a dangerously low ratio of cash assets to deposits (.014), when contrasted with the reserve requirement commercial banks are required to maintain. For institutions like mutual savings banks, however, this is not a dangerous ratio.

Mutual savings banks were initially set up to provide a safe place for keeping the funds of small savers. These funds were found to have a slow rate of turnover, and, as a consequence, the savings banks did not feel that they had to maintain a large volume of cash. Furthermore, the investment policy of these banks has traditionally been very conservative; they almost never make risky loans on which they could sustain a loss. Thus, although the assets of mutual savings banks are quite illiquid, the slow rate

[1] We use the term "surplus accounts" rather than "capital accounts" since mutual savings banks, like other *mutual* organizations, have no stockholders. Surplus arises when operations are profitable.

of deposit turnover and the fact that many of them have deposit insurance with the Federal Deposit Insurance Corporation preclude the probability of substantial losses on those assets during periods of relative prosperity.

Mutual savings banks have had an excellent record of performance. Even during the depression of the 1930's there were few failures. Yet despite this favorable record, mutual savings banks have not increased in numbers. Their assets have increased substantially, but they have not risen as quickly as those of other nonbank financial institutions. Table 8–2 shows the recent growth in the financial assets of various types of financial institutions. Only commercial bank financial asset growth has been slower than that of mutual savings banks. What accounts for this relatively slow rate of growth? The principal reason is probably the regional character of the mutual savings banks.

Mutual savings banks are almost exclusively a phenomenon of the Middle Atlantic and New England states. They were first started in these states

TABLE 8–2. FINANCIAL SECTOR STATEMENT OF FINANCIAL ASSETS, 1945–68 AMOUNTS OUTSTANDING AT END OF YEAR (IN BILLIONS OF DOLLARS)

YEAR	COMMER-CIAL BANKS	MUTUAL SAVINGS BANKS	SAVINGS AND LOAN ASSOCIA-TIONS	CREDIT UNIONS	LIFE INSURANCE COM-PANIES	PRIVATE PENSION PLANS	OTHER INSURANCE COM-PANIES	OTHER FINANCIAL INSTITU-TIONS
1945	143.8	17.0	8.7	0.4	43.9	1.8	6.9	12.6
1946	133.3	18.7	10.2	0.4	47.5	2.4	7.7	11.6
1947	136.8	19.7	11.7	0.5	50.9	3.1	8.8	11.5
1948	137.8	20.5	13.0	0.6	54.5	3.8	9.9	13.4
1949	139.9	21.5	14.6	0.7	58.4	4.5	11.3	15.4
1950	147.8	22.4	16.9	0.9	62.6	6.3	12.6	18.0
1951	156.8	23.5	19.2	1.1	66.7	7.4	13.8	19.1
1952	166.1	25.3	22.7	1.4	71.4	9.1	15.4	22.3
1953	170.5	27.2	26.7	1.7	76.6	11.1	16.8	24.5
1954	179.7	29.4	31.6	2.0	82.1	13.3	19.2	28.0
1955	185.1	31.3	37.7	2.4	87.9	17.7	21.0	34.2
1956	191.1	33.4	42.9	2.9	93.2	20.2	21.8	36.1
1957	197.0	35.2	48.1	3.4	98.3	22.5	22.1	37.5
1958	211.7	37.8	55.1	3.9	104.3	28.3	24.8	42.4
1959	216.9	38.9	63.5	4.4	110.1	33.1	27.1	48.7
1960	226.0	40.6	71.5	5.0	115.9	36.9	28.2	53.0
1961	243.0	42.8	82.1	5.6	122.8	44.9	31.6	60.6
1962	263.6	46.1	93.6	6.3	129.2	45.8	32.1	62.3
1963	283.1	49.7	107.6	7.2	136.9	53.8	35.2	70.8
1964	306.5	54.2	119.3	8.2	144.8	62.3	37.5	79.5
1965	337.1	58.2	129.4	9.1	153.1	70.0	38.5	90.5
1966	356.9	61.0	134.0	10.0	161.7	71.5	40.0	105.2
1967	396.0	66.4	143.6	11.2	173.2	86.9	45.0	119.2
1968	438.8	71.0	152.8	12.2	182.5	94.7	48.0	n.a.*

* Not available as of October 1969.

SOURCE: Board of Governors of the Federal Reserve System, *Flow of Funds Accounts, 1945–65*, May 3, 1966, pp. 14–20. *Federal Reserve Bulletin*, February 1968, pp. A–66 and 67; May 1968, pp. A–67.10 and 67.11; July 1969, pp. A–19 and A–35 and 36; *International Credit Union Yearbook*, 1969, p. 9.

in the early 1800's. As the economy expanded in the nineteenth and twentieth centuries, the mutual savings form of financial institution did not move geographically.

Another limiting factor in the growth of mutual savings banks has been competition from savings and loan associations. As indicated above, mutual savings banks were initially formed to provide a place for safe-keeping for the funds of small savers. Safety was the primary consideration, and little thought was given to the investment of funds for earnings. As a consequence, mutual savings banks preferred to make short-term mortgage loans and required relatively large down payments. Today, many mutual savings banks have departed from this tradition. In New York State, many will make thirty-year mortgage loans on as little as 10 percent down payments. This is clearly competitive. However, savings and loan associations had come to dominate this field of lending long before mutual banks became competitive. Savings and loan associations have also offered strong competition to mutual savings banks in obtaining deposits. The dividend return on savings and loan share accounts is usually about .5 percent higher than the interest return from the competing mutual savings bank deposit accounts.

Savings and Loan Associations

In contrast to mutual savings banks, savings and loan associations are specifically organized for the purpose of making mortgage loans. Table 8–3 shows that out of a total of $155.7 billion in assets in 1969, $133.0

TABLE 8–3. SAVINGS AND LOAN ASSOCIATIONS, SOURCES
AND USES OF FUNDS, MARCH 31, 1969
(IN BILLIONS OF DOLLARS)

Assets (uses of funds)	
Mortgages	133.0
U.S. government securities	10.1
Cash	2.6
Other	10.0
Total	155.7
Liabilities (sources of funds)	
Savings capital	133.5
Reserves and undivided profits	10.3
Borrowed money	5.6
Loans in process	2.6
Other	3.7
Total	155.7

SOURCE: *Federal Reserve Bulletin*, May 1969, p. A–36.

billion was in the form of mortgages. Cash assets amounted to 1.7 percent of all assets. Savings and loan share accounts are their principal source of funds. Purchasers of these accounts often believe that they are the same as savings accounts with commercial and mutual savings banks. This is not usually true, however. In a savings and loan association a depositor usually owns *a share of the assets* of the association. Fortunately, this ownership is not the same as ownership in a corporation. To get cash for one's stock in a corporation the owner must sell the stock. Since the market price of corporate securities varies, the owner may sustain a loss. This is not usually possible with the shares of a savings and loan association, which ordinarily carry some type of insurance. Those associations regulated by the Federal Home Loan Bank Board, for example, have their share accounts insured by the Federal Savings and Loan Insurance Corporation.

It should be observed that a few savings and loan associations do have a corporate form of ownership. These institutions issue stock that is regularly traded in the securities market. The savings accounts that are sources of funds for these corporations are liabilities and are thus comparable to the savings deposits created by commercial and mutual savings banks.

Like mutual savings banks, savings and loan associations receive their funds in the form of cash or checks drawn on commercial banks. When the associations accept these deposits and create savings and loan share accounts, the volume of near money in the economy is increased. The funds received by the associations are then deposited in their checking accounts at commercial banks and are subsequently used to make mortgage loans or to purchase some other type of asset, such as U.S. government securities.

When mortgage loans made by savings and loan associations are received by borrowers, the funds become active money and stimulate demand and spending. Thus, these associations act as financial intermediaries; they help to transfer funds from those who save, the holders of savings and loan share accounts, to those who borrow, the mortgagors. In this fashion, funds pass from less active to more active spenders. In the process, the volume of liquid wealth and the claims to money in the economy increase.

Table 8–2 shows that savings and loan associations until 1965 grew faster in recent decades than almost any other type of financial institution. This is probably attributable to their active lending habits and to the fact that their dividend rates are usually higher than the interest rates paid by competing mutual savings banks and commercial banks.

Another reason often suggested for the rapid growth of savings and loan associations in recent years is the fact that they are not subject to the same type of reserve requirements as commercial banks. There is quite a bit of truth in this argument. Savings and loan associations use cash holdings directly when redeeming share accounts. When additional funds are needed to redeem share accounts, the associations can either sell U.S. government security holdings or secure loans from a Federal Home Loan bank (if the association is a member of the Federal Home Loan Bank System), using their mortgage holdings as collateral. Furthermore, savings and loan associations seem to have little reluctance toward borrowing. In March 1969, borrowings amounted to $5.6 billion, 3.6 percent of assets, and even exceeded cash assets in volume. Commercial bank borrowings, on the other hand, were $140.4 billion, or 3 percent of assets; and bank borrowings were far exceeded by cash assets, which totaled $73.1 billion.[2]

At the present time, savings and loan associations that are members of the Federal Home Loan Bank System operate under a reserve requirement of 6.5 percent. The Federal Home Loan Bank Board is authorized to vary this requirement from 4 to 8 percent of each association's savings and loan share accounts. Of the 6.5 percent reserve requirement, 2.5 percent must be in U.S. government securities of up to 18 months maturity. The remainder may be in cash, long-term securities, bonds of other government agencies, and so forth. Prior to 1966, if a savings and loan association's actual ratio of reserves to savings capital dropped beneath the requirement, it was forced to stop making loans. This regulation was dropped in 1966, making savings and loan mortgage lending more comparable to commercial bank lending behavior. In addition, the lending territory of savings and loan associations has been extended from 50 to 100 miles. However, this still does not make savings and loan associations comparable to commercial banks, which make a variety of loans and have different reserve requirements.

Cash deposits with a Federal Home Loan bank and U.S. government securities are the principal assets used to meet the FHLB requirement. Were savings and loan associations subject to the same reserve requirements as Federal Reserve member banks, however, only cash assets could be used as reserves. This means that in 1969 savings and loan associations would have needed $10.7 billion in cash assets instead of $2.6 billion.[3] This would seem to give savings and loan associations some competitive advantage over commercial banks. The manipulation of Regulation Q by the Federal Reserve in the mid-1960's reduced this advantage. In addition, since 1964 the Federal Home Loan Bank Board has gradually moved toward a position of supplementing Federal Reserve control policies.

Life Insurance Companies

Life insurance companies, with $190.8 billion in assets as of March 31, 1969, are the second most important financial subsector of the economy.[4] Only commercial banks, which had total assets of $482.9 billion at the end of the same month[5] are more important.

Like other savings institutions, life insurance companies are financial intermediaries. They collect savings and then put these funds to use by

[2] *Federal Reserve Bulletin,* July 1969, p. A–19.
[3] Assuming that the average reserve requirement on commercial bank time and demand deposits for member banks in 1969 was 12 percent.
[4] See Table 8–4.
[5] *Federal Reserve Bulletin,* July 1969, p. A–19.

making investments. Thus, the process of getting funds from the ultimate lenders (savers) to borrowers is considerably eased.

The principal sources of life insurance company funds are the premiums they collect from the sale of life insurance, annuities, and accident and health insurance. Term life insurance and accident and health insurance policies provide the insured with protection. Annuities and nonterm life insurance not only provide protection but also add to the volume of near monies in the economy as the policies acquire a cash surrender value. Thus, total claims to the stock of money are increased.

Life insurance companies generally put their funds to work in long-term investments, primarily mortgage loans and corporate bonds. Table 8–4

TABLE 8–4. LIFE INSURANCE COMPANY ASSETS, MARCH 31, 1969
(IN BILLIONS OF DOLLARS)

Government securities	
United States	4.4
State and local	3.2
Foreign	3.2
Total	10.8
Business securities	
Bonds	69.9
Stocks	11.5
Total	81.4
Mortgages	70.5
Real estate	5.7
Policy loans	11.7
Other assets	10.7
Total assets	190.8

SOURCE: *Federal Reserve Bulletin*, July 1969, p. A–36.

shows that life insurance company holdings of mortgages in March 1969 totaled $70.5 billion, some 37 percent of total assets. Holdings of corporate bonds amounted to $69.9 billion, or 36 percent of assets. Life insurance companies put a large percentage of their funds into these long-term assets because they provide a steady source of revenue that can be used to meet benefit payments. Mortality tables enable insurance companies to predict approximately how much in benefits they will have to pay each year and reduce the need for a large volume of short-term assets that can quickly be converted into cash to meet unanticipated expenses.

The purchase of large quantities of long-term corporate securities by life insurance companies may well have a significant impact on the direction of growth in the U.S. economy. Long-term funds are used primarily for expansion of plant and equipment, a major source of economic growth. There are four main sources of such funds: retained earnings, depreciation, proceeds from the sale of bonds, and proceeds from the sale of stock.

What proportion of these funds is supplied by life insurance companies? In 1968, there was a net increase of $15.1 billion in outstanding corporate and foreign bonds. In that same year, life insurance companies added $3.9 billion to their portfolio holdings of corporate bonds.[6] The increase in life insurance company holdings of corporate securities thus accounted for 26 percent of the 1968 increase. In addition, of a total of $167.1 billion in outstanding corporate and foreign bonds in 1968, $71.4 billion were held by life insurance companies.[7]

Life insurance company holdings of corporate stock are comparatively small relative to bond holdings. Most states have legal prohibitions on the amount of stock a life insurance company may hold. In New York, for example, a life insurance company can invest no more than 5 percent of its assets in corporate common stock. Life insurance companies purchased $1.3 billion of net stock issues in 1968.[8]

In what types of businesses do life insurance companies tend to invest? In 1968, they held $3.6 billion in railroad bonds, $17.6 billion in public utility bonds, and $47.8 billion in industrial and miscellaneous bonds.[9] They also held $111 million in railroad stocks, $3.5 billion in public utility stocks, and $6.4 billion in industrial and miscellaneous stocks.[10] Clearly, life insurance companies direct their funds toward industrials and utilities. In industrials, they tend to invest in chemicals, machinery, and petroleum. The concentration in these areas depends largely on yield and the demand for funds by business. The issues purchased today tend to be direct placements; life insurance companies are purchasing fewer and fewer public issues.

OTHER NONBANK FINANCIAL INSTITUTIONS

There are a host of other financial institutions that provide funds for individuals and businesses. Some, like credit unions and pension funds, are principally savings institutions. Others, such as finance companies, do not collect savings but act as intermediaries between borrowers and savers nonetheless. In fact, finance companies themselves often borrow from other financial institutions, using the proceeds of the borrowings to lend to consumers.

---

[6] *Federal Reserve Bulletin,* February 1968, p. A–65.10; May 1968, p. A–67.7; and May 1969, pp. A–68 and A–69.7.
[7] *Federal Reserve Bulletin,* May 1968, pp. A–67.10 and A–67.11; and May 1969, pp. A–68 and A–69.7.
[8] *Federal Reserve Bulletin,* May 1969, p. A–69.7.
[9] Institute of Life Insurance, *Life Insurance Fact Book, 1969* (New York: 1969), p. 66. The total of these figures differs from the $71.4 billion mentioned above. This difference is attributable to different data sources and the fact that the $71.4 billion includes a small amount of foreign bonds.
[10] *Ibid.,* p. 81. Data include both common and preferred stock.

Credit Unions

A credit union is a savings institution that collects funds by selling shares to its members. This method of collecting funds is comparable to that employed by savings and loan associations. The uses to which credit unions put their funds, however, differ sharply from those of savings and loan associations. The latter will make loans, principally long-term mortgage loans, to many different qualified borrowers. Credit unions lend to a very restricted group of borrowers, and usually on a short-term basis.

Membership in a credit union is limited to a specific group of people. The group may consist of the members of a religious organization located in a particular community or members of the same occupational group. In the United States, 58 percent of all credit union members are industrial employees. An additional 15 percent are government employees.[11]

Group members are the principal source of funds for the credit union. Loans to members also represent the primary use to which these institutions put their funds; credit union lending is almost always restricted to members.

In recent years, these unions have experienced phenomenal growth. As Table 8–2 shows, their financial assets grew from $400 million in 1945 to $12.2 billion in 1968. No other type of savings institution, not even the rapidly growing savings and loan association, has had a faster rate of growth. Their relative importance as a financial institution is still minor, however.

Credit union assets consist primarily of short-term loans to members. Unlike other savings institutions, the credit unions concentrate on consumer installment debt. Out of a total $78.0 billion in installment credit held by financial institutions in March 1969, some $10.3 billion was held by credit unions. Only commercial banks (which held $37.3 billion) and sales finance companies ($18.3 billion) held more installment credit.[12] Most credit union lending takes the form of automobile, home-improvement, and debt-consolidation loans.

The major problem facing credit union members is the lack of savings protection comparable to that provided depositors in commercial and mutual savings banks by the FDIC and for shareholders in federal savings and loan associations by the Federal Savings and Loan Insurance Association. As a result, the risk attached to holding credit union shares is greater than for holding other forms of liquid wealth.

Pension Funds

Pension funds are designed to provide income for people after retirement. There are two types of pension plan: *insured* and *uninsured*. Insured

---

[11] *International Credit Union Yearbook,* 1969, p. 9.
[12] *Federal Reserve Bulletin,* May 1969, p. A–52.

plans are administered by insurance companies; uninsured plans are administered by corporations, unions, or trustees appointed by them. In either case, funds are supplied by employer and employee contributions. Uninsured plans have become increasingly popular in recent decades, largely because of legal limitations on insurance company investment in common stock. This has made the uninsured plans, which are not ordinarily subject to such legal regulations, more attractive.

Pension plans may be *funded* or *nonfunded*. Companies with nonfunded plans meet pension payment requirements out of current income; in funded plans, funds are collected and invested to help meet future benefit payments. If the plan is insured, these funds are put to the same uses as any other funds available to life insurance companies. Uses of funds in uninsured pension plans differ markedly, however. Table 8–5 lists the total

TABLE 8–5. INSURANCE SECTOR: FINANCIAL ASSETS AND LIABILITIES FOR PRIVATE PENSION PLANS AND NONLIFE INSURANCE COMPANIES, DECEMBER 31, 1967

(IN BILLIONS OF DOLLARS)

TYPE OF ASSET AND LIABILITY	PRIVATE PENSION PLAN	NONLIFE INSURANCE COMPANIES*
Financial assets		
Demand deposits and currency	1.2	1.3
Credit and equity market instruments		
Federal obligations	3.2	4.9
State and local obligations	—	13.7
Corporate bonds	25.5	4.0
Corporate stock	53.0	17.7
One-to-four family mortgages	3.9	—
Mortgages	—	.2
Other loans (policy loans)	—	—
Total	85.7†	40.5
Trade credit	—	3.2
Total financial assets	86.9	45.0
Total liabilities	86.9	25.0

* Fire and casualty companies, fraternal orders, and nonprofit medical plans.
† Totals may differ because of rounding.
SOURCE: *Federal Reserve Bulletin*, May 1968, p. A–67.11. Later data not available as of October 1969.

financial assets of uninsured private pension plans as of December, 1967. Out of a total $86.9 billion of financial assets, some $78.5 billion, or 90 percent, were in the form of corporate stocks and bonds. In the same year, by way of comparison, life insurance company holdings of corporate stocks and bonds amounted to only 46 percent of their total financial assets. The contrast is even more striking when we compare holdings of corporate stock. Life insurance company holdings of stocks were only 4 percent of financial assets; uninsured private pension plans, however, held $53.0 billion, or 61.0 percent, of their financial assets in this form.[13] The reasons for this difference, as previously indicated, are the legal restrictions imposed on life insurance company investment in stocks. In a period of relative prosperity, such as that of the post-World War II economic world, stocks will usually appreciate in value and hence are a more attractive investment than bonds. Thus, there is a strong inducement to invest pension plan funds in stocks.

Nonlife Insurance Companies

Nonlife insurance companies consist primarily of fire and casualty insurance firms. Like life insurance companies, their sources of funds are principally premium payments. Unlike life insurance companies, however, they also get substantial funds from capital accounts.

Fire and casualty insurance companies differ sharply from life insurance companies in their use of funds, too. Nonlife insurance company assets are, for the most part, highly liquid. As is shown in Table 8–5, a total of $6.2 billion, or 14 percent, of fire and casualty financial assets were in the form of demand deposits and U. S. government securities in 1967. In contrast, life insurance companies had only 4 percent of their financial assets in this form.[14]

This difference is largely attributable to the nature of the financial obligations that the respective institutions are likely to incur. Life insurance companies can predict their total future financial responsibilities with a high degree of accuracy on the basis of mortality tables. Hence, they need not keep large quantities of funds in a highly liquid form. Fire and casualty companies, on the other hand, cannot know in advance the claims that will be made in a given year as a result, for example, of fire or the vagaries of the weather. While one may expect increases in aggregate liability payments from year to year, this is of little assistance to the individual insurance company. Its power to predict the volume of future claims is limited. As a consequence, fire and casualty companies tend to concentrate their funds in assets that can quickly be converted into cash, such as demand deposits and government securities. They also invest heavily in corporate stock; this is permitted because of their relatively low debt/equity ratio.

Finance Companies

Finance companies differ from the other financial institutions we have discussed principally in their sources of funds. Commercial banks, savings banks, savings and loan associations, and credit unions all receive their funds from depositors and shareholders, and, in the process, create near

[13] *Federal Reserve Bulletin,* May 1968, p. A–67.11.
[14] *Ibid.*

monies. Life insurance companies receive their funds principally from premium payments; other insurance companies receive their funds from premium payments and capital accounts. Finance companies, however, get their funds principally from *borrowings* and *capital accounts.*

The two most important types of finance companies are consumer finance and sales finance companies. Consumer finance companies deal directly with the public; they usually make installment loans for the purchase of automobiles and consumer durables. Although the proceeds of the loans usually are used for a specified purchase, the actual loan is generally unsecured.

Sales finance companies, on the other hand, normally do not deal directly with the public. Instead, they purchase installment contracts from sellers of goods and services. The sale of these obligations to a finance company provides the retailer with funds that he can use immediately in his business operations and frees him from the expense and bother of collecting installment payments. Most installment-contract purchases are in the

TABLE 8–6. FINANCIAL ASSETS AND LIABILITIES
FOR FINANCE COMPANIES, SECURITY BROKERS AND DEALERS,
AND OPEN-END INVESTMENT COMPANIES, DECEMBER 31, 1967
(IN BILLIONS OF DOLLARS)

TYPE OF ASSET AND LIABILITY	FINANCE COMPANIES	SECURITY BROKERS AND DEALERS	OPEN-END INVESTMENT COMPANIES
Financial assets			
Demand deposits and currency	2.9	1.1	1.6
U.S. government securities	—	1.0	1.0
State and local obligations	—	0.5	—
Corporate bonds	—	0.7	3.0
Corporate stock	—	0.7	39.1
Mortgages	4.3	—	—
Consumer credit	24.3	—	—
Other loans	14.0	—	—
Security credit (to others)	—	8.7	—
Total	45.5	12.7	44.8*
Liabilities			
Corporate bonds	17.5	—	—
Bank loans	7.9	—	—
Other loans (open-market paper)	14.1	—	—
Security credit (to brokers and dealers)	—	10.6	—
Taxes payable	0.2	0.1	—
Stock: Corporation	—	—	44.8
Total	39.6*	10.7	44.8

* Totals differ because of rounding.
SOURCE: *Federal Reserve Bulletin*, May 1968, p. A–67.11. Later data not available as of October 1969.

field of auto financing. Sales finance companies frequently lend directly to automobile dealers at relatively low rates of interest, thus permitting the dealers to build up their stock of automobiles. Once the cars are sold, a dealer may extinguish the debt by paying cash or selling the installment contracts of his customers.

Table 8–6 shows the overwhelming importance of consumer credit as a use of funds for finance companies. At the end of 1967, their financial assets amounted to $45.5 billion, with 53 percent in consumer credit. Total assets, however, were actually somewhat higher because of land and building ownership. Financial liabilities at the end of 1967 were $39.6 billion.

As is shown in Table 8–7, in 1969 sales finance companies and consumer finance companies together accounted for over $27.2 billion in installment

TABLE 8–7. CONSUMER CREDIT, MARCH 31, 1969
(IN MILLIONS OF DOLLARS)

TYPE OF CREDIT AND INSTITUTION		AMOUNT
Installment credit		
Commercial banks		
Automobile paper	19,392	
Other consumer-goods paper	6,188	
Repair and modernization loans	2,670	
Personal loans	9,007	
Total		37,257
Sales finance companies		
Automobile paper	9,988	
Other consumer-goods paper	4,868	
Repair and modernization loans	70	
Personal loans	3,327	
Total		18,253
Credit unions		10,294
Consumer finance companies		8,927
Other financial institutions		3,275
Retail outlets		
Department stores	n.a.*	
Furniture stores	n.a.	
Appliance stores	n.a.	
Automobile dealers	320	
Other	n.a.	
Total		11,666
Total installment credit		89,672
Noninstallment credit		
Single payment loans		9,139
Charge accounts		6,340
Service credit		6,799
Total noninstallment credit		22,278
Total consumer credit		111,950

* Not available.
SOURCE: *Federal Reserve Bulletin*, May 1969, p. A–53.

debt, out of a total of $89.7 billion. Commercial banks, of course, held the largest amount, $37.3 billion. This is to be expected; commercial banks hold the largest volume of financial assets of any financial institution in the economy. Consumer credit is less important, however, for commercial banks than for finance companies. The former provide a wide variety of financial services for the public, whereas finance companies specialize in consumer credit.

Open-End and Closed-End Investment Companies

Open-end investment companies, commonly called *mutual funds,* are yet another economically important financial institution. They obtain funds by selling their stock directly to the public. The proceeds are then used to purchase stocks and bonds of other corporations.

Mutual funds issue new stock to meet the demands of the public. This stock may be purchased only from the investment company itself. When a stockholder wishes to redeem his shares, he does so by selling them back to the company. Thus, annual variations in the amount of open-end investment company stock outstanding depend upon the difference between new stock sales and stock redemptions. In 1968, open-end investment companies sold $6.820 billion of their own shares. They also retired $3.841 billion of their own shares, however. This left a net increase of $2.979 billion.[15]

Obviously, such an excess of sales over redemptions constitutes an increase in shares outstanding. It does *not* mean that the liquid wealth of mutual fund stockholders has increased, however. The value of mutual fund shares only increases when the company makes a profit on its investments in the stock of other companies.

Because of the large volume of funds received, open-end investment companies are able to purchase the stocks of diverse companies. Presumably this cuts down the possibility of loss attendant upon holdings concentrated in particular stocks. However, it is entirely possible that a falling market will undermine the greater part of an open-end company's portfolio of stock investments. Mutual funds took substantial losses in the stock market decline of 1962, for example. On the other hand, if the market is rising, as has been usual during recent decades, the value of an open-end investment company's stock investments will increase, and the value of its own stock will rise, too. Mutual fund investment company assets have risen in market value from $8.7 billion at the end of 1957 to $52.7 billion at the end of 1968. Part of this $44.0 billion increase is attributable to an increase in net sales of mutual fund stocks amounting to $21.7 billion. The remaining $22.3 billion increase in market value of assets, however,

---

[15] *Federal Reserve Bulletin,* May 1969, p. A–45.

is almost wholly due to the increased value of stock investments made by these companies.[16]

How liquid a form of wealth are mutual fund shares? Clearly, the possibility of loss and the lack of any federal insurance on this type of asset indicate a small degree of liquidity. Nonetheless, such stocks may be fairly good investments during an extended period of economic prosperity.

Closed-end investment companies are another type of investment company. They issue only a fixed amount of stock, which is not sold directly to the public (it is usually sold through an investment bank). Nor, once the stock has been purchased, can it be resold to the company; it can be resold only through some form of stock exchange to other individuals who are willing to purchase it. (The data on these companies are relatively incomplete, so none is presented here.) Closed-end and open-end investment companies are comparable, however, in that their fundamental purpose is to make earnings by wise investments in stocks of other corporations.

NONBANK FINANCIAL INSTITUTIONS AND THE ECONOMY

Most nonbank financial institutions are financial intermediaries that help channel funds from savers to borrowers. This is certainly a useful, and apparently an innocent, function. However, financial intermediaries create many problems for the economy.[17]

Weakening the Effectiveness of Monetary Controls

Nonbank financial institutions create forms of liquid wealth that compete with money. There are many forms of wealth; although real wealth and liquid wealth are the two inclusive categories, people are confronted with a choice between alternative forms of both liquid and nonliquid wealth. As Chapter 5 pointed out, the more successful nonbank financial institutions are in inducing people to maintain their liquid-wealth holdings in the form of savings bank deposits, savings and loan association share accounts, or life insurance policies instead of money, the weaker is the control of our monetary authorities over the economy. Monetary policy, until the recent use of Regulation Q by the Federal Reserve, operated directly only on commercial banks. This is one problem created for our economy by the operations of nonbank financial institutions: in the ab-

[16] *Ibid.*, p. A–45. Market value is the market value at the end of the period less current liabilities.

[17] Economists have discussed these problems extensively in the last two decades. Prominent among those associated with the ideas developed are John Gurley and Edward Shaw. For an excellent theoretical discussion of their views see John G. Gurley, and Edward S. Shaw, *Money in a Theory of Finance* (Washington, D.C.: Brookings Institution, 1960).

sence of effective monetary regulation, they may be responsible for an apparent weakening of our economic control mechanism.

Increased Velocity in Periods of Prosperity

A second problem arising out of increased nonbank financial institution operations is that of increased spending during periods of economic boom, when what is needed is a decrease in spending. Our monetary authorities, by limiting commercial bank lending activity, attempt to dampen spending and hence reduce the demand for goods. If, at the same time, savers are induced to switch from holding demand- or time-deposit accounts at commercial banks to the liquid-wealth forms created by nonbank savings institutions, however, funds may become activated. Savings institutions do not hold their increased money balances idle; they lend them to consumers in the form of installment loans, to home buyers for home construction and improvement, or to businesses for capital expenditures. When the borrowed funds are spent, spending and the demand for goods and services rise. In a relatively high-employment economy, spending and demand may rise faster than the ability of the economy to meet this demand. The result is an increase in prices rather than in the output of goods and services.

There does not have to be a change in the stock of money for this to occur, merely an increase in its use. A rise in the velocity of circulation of money has the same effect as does the spending of an increased stock of money—it raises total spending. Nonbank financial institutions contribute to these inflationary pressures by helping to transfer money balances from savers, who are not active spenders, to actively spending borrowers.

Evidence of the 1950's and 1960's. There is some evidence that increases in the velocity of money underlay a substantial part of the price rises and output increases of the 1950's. Consider the following two periods of rapid growth: 1951 and 1955–57. Wholesale prices increased 11 percent in 1951. The stock of money increased from $115.5 billion at the end of 1950 to $122.1 billion at the end of 1951. Gross national product rose from $284.6 to $329.0 billion. The income velocity of money, or the number of times that the stock of money is spent on gross national product during a year, is computed by dividing gross national product by a representative stock-of-money figure for the year in question. Applying this measure to the case at hand, we find that income velocity rose from 2.52 in 1950 to 2.77 in 1951. Thus, while gross national product increased 16 percent, the stock of money rose only 5 percent. This money therefore had to circulate more rapidly, and, indeed, velocity increased approximately 11 percent. This increase in velocity was twice as important for the growth in gross national product in 1951 as the increase in the stock of money.

In the second period, from the recession year of 1954 through prosperous 1957, the stock of money increased from an average stock of $130.0 billion in 1954 to $136.0 billion in 1957—again, an increase of only 5 percent. Wholesale prices in that period increased from 110.3 percent of the 1947–49 level in 1954 to 117.6 percent in 1957. Gross national product, meanwhile, rose from $363.1 billion to $442.8 billion, an increase of 22 percent. Income velocity rose from 2.79 in 1954 to 3.26 in 1957, an increase of 17 percent. Here again, increased velocity was more important than increased money balances as a means of financing the growth of gross national product—more than three times as important! This clearly illustrates that if increased money balances are not available to finance increased output, either the increase in output will stop or the existing money supply will be utilized more intensively.

Velocity continued to increase in the 1960's, particularly in the Viet Nam war period. From 1964 through 1968, gross national product increased from $632 billion to $860 billion, a 36-percent increase. At the same time, the money stock rose by more than 20 percent; velocity rose from 4.06 to 4.62.[18]

Conclusion. Much of the increase in velocity in this period was attributable to the increased funds available to nonbank financial intermediaries in the 1950's. Increased funds meant increased lending. The relatively rapid rate of growth of these institutions, as shown in Table 8–2, supports this view. After 1964, however, as indicated in Chapter 5, they grew more slowly than commercial banks, as a result of the effective use of Regulation Q by the Federal Reserve. Although nonbank financial institution growth contributed significantly to velocity increases in the 1950's, it was not as important in the period after 1964. It therefore appears that the nonbank public does respond to changing interest-rate differentials among financial institutions by altering the composition of its liquid-wealth holdings.

Obviously, increased loan activity by commercial banks in the periods of prosperity was another source of increased spending. Householders also tended to increase their rate of spending during these periods. What happened as a result? All this increased spending of a slowly rising money stock led to an increase in both output and the price of goods and services. As the economy approached full employment, the effects were concentrated more and more in price-level increases.

It should be emphasized that commercial banks and nonbank financial intermediaries affect the cyclical velocity of money in somewhat different ways. Nonbank intermediaries make relatively few changes in the composition of their earning-assets portfolios over the business cycle. Their acquisition of these assets is closely tied to current fund inflows, and these in turn reflect the reaction of the general public to interest rates and other factors that are set largely according to long-run growth considerations rather than cyclical ones. Although mutual savings banks and life insurance

[18] The data in this section are taken from various issues of the *Federal Reserve Bulletin.* The stock-of-money figure used in the computation of income velocity is the average of successive end-of-year figures.

companies may at first seem like exceptions with respect to their holdings of government securities, the percentage of assets held in this form does not show much cyclical variation. Thus, the destabilizing effects of nonbank financial intermediaries over the business cycle are primarily the result of an increase in the volume of their holdings of earning assets, rather than a change in the composition of these assets. Commercial banks, on the other hand, vary the composition of their portfolios with the cycle, thereby intensifying it. They switch from loans to investments on the downward part of the cycle, and vice versa on the upward part. They can do this because of the wide range of uses to which they are able to put their funds. Other financial intermediaries are more specialized in their use of funds.

Multiplication of Claims to Real Wealth

The third problem created by the growth of nonbank financial institutions is that of the multiplication of claims to real wealth in the economy. It has already been observed that the claims created by these institutions make monetary control of the economy more difficult. Actually, the enormous magnitude of these claims relative to the stock of money is itself a potential source of economic difficulty. Liquid wealth is only a claim to real wealth. While an increase in the volume of liquid wealth may induce increased spending, and hence increased output, the mere multiplication of claims does not itself increase the physical volume of real wealth in the economy.

Furthermore, real wealth can be purchased only with money. The more other forms of liquid wealth increase relative to money, the more difficult it may become to convert them into money. In the event of economic stress, people may want to convert the liquid wealth created by these institutions into money, since that is the most liquid of all assets. In periods of rapidly rising prices, people may come to expect a continuation of rising prices. As a consequence, most forms of liquid wealth, including money itself, will be losing purchasing power. There may then be an attempt to "get out of" other liquid wealth and into money, for the ultimate purpose of getting into goods. The total amount of liquid wealth, however, is several times the volume of money in the economy. Hence, not all claims to money can actually be redeemed. A concerted attempt by the American public to transform a major portion of their liquid-wealth holdings into money could conceivably result in financial chaos comparable to that of the early 1930's.

Fortunately, several forms of nonmoney liquid wealth, such as time deposits in commercial banks and mutual savings banks and savings and loan association share accounts, carry some form of federal insurance. Although the present assets of the federal insuring corporations are inadequate to meet all possible demands for converting insured liquid wealth into money, economists generally believe that the mere existence of this insurance may prevent the public from starting a financial panic. This "psychological" restraint on panics, however, applies only to recessions. What about "runs" on financial institutions that might occur with the expectation of sharply rising prices? Deposit insurance would do little good, because people would be demanding money in order to spend it. Thus, insurance would not restrain them from converting "near money" into money. Hopefully we shall not be confronted with this situation if the relatively conservative monetary-fiscal policies of the last decade are continued. It is usually only when a nation's spending and money-creating activities are unrestrained that great inflations take place and there is a general abandonment of both money and other liquid-wealth holdings.

SUMMARY

Sources and Uses of Funds

We have now briefly examined the sources and uses of funds of our major financial institutions. The results of this survey are summarized in Table 8–8. In general, those financial institutions that receive a large proportion of their funds from savers tend to put their funds into uses that yield a return over a long period of time. This is characteristic of mutual savings banks, savings and loan associations, and life insurance companies. Credit unions are a clear-cut exception. They appear to fill a gap left by other financial institutions; no other credit institution concentrates on ex-

TABLE 8–8. PRINCIPAL SOURCES AND USES OF FUNDS, BY TYPE OF FINANCIAL INSTITUTION

TYPE OF FINANCIAL INSTITUTION	PRINCIPAL SOURCES OF FUNDS	PRINCIPAL USES OF FUNDS
Commercial banks	Demand deposits Time deposits	Commercial and industrial loans Real-estate loans Consumer credit U.S. government bonds U.S. government short-term securities State and local government securities Cash assets
Mutual savings banks	Deposits	Mortgages
Savings and loan associations	Savings capital	Mortgages
Life insurance companies	Premium payments Earnings	Corporate bonds Mortgages Government securities
Credit unions	Savings capital	Consumer credit
Pension funds (noninsured)	Premium payments	Corporate stock Corporate bonds
Other insurance companies	Premium payments Capital accounts	Corporate stock State and local government securities U.S. government securities
Finance companies	Borrowings Capital accounts	Consumer credit
Investment companies	Capital accounts	Corporate stock

tending short-term credit to small savers in the relatively low-income groups.

Those financial institutions that receive a large fraction of their funds from capital accounts and borrowings tend to put their funds to uses that produce a high yield but are also highly liquid. Financial institutions that need funds on short notice to pay casualty claims (fire and casualty insurance companies), to repay borrowings (finance companies), or to redeem shares of stock (open-end finance companies) tend to invest their funds in highly liquid assets that can quickly be converted into cash. Of course, these assets are also somewhat risky, which accounts for their relatively high yield. Principal among these uses of funds are corporate stock and consumer credit. Uninsured pension funds are, to a certain extent, an exception. They receive their funds from premium payments and are able to predict with considerable accuracy their annual need for funds. Nevertheless, they tend to invest in both stocks and bonds. One important reason for this is probably the high yield obtained from stocks in our relatively prosperous postwar era.

The sources and uses of commercial bank funds differ sharply from those of other financial institutions. The main reason for this is the wide range of services that banks in the United States provide for their customers. Demand-deposit accounts, which can be converted into cash on demand, force banks to hold large amounts of highly liquid assets, such as short-term government securities, commercial and industrial loans, and consumer credit. On the other hand, time-deposit accounts, such as savings deposits, which have a relatively slow turnover rate, permit them to invest in relatively safe, long-term, interest-yielding assets, such as real-estate loans and U.S. government bonds.

Problems Posed by Financial Intermediaries

These problems—a weakening of the effectiveness of monetary controls, an increase in the velocity of money in periods of prosperity, and the multiplication of claims to real wealth—are not problems created by the nonbank financial institutions alone. Commercial banks, individuals, and government are all to some extent "responsible." A further exploration of these problems is reserved for the theory and policy discussion of Parts III and IV.

Supplementary Readings

Gurley, John G., and Edward S. Shaw. *Money in a Theory of Finance.* Washington, D.C.: Brookings Institution, 1960.

Simons, Henry C. "Rules Versus Authorities in Monetary Policy," reprinted in American Economic Association, *Readings in Monetary Theory,* Homewood, Ill.: Irwin, 1951, pp. 337–68.

Tobin, James, and William C. Brainard. "Financial Intermediaries and the Effectiveness of Monetary Controls." *American Economic Association Papers and Proceedings* (1963), pp. 383–400.

PART II

Money and Government

CHAPTER 9

The Historical Development
of Banking in the United States

Money consists of currency created by the federal government and demand deposits created by the commercial banking system. From the earliest days of our nation's history the American government has attempted to regulate money. At various times in our history Congress has placed the United States on bimetallic, gold coin, paper, and modified gold monetary standards. Congress has also created the First Bank of the United States, the Second Bank of the United States, the National Banking System, and, finally, our present Federal Reserve System. This chapter briefly examines the historical development of monetary standards and banking in the United States, with emphasis on the shaping influence of the government. The intent is to give some flavor of the historical problems we have faced and to set the stage for a consideration of contemporary monetary problems.

MONETARY STANDARDS
IN THE UNITED STATES

It will be recalled that the dollar is the unit of account in the United States. All debts, prices, and types of money are counted in terms of the dollar. Once a price for a good is established, we know how much money must be given up to acquire the good. Today this unit of account, the dollar, is an abstract measure of value; it is no longer domestically tied to a specific commodity. Officially the dollar is tied to gold: an ounce of gold is defined by law as being worth $35. However, no form of money, currency or deposits, can be redeemed in gold by citizens of the United States. Currency is our money of ultimate redemption. For this reason we say that the United States presently has an *internal paper standard;* that is, money can be redeemed only by currency, most of which is in the form of paper currency. Externally, of course, the United States is on the *gold standard,* since foreign government claims on the United States may be met in gold.

This distinction between our internal and external monetary standards has prevailed since the passage of the Gold Reserve Act of 1934. It has taken a long time for this characteristic of the contemporary American economy to be recognized by the general public, however. The Federal Reserve until recently printed currency bearing the designation, "will pay to the bearer on demand ———— dollars." Currently, however, Federal Reserve notes simply state, "———— dollars." The designation "will pay to the bearer on demand ———— dollars" has been dropped, in recognition of the fact that currency, not gold, is the actual money of ultimate redemption. Nonetheless, this change in the labeling of our currency caused considerable consternation among Congressmen.

U.S. currency and the unit of account have not always been divorced internally from specific commodities such as gold or silver. This is a comparatively recent development, which began on a permanent basis in 1934. For most of its history, the United States has been on some type of metallic standard.

The Period of Bimetallism

1792–1834. Under a bimetallic standard the unit of account is tied to two money metals, usually gold and silver. The first monetary standard in the United States was bimetallic. The *Coinage Act of 1792* defined the dollar as being equal either to 371.25 grains of silver or to 24.75 grains of gold. This meant that anyone bringing gold or silver to the mint could have it coined without charge. The legally defined mint ratio of silver to gold was 15 to 1 ($371.25/24.75 = 15$). A given amount of gold was, therefore, legally worth 15 times as much as an equal amount of silver. At that time, however, the actual market exchange ratio of silver to gold was about 15.5 to 1. Thus Congress undervalued gold and overvalued silver. As a consequence only one money metal, silver, circulated in the United States. The intent of Congress had clearly been that both gold and silver coin should circulate, however, since the amount of either metal in the United States was insufficient by itself to meet domestic currency needs. If the bimetallic standard had legally priced gold and silver closer to the market ratio, both metals would probably have circulated. The disparity between the mint and world ratios for gold and silver drove gold from circulation. Since gold in the United States was worth less silver at the mint than in the world market, little gold was brought to the mint for coinage. Silver, however, had a high price at the mint and a large amount of silver coinage took place.

Other circumstances combined to prevent even the freshly minted silver coin from having a wide circulation within the United States. American silver dollars found their way into the West Indies where Spanish and American silver dollars circulated side by side, each equally acceptable. Unworn Spanish dollars were actually heavier than American silver dollars, however, so a trade in Spanish and American silver dollars developed. American dollars were exchanged for the Spanish dollars with the heavier silver content and then were melted and minted in the United States into new American silver dollars. Thus there developed a flow of American silver dollars to the West Indies, and a return flow of a roughly equivalent number of Spanish dollars to the United States. Once these were melted, a greater number of American silver dollars were minted; these then flowed back to the West Indies. As a result, American silver dollars failed to circulate in the United States. Lower-denomination American coin and lightweight worn foreign coin circulated in the United States.[1] To put a halt to the outflow of silver caused by the failure of American silver dollars to remain in circulation in the United States, the Treasury stopped coining silver in 1805. This suspension continued until 1834, and even then silver dollars were not minted for general circulation until 1840. There was a general shortage of specie throughout this whole period.

Gresham's law. The reasons for the outflow of gold and high-denomination silver coin during this period may also be explained by reference to a principle called *Gresham's law,* which states that "bad money drives out good." This simply means that a money form will be used where its value is the greatest. Under the bimetallic standard, when the mint ratio departs from the market ratio, there will tend to be an outflow of one money metal to where its value is greatest. Gold was undervalued in the United States from 1792 to 1834, so it flowed abroad. Silver was overvalued in the United States during the same period, so it flowed into the United States. The heavier weight of Spanish silver dollars offset this inflow, however, and led to an outflow of the lighter-weight American dollars to the West Indies.

During the period *1792 to 1834,* therefore, the *United States was legally on a bimetallic standard,* but *in fact, it was on a silver standard.* The currency in circulation consisted of worn foreign coin, small-denomination American coin, and banknotes. (More will be said about banknotes in a subsequent section of this chapter.) Gold virtually disappeared from circulation, particularly in the last decade of the period.

1834–61. The United States continued on the bimetallic standard from 1834 to 1861, but during this period the standard became a *de facto gold standard.* This began in 1834 when Congress changed the legal ratio of silver to gold. Silver was kept at 371.25 grains to the dollar, but gold was changed to 23.22 grains to the dollar. This boosted the mint ratio to approximately 16 to 1. Congress hoped that the new mint ratio would return the United States to a de facto bimetallic standard, but again Congress miscalculated. The United States was too small a nation at the time to dominate the world price of gold and silver; changes in the American mint ratio had little influence on world gold and silver market prices. Since the market ratio of gold to silver was still approximately 15.5 to 1, gold

---

[1] At that time it was legally permissible for foreign coin to circulate freely in the United States. This privilege was gradually restricted and finally terminated in 1857.

became overvalued and silver undervalued in the United States. Some circulation of silver did continue in this period of a de facto gold standard, however.

Gold was now brought to the U.S. mint for coining instead of silver. The outflow of large-denomination silver coins increased. Small-denomination silver coins remained in circulation, but there was little new minting of silver coin. This contributed to a shortage of low-denomination coin. It was impractical to mint low-denomination gold coins. Since the mint price of gold was 16 times that of silver, a low-denomination gold coin would have had to be either very small in size or a mixture of a small amount of gold and a large amount of some other metal. Hence, to increase the amount of coins in circulation, Congress reduced the silver content of subsidiary silver coins in 1853. From that date to the present, our subsidiary silver coin has not contained an amount of silver equal in value to the face value of the coin.

1861–73. The United States officially continued on a bimetallic standard until 1873. From 1861 to 1879, however, we were actually on a *paper standard.* Faced with the necessity of financing the Northern war effort, Congress authorized the Treasury to issue $450 million in "greenbacks," an irredeemable paper currency designed to serve as legal tender. It was not until 1879 that redemption of these greenbacks in gold specie was permitted. Greenbacks are now known as "United States notes" and are still being issued today. (The total amount of outstanding United States notes is limited by law to $323 million, however.) Coins were also in short supply in this period. People hoarded coin during the Civil War, and for a time postage stamps were used to make change. Subsequently the Treasury issued fractional 3¢, 5¢, 10¢, 15¢, 25¢, and 50¢ notes to facilitate making change.

The Silver Question

The United States continued on a de facto paper standard from 1873 to 1879, but the period of the legal gold standard started prior to the resumption of specie payments in 1879. The Coinage Act of 1873 made no provision for coining silver dollars. In effect, this failure to provide for silver coinage put the United States on a legal gold standard, although low-denomination subsidiary silver coin could still be minted.

At the time this action meant little, since greenbacks were not being redeemed in either gold or silver. It came to have meaning, however, when, due to a sharp increase in world silver production, there was a fall in the market price of silver. This produced a clamor for "free silver" and a silver standard in the United States. The agitation was so strong that silver purchase acts were passed in 1878 and 1890. These acts provided that the

Treasury should purchase silver at a given price and issue silver coin and silver certificates.

The silver purchase acts of 1878 and 1890 were the first of a long series of acts designed to protect silver-producing interests in the United States. Additional silver purchase acts were passed in 1893, 1918, 1934, 1939, and 1946. These acts provided a firm market price for silver producers. Whenever the market price tended to fall beneath the Treasury buying price, producers could sell their output to the Treasury. This policy of protection continued until 1963, when Congress repealed the silver purchase acts and permitted the Federal Reserve to replace silver certificates with Federal Reserve notes. Silver is now used only in half-dollar coins. Actually, the concessions previously made to the silver interests by the various silver purchase acts were comparatively minor. Silver-backed currency and silver coin were generally a small part of our total currency supply.

The almost complete abandonment of silver as a money metal is related to the coin shortage of the early 1960's. Silver, as noted, was used as backing for silver certificates and in coin. Dimes, quarters, and half dollars contained 90 percent silver. There was heavy and increasing industrial use of silver in the 1960's. World market prices rose to as high as $1.75 per ounce of silver in 1967, whereas the Treasury support price was $.90 an ounce and its selling price was $1.29 an ounce. It paid to buy silver from the Treasury and sell it to industrial users. Treasury silver stocks dropped. Accordingly the government replaced silver certificates in circulation with Federal Reserve notes and passed the Coinage Act of 1965 which took all silver from dimes and quarters and reduced the silver content of the half dollar from 90 percent to 40 percent. It should be noted that the Treasury now makes a substantial profit, called *seigniorage,* on coin production. The cost of producing coin is less than the face value of the coin. Hence the Treasury makes a profit when it sells coin to the Federal Reserve at face value.

The Gold Standard

1873–1933. Although the United States was legally on the gold standard in 1873, the de facto paper standard continued until 1879. The Resumption Act of 1875 required that the U.S. Treasury begin the redemption of greenbacks in 1879. Actual resumption, the conversion of currency into gold on demand, started in 1879. It was this action that placed the United States on both *a legal and a de facto gold standard.* Gold coins were minted and gold certificates were issued that were fully backed by gold held in the Treasury.

Some doubt existed, however, concerning the legality of the gold standard. The widespread demands for "free silver" are indicative of this. The controversy was finally settled by the Gold Standard Act of 1900, which explicitly stated that the United States, like the leading European powers, was on a gold standard. The United States continued on this standard until 1933. With the exception of the World War I period, 1917 to 1919, U.S. currency could be redeemed in gold until 1933.

1933; 1934–69. Until 1933 gold coins, gold certificates, Federal Reserve notes, and the various forms of Treasury currency circulated in the United States. All were considered legal tender. The volume of gold coins and gold certificates in circulation, however, tended to diminish after the establishment of the Federal Reserve System. After 1917, member banks were required to keep all of their reserves in the form of deposits with the Federal Reserve banks. This caused a large transfer of gold from the vaults of member banks to those of the Federal Reserve banks. In addition, the Federal Reserve replaced gold certificates in circulation with its own Federal Reserve notes. These actions led to a reduction of the amount of gold and gold certificates in circulation.

In the 1930's it became increasingly difficult for the large industrialized nations to remain on the gold standard. The depression caused the principal trading nations of the world to abandon the gold standard in favor of monetary policies more conducive to internal economic stability (see Chapter 26 for a discussion of this point). By 1933 the United States was one of the few nations continuing on the gold standard. The widespread bank failures that accompanied the depression in 1933 then caused the United States to abandon the gold standard. The nonbank public and the commercial banks were required to turn in all holdings of gold coin, bullion, and certificates to the Federal Reserve banks (with the unpublished loophole of allowing private citizens to keep their gold coin in coin collections). This action took the United States off the gold standard internally. In addition, the United States stopped exporting gold; this took the United States off the gold standard externally as well. Thus, in 1933, the United States went on a *legal and de facto paper standard both domestically and externally.* Obligations could only be redeemed in paper currency.

In *1934* the United States returned to a gold standard, but one which may be more accurately described as a *modified gold standard.* Prior to 1934, an ounce of gold was legally worth $20.67. The new legal price of gold as set forth in the Gold Reserve Act of 1934 was $35 an ounce. It remains at this level today.

In addition, the Gold Reserve Act of 1934 prohibited any further gold coinage and declared all gold certificates to be the property of the Federal Reserve, and all gold coin and bullion the property of the U.S. Treasury. As a result, gold coin and certificates are no longer used for transactions within the United States.

Gold certificates, like silver certificates, are legal tender; however, this provision allows them to be converted only into Federal Reserve notes and prevents currency collectors from being in violation of the law. The private sector of the economy is prohibited from owning gold except as jewelry, in coin collections, or for industrial purposes. Paper currency is now the money of ultimate redemption. Thus the United States has been on *a de facto paper standard internally since 1934,* even though the dollar is legally defined as having a gold content.

The Gold Reserve Act of 1934 also authorized the Treasury to regulate the export of gold. Since that time the Treasury has used gold to settle international claims on American dollars. This means that the United States is on both *a legal and a de facto gold standard in international transactions.*

BANKING IN THE UNITED STATES FROM 1791 TO 1913

The First Bank of the United States, 1791–1811

Congress has often readjusted our monetary standard, the principal changes having come in 1834, 1861, 1873, 1879, 1933, and 1934. Similarly, the development of banking in the United States has been shaped largely by governmental action.

In 1791, Congress chartered the First Bank of the United States. The establishment of this bank was due largely to the efforts of Alexander Hamilton, our first Secretary of the Treasury, and other advocates of a central banking institution.

At the time, there were only three commercial banks in the United States. Their ability to issue currency was limited, and state governments were forbidden to print currency. The bimetallic standard was still in the process of being moved through Congress under Hamilton's guidance; coinage of gold and silver by the U.S. mint would not start until after the Mint Act of 1792. As a consequence, there was generally a shortage of money. The First Bank of the United States was designed to be a source of currency convertible into specie and to operate both as a commercial bank and as fiscal agent for the U.S. government.

The First Bank of the United States received its charter from Congress in 1791 and began operations with its head office in Philadelphia. In time it operated eight branches in important domestic trading centers. In brief, the principal provisions of the charter authorized the First Bank to (1) have a capitalization of $10 million (25,000 shares were to be issued with a value of $400 each, of which $2 million in stock was to be purchased by the government and the remaining $8 million was to be sold to the public; foreigners could own stock, but only U.S. citizens could vote their shares by proxy), (2) issue up to $10 million in paper currency in denominations of $5 and up (these notes were the equivalent of legal tender because they could be used to pay debts to the U.S. government), (3) receive deposits, (4) make loans, (5) act as fiscal agent for the federal government, and (6) act as a clearing mechanism for other banks. Among the restrictions placed on the Bank was the provision that forbade loans on real estate and com-modities. This prevented the Bank from engaging in speculative ventures that had frequently been the downfall of less well-managed state banks.

Opposition to the establishment of the Bank was strong. Thomas Jefferson was a leading opponent, for example, arguing that the Bank was unconstitutional. Others contended that the First Bank would inhibit the development of private banking in the United States, that it would be a monopoly and abrogate the powers of state governments. Even after its chartering, the First Bank of the United States encountered strong opposition. Rural interests that needed easy credit to meet the demands for funds in the expanding frontier areas, farm debtors, and commercial banks were particularly vocal in their opposition.

Commercial banks, for example, objected to the Bank's unwillingness to accept the notes of banks that refused to redeem their notes in specie (gold and silver). This policy made it difficult for many commercial banks to expand loans. Banks at that time created bank notes in much the same way as they create demand deposits today.[2] Each commercial bank could create paper currency (bank notes) when extending loans. Borrowers usually took the proceeds of their loans in the form of bank notes rather than in specie. As these bank notes were spent, they passed into circulation in the economy. The notes were liabilities of the issuing bank and were presumedly redeemable in gold and silver coin. If the issuing bank had a good reputation and adequate specie reserves to cover demands for specie, its notes achieved a wide circulation. On the other hand, a bank that was illiquid, made risky loans, overextended note issues relative to specie holdings, or made it difficult for noteholders to redeem its currency soon found that its notes had become generally unacceptable. By refusing to accept and redeem notes of overextended banks, the First Bank of the United States hoped to restrain excessive issues of state bank notes. This encountered strong state bank opposition.

In addition, the First Bank's combination of public and private functions aroused strong state bank resentment. They felt that this represented unfair competition. The First Bank was the only private commercial bank operating with a national charter. It also acted as a central bank by regulating state bank note issues and, as fiscal agent for the Treasury, it held federal funds.

There were also many who objected to the large volume of Bank stock held by foreigners, even though this stock did not carry voting privileges except by proxy. In sum, the opposition to the Bank was so strong that Congress failed to renew its charter in 1811. The First Bank of the United States, by assuming the responsibilities of a central bank in regulating the nation's currency, had run counter to rural interests, proponents of state rights, and commercial banks.

[2] Today, only the Federal Reserve and the U.S. Treasury can create paper money.

State Banking, 1811–16

When the First Bank of the United States closed its doors for the last time in 1811, the restraint on unsound bank note issues was eliminated. The United States then entered into a period of rapid state bank growth. The number of commercial banks rose from 88 in 1811 to 246 in 1816. Bank mismanagement also increased, however.

Speculative excesses occurred and inflation ensued. By 1814 state banks were no longer able to redeem notes in specie. Paper currency had been issued to excess. It has been estimated that the volume of state bank notes in circulation tripled from 1811 to 1816.[3]

Not all of this financial difficulty was caused by the closing of the First Bank. This was also the period of the Napoleonic Wars, in which the United States became involved through the War of 1812. Europe, like the United States, was experiencing currency problems. For example, from 1797 to 1821 the Bank of England refused to redeem its notes in specie; overissue of notes made it impossible to maintain redemption of notes in specie and inflation followed. The American experience was not unique.

The absence of a central bank hampered the financing of the War of 1812. The Treasury could have refused to accept depreciated state bank notes in payment of debt, but it did not choose to do so. Instead, it tried to persuade state banks to resume specie payments. This effort proved unsuccessful. It appears, therefore, that part of our difficulties arose from the failure of the Treasury to act as a monetary authority in the absence of a central bank.

The Second Bank of the United States, 1816–36

The drive for specie resumption led to the establishment of the Second Bank of the United States in 1816. The charter provisions passed by Congress were not unlike those of the First Bank. The major difference was that the Second Bank was larger. Its capitalization was greater, and it eventually operated a total of twenty-five branches.

The principal charter provisions authorized the bank to (1) have a capitalization of $35 million, 20 percent going to the government and 80 percent to the public; (2) issue up to $35 million in paper currency in denominations of $5 and up (these notes were to be legal tender for payments of debts to the United States government); (3) receive deposits; (4) make loans; (5) act as fiscal agent for the federal government; and (6) act as a clearing mechanism for other banks. The Bank's charter was to run for twenty years.

The Second Bank had an even stormier history than the First Bank. In

[3] Leon M. Schur, "The Second Bank of the United States and the Inflation after the War of 1812," *The Journal of Political Economy* (1960), pp. 118–34.

its early years, the Second Bank was badly managed. Loans were made to stockholders who used stock as collateral. Investments were expanded too swiftly; the Second Bank's own note issue was increased too quickly. The Bank's first president, William Jones, a political appointee who was not a banker, actually speculated in the Bank's stock. Jones finally resigned in 1818 and Langdon Cheeves, another nonbanker, became the Bank's second president. He succeeded in bringing some stability to operations, however.

Although the Second Bank of the United States was mismanaged in its early years, the principal charge against it was that it failed to prevent inflation in 1817 and 1818. It will be recalled that one of the primary reasons for establishing the Second Bank had been to put a stop to the inflation that had been caused by the excessive issue of state bank notes. This inflation was not halted by the founding of the Second Bank. Part of the blame, however, has to be placed upon the Secretary of the Treasury, William Crawford, who pressured the Second Bank into accepting the notes of banks with questionable reserves. Crawford was primarily interested in minimizing losses to the Treasury that could result from the closing of overextended state banks.[4]

The Second Bank finally began to follow a restrictive policy in the latter part of 1818. It refused to accept the notes of state banks that did not redeem in specie and it also restricted its own lending activity. It did this chiefly because its own specie reserve position was in danger. Unfortunately, the timing of this restrictive action was bad; it intensified a sharp economic contraction that subsequently occurred in 1818 and 1820. This depression of 1818–20 was probably initiated by a drop in the foreign demand for agricultural goods, but the decrease in the stock of money resulting from the Bank's restrictive policy certainly accelerated the depression. At the time, however, the Second Bank received almost all of the blame for the depression. The Bank's opposition even went so far as to instigate an unsuccessful attempt to have its charter revoked.

From 1820 on, the Second Bank operated on a relatively sound basis, particularly after Nicholas Biddle became the Bank's president in 1823. Biddle operated the Bank both as a private profit-making commercial bank and as a central bank for the nation. He tried to restrain excessive state bank note issues, particularly those of southern and western banks and, with increased Bank pressure, resumption of specie payments became fairly widespread.

With the election of Andrew Jackson to the U.S. Presidency in 1828, political difficulties again beset the Second Bank. Jackson was sympathetic to southern and western interests, which were mistrustful of eastern bankers, among other things.

In 1832, four years prior to charter expiration, Congress rechartered the Second Bank. Jackson vetoed the bill, however. In 1833, Jackson trans-

---

[4] *Ibid.,* p. 120.

ferred federal deposits from the Second Bank to various private "pet banks." Biddle countered this action by contracting the Second Bank's assets and demand liabilities.[5] The result was a nationwide economic contraction. Needless to say, there was no renewal of the Bank's charter when it expired in 1836.[6] This "bank war" between Biddle and Jackson spelled the end of central banking and the end of branch banking in the United States until the establishment of the Federal Reserve System in 1913.

State Banking, 1836–63

The period 1836 to 1863 was an era of state banking. Most legitimate banks operated on charters obtained from state legislatures or state banking authorities. There was no one central banking authority charged with supervising the stability of state bank notes or with regulating speculative lending operations by commercial banks.

As a result, there was financial chaos throughout most of this period. The number of banks increased rapidly in good times and decreased rapidly in recession; successive price inflations and deflations occurred. Many unsound loans were made, including illegal loans to stockholders. It was not uncommon for banks to have inadequate specie reserves, so that they were unable to redeem their bank note liabilities in specie. In fact, payment of specie was almost completely suspended from 1837 to 1842. The variety of bank notes in circulation ran into the thousands, many, as might be expected, being counterfeit. Books were published describing which notes were good and which were bad, but the books were out-of-date even before they were printed.

Attempts were made to reform and regulate the banking system, but these were primarily regional efforts that did little to improve the nationwide banking problem. The three main programs of reform were (1) the Suffolk System, (2) the Safety Fund System, and (3) free banking.

The Suffolk System was established in New England as early as 1824. Prior to 1824, the notes of banks outside of Boston had moved toward that city because of its financial importance in the New England area. Frequently, the notes of these outside banks did not circulate at par, whereas the notes of most Boston banks did. In fact, the more difficult it was for Boston banks to redeem the notes of outside banks, the greater the discount from par that these notes bore.

Thus, in conformity with Gresham's law, the good notes of the Boston banks were driven from circulation. People hoarded the notes of the

---

[5] For a discussion of this period see Jacob P. Meerman, "The Climax of the Bank War: Biddle's Contraction, 1833–34," *The Journal of Political Economy* (1963), pp. 378–88; and Peter Temin, "The Economic Consequences of the Bank War," *ibid.* (1968), pp. 257–74.
[6] For some years, the Bank tried to operate with a Pennsylvania charter, but it finally failed in 1841.

Boston banks and used the depreciated currency of distant banks in their daily transactions. To remedy this situation, the Suffolk System was set up. Under this system, banks outside of Boston that wished to have their notes redeemed at par within the Boston area were required to maintain at least a $2,000 redemption-fund account with the Suffolk bank. All notes of non-Boston banks received by the Boston banks were to be cleared by the Suffolk bank. If the "outside" banks refused to join the Suffolk System, the Suffolk bank would collect a large volume of their notes and then request redemption in specie. Naturally any bank with inadequate specie reserves was unable to meet such a sudden large demand for specie. In this fashion the Suffolk System rather effectively eliminated most speculative and excessive note issues from the New England area. Eventually almost all New England commercial banks became members of the system. It was only with the establishment of the National Banking System in 1863 that the need for the Suffolk System was eliminated.

The Safety Fund System was set up in 1829 by the New York State legislature. The principal function of this system was to protect depositors in the event of bank failure. Each bank in New York that was to receive a new charter or that requested renewal of its old one by the legislature was required to contribute an amount of money to the fund (to be held by the State Treasury) equal to 3 percent of its capital stock. Payments from the fund were to be made to creditors of banks that failed.

For a time the Safety Fund System worked successfully. This was during periods when bank failures were not widespread, however. With the demise of the Second Bank of the United States in 1836, bank failures became more extensive, particularly during the 1837–42 recession. The Safety Fund soon found that it did not have adequate funds to meet the claims of the creditors of all the banks that failed in this period. Legislation was then passed limiting insurance to the claims of noteholders only, not all creditors. The Fund continued to operate under the new arrangements for several decades, but it rapidly diminished in importance after 1846.

There are several reasons why the Safety Fund System gradually became less important. First, the bank failures from 1837 to 1842 demonstrated that a fund limited in scope to a small area of the country is unlikely to be able to stave off nationwide financial panic. Second, New York adopted "free banking" in 1838. Under free banking new banks were no longer required to get their charters from the state legislature, as banks that were members of the Fund had had to do. Finally, the establishment of the National Banking System in 1863 provided nationwide note stability.

Although the Safety Fund became relatively unimportant, it was the first major attempt in our banking system to insure bank creditors. Today, of course, Federal Reserve notes are legal tender, and for funds on deposit we have a nationwide system of deposit insurance under the auspices of the Federal Deposit Insurance Corporation.

Free banking was another answer to the excesses of state banking. Free banking started first in the State of New York with the passage of the Free Banking Act of 1838. A similar program was adopted at about the same time in Michigan. Under the New York plan any group of people could set up a bank, provided they deposited various state and United States bonds with the state comptroller in an amount equal to the volume of notes to be issued. In the event of bank failure, the comptroller was to pay the noteholders out of the proceeds of the sale of these assets deposited with him. The purpose of the act was to standardize procedures for the establishment of banks and to free banks from dependency upon the whims and political pressures of state legislatures. No longer, for example, could legislators demand bank stock in exchange for their vote in favor of granting a bank a charter.

Some fifteen states adopted free-banking laws prior to 1860. One difficulty with the free-banking system of this period was that frequently it was too easy for individuals to set up banks that complied with state requirements. Reserve requirements often did not exist, or were far too lenient. As a result, too many banks were established within a relatively short period of time, many with inadequate specie reserves, and too many risky loans were made.

Thus, *in the period of state banking from 1836 to 1863, the absence of a uniform currency and a central bank led to financial chaos.* There were a tremendous number of different bank notes in circulation, many of which were counterfeit. Charters came to be granted too freely. As a consequence, too many banks were weak and badly managed, and too many risky loans were made. Efforts at reform were regional in scope and thus unable to offer a solution to the national banking problem.

Much of this difficulty was caused by the closing of the Second Bank of the United States. At the time it was thought that the Treasury could regulate the banking system effectively by keeping federal funds in various "pet banks." These banks were supposed to maintain separate specie reserves to cover Treasury deposits. Frequently, however, these banks used Treasury deposits as a basis for expanding their own loans and note issues. Consequently, when these banks experienced financial difficulty, the Treasury often discovered that its funds could not be withdrawn.

Finally, the Treasury itself lost confidence in the "pet banks," and, after various abortive attempts at solutions, Congress set up the *Independent Treasury System* in 1846. Under this system, a series of subtreasuries were set up in various cities across the nation, where the Treasury could amass its funds. In this fashion, the Treasury gave up what few powers of monetary regulation it had had. Instead of using its deposits to keep state bank notes safe throughout the nation, it now confined itself to safeguarding its own funds. The Independent Treasury System did, in fact, safeguard federal funds, but in the process it left the banking system totally unregulated and it created some new difficulties.

For example, Treasury tax collections and Treasury expenditures did not coincide. When collections temporarily exceeded payments, a surplus would arise. Funds were withdrawn from the economy and held by the Treasury. This reduced the amount of specie reserves held by commercial banks and thereby lessened their ability to redeem notes. On the other hand, when Treasury payments exceeded tax collections, an increased amount of funds would flow to the banking system and provide the basis for bank-note and loan expansion, some of which was speculative.

The Independent Treasury System continued to operate until 1920. As early as 1863, however, the Treasury was again permitted to keep funds in commercial banks in addition to its own Independent Treasury System. Gradually the Treasury came to realize that it should use its deposits at commercial banks in a way that would not affect bank specie reserves adversely.

The National Banking System, 1863–1913

The shortcomings of state banking were obvious. The problem was how to rectify the situation. There was considerable pressure for bank reform, but it was not until the Civil War that this agitation brought positive results with the passage of the National Banking Acts of 1863 and 1864. These acts did not reinstate centralized regulation of banking, but they did correct some of the deficiencies of state banking.

The National Banking Acts were designed to meet two broad goals—(1) to establish a safe currency system, and (2) to assist the Treasury in financing the Civil War. It is probable that it was the financial pressure of the war that caused this banking legislation to be passed. According to the terms of these acts, national banks were to be established that would issue paper currency and provide a market for U.S. government securities. As it developed, the national banks did not purchase a large volume of U.S. government securities during the Civil War, and thus they never became a principal source of funds for the Treasury.

The national banks, which, taken together, constituted the National Banking System, did provide a safe currency system for the United States, however. This was accomplished by limiting the amount of notes that national banks could issue to a maximum of 90 percent of their holdings in U.S. government securities. Since the federal government had budget surpluses throughout much of the time in which the National Banking System existed, there were several reductions in national debt which limited the supply of notes and contributed to their safety.

Principal Provisions of the National Banking Acts

In addition to a provision for the issuance of bank notes based upon U.S. government security holdings, the National Banking Acts of 1863 and

1864 had provisions concerning the chartering of banks, capital requirements, reserve requirements, government security holdings, and bank lending operations.

The granting of charters. Under the National Banking Acts, any group of five or more persons could apply for a charter from the Comptroller of the Currency in Washington, D.C. In essence, this amounted to a new system of free banking, although the Comptroller was often strict in his granting of charters. Banks receiving their charters from the Comptroller were called "national banks," to distinguish them from "state banks," which received their charters from state banking authorities. This distinction between state and national banks remains with us today, as will be recalled from Chapter 4.

Capital requirements. The minimum capital requirements for the establishment of national banks were (1) $50,000 for banks in cities of under 6,000 inhabitants, (2) $100,000 for banks in cities from 6,000 to 50,000 inhabitants, and (3) $200,000 for banks in cities with still larger populations. These requirements still apply today to national banks.

Some 50 percent of the capital had to be paid to the bank's managers before the bank could begin operations. Each share had a par value of $100. Stockholders were subject to double liability; that is, if the bank failed, the stockholder could be required to pay an amount of money equal to his original stock purchase. The funds would be used to meet the claims of the bank's creditors. This provision is no longer in effect.

Government security deposits and bank notes. Prior to beginning operations, a bank was required to deliver a given volume of U.S. government securities to the U.S. Treasury. These securities had to have a value of $30,000 or one-third the value of the bank's capital stock, depending on which figure was larger. Once the bonds were delivered to the Treasury, the banks could start issuing national bank notes in an amount equal to 90 percent of the value of the securities. In 1900 banks were permitted to issue an amount of notes equal to a full 100 percent of the value of the securities. In addition, each national bank was obligated to redeem the notes of any other national bank at par.

Although each national bank was authorized to issue notes if it met the preceding requirements, the actual printing of the currency was done by the U.S. Treasury so as to minimize the risk of counterfeiting.

These notes were not legal tender, but since they could be used to pay federal taxes at par, they were the equivalent of legal tender, just like the earlier notes of the First and Second Banks of the United States. It was not until 1933 that Congress declared national bank notes to be legal tender. Today there are still a few national bank notes in circulation, but they are all in process of retirement; no national bank notes have been issued since 1935. Private commercial banks are no longer permitted to issue paper currency. Only the Federal Reserve and the U.S. Treasury are authorized to issue paper currency and coin money.

As further insurance for the safety of national bank notes, Congress provided in the National Banking Acts of 1863 and 1864 that no bank could issue notes in excess of the volume of its own stock and that the total volume of national bank notes could not exceed $300 million. A particular bank's share in the $300 million depended on its size and location. These limitations were removed in 1875.

In the event of the failure of a national bank, the Comptroller of the Currency was authorized to sell the securities that had been deposited by the bank and to use the proceeds to redeem its notes. In addition, the national banks were required to maintain a "redemption fund" with the Comptroller equal to 5 percent of their outstanding notes.

Reserve requirements. National banks initially had one set of reserve requirements for both currency and deposit liabilities. The reserve requirements stipulated that banks designated as *central reserve city* and *reserve city* banks maintain reserves equal in value to 25 percent of their bank-note and deposit liabilities. Banks in other cities were called *country banks.* They were to maintain reserves of 15 percent against notes and deposits. At first only New York was a central reserve city. In 1887, however, Chicago and St. Louis were also included in this category.

The reserves of central reserve city banks were to be vault cash in the form of "lawful money," by which was meant legal tender specie and Treasury currency. National bank notes, of course, could not be used as reserves. Reserve city banks, on the other hand, needed to keep only one-half of their reserve requirement in the form of vault cash. The remaining portion could be in the form of deposits with central reserve city banks. The terms were even more lenient for country banks; only 40 percent of their reserves had to be in the form of vault cash. The remaining 60 percent could be in the form of deposits with either reserve city or central reserve city banks.

In 1874 the reserve requirement for notes was dropped altogether; reserves were now only required for deposits. As we shall discuss in a moment, the composition of the assets used to satisfy the reserve requirement turned out to be one of the principal shortcomings of the National Banking System.

Other charter provisions. The major limitation on the lending activity of national banks was the banning of real-estate loans. This rule is no longer in effect. In addition, loans to any one borrower could not exceed 10 percent of the value of the capital stock of the bank. This regulation still applies to national banks. Finally, national banks were permitted to serve as fiscal agents of the U.S. government.

The Tax on State Bank Note Issues; Renewed Growth of State Banking

The National Banking Acts were successful in providing a safe, uniform currency. Although the number of state banks declined markedly in the face of competition from national banks, those remaining in operation continued to issue paper currency and many of these state banks issued excessive amounts of notes. Thus the National Banking Acts did not substantially improve the quality of *all* bank note issues. To correct this deficiency, Congress passed an act in 1865 that placed a 10 percent annual tax on all state bank note issues. This tax was so prohibitive that within a few years all state bank note issues were withdrawn from circulation. This also caused the number of state banks to decline sharply.

The National Banking System did not spell the end of state banking, however. Banks had always considered the right of note issue a fundamental prerequisite for banking, but a revolution was occurring in the banking habits of businesses and individuals, which soon invalidated that assumption. Following the Civil War, increasing use was made of deposit money; people found it more convenient to use demand deposits as a medium of exchange. State banks soon discovered that they could continue operations by creating deposits rather than currency. Bank customers seeking loans were willing to accept demand deposits in lieu of bank notes and, except for periods of financial panic, the turnover of deposits proved quite predictable. Thus, banks could operate much as they always had, now with reserves a fraction of deposits instead of a fraction of notes and deposits. Once banks became accustomed to operating under the new conditions, the number of state banks increased markedly. The number of national banks continued to mount also, but at a substantially slower rate than state banks.

Many new banks felt that it would be to their advantage to gain the right of note issue and prestige by becoming national banks. There were, nonetheless, several distinct advantages to a state charter. The rules and regulations of state authorities were more lax than those of the Comptroller of the Currency. Reserve requirements and required capitalization were usually lower for state than for national banks. State banks could make real-estate loans, whereas national banks could not.

Principal Defects of the National Banking System

Inelasticity of bank-note issue. The National Banking System did not provide for the needed seasonal, cyclical, or secular variation in currency. At seasonal peaks of business activity, for example, more currency and deposit money are needed. The volume of national bank notes was tied to the national debt, however, and the national debt is determined by federal surpluses and deficits, not by seasonal business activity. Thus, there was no room for a seasonal expansion of the currency supply.

More important than the seasonal inelasticity of national bank note issues was the cyclical and secular inelasticity of national bank notes. As the economy expands on the upward swing of the cycle, more currency is needed to carry on business activity. To the extent that expansion of business is in real output, an increase in money helps to finance the rise in economic activity. A growing economy needs additional currency and deposits to carry on a growing volume of transactions. Under the National Banking System, however, there was no mechanism for automatic note expansion. In point of fact, during the upward phase of the cycle, the federal government often found itself with a surplus which it used to retire part of the national debt. As national debt was retired, of course, the support for national bank notes decreased and their volume had to be reduced. Treasury surpluses were common throughout the 1880's and, as a consequence, the volume of national bank notes fell from $339 million in 1880 to a low of $165 million in 1891.[7] In later years surpluses were not as frequent, and by 1913 the volume of national bank notes had climbed to $745 million.[8] Thus national bank note variations were geared to national debt changes rather than to the economy's need for currency.

Other forms of currency did not have the desired elasticity in this period either. The volume of gold and silver coins in circulation depended upon foreign and domestic production of the money metals. This was also the case with gold and silver certificates, since they had to be backed fully by money metals. The greenbacks issued during the Civil War, which today we call United States notes, were limited in amount by act of Congress. These limitations, together with the limits placed upon national bank note expansion, effectively prevented the needed flexibility in our paper currency and coinage.

Pyramiding of reserves. Another major shortcoming of the National Banking System was that it made possible a pyramiding of reserves. It will be recalled that, legally, the reserves of national banks consisted of vault cash and deposits at other national banks. The *ultimate reserves* of all national banks, however, consisted of vault cash, not deposits at other banks, since only vault cash could be used to redeem deposit liabilities.

Nonetheless, as country and reserve city banks made cash deposits with either reserve city or central reserve city banks, the total volume of reserves held by national banks would increase, and, accordingly, the loan- and demand-deposit-creating ability of the banking system would rise also.

Assume, for example, that country banks had $1 million in vault cash and no deposits at other banks. Since country banks could maintain as

---

[7] Milton Friedman and Anna Schwartz, *A Monetary History of the United States, 1867–1960* (Princeton, N.J.: National Bureau of Economic Research, 1963), p. 131.
[8] *Ibid.*, p. 180.

much as three-fifths of their reserves as deposits at noncountry national banks, under these conditions country banks could transfer $600,000 in cash to reserve city banks. Assume that country banks deposit $600,000 in cash with reserve city banks. This is shown by entries labeled (a):

BALANCE-SHEET CHANGES FOR COUNTRY BANKS

ASSETS	LIABILITIES + CAPITAL ACCOUNTS
Reserves	
Vault cash − $600,000 (a)	
Deposits at reserve city banks	
+ $600,000 (a)	

BALANCE-SHEET CHANGES FOR RESERVE CITY BANKS

ASSETS	LIABILITIES + CAPITAL ACCOUNTS
Reserves	Demand deposits due country banks
Vault cash + $600,000 (a)	+ $600,000 (a)
Vault cash − $300,000 (b)	
Deposits at central reserve city	
banks + $300,000 (b)	

BALANCE-SHEET CHANGES FOR CENTRAL RESERVE CITY BANKS

ASSETS	LIABILITIES + CAPITAL ACCOUNTS
Reserves	Demand deposits due reserve city
Vault cash + $300,000 (b)	banks + $300,000 (b)

Country bank total reserves have not changed, but those of reserve city banks have risen by $600,000.

The process need not stop here. Reserve city banks were required to keep at least one-half of their reserves in the form of vault cash. Thus, reserve city banks could now transfer $300,000 in cash to deposit accounts at central reserve city banks. This transaction, as shown in the entries labeled (b) above, results in another increase in reserves; central reserve city bank reserves have increased by $300,000. Thus, the initial $1 million in vault cash reserves has been pyramided to $1 million in vault cash reserves and $900,000 in reserves in the form of deposits at other banks.

So far this caused no economic difficulties. However, if reserve city and central reserve city banks expand loans and deposits on the basis of these increased reserves, then in the event of a call for cash from other banks, there could well be a shortage of cash reserves. A shortage of cash reserves could force banks to suspend specie payments and this might precipitate financial panic. As knowledge of a lack of liquidity became general, people would fear for the safety of their deposits and demand more cash. This would place added strain on the resources of the banking system. The financial panics of 1873, 1884, 1893, and 1907 were in large part an outgrowth of such reserve pyramiding and excessive deposit creation by re-serve city and central reserve city banks. These panics were triggered by the currency drains that took place in periods of relative prosperity when banks were loaned up.

These difficulties could have been avoided if reserve city and central reserve city banks had kept enough vault cash on hand to back the deposit liabilities they owed other banks. Instead, as reserve city and central reserve city banks received cash deposits from other banks, they tended to con-sider this cash as part of their own reserves, and expanded loans and deposits as if they were receiving cash deposits from individuals. This is not to say that reserve city banks did not recognize their responsibility for maintaining funds to cover the deposits due other banks. The city banks were fully aware of this responsibility, particularly the large New York banks. They were private profit-seeking corporations in a highly competi-tive industry, however. As a result they felt obliged to keep their excess reserve positions low. Possible demands for cash by other banks were covered by the New York banks through call loans to stockholders. When pressed for funds from other banks, the New York banks could "call" back their funds from the brokers. These call loans were considered highly liquid.

The problem was, however, that if there were a widespread demand for cash throughout the economy, these call loans would prove to be non-liquid. Stockbrokers would not be able to get funds without selling stocks and causing a collapse of stock prices. Financial panic would follow in either case. Frequently these calls for cash would come when lending ac-tivity was high. Country banks would call for funds when farmers needed cash to help harvest and distribute crops in the fall. At the same time, how-ever, central reserve city and reserve city banks were faced with loan demands from their own seasonal borrowers. There was no central bank to provide additional funds at such times, either.

If this was the case, why didn't the banks keep all reserves in cash form? Primarily for two reasons. First, demand deposits, until 1934, earned inter-est. Therefore, these funds were a source of earnings for banks with tem-porarily idle funds. Second, country banks maintained deposits with re-serve city banks to secure the advantages of correspondent banking.

Another problem related to the pyramiding of reserves was the lack of any means of accumulating cash for the purpose of helping a bank in emergency. Each bank was prohibited from drawing down its vault cash beneath the required level. In effect, cash reserves were frozen at each na-tional bank. As a result, although one bank might have a large volume of vault cash, it could not send any substantial amount to a bank in difficulty if this would entail a reduction in its own vault cash beneath the legal minimum. Once a bank's vault cash had sunk to its legal minimum, it had to close its vaults even if it had more than enough cash to cover a bank run.

Thus, under the National Banking System, cash flowed toward central reserve city and reserve city banks and, as this occurred, the loans and deposits of these banks increased. When, however, the depositing country banks converted their deposits into cash, reserve city and central reserve city banks were forced to contract these loans and investments so as to reestablish a favorable reserve position. If they were unable to do so, they suspended cash payment and precipitated a financial panic.

Rigid reserve requirements. A third shortcoming of the National Banking System was that for the time that a bank was short of reserves, it was required to suspend the granting of new loans. This type of regulation created uncertainty for both borrowers and bank managers. Just when the demand for borrowing was strong, banks frequently had to halt the granting of new loans.

Inadequate check-clearing facilities. Finally, the clearing and collection mechanism for checks used by the National Banking System was archaic. There was no central check-clearing agency comparable to the system presently maintained by the Federal Reserve System (see Chapter 10). With a unit banking system consisting of thousands of banks, checks had to be cleared through an elaborate network of correspondent banking relationships. Had the United States had only a few banks with many branch offices like many European countries, the need for adequate check-clearing facilities would not have been so important. As it was, however, the correspondent clearing facilities were cumbersome. The cost of transferring funds between distant points was expensive, long delays frequently occurred in check clearing, and many banks did not redeem out-of-town checks at par.

Establishment of the Federal Reserve System

The shortcomings of the National Banking System became increasingly apparent with each successive financial panic. After the panic of 1907, a National Monetary Commission was set up to make a study of the situation. It made its report in 1910. On the basis of the findings in this report, a plan for bank reform called the *Aldrich Plan* was submitted to Congress. It called for the creation of a National Reserve Association that was to act as a central bank for the United States.

The Aldrich Plan, largely backed by the Republican party, encountered widespread opposition and was not brought out of committee by a Democratic House of Representatives. Reform legislation was needed, however, and Congress then passed the Federal Reserve Act in 1913 (largely a House bill) establishing the Federal Reserve System.

As originally conceived, the Federal Reserve System was designed not as a single strong central bank, but as a federation of largely autonomous regional central banks. Each regional bank was to be responsive to the unique needs of its area. It was hoped that this federated system could avoid the charge of "monopoly." People at that time feared centralization, as many do even today, equating it with authoritarianism and lack of individual freedom. In spite of the adverse experiences with state banking and the National Banking System, the public was not yet ready to accept central bank regulation. Many feared that under a centralized system our unit banks would be dominated by eastern banking interests; anything akin to either the First or Second Bank of the United States would have met fierce opposition.

This reluctance to accept a system of central banking, the purpose of which was to help provide the economy with safe banks and a sound currency, was a peculiarly American attitude. Other advanced nations of the Western world had long possessed central banks, some of which were even engaged in commercial banking, as the First and Second Banks of the United States had been. The Bank of England was established in 1694 and had a virtual monopoly of note issue very early in its history. The Bank of France, founded in 1800, has an extensive commercial banking operation, organized along branch banking lines. The German Reichsbank was set up in 1875, but it was actually an outgrowth of the Bank of Prussia, which was founded in 1765. Other European nations had long operated similar institutions.

The commercial banking systems of most of these nations differed from that of the United States, however, in that they were generally dominated by a few large banks with extensive branch networks. Europeans were accustomed to big, powerful banks, and this may have made it easier for them to accept regulation from a strong central bank. The American tradition of small unit banking, of laissez faire, of private enterprise, made us naturally suspicious of any agency that appeared to foster bigness and regulation.

Federal Reserve Correction of National Bank Deficiencies

The Federal Reserve System was initially set up to correct the deficiencies of the National Banking System; it was not specifically designed for purposes of economic stabilization, which is today the Federal Reserve System's most important function.

How did the Federal Reserve correct the shortcomings of the National Banking System? *First,* it introduced a mechanism for correcting inelasticity in the currency supply. Federal Reserve banks were authorized to issue a new type of bank note, Federal Reserve notes. Member banks could use their deposit accounts at Federal Reserve banks to acquire additional Federal Reserve notes as needed. If a bank's deposits at Federal Reserve banks were insufficient for this purpose, it could borrow from the Federal Reserve banks. Thus, commercial banks could always get additional currency from the Federal Reserve System. It was thought that this would help avoid the panics that had started when the customers of commercial banks feared that currency would not be available on demand. The new currency could also expand and contract to suit the demands of the public. The Federal Reserve Act did not eliminate other currency forms, however; it simply added a currency, Federal Reserve notes, which had the feature of elasticity. Today Federal Reserve notes have become our principal currency form.

Second, pyramiding of reserves became impossible for member banks. All national banks were required to become members of the new Federal Reserve System. Member banks maintained reserve deposit accounts with the Federal Reserve banks; deposits at other commercial banks no longer counted as member bank reserves. The Federal Reserve banks, in sharp contrast to central reserve city national banks, did not also operate as private commercial banks. Thus, when the district Federal Reserve banks received cash deposits from member banks, no expansion of loans and deposits could take place in the private sector of the economy.

Third, the Federal Reserve banks were to operate as banks for commercial banks. If commercial banks were short of reserves, they could borrow reserves from the Federal Reserve banks. This meant that member banks always had a source of additional reserves; they did not have to stop extending loans because they were temporarily deficient of reserves.

Fourth, the Federal Reserve banks provided an efficient mechanism for clearing and collecting checks throughout the country. This mechanism is briefly described in Chapter 10.

Early Shortcomings of the Federal Reserve System

Although the Federal Reserve System was able to solve many of the problems of the National Banking System, it also had some defects of its own. *First,* the Federal Reserve System did not make provisions for the safety of demand deposit money. It took the depression of the 1930's to bring this needed reform with the establishment of the Federal Deposit Insurance Corporation in 1934.

Second, according to the terms of the act it was not recognized that a central bank also has the important responsibility of stabilizing the economy. The Federal Reserve was originally viewed simply as a banker's bank. Federal Reserve banks were to be sources of currency and funds to meet the credit needs of the commercial banking system. This was a recurrent theme throughout the aforementioned corrections to the National Banking System. The Federal Reserve Act provided that the Federal Reserve banks "discount notes, drafts and bills of exchange issued or drawn for agricultural, industrial or commercial purposes, or the proceeds of which have been used for such purposes. . . ." [9] This feature was included not only

---

[9] Federal Reserve Board, *Annual Report* (1914), p. 17.

to protect banks and businesses in crisis, but also to take care of the ordinary needs of business for funds.

This amounted to an acceptance of the "real bills doctrine" or the "commercial loan theory of banking," which was briefly described in Chapter 3. In essence it was thought that the debts, or "paper," of its customers that a bank put up for borrowed funds should arise out of current production, since the production of real goods was believed to be the real source of funds for loan repayment. As was discussed previously, however, loans can prove illiquid in times of economic stress. Furthermore, expanding and contracting loans in accord with the "needs of trade" is a procyclical action. If full employment is reached, then the needed funds go to finance the operations of firms that successfully bid productive resources away from their competitors. Total output, however, remains unchanged. Thus, applying the real bills doctrine in periods of full employment only adds to inflationary pressures.

Fortunately, the Federal Reserve recognized the potential dangers of following the real bills doctrine as early as the 1920's. It was also during this period, as we shall discuss in some detail in Chapters 12 and 13, that the Federal Reserve began developing a sense of responsibility for the stabilization of economic activity.

Third, many economists believe that the depression of the thirties demonstrated that there was a shortage of contracyclical monetary tools at the disposal of the Federal Reserve. Accordingly, these powers were expanded to include reserve-requirement manipulation and open-market policy manipulation in the 1930's. As early as the 1920's it was made easier for member banks to borrow reserves. All of these techniques will be considered in Chapters 12 and 13.

Finally, the federated structure of the system created policy coordination problems. At first, the Federal Reserve Bank of New York tended to dominate the system, but the other district Federal Reserve banks sought to exercise more authority of their own. These organizational difficulties were resolved in the 1930's with the creation of our present Board of Governors.

As subsequent chapters will demonstrate, the Federal Reserve System has proved to be a valuable institution, which has been able to adapt successfully to changing economic circumstances. However much economists may disagree concerning the system's effectiveness, it can at least be said that the Federal Reserve has become aware of its responsibility for promoting economic stability.

Supplementary Readings

Friedman, Milton, and Anna Schwartz. *A Monetary History of the United States, 1867–1960.* Princeton, N.J.: National Bureau of Economic Research, 1963.

Hammond, Bray. *Banks and Politics in America from the Revolution to the Civil War*. Princeton, N.J.: Princeton Univ. Press, 1957.

Linke, Charles M. "The Evolution of Interest Rate Regulation on Commercial Bank Deposits in the United States." *The National Banking Review* (1966), pp. 449–69.

Martin, David A. "Bimetallism in the United States before 1850." *The Journal of Political Economy* (1968), pp. 428–42.

Spengler, Joseph J. "Coin Shortage: Modern and Pre-Modern." *The National Banking Review* (1965), pp. 201–16.

CHAPTER 10

The Structure
and Nonregulatory Functions
of the Federal Reserve System

The Federal Reserve as it is presently constituted acts as a central bank for the United States. Its primary function is to contribute to the stabilization of the domestic economy through the manipulation of money and credit. Its goals are stable prices, high employment levels, and economic growth. As subsequent chapters will show, however, these goals may be mutually contradictory. A fourth major objective of contemporary central-banking policy is to influence the flow of goods and money between domestic and foreign markets, but its overriding concern is to help achieve a prosperous and growing domestic economy. No longer is the Federal Reserve concerned merely with maintaining an elastic currency or being a banker's bank.

Later chapters discuss in detail how the Federal Reserve System attempts to achieve these goals through the administration of monetary policy. They will also summarize the contemporary controversy on economic policy. The scope of this chapter, however, is limited to an examination of the structure of the system and its nonregulatory functions.

THE STRUCTURE OF THE FEDERAL RESERVE SYSTEM

There are five principal elements in the organizational structure of the Federal Reserve System: (1) the Board of Governors; (2) the Federal Open Market Committee; (3) the Federal Advisory Council; (4) the twelve Federal Reserve banks and their branches; and (5) the member banks.

Board of Governors

The Board of Governors is the single most important part of the Federal Reserve System. It consists of seven men appointed to fourteen-year terms by the President of the United States with the approval of the U.S. Senate. The members of the Board are ultimately responsible for the operations of the entire Federal Reserve System. They formulate monetary policy and decide whether it will be restrictive or expansionary. In addition, the Board of Governors has more routine duties. It supervises the Federal Reserve banks and regulates member banks. It also interprets the Federal Reserve Act and issues various regulations under the Act.

The varied nature of the activities of the Board of Governors is well illustrated by the following résumé of some of its activities during 1968.[1]

Economic policy actions. 1. In January 1968, in a move designed to strengthen the U.S. balance of payments, the Board of Governors issued revised guidelines for the restraint of foreign credits by banks and other financial institutions. Banks and nonbank financial institutions were asked to reduce their outstanding loans to foreigners, and ceilings were set on the amount of foreign credit banks could extend.

2. In March, the Board adopted a number of regulatory changes to broaden the coverage of and tighten its control over the use of credit in stock-market transactions.

3. Also in March, the Board approved actions taken by the directors of the Federal Reserve banks to raise discount rates in order to limit the extension of credit.

4. In April, the Board adopted a new schedule of maximum rates of interest payable by member banks on large-denomination, single-maturity time deposits. No change was made in maximum rates payable on other types of time and savings deposits. The new rates, which were approximately .5 percent higher than the old rates, were part of a plan to restrict spending by raising the level of interest rates in the economy.

5. In June 1968, the Board again amended Federal Reserve regulations regarding stock-market credit. Effective June 8, margin requirements were increased from 70 to 80 percent on loans made on stocks and from 50 to 60 percent on loans made on convertible bonds. These margin increases were aimed at preventing excessive use of credit to finance security transactions.

6. In July, the Federal Reserve announced a $600 million increase in its reciprocal currency arrangement with the Bank of France. The increase enlarged the system's "swap network" with fourteen central banks and the bank for international settlements. This network, discussed in more detail in Chapter 25, is designed to assist countries that are experiencing temporary balance-of-payments deficits.

7. In August, the Board of Governors approved action by various Federal Reserve banks to reduce their discount rates to bring them into line with private market rates of interest, which had decreased as a result of the enactment of the 1968 surtax increase.

[1] Compiled from *Federal Reserve Bulletin*, 1968.

8. The Board of Governors amended Regulation D in September, 1968. All member banks were now to have a one-week reserve accounting period, with required reserves based upon deposits two weeks earlier. Vault cash counted as reserves was also to be lagged two weeks. Banks would be permitted to carry forward to the next reserve period excess reserves or reserve deficiencies of up to 2 percent of required reserves. This plan ostensibly was designed to ease bank adjustment problems at the end of reserve periods by reducing bank uncertainty concerning reserve positions, but it may also be viewed as a move by the Federal Reserve to ease credit.

Actions to enhance domestic competition in banking. The Board issued numerous orders under the Bank Merger Act approving and disapproving proposed mergers in 1968. It also issued orders under Section 3 of the Bank Holding Company Act approving and disapproving applications for the establishment of bank holding companies.

Routine administrative actions. 1. The Board admitted various state banks to membership in the Federal Reserve System.

2. It appointed Federal Reserve bank directors and branch directors. There were also a number of staff changes.

3. The Board of Governors announced a reorganization of functions. The Division of Examinations became known as the Division of Supervision and Regulation while the Division of Bank Operations became the Division of Federal Reserve Operations. The Division of Supervision and Regulation was assigned the responsibility of regulating securities credit and truth-in-lending regulations. The Division was also to continue to coordinate the commercial bank supervisory functions of the Federal Reserve System and to review examinations of state member banks by the Federal Reserve member banks. It also is to continue to process action by the Federal Reserve Board of Governors relative to such matters as bank mergers, bank holding companies, branches, and foreign banking corporations. The Division of Federal Reserve Bank Operations was assigned the duty of examining the Federal Reserve banks.

4. The Board of Governors regularly revised various regulations and gave interpretations of the Federal Reserve Act.

Bank examination and supervision. 1. The Board's Division of Supervision and Regulation examined all state member banks. Such examinations take place at least once a year. The Board does not normally examine national banks, since they are examined by the Office of the Comptroller of the Currency, which makes copies of its examinations available to the Board.

2. The Board's Division of Federal Reserve Bank Operations examined the Federal Reserve banks and their branches.

The Board and legislation. The chairman and members of the Board of Governors frequently appeared before Congress to give their opinions on proposed banking and economic policy legislation. For example, in June, the Board argued for a one year extension of statutory provisions giving the Fed the authority to regulate the maximum rates payable by federally insured financial institutions to attract savings funds. The Board felt that it would be difficult to limit interest rates paid by commercial banks for savings if their competitors—the savings and loan associations and mutual savings banks—were again permitted to set any rate they wished.

These were just some of the actions taken by the Board of Governors in 1968. In addition, the members of the Board served on the Federal Open Market Committee. As members of this committee, they exert a dominant influence over our most important instrument of monetary policy, the purchase and sale of U.S. government securities by the Federal Reserve banks.

Federal Open Market Committee

The Federal Open Market Committee, or FOMC, consists of twelve members, seven of whom are the members of the Board of Governors. Thus, the Board (if it is in agreement) has a controlling voice in FOMC deliberations. The remaining five members are the presidents of five of our twelve Federal Reserve banks. The president of the Federal Reserve Bank of New York is vice-chairman of the committee and serves as a permanent member because of the crucial role the New York bank plays in the purchase and sale of securities. The other four positions on the committee are rotated among the remaining presidents of Federal Reserve banks. The chairman of the committee is the chairman of the Board of Governors. Although only five presidents of Federal Reserve banks are members of the Federal Open Market Committee, in practice all twelve presidents attend committee meetings.

The FOMC meets approximately every three weeks for the purpose of determining Federal Reserve policy with respect to the purchase and sale of securities, principally U.S. government securities, on the open market. Open-market policy decisions are crucial for the economy because, as Chapter 11 will demonstrate, open-market transactions in government securities by the Federal Reserve banks strongly influence the reserve position of the commercial banking system; thus they are an important instrument of control over the money supply. In addition, the FOMC also directs the purchase and sale of foreign currencies by Federal Reserve banks.

The FOMC is a policy-setting organization. It does not itself execute the policies that it selects as most appropriate for the current economic situation. Responsibility for the actual purchase and sale of securities and currencies lies with the manager of the System Open Market Account and the special manager in foreign currency at the Federal Reserve Bank of New York. New York is the center of the government securities and foreign exchange markets in the United States. All private government securities dealers have their main offices there. Securities and currencies purchased by the New York bank are then apportioned among all the Federal Reserve banks according to each bank's share of total Fed assets.

Policy directives are formulated at each meeting of the FOMC. They are usually very broad in scope. For example, an economic-policy statement issued to the Federal Reserve Bank of New York on April 30, 1968, stated:

The information reviewed at this meeting indicates that over-all economic activity has expanded at a very rapid pace thus far in 1968, with prices rising substantially, and that prospects are for a continuing rapid advance in activity and persisting inflationary pressures in the period ahead. Since late fall, growth rates of bank credit, the money supply, and time and savings accounts at financial institutions have on balance moderated considerably. Market interest rates have risen in recent weeks, partly in reaction to the firming of monetary policy including the further increase in Federal Reserve discount rates. The U.S. foreign trade balance has worsened further, and the international payments position of the United States continues to be a matter of serious concern. In this situation, it is the policy of the Federal Open Market Committee to foster financial conditions conducive to resistance of inflationary pressures and attainment of reasonable equilibrium in the country's balance of payments.

To implement this policy, while taking account of the Treasury financing activity, System Open Market Operations until the next meeting of the committee shall be conducted with a view to maintaining firmer conditions prevailing in the money market; provided, however, that operations shall be modified to the extent permitted by Treasury financing, if bank credit appears to be deviating significantly from current projections.[2]

With such a broad directive, the account manager and special manager have a great deal of latitude with respect to how FOMC policies are executed. Since they are in day-to-day contact with the foreign-currency and government-securities markets, they are continually receiving information on the various forces directly affecting commercial bank reserve positions and the U.S. balance-of-payments situation. Consequently, within the context of current directives, they may need to make rapid adjustments to offset undesired changes in our reserve and currency positions. For example, the directive just quoted implies that for reasons of domestic policy the Federal Reserve banks' holdings of U.S. government securities should be decreased. Yet, at a given time, the account manager actually may be expanding these holdings. Why? Because other forces may be operating to contract commercial bank reserves. What is needed, under such a directive, is not an actual contraction in Federal Reserve holdings of securities, but a *net contraction of commercial bank excess reserves.*

[2] *Federal Reserve Bulletin,* August 1968, p. 677.

This is just one aspect of Federal Reserve open-market operations; Chapters 11 and 13 will discuss these operations in detail.

Federal Advisory Council

The Federal Advisory Council consists of twelve members, one from each Federal Reserve district. Each member is selected by his district Federal Reserve bank. He is usually a representative banker from the district. The council is strictly an advisory group. It meets at least four times a year to survey general business conditions in the economy and formulate appropriate policy recommendations to be presented at its meetings with the Board of Governors. There is no obligation on the part of the Board to execute the recommendations of the council, however.

Today it can be argued that there is little reason for the continuation of the council, since it has no powers. Originally, however, there was some justification for its establishment. When the Federal Reserve Act was passed, many commercial banks opposed the formation of a Federal Reserve Board; bankers felt that the Board would not be responsive to their interests and needs. Consequently, the Federal Advisory Council was set up to provide the banking industry with a means of directly informing the Federal Reserve Board of its needs and wishes.

The Federal Reserve Banks

The Federal Reserve System is composed of the Federal Reserve banks and their branch offices. Geographically, the United States is divided into twelve Federal Reserve districts, each with a Federal Reserve bank and branches. There are twenty-four branch offices, scattered throughout the various districts.

The location of these banks and their branches is shown in Figure 10–1. There are Federal Reserve banks in Boston, New York, Philadelphia, Cleveland, Richmond, Atlanta, Chicago, St. Louis, Minneapolis, Kansas City, Dallas, and San Francisco. The banks vary greatly in size. As Table 10–1 shows, the Federal Reserve Bank of New York is the largest, with total assets of $19.2 billion in 1969. This is to be expected, since New York is the money market center of the nation. The Federal Reserve banks of Chicago and San Francisco are next, with $13.0 and $10.2 billion in assets, respectively. The smallest is the Federal Reserve Bank of Minneapolis, with $1.7 billion in assets. This difference in capitalization among district Reserve banks conforms roughly to the percentage of total commercial bank assets held by the commercial banks within each district. Although initially it was hoped that the Federal Reserve banks would be approximately equal in size, it has not been possible to achieve this equality in size because of the concentration of financial business in a limited number of cities.

FIGURE 10–1. Boundaries of the Federal Reserve districts and their branch territories

Boundaries of Federal Reserve districts
Boundaries of Federal Reserve branch territories
Board of Governors of the Federal Reserve System
Federal Reserve bank cities
Federal Reserve branch cities

SOURCE: Board of Governors of the Federal Reserve System, Washington, D.C.

The decentralized character of the Federal Reserve System is an outgrowth of the traditional conflict between those who advocate local banking autonomy and those who argue for a more efficient centralized system. Local banking interests were quite vocal when the Federal Reserve Act was passed in 1913, and it was thought that local needs would be served best by regional Federal Reserve banks that were loosely federated under the

TABLE 10-1. FEDERAL RESERVE BANK ASSETS, MARCH 31, 1969
(IN MILLIONS OF DOLLARS)

DISTRICT NUMBER	FEDERAL RESERVE BANK	ASSETS
1	Boston	4,203
2	New York	19,263
3	Philadelphia	4,066
4	Cleveland	6,034
5	Richmond	5,868
6	Atlanta	4,679
7	Chicago	13,013
8	St. Louis	2,923
9	Minneapolis	1,745
10	Kansas City	3,314
11	Dallas	3,452
12	San Francisco	10,212
	Total	78,772

SOURCE: *Federal Reserve Bulletin*, April 1969, p. A-13.

Federal Reserve Board. Thus, at one time, each Federal Reserve bank had a substantial amount of authority in its district. This gradually changed as the need for more centralized operations became apparent. The Banking Act of 1935 recognized the need for centralization by giving the new Board of Governors of the Federal Reserve System strong powers.

Today, the principal function of each Federal Reserve bank is to supervise the operations of the member banks within its own district. The district Federal Reserve banks maintain member bank reserve deposits, clear and collect checks for member banks, lend them reserves, and supply them with currency. In addition, each district bank sets the discount rate for its district. This power, however, is subject to review by the Board of Governors.

Each Federal Reserve bank has the same type of administrative structure. Each is supervised by Class A, Class B, and Class C directors. There are a total of nine directors, three of each class. Class A and B directors are selected by the member banks of the district. Two directors, one Class A and one Class B, are chosen by the small banks of the district, two are chosen by the medium-sized banks, and two by the large banks. Class A directors may be bankers. Class B directors must not be bankers, but should be actively engaged in commerce, agriculture, or industry in the district. The remaining three directors (Class C) are chosen by the Board of Governors, which appoints a Class C director as chairman and another as deputy chairman of the board of directors. Class C directors cannot be actively engaged in the banking business. The directors of each district bank formulate policy for the bank and appoint its president and vice-president, as well as certain other employees. The appointment of these bank officials, however, is subject to approval by the Board of Governors.

Each Federal Reserve bank is a corporation chartered by the federal government. Its stockholders are the member banks. Ownership of stock of the district Federal Reserve bank is a requirement for commercial banks that wish to be members of the system. The amount of stock held by a member bank must, at present, equal 3 percent of its capital accounts. Thus, the amount of Federal Reserve bank stock subscribed to by member banks varies as member bank capital accounts change and as the number of member banks in the system changes.

Although a Federal Reserve bank is in fact a corporation, it is unlike a private corporation in many ways. A Federal Reserve bank's fundamental purpose is to regulate the operations of the member banks in its district within the confines of the monetary policies articulated by the Board of Governors. Hence, Federal Reserve banks are not profit-seeking corporations. True, a Federal Reserve bank in the course of its operations does make profits. Stockholders (member banks), however, by law, receive dividends equal to only 6 percent of the value of their subscription to Federal Reserve bank stock; member banks have no claim to additional dividends. Nor do they have a residual claim to the assets of a Federal Reserve bank. In addition, ownership of Federal Reserve bank stock, unlike the common stock of most corporations, is not transferable; there is no market for the stocks of the Federal Reserve banks. In the event of liquidation, the total value of the surplus and the par value of the common stock (assuming the Federal Reserve bank assets would yield their book value) would go to the U.S. government. Such a liquidation, however, is highly unlikely, given our tradition of at least some decentralization in central banking activities.

Member Banks

The last and most numerous component of the Federal Reserve System is, of course, the member banks themselves. Member banks are private, profit-seeking corporations, which, like all commercial banks, possess the unique ability to create and destroy money in the process of making loans and investments. Although they constitute only 43 percent of all commercial banks in the United States, member banks account for 82 percent of bank demand-deposit liabilities. To obtain member bank status, a bank must meet the requirements set forth by the Federal Reserve Act.

NONREGULATORY FUNCTIONS
OF THE FEDERAL RESERVE BANKS

Many of the functions performed by the Federal Reserve banks are not directly connected with the implementation of monetary policy. Three of these services have already been mentioned: (1) creating reserves for member banks; (2) supplying member banks with currency; and (3) clearing and collecting checks. All these functions are part of the main job of a Federal Reserve bank, the maintenance of member bank reserve deposits. A fourth nonregulatory function of the Federal Reserve banks is to act as fiscal agents of the U.S. government.

Maintenance of Member Reserve Accounts

Each member bank is required to maintain reserves in the form of vault cash and deposits at its district Federal Reserve bank. These deposits are used for more than merely meeting legal reserve requirements. Far from lying idle, the funds in these accounts are very active. Reserve deposits at Federal Reserve banks are constantly increasing and decreasing. The activity of these accounts demands careful supervision by both the member banks and the Federal Reserve banks to ensure that minimum member bank reserve requirements are met.

How are the funds in these accounts employed? First, they are used in the *creation of reserves* for member banks by the Federal Reserve banks. Member banks are usually able to borrow from their district Federal Reserve bank to meet temporary shortages of reserves, provided they have the proper collateral. Frequent trips by a member to the "discount window," however, may cause the Federal Reserve bank to restrict the amount it will loan a particular bank.[3] When it lends reserves, the Federal Reserve bank simply increases the member bank's deposit balance. *These reserves are created by the Federal Reserve bank, just as commercial banks create demand deposits when they extend loans. The Federal Reserve banks do not lend the reserves of one commercial bank to another; this is impossible, because a liability is a recognition of what one owes others.* When the member bank repays the loan, it uses its reserve account. Member bank borrowing of reserves is discussed at greater length in Chapter 11.

Second, *member bank reserve deposit accounts are the mechanism through which the economy is supplied with currency.* As described in Chapter 2, when the nonbank public's demand for currency increases, commercial bank demand deposit liabilities and vault cash holdings are reduced. Where do the commercial banks get currency to meet the increased demand? Nonmember banks buy it from member banks, who in turn purchase it from the Federal Reserve banks. Member banks "purchase" currency by accepting a decrease in their reserve accounts at Federal Reserve banks. When, subsequently, there is an influx of currency into the banking system, the excess currency is returned to the Federal Reserve banks, and member bank reserve deposits are increased.

---

[3] Federal Reserve banks do not normally discount eligible paper or make advances to member banks automatically; the time-honored position of the Federal Reserve has been that the discount facilities are available to member banks as a privilege and not as a right. During 1968, however, the Federal Reserve proposed an extensive redesign of its discount mechanism. As a result, some Federal Reserve lending of reserves to commercial banks will become automatic. A more extensive discussion of these changes in the discount mechanism will be found in Chapter 12.

Third, *banks with excess funds in their reserve accounts may lend this excess to banks with a shortage of reserves.* Negotiations of this sort take place in the *federal funds market.* The reserve accounts of lending banks are reduced, and those of borrowing banks increased. (For an explanation of how the federal funds market operates, see Chapter 5.)

Fourth, when overseas branches place Euro-dollars with their home offices in the United States, these banks' reserve positions are enhanced. *The Federal Reserve increases the accounts of American banks by the amount of the Euro-dollar placement.* (For a discussion of the Euro-dollar, see Chapter 7.)

Fifth, when *the Treasury transfers funds* from its accounts at member banks to its general accounts at Federal Reserve banks, member bank reserve deposits are decreased. This is discussed more fully in Chapter 11.

Finally, it is through member bank reserve accounts that many *checks are cleared and collected.* This is one of the most valuable functions that a Federal Reserve bank performs for member banks. A member bank's reserve deposits are increased when it sends checks drawn on other banks to the Federal Reserve bank for collection. Conversely, its reserve account is decreased when checks written by its depositors are presented for collection to the Federal Reserve banks by other member banks.

Check-clearing and Collection Operations by the Federal Reserve System

The volume of Federal Reserve bank check-clearing operations is almost staggering. In 1968, Federal Reserve banks handled 5,904,929,000 packages of non-U.S. government checks, valued at $2,350,761,951,000.[4] The bulk of these checks are now processed electronically.

The nationwide clearing and processing of checks was one of the principal functions the Federal Reserve System was designed to perform under the Federal Reserve Act, and it has been quite successful in fulfilling this task. Here is how the process works. Assume that an individual in New York has sold goods valued at $1,000 to someone in Chicago. The buyer pays for the goods with a check drawn on a Chicago member bank. The New York businessman then deposits the check with his bank in New York City. Assuming that the New York bank is also a member bank, there are several changes that may occur on its balance sheet.

If the Chicago bank is a customer bank, then the New York bank may simply increase the deposit account of the seller who presented the $1,000 check and, at the same time, reduce the deposit account of the Chicago bank. The check is then returned to the Chicago bank, which in turn reduces the account of the person who wrote the check. The net result of this transaction for the commercial banking system is that the Chicago bank will have lost an asset—deposits with the New York bank.

[4] Board of Governors of the Federal Reserve System, *Annual Report* (1968), p. 378.

If the Chicago bank is not a customer bank, the check-clearing and collection procedure is considerably more complicated. First, there are the balance-sheet changes that occur upon deposit of the check by the seller. These are shown as entries (a) below:

BALANCE-SHEET CHANGES FOR NEW YORK CITY MEMBER BANK

ASSETS		LIABILITIES + CAPITAL ACCOUNTS	
Due from banks	+$1,000 (a)	Demand deposits	+$1,000 (a)
Due from banks	−$1,000 (b)		
Reserves	+$1,000 (b)		

In order to collect on the check, the New York bank sends it to the Federal Reserve Bank of New York. This results in a change in the balance sheet of the Federal Reserve Bank of New York.

BALANCE-SHEET CHANGES FOR THE FEDERAL RESERVE BANK
OF NEW YORK

ASSETS	LIABILITIES + CAPITAL ACCOUNTS
Cash items in process of collection +$1,000 (a)	Deferred availability cash items +$1,000 (a)
	Deferred availability cash items −$1,000 (b)
	Member bank reserve deposits +$1,000 (b)

Entries labeled (a) show that the Federal Reserve Bank of New York has received a check (cash items in process of collection) the value of which has not yet been credited to the account of the New York member bank (deferred availability cash items). Shortly after the Federal Reserve Bank of New York receives the check, it increases the reserve account of the New York member bank.[5] The balance sheet of the New York bank is now adjusted to show that its reserve position has increased. This is recorded as entries (b) on the New York member bank balance sheet. The balance sheet of the Federal Reserve Bank of New York has also changed. These are recorded as entries (b) on the balance sheet of the Federal Reserve Bank of New York.

The Federal Reserve Bank of New York must still collect on the $1,000 check. If the member bank on which the check is drawn were a member bank in District Number 2 (the district of the Federal Reserve Bank of

---

[5] Usually, a Federal Reserve bank increases the reserve deposit account of member banks before it collects on the checks. As a result, cash items in process of collection are normally greater than deferred availability cash items. The difference between these two items, known as "Federal Reserve float," affects commercial bank reserve positions. The influence of "float" on the economy is discussed more fully in Chapter 11.

New York), it would have a reserve deposit account with the Federal Reserve Bank of New York. The reserve account of the member bank would be reduced, as would cash items in process of collection. But, in our example, the member bank on which the check is drawn is in District Number 7. Under these circumstances, the Federal Reserve Bank of New York must send the check to the Federal Reserve Bank of Chicago for collection. The Federal Reserve Bank of Chicago in turn lowers the reserve deposit account of the Chicago member bank and forwards the check to it. The Chicago member bank lowers the deposit account of the businessman who first wrote the check. The balance-sheet changes for this member bank are as follows:

BALANCE-SHEET CHANGES FOR THE CHICAGO MEMBER BANK

ASSETS		LIABILITIES + CAPITAL ACCOUNTS	
Reserves	− $1,000	Demand deposits	− $1,000

Thus the check has traveled from the Chicago businessman to the New York businessman, to the New York member bank, to the Federal Reserve Bank of New York, to the Federal Reserve Bank of Chicago, to the Chicago member bank, and back again to the Chicago businessman. The demand deposits of the New York businessman have increased; those of the Chicago businessman have decreased. The New York member bank has gained reserves; the Chicago member bank has lost reserves.

There is still one debt created during this process that remains unresolved. The Federal Reserve Bank of New York sent the check to the Federal Reserve Bank of Chicago for collection. Since the check was written on a bank in District 2, the Federal Reserve Bank of Chicago now owes $1,000 to the Federal Reserve Bank of New York. Debts of this type among Federal Reserve banks are cleared through the System's *Interdistrict Settlement Fund*. Each Federal Reserve bank owns gold certificates on deposit with the Interdistrict Settlement Fund in Washington, D.C. When one Federal Reserve bank is in debt to another, its gold-certificate fund is reduced by the amount of the debt. In turn, the creditor Federal Reserve bank has its gold-certificate holdings increased. This transaction is recorded on the balance sheets of the Federal Reserve banks and the Interdistrict Settlement Fund as follows:

BALANCE-SHEET CHANGES FOR THE FEDERAL RESERVE BANK
OF CHICAGO

ASSETS		LIABILITIES + CAPITAL ACCOUNTS	
Gold certificate account	− $1,000	Member bank reserve deposits	− $1,000

BALANCE-SHEET CHANGES FOR THE FEDERAL RESERVE BANK
OF NEW YORK

ASSETS	LIABILITIES + CAPITAL ACCOUNTS
Gold certificate accounts +$1,000	Member bank reserve deposits +$1,000

BALANCE-SHEET CHANGES FOR THE INTERDISTRICT
SETTLEMENT FUND

ASSETS	LIABILITIES + CAPITAL ACCOUNTS
	Gold certificate accounts Federal Reserve Bank of Chicago −$1,000 Federal Reserve Bank of New York +$1,000

Gold-certificate assets and member bank reserves have decreased at the Federal Reserve Bank of Chicago; they have increased at the Federal Reserve Bank of New York.

The preceding illustration of check-clearing procedures, as complicated as it may seem, is really simple compared to the overall check-clearing process. Remember that trillions of dollars worth of checks are cleared by the Federal Reserve banks each year. Checks are continually flowing back and forth in the economy. Our illustration merely showed the movement of one check through the clearing system. In practice, each member bank presents checks to its Federal Reserve bank daily for collection and also has checks presented to it. Thus, member bank reserve changes reflect *net flows* of checks. If the value of the checks a member bank presents for collection is greater than the value of the checks forwarded to it for collection, its reserves increase. If not, it loses reserves.

Similarly there are continual shifts of gold-certificate funds from one Federal Reserve bank to another. Each Federal Reserve bank daily forwards checks to the other eleven Federal Reserve banks, and in turn has checks presented to it. When the total value of checks forwarded by one Federal Reserve bank to other Federal Reserve banks exceeds the value of those presented, it gains gold certificates.

The clearing and collection of checks by the Federal Reserve are not the only check-clearing mechanisms in the economy. There is often a clearinghouse for banks having head offices within a particular city. Representatives of these banks meet daily in the clearinghouse and present checks to one another for collection. Debts that exist between the banks are then extinguished by a transfer of reserve balances from debtor to creditor banks. If the clearing is not done with Federal Reserve funds, the payment may be made to a city correspondent; this increases the accounts of creditor banks and lowers those of the debtor banks.

The Federal Reserve clears and collects checks not only for member banks but for nonmember banks. Typically, when a Federal Reserve bank receives checks written on accounts in nonmember banks, it increases the account of the depositing member bank. The checks are then forwarded to those member banks that serve as correspondents for the nonmember banks. The reserve deposits of these member banks are decreased. In turn, the correspondent member bank decreases the demand-deposit balances of the nonmember banks. As indicated in Chapter 4, a Federal Reserve bank will perform this function for a nonmember bank only when the nonmember bank is on the par list.

A checkless society? Developments of recent years may portend the demise of checks as the means of transferring demand-deposit liabilities and may well make the check-clearing process just described an anachronism. These developments are, first, the increased use of credit cards and, second, the introduction of computer technology into banking.

At present, credit cards are used simply as another form of charge account. Both are means of regularizing payments. Without the charge privilege, transactions must be completed immediately, using either cash or checks. With the charge privilege, a debt is created that is subsequently extinguished, again using either currency or demand-deposit money. Most firms have regular billing procedures; hence, debtors can predict when payments must be made, and creditors can forecast receipts with some degree of accuracy. This means, of course, that increased use of credit cards and charge accounts leads to a greater regularization of payments and receipts and less of a need to accumulate cash to meet unforeseen contingencies. This in turn means a decrease in the amount of money needed, an increase in the velocity of circulation of money, and a rise in the demand for goods and services. Overall this has been the trend for some time in the United States.

The credit card combined with the computer can change this payment technique, in addition to further regularizing the payments process. Bank computer systems can maintain the payments into and out of demand-deposit accounts for all bank customers in the economy. This should make it possible to eliminate checks as a means of transferring deposit balances. For example, a customer making a purchase would present his credit card and, using the seller's computer (which will be tied into the banking system computer), make immediate payment, by directing the computer to transfer funds from his demand-deposit account to that of the payee; he can charge the purchase and/or arrange for installment credit by instructing the computer to transfer funds at the end of the charge period or when installments are due. No check will be sent to the payee, whose account is automatically increased at the time specified. The computer will record the transaction and continuously update the customer's account.

A similar procedure takes place today when individuals instruct their creditors, such as the telephone company, to forward bills directly to their bank. Checks are not used since the creditor is paid automatically by the bank.

Business payments can also be made using computers. Credit cards need not be involved; business computers can be tied into banking computers. Thus, when one business needs to make payment to another, all it need do is instruct its bank through the computer to transfer funds from its account to the account of the creditor business.

In addition, bank computers can be tied into Federal Reserve bank computers. When commercial bank computers report to the Federal Reserve that net claims against other banks have increased, the Fed's computers can automatically increase the reserve account of the creditor banks and decrease those of the debtor banks. All this information on payments will automatically be fed into each bank's equipment. There will be no need for "float." [6]

Such a system is obviously far in the future. With a unit-banking system of 13,700 commercial banks, it would obviously be difficult to tie all banks in the country into a centralized clearing and payments system. But it is feasible for large businesses and large banks in major financial centers to develop computerized communications systems. Many European banking systems, where there are only a few commercial banks maintaining widespread branch bank networks, have operated on a comparable basis for decades. These European systems are not computerized. Rather, theirs is what is called a "giro" system, where the payer instructs his bank whom to pay and in what amounts. If a bank computer system ever comes about in the United States, the first step will probably be the computerization of all check clearing and collections by the Federal Reserve banks for member banks, as described in the preceding paragraph.[7]

Fiscal and Foreign Agent Functions of the Federal Reserve Banks

The Federal Reserve banks also serve as fiscal agents and depositories for the U.S. government. In this capacity, they maintain checking-deposit accounts for the Treasury department, which makes almost all its payments by drawing down these accounts. As treasury payments are made, the deposit accounts of the nonbank public are increased. As member banks forward government checks to the Federal Reserve for collection, member bank reserves are increased.

On the other hand, when the Treasury receives tax revenues and funds from the sale of government securities, this money is placed in its tax and

[6] See Chapter 11 for a discussion of "float."
[7] The developments discussed here are examples of institutional influences on the velocity of money. A more complete discussion of these forces will be found in Chapter 17.

loan accounts at commercial banks. Subsequently, as funds are needed to cover government payments, money is periodically transferred to the Treasury deposit accounts with the Fed. When this happens, member bank reserves are decreased and Treasury deposit accounts increased.

Treasury payments and receipts do not coincide; this is the principal reason for the maintenance of tax and loan accounts by the Treasury at commercial banks. If all tax receipts were placed immediately in the Treasury's general accounts with the Federal Reserve banks, a serious drain would occur in commercial bank reserves as depositors made tax payments. In the absence of open-market purchases by the Federal Reserve banks, this would force a contraction in commercial bank lending operations.

Not only do the Federal Reserve banks clear and collect checks for the Treasury, they also assist in public debt transactions. Federal Reserve banks act as agents in the sale of new U.S. government securities; they process the applications of purchasers of new security issues, deliver the securities, and receive payment for them.

The Federal Reserve's responsibilities as the fiscal agent and depository for the U.S. government extend beyond handling financial transactions of the U.S. Treasury. The Federal Reserve banks also act as depositories and fiscal agents for such agencies as the FDIC, Federal Home Loan Banks, Federal Savings and Loan Insurance Corporation, Public Housing Administration, Small Business Administration, Federal National Mortgage Association, and Commodity Credit Corporation. In addition, they act as fiscal agent for those government agencies that guarantee loans to contractors and subcontractors engaged in the production and delivery of goods vital to national defense.

The activity of the U.S. government deposit accounts maintained with the Federal Reserve banks is intense. In 1968, the Federal Reserve banks handled 544,813,000 packages of Treasury checks having a total value of $190,653,523 million.[8] In the same year, the general accounts of the U.S. government averaged $878 million.[9] Dividing the value of U.S. government check handlings by the average size of the U.S. general accounts gives us a measure of the turnover of federal government balances—217. This is a very high turnover rate, many times that of individual deposit accounts at commercial banks. The annual rate of demand-deposit turnover in New York, the most active financial center, was 131 in June of 1968.[10]

Finally, the Federal Reserve banks perform valuable services in the area of international economic relations. They are authorized to act as depositories for the International Monetary Fund, International Development Association, Inter-American Development Bank, and International Fi-

---

[8] Board of Governors of the Federal Reserve System, *Annual Report* (1968), p. 378.
[9] Computed by adding the end-of-month U.S. Treasurer general-account deposits for the period December 31, 1967 through December 31, 1968 and dividing the total by 13. Source of data is the *Federal Reserve Bulletin* tables on the consolidated statement of condition of all Federal Reserve banks.
[10] *Federal Reserve Bulletin,* July 1969, p. A–15.

nance Corporation. In addition, they are empowered to accept deposits of foreign monetary authorities. In practice, most foreign operations are carried on by the Federal Reserve Bank of New York for all the Federal Reserve banks; foreign deposits are recorded on the balance sheet of each Federal Reserve bank in proportion to its share of total Fed assets.

The Federal Reserve Bank of New York also buys and sells foreign currencies for the U.S. government. Until recently, this type of intervention in the exchange market was done not to influence exchange rates, but simply to provide the government with foreign currency needed in its operations abroad. Now, however, there is an economic regulatory purpose as well: to alleviate the pressure on the U.S. balance of payments. The special-accounts manager handles all purchases and sales of foreign currency for the FOMC. (More will be said of this in later chapters.)

SUMMARY

This chapter has described the structure and nonregulatory functions of the Federal Reserve. We have seen that the Board of Governors is the most important regulatory body of the Federal Reserve System; it is ultimately responsible for the determination of national monetary policy. The various Federal Reserve banks carry out its economic and regulatory policies and, in turn, regulate the operations of the member banks. Actually, it is the member banks that are the most important component of the Federal Reserve System, for they alone deal with the American public. In extending credit and creating money in their daily operations, they become the instrument whereby Federal Reserve policy is executed.

Of the various Federal Reserve banks, the New York bank is the most important. Because of its location in the nation's principal financial center, it acts for the other Reserve banks and the FOMC in the purchase and sale of U.S. government securities and foreign exchange.

All Federal Reserve banks provide member banks with important services, too. These are (1) the maintenance of member bank reserve deposit accounts; (2) the clearing and collection of checks; (3) the supplying of currency; and (4) the lending of reserves.

The Federal Reserve banks are the fiscal agents of the U.S. government. Member banks also provide services for the government. They maintain tax and loan accounts for the Treasury and assist in the sale and payment of interest on government securities.

Supplementary Readings

Board of Governors of the Federal Reserve System. *The Federal Reserve System: Purposes and Functions.* Washington, D.C., 1963, Chapters 2 and 17.
———. *Bank Credit-Card and Check-Credit Plans.* July 1968.
Mitchell, George W. "Effects of Automation on the Structure and Function of Banking." *American Economic Association Papers and Proceedings* (1966), pp. 159–67.

CHAPTER 11

Assets and Liabilities
of the Federal Reserve Banks

Chapter 7 stressed the importance of the reserve position of commercial banks as the basis for credit extension and money creation. This chapter discusses how variations in the assets and liabilities of the Federal Reserve banks may alter commercial bank reserves and hence the lending ability of the commercial banking system. The emphasis is not upon how the Board of Governors, through a manipulation of the Federal Reserve bank assets and liabilities, may affect commercial bank reserves and hence economic activity, however. Instead, we are concerned with the alterations in commercial bank reserves that are caused by changes in Federal Reserve bank assets and liabilities. Chapters 12 and 13 then examine the instruments of Federal Reserve policy and explain how they may be manipulated so as to effect alternative policy goals.

FEDERAL RESERVE BANK ASSETS

Gold Certificates

Table 11–1 is a detailed balance sheet for all Federal Reserve banks as of December 31, 1968. The first asset of major importance on the balance sheet is that of gold certificates.

Gold certificates formerly were used to satisfy a reserve requirement for Federal Reserve notes and deposits. Each Federal Reserve bank was required to maintain reserves in gold certificates of not less than 25 percent against its deposits and reserves in gold certificates of not less than 25 percent against its Federal Reserve notes. The first reserve requirement was eliminated in early 1965. The second requirement was eliminated in 1968. These requirements were eliminated because a diminishing U.S. gold supply had led the excess reserve position of the Federal Reserve to be virtually eliminated. Today gold certificates along with U.S. government securities serve as collateral for Federal Reserve bank liabilities. There is no requirement that these gold certificates must be equal in value to a required percentage of Federal Reserve bank liabilities, however. In addition to serving

TABLE 11-1. DETAILED STATEMENT OF CONDITION OF ALL
FEDERAL RESERVE BANKS COMBINED, DECEMBER 31, 1968

(IN THOUSANDS OF DOLLARS)

ASSETS			
Gold certificates on hand		1,278	
Gold certificates due from U.S. Treasury:			
Interdistrict settlement fund		5,967,237	
F.R. agents' fund		4,057,000	
Total gold certificate account			10,025,515*
F.R. notes of other F.R. banks			784,712
Other cash:			
United States notes		3,846	
Silver certificates		65	
National bank notes and F.R. bank notes		73	
Coin		201,619	
Total other cash			205,603
Discounts and advances secured by U.S. Govt. obligations:			
Discounted for member banks	163,580		
Discounted for others		163,580	
Other discounts and advances:			
Discounted for member banks	25,000		
Foreign loans on gold		25,000	
Total discounts and advances		188,580	
Acceptances:			
Bought outright		57,715	
Held under repurchase agreement			
Federal agency obligations:			
Held under repurchase agreement			
U.S. Govt. securities:			
Bought outright			
Bills	18,756,205		
Certificates			
Notes	28,706,122		
Bonds	5,474,502		
Total bought outright	52,936,829		
Held under repurchase agreement			
Total U.S. Govt. securities		52,936,829	
Total loans and securities			53,183,124
Cash items in process of collection:			
Transit items		10,946,517	
Exchanges for clearing house		199,019	
Other cash items		670,719	
Total cash items in process of collection			11,816,255
Bank premises:			
Land		31,769	
Buildings (including vaults)	123,682		
Fixed machinery and equipment	67,729		
Total buildings	191,411		
Less depreciation allowances	109,904	81,507	
Total bank premises			113,276

TABLE **11–1.** (*Continued*)

ASSETS (*Continued*)		
Other assets:		
Claims account closed banks	0	
Denominated in foreign currencies	2,060,664	
Gold due from U.S. Treasury for account International Monetary Fund	230,118	
Reimbursable expenses and other items receivable	4,206	
Interest accrued	455,801	
Premium on securities	1,294	
Deferred charges	3,174	
Real estate acquired for banking-house purposes	4,299	
Suspense account	9,589	
All other	3,035	
Total other assets		**2,772,180**
Total assets		**78,900,665**

LIABILITIES		
F.R. notes:		
Outstanding (issued to F.R. banks)		47,560,111
Less: Held by issuing F.R. banks	2,037,493	
Forwarded for redemption	11,854	2,049,347
F.R. notes, net (includes notes held by U.S. Treasury and by F.R. banks other than issuing bank)		45,510,764
Deposits:		
Member bank reserves		**21,737,916**
U.S. Treasurer—General account		**702,795**
Foreign		**215,966**
Other deposits:		
Nonmember bank—Clearing accounts	66,681	
Officers' and certified checks	20,969	
Reserves of corporations doing foreign banking or financing	75,840	
International organizations	321,458	
All other	262,212	
Total other deposits		**747,160**
Total deposits		**23,403,837**
Deferred availability cash items		**8,334,396**
Other liabilities:		
Accrued dividends unpaid		
Unearned discount	491	
Discount on securities	380,744	
Sundry items payable	9,126	
Suspense account	1,768	
All other	1	
Total other liabilities		**392,130**
Total liabilities		**77,641,127**

CAPITAL ACCOUNTS	
Capital paid in	**629,769**
Surplus	**629,769**
Other capital accounts†	
Total liabilities and capital accounts	**78,900,665**
Contingent liability on acceptances purchased for foreign correspondents	**109,198**

TABLE **11–1.** (*Continued*)

* Amounts in boldface type indicate items shown in the Board's weekly statement of condition of the F.R. banks.
† During the year this item includes the net of earnings, expenses, profit and loss items, and accrued dividends which are closed out on Dec. 31; see Table 11–2, p. 186.
SOURCE: Board of Governors of the Federal Reserve System, *Annual Report* (1968), pp. 364–65, Table 1.

as collateral, gold-certificate funds continue to be used in the *interdistrict settlement fund,* as described in Chapter 10.

How do the Federal Reserve banks get gold certificates? By purchasing them as they are issued by the U.S. Treasury. How do Federal Reserve banks lower their holdings of gold certificates? In effect, by selling them back to the Treasury. The Federal Reserve banks may not legally own gold; they may only have gold certificates, which are claims to the gold held by the U.S. Treasury. As a rule, Federal Reserve bank holdings of gold certificates increase and decrease in volume according to the amount of gold owned by the Treasury. Commercial bank reserves also usually increase and decrease in proportion to Treasury gold holdings.

Increases in Treasury gold holdings occur when the U.S. government buys gold from foreign governments. When a foreign government sells gold to the U.S. Treasury, Federal Reserve banks decrease the checking-deposit account of the Treasury and raise that of the foreign government.[1] Assume, for example, that gold is purchased by the Treasury at a cost of $1 million. The effects on the Federal Reserve banks are shown by the entries labeled (a) on the balance sheet below:

BALANCE-SHEET CHANGES FOR THE FEDERAL RESERVE BANKS

ASSETS	LIABILITIES + CAPITAL ACCOUNTS

Gold-certificate account +$1,000,000 (b)	Deposits
	  U.S. Treasurer −$1,000,000 (a)
	  Foreign +$1,000,000 (a)
	  U.S. Treasurer +$1,000,000 (b)
	  Foreign −$1,000,000 (c)
	Member bank reserves +$1,000,000 (c)

The Treasury then issues gold certificates in an amount equal to the value of the gold purchase. These certificates are added to the gold certificates that the Treasury already holds for the Federal Reserve banks, and the banks in turn increase the deposit accounts of the Treasury. These transactions are recorded by the entries labeled (b) above.

So far there has been no change in commercial bank reserves. A change occurs only as the foreign government spends the funds in the United

[1] Actually all transactions of this type are handled by the Federal Reserve Bank of New York.

States or transfers them to deposit accounts with U.S. commercial banks. There is a decrease in foreign deposits and a corresponding increase in member bank reserves—entries (c) above. Member bank deposit liabilities also increase. These deposits will be held either by foreigners or by U.S. citizens who have sold goods and services to foreigners.

Until 1968 the Treasury also bought gold from domestic producers. The balance-sheet entries were roughly the same as in the preceding illustration. There was one difference, however. Because the gold producers deposited the checks they received from the Treasury in deposit accounts at commercial banks, which in turn collected on the checks by forwarding them to the Federal Reserve banks, member bank reserves increased directly. When the Treasury issued the gold certificates, gold-certificate reserves and Treasury deposits again increased.

The Treasury also experiences drains on its gold supply. A foreign government, for example, may choose to convert its holdings in U.S. currency on deposit with commercial banks into gold, for the purpose of switching this money into another currency. Using checks written on deposit accounts with commercial banks, the foreign government will probably first build up its deposit accounts at the Federal Reserve Bank of New York. This will decrease both commercial bank deposit liabilities and reserves by an equal amount, thereby reducing both commercial bank required and excess reserves. Subsequently the foreign government will use its increased deposit accounts at the Federal Reserve Bank of New York to purchase the desired gold from the Treasury. Thus, foreign deposits with the New York bank are reduced and Treasury deposits increased. Lower Treasury gold holdings mean reduced gold certificate claims to gold, however. Consequently, the Treasury withdraws gold certificates in an amount equal to the gold drain and Treasury deposits decrease. The results of a $1 million purchase of gold by foreigners can be shown as balance-sheet changes by reversing the plus and minus entries on the preceding balance sheet.

The gold-certificate holdings of the Federal Reserve banks increase and decrease according to the amount of gold held by the U.S. Treasury. This, in turn, means that commercial bank reserves generally increase as Treasury gold holdings increase, and decrease as those Treasury gold holdings decrease. Hence, if the effects of a change in the gold supply upon commercial bank reserves are viewed as undesirable in light of the general economic situation, the Federal Reserve will take action to offset these efforts, usually through the purchase and sale of U.S. government securities. As a matter of fact, the Fed usually takes such action whenever commercial bank reserves fluctuate beyond a certain point because of forces over which the Federal Reserve banks have no direct control. A change in our gold stock is merely one of these forces.

Our gold stock has directly affected our balance of payments.[2] In

---

[2] See Chapter 24 for a discussion of the balance of payments.

the 1960's, foreign dollar claims against the United States exceeded the claims of the United States against foreign countries. As a result, some foreign nations chose to take part of their additional claims in the form of gold rather than increased holdings of dollars in U.S. commercial banks. Thus, we experienced gold loss and gold certificate reductions. Had the Federal Reserve not taken action, these forces would have reduced commercial bank reserves and lending ability.

Other Cash

"Other cash" consists of Federal Reserve bank holdings of Treasury currency. Two circumstances may lead to an increase in this balance-sheet item: (1) an issuance of new currency by the Treasury, which is purchased by the Federal Reserve banks; or (2) a return of Treasury currency to the Federal Reserve banks by member banks. On the other hand, a retirement of currency by the Treasury or a demand for Treasury currency by commercial banks would lead to a decrease in Federal Reserve holdings of "other cash."

When the Federal Reserve banks purchase currency from the Treasury, they make payment by increasing Treasury deposit accounts. Similarly, when the Treasury retires currency, it does so by drawing down its deposit accounts at the Federal Reserve banks. At present, a substantial volume of Treasury currency is in the process of being retired. Most Treasury paper currency, silver certificates, has been replaced by Federal Reserve notes. This action, as we pointed out in Chapter 9, has virtually eliminated silver as a money metal in the United States.

These actions, the issuance and retirement of Treasury currency, have no direct effect on member bank reserves. Indirectly, however, there is some effect. When the Treasury spends the deposits it receives from a sale of currency to the Federal Reserve banks, the deposit liabilities and reserve deposits of member banks increase. The checks written by the Treasury are received by the nonbank public and deposited in commercial bank demand-deposit accounts. Commercial banks then send the checks to the Fed for collection. Federal Reserve banks in turn increase member bank reserve deposits and lower Treasury deposits.

On the other hand, when member banks ask for additional Treasury currency or send unneeded Treasury currency to the Federal Reserve banks, the total value of member bank reserves is in no way affected. Only a change in the composition of member bank reserves takes place. Member bank reserves consist of both vault cash and reserve deposits at the Federal Reserve banks. A shipment of Treasury currency to the Federal Reserve banks by member banks decreases the amount of reserves held in the form of vault cash, but the Federal Reserve banks make payment by increasing member bank reserve deposits.

Fluctuations in the amount of Treasury currency holdings at the Federal

Reserve banks, like changes in gold-certificate holdings, are variables over which the Federal Reserve has no direct control.

Discounts and Advances

Federal Reserve bank holdings of discounts and advances, on the other hand, are a factor over which the Reserve banks do have some control. Discounts and advances usually arise when member banks borrow reserves. There are three principal types: (1) discounts and advances secured by eligible paper; (2) advances secured by U.S. government securities; and (3) advances secured to the satisfaction of the lending Federal Reserve bank.

Discounts are made when member banks sell "eligible paper" to a Federal Reserve bank. Eligible paper consists of notes, drafts, and bills of exchange arising out of agricultural, industrial, and commercial loans made by the borrowing bank. Such paper, at the time of discount, must have a maturity of less than ninety days, except for agricultural paper, which may have a maturity of nine months. For instance, if the paper has a value of $1 million and the current discount rate is 3 percent, the Federal Reserve bank pays for the paper by increasing the member bank's reserve deposits by $992,500. If the member bank wants an *advance,* rather than a discount, secured by eligible paper, the member bank's reserve deposits are still increased by $992,500.[3] The member bank must subsequently repay the advance, however, since it still owns the paper.

The total volume of discounts and advances based on eligible paper is actually very small. Almost all member bank borrowing of reserves takes the form of advances secured by U.S. government securities. Here, the security is a promissory note signed by the bank, which deposits U.S. government securities as collateral with the lending Federal Reserve bank. The reserve deposit account of the member bank is increased by the amount of the loan less the interest charged. Thus, discounts of eligible paper and advances secured by government securities are mechanically identical.

The third way in which a member bank may borrow reserves is through advances secured "to the satisfaction of the lending bank." This means that member banks may borrow reserves even if they do not wish to secure the advances with eligible paper or U.S. government securities. The lending Federal Reserve bank will determine what other assets are acceptable as collateral. The maximum maturity of such a loan, however, is four months. Advances of this sort also carry a penalty rate of interest, which is usually $\frac{1}{2}$ percent higher than the discount rate of advances secured by U.S. government securities. When the Federal Reserve banks received authority, in 1935, to make this type of loan to member banks, it was expected that such borrowing would only be done under exceptional circumstances. Instead, it has now become a normal procedure.

---

[3] An annual discount cost of 3 percent will amount to $7,500 for ninety days.

Generally, banks apply for one of these three types of loan either to meet a deficiency of reserves or to increase their level of reserves prior to expanding loans and investments. Many banks make frequent trips to the "discount window" for these reasons. As mentioned in Chapter 10, the Federal Reserve banks are usually ready to grant such loans to member banks, but the loans are not extended automatically. In practice, the Fed does not control the volume of member bank borrowings so much by loan limitation as by manipulation of the discount rate. If the Board of Governors believes that the lending activity of the commercial banking system should be restricted, it increases the discount rate. On the other hand, if an increase in spending seems appropriate, the Board will reduce the discount rate. Chapter 12 will discuss in more detail how discount-rate manipulation is used as an instrument of monetary policy.

In addition to lending reserves to member banks, the Federal Reserve banks may also make advances to individuals, partnerships, and corporations when alternative lending sources are unable to do so. These advances have a maximum maturity of ninety days and must be secured by U.S. government securities. The rate charged for such loans varies depending on economic conditions in the various Federal Reserve districts. It is usually $\frac{1}{2}$ to $1\frac{1}{2}$ percent higher than the discount rate on advances to member banks secured by U.S. government securities. Direct loans of this type are very rare in today's prosperity economy. As a matter of fact, Table 11–1 shows that, as of December 31, 1968, there were no loans of this type outstanding. When they are made, however, they tend to increase commercial bank reserves. As the borrowers use the proceeds of the loans, member banks acquire checks drawn on the Federal Reserve banks. When member banks present these checks for payment, the Federal Reserve banks increase member bank reserve deposit accounts. Conversely, loan repayments reduce member bank reserve deposits.

Acceptances

The purchase and sale of bankers' acceptances in the open market is one of the functions performed by the Federal Reserve Bank of New York for all the Reserve banks and for the FOMC. A bank or a business may draw up an order for a commercial bank to pay. The credit of the firm serves as collateral here. If the bank accepts the order to pay, the document becomes a *bankers' acceptance*. Since the bank has accepted the order, it is obligated to pay, and the acceptance becomes fully negotiable. These bankers' acceptances are often created when importers want to facilitate their purchase of goods and services abroad. In foreign trade, the seller may know little about the credit of the buyer but be willing to accept the credit of a commercial bank. The importer, of course, will supply the bank with the necessary funds before maturity of the acceptance. An importer under these circumstances will have the foreign exporter draw a bill on the importer's bank. Once the bank accepts the bill, the bankers' acceptance that has been created can be sold by the exporter. This is how he receives payment for the goods and services sold.

How does the purchase and sale of bankers' acceptances affect commercial bank reserves? When the Federal Reserve Bank of New York purchases these acceptances, it pays for them with checks drawn on itself. The checks are deposited by the recipients in their deposit accounts at commercial banks, and these banks present the checks for payment to the Federal Reserve Bank of New York. Payment is made on the checks by increasing the reserve accounts of the member banks. On the other hand, when the Federal Reserve Bank of New York sells bankers' acceptances, purchasers pay for them with checks written on commercial banks. The Federal Reserve Bank of New York collects on these checks by decreasing member bank reserve deposits.

Federal Reserve purchases and sales of bankers' acceptances are called "open-market operations." This is not the only type of open-market operation conducted by the FOMC. In fact, most of its dealings involve U.S. government securities, rather than bankers' acceptances. More will be said of open-market operations in U.S. government securities both later in this chapter and in Chapter 13.

Quantitatively, Federal Reserve bank holdings of bankers' acceptances amounted to only $57.7 million at the end of 1968. However, this represents a substantial increase in such holdings over other years in the recent past.

U.S. Government Securities

Quantitatively, U.S. government securities are the most important asset held by the Federal Reserve banks. Of a total $78.9 billion in assets held by the Reserve banks at the end of 1968, some $52.9 billion was in the form of U.S. government securities. These securities are purchased by the account manager at the Federal Reserve Bank of New York for all the Federal Reserve banks. Purchases are made either directly or on a repurchase-agreement basis from government securities dealers. Under a repurchase agreement, the securities dealer agrees to repurchase securities sold to the Federal Reserve within a specified period of time, normally fifteen days or less. Purchases of this sort by the Fed are generally designed to provide banks with additional reserves in periods of temporary reserve shortages.

The securities issues bought and sold by the Federal Reserve are almost always old U.S. government securities. Rarely do the Federal Reserve banks acquire new security issues directly from the U.S. Treasury. In fact, the Federal Reserve Act provides that the Federal Reserve banks cannot hold more than $5 billion in securities purchased directly from the Treasury at any time. This stipulation presumably limits the ability of the Fed to assist the Treasury in inflationary financing of Treasury deficits. Actually, when such purchases are made, they are usually for the purpose of helping the Treasury adjust to a lack of synchronization between its tax receipts and payments. As Chapter 13 will show, the purchase of old securities can also lead to inflationary pressures.

The securities purchased today by the Federal Reserve System are of varying maturities. For the period 1951 to 1961, Federal Reserve purchases were concentrated in short-term securities. Since February, 1961, however, the Federal Reserve banks have acquired both short- and long-term government securities. These purchases of longer-termed securities are designed to help bring about two policy ends: a stable domestic economy and a favorable balance of payments. In a less than full employment economy, Federal Reserve open market operations, if concentrated in securities with short maturities, can only tend to satisfy the requirements of policies designed to achieve economic stability. Purchases of short-term securities at this time tend to increase reserves (as we shall demonstrate in succeeding paragraphs), lower short-term interest rates, and induce an outflow of dollars from the U.S. economy (see Chapters 24 and 25). To compensate for this maladjustment in policy, the Board of Governors decided in 1961 that the Federal Reserve banks should buy and sell throughout the maturity range of U.S. government securities. By expanding long-term instead of short-term holdings, bank lending ability should expand and short-term interest rates be maintained, thus presumably reducing a possible flow of funds abroad.

How do Federal Reserve operations in U.S. government securities affect member bank reserve positions? In precisely the same manner as the purchase and sale of bankers' acceptances by the Federal Reserve. The Fed buys U.S. government securities from dealers who specialize in the trading of these securities and pays for them with checks written on itself. When a government securities dealer deposits this Federal Reserve check in his deposit account at a commercial bank, his deposits are increased. When his bank presents the check to the Fed for collection, it receives an increase in its reserve deposits. The following balance sheets show the effects of a purchase of $1 million in securities:

BALANCE-SHEET CHANGES FOR THE FEDERAL RESERVE BANKS

ASSETS	LIABILITIES + CAPITAL ACCOUNTS
U.S. government securities +$1,000,000	Deposits Member bank reserves +$1,000,000

BALANCE-SHEET CHANGES FOR THE COMMERCIAL BANKING SYSTEM

ASSETS	LIABILITIES + CAPITAL ACCOUNTS
Reserves +$1,000,000	Demand deposits +$1,000,000

The increase in the demand deposits of the securities dealer are only temporary, however, since he in turn must pay whoever sold him the securities purchased by the Federal Reserve System.

When the Federal Reserve sells government securities, just the reverse of this procedure takes place. The account manager tells the securities dealers that he wishes to sell. Buyers of the securities pay their brokers with checks written on their demand-deposit accounts at commercial banks. The securities dealers deliver the securities to the buyers and pay the Federal Reserve System with checks drawn on their accounts at commercial banks. The Fed then collects on the checks by lowering the reserve deposits of the commercial banks.

Thus, a sale of securities by the Federal Reserve means a decrease in commercial bank reserves, and a purchase means an increase in reserves. As we shall see later, the Federal Reserve is continually buying and selling securities. What is important for commercial banks and economic policy is the net effect of these transactions on commercial bank reserves and lending.

Float

Federal Reserve "float" is not an asset. It is simply the difference between an asset, cash items in process of collection, and a liability, deferred-availability cash items. Cash items in process of collection are checks that the Federal Reserve banks have received but not as yet collected on by decreasing member bank reserves. Deferred-availability cash items are checks that the Federal Reserve banks have received and not as yet paid by increasing member bank reserves. Theoretically, these two items should equal one another. In point of fact, however, they do not, since the Federal Reserve banks generally increase the accounts of depositing banks prior to collecting from the banks on which the checks were drawn. As a result, there is a time gap, and cash items in process of collection are larger than deferred-availability cash items. This difference is termed the "float." Variations in the float can significantly affect member bank reserve positions.

Deferred-availability cash items are paid within one day if the checks are drawn on local banks and within two days if they are drawn on distant banks. This is done almost automatically. It usually takes longer than this to collect on checks, however, since the checks received may have been written on banks in another Federal Reserve district. If so, they must be mailed to that district's Federal Reserve bank and then to the bank on which the check was drawn. This takes time. If for some reason the mails are delayed, the accounts of the depositing banks will still be increased within two days, even though the collection of the cash items has been delayed. The result is an increase in member bank reserves.

An increase in the volume of checks being written, and hence being cleared, will also increase float and reserves. A larger volume of checks being cleared strains the check-clearing mechanism of the Federal Reserve banks and slows up the collection process. Such increases in check payments occur regularly at mid-month and year end. Increased collection of checks, on the other hand, will reduce float and, accordingly, member bank reserves.

Other Assets

Other Federal Reserve bank assets consist primarily of the physical property comprising bank premises, holdings of foreign currencies, and accrued interest. The value of bank premises changes slowly. Any increase in these assets would involve an increase in member bank reserves, since the assets would be paid for by checks drawn on the Federal Reserve banks. When these checks are deposited in commercial bank deposit accounts, they are forwarded to the Federal Reserve for payment in the form of increased reserve deposits.

Federal Reserve holdings of foreign currencies increase and decrease in response to purchases and sales by the account manager at the Federal Reserve Bank of New York. These purchases and sales will generally result in a corresponding increase or decrease in foreign deposits with the Fed. Member bank reserves will be affected only when foreigners use these accounts in their dealings with domestic commercial banks and the nonbank public.

Accrued interest is a somewhat different matter. This item consists principally of interest that has accrued on Federal Reserve holdings of U.S. government securities. Changes in this asset will not normally affect commercial bank reserve positions. As accrued interest increases, Federal Reserve surplus accounts increase. When the interest is paid, Treasury deposit accounts and accrued interest decrease. Commercial bank reserves are unaffected by these transactions. To the extent, however, that the Treasury has to transfer funds from its tax and loan accounts at commercial banks in order to meet the interest payments, commercial bank reserves decrease.

FEDERAL RESERVE BANK LIABILITIES

Federal Reserve Notes

Federal Reserve notes were described in Chapter 2. They are the principal liability of the Federal Reserve banks that issue them. What are the effects of note increases on member bank reserves? There is no direct effect until member banks distribute them to the nonbank public. Member banks purchase currency (both Treasury and Federal Reserve currency) by drawing down their reserve deposit accounts. At this point, they have merely switched reserves from one form, reserve deposits, to another, vault cash. However, as soon as the nonbank public demands the currency, commercial bank vault cash reserves will be reduced. Conversely, return of currency to the banks will lead to an increase in reserves. Chapter 7 explained the effects of cash drains and inflows on bank lending capacity; this topic will be raised again in Chapter 15, where the various factors that determine bank reserves and the money supply are summarized.

Deposits

Member bank reserves. After Federal Reserve notes, member bank reserve deposits are the main liability of the Federal Reserve banks. At the end of 1968 these reserves amounted to $21.7 billion and supported $332.8 billion in member bank deposit liabilities.

Movements in member bank reserve deposits do not occur independently of changes in other items on the balance sheet of the Federal Reserve banks. On the contrary, member bank reserves increase and decrease *in response to* changes in other balance-sheet assets, liabilities, and capital accounts. Thus, they are the residual item that the Federal Reserve System attempts to regulate in order to promote domestic economic stability.

U.S. Treasurer general account. Earlier chapters have discussed the meaning of the general account of the U.S. Treasurer. It is principally through these deposit accounts that the federal government makes expenditures. Variation in the size of these Treasury accounts at Federal Reserve banks will usually affect member bank reserve positions.

Whenever the Treasury uses its balances at the Federal Reserve banks to make payments to the nonbank public or to the commercial banking system, there is an increase in member bank reserves. Assume, for example, that the Treasury uses $1 million of its deposits at Federal Reserve banks to retire U.S. government securities held by members of the nonbank public. The Treasury retires the securities with checks drawn on its accounts at the Federal Reserve banks. When the nonbank public deposits these checks in its checking accounts, the demand deposit liabilities of the commercial banking system increase by $1 million. Assuming a 15 percent reserve requirement, required reserves increase by $150,000. Excess reserves also increase, however. When the Treasury checks deposited by the nonbank public are presented to the Federal Reserve banks for collection, member bank reserves are increased by $1 million. Since required reserves amount to only $150,000, excess reserves have increased by $850,000. This permits a substantial increase in the lending activity of commercial banks. The changes resulting from such a debt retirement operation are summarized in the following balance sheets:

BALANCE-SHEET CHANGES FOR THE FEDERAL RESERVE BANKS

ASSETS	LIABILITIES + CAPITAL ACCOUNTS
	Deposits
	Member bank reserves +$1,000,000
	U.S. Treasurer −$1,000,000

BALANCE-SHEET CHANGES FOR THE COMMERCIAL BANKING SYSTEM

ASSETS		LIABILITIES + CAPITAL ACCOUNTS	
Reserves	+$1,000,000	Demand deposits of the nonbank public	+$1,000,000

Precisely the same balance-sheet changes occur when goods and services are purchased by the U.S. government from the nonbank public. There would be some difference, however, if the Treasury used its balances with the Federal Reserve banks to retire government securities held by commercial banks or to make other types of payments to the commercial banks. Then there would be no direct effect upon demand deposit liabilities of the commercial banking system. Commercial bank reserves would increase, however, because when Treasury checks are presented to the Federal Reserve for collection, payment is made by increasing member bank reserves.

On the other hand, not all decreases in Treasury deposits with the Fed will affect commercial bank reserves. There are transactions that take place between the Federal Reserve banks and the Treasury that may not initially involve either the commercial banks or the nonbank public. For example, if the Treasury uses its deposit balances to retire public debt held by the Federal Reserve banks, Reserve bank assets in the form of U.S. government securities are reduced, as are liabilities in the form of U.S. government deposits. The commercial banking system is in no way involved.

How do increases in Treasury deposits at the Fed affect member bank reserves? If the transaction involves only the Federal Reserve banks and the Treasury, there is no direct effect. As previously mentioned, an issuance of gold certificates by the Treasury will increase both holdings of these certificates and Treasury demand deposits at the Federal Reserve banks. It must be remembered, however, that until 1968 a gold-certificate issue may have involved the purchase of gold from gold producers who were members of the nonbank public. If this was the case, the gold purchase entailed a payment to the nonbank public and hence an increase in member bank demand and reserve deposits.

If an increase in Treasury deposits with the Fed involves the commercial banking system, a decrease in member bank reserves takes place. If, for example, the Treasury decides to transfer $1 million from its tax and loan accounts at commercial banks to its general accounts with the Federal Reserve banks, the reserves of the banks decrease by $1 million, and so do their deposit liabilities. The reduction in deposit liabilities means a decrease in required reserves, but since actual reserves have decreased by an equal amount, the net effect is a reduction of some magnitude in member bank excess reserves. Assuming a 15 percent reserve requirement, a $1 million decline in member bank demand deposits and reserves means an $850,000 decrease in excess reserves.

Foreign deposits. Foreign governments and foreign central banks maintain deposit accounts with our Federal Reserve banks and with commercial banks. (Some mention of this was made in Chapter 10.) When foreigners need money to purchase goods and services in the United States, there is a transfer of funds from foreign dollar holdings at the Federal Reserve banks to commercial banks. This results in an increase in member bank deposit liabilities and a simultaneous increase in reserves. A reverse flow, from checking-deposit accounts at member banks to Federal Reserve foreign accounts, means a reduction in commercial bank deposit liabilities and reserve deposits.

Other deposits. "Other deposits" consist primarily of nonmember bank clearing accounts, deposits of businesses engaged in foreign banking, deposits of various international organizations, and deposits of some government agencies. An increase in the total of "other deposits" usually decreases member bank reserves.

Nonmember banks that remit at par may maintain checking-deposit accounts with the Federal Reserve banks. These accounts are maintained primarily to facilitate the clearing of checks for the nonmember banks, although it is not necessary for a nonmember bank to have such an account in order to have access to the Federal Reserve clearing process. Large city correspondent banks will handle the clearing of checks for the nonmember banks.

An increase in nonmember bank deposits with the Federal Reserve banks will tend to decrease member bank reserves, but not necessarily all commercial bank reserves. In Connecticut, for example, nonmember banks may keep part of their reserves with Federal Reserve banks and part with commercial banks. If a Connecticut nonmember bank transferred some of its reserve deposits from member banks to Federal Reserve banks, a decrease in the reserves of the member banks would occur, but there would be no change in nonmember bank reserves. However, if the same bank transferred to a Federal Reserve bank its deposits in a member bank that was not authorized by the state's commissioner to hold nonmember bank reserves, there would be an increase in nonmember bank reserves and a decrease in member bank reserves. The precise effects on all bank reserves of changes in the location of nonmember bank reserves and deposits with other banks depend on the various state statutes governing the reserves of nonmember banks.

It is also difficult to know precisely how the remaining components of "other deposits" will affect bank reserve positions. Nor are the changes that take place in these deposits subject to direct control by the Fed. Fortunately, the relative importance and activity of these accounts is not great. Changes affecting commercial bank reserves in an undesired manner can usually be offset by open market operations undertaken by the Federal Reserve.

CAPITAL ACCOUNTS

Capital Paid In

Capital paid in refers to the par value of the stock of the Federal Reserve banks that has been purchased by the member banks. When banks become members of the Federal Reserve System, or as members become larger, they must purchase stock in their district Federal Reserve bank. To the extent that member banks use reserve deposits to purchase Federal Reserve bank stock, their reserves decrease. A retirement of stock, on the other hand, means an increase in member bank reserves.

Surplus

Surplus changes as Federal Reserve bank earnings change. These earnings are substantial because receipts from the interest on Federal Reserve bank U.S. government security holdings and discounts and advances are far in excess of their operating expenses.[4] Table 11–2 shows the earnings and expenses of the Federal Reserve banks in 1968. Current net earnings were $2.5 billion. Most of this, however, instead of being transferred to surplus, was paid to the Treasury. The Federal Reserve banks, at present, pay a 6 percent statutory dividend to member banks and increase the surplus by enough to keep the surplus account approximately equal to the value of the capital stock paid in. All remaining earnings are paid to the Treasury, technically in the form of interest on Federal Reserve notes. Thus, most of the interest earned on U.S. government securities is turned back to the Treasury. In 1968, the Treasury paid more than $2.7 billion in interest to the Federal Reserve banks, and received almost $2.5 billion back.

The net effect of this Federal Reserve policy is that there are only small yearly changes in surplus. Nevertheless, any increase in surplus means a decrease in member bank reserves, since it reflects an excess of receipts over payments. Payments by the Federal Reserve banks to employees, the U.S. Treasury, and member banks increase reserves, but the receipts remaining after these payments have been made tend to decrease reserves.

SUMMARY

In this chapter we have studied the components of the balance sheet of the Federal Reserve banks. The focus has been upon the effect of changes in these items on the reserves of commercial banks. Although our discussion has been almost exclusively in terms of member banks, it should be remembered that the reserves of nonmember banks will be affected in a manner similar to those of member banks.

[4] Surplus, as Chapter 5 explained, is a general category that usually includes capital surplus, undistributed profits, and reserves.

ITEM	TOTAL
CURRENT EARNINGS	
Discounts and advances	29,702,022
Acceptances	4,153,633
U.S. Govt. securities	2,653,503,692
Foreign currencies	76,539,434
All other	547,163
Total	2,764,445,942
CURRENT EXPENSES	
Salaries:	
Officers	9,965,527
Employees	119,117,557
Retirement and other benefits	20,933,715
Fees—Directors and others	1,237,972
Traveling expenses	2,831,590
Postage and expressage	28,688,476
Telephone and telegraph	2,495,618
Printing and supplies	10,369,493
Insurance	426,780
Taxes on real estate	6,184,251
Depreciation (buildings)	5,955,960
Light, heat, power, and water	2,400,885
Repairs and alterations	1,657,983
Rent	193,349
Furniture and equipment:	
Purchases	4,178,220
Rentals	10,061,483
All other	4,017,802
Inter-bank expenses	
Subtotal	230,716,663
F.R. currency	20,474,404
Assessment for expenses of Board of Governors	14,198,198
Total	265,389,265
Less reimbursement for certain fiscal agency and other expenses	23,038,895
Net expenses	242,350,370
PROFIT AND LOSS	
Current net earnings	2,522,095,572
Additions to current net earnings:	
Profits on sales of U.S. Govt. securities	792,717
Profits on foreign-exchange transactions	8,049,430
All other	154,073
Total additions	8,996,220
Deductions from current net earnings	476,222
Net addition to or deduction from (−) current net earnings	8,519,994
Net earnings before payments to U.S. Treasury	2,530,615,568
Dividends paid	36,959,336
Payments to U.S. Treasury (interest on F.R. notes)	2,463,628,983
Transferred to surplus	30,027,250
Surplus, January 1	599,741,400
Surplus, December 31	629,768,650

Note: Details may not add to totals because of rounding. SOURCE: Board of Governors of the Federal Reserve System, *Annual Report* (1968), pp. 374–75, Table 7.

In general, when Federal Reserve assets increase and there is no offsetting increase in other liabilities (defined as total liabilities less member bank reserve deposits) or capital accounts, member bank reserves will increase. If Federal Reserve assets decrease and there is no corresponding decrease in other liabilities or capital accounts, member bank reserves decrease. If, on the other hand, Federal Reserve bank assets remain constant and the total of other liabilities and capital accounts increases, there is a decrease in member bank reserves. Conversely, a decrease in other liabilities and capital accounts means an increase in member bank reserves.

This summary, however, merely reflects the truisms inherent in the construction of the balance sheet. What is more relevant is the impact on reserves of a change in a specific balance-sheet item. As the preceding analysis has shown, it cannot be predicted precisely that a change in a specific asset, another liability, or a capital account will necessarily affect member bank reserves; possibly some other balance-sheet asset, liability, or capital account will change instead. In spite of these difficulties, however, some specific conclusions can be derived.

First, an increase in discounts and advances to member banks will increase member bank reserves and a repayment of discounts and advances by member banks will decrease member bank reserves.

Second, a purchase of bankers' acceptances in the open market by the Fed will increase member bank reserves and a sale of bankers' acceptances in the open market will decrease member bank reserves.

Third, a purchase of U.S. government securities in the open market by the Fed will increase member bank reserves and a sale of these securities will reduce member bank reserves. *Fourth,* in increase in float will increase member bank reserves and a decrease in float will decrease member bank reserves.

Concerning changes other than those just mentioned, the most we can say is that changes in assets, other liabilities, and capital accounts will be associated with certain types of changes in member bank reserves. The more important of these changes are summarized as follows: (1) increases and decreases in gold-certificate holdings (a Federal Reserve asset) tend to be associated with increases and decreases in member bank reserves; (2) increases and decreases in Federal Reserve notes (a Reserve bank liability) result in equivalent decreases and increases respectively in member bank reserve deposits, without changing the total of member bank reserves; and (3) increases and decreases in U.S. Treasurer general-account deposits (also a Federal Reserve liability) tend to cause decreases and increases respectively in member bank reserve deposits.

Supplementary Readings

Board of Governors of the Federal Reserve System. *The Federal Reserve System: Purposes and Functions.* Washington, D.C., 1963, Chapter 11.

"Collateral for Federal Reserve Credit," *Federal Reserve Bulletin* (September 1963), pp. 1235–36.

Federal Reserve Bank of Chicago. *Modern Money Mechanics: A Workbook on Deposits, Currency, and Bank Reserves.* Chicago, May 1961.

CHAPTER 12

The Development
of Federal Reserve Instruments
# of Monetary Control, Part I

At present the Federal Reserve has five broad tools at its disposal that it may use to implement monetary, fiscal, and international economic policy. These instruments of control are (1) the reserve requirement, (2) the discount rate, (3) open market operations, (4) Regulation Q, and (5) the margin requirement. The first four are *general monetary controls.* They do not directly affect commercial bank lending operations in specific types of credit extension. The banks still have a free hand in determining which types of loans and investments they will make. The fifth policy instrument, the manipulation of margin requirements for the purchase and carrying of securities, is a *selective credit control.*

Chapters 12 and 13 examine these Federal Reserve instruments of monetary control in some detail. *First,* we shall consider how the Board of Governors may be expected to use these instruments of policy in alternative economic situations. *Second,* we shall examine the history of each policy instrument to see how it has actually been employed; some attempt will be made to assess whether or not the uses of each instrument, considered by itself, have been appropriate. The purpose here is to master a basic understanding of each instrument and the difficulties inherent in its use. *Finally,* we shall attempt an overall assessment of monetary policy. Clearly it is dangerous to consider each tool in isolation from every other instrument of monetary and fiscal policy. To reach a judgment concerning the merits of Federal Reserve monetary action, we must consider the net effect of all instruments of policy upon commercial bank credit and money creation.[1]

---

[1] Some instructors may prefer to postpone a study of the actual use of Federal Reserve policy instruments until Part IV, which treats alternative economic policies. This is certainly an acceptable pedagogical procedure. I prefer the present outline, since it (1) avoids a mechanical ticking off of the policy instruments divorced from the historical world in which we live and (2) provides some introduction to the theoretical apparatus considered in Part III—this is particularly important in courses where time prohibits an extensive elaboration of Parts III and IV.

APPROPRIATE USE OF FEDERAL RESERVE
MONETARY CONTROLS

Recession Policy

A period of recession, when human and nonhuman resources are less than fully employed, calls for increased spending. An increase in spending, in either the public or private sector of the economy, will expand the demand for goods and services, raise incomes, and stimulate employment of resources. However, before any additional spending can take place, funds are needed. A desire to spend will affect the economy only to the extent that it is financed, either by (1) an increase in the supply of money or (2) a more intensive utilization of the present supply of money—that is, an increase in the velocity of circulation. In the absence of these two conditions, an increase in the desire to spend cannot be implemented, and hence will not lead to higher employment levels.

Encouraging an increase in total spending can be difficult; increased spending depends in part on how the increase is financed. For example, an increase in federal government expenditures will be financed through increased taxes or through borrowing. If increased government spending is financed through taxation, its effects may be cancelled out, at least in part, by reductions in spending by taxpayers. If increased expenditures are financed by the sale of government securities, the effects of the increased spending will depend on who purchases the securities. If the nonbank public buys them, using idle funds, total spending will actually rise in the economy. However, if the nonbank public makes the purchase with funds that would otherwise have been spent on goods and services, the impact of the increased government spending will be lessened. If Federal Reserve banks buy the securities, public spending will be strongly stimulated, since the use of funds provided by the Federal Reserve will lead to an increase in the total money supply and in commercial bank reserves.[2]

An increase in private spending can be induced only by manipulating the determinants of private spending (these determinants are examined in detail in Chapter 19). In general, however, a drop in interest rates charged consumers and businesses for borrowing tends to lead to increased borrowing and spending. A general increase in income brought about by increased government spending tends to induce an increase in private spending, and improved profit expectations by businesses often lead to greater investment spendings. Finally (a tricky thing to establish empirically, but important analytically), increased liquid wealth holdings, particularly in the form of money and near monies, tend to induce people to spend more liberally.

---

[2] The potential effects of federal government spending on the stock of money and commercial bank reserve positions are discussed in Chapter 14. The theory behind this analysis of how effective demand increases by the federal government affect the economy is outlined in the model of economic activity developed in Part III.

The Federal Reserve plays a significant role in this process of economic stimulation. Appropriate use of Federal Reserve instruments of monetary control can directly increase commercial bank lending ability and the supply of money. With increased borrowings from commercial banks by business firms and consumers, more funds are made available to the economy, thereby providing a base for additional spending.

Some economists argue that Federal Reserve action in periods of recession is inadequate to actually reverse an economic decline. This may be true in many instances, but appropriate monetary policies during a recession will at least ease the path taken in recovery. Although expansionary policies may not be able to reverse a downward trend in the economy, they can intensify the speed of recovery once it is under way. On the other hand, inadequate creation of reserves by the Federal Reserve banks during recession and economic upturn can slow down the process of economic recovery.

What, then, are some of the possible uses of the instruments of central-bank policy during recession?

First, reserve requirements may be lowered. A reduction of reserve requirements will increase excess reserves and hence the lending ability of the commercial banking system.

Second, discount rates may be reduced. A drop in discount rates will make it easier for commercial banks to borrow reserves for the purpose of expanding lending operations.

Third, the Federal Reserve Bank of New York may purchase U.S. government securities and bankers' acceptances in the open market. Purchases of securities and acceptances will directly increase the volume of commercial bank reserves. More important, they will also increase the excess reserves of the commercial banking system. To the extent that the securities purchased were originally held by the nonbank public, the money stock will be increased.

Fourth, no action need be taken to adjust the maximum interest rate payable by member commercial banks on time deposits under Regulation Q. During recession, the rates actually paid by commercial banks are likely to be already below the permissible maximum.

Fifth, the Federal Reserve can lower margin requirements for the purchase and carrying of securities. Most economists today do not consider margin requirement changes an effective means of inducing increased spending in the economy. Instead, the consensus is that this instrument should be used primarily to minimize the use of borrowed funds to finance speculation in stock.

All these actions make it easier for banks and other financial institutions to lend. Given funds to do so, people will spend more. Interest rates too will ease because of abundant reserves and a plentiful money stock, and this will further stimulate borrowing and spending. True, the interest rate structure of the economy during a recession will probably be low already;

monetary policy can keep it low during an economic upturn; this will speed up the recovery process.

Neither the effectiveness nor even the advisability of monetary controls can be taken for granted in every situation, however. As we shall see later, they are subject to a number of limitations. Also, some instruments are more difficult to employ than others. In fact, open market operations are the only instrument whose power can be regulated with some degree of precision. Caution must be exercised in the use of the other instruments; otherwise, open market operations may be necessary to compensate for errors of judgment made in applying the other tools of monetary policy.

Different types of recession call for different types of monetary action. A deep depression clearly calls for an aggressive use of all policy tools. A very mild recession, on the other hand, may necessitate only a very small increase in Federal Reserve bank holdings of U.S. government securities and bankers' acceptances. It is even possible that no acquisition of securities and acceptances would be needed at all, since by the time the effects of the purchase are felt in the economy, a recovery may be under way. Thus, a purchase in a mild recession may serve only to intensify inflationary tendencies in the next economic boom.

Qualifications such as these raise serious questions concerning the effectiveness of our policy instruments. Some economists even go so far as to argue that the Federal Reserve should engage in no discretionary use of monetary controls at all. Instead, they believe that some type of automatic policy may be needed, one that would eliminate perverse variations in the stock of money as a source of economic instability. Such policies might include the automatic use of monetary tools to maintain price stability or the use of open market operations only to maintain a steady increase in the money stock at some low predetermined rate. Several of these alternative policy proposals are evaluated in the discussion of the relationship between money and financial policy in Part IV.

The instruments recommended by monetary policy for recession—the lowering of reserve requirements, the reduction of discount rates, and the purchase of U.S. government securities and bankers' acceptances—should not, therefore, be advocated without qualification. We mention them here simply to indicate the nature of the policies that might serve to mitigate a recession.

Economic Boom Policy

As long as there are unemployed resources available in the economy, increases in the money stock and thus in the demand for goods and services should not normally lead to substantial price level increases. Once productive resources are fully utilized, however, in the absence of countermeasures, money stock increases and excess demand will lead to rising prices. The rise in output that occurs during the early part of a boom, before resources are fully employed, is usually desirable. However, the increased price level and the consequent deterioration in the purchasing power of most liquid wealth, which are apt to result from a further extension of the boom, are in themselves undersirable. If the inflationary problem becomes sufficiently serious, countermeasures should be taken. These measures may take several forms. Wage or price controls may be imposed, for example. Such measures deal only with the symptoms, not the causes, of inflation, however. Prices have risen because of excess spending and increased costs. The full employment output of goods and services has produced a low supply relative to the effective demand. To halt a serious inflation either the source of the excessive spending must be eliminated or the price controls must be supplemented by a second pricing mechanism—a rationing system.

If the inflationary period occurs during wartime, when the increased spending that produces the inflationary pressures is made up of government military outlays that cannot be reduced, taxes may have to be increased— an unpopular measure at any time—in order to decrease demand in the private sector of the economy. In the absence of increased taxation, the only alternative is to enforce controls that will prevent the increased wartime incomes from being spent.

In peacetime, many economic controls are politically unacceptable in a democracy like the United States, and hence different ways must be found to reduce spending. Public pressure can force the government to reduce its expenditures. Pressure may also be brought against business and consumers to decrease expenditures. Labor unions may be persuaded to postpone demands for wage increases.

Generally, however, aside from increased taxation, the most frequently employed restrictive policy is some form of monetary control. To succeed in reducing the effective demand for goods and services, either the money stock or its velocity must be decreased.[3]

There are five basic ways in which monetary policy can attack this problem:

First, reserve requirements may be raised, thereby reducing commercial bank excess reserves and lending ability.

Second, discount rates may be increased, making it more difficult for commercial banks to borrow additional reserves and reducing the spread between the interest rate that commercial banks earn on loans and the amount they pay on borrowed reserves.

Third, the Federal Reserve Bank of New York may sell bankers' acceptances and U.S. government securities, thereby reducing the money stock and the bank reserves directly.

Fourth, when nonbank financial-institution lending has expanded during the boom, *the Federal Reserve may raise the maximum rate of interest pay-*

[3] It would be well to keep in mind that economic boom must be financed in some manner. Thus, increased spending may well have resulted from a too liberal use of expansionary policy instruments during the preceding period of economic recovery.

able on time deposits by commercial banks under Regulation Q to woo funds away from these institutions and hence decrease their lending ability.

Fifth, the Federal Reserve may raise margin requirements, thereby halting any speculation in stocks that is taking place on the basis of borrowed funds.

These policy actions collectively raise interest rates, making it more difficult for businesses and individuals to borrow. In addition, they may decrease the rate of increase in the stock of money and the volume of near monies. These measures should reduce spending in the economy.

The preceding section argued that a policy of monetary ease might not actually be able to bring about an economic recovery by itself. The converse of this statement is not true, however. A policy of monetary restriction *can* generally bring inflation to an end. The tools of monetary policy *are* strong enough to reverse almost any type of boom, other than the one caused by excessive federal budget deficits accompanied by sharp money stock increases. In fact, the danger of applying our monetary instruments to curb inflation is not that they will not be able to halt an inflation, but rather that they may throw the economy into a sharp recession if used improperly. Whereas an increase in excess reserves *may* cause banks to expand credit, a deficiency of reserves *must* cause them to curtail credit, and even to contract loans, investments, and demand deposit liabilities. Too sharp a reduction in reserves, therefore, may curtail spending drastically. For this reason, just as caution must be used in employing monetary techniques to ease credit, even more care must be taken in using devices to restrict credit. One example of an apparently inappropriate application of a restrictive measure was the doubling of reserve requirements from 1936 to 1937. Another was the increase of the discount rate in 1957. More will be said of these errors in discretionary monetary policy in subsequent sections of this chapter.

GENERAL MONETARY CONTROLS

The five basic tools of monetary policy are all designed to regulate the lending ability of the financial sector of the economy. Of these policy instruments, three, the reserve requirement, the discount rate, and open market operations, are principally aimed at manipulating the reserve position of the commercial banking system. These three instruments are considered first. The first two of these instruments are considered next. For open market operations, see Chapter 13.

The Reserve Requirement

An increase in member bank excess reserves expands the lending and investment capacity of the banking system. In the process, the ability of the system to create demand deposit money is increased. Conversely, a decrease in commercial bank excess reserves diminishes the ability of banks to lend, invest, and create money; a substantial deficiency of reserves will force a contraction in the economy.

Changes in the reserve requirement can be used to affect commercial bank reserve positions by altering the composition of commercial bank reserves. An increase in the reserve requirement means that some reserves formerly classified as excess become required reserves. A decrease in the reserve requirement, on the other hand, reduces required and raises excess reserves.

Table 12–1 lists the changes that have taken place in the reserve require-

TABLE 12–1. MEMBER BANK RESERVE REQUIREMENTS
(PERCENT OF DEPOSITS)

	THROUGH JULY 13, 1966				
	NET DEMAND DEPOSITS†			TIME DEPOSITS§	
EFFECTIVE DATE*	Central reserve city banks‡	Reserve city banks	Country banks	Central reserve and reserve city banks‡	Country banks
1917—June 21	13	10	7	3	3
1936—August 16	19½	15	10½	4½	4½
1937—March 1	22¾	17½	12¼	5¼	5¼
May 1	26	20	14	6	6
1938—April 16	22¾	17½	12	5	5
1941—November 1	26	20	14	6	6
1942—August 20	24				
September 14	22				
October 3	20				
1948—February 27	22				
June 11	24				
September 24, 16	26	22	16	7½	7½
1949—May 5, 1	24	21	15	7	7
June 30, July 1		20	14	6	6
August 1			13		
August 11, 16	23½	19½	12	5	5
August 18	23	19			
August 25	22½	18½			
September 1	22	18			
1951—January 11, 16	23	19	13	6	6
January 25, February 1	24	20	14		
1953—July 9, 1	22	19	13		
1954—June 24, 16	21			5	5
July 29, August 1	20	18	12		
1958—February 27, March 1	19½	17½	11½		
March 20, April 1	19	17	11		
April 17	18½				
April 24	18	16½			
1960—September 1	17½				
November 24			12		
December 1	16½				
1962—July 28	(‡)			(‡)	
October 25, November 1				4	4

TABLE 12–1. (*Continued*)

BEGINNING JULY 14, 1966

EFFECTIVE DATE*	NET DEMAND DEPOSITS†				TIME DEPOSITS§ (ALL CLASSES OF BANKS)		
	Reserve city banks		Country banks			Other time deposits	
					Sav-ings depos-its		
	Under $5 mil-lion	Over $5 mil-lion	Under $5 mil-lion	Over $5 mil-lion		Under $5 mil-lion	Over $5 mil-lion
1966—July 14, 21	16½‖		12‖		4‖	4‖	5
September 8, 15							6
1967—March 2					3½	3½	
March 16					3	3	
1968—January 11, 18	16½	17	12	12½			
In effect April 17, 1969	17	17½	12½	13	3	3	6
Legal requirements							
Minimum	10		7		3	3	3
Maximum	22		14		10	10	10

* When two dates are shown, the first applies to the change at central reserve or reserve city banks and the second to the change at country banks.

† Demand deposits subject to reserve requirements, which, beginning with August 23, 1935, have been total demand deposits minus cash items in process of collection and demand balances due from domestic banks (also minus war loan and Series E bond accounts during the period April 13, 1943 to June 30, 1947).

‡ Authority of the Board of Governors to classify or reclassify cities as central reserve cities was terminated effective July 28, 1962.

§ Effective January 5, 1967, time deposits such as Christmas and vacation club accounts became subject to same requirements as savings deposits.

‖ See columns above for earliest effective date of this rate.

Note: All required reserves were held on deposit with Federal Reserve banks, June 21, 1917, until late 1959. Since then, member banks have also been allowed to count vault cash as reserves, as follows: country banks—in excess of 4 and 2½ percent of net demand deposits effective December 1, 1959, and August 25, 1960, respectively; central reserve city and reserve city banks—in excess of 2 and 1 percent effective December 3, 1959, and September 1, 1960, respectively; all member banks were allowed to count all vault cash as reserves effective November 24, 1960.

SOURCE: Board of Governors of the Federal Reserve System, *Annual Report* (1968), pp. 382–83, and *Federal Reserve Bulletin*, May 1969, p. A–10.

ments of member banks since 1917. Reserve requirements were fixed by statute until the passage of the Banking Act of 1935, which gave the Board of Governors the authority to vary reserve requirements within legally prescribed limits. From 1935 to 1959 those limits, for demand deposits, were from 7 to 14 percent for country banks, 10 to 20 percent for reserve city banks, and 13 to 26 percent for central reserve city banks. Since that time the designation "central reserve city bank" has been eliminated. As the commercial banking system has developed, financial centers other than the former central reserve cities have assumed greater responsibility for the finances of the nation. Thus, member banks are now either reserve city or country banks. The legally prescribed limits for the reserve requirements on demand deposits for country banks are still 7 to 14 percent, but for reserve city banks they are now 10 to 22 percent. The reserve requirement limits for time deposits are 3 to 10 percent for all classes of banks.

The Board of Governors has generally exercised its authority to vary reserve requirements in a manner that would be considered appropriate in terms of the preceding policy discussion. However, manipulation of reserve requirements is used only infrequently for curbing inflation.

Increases in reserve requirements. The first case of a discretionary increase in reserve requirements occurred in 1936–37. From August 1936 to May 1937, all reserve requirements were raised to their legally permissible maximum. This amounted to a doubling of the requirements existing on August 15, 1936, and the move evoked considerable controversy. Many economists today regard it as an example of the inappropriate exercise of monetary policy by the Board. The economy had improved relative to the severe depression years of 1932 and 1933, when over twelve million persons were unemployed. We still did not have a full employment economy, however. There were nine and one-half million people unemployed in 1936, close to eight million in 1937, and more than ten million in 1938.[4] It is entirely possible, therefore, that the increases in the reserve requirements in 1936 and 1937 aggravated, if they did not cause, the recession that followed in 1937 and 1938.

The official justification for the reserve requirement increases in 1936 and 1937 was that the "Board's action was in the nature of a precautionary measure to prevent an uncontrollable expansion of credit in the future." [5] Commercial banks had accumulated $3 billion in excess reserves by the mid-thirties, and the Board of Governors feared that use of these excess reserves to expand credit in the economic upswing then under way might cause a price inflation. Hence, it took restrictive action, which was soon followed by a substantial decline in the stock of money.

It is difficult to appraise the wisdom of the Board's decision. If the large volume of excess reserves existed because of lack of demand for bank loans, the restrictive action could have had little direct effect on bank money creation and the 1937–38 recession. Thus the Federal Reserve may have been correct in moving to reduce the inflationary potential of these unused reserves. Proponents of this view at most concede that "the timing of the increase in requirements proved unfortunate. For various extraneous reasons, there followed a sharp decline in business and prices." [6]

[4] U.S. Department of Commerce, *Statistical Abstract of the United States* (Washington, D.C., 1953), p. 186.
[5] Board of Governors of the Federal Reserve System, *Annual Report* (1936), p. 2.
[6] E. A. Goldenweiser, *American Monetary Policy* (New York: McGraw-Hill, 1951), p. 180.

On the other hand, if one accepts the view that the banking system did not regard these reserves as excess reserves available for credit expansion, then the restrictive action *was* a significant factor in the 1937–38 contraction. It has been argued, for example, that

experience during the years from 1929 to 1933 had taught banks that it was not enough to keep in the form of high-powered money only the minimum amount required by law; legally required reserves could not be drawn on to meet emergency demands without the banks being liable to closure. . . . Doubling of required reserves . . . reduced drastically the cushion of effective reserves, as the banks viewed them, available against liabilities needing protection . . . the result was to induce banks to seek to rebuild their so-called excess reserves, thereby producing downward pressure on the money supply.[7]

The years 1936 and 1937 gave us our first experience with increases in the reserve requirement. Other increases occurred in 1941, 1948, and 1951. The increases in 1941 and 1951 were designed to help restrict credit extension in the private sector during a period of impending war, in the first instance, and of actual war in the second. The 1948 increase was a move to help restrain inflationary forces already at work in the economy. The effects of the 1948 and 1951 actions, however, were in part offset by another Federal Reserve policy, support of the government securities market. During this same period commercial banks were selling securities to the Federal Reserve banks, thereby adding to member bank reserves. It will be recalled that the sale of government securities by the Federal Reserve causes member bank reserves to decline. Aside from the conflicting effects of other Federal Reserve actions, however, these three reserve requirement increases were economically appropriate and timely.

Since 1951 there have been only four increases in reserve requirements, and one of these was not intended as a contracyclical measure. In November of 1960, the reserve requirement for the demand-deposit liabilities of country banks was increased from 11 to 12 percent. Simultaneously, it was announced that all member banks would be permitted to count vault cash as part of their legal reserves. Since country banks had substantial volumes of vault cash, the increase in reserve requirements for these banks was necessary to avoid a sharp increase in their excess reserves.

The year 1966 saw the Federal Reserve raise reserve requirements for member bank holdings of time deposits (other than savings deposits) in excess of $5 million from 4 percent to 5 percent. The overall effect of this action was to increase required reserves, particularly for those banks that issued savings certificates and other certificates of deposits in large volume. Large banks that aggressively sold CD's, paying the maximum interest allowable on them, had attracted deposits and hence reserves away from other commercial banks in the system. The increase in the reserve

---

[7] Milton Friedman, *A Program for Monetary Stability* (New York: Fordham University Press, 1960), p. 46.

requirement caused a deterioration in the reserve position of member banks, particularly reserve city banks. At the same time the Federal Reserve reduced the rate payable by member banks on CD's. This helped reduce the flow of funds to large reserve city banks, since other interest rates in the economy were climbing. Banks sold investments in order to find funds to enable them to expand loans. Overall lending activity, as a result of this aggressive contracyclical policy, was restricted. Whether all these actions, in particular the rise in the reserve requirement, were economically appropriate is highly problematical. As we shall see in Chapter 13, the restrictive policies of late 1965 and the first three quarters of 1966, though in the right direction, may well have been too harsh. Evidence of this is found in the leveling off of construction activity in 1966.

In January 1968 the Federal Reserve increased the reserves member banks are required to maintain against demand deposits in excess of $5 million. This was the first increase made in reserve requirements for demand deposits since the readjustment of 1960. The action markedly increased total required reserves, particularly for reserve city banks. In view of the very high employment levels prevailing, rising prices, and rising Viet Nam war expenditures, it would appear that this action was appropriate.

Finally, in April 1969, the Fed raised all reserve requirements against demand deposits by $\frac{1}{2}$ percent. This action was designed to restrict bank lending and private spending, which had not yet responded to the surtax of July 1968. With rising prices the Fed felt it necessary to further restrict credit in a wartime high employment economy.

Overall, aside from periods of war, the Fed has been reluctant to use increases in reserve requirements to combat expansion forces in the economy. There are several reasons for this attitude.

First, commercial bankers feel the direct impact of reserve requirement increases and are forced to readjust their loan and investment activities. Other tools of Federal Reserve policy, such as open market operations, do not have such a direct impact. A sale of securities by the Federal Reserve banks reduces total and excess reserves, but no one commercial bank can directly blame the Federal Reserve for the stringency of its reserve position. It is the purchase of securities by bank customers that affects the reserve position of the bank directly, not their sale by the Federal Reserve. A bank adjusts to customer actions of this sort in the course of everyday business. Furthermore, reserve requirement increases may encounter substantial resistance from bankers. Political pressure may be exerted on the Board to reverse itself, particularly if member bank profit positions are threatened.

Second, frequent reserve requirement changes can create difficulties for the managers of small banks. These banks are not equipped to make the rapid changes in the composition of their portfolios that such changes necessitate. In addition, the fact that changes in reserve requirements usually are announced in advance of the date on which they are to become effective causes a simultaneous attempt by all the affected banks to adapt in advance, further complicating the adjustment process. For example, an announced increase in reserve requirements may induce many banks to sell U.S. government securities immediately to get additional reserves before the increase takes effect. This may cause a sharp drop in the price of those securities and substantial capital losses for the selling banks. The adjustment process is difficult for banks whether the reserve requirement increases or decreases, but the increases cause more difficulty. Decreases are favorably received by banks.

Third, the most important reason that reserve requirement increases are used infrequently is because they have an extraordinarily strong contractionary effect. The Federal Reserve has never raised reserve requirements less than $\frac{1}{2}$ percent. Offhand, this amount may seem minimal, but even this small an increase has a significant impact on the commercial banks' money-creating potential.

Effects of a $\frac{1}{2}$ percent increase in reserve requirements. Assume, for example, that a $\frac{1}{2}$ percent increase in the reserve requirement for demand deposits is contemplated. By how much would this reduce the money-creating ability of the member banks? To solve this problem we can use the following equation, developed in Chapter 7:

$$D = \frac{R - r'(TD)}{r + i'} \qquad [7\text{–}5]$$

The factors included in equation 7–5 are D, the amount of demand deposits the member banks are capable of supporting, given the other factors; R, the volume of member bank reserves; r, the reserve requirement for demand deposits; r', the reserve requirement for time deposits; TD, the volume of member bank time deposits; and i', the ratio of excess reserves to demand deposits that member banks wish to maintain.

Assume that prior to any change in the reserve requirements, the following situation prevails:

$$\textit{If:} \quad \begin{aligned} R &= \$25.413 \text{ billion} \\ r' &= .0413 \end{aligned}$$

$$TD = \$152.274 \text{ billion}$$
$$r = 0.1513$$

$$\textit{Then:} \quad \begin{aligned} i' &= 0.0024 \\ D &= \$124.424 \text{ billion} \end{aligned}$$

If the actual volume of commercial bank demand deposit liabilities is equal to D—the volume that commercial banks can support—then the member banks cannot further expand loans, investments, and demand deposit money. However, this does not mean that they have no excess reserves. The fact that i' is greater than zero shows that in fact they do; under our assumptions, the member banks have $299 million in desired excess reserves. However, they cannot expand without switching some of these reserves needed to cover c (the desired ratio of currency to demand deposits discussed in Chapter 7) and i' to required reserves.

Now suppose there is a $\frac{1}{2}$ percent increase in required reserves and r becomes .1563. Assume further that there is no cash drain or inflow. This results in a decreased D of \$120.504 billion. In other words, an increase of $\frac{1}{2}$ percent in the reserve requirement for demand deposits would lead to a \$3.920 billion reduction in the money supply. In percentage terms, the forced contraction is equal to more than 3 percent of the original volume of demand deposits. This constitutes a rather sharp contraction in the money supply, and it is induced by only a small change in the reserve requirement.

Equation 7–5 is useful largely for pedagogical purposes, but it does bear a strong relationship to reality. The values chosen for r, r', and TD are close to the actual values of these factors for member banks during the four-week period ending June 19, 1968. Since a single value was necessary for r', it was assumed to be .0413, rather than the actual differential requirements of .03 and .06. Similarly, we assumed that the demand deposit liabilities for *all* member banks were subject to the 17 and $12\frac{1}{2}$ percent reserve requirements prescribed for reserve city and country banks at that date, not just those with deposits in excess of \$5 million. The value of r was then calculated as the ratio of required reserves for demand deposit liabilities to the sum of demand deposit liabilities for reserve city and country banks combined. Thus, .1513 represents the actual average reserve requirement for demand deposit liabilities of all member banks during this period, as limited by the foregoing assumptions. On the other hand, the assumption in the equation of a fixed value of 0.0024 for i' is unrealistic, since i' is unlikely to remain fixed under such conditions. It simplifies the example in this case, however, without destroying its validity for our purposes.

Whether conditions in the period on which these figures were based actually called for an increase in r is another matter. Most economists would agree that a tightening of credit in mid-1968 would have been desirable, but not the \$3.9 billion reduction in member bank demand deposit liabilities that a $\frac{1}{2}$ percent rise in reserve requirements would have necessitated. Smaller increases are feasible, but the Federal Reserve System does not normally change reserve requirements by less than $\frac{1}{2}$ percent. Thus, what apparently are small increases in the reserve requirement can exert a strong contractive force on the economy. If excess reserves are not large, this small increase can lead to a sharp contraction of loans and investments, and consequently (as Chapter 7 demonstrated) to a sharp reduction in the volume of demand deposit money.

It is for the reasons given here—(1) the disproportionately heavy impact upon banks, (2) the portfolio adjustment difficulties for banks, and (3) the severity of the resultant contractionary forces—that the Board of

Governors makes infrequent use of reserve requirement increases. The Board can soften the overall impact of this device by simultaneously purchasing U.S. government securities, however, a fact which suggests that open market operations are a superior anti-inflationary measure in the first place.

Decreases in reserve requirements. Decreases in reserve requirements have been more frequent than increases. The first decrease occurred in 1938. This action was clearly appropriate in light of the depressed condition of the economy at the time. The next decrease occurred in a war year, 1942, and was limited to central reserve city banks. This action was not contracyclical. Rather, it was intended to lessen the effect of large government security issues on bank reserves. The New York and Chicago banks had been experiencing reserve drains as large volumes of government securities issued to finance government defense expenditures were sold by the Treasury in Chicago and New York. As depositors drew down their accounts to buy these securities, reserves were lost. To compensate for this drain, the government reduced the reserve requirements for central reserve city banks.

Since the end of World War II, reserve requirements have generally been reduced in periods of recession or less than full employment. Thus reductions were made in the 1949, 1953–54, and 1957–58 recessions. During the 1960–61 recession, however, there was no lowering of reserve requirements for demand deposits; instead, the banks' lending capacity was increased by allowing all banks to count vault cash as part of their reserves. The reserve requirement for time deposits was decreased in the fall of 1962, however. The economy was expanding at this time, but there was still a substantial amount of unemployment. The purpose of the reduction was to provide reserves for long-term growth in deposits. Another reduction, this time in the reserve requirement for savings deposits, occurred in March 1967. Again, the stated purpose of the reduction was to provide for long-term growth in deposits.

How effective have reductions in reserve requirements been as a contracyclical monetary technique? The measures taken in 1949, 1953–54, 1957–58, and 1962 appear to have been theoretically in the right direction. Periods of less than full employment and recessions call for increased lending capacity. However, these decreases in reserve requirements were frequently accompanied by Federal Reserve bank sales of U.S. government securities, which tended to offset the expansive effects of the decreases. Apparently the Board of Governors felt that the increases in excess reserves caused by the reserve requirement decreases were too great. Subsequently, as the economy gained strength, the Board made open market purchases of U.S. government securities, so that additional reserves could be released gradually to the banking system. Again the point could be made that open market operations might have been a superior policy instrument in the first place.

The March 1967 decrease in reserve requirements against time deposits was not accompanied by a sale of securities. Despite low unemployment, the Federal Reserve followed a policy of aggressive ease, motivated perhaps by the slowdown of construction activity that started in 1966 and by a continuing decrease in automobile sales. In a further move, the Board lowered the discount rate in April. These actions led to rapid increments in the money stock. If the Federal Reserve's judgment was correct, its policy of monetary ease in late 1966 and much of 1967 may well have stopped a slowdown in economic activity from becoming a recession. On the other hand, as will be noted later, the Federal Reserve, by maintaining a policy of monetary ease for an excessive length of time in 1967, may have aggravated the inflationary pressures of late 1967 and 1968.

We can further illustrate how small decreases in reserve requirements lead to large increases in the ability of banks to expand deposit money by simply reversing the figures used in the preceding section. If r were initially .1563, then D could not exceed \$120.504 billion. If r were subsequently reduced to .1513, then D could expand to \$124.424 billion. Thus, if banks utilized all their increased lending capacity, a \$3.9 billion increase in the money stock, which is a substantial increase in any type of economic situation, would take place.

Evaluation of the reserve requirement as policy instrument. There is considerable doubt as to the merits of using variable reserve requirements as an instrument of economic policy. Contracyclical increases are unpopular, create management difficulties for bankers, and force banks to contract sharply in the absence of offsetting open market operations. Contracyclical reductions may not prove to be dependable in economic crises. For example, it is often argued that banks cannot be forced to expand loans and investments; hence almost any type of central-bank action designed to expand reserves, and thereby economic activity, will be ineffectual. The adage that you can bring a horse to water but cannot make him drink is often cited at this point as evidence of the weakness of all forms of monetary action. The economic history of the postwar period seems to give the lie to this adage, however. The cold war situation and an awareness of the economic and human loss associated with depression have helped to sustain comparatively high levels of employment and output. Recessions in this period have been mild. Banks have typically operated with small margins of excess reserves. Thus, it is reasonable to assume that, at least in mild recessions, banks will shortly make use of an increase in their money-creating abilities.

On the other hand, a reduction in reserve requirements is a powerful means of increasing bank lending ability. A full utilization of a \$3.9

billion increase in the loan and investment potential of the banking system, the figure given in the preceding sample, over a short period of time could create undesired inflationary pressures, making offsetting open market operations necessary. Only if variations in reserve requirements were substantially less than ½ percent could they be used without offsetting open market operations.

Is there then no justification for using reserve requirements as an instrument of economic policy? The Board of Governors some time ago recognized the difficulties inherent in the use of this policy instrument when it argued that "As an instrument of monetary management, changes in required reserve percentages are less flexible and continuously adaptable than the open market and discount instruments." [8] Nevertheless, the Board believes that reserve requirement reductions have a place among monetary management techniques today. Reserve requirement decreases immediately increase the excess reserves of *all* member banks, whereas open market operations first affect the reserve position of banks in New York City, where the U.S. government securities market is concentrated. Thus, the Board believes that the effects of a reduction in reserve requirements will be felt more quickly throughout the country than the effects of security purchases by the Federal Reserve Bank of New York would be. The fact that the Federal Reserve often sells securities at the same time that it lowers reserve requirements seems to cast suspicion on this line of reasoning, however. If the immediate effects of a sale of government securities are in fact concentrated in New York City, then how can this action effectively offset a reduction of reserve requirements? Nothing has been done to reduce the full expansion capabilities of banks outside New York. Only if banks in other areas adjusted to their increased excess reserves much more slowly than the New York banks would a countermeasure directed toward the New York banks alone be acceptable.

There is considerable evidence that banks outside New York respond only slightly more slowly to open-market-induced changes in excess reserves than New York banks. One recent study concluded that

the relative impact of open market operations on reserve city banks is close to unity, meaning that reserve city banks participate in open market sales or purchases according to their average share in total reserves . . . the relative short-run impact of open market operations on country banks indicates that 67 percent of the total impact will take place on such banks within one month. Thus, although country banks receive less than their share, the short-run impact is substantial.[9]

Thus it would seem that open market operations are a flexible instrument

[8] Board of Governors of the Federal Reserve System, *The Federal Reserve System: Purposes and Functions* (Washington, D.C., 1961), p. 54.
[9] Roy J. Ruffin, "An Econometric Model of the Impact of Open Market Operations on Various Bank Classes," *Journal of Finance*, September 1968, p. 636.

of monetary policy. Although reserve requirement changes do have some edge in this respect, since they affect the excess reserve positions of all member banks immediately, open market operations also transmit their effects rapidly.

The Discount Rate

The discount rate is the "price" that a district Federal Reserve bank charges member banks who borrow reserves.[10] Such borrowing is generally for a short period of time, about fifteen days. Each district Reserve bank sets its own discount rate, but the decision is subject to review by the Board of Governors. Although changes in rates do not occur frequently, rates are reviewed by the Federal Reserve every fourteen days. When changes are announced, the new rates are usually the same among the various Federal Reserve banks. This tendency has become more pronounced in recent decades as various sections of the nation have lost their regional character and, in financial matters, have become part of the national money market.

As pointed out earlier, member banks borrow to meet temporary shortages of reserves or to build up reserves prior to increasing their lending activity. The Federal Reserve banks and the Board of Governors change discount rates in order to affect member bank lending. Theoretically, increases in the rate restrict member bank borrowing of reserves and hence bank lending activity; conversely, decreases in the rate are believed to encourage borrowing of reserves and lending activity.

Unfortunately, matters are not quite that simple. The data show that Federal Reserve bank discounts and advances move in the same direction as the discount rate. Logically they should move in opposite directions if discount rate manipulations are to have their intended contracyclical effects. Banks, however, tend to borrow additional reserves on the upward part of the cycle, even with high discount rates—partly because of increased business and consumer demand for funds and partly because the earnings possible on loans exceed the discount costs. On the downward side of the cycle, the situation is reversed.

The behavior of discount rates and discounts and advances from 1917 through 1969. Figure 12–1 shows the movement in the discount rate of the Federal Reserve Bank of New York and the prime commercial paper interest rate from 1919 to 1969. The discount rate depicted on the graph represents advances secured by U.S. government securities and discounts and advances secured by eligible paper. Table 12–2 shows the present structure of discount rates, and Table 12–3 gives the volume of Federal Reserve bank discounts and advances from 1917 to 1969. These figures

---

[10] The term "discount rate" includes all three rates described in Chapter 11.

FIGURE 12–1. Short-term interest rates, 1919–69

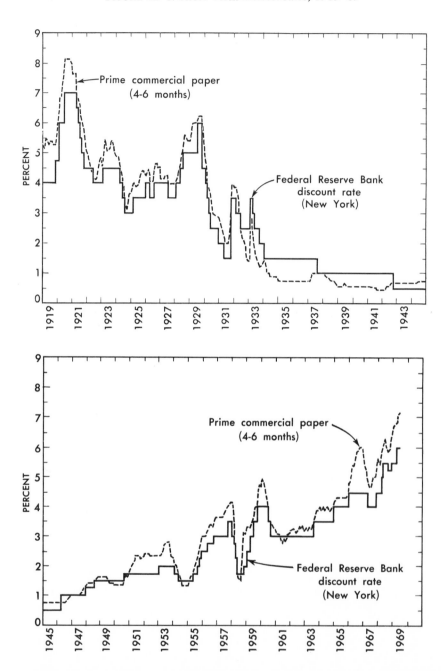

SOURCE: Board of Governors of the Federal Reserve System, *Federal Reserve Historical Chart Book*, 1967, pp. 26–27, and *Federal Reserve Bulletin*, 1968, 1969, p. A-31.

TABLE 12–2. FEDERAL RESERVE BANK DISCOUNT RATES

(PERCENT PER ANNUM)

DISCOUNTS FOR AND ADVANCES TO MEMBER BANKS

FEDERAL RESERVE BANK	Advances and discounts under Secs. 13 and 13(a)*			Advances under Sec. 10(b)†			Advances to all others under last par. Sec. 13‡		
	Rate on April 30, 1969	Effective date	Previous rate	Rate on April 30, 1969	Effective date	Previous rate	Rate on April 30, 1969	Effective date	Previous rate
Boston	6	April 8, 1969	5½	6½	April 8, 1969	6	7	April 8, 1969	6½
New York	6	April 4, 1969	5½	6½	April 4, 1969	6	7½	April 4, 1969	7
Philadelphia	6	April 4, 1969	5½	6½	April 4, 1969	6	7	April 4, 1969	6½
Cleveland	6	April 4, 1969	5½	6½	April 4, 1969	6	7½	April 4, 1969	7
Richmond	6	April 4, 1969	5½	6½	April 4, 1969	6	7	April 4, 1969	6½
Atlanta	6	April 4, 1969	5½	6½	April 4, 1969	6	7	April 4, 1969	6½
Chicago	6	April 4, 1969	5½	6½	April 4, 1969	6	7	April 4, 1969	6½
St. Louis	6	April 4, 1969	5½	6½	April 4, 1969	6	7	April 4, 1969	6½
Minneapolis	6	April 4, 1969	5½	6½	April 4, 1969	6	7½	April 4, 1969	6½
Kansas City	6	April 4, 1969	5½	6½	April 4, 1969	6	7	April 4, 1969	6½
Dallas	6	April 4, 1969	5½	6½	April 4, 1969	6	7	April 4, 1969	6½
San Francisco	6	April 4, 1969	5½	6½	April 4, 1969	6	7	April 4, 1969	6½

* Discounts of eligible paper and advances secured by such paper or by U.S. government obligations or any other obligations eligible for Federal Reserve bank purchase. Rates shown also apply to advances secured by obligations of Federal intermediate credit banks maturing within 6 months. Maximum maturity: 90 days except that discounts of certain bankers' acceptances and of agricultural paper may have maturities not over 6 months and 9 months, respectively, and advances secured by FICB obligations are limited to 15 days.

† Advances secured to the satisfaction of the Federal Reserve bank. Maximum maturity: 4 months.

‡ Advances to individuals, partnerships, or corporations other than member banks secured by direct obligations of, or obligations fully guaranteed as to principal and interest by, the U.S. government or any agency thereof. Maximum maturity: 90 days.

SOURCE: Board of Governors of the Federal Reserve System, *Federal Reserve Bulletin*, May 1969, p. A–9.

support the contention that the volume of discounts and advances fluctuates in the same direction as discount rates.

TABLE 12-3. FEDERAL RESERVE DISCOUNTS AND ADVANCES, ANNUAL AVERAGES OF DAILY FIGURES, 1917–69 (IN MILLIONS OF DOLLARS)

YEAR	AMOUNT	YEAR	AMOUNT	YEAR	AMOUNT
1917	376*	1935	7	1952	801
1918	1,134	1936	6	1953	777
1919	1,906	1937	14	1954	217
1920	2,523	1938	9	1955	666
1921	1,797	1939	5	1956	833
1922	571	1940	4	1957	850
1923	736	1941	5	1958	295
1924	373	1942	7	1959	812
1925	490	1943	25	1960	436
1926	572	1944	135	1961	83
1927	442	1945	376	1962	136
1928	840	1946	310	1963	269
1929	952	1947	219	1964	300
1930	272	1948	331	1965	474
1931	327	1949	231	1966	637
1932	521	1950	129	1967	209
1933	283	1951	293	1968	569
1934	36			1969	1,085†

* Based on data for August–December.
† Based on data for January–August.
SOURCE: 1917–60, Board of Governors of the Federal Reserve System, *Supplement to Banking and Monetary Statistics*, Section 10 (Washington, D.C., 1962), p. 14; 1961–68, computed from *Federal Reserve Bulletin*, various issues, 1961–69.

1917–32. There were five periods of economic decline between 1917 and 1932: late 1918 to early 1919, 1920 to mid-1921, mid-1923 to mid-1924, 1927, and late 1929 through 1932. The remaining intervals were periods of economic expansion. Theoretically, periods of decline call for discount rate decreases to encourage borrowing. Only in the first recession, 1918–19, were no decreases ordered, and there were good reasons for not altering the rates at that time. For one thing, the recession was very short-lived. For another, discount rates were already abnormally low relative to the rates commercial banks could earn on their loans and investments. The Federal Reserve had assisted the U.S. Treasury in financing the war effort by keeping discount rates low. This had facilitated the purchase of U.S. government securities with borrowed funds by both commercial banks and the nonbank public at comparatively low interest costs. It also enabled the Treasury to market securities with lower interest rates than would have been possible in a government bond market not supported by the Federal Reserve banks. As a result, we entered the short postwar recession with a low discount rate structure.

The mere fact that discount rates were lowered in four of the five cited recessions should not be taken as conclusive evidence that central-bank policy during all those periods was correct, however. Federal Reserve discount policy in 1920–21, for example, seems to have been inappropriate. Discount rates were raised sharply in late 1919 to counteract price rises. They were raised again in the first half of 1920 and maintained at the new level until well into 1921, when they were finally lowered. Thus, during most of this severe contraction, discount rates were very high.

Viewed from a present-day perspective, this was clearly inappropriate monetary action. Viewed from the perspective of 1920–21, however, it may have appeared to be appropriate action, since the Federal Reserve at that time was not so concerned with maintaining domestic economic stability as with maintaining our international gold position. The high discount rates of the period did help stem the outflow of gold. When a nation's internal rate of interest is low relative to rates abroad, it tends to lose gold as its citizens purchase the relatively high-yield foreign securities. On the other hand, when internal interest rates are high relative to rates abroad, not only do foreigners purchase the nation's securities, but its own citizens tend to increase their investments in domestic securities. This leads to an influx of gold. Federal Reserve discount rate manipulation in 1920 was thus designed to protect our gold reserves.

Following the events of 1920 and 1921, Federal Reserve discount rate changes during recession were appropriately contracyclical. The Federal Reserve came to adopt the position that monetary tools should be used to promote price stability and a high level of business activity. This policy was abandoned in 1929 and 1931, however. In an attempt to stem excessive stock market speculation, the Federal Reserve raised discount rates in mid-1929. Actually, other economic indicators had already turned down. Following the stock market crash of October 1929, discount rates were quickly reduced, reaching their historical low to that date in mid-1931. This was appropriate. In October of 1931, however, there came another discount rate increase, again designed to offset a drain of gold. This decision is difficult to justify in light of present-day knowledge of economic forces. There were about eight million people unemployed in the United States at the time, whose plight could only be worsened by restricted credit. Rates were subsequently reduced in 1932.

What happened to discount rates during the other years between 1918 and 1929? Rate increases occurred in 1919, 1920, 1923, 1925, 1926, and 1928. With the exception of 1920, these were all years of economic expansion, and the increases in the discount rate were called for.

In general, from 1917 to 1932, the Federal Reserve banks moved discount rates contracyclically. The principal exceptions were the low rates of World War I, the high rates prevailing through much of 1921, and the increases of 1929 and 1931. However, in spite of discount rate increases at both appropriate and inappropriate times, this was a period of easy money. As a look at Figure 12–1 will show, discount rates were typically below what commercial banks could earn on commercial paper.

Although the manipulation of discount rates was generally appropriate in this period in terms of the national economy, the movement of discounts and advances was not in the right direction. In every year when discount rates were increased, discounts and advances to member banks increased. In every year, except 1932, when discount rates were decreased, discounts and advances to member banks decreased. This is exactly the opposite of what is supposed to happen; a discount rate increase should *decrease* member bank borrowing of reserves and a discount rate decrease should *increase* member bank borrowing. Yet this did not occur.

It is usually argued, however, that discount rate increases and decreases are not intended to bring about absolute decreases and increases, respectively, in member bank borrowing of reserves. Instead, raising the cost of borrowing reserves during economic expansion is intended simply to hold down the increase in reserve borrowing that would have taken place in the absence of the rate increase. In periods of expansion there is a strong demand for funds by the nonbank public. Banks, as profit-seeking business enterprises, are anxious to satisfy that demand by expanding loans and investments. They tend to utilize their existing reserves more intensively at such a time and to expand their reserve base with borrowings from the Federal Reserve banks. Thus, discount rate increases had little apparent effect on borrowings because the high return on commercial bank alternative investment opportunities relative to discount rates during most of the period from 1919 to 1929 tended to sustain member bank borrowing. In such a situation, discount rate increases at best only hold down the rate of increase of member bank borrowing.

It is also argued that lowering the cost of borrowing reserves is intended simply to minimize the decrease in reserve borrowing that is expected to take place in a recession in the absence of the rate decrease. The demand for loans by the nonbank public is weak in such periods, and since it does not usually pay for banks to hold borrowed reserves that are not being utilized in profitable loan expansion, they will tend to repay outstanding borrowings. Discount rate decreases, therefore, only serve to minimize the decrease in the amount of member bank borrowing.

The preceding analysis is persuasive, but difficult to establish empirically, since it posits a knowledge of how banks would have reacted in the absence of the rate changes that actually took place. It is extremely difficult to predict how banks will react to changes in the discount rate; it is even possible that an increase in rates will encourage banks to increase borrowings and, accordingly, their own loans and investments. On the other hand, a decrease in rates may actually speed up repayment of borrowed reserves. (We shall return to these points later in the chapter.)

1933–51. Member bank borrowing of reserves declined to insignificant proportions in the 1930's. Member banks had substantial volumes of excess reserves throughout this period and, as a result, had no need to borrow reserves. Following a temporary rise in discount rates coincident with the nationwide closing of the banks from March 6 to March 13, 1933, there were reductions in the rates in April, May, and October of 1933, and further decreases in 1934, 1935, and 1937. From 1937 to 1942 there were no changes in discount rates; the rate on advances secured by U.S. government securities was at a historic peacetime low of 1 percent.

Although discount rates were very low in the 1930's, it does not necessarily follow that the period was one of easy money. Since banks had substantial volumes of excess reserves and few lending and investment opportunities, there was no serious need for trips to the discount window. The criterion of ease or restrictiveness of central-bank policy should not be the absolute level of discount rates; rather, it should be the level of discount rates relative to what banks can earn on their investment and lending opportunities. "The New York discount rate was never below the average 4- to 6-month commercial paper rate in any week in the eight years from 1934 through 1941. The result, of course, was negligible use of rediscounting facilities." [11] As Table 12–3 shows, Federal Reserve bank discounts and advances reached a low of $4 million in 1940. From this perspective, a policy of apparent monetary ease may actually be viewed as restrictive. Many economists would disagree with this view, but it merits some thought nevertheless.

Discount rates remained stable during World War II and the early postwar years. The discount rate on advances secured by U.S. government securities, however, was dropped to $\frac{1}{2}$ percent in 1942 and returned to 1 percent in 1946. These changes were the only ones made in this rate from 1937 to 1948. The main reason for this stability in discount rates is that decreases in rates during wartime are inappropriate from a contracyclical point of view. They encourage borrowing of reserves and credit expansion during a period of full employment, thus causing inflation.

On the other hand, to the extent that a war effort is financed through borrowing, a decrease in discount rates will encourage investment in government securities. As we shall see later, this type of financing effort is open to harsh criticism. A low discount rate was one means employed to assist the U.S. Treasury in financing American participation in World War II. Another was the support of the government bond market—a policy that is discussed in more detail in the next chapter.

The volume of discounts and advances made by the Federal Reserve banks increased during the war. From a prewar low of $4 million in 1940, they increased to an average of $376 million in 1945. Following the war, commercial banks continued to use the discount window with substantially greater frequency than they had during the depressed thirties, but the

---

[11] Milton Friedman and Anna Jacobson Schwartz, *A Monetary History of the United States, 1867–1960* (Princeton, N.J., Princeton University Press, 1963), p. 514.

volume of discounts and advances never approached that of the 1920's. A tendency on the part of banks to avoid borrowing reserves has always been part of our banking heritage. The 1930's merely reinforced this tradition and, except for the most prosperous postwar years, this tendency has remained evident to the present day. Another factor contributing to the small volume of discounting in the years 1933–51 was the open market policy of the Federal Reserve System. The Federal Reserve had committed itself to supporting the government bond market during World War II, and it continued this policy of support through early 1951. One way in which commercial banks may provide themselves with additional reserves to expand loans is to sell some of their holdings of U.S. government securities. Normally, widespread security sales would lead to a capital loss for the selling banks, since the increased supply of bonds would depress bond prices. With the Federal Reserve committed to maintaining bond prices, however, commercial banks were able to obtain reserves in this manner. Thus they had little need to get additional reserves through discounts and advances. To the extent that banks refrained from borrowing because of the Federal Reserve's open market policy, the effectiveness of contracyclical discount rate changes was reduced.

1951–69. Support of the government bond market by the Federal Reserve System ended with the Treasury–Federal Reserve Accord in March of 1951. Since that time discount rate changes have been used frequently to promote economic stability. Discount rates were lowered in the contractions of 1953–54, 1957–58, and 1960–61, and raised in the expansions of 1950–53, 1954–57, 1958–60, and 1961–69. During 1967, a year of economic expansion, rates were lowered in April. As we mentioned in discussing the reserve requirement, this decrease was apparently motivated by slack conditions in the automobile and construction industries. In addition, discount rates were temporarily lowered in the fall of 1968 as the Federal Reserve attempted to anticipate a possible drop in economic activity attributable to the 1968 surtax. The decreases were rescinded as soon as it became apparent that economic activity was continuing to move upward.

For the most part, contracyclical adjustments since 1951 appear to have been in the right direction. Nevertheless, in only one year, 1953, did discount rates and the volume of discounts and advances move in opposite directions. On the other hand, in 1955—a boom year—discounts and advances rose by more than $400 million. In 1956 they increased further, by almost $200 million. In fact, discounts and advances rose from a low of $217 million in 1954, the trough of the 1953–54 recession, to $850 million in 1957. In the same period, the discount rate for advances secured by U.S. government securities and for discounts and advances secured by eligible paper at the Federal Reserve Bank of New York rose 1.5 to 3.5 percent.

Furthermore, as Figure 12–1 shows, in periods of upswing, the discount rate was always below the rate for four- to six-month commercial paper, even when discount rates were being increased. At the bottom of each contraction the rate for four- to six-month commercial paper was less than the discount rate, even after discount rate decreases. Thus it appears that, in spite of the correct direction of discount rate changes, these changes in themselves have not been big enough to have the desired economic effect. At best, as in the 1920's, they may have decreased the volume of increased borrowings in economic expansion and minimized the decrease in borrowings in contraction. This, of course, is a contribution to maintaining economic stability, but it is very difficult to establish quantitatively how large a role rate changes actually played.

There is only one instance of a discount rate change in the 1950's that now appears to have been clearly inappropriate. The increases of August, 1957, were probably a miscalculation. The economy had reached its peak in June of 1957; a tightening of credit conditions in August thus appears not to have been necessary. However, it could be pointed out in defense of these changes that the rate on four- to six-month commercial paper at that time was substantially above the discount rate. In any case, in November 1957, several months after the recession of 1957–58 was well under way, the Federal Reserve banks reversed themselves and lowered discount rates.

The rate movements described for the period 1951–69 were nearly all designed to help stabilize the economy. The main exceptions were the rate increases of July 1963 and November 1964. These actions were taken principally to help reduce the adverse U.S. balance of payments and to protect the dollar against a gold outflow. Short-term interest rates abroad were higher than in the United States, thereby inducing an outflow of funds from the country. By raising discount rates, the Board of Governors hoped to increase domestic interest rates and decrease the outflow.

Evaluation of the discount rate as a policy instrument. In general, discount rate manipulation does not appear to have been a particularly successful tool of economic policy. The contracyclical uses made of this instrument in the 1920's and since 1951 have, for the most part, been in the right direction. The ameliorative effects of these discount rate changes have not been quantitatively observable, however; discounts and advances have usually moved in the same direction as discount rates. This is largely because the rate on four- and six-month commercial paper remained above discount rates in periods of economic expansion and below them in recession. Whenever discount rates are below market yields on assets such as commercial paper, on which commercial banks are able to make substantial earnings, the banks are encouraged to borrow reserves to expand their investment in these assets. Thus, in economic upswing, when this type of differential has tended to exist, Federal Reserve discounts and advances increased. One way in which the Fed could avoid this contradictory effect, of course, would be to make larger increases in the discount rates.

On the other hand, when discount rates are above market yields on assets such as commercial paper, banks are discouraged from borrowing reserves and expanding loans and investments. This type of differential has existed in recessions, and thus Federal Reserve discounts and advances have decreased. While it is true that some decrease may well be inevitable in recession because of a lack of demand for loans, it remains a legitimate question whether the fact that discount rates exceeded market rates aggravated the cyclical decline. Although discount rates were lowered, should they not have been reduced still further to bring them beneath market rates? The answer to these two questions is probably yes.

Thus, previous experience indicates that *discount rate changes, by themselves, have not been an effective instrument of monetary policy.* This conclusion is based primarily upon the movement of market rates, discount rates, and the volume of discounts and advances.

Other factors, largely nonquantitative, also tend to work against the success of discount rate policy:

1. The volume of discounts and advances is directly determined by member bank demands, not by Federal Reserve bank control.

2. Many member banks are reluctant to borrow reserves.

3. Announced discount rate changes may have adverse effects on member bank borrowing.

4. A change in the discount rate may not be a signal for a change in Federal Reserve policy.

5. No change in discount rates may itself become a policy tending to restrict or encourage credit changes.

First, the Federal Reserve banks have no direct control over the volume of discounts and advances. If banks meet the prescribed qualifications, they can almost always borrow reserves from their district Federal Reserve bank. This provides an escape for banks that wish to expand loans and investments in periods of full employment, rising prices, and a restrictive monetary policy. Even with large discount rate increases, banks that choose to pay the price for additional reserves can usually obtain them, and thereby circumvent Federal Reserve policy.

The Federal Reserve banks cannot directly change member bank reserves through discount rate policy. The most they can do is to encourage or discourage borrowing of reserves. Commercial banks may decide for themselves how much in reserves they wish to have. Thus, discount rate changes have the desired effect upon member bank reserve positions only when the Fed has guessed correctly about member bank reserve borrowing intentions. When it has guessed incorrectly, it must use other instruments of policy to offset undesirable movements in member bank borrowings. Typically, in such a situation, the Federal Reserve resorts to open market operations. Here is another instance in which one wonders why open market operations are not used in the first place to bring about desired changes in member bank reserve positions.

This criticism should not be taken to mean that there is no need for the discounting mechanism. Open market operations alone cannot take care of short-run needs for additional reserves of specific banks in specific communities:

First among the basic principles governing the use of Federal Reserve credit is that Federal Reserve System lending is to accommodate bank asset and liability adjustments over limited time periods and to meet essentially short-term fluctuations in member bank needs for funds. . . .

Federal Reserve Banks always stand ready to lend to any of their member banks caught in special regional or local adversities—such as droughts, drastic deposit drains, or other emergencies—for as long as reasonably needed for the bank to work out of these circumstances.[12]

Second, some member banks are apparently reluctant to borrow reserves. These banks usually maintain large volumes of excess reserves. Thus, if they wish to increase their credit holdings, they can do so even if the Federal Reserve raises discount rates in an economic upswing above market rates. Changes in the discount rate cannot restrict the lending operations of these banks; other tools in monetary policy must be used.

On the other hand, banks that typically operate with a narrow margin of excess reserves may be seriously affected by discount rate increases. To the extent that discount rates are raised sharply because of increasing bank loans (made by the banks with large excess reserves and a reluctance to borrow, the brunt of the contractionary policy is borne by the banks operating with a narrow margin of excess reserves. A discount rate increase, therefore, can be discriminatory and may unwittingly enhance the competitive position of one group of banks at the expense of another. Eventually, a contractionary discount rate policy will affect all banks; as the banks with excess reserves expand their loans and investments, their excess reserves will dwindle. Open-market operations could bring this about a good bit sooner, however.

Generally it is the smaller "country" banks that are reluctant to borrow reserves and the large reserve city banks that go most often to the discount window. In March of 1969, reserve city banks had a $12 million deficiency in reserves, whereas country banks had $189 million in excess reserves. Since country banks had borrowings of $306 million, they were left with −$117 million in free reserves (excess reserves minus borrowings at the Federal Reserve banks). Reserve city banks, on the other hand, had $612 million in borrowings and −$625 million in free reserves.[13] This difference in reserve positions is not attributable to the difference in size between coun-

---

[12] Board of Governors of the Federal Reserve System, *Reappraisal of the Federal Reserve Discount Mechanism,* July 1968, p. 1.
[13] *Federal Reserve Bulletin,* April 1969, pp. A–6 and A–7.

try and reserve city banks, since total reserve city bank assets were only about 1.7 times those of country banks.

To some extent the reluctance of country banks to borrow may be explained by a lack of investment opportunities. Reserve city banks are usually located in important financial centers and have opportunities for investment not available to the country banks. Furthermore, the smaller average size of the country banks precludes their extending loans to businesses of a large size. Finally, the reserve city banks, operating on a bigger scale than the country banks, have large staffs that are specialized in each of the many different facets of banking activity. This enables them to gauge their reserve positions more accurately and thus to be more economical in their use of reserves. All this suggests that the country banks' reluctance to borrow reserves is not built in; rather, their smaller size and less efficient operations force them to maintain relatively large volumes of excess reserves as safeguards. The fact that country bank borrowing of reserves increases during periods of strong cyclical upturn also supports this theory. In addition, country banks are encouraged to keep excess reserves by the return that can be earned on them in the federal funds market.

Whether small bank reluctance to borrow is built-in or forced in no way alters the conclusion that this reluctance weakens discount rate manipulation as an instrument of contracyclical economic policy. Increased discount rates cannot force banks that already have excess reserves to reduce loans and investments.

Third, announced discount rate changes may have undesired effects on member bank borrowing. For example, an increase in rates should normally discourage borrowing or reserves. However, if expectations concerning future economic trends are such that the announcement of a rate increase leads to public anticipation of further interest rate increases, there may well be an increased demand for loans by borrowers eager to obtain funds before increases occur. Commercial bankers may then have to expand their borrowings in order to meet the increased demands for credit.

Similarly, a decrease in rates should encourage bank borrowing of reserves; but if expectations are such that future rate decreases are anticipated, the demand for bank loans may decrease and bank borrowing of reserves may decline.

Fourth, a change in the discount rate may not be a signal for a change in Federal Reserve policy. For example, "when market rates of interest have moved away from close relationship with the existing discount rate, a change in the level of rates may represent merely a technical adjustment of discount rates to market rates so that the system's discount mechanism will function effectively in line with current policy." [14] If technical adjustments in discount rates are mistaken for signs of a change

---

[14] *The Federal Reserve System: Purposes and Functions*, p. 47.

in Federal Reserve policy, this misinterpretation may cause some degree of economic uncertainty. Suppose, for example, that a firm contemplating expansion considers a decrease in the discount rate as a signal that the Fed believes an economic slump imminent. The company may decide to postpone its expansion until the economic outlook is more favorable. A decrease in expenditures for expansion may then contribute to an actual economic downturn never anticipated by the Federal Reserve.

Fifth, failure to change existing discount rates may itself become a policy tending to discourage or encourage credit changes. It is the *difference* between market and discount rates that influences bank lending activity. If discount rates remain unchanged while market rates change, then, depending on the nature of the change in market rates, member bank borrowing and lending activity will either increase or decrease. This implies that if discount rate changes are to be effective as an instrument of contracyclical economic policy, they must be made frequently, in response to changing market rates of interest and the current economic situation.

Proposals to revise the Federal Reserve discount mechanism. The Federal Reserve recently completed a reappraisal of its discount mechanism. This study reaffirmed the principle that member banks should have access to the discount window, first, to meet short-term fluctuations in the need for funds and second, to meet special regional and local adversities. At the same time the Fed argued, as it always has, that member banks should not be continually in debt to the Federal Reserve banks.

The most important proposal by the Fed is to give each member bank a *basic borrowing privilege,* on a virtual no-questions-asked basis, that would be equal to a proportion of its capital stock and surplus. If followed by the Federal Reserve, the new procedure would be a marked departure from earlier lending practices. The reader may recall from the preceding section that banks qualifying "can generally" borrow reserves from their district bank. This borrowing privilege has never been unlimited. Obviously, loan officers at the Fed consider the size of the bank, its previous borrowing and repayment practices, etc., in determining the size of loans to individual member banks. Practice varies from one district to another and from one loan officer to another, however. As a result, commercial banks are sometimes uncertain about their ability to borrow from the Fed. This is another reason why some banks hesitate to use the discount window. Nevertheless, loan officers will as a rule try to accommodate what they consider "reasonable" requests by member banks. Aside from the latter part of 1966 there generally has been no attempt by the Federal Reserve to withhold funds from member banks.[15]

---

[15] During late 1966 it appeared that banks were borrowing reserves principally to meet sharp increases in the demand for funds by borrowers. Hence the Federal Reserve argued that "the System believes that a greater share of member bank adjustments should take the form of moderation in the rate of expansion of loans, and par-

The Federal Reserve justifies its proposed redesign of the discount mechanism by stating that

its chief objective is increased use of the discount window for the purpose of facilitating short-term adjustments in bank reserve positions. A more liberal and convenient mechanism should enable individual member banks to adjust to changes in fund availability in a more orderly fashion and, in so doing, should lessen some of the causes of instability in financial markets without hampering overall monetary control.

The Fed further argues that open market operations

in Government securities by the central bank serve effectively as the preponderant means of secular reserve provision and the leading edge of monetary policy implementation. The role of the discount mechanism, on the other hand, is to cushion the strains of reserve adjustment for individual member banks and, thereby, for financial markets.[16]

This line of reasoning may be contradictory, however. The evidence presented in Table 12–3 shows the procyclical character of Federal Reserve discounts and advances. Discounting actually runs counter to open market operations, providing an escape for banks that wish to expand loans and investments in periods of full employment, rising prices, and a restrictive monetary policy. Providing commercial banks with an automatic right to borrow reserves, even though in limited amounts as proposed, would further enable them to avoid the effects of restrictive monetary policy. It is exceedingly difficult to determine what portion of reserve borrowing is to cushion the strains of reserve adjustment for individual banks and what portion is to help finance expansion of loans to meet a strong demand for funds.

If banks individually increase their discounts and advances, their reserves increase and the Fed must sell still more government securities. Since the effects of open market operations are felt relatively quickly throughout the banking system, many banks would again, before long, be short of reserves and would again be induced to borrow more at the Fed.

The real bills doctrine once again. The discount mechanism was originally set up to meet the real and legitimate needs of trade, "to facilitate the production and orderly marketing of goods and not to finance the speculative holding of excess stocks of materials and merchandise." [17] This amounted to an acceptance by the Federal Reserve of the real bills doctrine, discussed in Chapters 3 and 9. One wonders if the suggested revision of the

---

ticularly business loans. Accordingly, this objective will be kept in mind by the Federal Reserve Banks in their extensions of credit to member banks through the discount window. Member banks will be expected to cooperate in the System's efforts to hold down the rate of business loan expansion—apart from normal seasonal needs—and to use the discount facilities of the Reserve Banks in a manner consistent with these efforts." *Federal Reserve Bulletin*, September 1966, p. 1339.

[16] Board of Governors of the Federal Reserve System, "Report of the System Committee," *Reappraisal of the Federal Reserve Discount Mechanism*, July 1968, p. 1.

[17] Federal Reserve Board, *Annual Report*, 1923, p. 5.

discount mechanism is not a return to this doctrine. A basic borrowing privilege, even though proportionately related to a bank's capital stock and surplus, theoretically could lead to a continual expansion of bank reserves. Commercial banks could decide to sell additional stock, thereby raising capital accounts. This would increase the amount of reserves they could borrow automatically and could lead to an increase in bank flows, money balances, and the demand for goods. In a full employment economy, this would mean rising prices, greater demand for loans by the non-bank public, still more bank borrowing of reserves, etc. The Fed, of course, could stop this via open market sales of U.S. government securities, but (at least theoretically) the Fed could ultimately run out of government securities. Or the Fed could also raise the reserve requirements, but this could be viewed as politically unpopular as a refusal to give banks additional reserves at the discount window. Admittedly it is highly unlikely that this sequence of events would occur in the real world. Nevertheless, it is interesting to speculate on what could happen if the basis of Federal Reserve reasoning on the discount mechanism were carried to what some economists consider its logical conclusion.

The Federal Reserve counters these speculations by arguing that it could limit borrowing by linking the discount rates to market rates of interest more closely. "The closer linkage of the discount rate to market rates will probably call for more frequent changes in the discount rate than have been made in recent years." [18] Still, it is hard to see how this would strongly limit borrowing. The Federal Reserve itself acknowledges that "market rates are likely to be somewhat above the discount rates so long as reserves are in scarce supply and rate relationships are allowed to seek their own levels." [19] *This is the way it has always been. The Federal Reserve discount rate has normally been above market rates of interest on the downward part of the cycle and below market rates of interest on the upward part of the cycle.* Thus it is difficult to see how the proposed revision of the discount mechanism could have an ameliorative economic effect.

Supplementary Readings

See end of Chapter 13.

[18] "Report of the System Committee," p. 20.
[19] *Ibid.*

The Development
of Federal Reserve Instruments
# of Monetary Control, Part II

GENERAL MONETARY CONTROLS (CONTINUED)

Open Market Operations

The most potent instrument of monetary policy the Federal Reserve has at its disposal is its ability to engage in open market operations. By purchasing U.S. government securities and bankers' acceptances from the nonbank public, it can directly increase both commercial bank reserves and the volume of demand deposit money. By selling U.S. government securities and bankers' acceptances to the nonbank public, it can directly decrease both commercial bank reserves and the volume of demand deposit money.

When properly used, open market operations can be of great help in stabilizing the economy. Since the purchase and sale of securities can be done in small or large amounts, it is possible to change the excess reserve position of the commercial banking system quickly or gradually and in limited amounts. As noted earlier, this is not the case with reserve requirement changes.

Open market operations are not subject to the shortcomings of discount rate changes, either. Since they change reserve positions directly, their effectiveness does not depend on the demands of the commercial banking system for reserves. In addition, open market operations do not generally suffer from the "announcement" shortcomings of the discount mechanism. As the FOMC continually engages in open market operations, commercial banks find it difficult to tell whether an increase in Federal Reserve holdings of securities is a normal adjustment in response to a seasonal need for additional bank reserves or an actual change in policy. Although the absence of a clear-cut announcement of change in Federal Reserve open market policy may cause some difficulty with respect to the use of this instrument, it does lessen the probability of adverse bank borrowing action like that which sometimes occurs when discount rate changes are announced.

The Use of the Open Market Tool

1917–35. The use of open market operations as an instrument of economic policy is comparatively recent. When the Federal Reserve System was set up in 1913, it was expected that holdings of U.S. government securities would simply be a source of earnings for the Federal Reserve banks. Although some open market operations in bankers' acceptances were envisioned, the initial purpose of these operations was to facilitate the role of the United States in international trade through the development of a bankers' acceptance market.

In practice, however, open market operations in bankers' acceptances have never played a significant role in the implementation of monetary policy, whereas those in government securities have assumed ever-increasing importance. Initially, each district bank was permitted to carry on its own open market operations, in accordance with the congressional intention that each Federal Reserve bank should have a substantial amount of local autonomy in regulating banking in its own district. It was soon discovered, however, that independent operations in government securities tended to have destabilizing effects on the economy. For example, if a Federal Reserve bank in one district sold securities that were purchased in another district, the result would be a loss of reserves by banks in the district where the securities were purchased, thereby leading to an unanticipated and frequently undesirable tightening of credit conditions in that district.

In addition, it was soon recognized that if open market operations were undertaken by the Federal Reserve purely for the purpose of making a profit, this could have a destabilizing effect not only on regional economies but on the national economy as well. In the early 1920's, for example, it was discovered that Federal Reserve bank purchases of U.S. government securities reduced the borrowing of reserves by member banks and that sales of securities increased borrowing. Hence, a contracyclical discount rate policy could be undermined by individual Federal Reserve banks as they purchased and sold government securities to increase earnings. Thus, even as early as the 1920's, the need for coordination between the discount mechanism, the principal instrument of monetary management at that time, and open market operations was obvious.

In 1922 a committee composed of men from various Federal Reserve banks was set up to coordinate purchases and sales of U.S. government securities by the district banks. The following year, this committee was disbanded. It was replaced by the Open Market Investment Committee, which was to buy and sell securities for all Federal Reserve banks. Technically, individual district banks still had the power to buy and sell securities, but they did so in very limited amounts.

One shortcoming of the Open Market Investment Committee was that its membership did not include representatives from all the Federal Reserve banks. Accordingly, in 1930 membership in the committee was broadened to include a representative from each bank. At the same time it was renamed the Open Market Policy Conference. The Banking Act of 1933 formalized this arrangement and renamed the conference the Federal Open Market Committee. It also denied each Federal Reserve bank the right to engage in open market operations on its own account, although an individual bank could still refrain from participation in FOMC operations if it wished. The Banking Act of 1935 removed this last right of individual Federal Reserve banks and established the FOMC in its present form.

Thus, only since 1935 have open market operations as we know them been carried on. Throughout most of the 1920's and early 1930's, however, some attempt was made to coordinate the administration of policy instruments, and the various committees in charge of security purchases and sales did make an effort to avoid conflict with discounting policy.

How effective were open market operations as a contracyclical device prior to 1935? This is a tricky question. We tend to judge the use of this policy instrument in terms of our current policy that security purchases and sales should be used to influence the expansion and contraction of the economy. During the early part of the period being considered, however, this was not an established objective of open market operations. Instead, the policy was simply to coordinate discounting and open market operations. In addition, most of the security sales and purchases during this period were primarily aimed at adjusting bank reserve positions to seasonal and temporary reserve needs. This is true even today; it is the main reason why the account manager buys and sells securities on a daily basis. Contracyclical purchases and sales of securities are only a small part of overall market operations. In the 1920's and early 1930's they were even less significant.

Nevertheless, small variations in Federal Reserve security purchases and sales can have a contracyclical effect, even though the bulk of the operations have no contracyclical purpose. Table 13–1 shows the annual average amount of U.S. government security and bankers' acceptance holdings of the Federal Reserve banks from 1917 through early 1969. From the beginning of the period through 1935, there was an increase in Federal Reserve security holdings (U.S. government securities plus acceptances) every year except 1921, 1923, 1926, 1928, 1929, and 1935. There were business contractions from late 1918 to early 1919, 1920 to mid-1921, mid-1923 to mid-1924, in 1927, and from late 1929 onward. Of the six years in which Federal Reserve bank security holdings decreased, four—1921, 1923, 1929, and 1935—were years of economic contraction; these appear

TABLE 13–1. FEDERAL RESERVE HOLDINGS OF U.S. GOVERNMENT
SECURITIES AND ACCEPTANCES, 1917–69
ANNUAL AVERAGES OF DAILY FIGURES
(IN MILLIONS OF DOLLARS)

YEAR	U.S. GOVERNMENT SECURITIES	ACCEPTANCES	YEAR	U.S. GOVERNMENT SECURITIES	ACCEPTANCES
1917*	100	188	1944	14,772	—
1918	134	287	1945	21,363	—
1919	254	324	1946	23,250	8
1920	324	385	1947	22,330	—
1921	254	91	1948	21,511	—
1922	455	159	1949	19,560	—
1923	186	227	1950	18,410	—
1924	402	172	1951	22,756	—
1925	359	287	1952	23,066	—
1926	350	281	1953	24,661	—
1927	417	263	1954	24,646	—
1928	297	328	1955	23,891	13
1929	208	241	1956	23,709	23
1930	564	213	1957	23,345	27
1931	669	245	1958	24,654	40
1932	1,461	71	1959	26,194	35
1933	2,052	83	1960	26,373	39
1934	2,432	25	1961	27,393	—†
1935	2,431	5	1962	29,522	—†
1936	2,431	4	1963	31,764	—†
1937	2,504	3	1964	34,618	—†
1938	2,565	1	1965	38,661	—†
1939	2,584	—	1966	41,856	—†
1940	2,417	—	1967	46,134	—†
1941	2,187	—	1968	51,303	—†
1942	3,191	—	1969	52,822‡	—†
1943	7,724	—			

* Based on data for August–December.
† Not shown separately in data source.
‡ Based on data for January–June.
SOURCE: 1917–60, Board of Governors of the Federal Reserve System, *Supplement to Banking and Monetary Statistics*, Section 10 (Washington, D.C., 1962), p. 14; 1961–68, computed from *Federal Reserve Bulletin*, various issues, 1961–69.

to have been instances of the incorrect application of contracyclical policy. However, the action of 1921 may be excused on the grounds that it was not until 1922 and 1923 that the Federal Reserve System acknowledged some responsibility for maintaining economic stability. Not until 1923 did it attempt to centralize open market security purchases by the twelve Federal Reserve banks. It may also be claimed that 1935 was not a year of contraction, but of expansion. This is true, but it was an expansion in the midst of a deep depression; some increase in security holdings was called for rather than the contraction that actually took place, even if the latter only amounted to $21 million.

In terms of our current conception of the function of open market operations, decreases in Federal Reserve bank security holdings were inappropriate in four of the six years in which they occurred between 1917 and 1935. Only in two years, 1926 and 1928, did the decrease in security holdings coincide with a business expansion, and in both cases the reduction in holdings was comparatively small—$15 and $55 million respectively.

Were the increases in Federal Reserve bank security holdings during this period any more meaningful? Security holdings were increased in twelve of these years. Five of these increases were in the depression years of 1930 through 1934; of the remaining seven increases, four occurred in years that were primarily periods of business contraction—1918, 1920, 1924, and 1927. The beneficial effects of the 1924 and 1927 increases, however, were offset by discount and advance decreases. On three occasions—in 1919, 1922, and 1925—increases took place during economic expansion, an inappropriate time for the monetary authorities to expand security holdings. The 1922 increase, however, was accompanied by discount and advance decreases that more than offset the economic effects of the expansion in security holdings.

In general, in the eighteen years from 1918 to 1935, security purchases moved in the wrong direction on seven occasions. The contracyclical action associated with security purchases from 1930 to 1934 was quite impressive, however. Holdings increased from $449 million in 1929 to $2.457 billion in 1934. Unfortunately, other actions by the monetary authorities during this period offset the effects of these vigorous and appropriate purchases. In judging the merits of Federal Reserve monetary actions, we must consider the net effect of all instruments of policy upon commercial bank reserve positions. In this section, however, we have discussed only whether Federal Reserve security purchases and sales, by themselves, were in the correct contracyclical direction.

1935–45. Federal Reserve open market operations had developed into an important instrument of contracyclical monetary policy by the 1920's and early 1930's. Starting in 1935, however, with a slight decrease in Federal Reserve bank security holdings, this use of open market operations was abandoned, and from 1935 through 1940 the level of securities held by the System stabilized. There were some year-to-year variations, but these were relatively insignificant compared with the substantial increases of the early 1930's. The apparent goal of policy during this time was to maintain an orderly market for government securities.

Beginning in 1937, the maintenance of an orderly government securities market became an increasingly important goal of open market operations. Maintaining an orderly market meant stabilizing U.S. government security prices. The first direct action of this sort came in 1937, when the Federal Reserve began buying long-term securities to prop up their declining prices. Short-term securities were sold at the same time so that member bank reserve positions would not be increased by the purchase of the long-term issues. The Federal Reserve again entered the market with a view to propping up government bond prices in September of 1939 with the beginning of World War II. Subsequent entries were made in early 1940 and immediately after Pearl Harbor in 1941.

With the start of World War II, the Federal Reserve firmly committed itself to supporting the government bond market. The *Annual Report* of the Board of Governors for 1941 stated:

The System is prepared to use its powers to assure that an ample supply of funds is available at all times for financing the war effort and to exert its influence toward maintaining conditions in the United States Government security market that are satisfactory from the standpoint of the Government's requirements.[1]

To implement this policy, the Fed stood ready to buy any amount of government securities that commercial banks and the nonbank public wished to sell. Since the government was issuing large volumes of securities to finance the deficit created by our huge armament expenditures, bond prices would have declined without Federal Reserve support. The increased supply would have forced the Treasury to offer higher interest rates in order to sell additional securities. This, in turn, would have meant increased government expenditures in the form of interest payments—funds for which would have had to come either from taxes or additional bond sales. Money would have had to have been diverted from armament expenditures to pay the increased interest. Federal Reserve support of the government bond market, in effect, increased the demand for the securities and thereby helped to maintain their price and hold down the interest burden of the Treasury. The effects of this policy on Federal Reserve holdings may readily be seen in Table 13–1. U.S. government security holdings increased from $2.187 billion in 1941 to $21.363 billion in 1945.

The money stock also increased substantially, from $45.5 to $94.2 billion, in the same period, as a result of this policy.[2] This happened as the U.S. government sold securities to the nonbank public and the commercial banking system. To the extent that the nonbank public purchased the securities, no new money was created. The Treasury simply received the money balances of the nonbank public and then spent those funds for wartime armaments, thereby returning the money to circulation. When members of the nonbank public sold their security holdings to the Federal Reserve or the commercial banks, however, there was an increase in demand deposit money. Furthermore, to the extent that securities sold by the Treasury were purchased by the commercial banking system, there was also an increase in the money supply. Initially there was an increase in Treasury demand deposits; as the proceeds of the security sales were spent

[1] *Annual Report,* 1941, p. 1.
[2] The data are for June 30, 1941, and June 30, 1945. Data source: Board of Governors of the Federal Reserve System, *Supplement to Banking and Monetary Statistics,* Section 1 (Washington, D.C., 1962), p. 15.

by the Treasury, the funds were received by the nonbank public, thereby increasing the money supply.

The commercial banking system was an important cog in this process. Whenever it purchased securities, deposit liabilities increased. As deposit liabilities increased, however, excess reserves decreased and so did the lending ability of the banking system. This could well have been a serious problem. During World War II, however, the commercial banks did not experience any limitation of their money-creating powers. The FOMC, by buying securities, created the reserves needed for expansion.

1946–51. The Federal Reserve continued to support the government bond market during the early postwar years. The Treasury was no longer confronted with finding a market for an expanding government debt; the war was over and government expenditures had decreased. However, it was confronted with the problem of refunding the large national debt built up during the war. Large volumes of new securities had to be sold in order to get the funds needed to retire old securities as they came due. After the war people demanded the goods and services they had been denied during the war. They neither wanted nor demanded government bonds. Without continued Federal Reserve support, bond prices would have dipped and interest costs increased.

The economy showed inflationary tendencies from 1946 through mid-1948. The commercial banking system tended to abet the price rises of these years by actively expanding loans, although deposit money increased only in 1946 and 1947. It was the security price support program of the Federal Reserve that enabled commercial banks to switch from U.S. government securities to loans without incurring capital losses.

One would imagine, given this set of circumstances, that the Federal Reserve would have sharply increased its security holdings from 1946 to 1948. Actually, these holdings increased only in 1946; decreases occurred in 1947 and 1948, due in large part to Treasury debt retirement practices. Federal government tax receipts exceeded expenditures in these years and yielded a large cash surplus. This surplus was used by the Treasury to retire federal debt, much of which was held by the Federal Reserve banks. Thus, although actual Federal Reserve open market policy during these years of inflation was basically expansive, nevertheless, in 1947 and 1948, debt retirement induced a decrease in Reserve bank security holdings—the right direction for Federal Reserve security holdings to move in periods of full employment and inflation. Had the Fed followed an aggressive contracyclical monetary policy, there would have been significant additional decreases in Federal Reserve bank security holdings. In practice, however, the Treasury surplus was the principal deflationary force at work in the economy; Federal Reserve policy was expansive, and the result was inflation. From 1946 to 1948, commercial bank reserves rose from $16 to $18 billion; excess reserves, despite a reserve requirement increase in 1948, were never less than $740 million in any month of the three-year period.[3]

In 1949, the situation was substantially different. Businesses found themselves with excessive inventories and proceeded to reduce them. This helped set contractionary forces in motion and a recession developed. Open market operations at this time were again perverse. Instead of buying more government securities, the Federal Reserve sold them. Its holdings of government securities decreased by $4 billion in 1949, causing member bank reserves to fall by $2.6 billion.[4] In a recession, there is generally a strong demand by commercial banks and financial investors for government securities because they represent a safe investment. This increased demand usually causes bond prices to rise. Federal Reserve sales of securities in 1949 prevented these price rises from taking place.

The beginning of the Korean conflict in June 1950 triggered a sharp economic expansion. The Fed attempted to restrain inflationary forces by raising reserve requirements and discount rates. The commitment to support government bond prices interfered with these contracyclical moves, however. From June 1950 to March 1951, Federal Reserve holdings of government securities actually expanded by $4.5 billion; member bank reserves and the money stock each rose by $3 billion.[5]

Throughout most of the 1940's, the members of the FOMC had generally agreed with the policy of supporting the price of government bonds. By 1950, however, many of them had become quite dissatisfied with the policy. This produced some dissension between the Federal Reserve System and the U.S. Treasury. The FOMC felt that it was unwise to continue supporting government bond prices; the Treasury, on the other hand, wanted this easy-money policy continued so as to keep the interest burden of the national debt low. After considerable controversy, which even involved President Truman, the Federal Reserve and the Treasury reached an accord in March of 1951. The issue was resolved in favor of the Federal Reserve and for the first time in almost ten years, it was allowed to follow a restrictive monetary policy without having to undercut that policy by buying government securities at fixed prices whenever commercial banks were short of reserves.

March 1951–64. Following the Treasury–Federal Reserve Accord of 1951, the Fed's use of open market operations was for the most part in an appropriate contracyclical direction. Federal Reserve bank holdings of securities expanded in 1951, 1952, and 1953 and remained roughly constant in 1954. Of the increases, those of 1951 and 1952 would appear at first glance to have been inappropriate. After more careful consideration, however, it becomes apparent that they may have been wise after all.

[3] *Supplement to Banking and Monetary Statistics,* Section 10, p. 16.
[4] *Ibid.,* p. 17.
[5] *Ibid.,* pp. 15, 17.

Most of the increase of 1951 occurred prior to the Treasury–Federal Reserve Accord, and it was timed to coincide with the 1951 reserve requirement increases. The overall increase in security holdings from 1951 to 1952 was only $300 million, in any case.

The increase of 1953 was an appropriate contracyclical action. The large volume of security purchases coincided with the first six months of the 1953–54 recession. Following this recession the nation experienced a sharp economic upturn in 1955–57. Federal Reserve policy then changed to one of increasing restraint. Security holdings decreased somewhat in 1955, remained roughly constant during 1956, and decreased again in early 1957. Additional restraint was simultaneously applied through increased discount rates.

The 1957–58 recession was sharp, but comparatively short-lived. Open market operations did not begin to function contracyclically until March 1958, just prior to the economic upturn, although reserve requirements and discount rates had been reduced earlier. Once the purchase of government securities by the account manager began, it continued each month, except for a seasonal adjustment in January and February 1959, straight through December 1959. These purchases, by themselves, were not contracyclical because there was no longer a recession. Significant sales of securities followed in early 1960. In midyear there came another reversal of policy, and security purchases resumed. Discount rates were lowered at the same time. Since this occurred just prior to the onset of the 1960–61 economic downturn, it appears that the Federal Reserve may have attempted to anticipate the downturn by returning to a policy of monetary ease.

The easing of monetary conditions that started in 1960 continued through 1964. Aside from seasonal decreases in early 1961, 1962, 1963, and 1964, Federal Reserve bank holdings of securities increased in every month except December 1960 and September and November 1962. The decrease that occurred in December 1960 was in part designed to offset the substantial increase in member bank reserves that resulted from the new Federal Reserve ruling that all vault cash could be counted as part of reserves from November 24, 1960, onward. The two decreases in 1962 were very small, amounting to $67 and $46 million for September and November, respectively.[6]

The recession of 1960–61 ended in February 1961. Logically, it would seem that there should then have been a decrease in Federal Reserve holdings of securities. The economy seemed to be improving rapidly throughout the period 1961–64. Gross national product increases were substantial and there were significant increases in the stock of money as a result of the Fed's easy-money policies. Unemployment was persistent, however. Although the number of people employed was at a record level, the

[6] *Federal Reserve Bulletin,* February 1963, p. 206.

civilian work force was growing so rapidly that the unemployment rate during this period was usually close to 6 percent. Unemployment did not begin to approach 5 percent until mid-1964. Apparently the Board of Governors and the FOMC considered this statistic important enough to warrant a continuation of a policy of moderate ease.

1965–69. On the basis of the raw data on the movement of Federal Reserve holdings of government securities, one would be forced to conclude that open market operations were inappropriate in every year from 1965 through 1968. *However, as must now be evident from the analysis of preceding periods, it is exceedingly difficult to interpret the net expansive or contractive effects of these operations.* Increases in Federal Reserve security holdings are not necessarily indicative of a policy of monetary ease, and decreases do not always imply a policy of restraint. Open market operations are often used to make adjustments for seasonal or unanticipated changes in commercial bank reserves. They are also used as a contracyclical instrument of economic policy, and partly to cushion the contracyclical effects of other policy instruments. The data for 1965–69 reflect such diverse ends.

The employment rate steadily decreased to less than 5 percent of the civilian labor force in 1965, and in 1966 to less than 4 percent, the level at which it remained throughout 1967 and 1968. On this basis, some expansion of Federal Reserve government security holdings was possibly called for, at least in 1965. Aside from seasonal decreases in January and September of 1965, such expansion did take place. The system's holdings of government securities rose by $4 billion. Only about $1 billion of this money wound up as additional commercial bank reserves, however; the remaining $3 billion served to offset decreases in reserves generated by our dwindling gold stock and the expansion in the demand for currency.

Although the unemployment rate in 1965 seemed to justify an expansive policy, there is no such justification for the expansion of Federal Reserve holdings of government securities by more than $3 billion in 1966, when unemployment was less than 4 percent. Are there other justifications? Due to gold flows and an increased demand for currency, the net increase in member bank reserves in 1966 was only about $1 billion, and the Federal Reserve itself argues that it followed a policy of restraint through most of the year.[7] Some of the data bears out this contention. Federal Reserve holdings of government securities declined in January, February, and March, and the overall increase in security holdings by the Fed was less than in the preceding year. In addition, in December 1965 discount rates had been increased and Regulation Q invoked; various classes of reserve requirements were raised in June and August of 1966, and in

[7] Board of Governors of the Federal Reserve System, *Annual Report,* 1966.

September the Federal Reserve requested that member banks voluntarily restrain their expansion of business loans.

Mid-1966 saw an apparent contradiction in this asserted policy of restraint. In July and September, the Fed exercised its power under Regulation Q to lower the maximum rates of interest payable on various classes of time deposits. The purpose of these decreases was to offset some of the competitive edge that had been gained by commercial banks over nonbank financial intermediaries following the use of Regulation Q in December of 1965. Savings and loan associations, finding it difficult to attract funds as a result of this action, had been forced to restrict mortgage loans. A sharp decrease in new construction contracts followed. The decrease in construction activity continued into late 1966. There was also some slack in auto demand. Because of this the Federal Reserve changed direction and instituted a policy of monetary ease in the last quarter of 1966. Open market operations became decidedly expansive at that time.

On balance, it appears that the expansion of government security holdings by the Federal Reserve was justified by current economic conditions during 1966. However, as we shall see later in the chapter, this should not be taken to mean that overall Federal Reserve policy was correct.

Federal Reserve holdings of U.S. government securities expanded by approximately $4\frac{1}{2}$ billion during 1967, the biggest increment since World War II. About $3 billion of the increase went to cover reserve losses attributable to gold flows and increased currency in circulation. The remainder represented an increase in member bank reserve deposits. At the same time, the consumer price index rose 3.2 percent, unemployment rates remained low, and the stock of money increased by 4 percent. Construction activity recovered early in the year. The Federal Reserve took no restrictive economic action until late 1967, when it raised discount rates. Even then there was no contraction of government securities holdings. The only curtailment in a continual expansion of Federal Reserve holdings of government securities occurred in the months of August and September, and represented principally a seasonal decrease. Open market operations in 1967 thus appear to have been procyclical and inappropriate.

Economically, 1968 was much the same as 1967. Unemployment remained low, while the consumer price index went up 5 percent. Again the Federal Reserve banks expanded their holdings of U.S. government securities, this time in excess of $5 billion, with almost all the expansion designed to compensate for member bank reserve decreases resulting from gold and currency drains. On the surface it appears that central bank policy was contracyclical and therefore appropriate. The increased reserve requirements, increased discount rates, and an increase in the income tax rate in 1968 indicate an overall governmental policy of restriction.

On the other hand, these moves were more than offset by the expansionary effects of government military spending, float increases, discount and advance increases, and drops in Treasury cash holdings and other federal reserve accounts. (Chapter 15 shows how the forces cited combine to expand money and reserves.)

Federal Reserve holdings of government securities stabilized in the first half of 1969, when they remained at the same level as in the last half of 1968. Discounts and advances expanded, but only enough to cover increased currency holdings of the public. This was all part of an economic policy of restriction designed to cope with rising prices. As such it appears to have been appropriate, but by August 1969 some economists were already voicing fears that the policy was overly restrictive and would "overkill" the inflation by creating too much unemployment.

Evaluation of the open market policy instrument. There are four principal advantages to the open market instrument. Increases or decreases in Federal Reserve bank security holdings may (1) be made slowly or rapidly and (2) be made in limited or in large amounts. In addition, these open market operations (3) enable the FOMC to directly manipulate the reserve positions of member banks and (4), when they involve the nonbank public, directly affect the stock of money. These four factors make open market operations a swift and flexible corrective for economic instability. They also permit the Federal Reserve to compensate for inappropriate uses of monetary tools, including the open market instrument itself.

This does not mean that it is easy to use open market operations as an instrument of monetary policy. Just as reserve requirement changes and discount rate manipulation pose problems for the monetary authorities, so does the purchase and sale of securities. Fortunately, however, the problems posed by the open market instrument are not as great as those posed by the other policy instruments.

Problems posed by the use of open market operations. First, we may be attempting to accomplish too much by using open market operations in both a dynamic and a defensive manner. We use open market operations "defensively" to make adjustments for seasonal or unanticipated changes in commercial bank reserves. We use them "dynamically" as an instrument of contracyclical economic policy. This duality of objectives often complicates the job of the account manager. For example, there is normally an influx of currency into the banking system from the nonbank public around the first of the year. Since this tends to increase bank reserves and lending ability and since such large increases in lending capacity are considered undesirable by the FOMC, the account manager sells securities.

The problem at first appears simple enough. The sale of securities must be sufficiently high to offset the undesirable increase in reserves, thereby neutralizing its effect on the economy. It is very easy to miscalculate in such matters, however. The account manager may overestimate the extent of the expected cash inflow and sell too many securities. The result will be an unintended tightening of credit conditions. Banks may interpret the tightness of their reserve positions as a sign of a change in Federal Reserve policy and accordingly reexamine their lending and investment policies.

To help him avoid miscalculations of this kind, the account manager has a great deal of statistical information available. He has detailed records of how the forces over which the Federal Reserve usually has no direct control (e.g., changes in vault cash, foreign accounts, or the balance of payments) have behaved in the past. He has been informed by the Treasury of impending security sales, tax receipts, and the expected future rate of government expenditures. He knows the extent to which banks have been borrowing reserves, either from the Federal Reserve banks or in the federal funds market. All this information helps him reach his daily decision on security purchases and sales for defensive purposes. Various statistical indicators, such as changes in the stock of money, the unemployment rate, or the gross national product, also help him decide how much dynamic action is required to carry out the current FOMC directive. In addition, of course, his long experience in the securities market gives him a "feel" for market conditions. Thus, he combines the quantitative and qualitative information available to him and makes his overall decision whether to buy or sell.

Nevertheless, miscalculations can occur. The data may have been interpreted incorrectly. Knowledge of the past is usually reliable as a basis for prognostication, but each new statistic has a way of altering past performance records. All this suggests that it might be simpler to use open market operations for dynamic purposes alone. Commercial banks would then be forced to resort to the discount window and the federal funds market to get the reserves needed to meet seasonal and unanticipated shortages. These borrowings could be repaid when seasonal and unanticipated reserve increases occurred. This is not a specific policy recommendation; it is merely one of a number of alternative ways of handling monetary problems that should be considered if the Federal Reserve is to be the viable and adaptive institution it has striven to be since the Accord of 1951.

Second, the variety of purposes for which we use open market operations makes it difficult to interpret the significance of these transactions. The defensive measures just mentioned, for example, could lead to decreases in the quantity of securities held by the Federal Reserve in a period when a dynamic approach calls for an increase in security holdings. The actual movement of total security holdings may be quantitatively correct, but imply, from a reading of the data change, a modification in policy that has not actually taken place. This, in turn, may set off a change in bank expectations. *Changes in the absolute level of reserves and Reserve security holdings, therefore, are difficult to interpret and should not always be taken as indicative of the degree of tightness in monetary policy.*

In addition, since the Accord of 1951, Federal Reserve use of open market operations has been coordinated, for the most part, with discount rate and reserve requirement changes. This further complicates the task of interpreting Federal Reserve policy from its open market operations alone. It is not possible to look at these operations in isolation and determine whether they were appropriate. A purchase or sale of securities may have been made to compensate for undesired changes in commercial bank reserves resulting from incorrect applications of other instruments of policy. Reserve requirement changes, for example, can lead to extreme changes in member bank reserve positions; open market operations may be used to correct this situation. Thus, to evaluate the open market instrument properly, we must consider it within the context of overall Federal Reserve policy.

Third, the fact that the federal debt is composed of varying maturities complicates the open market policy of the Federal Reserve. Decisions must be made not only about the amount of securities to be held, but also about their maturity distribution.

Shortly after the Treasury–Federal Reserve Accord of March 1951, the Board decided that the FOMC should confine its intervention in the securities market to a minimum—that it was preferable to allow the forces of a free competitive market to set the price and interest rates for both private and government securities. Nevertheless, it emphasized that some intervention would be necessary since open market operations were our most flexible policy instrument. Thus, the question was how best to keep intervention in free market forces to a minimum and simultaneously stabilize the economy through bank reserve manipulation. The solution decided upon was to confine open market operations to one portion of the government securities market, short-term securities. As a result, in 1952 and 1953, open market operations were restricted principally to Treasury bills.

Treasury bills are obligations of the U.S. Treasury that have maturities from three months to a year. Most issues consist of 91- and 182-day bills, however. Because of the shortness of maturity, there is a continual market for these securities. Trading in Treasury bills is more active than trading in any other type of securities. For this reason, the FOMC believed that open market operations could be conducted with the "least impact" in this part of the government securities market.

This policy of confining open market operations principally to Treasury bills was known as the "bills only" policy. Actually, the FOMC did not confine itself entirely to Treasury bills. Other government securities that had a maturity of less than fifteen months were also bought and sold, and, on a few occasions, the Federal Reserve was again called upon to support other sectors of the government securities market. This occurred briefly in December 1955 and July 1958.

Apparently, the Fed felt that restricting security purchases to short-term government securities would be an important step toward simplifying the decision-making process. The FOMC had to be concerned only with the volume of open market operations and their influence on bank reserve positions. It no longer had to worry about choosing among a variety of maturities. Staying out of the longer-term securities market would permit private demands for government securities to determine their prices and interest yields. Federal Reserve purchases and sales of short-term securities would not have a particularly destabilizing effect on security prices because of the large volume of private dealings in this market. In addition, much was made of the point that if

. . . Federal Reserve operations were regularly conducted in all maturity sectors of the Government securities market, the portfolio managers of financial institutions, other investors, and professional traders might well become unduly sensitized to possible changes in monetary policy. A particular hazard, for instance, would be that the trading in the longer term area of the market, which normally experiences the widest price swings, might become overly influenced by guesses about the maturities that might be involved in System operations.[8]

There was considerable opposition to this "bills only" policy. There were many within the Federal Reserve System and the U.S. Treasury who felt that the FOMC should not manipulate the economy only by influencing member bank reserve positions, but that it should also help set short-term and long-term rates of interest. This could only be done, it was thought, if the FOMC dealt in issues of all maturities. Was it not desirable on occasion to reduce long-term interest rates, for example? Would this not induce decreases in private long-term rates and thereby serve to stimulate business investment in plant and equipment?

Changes in economic conditions have a way of forcing changes in the way policy instruments are used! An adverse U.S. balance of payments developed in the late 1950's and early 1960's. This led to a reduction of U.S. gold reserves as foreigners chose to take gold instead of building up their claims to American dollars. Under the "bills only" policy, Federal Reserve security purchases in the 1960–61 recession were heavily concentrated in short-term issues. With increased demand, short-term interest rates tended to go down. Part of the adverse balance of payments of this period was due to the difference between U.S. and foreign short-term rates of interest. Higher short-term yields abroad induced individuals, businesses, and financial institutions in the United States to invest idle funds in foreign short-term securities rather than in domestic issues. Foreigners were also

---

[8] Board of Governors of the Federal Reserve System, *The Federal Reserve System: Purposes and Functions* (Washington, D.C., 1961), pp. 40–41.

induced to restrict their purchases of U.S. securities. As a result, there was an increased short-term capital outflow from the United States, and foreign claims to American dollars and gold rose. It was decided that heavy Federal Reserve purchases of short-term government securities aggravated this situation, inasmuch as they tended to hold down our short-term interest rates.

As a consequence, the "bills only" policy was abandoned in favor of a new policy that, while inducing easy-credit conditions in the U.S. by providing banks with ample lending capacity, might at the same time lead to short-term interest rate increases, thereby reducing the gold out-flow. Under this new policy, called "Operation Twist," the Federal Reserve would sell some short-term government securities so as to raise the yields and thus eliminate short-term capital outflows; simultaneously, it would buy long-term government securities so as to provide banks with greater lending ability. The purchase of long-term securities would also depress long-term interest rates and thereby possibly lead to investment demand increases that could help sustain domestic employment levels.

The "bills only" policy was officially abandoned in February 1961. Thus, the decisions of the account manager have again become complicated by a choice of maturities. He must now operate with possibly conflicting objectives in mind (domestic stability, a favorable balance of payments, and the financing of military expenditures), and he must determine not only the amount but also the kinds of securities that he is to purchase.

The Use of Regulation Q

Regulation Q enables the Federal Reserve to set the maximum rate of interest payable by member banks on various classes of time deposits. The Fed argues that it uses this monetary control to keep the rates paid by member banks in line with yields on other types of near monies and thus to "forestall excessive interest rate competition among financial institutions for consumer-type time deposits." [9]

Theoretically, the yield on one type of liquid asset relative to yields on other types of liquid assets influences the demand for that asset. For example, should the yield on time deposits rise relative to yields on competing financial assets, the volume of time deposits demanded will rise and the demand for other liquid assets will decline. Because the higher yield on time deposits makes them more attractive as a savings form, more of these deposits will be demanded—more time deposits and fewer other liquid assets will be purchased. Conversely, a relative decline in yield on a financial asset will decrease the amount demanded. *Hence it can be argued that the demand for a liquid asset is an increasing function of its own yield and a decreasing function of other yields.* Should the yield on competing liquid assets remain the same relative to that on time

[9] *Annual Report,* 1966, p. 10.

deposits, we would expect little substitution to occur. The presumed objective of the Federal Reserve's use of Regulation Q has been just this —namely, to allow time deposit rates to keep pace with yields on other short-term liquid assets. Had this policy been successful, we would have had to find other explanations for changes in the composition of near monies in the economy. As Chapter 5 demonstrated, the Federal Reserve has not managed to keep the yield on time deposit liabilities of member banks the same relative to yields on competing financial assets, however.

1936–69. Let us examine the actual use made of Regulation Q by the Fed. Table 13–2 shows the maximum interest rates payable on time and savings deposits from 1936 through 1969. The rates apply to all insured commercial banks. (The Federal Reserve sets the rates for member banks, and the FDIC has established identical rates for nonmember insured commercial banks.) The rates payable remained the same from 1936 until 1957, when all classes of rates, except those on time deposits payable in less than 90 days, were raised by $\frac{1}{2}$ percent. Following the 1957 increase, rates again remained constant, this time for five years. Since 1962, rate changes have come more frequently, changes having been made in 1962, 1963, 1964, 1965, 1966, and 1968. Only during this latter period, 1962–68, did the Fed actually attempt to keep commercial bank rates payable on time deposits in line with the yields on competing financial assets. The Federal Reserve's failure to use Regulation Q aggressively prior to 1962 should be clearly recognized, despite such a claim to the contrary as that made in a recent Federal Reserve pamphlet, which argued that "from January 1957 through December 1965 the Regulation Q ceilings were raised four times to allow CD rates to keep pace with yields on other short-term instruments." [10] This is obviously a misleading statement.

Not until 1964 did the growth rate of commercial bank assets first equal and then exceed that of the banks' principal rivals for consumer-type time deposits, the savings and loan associations. The inability of the commercial banking system to compete for time deposits, particularly in the 1950's and early 1960's was one result of the Fed's failure to make more frequent adjustments in the maximum rates payable under Regulation Q. This in turn contributed to increases in the velocity of money and in spending. It was in 1964 that the Federal Reserve first increased the yield payable on time deposits with a maturity of less than 90 days from its traditional 1 percent to 4 percent.

Prior to 1964, most of the activity in nonsavings-type time deposits was carried on by large money market banks in New York, which sold CD's to business enterprises having temporarily idle funds. This, of course, increased the reserves of these banks. Thus, activity in the CD market was and still is one way for individual commercial banks to acquire additional

[10] Jimmy R. Monhollon, ed., *Instruments of the Money Market,* Federal Reserve Bank of Richmond, February 1968, p. 54.

TABLE 13–2. MAXIMUM INTEREST RATES PAYABLE ON TIME AND SAVINGS DEPOSITS, 1933–69

(PERCENT PER ANNUM)

NOVEMBER 1, 1933–JULY 19, 1966

TYPE OF DEPOSIT	EFFECTIVE DATE: *Nov. 1, 1933*	*Feb. 1, 1935*	*Jan. 1, 1936*	*Jan. 1, 1957*	*Jan. 1, 1962*	*July 17, 1963*	*Nov. 24, 1964*	*Dec. 6, 1965*
Savings deposits:								
12 months or more	3	2½	2½	3	4	4	4	4
Less than 12 months					3½	3½		
Postal savings deposits:								
12 months or more	3	2½	2½	3	4	4	4	4
Less than 12 months					3½	3½		
Other time deposits:*								
12 months or more	3	2½	2½	3	4			
6 months to 12 months					3½	4	4½	
90 days to 6 months	3	2½	2	2½	2½			5½
Less than 90 days	3	2½	1	1	1	1	4	
(30–89 days)								

RATES BEGINNING JULY 20, 1966

TYPE OF DEPOSIT	EFFECTIVE DATE: *July 20, 1966*	*Sept. 26, 1966*	*April 19, 1968*
Savings deposits	4	4	4
Other time deposits:			
Multiple maturity:			
90 days or more	5	5	5
Less than 90 days	4	4	4
(30–89 days)			
Single-maturity:			
Less than $100,000	5½	5	5
$100,000 or more:			
30–59 days			5½
60–89 days	5½	5½	5¾
90–179 days			6
180 days and over			6¼

* For exceptions with respect to foreign time deposits, see *Annual Report* for 1962, p. 129, and 1965, p. 233.

Note: Maximum rates that may be paid by member banks as established by the Board of Governors under provisions of Regulation Q. Under this regulation the rate payable by a member bank may not in any event exceed the maximum rate payable by state banks or trust companies on like deposits under the laws of the state in which the member bank is located. Effective February 1, 1936, maximum rates that may be paid by insured nonmember commercial banks, as established by the FDIC, have been the same as those in effect for member banks.

SOURCE: Board of Governors of the Federal Reserve System, *Annual Report*, 1967, p. 363 and *Federal Reserve Bulletin*, April 1969, p. A–11.

reserves. Following the action of 1964 by the Federal Reserve in raising maximum rates of interest payable on commercial bank time deposits, consumer-type time deposits (other than savings deposits) began a marked rate of growth. This contributed to the relative decline of nonbank financial-institution growth rates. Subsequently, in December 1965, the Federal Reserve again increased the maximum rates payable by commercial banks on time deposits. This increase was particularly marked. Funds were drawn from other savings institutions. As mentioned in Chapter 5, the funds drawn from savings institutions are their deposits at commercial banks. These are cash reserves of savings institutions, and any reduction constitutes a decrease in their reserves and lending ability. The result, therefore, of the 1965 action by the Fed was a reduction in the lending ability of nonbank financial institutions, particularly savings and loan associations. Since savings and loan associations are a major source of funds for the construction industry, mortgage funds became very limited in 1966, and there was a slump in the housing industry. Increased Viet Nam war expenditures, no federal tax increases, and high employment levels in 1966 justified some monetary restraint. The action of the Fed was officially intended to keep commercial bank rates in line with other yields and "to enable banks to attract and retain time deposits of businesses and individuals and thus to assure an adequate flow of funds." [11] Actually, the action of the Fed turned out to be contracyclical.

Why did the savings institutions choose not to retaliate and raise their rates? After all, savings and loan association dividend rates at that time were directly determined by the individual associations, not by monetary authorities. They did not raise their rates principally because the Federal Home Loan Bank Board, for almost the first time in its history, began to exercise some contracyclical monetary power. The FHLB Board exercised indirect control over savings rates paid by federal savings and loan associations in 1966 by restricting the volume of advances its regional banks could make to savings and loan associations that had increased their dividend rate excessively. This policy was enforced from 1965 through mid-1966.

The contracyclical use of Regulation Q in December 1965 proved so effective that the Federal Reserve had to take action in mid-1966 to reduce the strong competitive edge that had been gained by commercial banks. The Fed raised reserve requirements against time deposits and reduced the maximum rates payable on new multiple maturity time deposits of 90 days or more from $5\frac{1}{2}$ to 5 percent and from $5\frac{1}{2}$ to 4 percent on similar deposits with maturities of less than 90 days. The FHLB Board at the same time ended its advance restriction policy, and savings and loan associations began to increase their dividend rates. These actions of monetary ease may have been appropriate because one industry,

---

[11] *Annual Report,* 1965, p. 13.

housing, was being so sharply affected by contracyclical monetary policy.

Regulation Q was not used in 1967. Overall policy in that year, as noted in earlier portions of this chapter, was one of monetary ease. During April 1968 the maximum rates of interest payable by member banks on large-denomination, single-maturity time deposits were increased. Consumer-type time deposits were not involved. This action was clearly aimed at keeping commercial bank rates competitive with other short-term rates.

Evaluation of Regulation Q. This is a comparatively new instrument of policy, one that the Federal Reserve itself has not yet officially recognized as a tool of contracyclical monetary policy. If the Fed were to raise yields paid on consumer-type time deposits by commercial banks relative to those paid by nonbank financial institutions, then the lending activity of nonbank financial institutions could be restricted on the upward part of the cycle. Any potential expansion of the lending capacity of commercial banks could be eliminated at the same time via open market operations. On the other hand, on the downward part of the cycle, if the Fed were to lower the yields paid by commercial banks relative to those paid by nonbank financial institutions, then savings institutions' reserves would increase and their lending ability would be expanded. Any contraction of individual bank lending ability at such a time could be offset by Federal Reserve purchases of government securities on the open market.

This line of analysis assumes that other regulatory agencies such as the FDIC and FHLB Board would cooperate with the Federal Reserve in allowing relative yields on time deposits to change. Today the FDIC and the FHLB Board have temporary authority to regulate the maximum rates of interest and dividends payable on deposits or share accounts. The official policy of these agencies is one of cooperation to eliminate rate competition among various types of financial institutions. Since this means keeping relative yields on all time deposits approximately the same, a contracyclical use of Regulation Q to manipulate relative yields seems highly unlikely. A policy of maintaining relative yield levels may have some virtue, however, since it would tend to eliminate, at least in part, such undesired increases in the velocity of money as occurred in the 1950's and early 1960's. (See Chapter 5.)

SELECTIVE CREDIT CONTROLS

Selective credit controls regulate the terms on which one may borrow for specific spending purposes. The presumption on which these controls are based is that certain types of spending are more important as sources of economic instability than others. By regulating the relative ease of borrowing for these spending purposes in recession or inflation, monetary authorities hope to dampen undesired cyclical instability.

Real-Estate Credit Controls

Borrowing for residential construction can be controlled in a number of ways. The amount required as a down payment may be varied, the interest rates charged for mortgage loans may be manipulated, and the time allowed for repayment may be shortened or extended. For example, if monetary authorities believe that increased expenditures on residential construction during a period of full employment represent a primary source of rising prices, repayment periods can be shortened for new construction loans and interest rates and required down payments increased. This should cause spending on residential construction to decrease and the inflationary forces extant in the economy to diminish.

Real-estate credit controls were imposed for the first time during the Korean conflict. While in effect, they fixed minimum down payments and the maximum maturities for mortgage loans. It was hoped that higher down payments and shorter maturities would restrict the expansion of real-estate credit that had been taking place in 1950. However, the effectiveness of these controls was hampered by the backlog of construction orders that had been placed prior to the time the controls were scheduled to take effect. They also encountered considerable resistance from builders, the public, and veterans' groups. They expired in 1953.

Consumer Credit Controls

Controls over borrowing for residential construction purposes are only one set of selective credit controls that have been designed to regulate specific forms of spending. In addition to real-estate credit controls, we have also had experience with consumer credit and stock market credit controls. Consumer credit controls are usually designed to regulate spending on consumer durable goods because this type tends to fluctuate with the business cycle. Normally the purchase of such consumer durables as refrigerators and washing machines increases during the upward part of economic fluctuations and decreases during the downward part. This type of spending behavior in itself will tend to intensify whatever type of economic fluctuation is current. To the extent that consumers borrow to make these purchases and are sensitive to changes in the terms on which they may borrow, the use of consumer credit controls may tend to lessen economic instability.

Consumer credit controls were imposed in World War II, from 1948 to 1949, and during the Korean conflict to relieve the inflationary pressure of increased expenditures on consumer durables. Minimum down payments were fixed and the term of installment contracts limited. During World War II, the volume of consumer credit decreased, but this might have occurred even without credit controls. Increased incomes during the war encouraged debt repayment, and the lack of available consumer durables naturally restricted the total volume of expenditures for these items. One of the principal difficulties with this form of control was the enforcement problem; the number of business establishments and the variety of goods covered by the controls was enormous.

Many economists in the past felt that consumers were not sensitive to interest rate changes but were responsive to the other terms upon which consumer goods were purchased. Hence they argued that general credit controls, which tended to affect interest rates, were ineffective as a means of regulating consumer spending. If this argument is correct, then direct control of consumption expenditures is a logical alternative. A more recent view "is that monetary variables have a significant effect on consumer purchases of durable goods and that the most appropriate measures of these variables are interest rates." [12] If this view is correct, and if consumer demand does respond to interest rate changes without too great a lag, then there should be no need for consumer credit controls. General credit controls, by affecting interest rates, would soon lead to changes in the amount of consumer durables demanded. The recently enacted "truth in lending" bill is designed to make consumers more aware of the true interest cost of borrowing.

Margin Requirements

Regulations over stock market credit are not designed to affect the volume of spending on real economic goods as are consumer and real-estate credit controls. Instead, selective credit controls over the purchase and sale of stock are designed to lessen speculation in stocks. For example, a margin requirement of 80 percent means that a lender may lend an amount up to 20 percent of the current market value of the stock that the proceeds of the loan will be used to purchase. Therefore, an increase in the margin requirement will decrease the amount that may be loaned for the purchase of stock. Theoretically, this should reduce the amount of borrowing for the purpose of purchasing stock and at the same time reduce speculation in securities. Furthermore, a reduction in borrowing to acquire stock should tend to reduce the demand for stocks and, consequently, to reduce upward pressures on stock prices. This is regarded as a significant move in a period of high stock speculation such as occurs in an inflation, since rising stock prices increase the amount that can be borrowed for stock purchase purposes, given a fixed margin requirement. Increased borrowing can then lead to additional increases in the price of stock and a "pyramiding" of borrowing can take place.

Stock speculation in itself has little direct effect on spending for real

[12] Michael J. Hamburger, "Interest Rates and the Demand for Consumer Durable Goods," *American Economic Review,* 1967, p. 1131.

goods and services in the economy. The danger of stock speculation lies in its influence on expectations. Rising stock prices may lead to favorable expectations concerning the economic outlook that are wholly unwarranted. Those whose stock holdings have sharply increased in value on paper may be induced by this to increase their borrowings and spendings on real goods and services. In a period of full employment, this can contribute to price inflation. In addition, suppose that many holders of stock then decide to take their profits. This might cause a collapse of stock prices. Those who borrowed to purchase stocks or goods and services will be forced to liquidate asset holdings to repay their loans as they come due. This will cause stock prices to fall even further; lower stock prices and credit reduction may then lead to the expectation of an economic decline. If this occurs, spending plans will be reexamined and actual spending, income, and output will decline. Hence there is a definite need for controls designed to lessen stock speculation.

Margin requirements are set by the Board of Governors in accordance with the Securities Exchange Act of 1934. Their purpose is to limit the amount of credit that may be extended on a security by prescribing its maximum loan value, which is calculated as a specified percentage of its market value at the time of credit extension. The *margin requirement* is thus the difference between the market value of the security and its maximum loan value. For example, if a security has a market value of $100 and if the margin requirement is 70 percent, then the maximum amount that may be loaned for the purchase of the security is $30.

Margin requirement control was given to the Federal Reserve to avoid the recurrence of stock market speculation such as that which occurred in the late 1920's. It was common practice during this period to purchase stocks almost entirely with borrowed funds. This technique created a strong demand for stocks and buoyed up their prices. Once stock prices broke, however, those who had borrowed were unable to cover their debts. When the value of stock fell beneath the volume of borrowings, borrowers could no longer get enough funds from the sale of stock to cover their debts. With the stock market crash of 1929, stock values declined so markedly that hundreds of thousands of people were financially ruined. Borrowers could not repay their loans, and lenders were unable to collect. The outcome of this financial chaos was a complete revamping of our laws governing the sale of stocks, the establishment of the Securities and Exchange Commission, and the granting of margin requirement control to the Federal Reserve.

Three specific regulations of the Fed cover the extension of credit for the purchase and carrying of securities: Regulations T, U, and G. Regulation T applies to lending by brokers and dealers in corporate securities; Regulation U applies to lending by commercial banks on stocks listed on national stock exchanges; and Regulation G applies to lending by persons other than banks, brokers, or dealers for purposes of purchasing registered

TABLE 13-3. MARGIN REQUIREMENTS, 1945–69*
(PERCENT OF MARKET VALUE)

| | EFFECTIVE DATE | | | | | | |
	2/5/45	7/5/45	1/21/46	2/1/47	3/30/49	1/17/51	2/20/53
Regulation T							
For extension of credit by brokers and dealers on							
listed securities	50	75	100	75	50	75	50
For short sales	50	75	100	75	50	75	50
Regulation U							
For loans by banks on							
stocks	50	75	100	75	50	75	50

| | EFFECTIVE DATE | | | | | | | |
	1/4/55	4/23/55	1/16/58	8/5/58	10/16/58	7/28/60	7/10/62	11/6/63
Regulation T								
For extension of credit by brokers and dealers on								
listed securities	60	70	50	70	90	70	50	70
For short sales	60	70	50	70	90	70	50	70
Regulation U								
For loans by banks on								
stocks	60	70	50	70	90	70	50	70

| | EFFECTIVE DATE | | | | EFFECTIVE DATE | |
	3/11/68	6/8/68			3/11/68	6/8/68
Regulation T			*Regulation G*		
For credit extended by brokers and dealers on			For credit extended by others than brokers and dealers and banks on		
Listed stocks	70	80				
Listed bonds convertible into stocks	50	60	Listed stocks		70	80
For short sales	70	80	Bonds convertible into listed stocks		50	60
Regulation U						
For credit extended by banks on						
Stocks	70	80				
Bonds convertible into listed stocks	50	60				

* Regulations G, T, and U, prescribed in accordance with the Securities Exchange Act of 1934, limit the amount of credit to purchase and carry registered equity securities that may be extended on certain securities by prescribing a maximum loan value, which is a specified percentage of its market value at the time of extension; margin requirements are the difference between the market value (100 percent) and the maximum loan value.

Regulation G and special margin requirements for bonds convertible into stocks were adopted by the Board of Governors, effective March 11, 1968.

SOURCE: Board of Governors of the Federal Reserve System, *Annual Report*, 1960, p. 160; and *Federal Reserve Bulletin*, April 1969, p. A–10.

stocks. The margin requirements for all three types of lenders are the same.

The Federal Reserve frequently employs margin requirements as an instrument of contracyclical economic policy. Table 13–3 shows the use made of this power since the end of World War II. Margin requirements have been increased nine times, in each case during a period of economic upturn. They have been decreased six times. All decreases except those of 1947 and 1962 coincided approximately with an economic downturn. The 1947 decrease followed an earlier 1946 increase to 100 percent. The 1962 decrease followed a sharp break in the price of stocks on the various U.S. stock exchanges in May 1962.

Evaluation of Selective Credit Controls

All forms of selective credit controls suffer from one main defect: *In the absence of direct controls on the manner in which individuals may spend their funds, there is almost no way in which credit controls can be made to produce the desired type of spending restriction.* It is always possible to borrow for one purpose and use the proceeds of the loan for some other purpose. When an individual borrows, the funds are simply placed in his checking account. No distinction is made between the borrowed funds and the other funds in the account. Thus, it would be possible to get an unsecured consumer loan and to use the entire proceeds for the purchase of stock. Even if the proceeds of the loan are actually used for some specified purpose, such as debt consolidation, the loan may still result in the freeing of other funds for speculation in real estate or stock.

This shortcoming inhibits the effectiveness of most selective credit controls. Although we still use them to some extent, they function at present as a minor tool of general monetary policy. Manipulation of the margin requirements for the purchase of stock is the only form of selective credit control still at the disposal of the Board of Governors.

EVALUATION OF MONETARY CONTROLS

Have monetary controls been used in a contracyclical manner? The preceding discussion has reached the following broad conclusions, based on the historical effectiveness of each of the instruments of monetary policy:

First, the Federal Reserve has had the power to change reserve requirements only since 1935. From 1935 through 1969, the only move in the wrong direction was the doubling of reserve requirements from 1936 to 1937. Other changes in the reserve requirement seem to have been correct in light of prevailing economic conditions.

Second, discount rate changes have generally been in the right contracyclical direction, particularly since 1951. However, the movement of discounts and advances, and the relation between the discount rate set by the Federal Reserve Bank of New York and the interest rate on four- to six-month commercial paper, seem to indicate that the changes made were frequently too mild. The increases in discount rates in August 1957 were probably a miscalculation. The decrease in rates in April 1967 and September 1968 were likewise inappropriate.

Third, open market operations have been a formal instrument of policy only since 1935, although they were used to some extent in the 1920's and early 1930's. Movements in security holdings of the Federal Reserve banks, although often inappropriate in the 1920's, were definitely used in an appropriate contracyclical manner in the early 1930's. The commitment to support prices in the government bond market eliminated open market operations as an instrument of contracyclical policy from 1935 until March 1951. Since that time, open market operations have resulted in correct contracyclical movements of Federal Reserve bank holdings of securities in all years except 1952, 1959, and 1967. References made earlier in the chapter to monthly movements in Federal Reserve security holdings indicate that our use of this instrument has become increasingly skillful.

Fourth, the use made of Regulation Q in December 1965 to raise the maximum interest rates payable on time and savings deposits was clearly appropriate. The effects were so strong, however, that they caused some slack in the residential construction industry. This in turn brought about compensatory action by the Fed in 1966. It should be emphasized that the Federal Reserve itself does not regard Regulation Q as an instrument of contracyclical monetary policy.

Fifth, margin requirement changes have been appropriate since the end of World War II.

The preceding summary is based on the effectiveness of each policy instrument used separately. How well do these controls work together, however? Table 13–4 lists the various uses made of the major policy instruments in recent years and the effect of this combination of forces on the money stock. The last column shows the overall ease or tightness of Federal Reserve policy during each of the economic expansions and contractions since October 1949. Table 13–5 shows the movements in both the stock of money and in free reserves, which are also regarded as an important indicator of the ease or restrictiveness of Federal Reserve policy. Finally, Figure 13–1 shows movements in the money stock since 1959.

An Evaluation of Federal Reserve Policy Since 1951

Before evaluating the general implementation of monetary policy, some comment on the stock of money and free reserves as indicators of the

TABLE 13–4. THE USE MADE OF MONETARY INSTRUMENTS OF POLICY, 1949–69

REFERENCE DATES FOR U.S. BUSINESS CYCLES	USE OF RESERVE REQUIREMENTS	USE OF DISCOUNT RATES	DISCOUNTS AND ADVANCES	FEDERAL RESERVE BANK SECURITY HOLDINGS	GROWTH IN STOCK OF MONEY	OVERALL POLICY
Expansion following October 1949 trough, through July 1953 peak	+January, February 1951	+August 1950, January 1953	−1950; +1951 through July 1953 peak	+through whole expansion	+through whole expansion	Ease
Contraction through August 1954 trough	−July 1953; June, July, August 1954	−February, April, May 1954	−through whole contraction	−gradual decline in contraction	Slower than required growth	Ease
Expansion through July 1957 peak		+April, May, August, September, November 1955; April, August 1956	−remainder 1954; +1955–56	−1955; February–June 1957	Slower than required growth	Increasing tightness
Contraction through April 1958 trough	−February, March, April 1958	+August 1957; −November, December 1957; January, March, April 1958	−through whole contraction	+March–April 1958	Almost no change	Tight in early part, ease in latter part
Expansion through May 1960 peak	−December 1959	+September, October, November 1958; March, May, June. September 1959	−remainder 1958; +1959; −March to May 1960	+May 1958–December 1959; −January 1960	At required growth in early part, decrease in latter part	Tight
Contraction through February 1961 trough	−August, September, November, December 1960	−June, August, September 1960	−through whole contraction	+through whole contraction	No growth	Tight
Expansion through 1964	−October, November 1962	+July 1963; November 1964	−remainder 1961; +1963	+through 1964	Slow in early part, at required growth in latter part	Ease
Expansion through 1969	+July, September 1966; −March 1967; +January 1968; April 1969	+December 1965; −April 1967; +November 1967; +March, April 1968; −August 1968; +December 1968; +April 1969	+1965–66; −1967; +1968–69	+through 1969	Greater than required growth through 1968; slow growth in 1969	Ease through 1968, tight in 1969

TABLE 13-5. PERCENTAGE CHANGE IN THE STOCK OF MONEY
AND DOLLAR CHANGE IN FREE RESERVES, 1949–69

YEAR	PERCENTAGE CHANGE IN THE STOCK OF MONEY	FREE RESERVES (IN MILLIONS OF DOLLARS)
1949	−0.9	706
1950	2.6	675
1951	4.5	467
1952	5.0	− 66
1953	2.5	− 91
1954	1.6	627
1955	3.1	− 20
1956	1.2	−270
1957	0.5	−323
1958	1.2	297
1959	3.2	−353
1960	−1.3	116
1961	1.6	520
1962	2.1	421
1963	3.0	197
1964	3.8	107
1965	4.0	− 90
1966	4.5	−276
1967	3.9	194
1968	6.3	−206
1969	1.1*	−803*

* For January to June.
SOURCE: Board of Governors of the Federal Reserve System, *Supplement to Banking and Monetary Statistics:* Section 1, p. 20; Section 10, p. 56; Section 12, p. 37 (Washington, D.C., 1962); and various issues of the *Federal Reserve Bulletin.*

ease or restrictiveness of policy is in order. It is the results of monetary policy that count, not whether individual policy instruments were used appropriately. Some economists, in particular the quantity theorists (discussed in Parts III and IV), contend that changes in the money stock and economic activity are closely related. They judge the effectiveness of Federal Reserve policy by observing the rate of change in the stock of money. A greater than normal increase in the money stock is seen as indicating a policy of ease, and a less than normal increase as indicating restriction. On the other hand, Federal Reserve action affects member bank reserve positions more directly than it does the stock of money. Thus it can be reasoned that changes in member bank free reserve positions should be interpreted as indicative of policy change.

Free reserves are defined as member bank excess reserves less member bank borrowed reserves. A large volume of free reserves is interpreted as indicative of an easy-money policy. Net borrowed reserves (negative free reserves) are taken as a sign of a tight-money policy. This measure, free reserves, has sometimes been used by the FOMC as a guide to open market operations. Actually, a given level of free reserves can produce either easy- or tight-money conditions, depending on the relation between

FIGURE 13–1. United States money stock, 1959–69 *

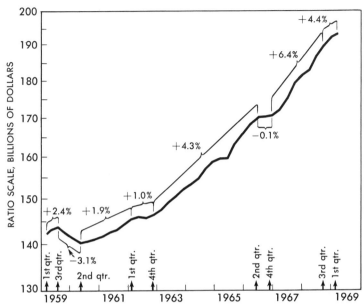

* Percentages are annual rates of change between periods indicated.

SOURCE: Federal Reserve Bank of St. Louis, *Rates of Change in Economic Data for Ten Industrial Countries,* May 15, 1969, p. J-1.

commercial bank desired free reserves and the level deemed appropriate by the Fed.[13] Thus one Federal Reserve economist recently argued

the Committee has come to rely less than in the 1950's on any single measure, such as free reserves. It tries instead with the aid of its staff to specify for a constellation of variables the ranges of short-term variation that are believed to be consistent with a projected rate of growth in total bank deposits over the next month or so.[14]

Some objective measures are needed, however. In the analysis that follows, we shall use both the rate of change in the stock of money and free reserves as indicators of the actual course of Federal Reserve policy.

1951–65. Our previous analysis of the use of each individual policy instrument indicates that during the years since 1951 the Federal Reserve has frequently followed a correct contracyclical policy. Since the Accord of March 1951 occurred in the midst of an economic expansion, we shall

[13] See William G. Dewald, "Free Reserves, Total Reserves, and Monetary Control," *The Journal of Political Economy,* 1963, pp. 141–53; and A. P. Meigs, *Free Reserves in the Money Supply* (Chicago: University of Chicago Press, 1962).
[14] Paul Meek, "Discount Policy and Open Market Operations," prepared for the Steering Committee for the Fundamental Reappraisal of the Discount Mechanism Appointed by the Board of Governors of the Federal Reserve System, February 26, 1968, p. 9.

start our discussion with an earlier reference point, the beginning of this expansionary period, in October 1949.

Normally, economic expansion during periods of high employment calls for a restrictive monetary policy, and economic contraction calls for monetary ease. In terms of the reference dates for United States business cycles listed in Table 13–4, this means that there should have been a policy of ease in the contractions of 1953–54, 1957–58, and 1960–61. The expansions of 1949–53 and 1955–57 called for some tightening of money and credit conditions, whereas those of 1958–60 and 1961–64 called for some ease in money and credit conditions, since the unemployment rate continued high after the 1957–58 recession. The expansion of 1965–68 called for restraint, since the period was one of rising prices, high employment, and increased military expenditures.

Tables 13–4 and 13–5 and Figure 13–1 show that our experience with Federal Reserve policy has been mixed. *During the expansion following the October 1949 trough through the cyclical peak reached in July 1953,* the Fed generally followed a policy of monetary ease. While reserve requirements were raised in early 1951 and discount rates increased in August 1950, these movements were offset by Federal Reserve security purchases. The year 1952 was also one of monetary ease—witness the 5 percent increase in the stock of money. Nevertheless, member bank borrowings had increased substantially in 1952, with the result that free reserves had become negative for the first time in twenty years. This may be taken as a sign that late in the period the Fed moved toward a policy of some restraint as the threat of inflation became apparent.

The expansion of this period had been unique until early 1953. Employment levels were extremely high and prices were very stable. Prices had not yet increased, but the Federal Reserve feared that they would. As a consequence, the Fed sought to halt the incipient price inflation that might have started from bank credit expansion in a period when industry was operating close to capacity. As noted, free reserves became negative in 1952. Action was taken in January 1953 to raise discount rates in order to pressure banks into reducing their borrowings. Interest rates increased, and member banks attempted to improve their reserve position by reducing investments. This reaction of the banking system led the Federal Reserve to believe that its restrictive action had been too severe. A quick reversal of policy was made in May 1953, when the Federal Reserve increased its holdings of government securities. This action did not immediately result in a substantial easing of credit conditions but the member banks' borrowed reserve position did decrease from −$631 to −$303 million from April to May 1953.[15]

How effective was Federal Reserve policy in controlling the expansion just discussed? In isolation, the use made of the reserve requirement and

[15] *Supplement to Banking and Monetary Statistics,* Section 10, p. 14.

discount rate mechanisms was appropriate through the whole period; the actions taken were in the right direction. However, the movement of the stock of money and member bank free reserves indicates a policy of monetary ease through most of the period. This was clearly inappropriate, in view of the high employment levels prevailing, and it is surprising that we did not have a price inflation in 1952. Restrictive action in early 1953, late in the expansion, was also inappropriate. On the other hand, the rapid change in policy from restriction to ease in May 1953 was clearly correct because it preceded the cyclical peak of July 1953 and the subsequent economic contraction.

The Federal Reserve tried to follow a policy of monetary ease throughout the *1953–54 contraction*. Reserve requirements and discount rates were lowered. There was a very small contraction in Federal Reserve bank security holdings, but it was not restrictive in character, the decrease in credit coinciding primarily with the 1954 rather than the 1953 reserve requirement decreases. Thus, the impact of the July 1953 reserve requirement decrease was not undermined by offsetting reserve credit decreases. As a consequence, credit conditions remained relatively easy through much of the 1953–54 contraction. Member bank free reserves changed from a net borrowed position early in the contraction to a large free reserve position in the latter part. The stock of money grew at a much slower rate than it had in the preceding expansion, however.

Federal Reserve policy became increasingly restrictive during the *1954– 57 economic expansion*. Discount rates were increased and Federal Reserve security holdings decreased. Except in 1954, the money supply grew very slowly. For example, it increased only 1 percent in 1956, too small an amount to provide for the needs of a growing economy.

In economic expansion and boom, commercial banks need additional reserves to support increased lending. When those reserves are not provided by the Fed member banks are forced to borrow at the discount windows. Starting in early 1955, member bank borrowings increased sharply. Free reserves dropped, becoming negative in August 1955 and remaining that way through the remainder of the boom except for one month, January 1957. Member bank reserves, of course, did not increase. The borrowed reserves, and some increase in float, simply offset the decrease in member bank reserves that would otherwise have occurred as a result of the open market sales that were taking place. Member bank reserves, therefore, were not permitted to increase.

Without additional reserves to meet the demand for funds, banks had to reduce their investments to increase their lending activity. The net result of this action, as explained in Chapter 6, was a transfer of money balances from the less active part of the nonbank public to the more active borrowing and spending part. At the same time the banking activity of nonbank financial institutions increased. Increased inflationary pressures were therefore at work in the economy.

The period of the 1954–57 expansion was one of high employment levels, rising prices, increasing private investment outlays, and rapidly increasing gross national product; monetary policy at the time was, appropriately, one of restraint. It is ironic that prices increased in this period. However, increased lending, together with price and cost increases in the automobile and investment goods industry, helped offset the effects of restrictive monetary policy.

The *contraction* that followed the 1954–57 expansion was short, but sharp. Unemployment increased substantially. Our monetary authorities were slow to respond to the downturn in the economy. Discount rates were increased in August 1957 and were not reduced until November. Reserve requirements were reduced in early 1958, and some open market purchases were made in March. Free reserves did increase as reserve requirements were lowered. However, by this time, we were already in the latter stages of a recession. The stock of money actually dropped during the 1957–58 contraction. Monetary policy for this period, therefore, does not appear to have been appropriate.

Federal Reserve monetary action during the *1958–60 expansion* is more difficult to interpret. Discount rates were increased three times in 1958 and four times in 1959. Such restrictive action is often appropriate in a period of business expansion. In all but four months of this period, however, the unemployment rate was in excess of 5 percent. The lowest average unemployment rate for any full year, $5\frac{1}{2}$ percent, was in 1959.[16] On the basis of the unemployment statistics, a policy of monetary ease would probably have been preferable.[17] Instead, the discount rate increases were so prompt and strong that, at the time of each increase, the discount rate for the Federal Reserve Bank of New York almost equaled the prime rate on four- to six-month commercial paper. This was as close as the Federal Reserve System came in the post-Accord period to pushing the discount rate above the commercial paper rate in economic expansion. This action came, however, when we still had a large volume of unemployment! To make matters worse, the high discount rate set in September 1959 was kept for nine months; it was not lowered until six months after the commercial paper rate had begun to decrease.

Federal Reserve open market policy was significantly different from its discount rate policy. Security purchases began in May 1958 and continued through December 1959. This would seem to indicate a policy of monetary ease. Such was not the case, however; free reserves became negative in 1959. Most of the large increases in Federal Reserve security holdings were designed merely to offset other forces that were tending to

[16] *Federal Reserve Bulletin*, January 1960, p. 78, and January 1961, p. 88.
[17] It must be recognized, however, that if an easy money policy leads to demand increases in those sectors of the economy that have full employment, price inflation will follow. It is important that spending increase where unemployment exists. If many people are permanently unemployed due to a lack of proper job skills, then inflation and less than full employment may exist simultaneously.

decrease member bank reserves—namely, increases in currency in circulation and decreases in the gold stock. Federal Reserve security holdings increased from May 1958 through December 1959 by $3 billion, whereas the increase in currency in circulation and the decrease in gold stock were $2 billion and $2.3 billion respectively. Since discounts and advances, and float, had increased, member bank reserves in the same period increased by $0.7 billion.[18] The one contradiction to this picture of monetary restriction was an increase in the stock of money of 3.2 percent in 1959. It can be argued, however, that this increase represented merely a moderate "catching up" of the money stock to the legitimate needs of the economy. The average increase in this economic indicator had been only 1.6 percent during the period 1953–58.

With economic growth, a larger population, and increased real output in the economy, some expansion of commercial bank reserves and the stock of money was surely needed. Federal Reserve policy, however, apparently called for limiting the availability of new reserves to member banks and severely limiting the increment in the stock of money. *This policy was apparently based on the assumption that the expansion of 1958–60 was much like earlier expansions, with comparatively high employment levels and potential price level increases.* It is because this assumption was questionable that the policies of this period are difficult to interpret. First, the period was one of expansion, which theoretically calls for monetary restriction if inflation is to be avoided. Second, discount rates were increased, which is an appropriate action in light of the first point. Third, the Federal Reserve purchased securities, which is an expansionary action. However, because the increase in security holdings merely served to offset other forces tending to decrease member bank reserves, open market policy was basically restrictive, which is also appropriate in terms of the first point. Fourth, unemployment in this period was usually in excess of $5\frac{1}{2}$ percent, a level that theoretically calls for credit expansion and monetary ease. Hence, restrictive policies were inappropriate in light of the employment situation.

The *contraction* from *June 1960* through *February 1961* and the subsequent *expansion* as it continued into 1965 are generally believed to have been periods of monetary ease. Reserve requirements were lowered in the contraction. Discount rates were also lowered in the contraction, but were raised slightly in the expansion to reduce the gold outflow. Federal Reserve bank security holdings and free reserves both increased during the contraction and the early part of the expansion. Again security purchases were greater than the increase in member bank reserves. As in preceding periods, the decreases in gold stock and increases in currency in circulation tended to absorb some of the reserve-creating potential of Federal Reserve open market purchases. At no time, however, did it appear that member

---

[18] *Supplement to Banking and Monetary Statistics,* Section 10, p. 19.

banks were deficient in reserves. From June 1960 through December 1964 member bank free reserves were positive, although they were becoming comparatively low at the end of 1963 and finally became negative in 1965. All these forces indicate that monetary policy was expansive through both contraction and expansion in the first half of the 1960's.

In light of continued high unemployment levels, expansionary policy was appropriate. Unemployment did not drop below 4 percent until 1966. However, the data in Table 13–4 and Figure 13–1 belie the conclusion in the preceding paragraph concerning the ease of monetary policy during the early 1960's. The stock of money had begun to decline in the fourth quarter of 1959. This may well have been a source of the 1960–61 contraction. It continued to decline through the second quarter of 1960; not until the fourth quarter of 1961 did it again reach and finally exceed the 1959 high of $144 billion. Overall, the money stock decreased 1.3 percent in 1960 and increased only 1.6 percent in 1961. These figures show that policy actions of 1960–61 resulted in monetary restriction rather than the intended monetary ease. The following four years, 1962–65, brought average annual increases in the money stock of 3.2 percent. This figure is more nearly in accord with the long-run need of the economy for an annual increase in the supply of money equal to the rise in productivity.

1965–69. Expansion in the economy continued through 1969. Until September 1969 unemployment levels were always less than 4 percent.[19] The Fed switched to a policy of monetary restraint in 1965. Discount rates were increased in December, as were rates payable on time deposits; free reserves declined to a net borrowed position early in the year. The stock of money continued to grow, however. The rate of increase in the money stock was 6.3 percent for the second quarter of 1965 through the first quarter of 1966, the largest rate of increase in any four-quarter period since the Korean conflict.

Stock of money and free reserve figures both attest to a policy of restraint through most of 1966. The stock of money increased at a rate of −.1 percent from the second through the fourth quarters of 1966. Net borrowed reserves increased to −$431 million in October and then sharply declined.

Late 1966 gave rise to a policy of monetary ease, which continued through 1967. Unemployment rates, as we noted in earlier sections of the chapter, continued low. However, the use of Regulation Q in late 1965 had caused slack in the construction industry through much of 1966. We find that free reserves became positive in March 1967 and remained so through-

---

[19] This does not mean that all segments of the work force were prosperous. Unemployment rates for black Americans were substantially higher than those for whites. Teenage unemployment rates were particularly high—often reaching 25 percent —among Negroes and other minority groups. Generally, high levels of employment bring into sharper focus continuing pockets of poverty; this gives rise to social and economic disruption as people in these areas realize their plight and begin to demand a greater share in the economy's wealth.

out the year. From the fourth quarter of 1966 through the third quarter of 1967 the stock of money increased 6.4 percent. Overall, in 1967, the stock of money increased only 3.9 percent, however. Discount rates were lowered slightly in April. Reserve requirements against time deposits were lowered slightly in March. Although the consumer price index rose 3.2 percent, no restrictive action was taken until the discount rate was increased in November. This policy of monetary ease hardly seems justified in view of the economic situation during 1967. The strongest expansionary force in the economy was the Viet Nam war effort, which had already been sharply expanded in 1965. In addition, ever-increasing federal deficits and the failure of Congress to enact a tax increase contributed to rising interest rates, making it increasingly difficult for the Treasury to finance the deficit and to refinance old debt as it came due. Thus the Federal Reserve may have been forced into a policy of monetary ease in order to assist the Treasury in financing government expenditures. FOMC policy directives to the account manager at the Federal Reserve Bank of New York increasingly included the provisional clause "taking account of expected Treasury financing activity." [20]

More of the same was in store for the economy in 1968. Officially, the Federal Reserve followed a policy of monetary restraint. Free reserves finally moved into a net borrowed position in March. Discount rates were increased in March and April. Reserve requirements were increased in January; interest rates on certain classes of time deposits were increased in April; and margin requirements were increased in June. Yet the percentage growth in the stock of money for the first two quarters of the year was $4\frac{1}{2}$ percent, with the overall annual rate of change having been $5\frac{1}{2}$ percent since the third quarter of 1967. This was a rate of change hardly consonant with restraining a booming economy.

Congress finally passed an increase in the income tax rate in July 1968. Anticipating some slack in the economy following this increase, the Federal Reserve lowered discount rates slightly in August and made it easier for commercial banks to meet their reserve requirements through a change in the reserve accounting period. In addition, continued high military expenditures no doubt placed considerable pressure on the Federal Reserve to help in Treasury financing activities.

What was happening to economic indicators during this time? Unemployment rates continued low; the consumer price index continued to increase; and anticipated decreases in demand failed to materialize. Business demand for investment goods and services continued strong; residential construction actually increased; and consumer demand continued high. It may well be that the private sector of the economy anticipated continuing price increases, thereby offsetting some of the restraining effects of the tax surcharge.

[20] See, for example, *Federal Reserve Bulletin,* October 1967, p. 1720.

In view of these facts, a policy of monetary ease was hardly appropriate during 1968. Only if demand had actually leveled off following the tax increase would the move toward additional ease in the third quarter of 1968 have been appropriate.

As noted in our discussion of open-market operations, economic policy became very restrictive in the first half of 1969. Discount rates and reserve requirements were increased; government security purchases by the Fed were negligible; net borrowed reserves increased markedly; and the stock of money grew very slowly. All of these were signs of an appropriately restrictive monetary policy. On the other hand, the real rate of growth of the economy had slowed by mid-year, and some economists were predicting an economic decline by early 1970, a decline that would be accompanied by rising prices (as sometimes occurs early in a recession).

In general, an assessment of the appropriateness of Federal Reserve monetary policy since the Treasury–Federal Reserve Accord yields mixed results. Federal Reserve policy was appropriate, *for the most part,* in five periods—the contraction of 1953–54, the expansion of 1955–57, the contraction of 1960–61, and the 1961–65 and much of the 1969 parts of the expansion of 1961–69—although the stock of money changes tend to contradict this conclusion for the contractions of 1953–54 and 1960–61. In the remaining periods, the basic policy appears to have been incorrect. A number of monetary actions taken during these periods were correct, however, either on the basis of prevalent national economic trends or in light of what the monetary authorities took to be the major economic problems of the period. *Our use of general monetary instruments will continue to be imperfect as long as our knowledge of the present status of the economy, of the probable course of economic events, and of the effect our use of the instruments of monetary policy will have on the behavior of the economy is imperfect.*

Additional Problems in the Use of General Monetary Controls

The historical discussion thus far has shown that policy mistakes can occur even when the use of policy at first appears to be correct. The *timing* of policy changes can be of great importance, for example. The timing of credit restrictions in early 1953 and the summer of 1957 was bad. On the other hand, the reversals of policy in 1953 and 1960, when the Federal Reserve began expanding security holdings, were well timed to precede the economic downturn and may have helped to cushion its effects on the economy.

One thing almost all economists agree upon is that *general monetary controls can break the back of almost any inflation,* provided it is not being stimulated by increases in bank reserves and the money supply because of conflicting expansionary policy actions. An increase in reserve requirements or a sufficiently large sale of government securities by the Federal Reserve banks can wipe out member bank excess reserves as quickly as they are created through discounts and advances. These techniques, however, must be used in moderation, since there is always the danger of causing a sharp economic contraction rather than merely stemming rising prices.

As noted earlier, however, economists are by no means in agreement that an easing of credit and money conditions will produce economic recovery. The consensus is that, at best, monetary ease may encourage an economic upturn but that the true source of a recovery is an increased desire to spend. We shall examine this thesis further in Parts III and IV, where we consider monetary theory and alternative economic policies. The presumed inability of monetary instruments to cause an economic upturn is what most economists regard as the *principal shortcoming* of contemporary monetary policy.

There are other problems connected with the use of general monetary controls, too. An appropriate policy may be offset by other forces. For example, increased cold war pressures during a period of full employment may lead to an increase in government expenditures, a deficit, and rising prices, thereby offsetting a contractionary monetary policy. There may be little that can be done about such a situation in the absence of Congressional approval of needed tax increases—witness the situation caused by the delay in passing the 1968 surtax increase.

Also unfortunate is the fact that an appropriate policy may be partly offset by *forces that are touched off by the use of the instruments themselves*. There are basically three such forces: (1) velocity increases due to commercial bank lending and investing activity, (2) velocity increases due to the lending activity of nonbank financial institutions, and (3) velocity increases attributable to nonmember bank lending and investing activity.

First, commercial bank lending and investing activity may induce undesired changes in the velocity of money that would tend to offset an appropriate use of the instruments of monetary policy. In periods of economic expansion, banks try to offset the restrictions placed on their lending abilities by selling off investments. This draws down the comparatively idle demand deposits of the nonbank public, which purchases these securities. The banking system is then able to expand loans and create deposits in an amount equal to the reduction investments. The funds received by borrowers are active money balances and will be spent. Thus, if there is no change in the money supply, its utilization will have increased. This velocity increase adds to the demand for goods and services and, in a full employment economy, may lead to price inflation. The monetary authorities could then follow a more restrictive policy, but if it is applied too rigorously it might lead to an economic reverse. Furthermore, a tighter money policy might enhance the competitive position of nonbank financial institutions and, as some argue, further weaken the controls of the Federal Reserve System over the economy.

Second, velocity increases attributable to increased lending activity of nonbank financial institutions may also take place and thereby further weaken the effects of a restrictive monetary policy. Briefly, the funds that nonbank financial institutions attract come to them in the form of commercial bank demand deposits. When these funds are switched from inactive deposits at commercial banks to accounts of the nonbank financial institutions, these institutions will activate the money balances. The funds will be used to expand mortgage loans and corporate security holdings. Thus, there is increased spending of a given volume of money balances and a resultant increase in inflationary pressures.

It was previously mentioned that banks typically attempt to switch their assets from investments to loans during economic expansion so as to maximize their earnings. There is a limit, however, to the degree to which this switching may take place. For liquidity purposes, the Federal Reserve System insists that member banks maintain at least a certain amount of their assets in safe U.S. government securities in addition to required reserves. The limits imposed by the regulators of the nonbank financial institutions are typically weaker, however. Savings and loan associations that are members of the Federal Home Loan Bank System are presently operating under a 6.5 percent reserve requirement, most of which may consist of U.S. government securities. Therefore, the requirement that commercial banks must also maintain a large volume of safe U.S. government securities further restricts the shiftability of member bank assets. So long as nonbank financial institutions were able to attract deposits from commercial bank depositors and at the same time satisfy their own comparatively low reserve requirements, these institutions were able to continue expanding the velocity of the money supply and thereby counteract a restrictive monetary policy. Their ability to do so has declined markedly since 1965.

Third, the regulations of the Federal Reserve System do not extend to all commercial banks, only to member banks. The deposit liabilities of the member banks constitute better than 85 percent of the deposits of all commercial banks, yet, in terms of total numbers, nonmember banks represent the majority. The nonmember banks are subject to state banking laws, not the Federal Reserve Act. The state banking laws and regulations of most of the fifty states are sometimes laxer than the requirements of the Federal Reserve Act. As a result, the ratio of cash assets to deposits is frequently lower for state nonmember banks than for "country" member banks. Thus, nonmember bank loans increase proportionately more than those of "country" member banks during periods of monetary restriction. During periods of monetary ease, however, nonmember banks expand loans less than do member banks. This behavior pattern has led one economist to draw the "inference . . . that nonmember banks are less responsive than member banks to changes in the direction of Federal Reserve policy." [21]

Less stringent regulations make it possible for nonmember banks to offset the desired effects expected from a particular type of Federal Reserve monetary policy. If the lending activity of the member banks is being restricted by the Federal Reserve, borrowers may be able to get loans from the nonmember banks. Increased loans lead to an increased money stock, and thus cause increased spending. To offset this trend the Federal Reserve may have to tighten credit conditions even further for the member banks. This situation has not yet occurred to any measurable extent because the size of nonmember banks relative to member banks is still small. There is no guarantee that this will always be the case, however. This is one of the reasons economists sometimes contend that all commercial banks should be required to become member banks.

Conclusion

Our discussion of the instruments of general monetary control has tended to emphasize the difficulties inherent in policy implementation. The basic tools have sometimes been used correctly; other times there have been miscalculations. Rapid changes sometimes occur in the economy, and it is difficult to predict both the course of economic fluctuations and the response of consumers and business to policy changes. The Viet Nam war, like World War I, World War II, and the Korean conflict before it, reduced the Federal Reserve's freedom of action and forced it to follow a program of monetary ease. Nevertheless, the monetary instruments of policy discussed in Chapters 12 and 13 have been our principal weapons in combating cyclical movements since 1951. The Federal Reserve is constantly seeking to develop measures superior to those presently being used to forecast the future performance of the economy and its reaction to the discretionary instruments of monetary management. Perhaps, too, entirely new techniques of monetary management will be necessary in the future. We shall consider some possible alternatives to the present policy instruments in Part IV.

Supplementary Readings for Chapters 12 and 13

Board of Governors of the Federal Reserve System. *Reappraisal of the Federal Reserve Discount Mechanism.* "Research Studies Prepared for the Steering Committee." Washington, D.C., 1968.
Board of Governors of the Federal Reserve System. *The Federal Reserve System: Purposes and Functions.* Washington, D.C., 1963, Chapter 3.

[21] Clark Warburton, "Nonmember Banks and the Effectiveness of Monetary Policy," in the Commission on Money and Credit, *Monetary Management* (Englewood Cliffs, N.J.: Prentice-Hall, 1963), p. 337.

Friedman, Milton. *A Program for Monetary Stability.* New York, Fordham University Press, 1960, Chapter 2.

Friedman, Milton, and Anna Schwartz. *A Monetary History of the United States, 1867–1960.* Princeton, N.J., National Bureau of Economic Research, 1963, Chapters 6, 7, and 11.

Goldenweiser, E. A. *American Monetary Policy.* New York, McGraw-Hill, 1951, Chapters 8, 9, 10, and 11.

Mann, Maurice. "How Does Monetary Policy Affect the Economy?" *Journal of Money, Credit and Banking* (1969), pp. 538–48.

Roosa, Robert V. *Federal Reserve Operations in the Money and Government Securities Markets.* New York, Federal Reserve Bank of New York, 1956.

Saving, Thomas R. "Monetary-Policy Targets and Indicators." *Supplement to the Journal of Political Economy* (1967), pp. 446–56.

Smith, Warren L. "Reserve Requirements in the American Monetary System." In Commission on Money and Credit, *Monetary Management,* Englewood Cliffs, N.J., Prentice-Hall, 1963, pp. 175–315.

———. "The Instruments of General Monetary Control." *The National Banking Review* (1963), pp. 47–76.

Warburtin, Clark. "Nonmember Banks and the Effectiveness of Monetary Policy." In Commission on Money and Credit, *Monetary Management,* Englewood Cliffs, N.J., Prentice-Hall, 1963, pp. 317–60.

CHAPTER 14

Monetary Powers
of Other Government Agencies

The Federal Reserve is the only government agency that has both the responsibility of promoting general economic stability and the power to do so. Other federal agencies possess monetary powers, but none have as their primary function the regulation of the entire economy. The Treasury, for example, implements the fiscal policies articulated by Congress and the President. The extent to which it can operate independently of Congress and the President is very limited, however. The Treasury cannot increase spending or reduce tax rates in order to stimulate the economy in the same way that the Board of Governors can manipulate discount rates, reserve requirements, and open market operations. Other government agencies, like the Federal Housing Administration or the Commodity Credit Corporation, have the power to affect specific types of credit extension, but they do not operate to promote general economic stability and growth. Only to the extent that their operations in one specific area of credit extension are contracyclical do they contribute to overall economic stability. The Council of Economic Advisers, like the Federal Reserve, is concerned with general economic stability, but its powers are principally advisory. It attempts to set up wage-price guidelines, makes projections about the future course of the economy, and recommends economic policy actions to the President.

In this chapter we shall briefly examine the monetary powers of various federal agencies and how, potentially, they can affect money and the economy.

THE U.S. TREASURY

The Treasury may influence commercial bank reserves and the money stock (1) by buying and selling gold, (2) by issuing coin and currency, (3) by movements in its balances at commercial banks, and (4) by various debt management techniques. It must be emphasized, however, that the Treasury does *not* have the power to create government deficits or surpluses.

Congress and the President determine deficits and surpluses. The Treasury, through its debt management operations, merely determines how deficits will be financed, how tax surpluses will be used in debt retirement, and how debt will be refunded.

The Purchase and Sale of Gold

The influence of gold purchases on bank reserve positions was discussed in Chapter 11. It will be recalled that when the Treasury uses its funds at the Federal Reserve banks to purchase gold, there is generally an increase in member bank reserves and demand deposit liabilities. Conversely, the sale of gold by the Treasury tends to decrease member bank reserves and demand deposit liabilities.

However, since March 1968 Treasury transactions in gold have virtually ceased. Until then the Treasury bought and sold gold from foreign governments and in foreign private markets. In addition, it bought gold from domestic mines and sold it to domestic industrial users. All these actions, except for those with foreign governments, have ceased, and even these are so negligible that the U.S. gold stock has been almost constant since March 1968. The overall level of gold in major world treasuries has been frozen, with all new output being sold in the private gold market.

The Issue of Coin and Currency

When the Treasury issues coin and currency, Federal Reserve holdings of Treasury coin and currency increase, as do the Treasury deposit accounts at the Federal Reserve banks. As the Treasury uses its increased balances to purchase goods and services from the nonbank public, commercial bank reserves and the demand deposit component of the money supply increase. As the Federal Reserve banks put the currency into circulation, demand deposit money is reduced. Thus, only when the Treasury spends the proceeds from the sale of coin and currency to the Federal Reserve banks is there a direct effect upon the stock of money.

The Treasury puts additional coin and currency into circulation as it is needed by the public. In recent years, the demand for coins, in particular, has been running ahead of the ability of the Treasury mints to produce them. There is almost never a reduction of the total volume of Treasury coin and currency in circulation, although, as noted in Chapter 9, in 1963 the Treasury began withdrawing its silver certificates. Federal Reserve notes are now used in place of low-denomination Treasury notes .

As in the case of gold acquisitions and sales, the Treasury does not manipulate the volume of Treasury coin and currency outstanding so as to affect the volume of bank reserves and the money stock.

Location of Treasury Balances

The Treasury does have full control over the location at which it keeps its funds. They may be held in tax and loan accounts at commercial banks, in the general account with Federal Reserve banks, or in the Treasury's own vaults. As noted in Chapters 5 and 11, the Treasury usually makes payments out of its general account, places payments received into tax and loan accounts, and transfers funds from tax and loan accounts to the general account as expenditures come due.

The purpose of the tax and loan accounts is to soften the economic repercussions of Treasury tax collections and bond sales. Were such receipts to be placed immediately in the general account and held idle until such time as the Treasury needed them, serious deflationary forces would be set to work. By keeping tax and bond sale receipts in tax and loan accounts, bank reserve positions and total commercial bank demand deposit liabilities are left unaffected. The deposits are merely redistributed from the taxpaying public to the Treasury.

Although it is evident that the Treasury manipulates its balances so as to avoid affecting commercial bank money-creating abilities adversely, still, the location of these balances is a potential tool of monetary control. In the past the Treasury has usually left adjustment of commercial bank reserve positions to the Federal Reserve. However, if the Treasury decided to, it could exert a powerful force on bank reserves by changing the location of its funds. By transferring $1 million from its general account to tax and loan accounts, for example, it could increase commercial bank reserves by $1 million. Assuming a 12 percent reserve requirement, commercial bank required reserves would increase by $120,000 (because of the increase in demand deposit liabilities owed to the Treasury). Excess reserves, however, would increase by $880,000. In terms of the simple money-expansion formula introduced in Chapter 7,

$$D = \frac{R}{r} \qquad\qquad [7\text{-}1]$$

we have

$$D = \frac{\$880,000}{.12} = \$7,333,333$$

Thus, in the event of a $1 million transfer of Treasury deposits to commercial banks, the lending and money-creating abilities of the commercial banking system would increase by $7,333,333.

A transfer of deposits in the opposite direction—from tax and loan accounts to the general account—would have a strong contractionary effect. Total reserves, required reserves, and excess reserves would decrease by $1 million, $120,000, and $880,000 respectively. The ability of the banking system to support demand deposits would thus be reduced by $7,333,333.

Similarly, if the Treasury decreased the amount of cash in its own vaults by $1 million and placed these funds in tax and loan accounts, there would be an increase in commercial bank reserves of $1 million, which again would result in a multiple increase in the lending ability of the banking system. On the other hand, if the Treasury demanded cash in exchange for balances in its tax and loan accounts, a correspondingly large contraction would take place.

Debt Management

Manipulation of the composition of the national debt is termed debt management. Our present federal debt is in excess of $350 billion, and almost one-third of this amount is held by various federal agencies. The Federal Reserve banks alone held $52.4 billion in U.S. government securities in early 1969. Almost $230 billion in securities, however, is owned by the public. Table 14–1 gives a more complete picture of the ownership of the federal debt.

TABLE 14–1. OWNERSHIP OF DIRECT
AND FULLY GUARANTEED SECURITIES
(PAR VALUE IN BILLIONS OF DOLLARS)

HOLDER	AMOUNT AT END OF FEBRUARY 1969
U.S. government agencies and trust funds	78.7
Federal Reserve banks	52.3
Commercial banks	60.8
Mutual savings banks	3.6
Insurance companies	7.8
Other corporations	17.8
State and local governments	28.4
Individuals	
Savings bonds	51.5
Other securities	24.7
Foreign and international	12.0*
Other miscellaneous investors	21.1†
Total gross debt	358.7

* Includes investments of foreign balances and international accounts in the U.S.
† Includes savings and loan associations, dealers and brokers, nonprofit institutions, and corporate pension funds.
SOURCE: *Federal Reserve Bulletin*, April 1969, p. A–40.

Important decisions must be made periodically by the Treasury with respect to the handling of this enormous debt. Refunding decisions have to be made. If there is a budget surplus, the Treasury must decide how to handle it. If there is a deficit, its financing will need Treasury attention. These decisions will have a significant effect on the banking system and on economic activity.

Refunding. The term "refunding" is used to describe the issuance of new debt and the use of the proceeds to retire old debt. Almost 50 percent of U.S. government marketable securities have a maturity of less than one year.[1] As a consequence, a large volume of debt needs to be refunded annually. The Treasury must decide what type of security is to be used to replace old debt as it comes due. Since the ownership distribution of securities may be affected by the refunding decision, bank reserve positions may also be affected. For instance, if new issues are sold to the commercial banks, and the proceeds used to retire securities held by the Federal Reserve banks, commercial bank reserves will decrease. The balance-sheet changes for such a transaction are

BALANCE-SHEET CHANGES FOR THE COMMERCIAL BANKING SYSTEM

ASSETS	LIABILITIES + CAPITAL ACCOUNTS
U.S. government securities +$1,000,000 (a) Reserves −$1,000,000 (b)	U.S. government demand deposits +$1,000,000 (a) U.S. government demand deposits −$1,000,000 (b)

BALANCE-SHEET CHANGES FOR THE FEDERAL RESERVE SYSTEM

ASSETS	LIABILITIES + CAPITAL ACCOUNTS
U.S. government securities −$1,000,000 (b)	Member bank reserves −$1,000,000 (b)

Entries labeled (a) show the effects of the sale of the securities; entries labeled (b) show the effects of the retirement of securities held by the Federal Reserve banks.

On the other hand, had the new securities been sold to the Federal Reserve System and the proceeds used to retire old securities held by the commercial banking system, the situation would have been reversed. Commercial bank reserves would have increased and their ability to lend and create money would have been expanded.

In general, if new securities are sold to the commercial banking system or the nonbank public and the proceeds are used to retire debt held by government agencies, the result will be a decrease in commercial bank lending ability. If, however, new securities are sold to the Federal Reserve banks (this can be done only in very limited quantities) and the proceeds used to retire debt held by the nonbank public or the commercial banking system, then commercial bank reserve positions will be improved.

Surpluses. When the federal government collects more in taxes than it spends, a surplus is created. It is up to the Treasury to decide whether to hold the surplus idle or to use it to retire part of our debt. If it decides to

[1] *Federal Reserve Bulletin,* April 1969, p. A–41.

retire debt, then commercial bank reserves will be affected, depending on whose debt holdings are retired.

The surplus itself represents a decrease in nonbank public demand deposit holdings and an increase in Treasury accounts. If the debt retired is held by the nonbank public, then the surplus and debt retirement will have no effect on bank lending positions. Demand deposits will simply have been redistributed from one part of the nonbank public (taxpayers) to another (bondholders).

On the other hand, if the debt retired is held by the Federal Reserve banks, commercial bank reserves will be reduced. If it is held by commercial banks, there is no change in total bank reserves. Excess reserves are increased, however, because of an overall decrease in commercial bank demand deposit liabilities:

BALANCE-SHEET CHANGES FOR THE COMMERCIAL BANKING SYSTEM

ASSETS	LIABILITIES + CAPITAL ACCOUNTS
	Nonbank public demand deposits −$1,000,000 (a)
	U.S. government demand deposits +$1,000,000 (a)
U.S. government securities −$1,000,000 (b)	U.S. government demand deposits −$1,000,000 (b)

Entries labeled (a) show the effects of the tax surplus; entries labeled (b) show the effects of the security retirement on commercial banks.

Deficits. When the federal government spends more than it collects in taxes, funds must be found to meet the excess of expenditure. Two alternatives exist. The Treasury may print more currency and use it to meet the deficit, or it may borrow the funds. In the United States the first alternative has not been considered acceptable. Therefore, the Treasury resorts to borrowing: it issues new government securities. The principal purchasers of new securities are the nonbank public and the commercial banking system.

When funds are borrowed from the commercial banking system, there is initially an increase in commercial bank holdings of U.S. government securities and an equal increase in Treasury tax and loan accounts. Since the banks have used some of their capacity for loan and investment expansion to buy government securities, their abilities to make loans to the nonbank public is decreased. Subsequently, as the Treasury spends the proceeds of the loan, money balances will be transferred to the nonbank public. The net effect of financing a deficit in this manner is an increase in the demand deposit holdings of the nonbank public and thus in the stock of money.

A deficit need not always result in an increase in the stock of money, however. If the Treasury were to sell securities to the nonbank public, for example, there would be no change in the money stock. Instead, demand deposits would be transferred from one part of the nonbank public—those who bought bonds—to the U.S. Treasury, and then in turn to another part of the nonbank public—those who sell goods and services to the Treasury. Thus, money balances would simply be redistributed among the members of the nonbank public. The impact of this redistribution of deposit ownership, however, is not likely to be neutral. Those who produce goods and services for sale to the Treasury generally utilize their money balances more intensively than those who purchase securities. As a result, the velocity of the money supply will increase, thereby leading to increased expenditures in the economy.

It is very dangerous to finance a deficit in an inflationary period by selling new securities to the central bank. If the Treasury were to sell securities to the Federal Reserve banks and then spend the proceeds, commercial bank reserves and demand deposits would initially increase by an equal amount. Without offsetting action by the central bank, the banking system could then create deposits by a multiple of the volume of excess reserves created by the rise in total reserves. This would set in motion more inflationary forces. It is equally dangerous to finance a deficit by directing the central bank to support the government bond market by purchasing securities previously purchased by the nonbank public and the commercial banking system. The results are the same as if the central banking system had bought the securities in the first place—commercial bank reserves increase. It was in precisely this manner that a large part of our World War II deficits were financed, and the result was continued inflationary pressures in the economy.

Debt management and economic fluctuations. As we have seen, Treasury debt management techniques can affect commercial bank reserve positions and money-creating abilities in a variety of ways. Refunding may expand or contract reserves, depending on whose securities are retired and who purchases the new securities. To the extent that the central banking system buys new securities, bank reserves will probably increase. To the extent that the central banking system has its security holdings retired, bank reserves will probably decrease, unless the Federal Reserve also buys new securities. In addition, a Treasury surplus reduces bank reserves when it is used to retire securities held by the Federal Reserve. A deficit expands reserves when the Federal Reserve banks buy newly issued government securities.

Normally, however, the Treasury does not make debt management decisions for the specific purpose of regulating the economy through the banking system. It uses debt management to complement the activities of the Federal Reserve, not to interfere with them. However, *the principal job of regulation is left to the Board of Governors of the Federal Reserve System.* This is not to say that there is never any Treasury interference with Federal Reserve policy actions. The support of the government bond market by the

Federal Reserve during and after World War II is an excellent example of how a decision to manage the debt in a particular way—in this case to keep the interest burden low—can interfere with the monetary authorities' control of the banking system.

From the point of view of economic stability, it is advisable for the Treasury to avoid changes in the maturity, ownership, and interest yields of the federal debt that provoke procyclical reactions in the economy. Whenever possible, debt management decisions should be contracyclical.

What would be appropriate contracyclical Treasury debt management policy? In a *recession,* the following guidelines might be used: First, if there is a deficit and the recession is severe, then the debt should be financed through the sale of securities to the central banking system.[2] However, if the recession is mild, the securities should be sold either to the commercial banks or to the nonbank public. In a mild recession, the economy may be overstimulated by the sharp increase in reserves that arises from central bank security purchases. Second, if there is a tax surplus (which is unlikely in recession), it should not be used to retire securities held by the central banking system, since this would reduce commercial bank reserves. Instead, it should be employed to retire securities held either by commercial banks or by the nonbank public. This would help reduce somewhat the deflationary effects of the surplus itself. Third, new security issues and debt retirement should be manipulated in such a way that the *maturity structure of the debt is shortened.* The growth and prosperity of the economy are in large part dependent upon business investment expenditures. If the Treasury were to lengthen the maturity of the debt by selling long-term securities in a recession, it is possible that there would be a reduction of funds available for business investment. Government debt is virtually riskless in terms of the ability of the borrower to repay it. Since private securities, on the other hand, generally involve some element of risk, lenders may be more inclined to purchase long-term government securities in a recession than corporate bonds. It is therefore advisable for the Treasury to shorten the maturity of the debt, permitting long-term funds to be channeled into business investment.

In an inflation, these policies should be reversed. First, if there is a deficit, it should not be financed by selling securities to the central bank. Such a move would be extremely inflationary. Second, if there is a surplus, it should be used to retire securities held primarily by the central bank. This will draw down the reserves of commercial banks and thus reduce

[2] An even more efficient way of financing increased government expenditures during severe recession would be pure money creation. Were the central bank able to finance the increased expenditures by creating money without simultaneously purchasing new Treasury securities, there would be no increased interest burden on taxpayers and no accompanying problem of the deflationary aspects of possible future debt retirement. So drastic a measure would be advisable only for depressions of the magnitude experienced in the 1930's, however. Given an irresponsible legislature and executive, this policy could be disastrous in periods of full employment.

their money-creating potential. Third, the maturity structure of the debt should be lengthened. If the Treasury concentrates on the sale of long-term securities, long-term funds may be drawn away from business investment, thereby reducing inflationary pressures. Unfortunately, this is precisely the period in which the Treasury may find it difficult to market long-term issues. During periods of full employment and inflation, interest rates are bid up by competitors for funds. Since the Treasury is prohibited by law from marketing issues maturing in five or more years at interest yields in excess of $4\frac{1}{4}$ percent, it is difficult for government securities to compete with private enterprise for long-term funds.

The Treasury made some effort to lengthen the maturity structure of the debt during the 1960's. From the latter months of the 1960–61 recession to September 1964, the average maturity of U.S. government marketable securities held by the public increased from fifty-four months to sixty-six months.[3] Much of this change in the composition of the debt was accomplished through the use of a new technique, advanced refunding. Under this system, the Treasury offered owners of government securities new, longer-term issues in exchange for their old securities prior to the time they were due to mature. To induce bondholders to make the exchange, the new securities had a higher yield. However, starting in 1965 the Treasury found it increasingly difficult to use the advanced refunding technique. The expanded Viet Nam war effort required increased Treasury financing; competing domestic interest rates also increased. The net effect was to again reduce the maturity structure of the federal debt. From the middle of 1965 to the middle of 1968 the average maturity of marketable securities decreased from five years four months to four years two months.[4]

OTHER FINANCIAL PROGRAMS

The list of government agencies engaged in lending and insuring debt is almost too long to enumerate. We have noted in earlier chapters that the FDIC insures the deposit liabilities of commercial banks and mutual savings banks up to a maximum of $15,000 per account. The Federal Savings and Loan Insurance Association insures savings and loan share accounts up to the same amount. In addition, Federal lending and insurance programs are concentrated principally in three fields: agriculture, business, and housing. Federal activity in these fields involves both direct loans and participation in, or insurance of, private loans.

The Small Business Administration is the federal agency presently engaged in business lending. Various types of agricultural loans are made by the Rural Electrification Administration, the Farmers Home Administration, the Commodity Credit Corporation, and the Federal Land Banks.

[3] Thomas R. Beard, *U.S. Treasury Advanced Refunding* (Washington, D.C.: Board of Governors of the Federal Reserve System, 1966), p. 12.
[4] *Wall Street Journal*, March 31, 1969, p. 1.

In addition, the Federal Intermediate Credit Banks are a source of funds for other agencies that lend to agriculture. Finally, various federal agencies are extensively engaged in extending or insuring real-estate credit. There was $247.3 billion in mortgaged debt outstanding on nonfarm family-unit dwellings in 1968. One-third of this debt was either insured by the Federal Housing Administration or guaranteed by the Veterans Administration.[5] The Federal Home Loan Bank Board and the Federal National Mortgage Association also have a significant impact on real-estate credit. These two agencies will be discussed separately in the following section.

How important are these extensive federal loan and insurance programs for monetary stability? Because they are designed to help particular industries, individual home purchasers, and specific firms, they may have procyclical effects. For example, in periods of full employment and rising prices, it frequently becomes difficult for small businesses to borrow for purposes of expansion. As the Federal Reserve makes it increasingly difficult for commercial banks, which are an important source of funds for small business, to lend, they will lend only to their larger, and presumably more credit-worthy, customers. Small businesses then turn to the Small Business Administration for funds. As the lending activity of the SBA expands, total lending in the economy increases. Thus, by providing additional funds in a period of inflation, a federal agency may make it more difficult for the Federal Reserve to regulate economic activity.

On the average, it appears that the various federal credit programs have behaved perversely relative to economic activity. One study of these programs in the 1950's argued that "Since World War II they have created inflationary pressures in every year." [6] During the 1950's, the net change in total credit extended by federal agencies was positive in each year. Except for the recessions of 1953–54 and 1957–58, however, at least some *decrease* in credit extended was called for on contracyclical grounds. Thus, for the period through 1958, it seems reasonable to conclude that federal credit programs frequently had a procyclical effect.

The record for the 1960's is not much better. Table 14–2 summarizes the lending and insurance activity of various federal agencies since 1959. Agricultural loans by Banks for Cooperatives, a federal program, increased in 1959 but remained steady during the recession of 1960–61. Subsequently their loans increased every year through 1968. Federal Intermediate Credit Bank loans and discounts expanded in every year from 1959 to 1968. Mortgage loans of the Federal Land Banks likewise increased every year during that same period.[7] Thus the last two groups, the Federal Land Banks and Federal Intermediate Credit Banks, acted

---

[5] *Federal Reserve Bulletin,* April 1969, p. A–50.
[6] Warren A. Law, "The Aggregate Impact of Federal Credit Programs on the Economy," in Commission on Money and Credit, *Federal Credit Programs* (Englewood Cliffs, N.J.: Prentice-Hall, 1963), p. 310.
[7] *Federal Reserve Bulletin,* various issues 1960–68.

TABLE 14–2. BALANCE-SHEET ITEMS FOR VARIOUS FEDERAL CREDIT AGENCIES, 1959–68

(IN MILLIONS OF DOLLARS)

YEAR	Federal Home Loan Bank advances (end of period)	Federal Home Loan Bank advances (during period)	Federal National Mortgage Association mortgage holdings (end of period)	Banks for Cooperatives loans to cooperatives (end of period)	Federal Intermediate Credit Banks loans and discounts (end of period)	Federal Land Banks mortgage loans (end of period)	FHA insured residential loans made	VA guaranteed residential loans made
1959	2,134	2,067	5,531	622	1,397	2,360	7,694	2,787
1960	1,981	1,943	6,159	649	1,501	2,564	6,293	1,985
1961	2,662	2,882	6,093	697	1,650	2,828	6,546	1,829
1962	3,479	4,111	5,923	735	1,840	3,052	7,184	2,652
1963	4,784	5,601	4,650	840	2,099	3,310	7,216	3,045
1964	5,325	5,565	4,412	958	2,247	3,718	8,130	2,846
1965	5,997	5,007	4,731	1,055	2,516	4,281	8,689	2,652
1966	6,935	3,804	7,063	1,290	2,924	4,958	7,320	2,600
1967	4,386	1,527	8,870	1,506	3,411	5,609	7,150	3,405
1968	5,259	2,734	11,387*	1,577	3,654	6,126	8,275	3,774

* Includes mortgage holdings of Government National Mortgage Association and Federal National Mortgage Association. Since 1968, GNMA has carried on the former special assistance and liquidity and management functions of FNMA.

SOURCE: *Federal Reserve Bulletin*, September 1965, pp. 1314, 1321; and April 1969, pp. A–37, A–49, A–50.

procyclically except in the 1960–61 recession. Banks for Cooperatives operations were always procyclical.

FHA insured mortgages likewise behaved procyclically in the early 1960's, increasing prior to the 1960–61 recession, decreasing during the recession, and increasing through 1965. Although the FHA made fewer loans in 1966 and 1967, this was not due to a concern for contracyclical policy, but rather was due to the fact that interest yields on FHA insured mortgages were significantly lower than those on conventional mortgages. Hence there was a reluctance on the part of lenders to purchase them. This is reflected in the activity of the Federal National Mortgage Association, which sharply increased its holdings of FHA insured mortgages in 1966 and 1967. VA guaranteed mortgages behaved procyclically until 1964. The new GI Bill of Rights and the increased size of the Armed Forces during the Viet Nam conflict make it difficult to interpret the data concerning VA guaranteed mortgages following 1964.

The Federal Home Loan Bank Board [8]

The Federal Home Loan Bank System is composed of four groups: the Federal Home Loan Bank Board, eleven Federal Home Loan Banks, the member institutions, and the Federal Savings and Loan Insurance Corporation. The Board, which consists of three members appointed by the President for four-year terms, is the principal regulatory authority and controls the entire system. The Federal Home Loan Banks extend credit to member institutions, which are principally state-chartered and federal savings and loan associations. A few savings banks are members, and membership in the system is also open to insurance companies. The functions of the Federal Savings and Loan Insurance Corporation are similar to those of the FDIC.

Savings and loan associations are an important source of real-estate credit. As we noted in Chapters 8 and 13, mortgage loans are their principal asset. Increases in savings and loan share accounts provide most of the funds available to the associations for investment. However, borrowings from regional Federal Home Loan Banks are another source of funds. These borrowings can be used for emergencies, for balancing seasonal flows of funds, and for meeting the demand for mortgage funds when local increments in savings and loan share accounts are not sufficient to do so.

Borrowings from district banks. The maximum amount any member can borrow from the Federal Home Loan Banks is set by statute at 50

[8] E. Warren Shows, of the University of South Florida, has made available for the preparation of this section some material from his *The Performance of Savings and Loan Associations in a Metropolitan Market Area,* unpublished Ph.D. dissertation, Georgia State University, 1968.

percent of its liability for shares and deposits. Within this limitation, regional banks establish lines of credit for each member in the district. In addition to the statutory limitation, the Federal Home Loan Bank Board has established a basic limitation on borrowing for expansion purposes. Such borrowing cannot exceed $17\frac{1}{2}$ percent of a member's withdrawable accounts. Rates charged for new advances and existing loans are determined by the regional banks' cost of borrowing. A borrowing member must hold stock in its Federal Home Loan Bank equal to $\frac{1}{12}$ of 1 percent of its indebtedness to the bank, and all members must hold stock in the system equal in value to not less than 1 percent of the net balance of their mortgage loans.

One of the original objectives of the Federal Home Loan Bank System was to provide funds to member associations for expansion. Funds were to be made available to members where local savings were inadequate for such purposes. As Chapter 13 pointed out, this objective has since been modified. During the 1960's, the Federal Home Loan Bank Board discovered that many borrowers were making unsafe loans. As a result, it acted to restrict the use of system credit by members. Although the 50 percent statutory limitation on all borrowing and the $17\frac{1}{2}$ percent limit for expansion borrowing established the basic limits of member borrowing, the Board enacted further limitations and restrictions in 1964 and 1965. For example, in December 1964 it ruled that only savings and loan associations with scheduled items equal to less than 4 percent of assets could borrow up to $17\frac{1}{2}$ percent of savings capital for expansion. If this ratio exceeded 6 percent, expansion borrowing was limited to 5 percent of savings capital.

In September 1965 the Board issued a policy statement to regional banks forbidding advances to members for participation loans involving associations outside the borrowing member's normal lending area. In November 1965 the Board advised regional banks that member borrowing in anticipation of future needs violated the System's general policy on advances. In April 1965 the Board had recommended to the regional banks that the borrowing privileges of members that had raised dividend rates at the end of the preceding year be restricted. As a result of this policy, and the use of Regulation Q by the Federal Reserve in late 1965, the ability of savings and loan associations to compete for funds was severely diminished. The rate of growth of the associations began to decline, and lending for construction purposes was curtailed. The subsequent drop in construction activity, as we noted in Chapter 13, helped restrict spending. Thus, for the first time in its history, the Federal Home Loan Bank Board was following a contracyclical economic policy. For reasons discussed earlier, the Board abandoned this policy in July 1966. Since that time the Federal Reserve and the Federal Home Loan Bank Board have cooperated to reduce the competition among savings and loan associations and commercial banks for individual-type time deposits.

Evaluation. The Federal Home Loan Bank Board, like the U.S. Treasury and most government agencies other than the Federal Reserve, is not charged with the responsibility of regulating the stability of the economy. However, because its actions do affect credit conditions and the ability of savings and loan associations and commercial banks to lend, it is prudent for the Board to coordinate its policies with those of the Federal Reserve. It now attempts to do this.

The Federal National Mortgage Association

The Federal National Mortgage Association received its charter in 1938 with the passage of the National Housing Act. This act was intended to assist the home-construction industry at that time and to provide financing for mortgages. Until 1968 it operated as a quasi-governmental agency, but it now acts as a public stock company. Congress passed enabling legislation in 1968 to permit it to operate as a private enterprise.

The principal and best-known function of FNMA is its secondary market operations. These operations provide assistance to the home-mortgage market by increasing the liquidity of mortgages at times when the normal buyers of mortgages are not active in the market. The FNMA does not make mortgage loans directly, but offers to buy those held by other institutions. It also stands ready to sell mortgages from its portfolio.

Any institution wishing to sell mortgages to the FNMA must purchase common stock in the association in an amount equal to .5 percent of the funds to be committed by the FNMA. To be acceptable for purchase by the FNMA under its secondary market operations, each mortgage must cover residential property and must have been insured by the FHA or guaranteed by the VA on or subsequent to August 1954. The unpaid principal balance shall not be less than $5,000, and there must be a minimum unexpired term of ten years.[9]

At present there are 3,400 banks, mortgage companies, and realty firms authorized to do business with the FNMA. Since 1954, $11.4 billion in mortgages have been purchased. In 1968, $1.9 billion in mortgages were purchased and $0.4 million were sold.[10] *It is the intention of the FNMA to act as a temporary holder of mortgages. Theoretically, it buys at a time when there are no other buyers and sells when the demand for mortgages is on the increase.* It finances its operations through the sale of debentures in the private market, the sale of common stock, and the liquidation of holdings. The extent to which the association may borrow funds is set by statute at 20 times its total capital, surplus, reserves, and undistributed earnings.

When a mortgage is purchased and becomes part of its secondary market portfolio, the FNMA can service the mortgage directly or pay the seller

[9] "Sellers Guide Supplement," Federal National Mortgage Association, August 13, 1969.
[10] Federal National Mortgage Association, *Annual Report,* December 31, 1968.

of the paper to receive and transfer payments to it. The latter method is the prevailing practice, and the servicing firm receives a fee of .5 percent of the mortgage for handling this function. The home owner is never aware that his mortgage is owned by FNMA.

Evaluation. Table 14–2 shows the level of FNMA mortgage holdings from 1959 to 1968. These figures show the very dramatic role played by the FNMA in the 1966 money squeeze. During this period FNMA became a primary market for mortgages, as sellers scrambled to dump any available paper they had on the market. *The actions of FNMA can thus be procyclical.* Its purchase of low-yield mortgages in 1966 provided other institutions, such as commercial banks and savings and loan associations, with funds which these financial institutions used to make more lucrative high-yield mortgage loans at prevailing high-interest rates. The FNMA continued to expand its holdings into 1968; it held $11.4 billion in mortgages in December 1968, in contrast with only $8.9 billion twelve months earlier.

Supplementary Readings

Beard, Thomas R. *U.S. Treasury Advanced Refunding.* Washington, D.C.: Board of Governors of the Federal Reserve System, 1966.
Commission on Money and Credit. *Fiscal and Debt Management Policies.* Englewood Cliffs, N.J., Prentice-Hall, 1963.
————. *Federal Credit Agencies.* Englewood Cliffs, N.J., Prentice-Hall, 1963.

CHAPTER 15

Commercial Bank Reserves and the Money Supply

Although economists are agreed that variations in the money stock affect economic activity, there is some controversy as to the precise nature of the relationship. The following basic statement is generally considered axiomatic, however. *If an increase in the desire to spend is accompanied by either an increase in the stock of money or an increased turnover of a given money stock, then spending will rise and so will the level of general economic activity.* On the other hand, if a decreased desire to spend is accompanied by a decrease in the stock of money or its turnover, spending will decline and an economic recession will occur. Whether monetary changes *cause* spending changes or merely *accompany* them, variations in the money supply are clearly related to the level of economic activity. Because the volume of money is primarily dependent upon commercial bank reserve positions, the Federal Reserve seeks to stabilize the economy by regulating the level of reserves.

We shall examine the influence of the money supply on the economy in detail in Part III. To understand this influence, however, certain basic points on the quantitative determination of the money stock must first be studied. Thus it is advisable to review briefly the factors determining the money stock covered in Part I. We shall also examine in this chapter the quantitative determination of member bank reserves by the forces covered in Chapters 11 to 14.

REVIEW

We have said that money is anything generally acceptable as a means of extinguishing debt. It facilitates the exchange of goods and services and acts as a store of value. In the United States, money consists of currency and demand deposits owned by the nonbank public. Other liquid assets perform *some* of the functions of money, but none are as convenient for use in transactions or as completely free from the possibility of default.

The volume of currency depends largely on the demands of the public, since our central bank, the Federal Reserve, will supply almost any amount of currency demanded. Changes in the volume of currency outstanding are usually accompanied by opposite changes in the volume of demand deposit money. Because the U.S. government does not normally create currency to meet its own obligations, increases in the volume of currency occur only when individuals and businesses demand currency in exchange for demand deposit money. When this happens, commercial banks use their reserve accounts at the Federal Reserve banks to acquire the additional currency. Conversely, the amount of currency in circulation decreases when currency is exchanged for demand deposits. Commercial banks then deposit their excess currency holdings with the Federal Reserve banks and their reserve accounts are increased.

Shifts in the volume of demand deposits are more significant than currency changes. The largest increases in demand deposit money take place when commercial banks extend loans and make investments. In turn, demand deposits contract when loans and investments are retired.

The ability of an individual bank to create money (demand deposits) is limited by the volume of its excess reserves. The ability of the commercial banking system to create money also depends upon its excess reserve position. Because it operates under a fractional reserve requirement, however, the banking system can create a volume of deposits that is a multiple of its excess reserves. Similarly, when there is a deficiency of reserves, the banking system must contract deposits by a multiple of the reserve shortage.

Thus, the banking system's reserve position and its ability to create money depend upon (1) R, the volume of its reserves, (2) r, the reserve requirement for demand deposits, (3) TD, the volume of time deposits, (4) r', the reserve requirement for time deposits, (5) c, the ratio of currency to demand deposits that is currently desired by the public, and (6) i', the ratio of working balances of excess reserves to demand deposits desired by the banking system. Of these various factors, R, r, and r' depend principally upon Federal Reserve policies or, in the case of nonmember banks, upon state banking authorities. TD and c, on the other hand, depend upon the desires of the public. Only i' depends directly upon commercial bank policy. In Chapter 7 all these factors were combined into equations 7–4,

$$\Delta D = \frac{\Delta A}{r + c + i'} \qquad [7\text{–}4]$$

and 7–5,

$$D = \frac{R - r'(TD)}{r + i'} \qquad [7\text{–}5]$$

D is the volume of demand deposits the commercial banking system can support, given the other five factors; ΔD is the potential change in D given r, c, i', and some change in reserves, ΔA. Note that D refers to the volume of demand deposits the system *can* support, not the volume it will actually create.

To determine just how much money (currency and demand deposits) the economy has, it is not enough that we have information on just those factors that affect reserve positions. The amount of money in the economy depends on the interaction of the public's demand for money and the willingness and ability of the banking system to supply it.

THE QUANTITATIVE DETERMINATION OF MEMBER BANK RESERVES

Bank reserve positions cannot be considered the sole element determining the volume of demand deposit money in the economy. However, they are generally regarded as the most critical factor.

As noted in Chapters 10 through 13, the Federal Reserve is held responsible for promoting a stable and growing economy by manipulating member bank reserve positions. It does this by open market operations, reserve requirement changes, and discount rate manipulations. Of these techniques, open market operations are employed the most frequently. They are used to augment or decrease member bank reserves for dynamic contracyclical purposes, and they are also used for defensive purposes—to meet seasonal needs or unanticipated reserve difficulties.

Many forces directly affect the volume of member bank reserves. This section summarizes *all* the forces that quantitatively determine the volume of reserves—forces that the Federal Reserve must consider when engaging in open market operations. Although we shall focus here on member bank reserves, this does not mean that nonmember banks are unimportant; they are very important for the communities in which they are located. In the aggregate, however, the volume of demand deposits created by member banks is significantly larger. Member banks, as a group, also carry on a larger volume of banking activity. One note of caution applies to the following analysis: showing *how* member bank reserves change quantitatively in response to other factors does not explain *why* they change.

Factors Supplying Reserve Funds

Table 15–1 lists the various factors that tend to increase or decrease member bank reserves. Those that supply reserves are called *sources of funds*. When they increase, member bank reserves with Federal Reserve banks tend to increase. When they decrease, member bank reserves tend to decrease. This should not be taken to mean, however, that an increase or decrease in a source of funds *must* increase or decrease reserves. Other factors may offset its effect. For example, a gold-stock increase should lead to an increase in reserves, but if the increased reserves are not desirable from a contracyclical standpoint, the Federal Reserve may decide to sell government securities to depress reserves. In itself, an increase in a source of funds tends to increase reserves. However, this may not happen if there is an offsetting decrease in some other source of funds. Thus it is the *total* change in bank sources of funds that is important for the purpose of member bank reserve determination.

In addition to sources of funds, there are *uses of funds*. These uses compete with reserves in that they tend to absorb and thereby reduce them. When the uses of funds increase, member bank reserves with Federal Reserve banks tend to fall. When they decrease, member bank reserves with the Federal Reserve banks tend to increase.

As Table 15–1 shows, sources of funds increased by $4.219 billion from August 1967 through August 1968. Uses of funds, other than member

TABLE 15–1. FACTORS SUPPLYING RESERVE FUNDS,
AUGUST 1967 AND AUGUST 1968
(IN MILLIONS OF DOLLARS)

AVERAGES OF DAILY FIGURES— RESERVES AND RELATED ITEMS	AUGUST 1967	AUGUST 1968	CHANGES IN FACTORS FROM AUGUST 1967 TO AUGUST 1968
Factors supplying reserve funds			
(sources of funds)			
Federal Reserve credit			
U.S. government securities	46,612	52,646	+6,034
Discounts and advances	89	568	+ 479
Float	1,423	1,759	+ 336
Other	86	74	− 12
Total	48,210	55,047	+6,837
Gold stock	13,053	10,367	−2,686
Treasury currency outstanding	6,665	6,733	+ 68
Total	67,928	72,147	+4,219
Factors absorbing reserve funds			
(uses of funds)			
Currency in circulation*	45,011	48,193	+3,182
Treasury cash holdings	1,488	812	− 676
Treasury, foreign, and other deposits			
with Federal Reserve banks	1,617	1,592	− 25
Other Federal Reserve accounts	212	− 102	− 314
Total	48,328	50,495	+2,167
Member bank reserves with Federal			
Reserve banks	19,600	21,652	+2,052
Total	67,928	72,147	+4,219
Addendum			
Member bank reserves with Federal			
Reserve banks	19,600	21,652	+2,052
Currency and coin	4,191	4,409	+ 218
Total	23,791	26,061	+2,270

* Includes currency and coin held as vault cash by commercial banks.
SOURCE: *Federal Reserve Bulletin*, September 1968, p. A–4.

bank reserves with Federal Reserve banks, increased by \$2.167 billion in the same period, however. Subtracting the increase in the factors absorbing reserves from the increase in the sources of funds leaves a \$2.052 billion increase in member bank reserves with the Federal Reserve banks.

The relationship between member bank reserves held with the Federal Reserve banks and the sources and uses of funds can be conveniently summarized as follows:

> Member bank reserves
> with Federal Reserve = sources of funds − uses of funds [15–1]
> banks

Breaking this simple formula down into its components, we have:

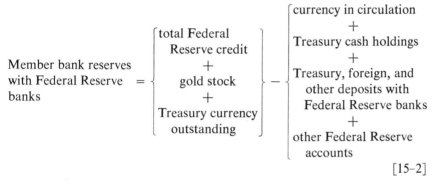

Member bank reserves with Federal Reserve banks =
{ total Federal Reserve credit + gold stock + Treasury currency outstanding }
−
{ currency in circulation + Treasury cash holdings + Treasury, foreign, and other deposits with Federal Reserve banks + other Federal Reserve accounts }

[15–2]

Almost all these factors were discussed in Chapter 11 in examining the influence of various Federal Reserve balance-sheet items on member bank reserves. Here, however, U.S. Treasury balance-sheet items are also considered.

Federal Reserve credit. The major source of funds is Federal Reserve credit. When the Federal Reserve purchases bankers' acceptances, makes discounts and advances, buys U.S. government securities, and finds that "float" is expanding, there is a direct increase in member bank reserves. Conversely, when these sources of funds decrease, member bank reserves decrease.

Gold stock. The second most important source of funds until 1968 was our gold stock. As the Treasury buys gold using its accounts at Federal Reserve banks, member bank reserves are increased; as it sells gold, reserves are diminished. The value of our gold stock differs somewhat from the total value of the gold certificate reserves of the Federal Reserve banks. When the Treasury buys or sells gold, it almost always issues or retires an equal amount of gold certificates. However, not all Treasury gold holdings are used as the basis of issues of gold certificates; the Treasury keeps a small volume of gold balances idle. For example, the gold stock at the end of August 1968 was $10.367 billion; total gold certificates held by the Fed amounted to only $10.025 billion.[1]

Treasury currency outstanding. The third source of funds is Treasury currency outstanding, the total value of currency issued by the Treasury. As noted in Chapter 11, when the Treasury issues additional currency, the Federal Reserve banks purchase it by increasing the Treasury's general account. Member bank reserves then increase as the Treasury spends its increased deposit balances. Although this factor accounts for approximately 10 percent of all sources of funds, changes in Treasury currency have been less dramatic than either Federal Reserve credit or gold stock changes. Only $68 million out of the total $4.219 billion change in sources of funds from August 1967 to August 1968 was attributable to changes in Treasury currency outstanding.

Currency in circulation. Uses of funds work in the opposite direction from sources. As uses increase, member bank reserve deposits decrease. The most important use of funds is currency in circulation outside the Treasury and Federal Reserve banks—that is, currency held by the non-bank public or the commercial banking system. Although commercial bank reserves move in the opposite direction from public currency holdings, they need not vary in the opposite direction from currency in circulation. That part of currency in circulation which is held by commercial banks is actually part of their total reserves. Hence, only member bank reserves held with the Federal Reserve banks vary with currency in circulation. Other things being equal, if the public wants additional currency or if commercial banks choose to hold a greater portion of their reserves in the form of vault cash, then member bank reserves with Federal Reserve banks must decline. On the other hand, a return of cash by the public to the banks or a decrease in the fraction of reserves banks wish to hold in the form of vault cash will increase member bank reserves with the Federal Reserve banks.

As can be seen in Table 15–1, currency in circulation is by far the principal competing use for funds. From August 1967 to August 1968, currency in circulation expanded by $3.182 billion; banks picked up $218 million of this increase as vault cash. This means that the currency holdings of the nonbank public increased by $2.964 billion. In the absence of preventative steps by the Federal Reserve, total member bank reserves would have been reduced by the same amount.

Treasury, foreign, and other deposits with Federal Reserve banks; other Federal Reserve accounts. The second most important use of funds competing with reserves is a composite of various Federal Reserve lia-

[1] *Federal Reserve Bulletin,* August 1968, p. A–12. Since 1968, Treasury gold holdings have been almost constant. See p. 261.

bilities and capital accounts—Treasury, foreign, and other deposits with Federal Reserve banks and other Federal Reserve accounts. These factors and their effects on bank reserves were described in some detail in Chapter 11.

Treasury cash holdings. The final competing use of funds is Treasury cash holdings—the cash held by the Treasury in its own vaults. If the Treasury draws down its cash holdings by increasing its cash payments, the nonbank public will receive the funds and part of them will find their way into the banking system, thereby building up commercial bank reserves. If the commercial banks do not wish to hold an increased amount of vault cash, they can send the cash to the Federal Reserve banks and have their reserve deposit accounts increased. In a similar manner, the increase of Treasury cash holdings will draw down member bank reserves with Federal Reserve banks.

THE QUANTITATIVE DETERMINATION OF THE STOCK OF MONEY

Just as we can describe the quantitative determination of member bank reserves, so we can also describe the quantitative determination of the stock of money. The same note of caution, however, applies; showing quantitatively *how* money stock changes in response to various factors does not explain *why* it changes.

Three institutions have the power to vary the money supply: the commercial banking system, the Federal Reserve, and the U.S. Treasury. The components of our money supply—demand deposits, Federal Reserve notes, and Treasury currency—are liabilities of these three institutions.

It will be recalled that assets must equal liabilities plus capital accounts. Those liabilities that are part of the money stock are called *monetary liabilities.* If monetary and nonmonetary liabilities are separated, we have

$$\text{Assets} = \text{Monetary liabilities} + \text{nonmonetary liabilities} + \text{capital accounts} \qquad [15\text{–}3]$$

and

$$\text{Monetary liabilities} = \text{Assets} - \text{nonmonetary liabilities} - \text{capital accounts} \qquad [15\text{–}4]$$

The quantity of the money stock is determined by subtracting the nonmonetary liabilities and capital accounts from the assets of the three institutions that create monetary liabilities. This is shown in Table 15–2.[2]

---

[2] This table is based upon, but not identical with, the "Consolidated Condition Statement" published monthly in the *Federal Reserve Bulletin.* The focus of Table 15–2 is on demand deposits and currency, whereas the "Consolidated Condition Statement" emphasizes total deposits and currency. A description of the "Consolidated Condition Statement" is contained in the Board of Governors of the Federal Reserve System's

TABLE 15–2. FACTORS TENDING TO INCREASE OR DECREASE
THE STOCK OF MONEY,
JULY 26, 1967, AND JULY 31, 1968
(IN BILLIONS OF DOLLARS)

FACTORS	JULY 26, 1967	JULY 31, 1968	CHANGE IN FACTORS FROM JULY 26, 1967 TO JULY 31, 1968
Factors supplying money (assets)			
Gold stock	13.1	10.4	− 2.7
Treasury currency outstanding	6.6	6.7	+ 0.1
Commercial bank loans and investments	338.6	372.1	+33.5
Federal Reserve loans and investments	46.7	52.1	+ 5.4
Total	405.0	441.3	+36.3
Factors absorbing funds supplying money *(liabilities and capital accounts)*			
Nonmonetary liabilities			
Time deposits of commercial banks	177.1	193.4	+16.3
Treasury cash holdings	1.5	0.8	− 0.7
Treasury deposits at Federal Reserve banks	1.2	1.0	− 0.2
Treasury deposits at commercial banks	5.9	5.7	− 0.2
Net foreign deposits	1.8	2.2	+ 0.4
Other nonmonetary liabilities and capital accounts*	44.2	52.1	+ 7.9
Total	231.7	255.2	+23.5
Monetary liabilities			
Currency outside banks	38.6	41.4	+ 2.8
Demand deposits	134.7	144.7	+10.0
Total	173.3	186.1	+12.8
Assets less liabilities and capital accounts	0	0	0

* Computed as the difference between assets and the sum of all other nonmonetary liabilities and monetary liabilities.
SOURCE: *Federal Reserve Bulletin*, August 1968, pp. A–4, A–5, A–18, A–19.

From the relationships established in equation 15–4 and Table 15–2, it can be seen that the money stock will vary directly with changes in assets and inversely with changes in nonmonetary liabilities and capital accounts. All the factors that tend to increase or decrease the stock of money have already been discussed in some other context, principally with respect to commercial bank reserve positions. As a result, the discussion at this point can be relatively brief.

Factors Tending to Supply Money

Commercial bank loans and investments are the greatest source of money. When commercial banks grant loans or make investments, they

---

Supplement to Banking and Monetary Statistics: Section 1—Banks and the Monetary System (1962). It should be noted that Table 15–2, like the "Consolidated Condition Statement," "is a consolidation rather than a combination of the accounts of the components. In the process of consolidation most of the relationships among the components are eliminated" (*Supplement,* p. 3).

either create deposits or put currency into circulation. Conversely, as loans are retired or holdings of investments reduced, commercial bank deposit liabilities are reduced. In addition, since some people repay loans with currency, currency outside banks may also be reduced.

The second largest source of money is Federal Reserve bank loans and investments. When the Federal Reserve buys bankers' acceptances and U.S. government securities from the nonbank public, the stock of money is directly increased. Bank reserves move in the same direction as the stock of money. On the other hand, when the Federal Reserve buys bankers' acceptances and U.S. government securities directly from commercial banks, only bank reserves are initially increased. Similarly, the extension of discounts and advances to commercial banks will directly affect only bank reserves, not the currency and demand deposit holdings of the non-bank public. This type of change in Federal Reserve loans and investments tends to affect "other nonmonetary liabilities and capital accounts" instead of monetary liabilities.

There is an indirect connection between Federal Reserve loans and investments and monetary liabilities even when the nonbank public is not directly involved in the loan and investment change. By purchasing securities from commercial banks or making discounts and advances, the Federal Reserve banks may prevent commercial banks from contracting their assets and, accordingly, the stock of money.

Changes in the gold stock and Treasury currency outstanding may also affect the stock of money. In the past when the buyers and sellers of gold to the Treasury were members of the nonbank public, the money supply varied in direct proportion to the gold stock. To the extent, however, that Treasury currency is issued in response to the need of the nonbank public, there will be an increase in currency in circulation, but no change in the total money stock. Instead, Treasury deposits at Federal Reserve banks will probably increase.

All the factors that tend to supply money expanded by $36.3 billion from July 1967 to July 1968, but the money stock rose by only $12.8 billion in the same period because of an increase in nonmonetary liabilities of $23.5 billion.

Factors Absorbing Funds Supplying Money; the Relationship between Assets and Nonmonetary Liabilities

The funds that are supplied when *assets supplying money increase* need not all go into monetary liabilities. They may also be absorbed by nonmonetary liabilities and capital accounts. As commercial bank loans and investments expand, for example, some borrowers may choose to increase their time-deposit holdings instead of currency or demand deposits. It is quite probable that many of those who receive payment from borrowing businesses will also build up time deposits. For instance, if commercial banks lend $10 million to businesses so that these firms may meet their payrolls, the employees, upon receiving the $10 million, may decide to put $8 million in demand deposits, $1 million in currency, and $1 million in time deposits. This would cause the stock of money to increase by $9 million instead of $10 million. The balance-sheet entries for this transaction would be

BALANCE-SHEET CHANGES FOR THE COMMERCIAL BANKING SYSTEM

ASSETS		LIABILITIES + CAPITAL ACCOUNTS	
Loans and investments	+$10,000,000 (a)	Demand deposits of borrowing businesses	+$10,000,000 (a)
		Demand deposits of borrowing businesses	−$10,000,000 (b)
Vault cash	−$1,000,000 (b)	Demand deposits of payroll recipients	+$8,000,000 (b)
		Time deposits of payroll recipients	+$1,000,000 (b)

Entries labeled (a) show the effects of borrowing, and entries labeled (b) show what happens when the funds are spent by the borrowing firms.

Similarly, if commercial bank loans and investments expand as a result of the purchase of securities from the U.S. government, Treasury demand deposits rather than the demand deposits of the nonbank public increase. Only when the Treasury spends the proceeds of the security sale will monetary liabilities increase.

Asset decreases may also be accompanied by nonmonetary liability decreases. For example, an individual may choose to repay a consumer loan by drawing down his time deposit account rather than his checking account. Thus, changes in the factors supplying money may change either monetary or nonmonetary liabilities.

Changes in money-creating assets are not the only factors that can cause a shift in monetary and nonmonetary liabilities. Changes in one type of liability can affect another type of liability without any change occurring in assets. As a rule, in the absence of asset changes, monetary liability increases and decreases tend to accompany nonmonetary liability decreases and increases, respectively. For example, as noted in Chapter 2, there are frequent transfers between time and demand deposits. A rise in interest rates payable on time deposits will usually induce depositors to build up these accounts and to maintain lower demand deposit balances. On the other hand, when consumers anticipate large capital expenditures they will frequently transfer funds from time to demand deposit accounts.

As Table 15–2 illustrates, time deposits are the principal nonmonetary liability competing with monetary liabilities for funds. In the year from July 1967 to July 1968, time deposits expanded by $16.3 billion, whereas all other factors absorbing funds expanded by only $7.2 billion.

SUMMARY, EVALUATION, AND PREVIEW

Reserve Fund Sources

As sources of funds increase, member bank reserves with Federal Reserve banks increase. As sources of funds decrease, member bank reserves with Federal Reserve banks decrease. In the absence of offsetting vault cash changes, when sources of funds change, total member bank reserves move in the same direction as member bank reserves with Federal Reserve banks.

As uses of funds increase, member bank reserves with Federal Reserve banks decrease. As uses of funds decrease, member bank reserves with Federal Reserve banks increase. Again, in the absence of offsetting vault cash changes, total member bank reserves move in the same direction as member bank reserves with Federal Reserve banks when uses of funds change.

The quantitative determination of member bank reserves should not be viewed mechanically. Actual bank reserve positions are determined by the influence of all the factors giving rise to or absorbing funds. In practice, a factor tending to increase reserves may well be offset by another factor tending to absorb reserves. Table 15–1 and equations 15–1 and 15–2 can be used to show the principal *quantitative reasons* for member bank reserve changes (movements in Federal Reserve credit, gold stock, and currency in circulation). Pinpointing the quantitative reasons for reserve changes, however, is not the same as explaining *why* there was a change. To do the latter, we need to explain the behavior of our monetary authorities (who determine Federal Reserve credit), our balance of payments (which helps determine the size of our gold stock), and the actions of the nonbank public (which determine the nonbank public part of currency in circulation). For example, from August 1967 to August 1968, member bank reserves increased only $2.3 billion, although Federal Reserve credit rose by $6.8 billion. What happened to the additional $4.5 billion in funds? A decrease in gold stock absorbed $2.7 billion, and an increase in currency in the hands of the nonbank public absorbed $2.9 billion. Two principal forces lay behind the changes in the gold stock and in the currency holdings of the nonbank public: (1) the Viet Nam conflict and (2) a Federal Reserve policy of monetary ease.

Money-Stock Sources

The money stock tends to increase as factors supplying money increase and decrease as they decrease. As factors absorbing funds supplying money increase, other things being given, the money stock decreases. As the same absorptive factors decrease, the money stock tends to increase.

Just as the quantitative determination of member bank reserves should not be viewed mechanically, neither should the quantitative determination of the stock of money. The actual stock of money is determined by all the supply-and-demand forces involved. A factor tending to increase the stock of money (such as increased loans and investments) can easily be offset by another factor (such as increased time deposits) that tends to decrease it. Table 15–2 and equations 15–3 and 15–4 merely list the forces that quantitatively determine the stock of money. As in the case of reserve-base determination, we must examine *why* the forces that quantitatively determine the stock of money vary. To do this satisfactorily, a theory of the money supply is needed.

Evaluation and Preview

Equations 7–4 and 7–5 are mathematical representations of the forces that determine reserves and the stock of money quantitatively.

$$\Delta D = \frac{\Delta A}{r + c + i'} \qquad [7\text{--}4]$$

$$D = \frac{R - r'(TD)}{r + i'} \qquad [7\text{--}5]$$

Thus they have the same failings as other descriptive techniques. They merely state relationships between these forces; they do not explain why the relationships exist. As previously noted, the actual amount of money in the economy depends on the interaction of the public's demand for money and the willingness and the ability of the banking system to supply it. In equations 7–4 and 7–5, R, r, and r' are principally supply forces determined by the Federal Reserve, TD and c are demand forces determined directly by the nonbank public, and i' is a supply force depending upon commercial bank policy.

Surprisingly, for a long time, the determination of the money stock has been taught simply in terms of such equations as 7–4 and 7–5 and Tables 15–1 and 15–2. In capsule form, most past explanations of money-stock determination may be stated as follows: money consists of currency outside banks and demand deposits. Since variations in currency can occur only at the expense of demand deposits, the total volume of money depends primarily on demand deposit variations. The ability of the banking system to create demand deposits depends on its reserve base, which in turn is controlled by the Federal Reserve. Depending upon the required reserve ratios, the volume of demand deposits will be some multiple of the reserve base. Hence, it is argued, the volume of money depends upon central-bank policy.

This line of analysis makes two rather untenable assumptions, however: (1) that the commercial banking system reacts passively to changes in its reserve base and (2) that the Federal Reserve selects a specific amount of money that it considers suitable for the economy and counters any move by commercial banks to create a different amount.

The discussions in Chapters 6, 12, and 13 show that these assumptions are not valid. First, commercial banks tend to economize on reserves during periods of economic upturn. They expand loans, the turnover of money, and the money stock in order to profit from rising interest rates. The growth of loans, the turnover of money, and the volume of demand deposits are reduced during economic contraction as interest yields to banks on loans and investments drift downward. Thus, banks react quite vigorously to changes in reserve positions. Furthermore, as shown in Chapter 13, the Federal Reserve sometimes uses free reserves, not the stock of money, as its target variable. More recently it has been argued that the Fed "tries . . . with the aid of its staff to specify for a constellation of variables the ranges of short-term variation that are believed to be consistent with the projected rate of growth and total bank deposits over the next month or so." [3] In addition, the Federal Reserve makes policy changes slowly. All these considerations allow commercial banks substantial latitude in money creation, which they exercise through varying i' in equation 7–4.

So far, in Parts I and II, we have been primarily concerned with the roles that private financial institutions and the government play in the quantitative determination of the money stock. The interaction of the supply and demand for money is first discussed explicitly in Part III, which deals with monetary theory, the study of the relationship of money to aggregate economic activity. Part III seeks to develop a basic understanding of contemporary monetary theory, so that we can see how the principal aggregate economic variables interact to determine income and output. The demand for money and the theory of the money supply are discussed at length in Chapter 20.

[3] Paul Meek, "Discount Policy and Open Market Operations," prepared for the Steering Committee for the *Fundamental Reappraisal of the Discount Mechanism* (Washington, D.C., 1968), p. 9.

PART III

Money and Aggregate Economic Activity

CHAPTER 16

An Introduction
to Monetary Theory

OBSERVATIONS ON THEORY

Like most scientific theory, economic theory may function as a framework of analysis or simply as a series of hypotheses subject to empirical verification. As an analytical framework, economic theory provides a *measure* against which to observe the real world; the framework may or may not correspond to the actual functioning of the economy. A set of economic hypotheses, on the other hand, attempts to *explain* how the world in which we live and work actually operates.

These two views of economic theory are obviously not completely distinct from each other. A set of hypotheses often leads to the formulation of a framework of analysis. Thus, in monetary theory, for example, what we now call the "Keynesian theory" led to the "Keynesian income-expenditure analytical framework," which any economist can use to help explain reality, no matter what set of hypotheses he tentatively accepts.

Most economists strive to make their framework of analysis correspond as closely as possible to reality. Thus, to some extent both aspects of theory have the same ultimate goal. It could be argued that it makes little difference whether economic theory bears a close relation to the real world, so long as it is useful in explaining and predicting the behavior of economic variables. This line of reasoning may be specious, however. It is somewhat like saying that we should continue to use the Ptolemaic system to explain the movements of the planets and stars because that system does a fairly good job of predicting the motions of some heavenly bodies. We have long since put aside the Egyptian astronomer's method because other systems seem to be closer to the reality of cause and effect and give even better results. Similarly, a particular economic theory may do an adequate job of predicting behavior, but it may be completely misleading about the causal forces behind the economic events it forecasts. To have value, economics must improve our understanding of the world. All science is dedicated to this end. Since economics is specifically concerned with the study of our economic and social environment, its framework of analysis and its hypotheses must continuously come closer and closer to an approximately correct interpretation of economic causes, effects, and interrelationships. This can be accomplished only by continual quantitative testing of hypotheses—testing designed not to prove hypotheses but to disprove them. If a proposition is not disproved, it is tentatively accepted until a better explanation is offered. This scientific method of testing theories is sometimes called the *falsification method.*[1] It involves the following steps: (1) formulation of a theory; (2) deduction of conclusions from the theory; (3) comparison of the theory with others; (4) quantitative testing of its conclusions; and (5) tentative acceptance of the theory, if it has not been proven false by the test.

MONETARY THEORY

Monetary theory may be approached in the manner described above. Contemporary economists, when handling problems of income determination, economic fluctuations, and economic growth, treat those problems almost exclusively within the Keynesian income-expenditure analytical framework. Even those economists who reject many of the Keynesian hypotheses concerning money and income nevertheless use the general Keynesian framework as a tool of analysis.

Monetary theory studies the influence of the demand for and supply of money upon prices, interest, output, and employment. Actually, monetary theory is part of a broader area of study—the theory of output and employment determination, sometimes called *macroeconomic theory.* Our purpose here is to place money in its proper perspective within the broader study of macroeconomic analysis. In so doing we will have to spend some time developing that framework of analysis, but our emphasis will be upon money and the demand for it within that framework. A thorough treatment of aggregate economic activity may be found in books on output and employment theory.

The role money plays in the economy is a subject of great controversy among contemporary economists. The disputes are of a theoretical and empirical nature. Most economists would agree that changes in the supply and in the demand for money play a significant role in determining the level of economic activity. The disagreement centers on the mechanism by which these changes influence the economy. Briefly, one position is that interest rates affect the demand for investment goods, which in turn helps determine income and employment. Variations in the stock of money and the demand for money change interest rates and hence affect income and employment. This is the view of many "Keynesian" theorists. Other economists, although they accept the view that money supply and demand

---

[1] Karl Popper, *The Logic of Scientific Discovery* (New York: Basic Books, 1959), Chapter 4.

determine the interest rate, believe in addition that a change in the money supply and in the demand for money may directly affect the demand for various forms of liquid and real wealth, and hence aggregate economic activity. This is the view of many contemporary "quantity" theorists. Ultimately, the differences between these two points of view may be resolved by empirical work.[2]

PREVIEW OF PARTS III AND IV

In Part III we shall first be concerned with the historical development of monetary theory, referring briefly to several economists who have made significant contributions to the development of contemporary theories and our framework of analysis. Having placed our current state of knowledge in historical perspective, we shall then study the Keynesian framework of analysis, using it to examine various contemporary hypotheses concerning the role that money plays in the economy. With this background in theory and analysis we shall then be able to come to grips with the economic policy issues discussed in Part IV.

Supplementary Reading

Popper, Karl. *The Logic of Scientific Discovery*. New York, Basic Books, 1959.

[2] See Chapter 22 for a fuller exposition of these alternative theoretical positions.

CHAPTER 17

The Historical Development of Monetary Theory

INTRODUCTION

In this chapter we shall attempt to summarize the historical development of monetary theory. Because any brief survey is necessarily incomplete, we shall emphasize a selected group of philosophers and economists whose work in some way constituted an advance in economic knowledge or synthesized a stream of analysis. By showing how earlier theorists visualized the relationship between monetary phenomena and the state of economic activity, we can view our contemporary framework of analysis in perspective.

The philosophers of the sixteenth, seventeenth, and eighteenth centuries were concerned with economic problems much like those of today—less than full employment, inflation, and lack of growth in the level of aggregate economic activity. The policy recommendations made then—to expand bank credit and the money stock during periods of depression and restrict the expansion of the money stock during periods of full employment and rising prices—were ones we still hear made today.

On the other hand, most economists of the nineteenth and early twentieth centuries concentrated on problems of the pricing process. They wanted to know how best to allocate productive resources among competing uses and were concerned with how the prices of productive resources and final products are determined. These economists tended to neglect problems of the economy as a whole, largely because they assumed full employment of resources. Although they were aware that less than full employment situations existed, they accepted the view that production creates its own demand. Under this assumption, depression is simply a temporary departure from normal full employment. In the long run, money supply-and-demand changes lead to price changes, but not output and employment, changes.

During the early part of the twentieth century there was a revival of interest in monetary economics and a renewed concern with crises affecting the level of economic activity. Economists sought to develop a framework of analysis that could explain both price behavior and cyclical movements in the economy. Thus, Irving Fisher developed the equation of exchange. Alfred Marshall, John Maynard Keynes, D. H. Robertson, Leon Walras, and A. C. Pigou formulated alternative cash balance equations. These equations, as we shall see, are still widely used by economists to explain not only price level behavior but also output and demand for money changes. Other economists placed greater emphasis on explaining the volatile nature of the economy, its cyclical ups and downs. Irving Fisher wrote on this problem, as did Knut Wicksell, Ralph Hawtrey, and others. They sought a complete theory of the cycle, focusing for the most part on the interest rate as the prime mover. As an economic policy, they advocated central-bank control over the interest rate in order to eliminate recurrent inflations and recessions.

The depression of the 1930's demonstrated the inadequacies of these theories, however. The economic models of the early twentieth century were too elementary to handle the complex problems of our technically advanced society. The old theories reasoned too simply from cause to effect, neglecting the manifold interrelationships between variables. As a result, we were ready for the "Keynesian Revolution" that completely changed our notions about the determination of overall economic activity. We shall analyze these developments at length in Chapters 18 through 21.

THE SIXTEENTH CENTURY

Jean Bodin (1530–96)

Those who write on economic subjects tend to do so within the context of the problems of their age. The fifteenth, sixteenth, and seventeenth centuries were periods of price revolution. Thus, many economic philosophers of the time were concerned largely with explaining why prices had risen.

In his "Reply to the Paradoxes of Malestroit Concerning the Dearness of All Things and the Remedy Therefor," for example, Jean Bodin argued that there were a number of reasons for the rise in French prices during the sixteenth century, the principal ones being the abundance of gold and silver, monopolies, scarcity, the pleasure of princes, and debasement of the coinage.

Bodin's "Reply" was a rebuttal to Malestroit's contention that prices in France were no higher than in the past since goods cost no more gold and silver than formerly. Bodin countered this by citing evidence that wine and wheat cost twenty times what they had a hundred years before and that the price of land, which he assumed to be fixed in quantity and quality, was three times what it had been fifty years earlier. Bodin, however, was not content merely to cite statistics to prove that prices had risen; he was fundamentally concerned with the *causes* of the price rise.

He lists the five causes just cited, the most important of which was the first—the abundance of gold and silver.

I find that the high prices we see today are due to some four or five causes. The principal and almost the only one (which no one has referred to until now) is the abundance of gold and silver, which is today much greater in this Kingdom than it was four hundred years ago, to go no further back.[1]

Bodin goes on to state that the amount of gold and silver, which was used as currency in his time, had increased substantially and that, as a consequence, prices had risen. Here we have one of the first statements linking price movements to movements in the money stock. Bodin also raises this question: if it is the abundance of gold and silver that causes high prices, where does the increase in gold and silver come from? It arises, he explains, from trade with foreigners who have mines of gold and silver at their disposal. Spain, for example, with gold and silver obtained from the mines of Peru, was able to demand increased quantities of goods and services produced in France—wheat, cloth, dyes, paper, and books. England had mines also and, since she could not produce wine, prunes, and dye, bought them from France. Thus, as we would say today, the increased supply of money caused an increased demand for French goods. Prices responded by increasing both at home and abroad.

THE SEVENTEENTH AND EIGHTEENTH CENTURIES

The economic problems of the late seventeenth and much of the eighteenth century were quite different from those of the preceding period in which Bodin wrote. Now the problems were boom and bust, economic distress, and less than full employment. In many ways these problems were much like those of the depression years of this century. Writers of the seventeenth and eighteenth centuries argued that economic activity and trade depended on money and its circulation. They concentrated on the interaction of the demand for goods and services, the stock of money, the quickness of circulation, the volume of employment, and the price level.

John Locke (1632–1704)

John Locke, writing in the 1690's, advanced monetary theory considerably beyond Bodin.[2] Whereas Bodin had been primarily concerned with

---

[1] Jean Bodin, "La Réponse de Jean Bodin aux paradoxes de Malestroit touchant l'encherissement de toutes choses et le moyen d'y remedier," as reprinted in Arthur E. Monroe, ed., *Early Economic Thought* (Cambridge, Mass.: Harvard University Press, 1924), p. 127.

[2] See John Locke, *Consequences of the Lowering of Interest, and Raising the Value of Money*, 1692; and *Further Considerations Concerning Raising the Value of Money*, 1696. For an excellent discussion of Locke and other writers of the eighteenth century,

the effects of money on prices, Locke expanded this discussion by studying the effects of money on trade, the role of the demand for money, and the importance of interest rates in the economy. He held, for example, that money is necessary to carry on trade. If it is not generally available and in circulation, then it is difficult to purchase goods and services. As a result, there is a stoppage of trade. Thus he posited a relationship between money and economic activity, although he did not explain precisely how the relationship operated.

To Locke, money was important in another respect: a certain amount was needed to carry on a specific amount of trade. The amount needed depended upon the "quickness of circulation" of money. Today we would say *"velocity"* of circulation rather than "quickness." Both terms refer to the number of times that the money in the economy is spent, or "turned over," during a given period. The more often money is spent, the more economic activity takes place. The less often it is spent, the lower is the volume of trade. To put it another way, the greater the amount of money people want to hold, the smaller its turnover (velocity) will be, and the greater the amount of money that will be needed to carry on a specific volume of trade. The relative need of the community for the necessities of life and the extent of its commerce thus determine how much money is demanded and consequently, its quickness of circulation. Here, Locke made a significant advance in monetary analysis; this is one of the first formulations of the velocity and the demand for money concepts.

Locke also had a relatively advanced notion of interest. He defined "interest" as the price for the hire of money. Its level is determined by the relationship between the amount of money needed and the amount available. Thus, if the amount needed for trade was great relative to the supply, the interest rate would be high. Furthermore, if the rate of interest were legally to be forced beneath this high level, no additional borrowing could take place because lenders would be unwilling to lend.

John Law (1671–1729)

John Law, aside from his reputation as a romantic adventurer, financier, and organizer of the Banque Royale in France, is best known as the author of *Money and Trade Considered* (1705). Writing in a period of high unemployment, Law argued that trade depends upon money. Hence, the more money there is in the economy, the more likely we are to have full employment.

In Law's time money consisted largely of gold and silver coin. Thus, the more coin there was in circulation, the greater the employment, according to Law's theory. He went further than this, however, and extended

see Douglas Vickers' *Studies in the Theory of Money 1690–1776* (Philadelphia: Chilton Company, 1959).

the argument to bank notes. The more "credit money" in circulation, he said, the more people will be employed. In a period of less than full employment, the monetary authority could get more money into circulation and hence induce a higher level of employment by allowing banks to issue paper currency.

Law did not propose an unlimited issue of paper currency, but a limited one suited to the needs of trade. Thus, there would be no danger of overextending currency. This argument is similar to the "commercial loan theory of banking," also called the "real-bills doctrine," [3] discussed in Chapter 3. Law proposed that the notes issued be secured by the value of land. Thus, the maximum amount of notes that could be issued would be limited by the total value of land. The actual amount in circulation, so long as it was less than the value of land, would depend on the need for money in trade. Hence there would be little change in the value of money, and the amount of money would always be adequate to keep trade and employment active.

The flaw in this argument is that the system depends entirely on a permanent valuation of land. If the price of land were to increase, then more currency could be issued. This would drive up the price of other goods and increase the need for additional money balances. Cumulative price inflation would follow. If, on the other hand, the value of land were to decrease, a reduction in the amount of money in circulation would be necessary, which in turn would reduce trade, the price of other goods, and the need for money. Cumulative price deflation would ensue.

Law's principal contribution to monetary analysis was his attempt to establish a positive relationship between employment, trade, and the amount of metallic and bank money in the economy.

Richard Cantillon (1680–1734)

Richard Cantillon, in his essay "On the Nature of Commerce in General" (written in 1734 and published in 1755), went far beyond Bodin, Locke, or Law in his examination of monetary principles. He did not argue as directly as had his predecessors from money changes to either price or employment changes, however. Instead he was concerned with the process by which money-stock changes affect price. He was apparently one of the first to argue that an increase in the quantity of money raises prices through its effect on demand. Cantillon's contributions, however, valuable as they were, did not directly affect economic thought until the latter half of the nineteenth century, when Stanley Jevons rediscovered his work.

Cantillon's theory of money was principally concerned with the rela-

---

[3] See Lloyd W. Mints' *A History of Banking Theory* (Chicago: University of Chicago Press, 1945), pp. 30–32, for the classic refutation of this doctrine.

tion between money and prices, although he did discuss employment changes to some degree. He wanted to discover how the money-price relation operates. "The great difficulty of this analysis consists in discovering by what path and in what proportion the increase of money raises the price of things." [4] The solution he arrived at was: "that in general an increase in the monetary stock causes in a State a proportional increase in consumption, which by degrees produces the rise of prices." [5] Thus, an increase in the money stock stimulates demand, which eventually leads to price increases.

How does this occur? Cantillon presents several examples, two of which are considered here. First, if the increase in money comes from mining, then the mine owners and those who work the mines will increase their expenditures on food, clothing, and other goods. This gives added employment to artisans, who, in turn, will increase their expenditures. Thus, there will be a multiple round of expenditure and employment increases. In the process, however, prices begin to rise, and those people who did not participate in the initial round of expenditure and employment increases will suffer from the higher prices. Cantillon regards these people as fixed-income recipients; they have only two alternatives—they can reduce their consumption or leave the country. "This, roughly, is how a considerable increase of money from Mines increases consumption; and while diminishing the number of inhabitants, brings about a greater expenditure among those who remain." [6] The increased domestic price level would then induce people to make more purchases abroad, where goods are cheaper. This would cause money to leave the economy, and a reverse cycle of lower money circulation, poverty, and misery would follow.

A second case discussed by Cantillon imagines an increased money stock resulting from a country selling more abroad than it purchases—what we now term a favorable balance of trade. With more money coming into the country than is leaving, there will be a gradual increase in expenditures, consumption, and prices. This time, however, the process will not reverse itself unless the favorable balance of trade is upset.

Thus Cantillon developed a relatively sophisticated theory of how money affects the economy. He did not limit himself to a discussion of the supply of money; he also examined its velocity: "an acceleration, or a greater speed, in the circulation of money in trade amounts to the same thing as an increase in standard money." [7] He showed that an increase in the velocity of money, given the money supply, would increase trade, just as an increase in the money supply, given constant velocity, would increase trade.

[4] Richard Cantillon, "On the Nature of Commerce in General," as reprinted in Arthur E. Monroe, *op. cit.*, p. 264.
[5] *Ibid.*
[6] *Ibid.*, p. 265.
[7] *Ibid.*, p. 264.

THE NINETEENTH CENTURY

There were relatively few developments in monetary theory in the nineteenth century. Economists turned away from the study of the economy as a whole to a study of commodity pricing and resource allocation. When discussing monetary phenomena, they generally assumed a full employment economy. This led them to discuss money changes in terms of price level effects. As a consequence, many of these economists developed what today we would call a "crude theory of money." In essence they maintained that money-stock changes lead to proportionate price level changes. Although they knew of the velocity concept, they usually assumed it to be constant.

Since they were primarily concerned with resource analysis, nineteenth-century economists did not consider short-run unemployment problems. They usually accepted Say's law that "production creates its own demand." According to this theory, when people work and create goods, they receive income, most of which is spent. That which is not spent is saved, but this does not cause demand to fall since funds that are saved will eventually be channeled into investment demand for such goods as plant equipment. Thus the demand for new goods is created by the supply. Because demand is always sufficient to take goods off the market, less than full employment cannot long persist. Today, of course, we have only to point to the depression of the 1930's to see the limitations of this concept.

Some nineteenth-century economists did write about money, however; and men like Thornton, Ricardo, and Mill made a number of contributions to monetary theory.

Henry Thornton (1760–1815)

Thornton wrote during the Napoleonic wars, when the Bank of England refused to convert paper currency into specie (metallic money). Prices rose because of "the restriction," as it was called, and a vigorous monetary debate followed. One group, the bullionists, argued that the value of paper currency had depreciated because it had been issued to excess. The other group, the antibullionists, did not believe that paper currency could be issued to excess if it were issued on the basis of the needs of trade. Here again is the real-bills doctrine. Notice also how this debate centered on the relation between money and prices, not on the relation between money and employment.

Henry Thornton was a bullionist. Here is his view of how money-stock changes lead to price change:

Let us, now, trace carefully the steps by which an encrease of paper serves to lift up the price of articles. Let us suppose, for example, an increased number of

Bank of England notes to be issued. In such case the traders in the metropolis discover that there is a more than usual facility of obtaining notes at the bank. . . . Every trader is encouraged by the knowledge of this facility of borrowing . . . is rendered, by the plenty of money, somewhat more ready to buy, and rather less eager to sell. . . . Thus an inclination to buy is created in all quarters, and an indisposition to sell. Now, since the cost of articles depends on the issue of that general conflict between buyers and sellers . . . it follows, that any circumstance which serves to communicate a greater degree of eagerness to the mind of one party than to that of the other, will have an influence on price.[8]

In Thornton's opinion, an increased money stock will lead to increased demand and consequently higher prices. He does not say that price need rise proportionately to the increase in the money stock. He was well aware that an increase in money may lead to the employment of idle factors of production and hence to more output but not necessarily higher prices. However, he argued that the number of unemployed persons is limited. Hence, once the idle are employed, prices will rise as long as the stock of money continues to increase:

An encreased quantity of articles can only arise from additional commodities either brought from abroad or produced at home through the exertion of new industry. . . .

When the Bank of England, enlarges its paper, it augments, in the same degree, as we must here suppose, its loans to individuals. These favoured persons immediately conceive, and not without reason, that they have obtained an additional though borrowed capital, by which they can push their own particular manufacture or branch of commerce. . . .

But, first, it is obvious, that the antecedently idle persons to whom we may suppose the new capital to give employ, are limited in number; and that, therefore, if the encreased issue is indefinite, it will set to work labourers, of whom a part will be drawn from other, and perhaps, no less useful occupations. . . .

. . . whatever view we take of the subject, we seem obliged to admit, that although additional industry will be one effect of an extraordinary emission of paper, a rise in the cost of articles will be another.[9]

Another of Thornton's contributions is the policy conclusion he draws from his analysis. He argues that the amount of paper money should be limited, that money should neither be issued to excess nor allowed to diminish sharply, in order to limit price variation. As the economy grows in productivity, however, some increase of money stock should be permitted.[10] Economists are still discussing proposals of this sort today.

[8] Henry Thornton, *An Enquiry into the Nature and Effects of the Paper Credit of Great Britain* (London, 1802), pp. 195–96.
[9] *Ibid.*, pp. 257–61.
[10] *Ibid.*, p. 295.

David Ricardo (1772–1823)

Ricardo, like Thornton, was a bullionist. His writing, however, is by no means as succinct as that of Thornton. If we were to judge Ricardo only on the basis of his work in *The Principles of Political Economy and Taxation* (1821), we would be forced to conclude that he was a crude quantity theorist. He argues that the value of paper money can be maintained by limiting its quantity.

In "On the High Price of Bullion," however, he introduces the notion of "rapidity of circulation."

The value of the circulating medium of every country bears some proportion to the value of the commodities which it circulates. In some countries, this proportion is much greater than in others, and varies, on some occasions, in the same country. It depends upon the rapidity of circulation, upon the degree of confidence and credit existing between traders, and above all, on the judicious operations of banking.[11]

In other words, given a constant stock of money and no change in productivity, an increase in the rapidity of circulation (velocity) will lead to a price level increase. When velocity increases, the money supply is being used more often because people demand more goods and services. To get more goods, each individual draws down his money holdings; but collectively money holdings remain the same. This is how velocity increases. People, however, do not get more goods, since more are not available. Hence the increased demand simply bids up the price of goods. Ricardo did not make this extension of the analysis, however. Like other bullionists, he assumed that velocity was as high as possible in Great Britain, and hence was a constant. Because of this erroneous assumption, his statement that the value of money depends on the rapidity of circulation is rendered meaningless.

With respect to economic policy, Ricardo too felt that the amount of paper money issued should be limited because its overissue would lead to price increases.

John Stuart Mill (1806–73)

The works of John Stuart Mill provide us with a synthesis of the classical economics of the nineteenth century. Although well aware of unemployment and business crises, Mill accepted Say's law. As a consequence, his monetary analysis, too, concentrated largely on the relation between money and prices.

Most of Mill's monetary theory is developed in Book III of his *Principles*

---

[11] David Ricardo, "On the High Price of Bullion," as reprinted in Piero Sraffa, *The Works and Correspondence of David Ricardo* (London: Cambridge University Press, 1951), Vol. 3, p. 90.

of Political Economy. He begins with a definition of money that is actually very close to the definition many textbooks use today.

Definition of money. Mill defines money as a medium of exchange and common measure of value. Money is useful because of the inconveniences of barter and the necessity of having something durable in circulation. Gold and silver, thought Mill, are particularly well suited to these purposes; they are portable, imperishable, divisible, and acceptable to all people. "Of all commodities they are among the least influenced by any of the causes which produce fluctuations of value." [12] Furthermore, any change in their value would not be sudden, since their quantity could not readily be diminished or increased.

Value of money. Mill considered money a commodity, the value of which was determined like that of other commodities—temporarily by supply and demand and in the long run by the cost of production. Cantillon and Ricardo had held similar positions.

According to Mill, the value of money depends, other things being equal, upon its quantity and its rapidity of circulation. The purchasing power of money depends first on supply and demand.

The supply of money, then, is the quantity of it which people are wanting to lay out; that is, all the money they have in their possession, except what they are hoarding, or at least keeping by them as a reserve for future contingencies. The supply of money, in short, is all the money in circulation at the time.[13]

This concept of money supply differs from our current understanding of the term in that we include monetary hoards. The demand for money he defines as "all the goods offered for sale." [14] Mill considered only real commodities to be money, whereas our present definition includes demand deposits.

How do demand and supply determine the value of money? "An increase of the quantity of money raises prices, and a diminution lowers them. . . ." [15] Thus, if other things remain unchanged, an increase in the supply of money will increase the demand for goods by an equal amount, and this will lead to a universal rise in prices.

The rapidity of circulation also helps determine the value of money. Mill defines it as "the average number of purchases made by each piece in order to effect a given pecuniary amount of transactions." [16] If the number of transactions and the amount of money is fixed, then the value of money varies inversely with the rapidity of circulation. That is, the higher the

[12] John Stuart Mill, *Principles of Political Economy*, Ashley Edition (London: Longmans Green, 1909), p. 485.
[13] *Ibid.*, p. 490.
[14] *Ibid.*
[15] *Ibid.*, p. 495.
[16] *Ibid.*

rapidity of circulation grows, the less the purchasing power of a particular amount of money will be and the higher the price of goods and services. This is a definition of velocity very much like that later used by Irving Fisher. The basic concept is that the more often money changes hands in the purchase of goods and services, given the amount of goods available, the greater the demand for goods will be and the higher the prices of those goods.

In general, Mill formulated what amounts to a relatively crude quantity theory of money. His other theory of the value of money—the cost of production theory—has been almost universally abandoned.

Credit. Mill does not ignore the importance of credit; on the contrary, he conceives of it as a major determinant of the price level. He feels that credit, no matter what form it takes (bank notes, bills of exchange, promissory notes, or deposits and checks), has an influence on the price level. In fact, it has the same influence on the price level as gold and silver money does. An increase in the volume of credit extension increases the demand for goods, and, accordingly, prices rise. Similarly, an increase in the amount of inconvertible paper currency (paper money that is not convertible on demand into gold and silver coin) causes price increases.[17]

THE EARLY TWENTIETH CENTURY

Economists of the early twentieth century continued in the tradition of nineteenth-century classical economics. They believed that the price level is determined by the volume of money, that relative prices are determined by the supply of and demand for commodities, and that full employment is the normal state of the economy. These scholars did advance monetary theory in two areas, however. First, they formulated alternative analytical approaches to explaining the economic role of money. The Fisher *transactions equation of exchange* and the various Cambridge *cash balance equations* are examples of this development of monetary theory as a framework of analysis. Second, they made a renewed attempt to understand the role of money in short-term cyclical fluctuations, although they usually made little effort to verify their hypotheses empirically. The remainder of this chapter examines these early twentieth-century contributions to monetary theory.

Irving Fisher (1867–1947)

Irving Fisher, an American mathematician and economist, formulated the *equation of exchange,* attempted a statement of the quantity theory of money in the early twentieth century, and developed a theory of the busi-

---

[17] *Ibid.,* Chapters 12 and 13.

ness cycle that was designed to explain economic fluctuations during periods of transition, when prices are rising or falling.

The equation of exchange. The equation of exchange formulated by Irving Fisher was

$$MV + M'V' = \Sigma pQ \qquad [17\text{--}1]$$

where M is the amount of currency in the economy during a given year, V is the velocity of circulation (turnover) of this currency, M' is the volume of demand deposits in the economy during the year, V' is the velocity of circulation of these demand deposits, and ΣpQ is the sum of (1) the average price, p, of a commodity purchased in the economy during the given year multiplied by the quantity, Q, of it purchased, (2) the average price, p', of another commodity purchased during the given year multiplied by the quantity, Q', of it purchased, and (3) so forth for all other goods exchanged. In other words, equation 17–1 is a simplified way of expressing the following equation:

$$MV + M'V' = pQ + p'Q' \ldots \qquad [17\text{--}2]$$

Fisher himself further simplified this equation to

$$MV + M'V' = PT \qquad [17\text{--}3]$$

where P is a weighted average of prices and T is the sum of all the Q's. Strictly speaking, this simplification is not legitimate, since it implies that one can add together such diverse commodities as eggs, guns, and oranges. If each of the symbols in equation 17–3 is expressed as an index number, however, then this criticism no longer applies. P and T would then be indices of prices and quantities respectively. The equation would then show the relative change in each of the magnitudes rather than their absolute values.

Contemporary versions of the equation of exchange. Today, many variants of equations 17–1, 17–2, and 17–3 are used by economists. One particularly popular version is

$$MV = PQ \qquad [17\text{--}4]$$

where M is the average amount of money in the economy during a specified period, such as a year, and V is the number of times this money is spent on PQ, which is the sum of the values of a specified group of goods.[18] There are two principal differences between Fisher's equation of exchange and this contemporary formulation. First, the contemporary definition of M includes both currency and demand deposit money, whereas Fisher's M includes only currency. Second, Fisher's PQ includes all goods and services exchanged during a given period, whereas contemporary

[18] See Chapter 18 for a complementary discussion.

economists usually define PQ in terms of the specific problem they are considering. When the relation between money and gross national product is being considered, for example, PQ refers to gross national product, the value of newly produced final goods and services. V, in this instance, is an *income velocity* concept, showing the number of times that the volume of money, M, is spent on gross national product. When used in this manner, equation 17–4 is sometimes restated as

$$MV = Y \qquad\qquad\qquad [17\text{–}5]$$

where Y is gross national product.

On the other hand, when economists study the relation of the expenditure of money to all goods and services bought and sold, all transactions are considered—dealings in new goods and services, the resale of used goods, financial transactions, and so on. In this case, PQ is much larger than gross national product, and V represents *transactions velocity,* the number of times money is spent on *all* types of goods and services during a given period. This type of velocity figure, of course, is much larger than the figure for income velocity. Fisher's V and V' both represent transactions velocity. Sometimes, when economists wish to emphasize that they are concerned with transactions velocity, they will use the following type of Fisher equation:

$$MV = PT \qquad\qquad\qquad [17\text{–}6]$$

Here M is the average amount of money in circulation during a period, V is the number of times that M is used in the purchase of PT, and PT is the monetary value of all transactions in the economy during the period in question.

The difference between equations 17–5 and 17–6 can be illustrated as follows. Assume that the average amount of money in a given year, t, is $200 billion and that gross national product, Y, is $900 billion. Then, since $MV = Y$ and $200 billion $\times V = $900 billion, V (income velocity) must equal 4.5 in terms of equation 17–5. Thus, the money stock was used 4.5 times in the purchase of gross national product. If in some subsequent time period, $t + 1$, M rises to $225 billion and Y to $1,125.0 billion, then V must also have increased to 5.0.

On the other hand, if M is $200 billion in time period t, and the value of all transactions is, say, $4,000 billion, then, since $MV = PT$, V must equal 20 in terms of equation 17–6. If M rises to $225 billion and PT to $4,200 billion, then V must have declined to 18.66.

One factor that should be stressed concerning the equation of exchange is that the equation itself is a mere truism. No matter what variant of the equation we use, we are merely summarizing what has occurred. The left-hand side, the money side of the equation, must always equal the right-hand side, the goods side. Thus, each side is simply a different way of describing the same phenomena, expenditures. The goods side expresses the value of expenditures; the money side expresses the volume of money multiplied by the number of times it is used so as to lead to the value of expenditures.

The equations themselves contain no statements of causality. Equation 17–4, for example, *does not explain why M, V, P, and Q possess certain values*. It does not tell us how a change in one of the four magnitudes will cause a change in the others. It merely summarizes in convenient form the result of the values of M, V, P, and Q. It is the task of theory, however, as hypothesis, to explain cause and effect. One of the functions of contemporary monetary theory, for example, as developed in Chapter 21, is to explain why velocity changes—whether it is a mere residual caused by changes in the right-hand side of the equation of exchange, or whether it may vary independently of the right-hand terms and thereby directly determine changes in PQ. Thus, monetary theory seeks to define causality. Does a change in V lead to a change in PQ, or does the change in PQ determine the change in V? The equations of exchange alone cannot resolve these questions.

Fisher's use of the equation of exchange. An equation of this sort is merely a *tool* economists use to help explain economic changes. Thus Fisher, having formulated equation 17–3, proceeded to use it to explain economic relationships.

On the basis of the equation of exchange, he gave a precise statement of the *quantity theory of money:*

The price level varies (1) directly as the quantity of money in circulation (M), (2) directly as the velocity of its circulation (V), (3) inversely as the volume of trade done by it (T). The first of these three relations is the most important. It constitutes the "quantity theory of money." [19]

However, he carefully hedges this statement:

The quantity theory . . . does not claim that while money is increased in quantity, *other* causes may not affect M', V, V', and the Q's, and thus aggravate or neutralize the effect of M on the p's. But these are not the effects of M on the p's. So far as M *by itself* is concerned, its effect on the p's is strictly proportional. . . .

We have emphasized the fact that the strictly proportional effect on prices of an increase in M is only the *normal* or *ultimate* effect after transition periods are over. The proposition that prices vary with money holds true only as between imaginary periods for each of which prices are stationary or are moving alike upward or downward and at the same rate.[20]

Thus, it would appear that the quantity theory of money, as formulated by Fisher, is valid only in the long run and when all quantities except M and P are constant.

[19] Irving Fisher, *The Purchasing Power of Money* (New York: Macmillan, 1911), p. 29.
[20] *Ibid.*, pp. 158–59.

As the quotation above shows, Fisher was well aware of how other causes could disturb the relation between money and prices. The factors that he felt would influence the volume of trade, T, are listed in Table 17–1. Fisher felt that historically these outside influences had usually tended to increase T and to decrease P. However, he looked upon them as long-run sources of change. Population, technical knowledge, and capital accumulation changed slowly, but over time would lead to increased T and possible price declines.

TABLE 17–1. FISHER'S OUTSIDE INFLUENCES
ON THE VOLUME OF TRADE

Conditions affecting producers
    Geographical differences in natural resources
    The division of labor
    Knowledge of the technique of production
    The accumulation of capital
Conditions affecting consumers
    The extent and variety of human wants
Conditions connecting producers and consumers
    Facilities for transportation
    Relative freedom of trade
    Character of monetary and banking systems
    Business confidence

SOURCE: Irving Fisher, *The Purchasing Power of Money* (New York: Macmillan, 1911), pp. 74–75.

Fisher also examined the outside causes that affect the velocities of circulation of money and deposits. His classification of these factors is given in Table 17–2. He believed that three sets of forces—individual habits

TABLE 17–2. FISHER'S OUTSIDE INFLUENCES ON THE VELOCITIES
OF CIRCULATION OF MONEY AND DEPOSITS

Habits of the individual
    As to thrift and hoarding
    As to book credit
    As to the use of checks
Systems of payments in the community
    As to frequency of receipts and of disbursements
    As to regularity of receipts and disbursements
    As to correspondence between times and amounts of receipts and disbursements
General causes
    Density of population
    Rapidity of transportation

SOURCE: Irving Fisher, *The Purchasing Power of Money* (New York: Macmillan, 1911), p. 79.

(thrift habits, the habit of charging, and the habit of using checks), the systems of payments in the community, and general causes (density of population and rapidity of transportation)—had tended historically to increase the velocity of circulation of money, and hence to increase prices. As in the case of variations in T, Fisher saw these influences on velocity as long-run factors. Although he seems to have been correct in observing the increase of T, some economists today believe that velocity has tended to decrease rather than increase in the long run. In short-run periods of transition, Fisher believed that there could be substantial variation in velocity.[21]

With respect to outside influences on the volume of deposits, M', Fisher felt that the substitution of checks for cash payments had exerted a powerful influence in the direction of raising prices. Since today we count demand deposits as part of the money stock, Fisher's argument, in modern terms, simply amounts to a statement that an increase in the money stock tends to increase prices. This is another way of stating the Fisher version of the quantity theory.

Fisher concluded that the long-run behavior of T tended to lower prices, but that the long-run effect of changes in V, V', and M' was to raise prices. The cumulative effects of these influences over time could well be significant for price level variation, but in the short run their effects would tend to be negligible. This does not mean that he believed that M and P must always move proportionately in the short run; as we have shown, he felt that M and P need not be proportional in periods of transition.

Fisher's theory of the cycle. Fisher recognized that the relation between money and prices was not rigid and that the economy is generally in a period of transition. He attempted to explain the behavior of prices and the state of economic activity during such periods, which we would term short-run cyclical fluctuations. His explanation is monetary, focusing on interest rate behavior as the source of economic instability: "the peculiar behavior of the rate of interest during transition periods is largely responsible for the crises and depressions in which price movements end." [22]

Economic fluctuations, according to Fisher, occur because the rate of interest fails to respond quickly enough to price changes. In brief, his conception of the business cycle may be described as follows: assume that prices are rising. Because of rising prices and widening profit margins, businesses increase their borrowings at commercial banks. Hence deposit money, M', expands. As these funds are spent, prices rise further, enabling profits to continue to increase and still more borrowing to take place. The cost of borrowing increases, but more slowly than prices. Disturbances in V, V', and the Q's also take place. Because of the apparent good times,

---

[21] Some of the sources of this short-run change in V are mentioned in our subsequent discussion of Fisher's transition-period theory of the cycle. Some contemporary sources of velocity change have already been discussed: (1) commercial bank loan and investment behavior, (2) the development of nonbank financial intermediaries, and (3) the increased use of the credit card.

[22] Fisher, *op. cit.*, p. 56.

increased spending occurs that is not financed solely by increased borrowing. Hence, V and V' increase. Output also rises. Some unemployed workers are drawn into the productive process, but the size of population, the rate of invention, and the efficiency of labor "pretty definitely limit the amount of trade that can reasonably be carried on." [23] Thus the Q's can only increase to a limited extent, and the primary effects of the rising M', V, and V' will be on prices.

This type of expansion cannot continue indefinitely, however. As the boom continues, banks will begin to run short of reserves. As a result, the increase of deposit money will stop, although the cost of borrowing will continue to increase. Profits relative to the cost of borrowing will decrease and borrowing will diminish. In addition, firms that borrowed heavily will find themselves unable to renew their loans at former rates of interest. Some firms may fail and so precipitate a financial panic. Because of the loss of business confidence, the cycle will reverse itself. There is a continuing contraction of loans and deposits, the velocity of money decreases, and people become sufficiently concerned with "solvency" to refrain from spending. All this leads to a decline in prices. Interest rate adjustments lag behind the decline of prices. Output tends to diminish somewhat, and a depression of trade occurs. Prices continue to fall until rates of interest diminish sufficiently. By the time this happens, however, weak firms will have been forced out of business. Once interest rates are low enough for borrowers to be in a position to resume borrowing, prices will stop falling and the previously described upward movement will begin anew.

From a present-day vantage point, the two greatest defects of this model of the business cycle are its overemphasis on the rate of interest as an economic determinant and the assumption that prices are flexible not only upward but downward. If the response of business borrowing to interest rate adjustments is negligible, as many contemporary economists contend (see Chapter 19), then the lag of interest rates behind price changes can no longer be considered the *modus operandi* of successive cyclical expansions and contractions. Furthermore, on the downward side of the cycle, businesses generally may refuse to accept lower prices in the face of decreased demand, preferring instead to reduce output (the Q's) and employment. In such a case, the decrease in Q's may not be temporary, as Fisher contended, and the cycle may therefore not be self-correcting.

Knut Wicksell (1851–1926)

Like Irving Fisher, Knut Wicksell was a quantity theorist concerned primarily with the relation between money stock, expenditure, price, and interest rate variations as sources of economic disturbance. He believed that changes in the quantity of money (which he defined as currency)

---

[23] *Ibid.*, p. 62.

would lead to variations in the demand for goods and services and consequently to changes in price and expenditures. Thus he argued that "the result of the increase in the quantity of money is a rise in the demand for commodities, and a fall in their supply, with the consequence that all prices rise continuously—until cash balances stand once again in their normal relation to the level of prices." [24]

Changes in the quantity of money are not the sole cause of economic disturbances, however. Wicksell felt that the source of changes in money, supply, expenditures, prices, and economic fluctuation lay in discrepancies between market and natural rates of interest. So long as these two rates are equal, he postulated, there will be no change in the price level. When the market rate of interest is less than the natural rate, however, then cumulative price inflation will occur until such time as the two rates are equal. On the other hand, when the market rate is above the natural rate, a cumulative price deflation will take place until such time as the two rates again coincide.

What is meant by the "natural" and "market" rates of interest? The *natural rate of interest* is much the same as what economists call the marginal efficiency of capital or investment; it is *the expected yield on newly created capital. The market rate of interest* is *the rate charged by banks.* Should the natural rate be above the market rate, profit margins will be high, and the demand for capital goods strong. Prices would increase. However, should the natural rate be less than the market rate, profit margins will be low, the demand for capital goods will be weak, and prices will decrease.

Wicksell thought that a discrepancy between these interest rates could set off cyclical disturbances. Commercial bank behavior can be one cause of a variance between the rates. For example, Wicksell indicates that banks

raise the rate when their gold stocks are threatened with depletion or their current obligations are so great that their disparity in relation to their gold holdings is regarded as dangerous, or, still more, where both of these things occur together, as is often the case. They lower their rates of interest under the reverse conditions: increased gold holdings or diminished commitments, or both.[25]

Conversely, *a fall in the market rate of interest as banks lower their rates* may lead to the following sequence of events:

In the first place saving will be discouraged and for that reason there will be an increased demand for goods and services for present consumption. In the second place, the profit opportunities of entrepreneurs will be increased and the demand for goods and services, as well as for raw materials already in the market for future production, will evidently increase to the same extent as it had previously been held in check by the higher rate of interest. Owing to the increased income thus accruing to the workers, landowners, and the owners of

[24] Knut Wicksell, *Interest and Prices,* translated by R. F. Kahn (New York: Macmillan, 1936), p. 41.
[25] Knut Wicksell, *Lectures on Political Economy* (New York: Macmillan, 1935), Vol. 2, p. 204.

raw materials, etc., the prices of consumption goods will begin to rise, the more so as the factors of production previously available are now withdrawn for the purposes of future production. Equilibrium in the market for goods and services will therefore be disturbed. As against an increased demand in two directions there will be an unchanged or even diminished supply, which must result in an increase in wages (rent) and, directly or indirectly, in prices.

. . . we are entitled to assume that all production forces are already fully employed, so that the increased monetary demand principally takes the form of rivalry between employers for labour, raw materials and natural facilities, etc., which consequently leads to an increase in their price, and indirectly, owing to the increased money income of labour and landlords and the increased demand for commodities, to a rise in the price of all consumption goods in addition to that which arises from diminished savings.[26]

Thus, according to Wicksell, an increased supply of money and decreased market rates of interest mean increased demand for consumption and capital goods, and, in a full employment economy, increased prices. This rise in prices will continue so long as banks can continue to lend and keep the market rate beneath the natural rate. Wicksell did not believe, however, that this type of fluctuation would continue to be cumulative. Instead, he felt that the economic system contained forces that tended to eliminate the differences between the natural and monetary rates of interest, self-corrective forces.

A rise in prices exerts its influence . . . on the demands of the monetary circulation. The quantity of coins and notes circulating in the hands of the public is usually much larger than the available reserves of the banks. It follows that quite a small rise in prices may bring about a very significant contraction of the banks' reserves.[27]

A loss of reserves, of course, means a reduction in the lending ability of the banking system. If bank solvency is threatened, banks will raise their lending rates. Once they approach the "natural" rate, the cumulative process of price inflation will stop.

On the other hand, a rise in the market rate above the natural rate, caused by a loss of bank reserves, for example, will cause this process to work in reverse. There will be a decrease in consumption, in the demand for capital goods, in profit opportunities, and in prices. This process will continue until a return flow of reserves to the banking system takes place, permitting banks to reduce their lending rates. "It is thus confidently to be expected that the bank rate, or more generally the money rate of interest, will always coincide *eventually* with the natural capital rate, or rather that it is always *tending* to coincide with an ever-changing natural rate." [28]

Although Wicksell believed that changes in market rates can set off eco-

---

[26] *Ibid.*, pp. 194–95.
[27] Wicksell, *Interest and Prices,* pp. 113–14.
[28] *Ibid.*, p. 117.

nomic disturbances, he did not view them as the principal initiating force behind business fluctuations. Actually, he thought that the difference between the money and natural rates was usually caused first by a change in the natural rate, and then by the typical slowness of the banking system in adjusting its lending rates.

In other words, the difference between the actual loan and normal rates, which we have already designated as a major cause of fluctuations in commodity prices, arises less frequently because the loan rate changes spontaneously whilst the normal or real rate remains unchanged but on the contrary because the normal rate rises or falls whilst the loan rate remains unchanged or only tardily follows it.[29]

Anything tending to change the expected return on new capital will cause changes in this natural rate. If the prospects for production improve, possibly because of technological advances, then the natural rate rises, and, with the lag of bank rates, a boom takes place. If, however, business expectations worsen or if few innovations occur, then the natural rate falls and we have "bad times."

Assuming this theory to be correct, is there some appropriate economic policy that would eliminate discrepancies between the market and natural rates of interest, and accordingly economic fluctuations? Wicksell thought that an appropriate central-bank policy could do the job. "The only possibility of a rational control of the price level must lie in . . . the proper regulation of the interest policy of the banks." [30] Ideally, he argues, a "spontaneous raising or lowering of the discount rate should in the long run have a more powerful influence on prices than any other cause." [31]

The Cambridge School

While Irving Fisher in the United States was developing the equation of exchange, stressing the relation between M, V, P, and Q, various English economists were developing alternative equations. These economists are usually called members of the "Cambridge School," and the equations they developed are known as *cash-balance equations*.[32]

The main difference in approach between Fisher and the members of the Cambridge School is that Fisher related the money stock to total expenditures (PQ) through the velocity of circulation, whereas the Cambridge School related the money stock to total expenditures through the demand for money. This alternative approach caused the Cambridge economists to

---

[29] Wicksell, *Lectures on Political Economy*, Vol. 2, p. 205.
[30] *Ibid.*, p. 216.
[31] *Ibid.*
[32] D. H. Robertson, Alfred Marshall, A. C. Pigou, and John Maynard Keynes are usually identified with the Cambridge School. Leon Walras, on the Continent, also made significant contributions to the cash-balance approach.

stress the reasons for *holding* money, whereas Fisher stressed the reasons for *spending* it. Actually, as we shall see, the velocity of money and the demand for it are simply reciprocals of each other.

The cash-balance equation. There are many different formulations of the Cambridge equations. The most frequently cited version is

$$M = KRP \qquad [17\text{--}7]$$

where M is the amount of money in circulation at a moment of time, R is the real national output of goods and services per unit of time, P is the price of R, and K is the proportion of RP that the community wishes to keep enough money to purchase.[33] The equation "can be read as follows: In a stable community the quantity of money in existence is also that which people wish to hold, having regard to the level of output, its price level, and their preferences as regards the form in which they hold their resources." [34]

This equation is closely related to the various equations discussed earlier. Consider equation 17–4, $MV = PQ$, in which PQ refers to gross national product. The PQ of this equation may be equated with RP in the Cambridge cash-balance equation cited above. It has the same meaning in both cases as long as the unit of time is a year. Thus, equation 17–7 may be rewritten as $M = KPQ$, and equation 17–4 may be restated as $M = PQ/V$. Then, since $PQ/V = KPQ$, it follows algebraically that $K = 1/V$. In other words, K and V are simply the reciprocal of one another; the demand for money to hold and the velocity of circulation of money are the inverse of each other. Assume for example, that the money supply, M, is used four times in the course of a year to purchase PQ. This is just another way of saying that in the course of a year people, on the average, held an amount of money equal to one-fourth of the value of their expenditures on PQ.

Stating the relationship between money and PQ in this manner enables us to focus on the motivations for demanding money to hold. Alfred Marshall, for example, stressed this when he reasoned:

The total value of a country's currency, multiplied into the average number of times of its changing hands for business purposes in a year, is of course equal to the total amount of business transacted in that country by direct payments of currency in that year. But this identical statement does not indicate the causes that govern the rapidity of circulation of currency: to discover them we must look to the amounts of purchasing power which the people of that country elect to keep in the form of currency . . . *changes in the rapidity of circulation of money are themselves incidental to changes in the amount of ready purchasing power which the people of a country find it advantageous to keep in their holding.*" [35]

[33] D. H. Robertson, *Lectures on Economic Principles* (London: Staples Press, 1959), Vol. 3, Chapter 1.
[34] *Ibid.,* p. 18.
[35] Alfred Marshall, *Money, Credit and Commerce* (London: Macmillan, 1923), p. 43. Italics are mine.

What factors determine the relative demand for money, *K*? They are actually much the same as the forces that determine Fisher's *V*. Dennis Robertson divides them into five groups:

1. Factors connected with business habits—the frequency and regularity with which payments are made, and so forth;
2. Factors connected with the structure of industry—in particular how far the production and sale of output are split up into stages in the hands of different firms between whom payments have to be made for the transfer of goods in process or in store;
3. The general conditions of social and business life, and hence the degree of certainty and confidence with which consumers and producers are making their plans . . . ;
4. The state of development of the markets for existing capital goods—land, houses, etc., and of paper titles thereto: this works both ways,—such things need money to exchange them with, but some of them are also partial substitutes for money;
5. The rate of return obtainable by employing resources otherwise than by tying them up in the form of money.[36]

The cash-balance equation as a tool of analysis. Given changes in any of the five groups of factors above, forces are set in motion that will lead to a change in *K*, the demand for money, and consequently to changes in any or all of the other three magnitudes in the cash-balance equation. For example, assume that adverse expectations concerning the business outlook lead to an increase in the demand for money relative to expenditures. In the absence of money-stock increases, there will be a decrease in spending, and hence a drop in gross national product (*RP*). This occurs because the only way in which people can increase their money holdings in such a situation is to refrain from spending. Thus the demand for goods and services decreases. There are fewer sales, incomes decrease, and people discover that they are not really able to increase their money holdings. Some individuals will have increased their holdings, but only at the expense of others. It is impossible for the community as a whole to acquire additional money holdings unless the monetary authority is willing to supply more.

An almost identical description of events can be made using the Fisher velocity approach. Here, however, we start by saying that people reduce the velocity of money circulation because of adverse expectations concerning the business outlook. Reduced spending means less demand for goods and services, and hence less gross national product (*PQ*). While both the "velocity" and "cash-balance" approaches are equally valid, the latter is generally considered more satisfactory because, as the last quotation from Alfred Marshall implies, the cash-balance equation relates more directly to individual motivation. In addition, it fits more conveniently the economist's basic concepts of supply and demand.

[36] Robertson, *op. cit.*, pp. 20–21.

SUMMARY AND EVALUATION

Economists have long recognized a relation between money and economic activity. The relation between money and price was first stressed in the *sixteenth century*. In the *seventeenth and eighteenth centuries* a fuller understanding of the relations between money, velocity, economic activity, and trade developed. It was argued that economic activity and trade depended on money and its circulation. Some distinction was made between the effects of money on trade (Locke) and on employment (Law).

In the *nineteenth century,* an era of comparatively high employment, there were few advances in monetary theory. Because economists tended to assume that full employment was the natural state of the economy, money-stock changes were generally related to changes in the price level rather than to employment and output.

The *early twentieth century* brought significant theoretical developments. Alternative analytical approaches were formulated, and comprehensive theories of the business cycle were developed. *Irving Fisher* was one of the most important monetary theorists of the period. His principal contribution is probably his statement of the equation of exchange, a tool of economic analysis that is used by economists of almost all theoretical leanings. In addition, his statement of the quantity theory of money is succinct and carefully qualified. Rephrased so as to make money-stock variations a principal cause of variations in gross national product rather than simply in prices, his statement of the quantity theory is viewed by some economists as a rough but relatively valid and current theory of income and output determination. Fisher was also one of the first economists to attempt to verify his hypotheses statistically. Close to one-quarter of his book, *The Purchasing Power of Money,* is devoted to an empirical verification of his views.

Fisher will probably not be remembered for his description of cyclical disturbances. He seems to have overemphasized the importance of interest rate variations and to have been too concerned with the relation of money to prices rather than to aggregate real output. Although he stresses the fact that cycles differ markedly, his analysis of the causes of cyclical disturbances relies too much on a unidirectional sequence of events. In this he does not differ substantially from other early twentieth-century economists like Ralph Hawtrey, who also developed theories of the business cycle. Economists today prefer to stress the interrelationship of these critical variables.

The monetary theory of the *Cambridge economists* was organized around the cash-balance equation. This equation, like Fisher's equation of exchange, provides us with a convenient framework for analyzing changes in macroeconomic behavior. By emphasizing the relation between K and RP, the Cambridge economists called attention to the motives for holding money. Their influence on contemporary thought has been substantial. The emphasis on the demand for money by the two current schools of economic thought, the "Keynesians" and the "Chicago School Quantity Theorists," indicates the importance of the Cambridge contributions.

Wicksell, like Fisher and the Cambridge economists, was a quantity theorist. While stressing the connection between money and prices, his analysis was not restricted to a mere treatment of a direct relation between the two. Instead, he developed a dynamic theory designed to explain price and business fluctuations, which stressed interaction among many variables. Wicksell argued that the forces that determine the market and natural rates of interest can set off discrepancies between each other and, accordingly, induce a price level change. A continued difference between these rates means either boom or bust, depending on whether the natural rate is higher or lower than the market rate. Thus, pressures on bank reserve positions could bring to a halt cumulative price inflation or deflation. As a principle of economic policy, he advocated central-bank action to regulate bank lending rates.

The principal shortcomings of this analysis are fairly obvious. Wicksell assumed a full employment economy. As a result, cyclical changes necessarily meant price rather than output changes. He also assumed that prices were equally flexible upward and downward. In these respects he made the typical early twentieth-century assumptions (see the earlier discussion of Irving Fisher). Also, like other monetary theorists of his period, he may have overemphasized the importance of the interest rate as a determinant of economic activity.

All the theories discussed so far proved inadequate as an explanation of the depression of the 1930's. Economists in the third decade of the century were forced to meet the crises of these years. The theories they advanced are discussed in Chapters 18 to 22. As we study these theories, which form the basis for our contemporary framework of analysis, it will be helpful to bear in mind that they, too, will eventually be improved by new approaches and hypotheses.

Supplementary Readings

PRE-TWENTIETH CENTURY

Law, John. *Money and Trade Considered,* 1705.
Locke, John. *Consequences of the Lowering of Interest, and Raising the Value of Money,* 1692.
———. *Further Considerations Concerning Raising the Value of Money.* 1696.
Mill, John Stuart. *Principles of Political Economy.* Ashley Edition. London, Longmans, Green, 1909, Book III, Chapters 7–13.
Mints, Lloyd W. *A History of Banking Theory.* Chicago, University of Chicago Press, 1945, Chapter 4.
Monroe, Arthur E. *Early Economic Thought.* Cambridge, Mass., Harvard University Press, 1924, Selections 6 and 11.
Spengler, Joseph J. "Richard Cantillon: First of the Moderns." *Journal of Political Economy* (1954).

Sraffa, Piero. *The Works and Correspondence of David Ricardo.* London, Cambridge University Press, 1951, Volumes 1 and 3.

Thornton, Henry. *An Enquiry into the Nature and Effects of the Paper Credit of Great Britain.* London, 1802, Chapters 8, 10, and 11.

Vickers, Douglas. *Studies in the Theory of Money, 1690–1776.* Philadelphia, Chilton, 1959.

EARLY TWENTIETH CENTURY

Fisher and the Transactions Approach

Fisher, Irving. *The Purchasing Power of Money.* New York, Macmillan, 1911, Chapters 1–6, 8.

The Cambridge School and the Cash-Balances Approach

Marshall, A. *Money, Credit, and Commerce.* London, Macmillan, 1923, pp. 38–50.

Pigou, A. C. "The Value of Money." In American Economic Association, *Readings in Monetary Theory,* Homewood, Ill., Irwin, 1951, pp. 162–83.

Robertson, D. D. *Lectures on Economic Principles.* London, Staples Press, 1959, Volume 3, pp. 9–30.

Keynes, J. M. *A Tract on Monetary Reform.* New York, Harcourt, Brace & World, 1923, Chapters 1–4.

The Swedish School

Wicksell, Knut. *Interest and Prices.* Translated by R. F. Kahn, New York, Macmillan, 1936, Introduction, Preface, and Chapters 5–9.

———. *Lectures on Political Economy.* New York, Macmillan, 1935, Volume 2, pp. 127–228.

Myrdl, Gunnar. *Monetary Equilibrium.* London, Saunders, 1939.

CHAPTER 18

A Model of Income Determination: Basic Concepts

INTRODUCTION

The monetary theories developed in the early part of the twentieth century proved inadequate as an explanation of the continued depression in the 1930's primarily because they rested on two assumptions no longer tenable in our economy. Most economists of the 1920's and early 1930's accepted Say's law that production creates its own demand. In addition, they assumed an upward and downward flexibility of wages and prices. From these assumptions they deduced that conditions of less than full employment could not continue for long. When goods and services are produced, they create income equal to the value of production; according to Say's law, all this income must be spent. If consumers do not spend all their income, then that portion which is saved will eventually be channeled to investors in plant and equipment. Thus the demand for and supply of goods always tend to be equal. Price and wage variations do not affect this conclusion. When prices rise, demand will be sufficient to take goods off the market, since wages are also rising. On the other hand, demand will be sufficient to take all goods off the market when wages are falling because with falling wages businesses will have decreasing costs and will thus be able to lower prices. Lower prices will stimulate demand and thereby eliminate any threat of a glut of goods on the market.

These arguments may have been plausible in the nineteenth century, but the depression of the 1930's clearly pointed to fallacies that made them inadequate for a modern economy. The number of people unemployed in the 1930's and the overall duration of unemployment proved conclusively that the depression was anything but a temporary dislocation from long-run full employment.

In his *General Theory of Employment, Interest, and Money*, published in 1936, John Maynard Keynes flatly denied the validity of Say's law, arguing that "effective demand associated with full employment is a special case." [1] In addition, it was demonstrated that there exist institutional rigidities (administered prices and labor unions) that often prevent downward movements in wages and prices. This disproved another fundamental assumption of earlier economists, that prices were fully flexible downward.

The abandonment of Say's law and early twentieth-century monetary theories was termed the "Keynesian Revolution." It caused economists to revise drastically both their *hypotheses* and their *framework of analysis*. We are going to study the developments at the second level of theory, the analytic level—what contemporary economists label the "Keynesian Income-Expenditure Framework." Although this approach is an outgrowth of Keynes' work, the theory presented here is actually a contemporary refinement developed by J. R. Hicks, Oscar Lange, Franco Modigliani, Alvin Hansen, Don Patinkin, Lloyd Metzler, Abba Lerner, and many other economists. [2]

This contemporary income-expenditure framework of analysis, which emphasizes the role of money in the economy, is studied in some detail in the two chapters which follow. This chapter lays the groundwork for succeeding chapters. The income-expenditure framework of analysis is designed to explain the factors that determine the economic well-being of the nation, and the measure that economists use to assess economic performance, gross national product. When gross national product indicates that output and employment are high and increasing, it is generally taken to mean that the economy is advancing, that standards of living are increasing, and people are better off than they have been. In order to understand the principles governing economic performance, we must first understand the uses and limitations of this measure of performance, gross national product.

CONCEPTS OF NATIONAL INCOME ANALYSIS

GNP as the Market Value of All Goods and Services

By gross national product we mean the market value of all final goods and services produced in an economy within some specified period of time, usually a year. Gross national product (GNP) is not a measure of the total *number* of units of output, only of their *value*. If the value of the production is increasing and the prices of the individual units of output remain constant, then we can say that the number of units of output produced has increased—that the economy is more productive than formerly and has more goods and services to distribute to the population.

This conception of gross national product as the total market value of

---

[1] John Maynard Keynes, *The General Theory of Employment, Interest, and Money* (New York: Harcourt, Brace & World, 1936), p. 28.
[2] See the list of supplementary readings at the end of Chapter 21 for specific references.

goods and services produced in a year's time may also be expressed in symbols:

$$GNP = PQ$$
$$= p_1q_1 + p_2q_2 + p_3q_3 + p_4q_4 \ldots + p_nq_n \qquad [18\text{-}1]$$

Here p_1 represents the price of product number 1; q_1 is the number of units of product number 1 that were produced in the economy. Similarly p_2, p_3, p_4, and p_n represent the prices of the second, third, fourth, and so on up to the nth product produced; q_2, q_3, q_4, and q_n are the respective quantities of these products produced. Gross national product is thus the sum of the price of each good or service multiplied by the amount produced. GNP has both a *price* and a *quantity* element and may increase or decrease as a result of a change either in price or output. For this reason we stated that when GNP increases, economic performance is thought to improve also, *barring a price increase.* GNP may be used as a measure of performance only if prices neither increase nor decrease. Prices change constantly, however. Column 1 of Table 18–1 shows that GNP was $124.5 billion in 1941 and $860.6 billion in 1968. This means that the *value* of all goods and services increased almost seven times in the twenty-seven year period. It does not mean, however, that *productivity* in the economy increased almost seven times, because as column 4 shows, prices increased 2.4 times. Thus the economy was only about 2.7 times as productive in 1968 as it was in 1941. Hence, *GNP must be adjusted for price change to be valid as a measure of performance.*

To arrive at a value of gross national product that reflects only output change over time, we divide the dollar figures for GNP in a given year (often called *current dollars*) by the price index for that year (often called the *price deflator*).[3] The resultant figure tells us what the output for a given year would have cost had prices remained unchanged from some particular year in the past. This figure is termed the *real gross national product,* or the *GNP in constant dollars.* Only when the real GNP figures for different years are compared, as in column 2 of Table 18–1, do we see the real output change.

The difference in the figures in columns 1 and 2 shows how price changes substantially alter the apparent performance record of our economy. For example, during the depression, 1930's output dropped markedly from the 1929 level, but not by as much as GNP in current dollars, which is distorted by price change. Similarly, although output has increased almost con-

---

[3] Division gives us this result because if GNP = PQ, then $Q = $ GNP$/P$. Since GNP and P are known, Q can be determined. Some texts treat the subject of index number construction more extensively. See, for example, W. H. Steiner, E. Shapiro, and E. Solomon, *Money and Banking,* 4th ed. (New York: Holt, Rinehart and Winston, 1958), pp. 392–401. For a discussion of some of the limitations to the accuracy of real output measures based upon price indexes, see John J. Klein, "Price-Level and Money-Denomination Movements," *Journal of Political Economy* (1960), p. 369.

TABLE 18–1. UNITED STATES GROSS NATIONAL PRODUCT,
REAL GROSS NATIONAL PRODUCT,
AND IMPLICIT PRICE DEFLATOR, 1929–69

YEAR	GROSS NATIONAL PRODUCT (IN BILLIONS OF CURRENT DOLLARS)	REAL GROSS NATIONAL PRODUCT, 1958 (IN BILLIONS OF CONSTANT DOLLARS)	IMPLICIT PRICE DEFLATOR (1958 = 100)
1929	103.1	203.6	50.6
1930	90.4	183.3	49.3
1931	75.8	169.2	44.8
1932	58.0	144.1	40.3
1933	55.6	141.5	39.3
1934	65.1	154.3	42.2
1935	72.2	169.6	42.6
1936	82.5	193.0	42.7
1937	90.4	203.3	44.5
1938	84.7	193.0	43.9
1939	90.5	209.4	43.2
1940	99.7	227.2	43.9
1941	124.5	263.7	47.2
1942	157.9	289.7*	54.5*
1943	191.6	304.1*	63.0*
1944	210.1	298.0*	70.5*
1945	212.0	284.6*	74.5*
1946	208.5	312.6	66.7
1947	231.3	309.9	74.6
1948	257.6	323.7	79.6
1949	256.5	324.1	79.1
1950	284.8	355.3	80.2
1951	328.4	383.4	85.6
1952	345.5	395.1	87.5
1953	364.6	412.8	88.3
1954	364.8	407.0	89.6
1955	398.0	438.0	90.9
1956	419.2	446.1	94.0
1957	441.1	452.5	97.5
1958	447.3	447.3	100.0
1959	483.6	475.9	101.6
1960	503.8	487.8	103.3
1961	520.1	497.3	104.6
1962	560.3	530.0	105.7
1963	590.5	551.0	107.2
1964	632.4	581.1	108.8
1965	684.9	617.8	110.9
1966	747.6	657.1	113.8
1967	789.7	673.1	117.3
1968	860.6	706.7	121.8
1969	935.0*	730.5*	128.0*

* Estimated by the author. See John J. Klein, "Price-Level and Money-Denomination Movements," *Journal of Political Economy* (1960). The real gross national product is estimated by dividing the figure in column 1 by the estimate of the price level in column 3.
SOURCE: *Survey of Current Business*, August 1965, pp. 24, 25, 26, 27, 52, and 53; and *Federal Reserve Bulletin*, December 1967, p. 2136, and April 1969, p. A–66.

tinuously in the last twenty-five years, it has not increased by as much as the GNP in current dollars indicated because prices have also increased.

GNP and the Time Period: Stock and Flow Concepts

GNP is what economists call a *flow* concept. It is a measure of the value of output *over a period of time.* Thus, when we say that the economy produced $935 billion worth of goods and services in the year 1969, for example, we are not saying that at any moment of time in 1969 there was $935 billion worth of goods and services available in the economy, but rather that the total value of goods and services produced *during the year* amounted to $935 billion.

GNP is also used to express a *rate,* rather than an *amount,* of output. It could be said, for example, that in the second quarter of 1969 production was at the rate of $935 billion per year. This does not mean that $935 billion in goods and services were actually produced but only that the economy might be expected to produce that amount of goods and services over the year if production continued at the same pace as in the second quarter. Thus in 1969 only one-fourth of the $935 billion was actually produced in the time period measured. To arrive at the estimated annual rate, we multiply the amount produced by the number of quarters in the year, four.

The concept of the rate of production is important in terms of economic policy considerations. Economic events move quickly. If the rate of output diminishes during one part of a year, it is important that appropriate offsetting action be taken without delay. Were the monetary authorities to permit a full year to pass in order to compare the different outputs for successive years before taking action, the whole economic situation might have worsened seriously. We study shorter time periods in order to be able to predict the future rate of production accurately.

We have said that GNP is a flow concept. As such, it may be contrasted with *stock* concepts. A stock of something is simply a quantity existing at a moment of time. Measures such as the stock of money, liquid wealth, and non-liquid wealth are stock measures.[4]

The importance of the distinction between stocks and flows cannot be overemphasized. Critical errors of analysis are often made because this distinction is not understood. For example, income and the amount of money on hand are often confused. A person may receive money payments over

---

[4] Sometimes stock measures are stated as averages over time rather than as totals at a moment of time. Thus, if we were to add up the end-of-the-month liquid-wealth holdings of the nonbank public for thirteen consecutive months starting with December 31, 1968, and ending with December 31, 1969, and divide the sum by thirteen, we would have the average liquid-wealth holdings of the nonbank public for the year 1969. This figure would be the amount of liquid wealth that people had, on the average, *at any moment of time during 1969.*

the year totaling $12,000; his income, in other words, is $12,000. This is a flow concept. The amount of his money holdings at the end of one year compared with his holdings at the end of the next is a stock concept, however, and depends only in part on the size of his income. Only if the income recipient makes no payments out of his income will his money *stock* increase by $12,000. On the other hand, if he purchases $12,000 in goods and services, there is no change in his money balances over the year. This illustrates an important relationship between stocks and flows: *a flow, other things being equal, will result in a stock change equal to the flow.*

This holds true for GNP also. If the economy produces $900 billion in final goods in a given year and only $700 billion are consumed, then the difference in the end-of-year stock of wealth figures for two consecutive years is equal to the value of the goods produced but not consumed during the year. This difference is termed *saving*. On the other hand, if an economy consumes more goods than it produces, there is a reduction of real wealth termed *dissaving*. These differences represent the connecting links between the flow (value of output) and the stock (real wealth) of goods in the economy.

The Identity of Income and Product

Equation 18–1 demonstrated that GNP has both a price and an output element. Thus

$$GNP = PQ \qquad [18\text{-}1]$$

GNP may also be interpreted as a measure of the nation's expenditures on its total product or as a measure of its income. In the first instance, emphasis is placed on the expenditures that are made on particular types of goods and services. The U.S. Department of Commerce, for example, calculates GNP as the sum of expenditures on consumption, investment, and government goods and services. Also included is the difference between the value of our production for export and our imports of goods and services. All this may be expressed mathematically:

$$Y = C + I + G + (X - M) \qquad [18\text{-}2]$$

where Y is gross national product, C is expenditures by households on consumer goods and services, I is expenditures on investment goods, G is government expenditures on goods and services, X is exports of goods and services, and M is imports of goods and services.[5]

Gross national product may also be a measure of income. Incomes are earned in the process of producing the goods and services for which expenditures are made. Individuals receive wages and salaries in exchange for

[5] From this point on, in accord with general practice, we shall refer to gross national product as Y.

their productive efforts. After taxes and other adjustments, they are left with *disposable personal income,* the amount of income that each is actually able to spend or save over a year's time. Businesses have profits after selling their output, meeting their costs of production, and paying taxes. Government collects the taxes for its income. Thus, the total value of the output is distributed to producers in the form of personal income, profits, and taxes. This may be expressed in symbols as[6]

$$Y = Y_d + S_b + T \qquad\qquad [18\text{--}3]$$

where Y is gross national income or product, Y_d is disposable personal income, S_b is business saving, and T is federal, state, and local government tax receipts.

TABLE 18–2. GROSS NATIONAL PRODUCT, 1968
(IN BILLIONS OF CURRENT DOLLARS)

Personal consumption expenditures (C)			
Durable goods		82.5	
Nondurable goods		230.3	
Services		221.0	
Total			533.8
Gross private domestic investments (I)			
Fixed investment			
Nonresidential			
Structure	29.2		
Producers' durable equipment	60.8		
Total		90.0	
Residential structures			
Nonfarm	29.3		
Other	0.6		
Total		29.9	
Total		119.9	
Change in business inventories		7.7	
Total			127.6
Net exports of goods and services (X − M)			
Exports	50.0		
Imports	−48.1		
Total			2.0
Government purchases of goods and services (G)			
Federal			
National defense		78.9	
Other		21.1	
Total		100.0	
State and local		97.2	
Total			197.2
Gross national product			860.6

SOURCE: *Federal Reserve Bulletin*, April 1969, p. A–66.

[6] The symbols in the equations are for the most part drawn directly from the term they represent; for example, T stands for *t*axes and S_p for *p*ersonal *s*aving.

Since

$$Y = C + I + G + (X - M) \qquad [18\text{--}2]$$

and

$$Y = Y_d + S_b + T \qquad [18\text{--}3]$$

it follows that

$$C + I + G + (X - M) = Y_d + S_b + T \qquad [18\text{--}4]$$

This equation can be simplified still further when we consider how individuals use disposable income. They either spend it or save it. Thus

$$Y_d = C + S_p \qquad [18\text{--}5]$$

where S_p is personal saving. Substituting equation 18–5 for Y_d in equation 18–4, we have

$$C + I + G + (X - M) = C + S_p + S_b + T \qquad [18\text{--}6]$$

C is the same on both sides of the equation. Therefore

$$I + G + (X - M) = S_p + S_b + T \qquad [18\text{--}7]$$

This equation must always hold true for the past performance of an

TABLE 18–3. GROSS NATIONAL PRODUCT AS INCOME, 1968
(IN BILLIONS OF CURRENT DOLLARS)

Disposable personal income (Y_d)			
Personal outlays (C)			
Personal consumption expenditures	533.8		
Consumer interest payments	13.7		
Personal transfer payments to foreigners	0.7		
Total		548.2	
Personal savings (S_p)		40.7	
Total			588.9
Disposable business corporate income (S_b)			
Corporate profits and inventory valuation			
Adjustments	89.2		
Dividends	−24.6		
Profit tax liability	−41.3		
Total		23.3	
Capital consumption allowances		74.3	
Total			97.6
Government taxes (T)			
Personal tax and nontax payments		96.9	
Indirect business tax and nontax liability		75.8	
Corporate profits tax liability		41.3	
Contributions for social insurance		46.9	
Government transfer payments		−55.3	
Net interest paid by government and consumer		−25.9	
Subsidies less current surplus of government enterprises		− 0.7	
Total			179.0
Statistical discrepancy			−4.8
Gross national product as income			860.6*

* Differences in total due to rounding.
SOURCE: Adapted from *Federal Reserve Bulletin*, April 1969, pp. A-66, A-67.

economy because of the equality of income and product. When product is produced, its value is distributed as income to its producers. Tables 18–2, 18–3, and 18–4 demonstrate this by giving the components of

TABLE 18–4. DISPOSABLE PERSONAL INCOME, 1968
(IN BILLIONS OF CURRENT DOLLARS)

Compensation of employees			
Wages and salaries			
Private	367.2		
Military	18.3		
Government civilian	78.1		
Total		463.5	
Supplements to wages and salaries		50.1	
Total			513.6
Proprietors' income			
Business and professional		47.8	
Farm		15.1	
Total			62.9
Rental income of persons			21.0
Net interest			26.3
Government transfer payments			55.3
Net interest paid by governments and consumer			25.9
Dividends			24.6
Business transfer payments			3.3
Personal tax and nontax payments			
Total			−96.9
Contributions for social insurance			−46.9
Disposable personal income (Y_d)			589.1

SOURCE: Adapted from *Federal Reserve Bulletin*, September 1968, pp. A–66, A–77.

gross national product and gross national income for a recent year, 1968. They show how the equations given relate to actual income statistics.

Money and GNP

In the preceding discussion we established that PQ, Y, $C + I + G + (X - M)$, and $Y_d + S_b + T$ are equivalent. No mention has been made of the financing of these magnitudes, however. Obviously money is the medium used when Y is purchased. As we indicated in Chapter 17, when the average amount of money in the economy during a specified period of time, such as a year, M, is multiplied by the number of times it is spent on final goods and services, V, the product is a measure of the value of the expenditures on final goods and services produced. That product, of course, is Y.

Hence it follows that

$$Y = C + I + G + (X - M) = Y_d + S_b + T = PQ = MV \quad [18\text{–}8]$$

Each section of this equation is simply a different way of looking at the same thing, Y. The significance of equations 18–1 through 18–8 for income determination will be developed more fully in the chapters that follow.

Supplementary Reading

Hawtrey, R. G. "Money and Index Numbers," reprinted in F. A. Lutz and Lloyd W. Mints, eds., *Readings in Monetary Theory*. Philadelphia, Blakiston, 1951.

Data Sources

U.S. Department of Commerce, Office of Business Economics. *The National Income and Product Accounts of the United States, 1929–1965 Statistical Tables*. Washington, D.C., U.S. Government Printing Office, 1966.

———. *Survey of Current Business*. August 1968.

National Bureau of Economic Research. *A Critique of United States Income and Product Accounts.* Studies in Income and Wealth, Vol. 22. Princeton, N.J., Princeton University Press, 1958.

CHAPTER 19

A Model of Income Determination: Demand for Product Forces

Monetary theory seeks to explain the role of monetary supply and demand forces in the determination of economic activity. However, many variables in addition to money help determine income and output. Monetary theory today is thus an integral part of macroeconomic theory. To appreciate the importance of money, we must understand how it works with and is affected by other economic variables.

This chapter and the next are concerned with contemporary macroeconomic theory. Specifically, the factors that cause change in our measure of economic performance, gross national product, are examined. The most important sources of economic change will be isolated within two frameworks, one using *graphs* and one using *general functional equations*. These abstractions from reality constitute a type of economic model. Despite the fact that our economic model is an abstraction, however, it will be fairly rigorous so that the complexities of the economy can be realistically described. The model should help us interpret income determination by depicting the interaction of the most important sources of economic change both visually and in general behavior equations. The development of the model is divided into two sections. This chapter will examine the determination of the factors in equation 18–6:

$$C + I + G + (X - M) = C + S_p + S_b + T$$

Chapter 20 then adds monetary supply and demand to the model and shows how it may be used to interpret the interaction of various economic forces.

INTRODUCTION TO THE MODEL

In essence, contemporary income theory argues that the interaction of demand and supply forces determines the level of economic activity.

When demand is less than supply, stocks of goods accumulate and businesses are forced to reduce Y, aggregate output. If prices do not subsequently decline when supply exceeds demand, then all of the drop in gross national product is in real output. On the other hand, when the demand for goods and services exceeds the supply, the stock of goods declines, business expectations improve, and firms are induced to increase their output. Hence gross national product increases. Should the economy already be operating at full employment, or capacity, however, all the increase in Y will be in prices; the value of output will grow but not the amount. Thus, the only time that Y will not change is when there is neither a shortage nor an excess of demand relative to output, when demand equals supply.

These are the essentials of modern income analysis. The demand for goods relative to the supply is of crucial significance and businesses respond to differences between demand and supply by adjusting aggregate output. This does not explain the fundamental sources of income and output change, however. For this we must examine the components of demand in more detail.

Equation 18–6 offers us some insight into the sources of demand determination. We have said that this equation is always accurate for past performance. Thus, when we say that the sum of C, I, G, and $(X - M)$ must equal the sum of C, S_p, S_b, and T, we are speaking after the fact; we are discussing what has occurred. This is what economists call *ex post* analysis.

Since investment, saving, and expenditure *plans* are made independently and by different individuals, there is no reason why the *planned* magnitudes should be equivalent. Thus the two sides of our equation may differ when the magnitudes of the variables represent plans that look to the future. The total amount of planned expenditures of businesses, of governing bodies, and of exporters and importers may differ, therefore, from the total amount of planned personal saving, expected business profits, and expected government tax receipts. When we say that the sum of the *plans* for C, I, G, and $(X - M)$ may differ from the plans for C, S_p, S_b, and T, we are speaking before the fact; we are looking ahead to what has not yet occurred. This is what economists call *ex ante* analysis.

When the plans for the magnitudes on each side of equation 18–6 *are* equal, then the economy is said to be in *equilibrium*: there are no forces at work tending to change income and output. Aggregate demand and supply will be equal; businesses will produce just enough goods to meet anticipated demands.

Therefore, it is the plans for C, I, G, $(X - M)$, S_p, S_b, and T that are sources of income determination. The remainder of this chapter examines each of these magnitudes in some detail and then places them in our model of income determination.

METHODOLOGY AND SYMBOLS

As previously noted, both graphs and general behavior equations are employed in constructing the model. In order to keep the pedagogical techniques as simple as possible, graphical relationships are usually shown as straight lines. This does not mean that real-world relationships are actually linear. In addition, some of the standard four-quadrant techniques used in national-income analysis texts are not used here. The four-quadrant techniques have limited applicability for a general model.

The general behavior equations introduced in this chapter describe the behavior of various groups in the economy. For example, the following section develops an equation for saving that shows how saving by households is related to various factors, the most important of which is disposable personal income. Specific forms of these equations are not developed, since we are concerned here with the general nature of the sources of economic change. Complex diagrams and specific equations will be found in the formal study of macroeconomic analysis.[1]

The following is a list of the symbols used in our model of income determination. They are presented now to provide a convenient listing and brief definitions that may be referred to throughout the coming chapters.

Y = gross national product

C = consumption expenditures

I = investment expenditures

G = government expenditures

F or $(X - M)$ = net foreign investment (the difference between exports and imports of goods and services)

Y_d = disposable personal income

S_b = business saving

T = tax receipts

S_p = personal saving

f = "a function of"

i = rate of interest

W = liquid wealth

X = all other factors that may influence C and S_p

Z = all the forces that cause the legislature to change the tax rate or government spending

U = any forces other than Y that may influence S_b

U' = forces other than Y that help determine the marginal efficiency of investment

[1] For an undergraduate approach to macroeconomic theory, see Edward Shapiro, *Macroeconomic Analysis,* 2nd ed. (New York: Harcourt, Brace & World, 1969). A graduate-level approach is found in R. D. G. Allen, *Macroeconomics* (New York: St. Martin's Press, 1965).

J = all the forces that cause F to change

M_d = the demand for money

W' = total wealth

X' = other variables that may influence demand for money

M_s = the supply of money

H = high-powered money: currency plus reserves for demand deposits

Z' = other variables that may influence the supply of money

PERSONAL SAVING AND CONSUMPTION DEMAND

Individuals may either spend or save personal disposable income. Thus a decision to save may also be looked upon as a decision not to make a consumption expenditure. Hence

$$Y_d = C + S_p \qquad\qquad [18\text{--}5]$$

where Y_d is disposable personal income, C is consumption demand, and S_p is personal saving. Changes in decisions to save and spend lead to changes in spending and therefore to changes in gross national product. Since consumption spending is, quantitatively, the single most important component of Y, we shall first examine those variables that economists consider most likely to influence behavior in this area.

Disposable Personal Income

The principal determinant of personal saving and consumption demand is generally believed to be the level of disposable personal income. The logic of this view is quite simple: increased incomes enhance the spending ability of individuals; with more to spend people tend to raise their standards of living, saving just a portion of the increased income. Decreased incomes decrease the spending ability of individuals. People are forced to reduce their actual spending, but the reduction will not usually equal the decrease in income, because people typically attempt to maintain their prior living standards under such conditions. This analysis applies not only to the individual but also to the aggregate of individuals. For example, income and output may increase without actually raising the income of anyone already working. This is what happens when more people are employed. As the unemployed are drawn into the work force, their disposable incomes rise and they increase their expenditures and saving. Whether the increased incomes are of those already working or of the newly employed, the economy still feels the impact of the consumption expenditure and saving increases.

This contention seems to be supported by the data given in Table 19–1 and Figure 19–1 which show consumption to be closely related to changes

TABLE 19–1. GROSS NATIONAL PRODUCT
AND ITS COMPONENTS, 1929–68

	GNP AND ITS COMPONENTS (IN BILLIONS OF DOLLARS)						COMPONENTS OF GNP AS PERCENTAGES OF GNP*				
YEAR	GNP	C	I	G	$(X - M)$	Y_d	C	I	G	$(X - M)$	$\dfrac{C}{Y_d}$
1929	103.1	77.2	16.2	8.5	1.1	83.3	74.9	15.7	8.2	1.1	92.7
1930	90.4	69.9	10.3	9.2	1.0	74.5	77.3	11.4	10.2	1.1	93.8
1931	75.8	60.5	5.6	9.2	0.5	64.0	79.8	7.4	12.1	0.6	94.5
1932	58.0	48.6	1.0	8.1	0.4	48.7	83.8	1.7	14.0	0.7	99.8
1933	55.6	45.8	1.4	8.0	0.4	45.5	82.4	2.5	14.4	0.7	100.6
1934	65.1	51.3	3.3	9.8	0.6	52.4	78.8	5.1	15.0	0.9	97.9
1935	72.2	55.7	6.4	10.1	0.1	58.5	77.1	8.9	14.0	0.1	95.2
1936	82.5	61.9	8.5	12.0	0.1	66.3	75.0	10.3	14.5	0.1	93.4
1937	90.4	66.5	11.8	11.9	0.3	71.2	73.6	13.0	13.2	0.3	93.4
1938	84.7	63.9	6.5	13.0	1.3	65.5	75.4	7.7	15.3	1.5	97.6
1939	90.5	66.8	9.3	13.3	1.0	70.3	73.8	10.3	14.7	1.1	95.0
1940	99.7	70.8	13.1	14.0	1.7	75.7	71.0	13.1	14.0	1.7	93.5
1941	124.5	80.6	17.9	24.8	1.3	92.7	64.7	14.4	19.9	1.0	86.9
1942	157.9	88.5	9.8	59.6	0.0	116.9	56.0	6.2	37.7	0.0	75.7
1943	191.6	99.3	5.7	88.6	−2.0	133.5	51.8	3.0	46.2	−1.0	74.4
1944	210.1	108.3	7.1	96.5	−1.8	146.3	51.5	3.4	45.9	−0.9	74.0
1945	212.0	119.7	10.6	82.3	−0.6	150.2	56.5	5.0	38.8	−0.3	79.7
1946	208.5	143.4	30.6	27.0	7.5	160.0	68.8	14.7	12.9	3.6	89.6
1947	231.3	160.7	34.0	25.1	11.5	169.8	69.5	14.7	10.9	5.0	94.6
1948	257.6	173.6	46.0	31.6	6.4	189.1	67.4	17.9	12.3	2.5	91.8
1949	256.5	176.8	35.7	37.8	6.1	188.6	68.9	13.9	14.7	2.4	93.7
1950	284.9	191.0	54.1	37.9	1.8	206.9	67.0	19.0	13.3	0.6	92.3
1951	328.4	206.3	59.3	59.1	3.7	226.6	62.8	18.1	18.0	1.1	91.0
1952	345.5	216.7	51.9	74.7	2.2	238.3	62.7	15.0	21.6	0.6	90.9
1953	364.6	230.0	52.6	81.6	0.4	252.6	63.1	14.4	22.4	0.1	91.1
1954	364.8	236.5	51.7	74.8	1.8	257.4	64.8	14.2	20.5	0.5	91.9
1955	398.0	254.4	67.4	74.2	2.0	275.3	63.9	16.9	18.6	0.5	92.4
1956	419.2	266.7	70.0	78.6	4.0	293.2	63.6	16.7	18.8	1.0	91.0
1957	441.1	281.4	67.8	86.1	5.7	308.5	63.8	15.4	19.5	1.3	91.2
1958	447.3	290.1	60.9	94.2	2.2	318.8	64.9	13.6	21.1	0.5	91.0
1959	483.6	311.2	75.3	97.0	0.1	337.3	64.4	15.6	20.1	0.0	92.3
1960	503.8	325.2	74.8	99.6	4.0	350.0	64.5	14.8	19.8	0.8	92.9
1961	520.1	335.2	71.7	107.6	5.6	364.4	64.4	13.8	20.7	1.1	92.0
1962	560.3	355.1	83.0	117.1	5.1	385.3	63.4	14.8	20.9	0.9	92.2
1963	590.5	375.0	87.1	122.5	5.9	404.6	63.5	14.8	20.7	1.0	92.7
1964	632.4	401.2	94.0	128.7	8.5	438.1	63.4	14.9	20.4	1.3	91.6
1965	683.9	433.1	107.4	136.4	6.9	472.2	63.3	15.7	19.9	1.0	91.7
1966	743.3	465.9	118.0	154.3	5.1	508.8	62.7	15.9	20.8	0.7	91.6
1967	789.7	492.2	114.3	178.4	4.8	546.3	62.3	14.5	22.6	0.6	90.1
1968	860.6	533.8	127.6	197.2	2.0	589.1	62.0	14.8	22.9	0.2	90.6

* Figures may not total 100.0 because of rounding.
SOURCE: *Survey of Current Business*, August 1965, pp. 24, 25, 32, and 33; *Federal Reserve Bulletin*, December 1967, pp. 2136–37; and April 1969, p. A–67.

Y and Y_d.[2] When gross national product and disposable personal income rise, consumption also increases. When they decline, consumption

---

[2] The relationship between S_p and Y_d is not shown, since, according to equation 18–5, S_p is simply the difference between C and Y_d.

FIGURE 19–1. Gross national product, consumption expenditures,
and disposable personal income, 1929–68
(in billions of dollars)

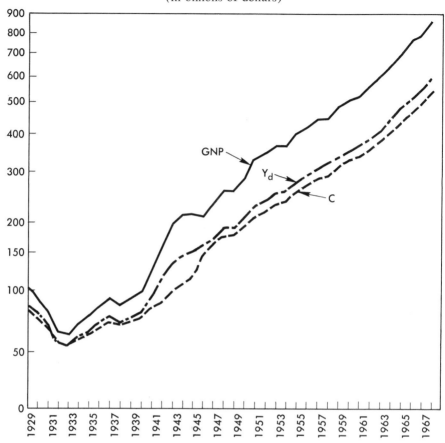

SOURCE: Table 19–1.

declines. During the depression of the 1930's, for example, Y, Y_d, and C all decreased, although consumption as a percentage of Y and Y_d actually increased. This is also evidence for the theory that people will try to maintain their customary level of expenditures despite decreased incomes.

As incomes increased after 1933, C also increased, but the ratio of C to Y and Y_d decreased, apparently as a result of higher income tax rates in the 1930's.

World War II raised incomes sharply, but again consumption failed to rise proportionately. Increased taxes and the general unavailability of major consumer durable goods such as automobiles and major household appliances restricted consumption expenditures. Immediately after the war, although Y decreased, consumption expenditures rose thanks to lower tax rates and higher disposable income. Through the last part of the 1940's, these expenditures increased proportionately with gross national product and disposable personal income. Since 1950, changes in C have continued to parallel Y and Y_d changes, but at a slightly lower level. Apparently, the pent-up demand for consumer goods and services that had accumulated during the depression and war years was, for the most part, satisfied in the latter half of the 1940's. People were thus able to lower their rate of consumption and increase their rate of saving in the 1950's and 1960's. In general, however, the movement in Y, Y_d, and C has been upward, although recession years have witnessed a slight reduction in the amount of income and consumption expenditure increase in comparison with more prosperous times.

The effects on C/Y_d of the 1964 income tax decrease are evident in the decreased ratio for that year. The lower tax rates caused an increase in disposable income, but due to an increase in personal saving, consumption expenditures increased by less than disposable income did. C/Y_d dropped further to almost .90 in 1967, most probably as a result of (1) a rise in interest rates, which contributed to an increase in the personal saving rate, and (2) additional increased saving in anticipation of the 1968 income tax surcharge. The second force contributed to the inability of the tax surcharge to reduce consumption further in 1968. An additional factor in the failure of the tax surcharge to reduce consumption significantly was that by the second half of 1968, households were anticipating continued inflation. Hence there was a strong desire to spend prior to additional price-level increases.

The relationship between Y, Y_d, and C appears to have been fairly close, however. This supports the view that income is an important determinant of consumption demand and spending. It should be noted, however, that consumption is directly determined by Y_d rather than Y, because the full amount of Y is not available to the spender. The chain of causation, in other words, runs from Y to Y_d and then to C.

Wealth as a Source of Consumption and Saving Change

The volume of liquid wealth may also exert an influence on consumption demand and personal saving. At any given level of disposable personal income, the greater the volume of liquid wealth, the greater will be the demand for consumption goods and services. The logic on which this assertion is based is that more liquid wealth means more command over goods and services and less need to save out of current income to meet contingencies. The lower the level of liquid wealth, the less ability individuals have to make high-level consumption expenditures and the greater is the need to save.

The total volume of liquid wealth is influenced by saving. When a person saves and does not spend, his liquid-wealth holdings increase. Initially, as disposable income exceeds consumption expenditures, money receipts will exceed money expenditures and liquid-wealth holdings in the form of money balances will increase. Subsequently, however, the saver may decide to keep his increased liquid-wealth holdings in another form. Thus he may choose to increase his holdings of savings deposits, government securities, corporate stocks, privately issued bonds, or insurance policies. As these forms of wealth increase in volume while holdings of physical wealth remain unchanged, it becomes more and more likely that he will increase his rate of expenditure on consumption goods and services and decrease his saving rate, S_p. His ability to meet future expenditures, both foreseen and unforeseen will have increased, and consequently he will have less need to maintain the same saving rate as at a lower level of liquid wealth.

The situation is different when consumption expenditures exceed disposable income and S_p is negative; dissaving occurs then. An excess of expenditures over income can only be financed by borrowing or drawing down liquid-wealth holdings. Thus the ability to make future expenditures and meet unforeseen contingencies is reduced, and to recoup these holdings, a reduction in expenditures is necessary.

Empirical evidence tends to support this analysis. "As a general rule, the saving rate for individual households appears to vary inversely with the ratio of liquid assets to income, and the influence of liquid assets on saving tends to diminish as the level of income rises." [3]

So far the discussion of the influence of liquid wealth on expenditures and saving has made no mention of prices. We have assumed that they are constant. What happens if they vary? Assume, for example, there is an increase in the price level. When this occurs, there is a corresponding decrease in the purchasing power of most forms of liquid wealth; about the only forms of liquid wealth that will increase in value are stocks, the price of which usually fluctuates along with the general price level. Other forms of liquid wealth usually have a fixed nominal value. Thus $1,000 in money or savings deposits continues to be $1,000 regardless of changes in the price level; a bond with a maturity value of $1,000 will continue to have that same maturity value, although its market price will probably decline. The decreased purchasing power of bonds and the availability of favorable alternative financial investments, such as corporate stocks, generally leads to a decline in the price of bonds that have already been issued.

On balance, with a price-level increase, the purchasing power of liquid wealth tends to decrease. What influence will this have on consumption expenditures? In order to regain the ability to meet unanticipated expenditures, people will increase saving out of income. Consequently, consumption expenditures will fall.

Liquid wealth and the real value of liquid wealth have been introduced as possible influences on consumption demand. *Real wealth* should also

[3] Robert Ferber, "Research on Household Behavior," *American Economic Review* (1962), p. 37.

be considered. The amount of physical goods in the economy may help to determine expenditures on consumer durables. The more physical goods are owned, presumably, the less the need for additional units of them, and hence the lower the expenditures on them.

This only applies if the average age of physical goods is constant over time, however; it is also true that the greater the average age of physical goods, the more likely there is to be an extensive demand for replacements, regardless of the total volume of real wealth then extant. The increasing age of the stock of consumer durables during the depression and World War II underlay at least part of the strong postwar consumer demand for durables, which occurred despite the fact that there was a large amount of physical goods in American households. Overall, the average age of real wealth owned by individuals in the United States tends to vary as consumer expenditures on durable goods fall off in recession and increase in more prosperous periods.

The Rate of Interest

The rate of interest affects consumption demand in several ways. For example, an increase in the rate of interest may usually be expected to lead to an increase in the rate of saving and, other things being equal, to a decrease in consumption spending. Since interest is paid to savers to compensate them for giving up current consumption, the higher the interest return, the more people are induced to save. Conversely, the lower the interest return, the less saving occurs.

The relationship between the rate of interest and consumption demand should also be considered from the borrower's point of view. The individual who finds that he may borrow a given amount of money at a reduced interest cost may be induced to borrow more and so increase his spending base. Similarly, when banks expand loans because of increased excess reserves and leave their lending rates unchanged, credit conditions are easier. Borrowers who previously did not qualify for loans may now be able to obtain them. When they do, their spendings will increase.

Changes in the interest rate and consumption demand may also be in the same direction, however. Those people who only feel it necessary to get a specific dollar yield on their financial investments will save less if interest rates increase, since less savings will give the same total yield. Hence consumption demand may increase. For example, a person who wants $30 in interest income needs $1,000 in savings when the interest rate is 3 percent but only $500 in savings when it is 6 percent.

There are still other possibilities. A rise in the rate of interest paid on newly issued securities relative to that paid on already existing securities will cause the market price on the old securities to decline. If a potential bond purchaser is to be induced to buy an old security instead of a new one, he must be offered an *effective yield* on the old security comparable to that on the new security. Assume, for example, that an old bond has a par value of $1,000 and a 3 percent rate of return, while a comparable new security yields 4 percent. The price of the old security must drop in order to meet this competition. To give the investor an effective 4 percent return on his investment when the dollar yield on the old bond is $30, the seller must ask himself: $30 is 4 percent of how large a financial investment?

$$(x) \ (.04) = \$30$$

or

$$(\$750) \ (.04) = \$30$$

Thus, the price of old bonds declines during periods of generally rising interest rates. This means that the volume of liquid wealth in the form of old securities has declined and that, accordingly, an increase in saving and a decrease in consumption demand have been induced.

In general, economists who accept the Keynesian hypotheses often tend to minimize the influence of interest on consumption and saving. Lawrence Klein is representative of this group when he states

There is no empirical evidence, so far, that shows significant interest effects on total spending or saving by consumers after income effects are taken into account. That is not to say that wide movements of interest rates and relative prices, much wider in the short run than have been observed, will have no influence on the total spending or saving.[4]

On the other hand, economists schooled in the quantity theory tradition or the new "portfolio" approach more often emphasize the interest rate as an important economic variable. These two groups of economists believe that interest-rate increases tend to increase saving and to lower consumption and that interest-rate decreases have the reverse effect. However, it is difficult to make a reasonably accurate quantitative prediction as to the potential effects of interest-rate changes on the rate of saving and consumption expenditures. There are many variables at work here, and the effects of interest rate changes are difficult to disentangle from the effects of other forces affecting consumption and saving. Evidence seems to be more concrete that interest rates do affect the demand for one type of consumer good—consumer durables, which are really a form of investment goods. Michael Hamburger, as we noted in Chapter 13, has demonstrated "that monetary variables have a significant effect on consumer purchases of durable goods and that the most appropriate measures of these variables are interest rates."[5]

---

[4] Lawrence R. Klein, *The Keynesian Revolution*, 2nd ed. (New York: Macmillan, 1966), p. 201.
[5] Michael J. Hamburger, "Interest Rates and the Demand for Consumer Durable Goods," *American Economic Review* (December 1967), p. 1131.

Additional Explanations of Personal Saving and Consumption

In addition to the factors mentioned earlier, age, education, distribution of income, and price expectations are often mentioned as determinants of consumption demand and saving. It is often argued, for example, that the older the population, the less the need for consumer durable goods. Furthermore, the less education people have, the less income they may be expected to earn, and the lower their level of spending will be. In addition, the greater the proportion of income going to high-income groups, the less tendency there will be to spend on consumption overall. Because their standards of living are already high, those with large incomes tend to save more and spend a smaller fraction of additions to their income than those with lower incomes. Finally, the greater the expectation that prices will increase, the greater the apparent need to buy before prices actually rise and the purchasing power of income deteriorates.

These are just a few of the other factors economists take into consideration in explaining consumer spending and saving. The explanation of spending behavior is a complicated affair, and many of the problems are not even touched upon here. For example, consumption behavior seems to be affected differently by short-run income changes than by long-run changes. Economists have offered numerous explanations for this paradox, but none that are completely satisfactory.

An Equation for Personal Saving

Having examined separately a number of determinants of saving and consumption, we must now attempt to describe in some way the combined effect of these various factors on consumption and saving behavior. Selecting those factors that seem most relevant on the basis of empirical study and careful a priori reasoning, we have Y_d, disposable personal income; i, the rate of interest; W, liquid wealth; and X, all the other factors that may influence C and S_p. Putting this into equation form, we have

$$S_p = \mathrm{f}(Y_d, i, W, X) \qquad [19\text{--}1]$$

and, since $Y_d = C + S_p$ (equation 18–5), then, substituting, we have

$$Y_d = C + \mathrm{f}(Y_d, i, W, X); \quad C = Y_d - \mathrm{f}(Y_d, i, W, X) \qquad [19\text{--}2]$$

These equations tell us that consumption demand and personal saving are a function, f, of, or determined by, disposable personal income, liquid wealth, the rate of interest, and other relevant variables. If X remains constant, we may assume that the *saving* rate increases with a rise in disposable personal income, a drop in liquid wealth, and a rise in the rate of interest. Thus the relationship between saving, disposable income, and the rate of interest is direct, whereas the relationship between saving and liquid wealth is inverse. On the other hand, *consumption* rises with an increase in disposable income, an increase in liquid wealth, and a drop in rate of interest. Thus the relationship between consumption, disposable income, and liquid wealth is direct, whereas the relationship between consumption and the rate of interest is inverse.

In developing a diagrammatic representation of Y changes, we shall concentrate on the saving equation, 19–1, rather than the consumption equation, 19–2, in order to keep the analysis comparatively simple. In a sense, the analysis illustrates consumption determinants too, however, for C and its determinants may be derived readily from equation 19–1. Once we determine S_p, we can easily compute C from $C = Y_d - S_p$. This also means that we can deal with equation 18–7, $I + G + (X - M) = S_p + S_b + T$, instead of equation 18–6, $C + I + G + (X - M) = C + S_p + S_b + T$. C is identical on both sides of the equation and thus cancels out.

The relation between the variables of equation 19–1 is illustrated diagrammatically in Figure 19–2. Planned personal saving at any level of Y

FIGURE 19–2. The relationship between S_p and Y

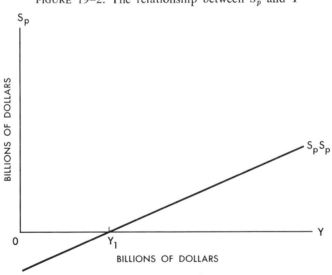

is measured along the vertical axis; Y is measured along the horizontal axis. Y rather than Y_d is used as the horizontal axis because, ultimately, a model of income determination must be designed to explain changes in Y. Thus in Figure 19–2 *the line* S_pS_p *shows the relationship between S_p and Y.* This line records the total amount of personal saving that people plan to do at various levels of Y. The greater the level of Y, the greater is the volume of personal saving that people feel is necessary. Thus at any point above an output of Y_1 people want to save. At any level of output below that there will be dissaving; people will tend to spend more on consumption goods than they receive in income.

The line S_pS_p also shows the relationship between changes in personal saving and changes in gross national product. Let the symbol Δ, delta, refer to a small change. By moving from any point on the line S_pS_p to another we can observe the change in S_p that is induced by a change in Y. Thus, the ratio $\Delta S_p/\Delta Y$ is a measure of how changes in Y induce changes in S_p. In terms of the diagram, it is also a measure of the slope of the line S_pS_p (which we have drawn as a straight line to keep the analysis simple). The fact that the slope is less than one (since the angle made by S_pS_p and Y is less than $45°$) reflects the desire of the public both to save and to spend when a change in Y occurs; thus, as Y increases, the amount of saving also increases, but by less than the increase in Y. The remainder of the change in Y goes into consumption expenditures, government tax collections, and business income.

This last point requires some further explanation. It will be recalled that Y_d, and not Y, is the direct determinant of C and S_p. The ratio of a change in personal saving induced by a change in disposable personal income is $\Delta S_p/\Delta Y_d$; this is called the *marginal propensity to save*. The remainder of any change in Y_d goes into consumption change. The ratio of the change in consumption expenditures induced by the change in disposable personal income is $\Delta C/\Delta Y_d$, the *marginal propensity to consume*.

The marginal propensity to save, $\Delta S_p/\Delta Y_d$, necessarily differs from $\Delta S_p/\Delta Y$. As gross national product increases, disposable personal income increases but so do business saving and government tax collections. In our economy, the tax structure is geared to the level of income and output. The higher Y becomes, the greater is the amount of taxes collected by the government. For these reasons the marginal propensity to save must differ from the ratio of the change in personal saving to a change in gross national product. The marginal propensity to save, $\Delta S_p/\Delta Y_d$, must be *greater* than the ratio $\Delta S_p/\Delta Y$. Assume, for example, that 80 percent of the changes in Y go into a Y_d change, 10 percent into a change in business saving, and 10 percent into a change in government tax collections. Assume further that the marginal propensity to save is .20. Given these conditions, an increase of $50 billion in Y will become a $40 billion increase in Y_d, a $5 billion increase in government tax collections, and a $5 billion increase in business saving. In turn, the $40 billion rise in Y_d results in a $32 billion increase in consumption expenditures and an $8 billion rise in personal saving, S_p. In other words, for every dollar change in Y there will be a 16 percent change in S_p. Thus the ratio of ΔS_p to ΔY is .16, in contrast to the marginal propensity to save of .20.

What about the other determinants of consumption and personal saving? How do they fit into this picture of the relation between S_p and Y? Since a two-dimensional diagram can only show the relationship between two variables along any one given line such as S_pS_p, the other variables must be assumed to be fixed. If other variables do change, however, then the position of the line S_pS_p must change to show the relationship between S_p and Y given the new values of the other variables. Thus in terms of Figure 19–2, S_pS_p will move upward if, at any given level of Y, there is a decrease in liquid wealth or a rise in the rate of interest. In addition, anything that would cause X to change would also lead to a change in S_pS_p.

Business Saving and Taxes Added to Personal Saving

We have said that when the total of the plans for $S_p + S_b + T$ differs from the total of the plans for $I + G + (X - M)$, economic change occurs. What do the totals of the plans for S_p, S_b, and T look like at any given level of gross national product? This relationship is depicted in Figure 19–3.

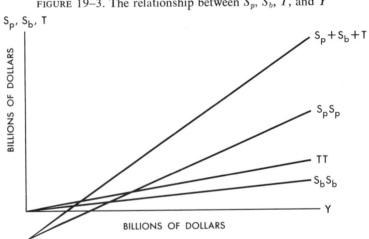

FIGURE 19–3. The relationship between S_p, S_b, T, and Y

The tax line, TT, shows the relationship between the tax receipts at all levels of government and the level of gross national product. This line is drawn sloping upward and to the right, since the various governmental bodies collect more taxes as incomes increase. For the sake of simplicity, we have assumed that the government tax collections are a constant proportion of Y changes. Because the position of line TT is determined by the actions of the legislatures, it will not be directly influenced by economic variables such as Y_d, i, and W. The legislatures are influenced by economic conditions indirectly, of course.

T may be defined as follows:

$$T = f(Y, Z) \qquad\qquad [19\text{–}3]$$

This equation tells us that T, the total of government tax collections, is a function of Y, the level of gross national product, and Z, a general variable standing for all those forces that cause the legislature to change the tax rate. As already indicated, in Figure 19–3 the relationship between T and Y is assumed to be positive.

In Figure 19–3, S_bS_b, the business saving line, shows the relationship between the level of business saving, S_b (consisting of disposable corporate income and capital consumption allowances), and gross national product.[6] This relationship is positive, for businesses expect to have higher earnings as the level of income in the economy rises. For the sake of simplicity, we have assumed that the relationship between changes in the amount of business saving and Y are always proportionate. Thus the equation for S_b is

$$S_b = f(Y, U) \qquad\qquad [19\text{–}4]$$

U stands for any forces tending to change S_b at any given level of Y, such as government taxes on business, corporate dividend policies, and capital consumption allowances. Decreases in business taxes, higher capital consumption allowances, and reduced dividend rates will all tend to raise S_bS_b. Hence business saving may be increased at all levels of Y. As before, however, a given line such as S_bS_b in Figure 19–3 assumes other factors to be fixed. Assuming that all determinants of S_p, S_b, and T other than Y are fixed, we may depict the combined impact of the three lines, S_pS_p, S_bS_b, and TT. This is represented by line $S_p + S_b + T$, which shows the expected total of S_p, S_b, and T at various levels of Y. The relationship is positive, with a slope less than one but greater than zero.

Shifts in the $S_p + S_b + T$ Line

A shift in S_pS_p attributable to W and i changes will usually cause the entire line $S_p + S_b + T$ to shift by the same amount. Shifts in the S_bS_b and TT line, however, may not move $S_p + S_b + T$ by the same amount, since these changes affect the level of disposable personal income. For example, if the distribution of gross national product changes as income rises, so that a greater proportion goes into business saving and taxes, the net effect will be a reduction in disposable personal income. Personal saving will also be affected; S_pS_p will rotate down. As a result, the total line $S_p + S_b + T$ will rotate up somewhat, but the rotation in the total line will be less than the rotation in TT and S_bS_b. This is illustrated in Figure 19–4. We assume an increase in tax rates. S_bS_b and TT are added together to simplify our analysis. The solid lines represent the original positions of $S_bS_b + TT$, S_pS_p, and $S_p + S_b + T$. The distance between the old $S_p + S_b + T$ and the new total line is equal to the difference between the rise in $S_bS_b + TT$ and the decrease in S_pS_p.

---

[6] The data published by the U.S. Department of Commerce for business saving covers only corporate enterprise. The earnings of unincorporated enterprises are included in disposable personal income.

FIGURE 19–4. The relationship between S_pS_p, $S_bS_b + TT$, and changes in the tax rate

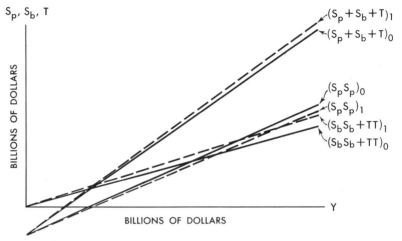

Summary of Forces Affecting the $S_p + S_b + T$ Line

The $S_p + S_b + T$ line will shift whenever determinants of S_p, S_b, and T, other than Y, change. Thus

1. S_pS_p, and hence $S_p + S_b + T$, will fluctuate inversely with movements of liquid wealth.[7] It will rise with a decrease in individual holdings of the components of liquid wealth—the stock of money, time deposits, savings and loan share accounts, U.S. government securities, corporate stocks, bonds, and life insurance policies. Conversely, S_pS_p, and hence $S_p + S_b + T$, will fall with an increase in those liquid-wealth holdings.

2. S_pS_p, and hence $S_p + S_b + T$, vary directly with price-level changes because of the change in the purchasing power of liquid wealth. On the other hand, S_pS_p and $S_p + S_b + T$ vary inversely with price expectations.

3. S_pS_p, and hence $S_p + S_b + T$, vary directly with the interest rate.

4. S_pS_p falls whenever the tax rate is increased, but $S_p + S_b + T$ rises. The rise in $S_p + S_b + T$ is less than the increase in TT, however. Conversely, lower tax rates cause a downward turn in $S_p + S_b + T$, but by less than the decrease in TT.

5. S_pS_p varies inversely with changes in business saving, but $S_p + S_b + T$ moves in the same direction as business saving changes. Hence change in $S_p + S_b + T$ is less than the change in S_bS_b.

6. TT changes with legislative actions that alter the tax rate. $S_p + S_b + T$ varies as described in number 4 above.

[7] That is, at any given level of income, personal saving will increase with a drop in liquid wealth. This ignores the fact, discussed earlier, that as saving takes place liquid wealth increases. What happens is that liquid wealth accumulates as saving occurs and this subsequently will enable S_pS_p, the *rate* of saving, to fall and consumption to increase at all levels of income.

7. S_bS_b varies inversely with changes in the tax rates on business and corporate dividend payments but directly with capital consumption allowances.

INVESTMENT BEHAVIOR

The Importance of Investment

A major role in bringing about economic prosperity is usually ascribed to investment expenditures. A high level of expenditure on plant and equipment, inventories, and residential construction is generally considered to be a sign of a healthy and growing economy. For instance, an increase in the amount of productive plant and equipment enhances the output capabilities of the work force and thus enables any given amount of labor to produce more goods for the economy. Higher output should lead to higher consumption levels and a higher standard of living. Even if there is no increase in the amount of plant and equipment, the maintenance of

FIGURE 19–5. Investment and government expenditures for the United States, 1929–68
(in billions of dollars)

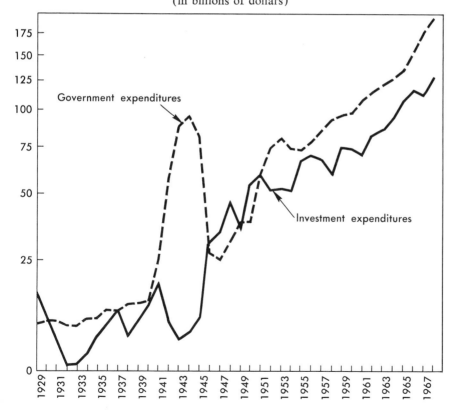

SOURCE: Table 19–1.

a given amount by means of capital replacement may have similar beneficial effects on the economy, since old plant and equipment are normally replaced by new, higher quality products.

Investment expenditures do not exhibit the same stability relative to gross national product as consumption expenditures. Table 19–1 and Figure 19–5, for example, show that investment expenditure as a percentage of gross national product has varied in recent decades from a low of 1.7 percent in 1932 to a high of 19.0 percent in 1950. Similarly, the volume of investment expenditure went from a low of $1 billion in 1932 to a high of $127.6 billion in 1968. Year-to-year variations in *I* are substantial.

The data suggest that investment expenditure change may well be a source of income and output change, which in turn may induce a change in the amount of consumption expenditures. As can be seen in Table 19–2,

TABLE 19–2. INVESTMENT, CONSUMPTION, GOVERNMENT EXPENDITURE, AND GROSS NATIONAL PRODUCT CHANGES FROM THE PRECEDING YEAR FOR THE UNITED STATES, 1948–68 (IN BILLIONS OF DOLLARS)

YEAR	INVESTMENT CHANGE	CONSUMPTION CHANGE	GOVERNMENT EXPENDITURE CHANGE	$(X - M)$ CHANGE	GNP CHANGE
1948	+12.0	+12.9	+6.5	−5.1	+26.3
1949	−10.3	+3.2	+6.2	−0.3	−1.1
1950	+18.4	+14.2	+0.1	−4.3	+28.4
1951	+5.2	+15.3	+21.2	+1.9	+43.5
1952	−7.4	+10.4	+15.6	−1.5	+17.1
1953	+0.7	+13.3	+6.9	−1.8	+19.1
1954	−0.9	+6.5	−6.8	+1.4	+0.2
1955	+15.7	+17.9	−0.6	+0.2	+33.2
1956	+2.6	+12.3	+4.4	+2.0	+21.2
1957	−2.2	+14.7	+7.5	+1.7	+21.9
1958	−6.9	+8.4	+8.1	−3.5	+6.2
1959	+14.4	+21.1	+2.8	−2.1	+36.3
1960	−0.5	+13.0	+2.6	+3.9	+20.2
1961	−3.1	+10.0	+8.0	+1.6	+16.3
1962	+11.3	+19.9	+9.5	−0.5	+40.2
1963	+4.1	+19.9	+5.4	+0.8	+30.2
1964	+6.9	+26.2	+6.2	+2.6	+41.9
1965	+13.4	+31.9	+7.7	−1.6	+51.5
1966	+10.6	+32.8	+17.9	−1.8	+59.4
1967	−3.7	+26.3	+24.1	−0.3	+46.4
1968	+13.3	+41.6	+18.8	−2.8	+70.9

SOURCE: Table 19–1.

a decline in investment spending is often accompanied by a small increase in consumption. From 1948 to 1949, *I* dropped by $10.3 billion and consumption rose by $3.2 billion; from 1953 to 1954, *I* fell $0.9 billion, while *C* increased $6.5 billion. From 1957 to 1958, *I* dropped by $6.9 billion and, from 1960 to 1961, by $3.1 billion; during those same years, *C* rose by $8.4 billion and $10.0 billion respectively. More recently, *I* fell by $3.7 billion in 1967, principally because of a drop in business inventories. At the same time, *C* continued to expand sharply as a result of heavy Viet Nam war expenditures. However, the increase in consumption in 1967 was less than in 1966 and 1968, when both investment and consumption moved upward sharply.

On the other hand, when *I* increased markedly in 1950, 1955, 1959, 1962, 1965, 1966, and 1968, there were also very sharp rises in *C*. These last statistics are particularly significant in terms of the consumption-investment relation because, except for 1966 and 1968, changes in government expenditure in those years were relatively small. Consequently, the relationship between *C* and *I* is more visible.

In short, the association between *C* and *I* is by no means neat, historically. Changes in *C* and *I* are clearly not proportionate, and as a consequence the relationship between *I* and *Y* changes. The effects of changes in tax receipts and business saving must be considered. Changes in the other determinants of *C* and S_p may also occur. Thus it is the overall effect of the interaction between $S_p + S_b + T$ and $I + G + (X - M)$ that must be examined.

At present, however, we are concerned with investment demand as a source of economic change. The *importance* of *I* change to economic progress and income change is clear, but how do economists explain the fluctuations in investment behavior itself? This is the crucial question. For instance, from the perspective of economic policy, if it is felt that *I* is the variable that should be manipulated, then our analysis must provide clues to the ultimate determinants of *I* so that they may be properly manipulated to bring about the desired *I* change.

The Determinants of Investment Expenditure

The following discussion describes the behavior of gross private domestic investment. It is not concerned with components of gross private domestic investment, but rather with determinants of total investment expenditures. A separate analysis could be made of the various types of investment expenditures, but in order to keep our economic model relatively simple and free of the complexities caused by a plethora of variables we shall treat only the determinants of the aggregate *I*. Hence for the most part our analysis assumes that the behavior of most forms of investment is comparable to that of investment in capital assets, especially productive plant and equipment.

The investment criteria: the MEI and the rate of interest. Two forces are generally thought to determine investment: the marginal efficiency of investment and the rate of interest. *The marginal efficiency of investment (MEI) is that rate of return which will cause the present value of expected future yields from new investment to equal the actual outlay for new invest-ment.* Suppose, for example, that a firm expects to increase its annual sales by $50,000 from the sale of a product it could make on a new machine. Then suppose that the annual increase in costs (principally labor and materials) of producing the additional sales is expected to be $25,000 and that the firm is in a 50 percent tax bracket. The average annual ex-pected change in after-tax profits is thus $12,500. If the total cost of the new machine is $100,000 and it is expected to yield this income stream of $12,500 in perpetuity, we can calculate r, the marginal efficiency of investment, using the formula

$$r = \frac{R}{P} \qquad [19\text{--}5]$$

where R is the after-tax profit expected in perpetuity and P is the actual cost of investment. Thus

$$r = \frac{12,500}{100,000} = 12\frac{1}{2}\%$$

This theory of investment expenditures assumes that entrepreneurs seek profit and are profit maximizers. The illustration above shows that, for a $100,000 investment in a machine, the firm can increase its annual profits by $12,500. But this does not mean that the firm will accept the project or will actually spend $100,000 on new investment. One important item has been omitted—the cost of funds. It is this cost that determines the cutoff point on new investments. Firms are continually considering alterna-tive investments in plant and equipment, each of which is expected to yield a particular income stream. The profit-maximizing firm will rank alternative investment projects by rates of return and will accept new projects until a point is reached where the *marginal efficiency of investment is equal to the cost of getting the funds to finance the investment project.* This "cost of funds" is, of course, *the interest rate.* Thus, in our example, if the cost of getting the funds to buy the new machine were 10 percent, it would pay the firm to go into the project, since total profits would increase by the $2\frac{1}{2}$ percent spread. It would not pay the firm to make investments yielding less than a 10 percent return, since interest costs would then exceed ex-pected profits.

Let us modify equation 19–5 by substituting the current rate of interest, i, for the marginal efficiency of investment, r, and V, the present value of the income stream expected from an investment project, for P, the actual cost of investment. R is again the after-tax profit expected in perpetuity. We now have

$$V = \frac{R}{i} \qquad [19\text{--}6]$$

or

$$\frac{\$12,500}{10\%} = \$125,000$$

Here we see that the $12,500 income stream discounted at the interest cost of 10 percent gives rise to a present value of $125,000 for the machine. Since the actual cost of investment is only $100,000, there is a net gain of $25,000 and it clearly pays to invest in the machine. Thus the investment-cutoff criterion can be stated in two ways, each of which is equivalent to the other. In order to maximize profits, a firm should

1) Accept investment projects for which the marginal efficiency of investment is greater than or equal to the interest cost, or

2) Accept investment projects for which the actual cost of investment is less than or equal to the discounted present value of the expected future yields.

Shortcomings of the analysis. The preceding analysis makes two assumptions that limit its applicability: (1) that an investment project yields a constant income stream and (2) that this income stream is yielded in perpetuity. If the income stream is *not* constant, which is generally the case, then the firm must estimate the expected return for each year of the estimated life of the project. We must replace equations 19–5 and 19–6 with another equation,

$$V = \frac{R_1}{1 + i} + \frac{R_2}{(1 + i)^2} + \cdots + \frac{R_n}{(1 + i)^n} \qquad [19\text{--}7]$$

Here V and i are defined in the same way as in equation 19–6, R_i is the ith expected return, and R_n is the final return. Assume, for example, that a proposed investment is expected to yield $10,000 ($R_1$), $20,000 ($R_2$), and $10,000 ($R_3$) for each of three years, at the end of which time the project will be scrapped. If the interest cost is 10 percent, then

$$V = \frac{\$10,000}{1.10} + \frac{\$20,000}{(1.10)^2} + \frac{\$10,000}{(1.10)^3} = \$33,207$$

Unless the actual cost of investment is equal to or less than $33,207, it will not pay the firm to invest in the project.

Another shortcoming of the earlier analysis is the treatment of the cost of funds (or capital) as constant interest cost. Firms have alternative sources of funds—retained earnings, depreciation, new stock sales, and new bond sales—each of which has a different annual cost. Some investment projects cost so much that they force firms to use all available sources of funds; others can be financed from just one source. Usually firms will use internally generated funds (retained earnings and depreciation) prior to selling new stocks and bonds. The cost of funds can be expected to increase as the amount of funds needed expands. Only in the simplest of circumstances can we assume a constant interest rate. Nevertheless, for the sake of simplicity we will do just this. (It is actually more reasonable to assume a constant interest cost for the economy as a whole than for the individual firm, since different interest costs generally seem to be functionally related. We shall return to this point in Chapter 20.)

The MEI for the economy. The preceding paragraphs have analyzed the MEI in terms of how a profit-seeking firm arrives at investment decisions. For the economy as a whole, the same line of reasoning applies. To arrive at an investment demand function we simply add the investment demand of individual firms.

Conceptually we may visualize the relationship between the marginal efficiency of investment and the amount of desired investment for the economy as an investment schedule like that shown in Figure 19–6. Invest-

FIGURE 19–6. The investment demand schedule

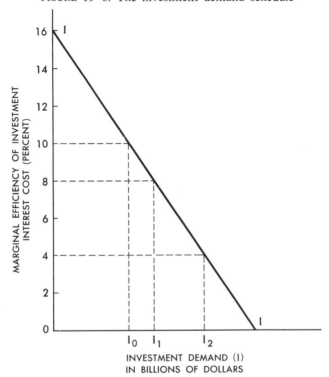

INVESTMENT DEMAND (I)
IN BILLIONS OF DOLLARS

ment demand is measured along the horizontal axis, and the marginal efficiency of investment along the vertical axis. The investment demand schedule, line *II,* shows that the relationship is an inverse one; in mathematical terms, the slope of the demand schedule is negative. This is because alternative investment projects are ranked in order of their desirability, that is, in order of their marginal efficiency of investment. All projects to the left of I_1, for example, yield better than 8 percent returns. Projects between I_1 and I_2 yield between 8 and 4 percent. We assume that firms in the economy prefer to invest in projects with high yields. It is unlikely that they would give priority to investment in a low-yield project unless it were somehow required for business survival (in which case its yield must, in an ultimate sense, be very high indeed). In the aggregate, however, this latter consideration is not likely to be particularly important in determining overall investment demand.

Now let us approach the topic in terms of the rate of interest on the vertical axis. If the interest cost is 8 percent, then businesses and individuals will plan to make investment expenditures of only I_1 billions of dollars. Additional investment expenditure is not apt to take place because the interest cost of getting the funds to invest in real plant and equipment would be greater than the expected return.

Given this investment schedule, changes in investment expenditure will take place only when there are variations in the rate of interest. If the interest rate should rise to 10 percent, for example, the level of planned investment expenditures would drop from I_1 to I_0. Many projects that were considered profitable when the interest cost was 8 percent are no longer so and must be dropped. On the other hand, a decrease in interest costs to 4 percent should lead to a rise in investment expenditures to I_2. There are now more projects that yield returns in excess of the interest cost, and hence there is a rise in investment.

On the basis of this line of reasoning, interest costs are clearly an important factor in determining the amount of investment in the economy. If this is true, then such determinants of interest rates as bank lending practices, central-bank monetary policy, fiscal policy, the money supply and money demand are also significant in determining the amount of investment demand, and hence the overall level of expenditures and gross national product.

Some economists during the 1930's and 1940's argued that interest rates were not important determinants of investment. It was said, for example, that "remarks about the interest inelasticity of investment have been well substantiated by different types of empirical investigation," [8] and that "since the late 1930's there has been a general tendency to suppose that investment is relatively insensitive to the interest rate." [9]

On the other hand, studies in the 1950's and 1960's tended to support the more traditional view presented here. Frank de Leeuw, for example, has demonstrated that the rate of interest and investment by manufacturers is inversely related.[10] Some economists who previously minimized the importance of interest rates even reversed their position:

Conclusions from [earlier studies] may have been premature, for results obtained

[8] Klein, *op. cit.*, p. 65.
[9] J. S. Duesenberry, *Business Cycles and Economic Growth* (New York: McGraw-Hill, 1958), p. 49.
[10] Frank de Leeuw, "The Demand for Capital Goods by Manufacturers: A Study of Quarterly Time Series," *Econometrica* (1962), pp. 407–23.

since 1952 in samples that contain several observations at widely varying interest levels show that interest is a significant variable in equations of investment behavior. The new results show statistical significance for interest variables; they do not necessarily show high elasticity.[11]

And again:

In order of statistical significance, variations in yields on industrial funds, on Treasury bills, and on government bonds appear to have an effect on manufacturers' fixed investment, but only with a one-year lag. The explanation offered for the relationship is that considerable time elapses between initial planning and carrying out of investment, and that interest rates serve as indices of credit availability.[12]

Thus, evidence concerning the influence of interest rates on investment is contradictory. For purposes of analysis, however, we shall treat investment as a function of the rate of interest. As subsequent chapters will demonstrate, the model of income determination we are developing can cope with a situation where investment is either responsive or completely nonresponsive to interest-rate changes.

The MEI and other influences on investment demand. Influences on investment demand, other than the interest rate, are taken into account by the marginal-efficiency-of-investment concept. Anything that can cause a change in MEI will lead to a change in the amount of investment at any given rate of interest. For example, if there is an increase in MEI, the expected rate of return for any given amount of investment will have increased. Also, at any given interest cost, entrepreneurs will be willing to spend more on investment goods and services than formerly because more projects are profitable than formerly.

Figure 19–7 illustrates a shift of this sort. Line II is the original investment schedule. Line $I'I'$ represents the new investment schedule. In terms of investment I_1, this shift increases the return over cost from i_1 to i_2. If the interest cost is originally i, and remains unchanged, then the differential between the rate of interest and the expected return permits an increase in investment expenditures from I_1 to I_2.

Some of the more important forces that influence the marginal efficiency of investment and hence the investment schedule are (1) income, (2) technology, (3) cost of labor and materials, (4) government tax policies, and (5) business expectations.

The *general level of income, Y,* is an important source of investment change. As income grows, demand for products grows too. Thus it is likely that businesses will expand their demand for productive plant and equipment in order to tool up to meet the anticipated demand. The closer to capacity a business enterprise operates, the more likely it is

[11] Klein, *op. cit.,* p. 204.
[12] Franz Gehrels and Suzanne Wiggins, "Interest Rates and Manufacturers' Fixed Investment," *American Economic Review* (1957), p. 91.

FIGURE 19–7. Changes in the investment demand schedule

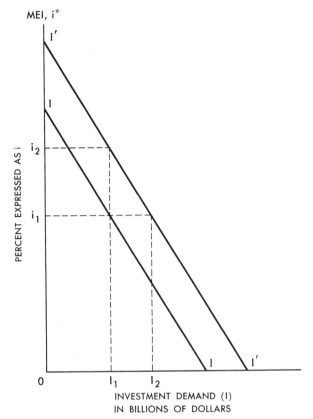

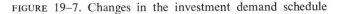

* MEI = marginal efficiency of investment; *i* = rate of interest.

that there will be investment expenditure increases as final product demand continues to exert a strong pull on the economy. On the other hand,
when there is a decline in the economy, there is excess productive capacity,
and anticipated final product demand and planned investment expenditures
will be low. For instance, Table 19–2 shows that the years of greatest
investment increase were in periods of prosperity, whereas the largest investment decreases occurred in recessions. This would seem to indicate
that investment is dependent on the level and rate of increase of income.
The larger the growth of income, the greater is the need for plant and
equipment to meet increasing consumption demand.

Technological change is another important factor that may be a source
of change in the marginal efficiency of investment. When a cost-saving
innovation takes place, the rate of return from investment increases. For
instance, in our simple example on page 348, if a technological advance
permits the firm to produce more product, say $60,000 worth, at the
same cost of labor and materials and if the price of the machine is the

same, then the marginal efficiency of investment is $17\frac{1}{2}$ percent. The cost per unit of output will have been reduced, allowing greater production, or the same production but at a lower total cost. Either way the expected rate of return has increased.

Variations in the *cost of labor and materials* will also influence investment demand. If union pressures raise labor costs, for example, then expected costs on investment projects will also rise and the expected rate of return will diminish. An increase in raw material costs would have the same effect.

Government tax policies are also important. If taxes on business enterprise decrease, the after-tax profits accruing from any investment project increase, raising the expected rate of return. Similarly, government revision of depreciation schedules and depletion allowances also affects investment demand. If businesses are allowed to write off the cost of plant and equipment over a shorter period of time, during any given year while plant and equipment are being depreciated, for example, more funds are available to the firm for investment. Shorter depreciation periods and investment tax credits following 1961 markedly increased investment in the 1960's.

Business expectations of future trends in the economy are especially significant as a determinant of investment demand. In some ways this factor is related to the current level of income and output. If Y is high and rising, expectations will probably be favorable for investment spending. On the other hand, a declining Y may generate adverse expectations and lead to a decline in investment expenditures. Expectations may be influenced by many considerations, however. The prospect of war may lead equipment producers to expect government orders and induce preparations for capacity expansion, for example. Legislative talk of tax revision may cause businesses to postpone investment outlays until the precise nature of the reforms is known. In this respect, uncertainty and anticipation concerning the future clearly influence investment. Expected increases in the cost of equipment will cause investment expenditures to be made prior to the time they would otherwise have occurred. Similarly, falling stock prices may cause concern about the future and induce investment decreases even in a healthy economy.

In general, the factors that increase expected receipts or reduce expected costs lead to an increase in the marginal efficiency of investment; they cause a shift of the investment demand schedule upward and to the right. The factors that decrease the marginal efficiency of investment cause a shift downward and to the left.

The Investment Demand Equation

We have said that investment is determined by the interaction of the rate of interest and the marginal efficiency of investment and that the latter is determined primarily by income, technology, the cost of labor and materials, government tax policies, and business expectations. Of these five forces one—income—is so important that it is often studied separately. Thus it can be said that investment is determined by i, the rate of interest, Y, gross national product, and U', the forces other than Y that also help determine the marginal efficiency of investment. In equation form

$$I = f(i, Y, U') \qquad\qquad [19\text{–}8]$$

The relationship between interest and investment is inverse. The higher the level of interest costs, the smaller investment demand becomes; the lower the level of interest costs, the greater investment demand becomes. The relationship between investment and income is positive, however. The higher the level of income, the greater is the investment demand; the lower the level of income, the lower is the investment demand. Similarly, when other forces (U') increase the marginal efficiency of investment, investment demand increases; when they decrease the marginal efficiency of investment demand decreases.

The relationship beween income and investment is shown diagrammatically in Figure 19–8. I, investment demand, is measured on the

FIGURE 19–8. The relationship between investment and income

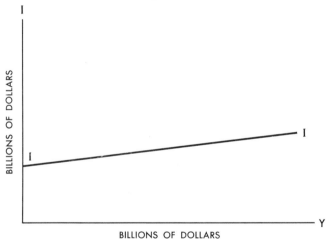

BILLIONS OF DOLLARS

vertical axis and Y on the horizontal axis. Line II slopes upward and to the right, indicating that the higher the level of income and output is, the greater is the investment demand. Again, for simplicity, the investment demand schedule is shown as a straight line.[13]

[13] This investment demand line differs from that in Figures 19–6 and 19–7, where we were concerned with the relationship between investment and the rate of interest. In Figure 19–8 we are simply demonstrating the positive relationship between I and

ADDING GOVERNMENT EXPENDITURES AND THE
BALANCE OF TRADE TO THE EQUATION

We have said that when plans for $S_p + S_b + T$ differ from the plans for $I + G + (X - M)$, changes in income will take place. Earlier in the chapter we discussed the relationship between $S_p + S_b + T$ and Y; to complete our discussion, we need to show the relationship between $I + G + (X - M)$ and Y.

Line *GG* in Figure 19–9, parallel to the horizontal axis, shows the

FIGURE 19–9. The relationship between *I*, *G*, *F*, and *Y*

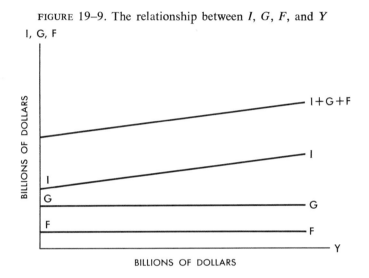

relationship between government expenditures and GNP. There is no change in *G* as *Y* increases along the horizontal axis because the level of government spending is assumed to be dependent on legislative action rather than on the level of income and output. An increase in government spending shifts the line upward; a decrease moves it down.

Like tax receipts, government expenditures are determined by the legis- lature, which is influenced principally by considerations other than the current level of income and employment. During inflation, it is true, there is considerable talk of the need to hold down government expenditures, while in a recession expenditure increases are urged upon the legislature. For the most part, however, federal expenditures on final goods and services are influenced primarily by considerations of national defense and state and local expenditures by the need for social goods and services such as highways and schools. Thus noneconomic factors are more crucial, in general, than economic ones.

Y, and hence it is assumed that *i* and *U′* are fixed. If *i* increases, then line *II* in Figure 19–8 must shift downward because of the inverse relationship between *I* and *i*. If the marginal efficiency of investment decreases, line *II* must also shift downward.

Tables 19–1 and 19–2 and Figure 19–5 show the growth of government expenditures in recent decades. As might be expected, the greatest increase came during World War II. In 1943 government expenditures as a percentage of GNP reached a high of 46 percent. Immediately after the war there was a sharp decline in defense spending, and government spending as a percentage of GNP fell back to the levels of the 1930's. During the first five postwar years, government expenditures averaged 12.8 percent of GNP. With the advent of the Korean conflict, defense expenditures again rose, and in 1953 government expenditures as a percentage of GNP reached 22.4 percent. Following the Korean conflict there was some reduction in defense spending, but not enough to bring government spending as a percentage of GNP back to the level of the 1930's and late 1940's. From 1954 through 1966 government spending as a percentage of GNP varied between 18.6 and 21.1 percent. Government expenditures increased to 23 percent of GNP in 1968, as the Viet Nam war again raised defense outlays. Thus federal expenditures have been somewhat volatile, largely because of variations in our defense needs. In contrast, state and local expenditures in the post-World War II period have grown steadily in volume year in and year out.

Putting these considerations in equation form, we have

$$G = \text{f}(Z) \qquad\qquad [19\text{--}9]$$

which tells us that G, total government expenditures, is a function of Z, a variable representing those forces that cause legislatures to change government spending. (This variable is the same as the Z variable that stood for all the forces that cause the legislature to change the tax rate.)

The difference between exports and imports, $X - M$, is also assumed to be independent of the level of income. Let F be $X - M$. Line FF in Figure 19–9 then represents F, the difference between exports and imports, and illustrates the independence of Y and F. It shifts with changes in the forces that determine the volume of imports and exports. Line FF is above the horizontal axis when exports exceed imports and beneath it when imports exceed exports.

The equation for the difference between exports and imports, F, is

$$F = \text{f}(J) \qquad\qquad [19\text{--}10]$$

where J is a variable representing the forces that cause F to change.

In some ways the assumption that F is independent of the level of income is rather unrealistic; imports do depend on the level of income in one's own country. When income and output increases at home, people may be expected to increase their consumption of domestic goods and services *and* their consumption of imported goods. Likewise, if incomes decrease at home, the public will probably purchase less of both domestically produced and foreign goods and services. Thus if exports remain constant and if the other determinants of imports remain unchanged, F

should increase during recession and decrease with prosperity and rising incomes.

The data available seem to support this line of reasoning. Table 19–3 lists the volume of exports and imports for the post-World War II period. Imports tended to decrease slightly or remain the same in the recessions of 1949–50, 1953–54, 1957–58, and 1960–61. Conversely, during the prosperous periods, imports increased. The effects of these changes in imports on F, however, are barely discernible because exports did not

TABLE 19–3. EXPORTS, IMPORTS, AND NET EXPORTS OF GOODS
AND SERVICES FOR THE UNITED STATES, 1946–68
(IN BILLIONS OF DOLLARS)

YEAR	EXPORTS	IMPORTS	NET EXPORTS
1946	14.7	7.2	7.5
1947	19.7	8.2	11.5
1948	16.8	10.3	6.5
1949	15.8	9.6	6.2
1950	13.8	12.0	1.8
1951	18.7	15.1	3.6
1952	18.0	15.8	2.2
1953	16.9	16.6	0.3
1954	17.8	15.9	1.9
1955	19.8	17.8	2.0
1956	23.6	19.6	4.0
1957	26.5	20.8	5.7
1958	23.1	20.9	2.2
1959	23.5	23.3	0.2
1960	27.2	23.2	4.0
1961	28.6	23.0	5.6
1962	30.3	25.1	5.2
1963	32.3	26.4	5.9
1964	37.1	28.6	8.5
1965	39.2	32.3	6.9
1966	43.1	38.1	5.0
1967	45.8	41.0	4.8
1968	50.0	48.1	2.0*

* Differences in net figures are due to rounding.
SOURCE: Office of Business Economics, U.S. Department of Commerce, *The National Income and Product Accounts of the United States, 1929–1965 Statistical Tables: A Supplement to the Survey of Current Business*, 1965, pp. 74–75; *Federal Reserve Bulletin*, June 1969, p. A–66.

remain constant. Just as U.S. imports depend on national income levels, so our exports depend on income levels abroad. If incomes increase abroad, foreigners will demand more of their own goods and also more U.S.-produced goods. Thus, variations in foreign incomes may cause changes in U.S. exports and in F that cancel out any inverse relationship between F and Y in the United States arising from the positive relationship between imports and Y.

Furthermore, American imports and exports are also related. When imports increase because of income increases, exports eventually increase also because an increased demand for foreign goods by U.S. citizens induces other nations to increase their production. As this happens, income and output abroad increase, enabling foreigners to demand more American goods. This leads to increased U.S. exports and incomes. Thus, the greater the extent to which American purchases are concentrated in countries that in turn make heavy purchases in the United States, the more likely it is that increases in domestic output will lead to both import and export increases for the United States. For these reasons, it is difficult to establish a definite relationship between F (the difference between exports and imports) and the level of output. If exports change as discussed above, then either a direct or an inverse relationship between F and Y is equally possible.

Relative prices between countries and official trade policies are some of the other factors that also affect the position of line *FF*. If prices in the United States decline relative to those abroad, both U.S. citizens and foreigners will demand more American goods. On the other hand, if prices in the United States rise relative to those abroad, demand for goods produced outside the United States, which are now less expensive, will rise.

Changes in national trade policies will also affect the shape of the *FF* line. If the United States were to impose trade restrictions making it more difficult for Americans to buy abroad, imports would decline and, other things being equal, the *FF* line would rise. Of course, other things do not always remain the same. If we were to make it more difficult for Americans to import, other nations would probably retaliate by restricting their imports from us. On the other hand, relaxing trade barriers can lead to a general increase in trade and a corresponding rise in both exports and imports.

The $I + G + F$ Line

The line $I + G + F$ in Figure 19–9 represents the sum of the three separate lines *II*, *GG*, and *FF*. It is parallel to *II* because investment is the only variable that changes with income and output. This line will shift upward with upward movements in any of the lines that represent its components and downward with downward movements in these lines. The component lines in turn will shift when changes occur in their determinants other than Y.

INCOME DETERMINATION

Figure 19–10 shows how the $S_p + S_b + T$ and $I + G + F$ lines interact to determine the income levels in the economy. In drawing these lines we are assuming, of course, that the determinants of each line (and consequently of Y) other than those listed are fixed.

FIGURE 19–10. Income determination

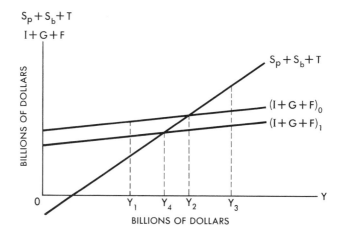

Given lines $S_p + S_b + T$ and $(I + G + F)_0$, assume that the economy is initially producing at a rate of Y_1 billion dollars per year. At that rate of output, the planned expenditures on $I + G + F$ exceed $S_p + S_b + T$, the planned withdrawals from the income stream. Under these circumstances, a strong force for income change exists—excess demand. More goods and services are wanted than are being produced, and inventories are being depleted. Businesses usually respond to this situation by increasing output, which in turn leads to increased incomes, consumption, personal saving, business saving, government tax takes, and investment. Thus C, S_p, S_b, T, and I have all increased because each is partly determined by Y. These forces tend to increase income to Y_2, at which point demand equals supply and the economy is in a state of equilibrium.

On the other hand, if the rate of output is Y_3, then the planned income withdrawals, $S_p + S_b + T$, exceed expenditures on $I + G + F$. Again, a force for change exists—this time, excess supply. Not all that is produced by business will be sold, and a contraction will occur. Businesses will tend to cut back production until the excess supply is eliminated—again, until the equilibrium income, Y_2, is reached.

The critical assumption for the preceding analysis is that other things remain the same. In the real world, however, other things are in almost continuous flux. Fortunately, our model of income determination enables us to predict the direction of economic change with some semblance of accuracy in spite of the almost continual variation in real world conditions, since changes in these conditions usually occur slowly and in limited magnitudes.

Any of the forces that lead to a shift of either $S_p + S_b + T$ or $I + G + F$ may cause a change in Y. The nature of these changes was discussed earlier in this chapter and will be summarized briefly again at its conclusion. Let us examine one change in detail, however: a decrease in government expenditures. Assume that the economy is initially in equilibrium at Y_2. A decrease in G will then shift the $I + G + F$ line down to $(I + G + F)_1$. Now there is excess supply at Y_2. Investment and consumption spending contract, and actual personal saving, business saving, and government tax receipts decrease also. A new equilibrium income level is reached at Y_4.

Looking a bit more closely at this situation, we see what happens as the government decreases its rate of expenditures. With a smaller demand for output, business must reduce its rate of production or face mounting inventories. With reduced output, employment declines, payments of wages and salaries drop, and disposable personal income decreases. With lower incomes, individuals must reduce their rate of consumption expenditures. People are reluctant to accept a drop in their standard of living, however; because of this, when they reduce their consumption expenditures, they will not reduce them by as much as their disposable income has fallen. Consequently their rate of personal saving also falls. Investment by businesses decreases because of reduced orders and lower Y. The induced consumption and investment expenditure decreases will cause income and output to fall even further. Business saving also decreases because of inadequate demand and the probability of falling profit margins as businesses produce at substantially less than optimum levels. Finally, government tax collections decrease because they are geared to the level of income. Ultimately, Y will have dropped by some *multiple* of the reduction in government expenditures.

The overall drop in Y from Y_2 to Y_4 is greater than the drop in government expenditures because a drop in Y induces decreases in consumption demand and investment expenditures. Thus there is a series of decreases in Y, C, and I. Each successive decrease, however, is smaller than the preceding one. The fact that people divide their falling incomes between consumption and saving decreases reduces the size of the successive income decreases arising out of the induced consumption expenditure decreases. Similarly, businesses drop their investment expenditures by only a small portion of their income decreases, since they are interested in maintaining their productive capacity.[14]

[14] Economists frequently employ what is called *multiplier analysis* to predict Y changes from changes in government spending, changes in investment arising out of U' changes, or changes in consumption arising out of W and X changes. This multiplier analysis makes the assumption, however, that there are no rate-of-interest changes. This very unrealistic assumption significantly impairs the usefulness of the comparatively simple multiplier analysis employed in the classroom.

The concept of the multiplier may be briefly described as follows. Assume that taxes and business saving are zero and are not geared to level of income. Further assume that there is no F, and that I and G are fixed. The marginal propensity to consume, $\Delta C / \Delta Y_d$, is then equal to $\Delta C / \Delta Y$ and $\Delta S_p / \Delta Y_d$ equals $\Delta S_p / \Delta Y$. If this is the case, the ratio of the change in Y to a change in autonomous spending (ΔI or ΔG) will be equal to $1/1 - \Delta C / \Delta Y$. This is known as the *simple spendings multiplier* and can help us predict Y changes from I and G changes. The difference between ΔY and ΔI or ΔG would be induced consumption expenditure

THE RELATIONSHIP BETWEEN Y AND i
(THE *IS* CURVE)

The income determination process just described assumed one very important variable to be constant: the rate of interest. Because both personal saving and investment are a function of interest-rate changes, a different amount of saving and investment takes place at every different rate of interest. Consequently, equilibrium income varies with the interest rate also.

Figures 19–11 and 19–12 illustrate this relationship. In Figure 19–11,

FIGURE 19–11. Income determination when the interest rate changes

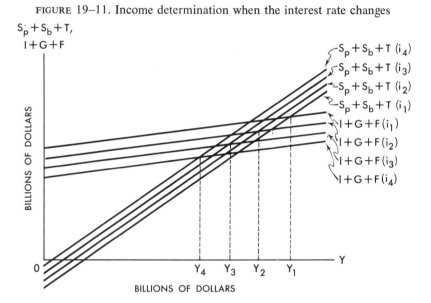

i_1, i_2, i_3, and i_4 represent successively higher interest rates. Each higher rate of interest leads to a successively lower $I + G + F$ line. On the other hand, each higher rate of interest leads to a successively higher $S_p + S_b + T$ line and, as a consequence, equilibrium income levels become successively lower. If, for example, the rate of interest is initially i_1, equilibrium income is Y_1. If i is increased to i_3, other things being given, there is excess supply. Income and output contract toward Y_3. For any level of Y to be one of stable equilibrium, the slope of the $I + G + F$ line must be less than the slope of the $S_p + S_b + T$ line.

---

change. For example, assume that the marginal propensity to consume is .8. Substituting into the multiplier formula, we get $1/1 - .8$, or 5. This tells us that if government expenditures decrease, for example, by $1 billion, the overall decrease in income induced will be $5 billion, $1 billion in the form of reduced government expenditures and $4 billion in reduced consumption spending. In terms of Figure 19–10, if the slope of the lines were drawn according to these assumptions Y_4 would be $5 billion less than Y_2.

FIGURE 19–12. The relationship between the rate of interest and the equilibrium level of income

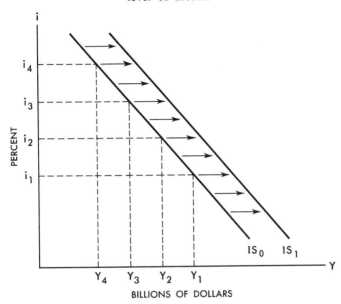

BILLIONS OF DOLLARS

The relationship between these alternative rates of interest and the equilibrium income levels that correspond to them is plotted in Figure 19–12 as IS_0. The relationship is inverse; the higher the rate of interest rises, the lower the level of equilibrium income sinks. The line illustrating this relationship is called the *IS line*. At every point on this line, income is in equilibrium; that is, planned $I + G + F$ equals planned $S_p + S_b + T$. This type of equilibrium is frequently called *commodity market equilibrium* because the demand for *C, I, G,* and *F* type commodities equals the supply of those products.

The *IS* line is an important link in our model of income determination. Given the personal saving, business saving, tax, government spending, and net export functions, *the level of income is determined by the investment function*. Given the marginal efficiency of investment, *the rate of interest determines investment spending*. This further illustrates the economic importance of the rate of interest. Given the *IS* line, there is a different possible level of equilibrium income for every different rate of interest. We cannot determine the actual equilibrium *Y* until we know the rate of interest and how it is determined, however. This will be taken up in Chapter 20.

SUMMARY OF FORCES AFFECTING *IS*

By bringing together the various functions described in this chapter, we are able to illustrate what happens to the *IS* line given various changes in the economy. In general, anything other than i that causes $I + G + F$ to shift upward or $S_p + S_b + T$ to shift downward will move the position of the *IS* line to the right. For example, in Figure 19–11, all the $I + G + F$ lines will rise with an increase in government spending. Hence equilibrium income, as determined by the intersection of the $S_p + S_b + T$ and $I + G + F$ lines for a particular rate of interest, will be attained at a point farther to the right. This means that there is a new *IS* line to the right of the old one. The line IS_1 in Figure 19–12 illustrates one possible new location for *IS*. The new position tells us that equilibrium income will now be higher at any given rate of interest. The new income and output will, of course, be some multiple of the government spending increase. Induced expansions of consumption and investment will have occurred.

On the other hand, anything that lowers $I + G + F$ or raises $S_p + S_b + T$ shifts *IS* to the left, causing a contraction in Y at any given rate of interest.

More specifically:

1. $$S_p = f(Y_d, i, W, X) \qquad [19\text{–}1]$$

Given X, S_p varies directly with Y_d (disposable personal income) and i (rate of interest), and inversely with W (liquid wealth). When liquid wealth increases or decreases, *IS* shifts to the right or left respectively.

2. $$T = f(Y, Z) \qquad [19\text{–}3]$$

Government taxes are determined by legislative action (Z). Given Z, T (the government tax take) varies directly with Y. A change in Z leads to a change in tax rates. If tax rates increase, T increases at all income levels and *IS* shifts to the left. A decrease in tax rates moves the *IS* line to the right.

3. $$S_b = f(Y, U) \qquad [19\text{–}4]$$

Given U, S_b varies directly with Y. A change in U (all those forces other than Y that affect business saving) leads to a change in S_b. If, because of U changes, S_b increases at any given income level, *IS* moves to the left. If S_b decreases at any given income level, *IS* moves to the right.

4. $$I = f(i, Y, U') \qquad [19\text{–}8]$$

I (investment demand) varies inversely with i (rate of interest) and directly with Y (level of income). U' stands for the forces that change the marginal efficiency of investment. If these determinants of MEI cause it to increase, the *IS* line moves to the right. Thus a decrease in the costs of production or enhanced profit expectations lead to increases in *IS*. On the other hand, an increase in the costs of production or worsened profit expectations decrease *IS*.

5. $$G = f(Z) \qquad [19\text{–}9]$$

Government expenditures are determined by legislative action (Z). Increases and decreases in G will move *IS* to the right and left respectively.

6. $$F = f(J) \qquad [19\text{–}10]$$

IS moves to the right or left with increases or decreases respectively in F (the difference between exports and imports) caused by changes in J (the forces that lead to import and export changes).

Supplementary Readings

See end of Chapter 21.

CHAPTER 20

A Model of Income Determination: The Demand for and Supply of Money

Chapter 19 demonstrated that, given the commodity market equilibrium line *IS,* there is a different level of equilibrium income for each different rate of interest. Thus, to determine equilibrium income, an equilibrium rate of interest must be determined. This chapter adds monetary supply and demand to our contemporary model of income determination and demonstrates how they interact with the $I + G + F$ and $S_p + S_b + T$ lines to establish equilibrium income, Y, and equilibrium interest, i. We shall see that to establish equilibrium income we must simultaneously establish a monetary equilibrium.

THE SUPPLY OF MONEY

Chapter 15 mentioned that most theories of money supply determination today actually take the supply of money as fixed. Money consists of currency outside banks and demand deposits. Since variations in currency can occur only at the expense of demand deposits, the total volume of money depends primarily on demand deposit variations. The ability of the banking system to create demand deposits depends on its reserve base, which in turn is controlled by the Federal Reserve. Depending on the required reserve ratios, the volume of demand deposits will be some multiple of the reserve base. Those who take the money supply as fixed argue that the Reserve's powers are such that it can cause the reserve position of the commercial banks to be whatever it desires. It follows then that the volume of money depends on central-bank policy. Put another way, this means that the Federal Reserve can autonomously determine the stock of money independent of conditions that are endogenous to (produced from within) the economic system.

As noted earlier, this line of analysis makes two untenable assumptions:

(1) that the commercial banking system reacts passively to changes in its reserve base and (2) that the Federal Reserve selects a specific amount of money which it considers suitable for the economy and counters any move by commercial banks to create a different amount. In fact, commercial banks react quite vigorously to changes in reserve positions. Furthermore, since the Federal Reserve makes policy changes slowly, commercial banks have substantial latitude in money supply creation. Our analysis of the effectiveness of various monetary controls shows that *the money supply actually tends to change procyclically, increasing on the upward part of the cycle and decreasing or increasing at a decreasing rate on the downward part of the cycle.* Thus it cannot be argued that the Federal Reserve autonomously determines the stock of money.

A Contemporary Theory of the Money Supply

There have been few studies designed to specify a money supply function. As previously indicated, the usual assumption is that the money stock is exogenously determined by the monetary authority. Recently there have been several attempts to estimate money supply functions for the United States. (See the references on money supply at the end of Chapter 21.) All these studies work within what are roughly comparable conceptual frameworks. The formal theory usually assumes that the money supply, M_s, is the product of high-powered money, H (currency plus bank reserves for demand deposits), and a money multiplier, m. Expressed mathematically, this relation is

$$M_s = Hm \qquad [20\text{--}1]$$

High-powered money, H, is determined exogenously by the Federal Reserve when it determines R, the reserve base of the banking system. The money multiplier in turn depends on r, the reserve requirement on demand deposits, on c, the nonbank public's desired ratio of currency to demand deposits, and on i', the commercial banking system's desired ratio of minimum excess reserves to demand deposits.

These factors are summarized in equation 20–2:

$$m = \frac{1 + c}{r + c + i'} \qquad [20\text{--}2]$$

This equation is closely related to our earlier equation 7–5, $\Delta D = \Delta A / r + c + i'$. Because equation 7–5 was designed to show how demand deposits of the banking system would respond to changes in the reserve base, the multiplier was simply $1/r + c + i'$. Equations 20–1 and 20–2, however, are intended to predict the total money supply, inclusive of demand deposits and currency.

Equations 20–1 and 20–2 include both demand-for-money and supply-of-money forces. The supply-of-money forces are H, r, and i', whereas c is a demand-for-money force. Assuming H, r, and c to be constants, there is an inverse relationship between i' and M_s. The desired ratio of excess reserves to deposits is assumed to depend on the earnings of commercial banks. Thus i' is expected to vary inversely with the interest commercial banks can earn on loans and investments, i. *The hypothesis is that commercial banks are willing to economize more and more on their reserves as the interest yields on loans and investments increase.* If this is so, then an increase in i will lead to an increase in the size of the money multiplier, m, and thereby to an increase in the nominal stock of money. Ultimately i' will become zero, at which point the relationship between the money supply and the rate of interest becomes perfectly inelastic. At this point, commercial banks have no excess reserves and the money supply is at a maximum.

Figure 20–1 shows diagrammatically the relationship between i and M_s, given H and the forces behind m. The money supply line is called MM. High-powered money, H, is assumed to be fixed by the central bank. Quadrant I depicts the inverse relationship between the interest rate, i, and i'. Quadrant II shows how m varies inversely with i'. Quadrant III then shows how the money supply will vary positively in response to m. Finally,

FIGURE 20–1. The relationship between the money supply and the rate of interest

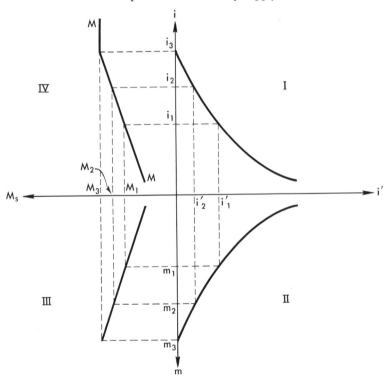

Quadrant IV shows the results of variations in i on M_s. The chain of causation runs from i to i', to m, and then to M_s, thereby establishing a positive relationship between i and M_s. For example, if the rate of interest is i_1, then M_1 is the stock of money. When the rate of interest rises to i_2, i' becomes i'_2, m rises to m_2 and the money stock rises to M_2. When the rate of interest becomes i_3, m rises to its maximum, m_3, and the money supply, M_3, is the maximum amount that the economy can have, since bank excess reserves are zero. From this point on, no matter how high the interest rate is, the money stock cannot change so long as the other conditions given remain fixed.

Putting all these forces together into one general behavior equation gives us

$$M_s = f(H, i, Z') \qquad [20\text{-}3]$$

where M_s stands for the money supply, H for high-powered money determined by the Fed, i for the rate of interest to which the banking system responds (by changing i' and hence m), and Z' for all the other forces that affect m and thereby the money supply.

Changes in *MM*

The line *MM* assumes a given high-powered money, H. In addition, other factors controlled by the central bank, such as r, are assumed to be unchanged. These forces are included in Z'. What happens if the various forces controlled by the central bank are permitted to change? If bank reserves increase because of open market operations, for example, or if r decreases, then, at any given rate of interest, commercial banks have more excess reserves and consequently can create additional money balances. The line $M'M'$ in Figure 20–2 shows the effects of such changes. The

FIGURE 20–2. Changes in the supply-of-money schedule.

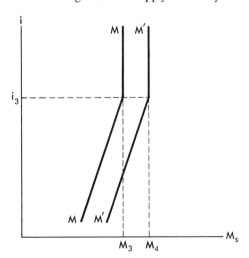

money supply line has shifted to the right from *MM*. If *H* should decrease, or *r* rise, however, the banking system will no longer support as much money. The money supply schedule will shift to the left.

Changes in these forces will also affect the maximum amount of money that the economy can have. For example, a decrease in *r*, or an increase in *H*, will expand the maximum amount of money. In Figure 20–2, this is demonstrated by the rise from M_3 to M_4 at i_3.

If the discount rate decreases, the spread between the return that can be earned by commercial banks on loans and investments and the cost of borrowing reserves widens. This may induce banks to lend more money. Knowing that the cost of borrowing reserves is lower, they may be more willing to take risks; accordingly, they may expand loans and thus the stock of money. The results of a discount-rate drop are shown in Figure 20–3 as a movement from *MM* to *MM'*. Note that the amount of money

FIGURE 20–3. Changes in the supply-of-money schedule caused by discount-rate changes

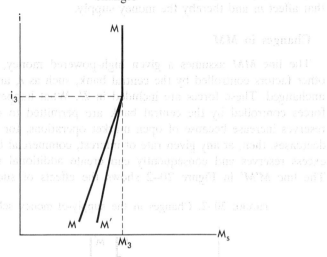

that banks can create will expand only at interest rates beneath i_3. This is because the maximum amount of money that can be created under a given reserve base is not expanded. The discount rate has been permitted to change in this illustration, but not the reserve base. Conversely, a rise in the discount rate would cause a movement to the left without changing the maximum money supply figure, M_3. The interest rate at which we now get this maximum amount of money, however, is still i_3.

Another element in equations 20–2 and 20–3 must be considered—*c*, the ratio of currency to demand deposits. This force is included in *Z'*. It will be recalled that as *c* increases, the ability of the banking system to create money decreases. In the absence of offsetting forces, the potential amount of money that banks can create is reduced by a multiple of the currency drain. Thus an increase of c would lead to a reduction of the money multiplier, m, and shift the money supply line to the left, possibly from $M'M'$ to MM in Figure 20–2.

One force not included in equations 20–2 and 20–3 is the volume of time deposits, TD. Should the volume of time deposits increase, more reserves would be needed to cover time deposits and less could be used as backing for demand deposits. Hence H would decrease and the money supply line would shift to the left. Likewise, should r', the reserve requirement for time deposits, increase, there would be a drop in H and a shift to the left in MM.

Summary of forces affecting **MM.** All these factors influence the MM line. An analysis of their combined impact will yield a theory of money supply determination:

1. The money supply schedule slopes upward and to the right with respect to the rate of interest; this means that the money supply and the rate of interest are directly related. The higher the rate of interest, the greater is the potential supply of money; the lower the rate of interest, the lower is the potential supply of money.

2. The money supply varies in direct proportion to H, high-powered money. As H increases and decreases, MM shifts to the right and left respectively.

3. The money supply varies inversely with r (the reserve requirement for demand deposits), r' (the reserve requirement for time deposits), and the discount rate. Increases in these variables will cause MM to shift to the left; decreases in these variables cause MM to shift to the right.

4. The money supply varies inversely with c and TD. Increases in c, the ratio of currency to deposits, and TD, time deposits, cause MM to move to the left. Decreases in these forces cause MM to move to the right.

THE DEMAND FOR MONEY

The MM line shows how much money it is *possible* to have at varying rates of interest (other things being given)—but how much money will there *actually* be at any given time? To determine the amount of money the economy has at any point in time, information about the demand for money as well as the money supply schedule is needed. For example, given MM, if at i_1 in Figure 20–4 people want only M_0 and not M_1, there is an excess supply of money. If at i_2 people want M_3 and not M_2, there is an excess demand for money; that is, there is a shortage of money relative to individual and business demands. The following pages examine the demand for money in some depth. The position presented here is a synthesis of currently held views. Chapter 22 examines alternative contemporary theories on the demand for money in more detail.

FIGURE 20–4. The supply-of-money schedule

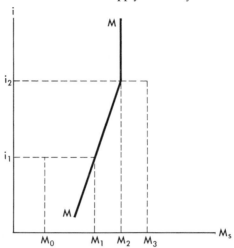

The Demand-for-Money Equation

People want money for many reasons. Households demand it to purchase goods and services, to hold for future purchases, to meet unforeseen contingencies, to avoid the loss that is possible on other forms of liquid wealth, and to have funds ready to make financial investments when suitable profit opportunities arise. Businesses demand money for the same reasons but are more likely to minimize cash balances in an effort to maximize profits. Governments also demand money, primarily to buy goods and services. It is customary to exclude federal government money holdings from the money stock, however.[1]

Liquid assets are not the only assets that can satisfy these motives for holding money. At any point in time, an individual may hold his wealth in the form of money, other liquid assets, or real wealth. Only one of these assets, of course, can serve directly as a medium of exchange in the purchase of goods and services—money itself. Thus a decision to hold money necessarily involves a decision not to hold that amount of wealth in other assets. When a householder or business enterprise decides to increase expenditures, wealth holdings are redistributed from money to goods. The composition of the wealth holdings of both the purchaser and the seller of goods changes.

Generally, other things being given, *the demand for money,* and hence the asset composition of total wealth, *is determined by* **Y,** *the rate of ex-*

---

[1] It will be recalled that the money stock consists of currency and demand deposit holdings of the nonbank public. When the government taxes and spends, both the velocity and amount of money held by the nonbank public may vary.

penditures on gross national product, i, *the rate of interest, and* W', *total wealth.* Putting this in equation form, we have

$$M_d = f(Y, i, W', X') \qquad [20\text{-}4]$$

where M_d is the demand for money, Y is gross national product, i is the rate of interest, W' is total wealth, and X' represents other variables that may influence the demand for money.

The Relationship Between the Demand for Money and Y

Other things being given, the relationship between the demand for money and the rate of expenditures is positive. The greater the expenditures are, the more money is needed to make them. The smaller the rate of spending becomes, the less money is needed. The demand for money, however, will always be a fraction of the rate of expenditures. Since expenditures and income receipts occur over a period of time, the average amount of funds held during a period of time will usually be less than the total amount of expenditures.

If the rate at which funds are received and the rate at which expenditures are made remain unchanged, then the demand for money should remain the same. If expected expenditures increase, however, and the rate of income remains the same, then the amount of money demanded will increase; otherwise the expected expenditure increases will not take place. The additional funds will be acquired by selling security holdings, converting time deposits into money, or borrowing from banks. Should expected expenditures decline, on the other hand, there is less need for money to carry out transactions. Money will grow idle, and there may be an effort by the holders of idle balances to lend to others, convert demand deposits into time deposits, or make profitable use of the funds in some other way.

Although M_d is directly related to transactions, it should be emphasized that the measure of transactions being used in our analysis is Y, gross national product. As was explained in Chapter 17, total transactions in the economy are greater than gross national product. Money is used to effectuate many types of transactions that do not involve the purchase of newly produced final goods such as the purchase and sale of intermediate goods, the purchase and sale of goods produced in earlier income periods, and the purchase and sale of stocks and bonds.

The direct relationship between the demand for money and Y is frequently ascribed to the *transactions motive* for holding money. By this we mean "the need of cash for the current transactions of personal and business exchanges." [2] Another motive for holding money that is generally assumed to depend on the level of income and output is the *precautionary*

[2] J. M. Keynes, *General Theory of Employment, Interest, and Money* (New York: Harcourt, Brace & World, 1936), p. 170.

motive. This refers to the "desire for security as to the future cash equivalent of a certain proportion of total resources." [3] These funds presumably are held to meet unforeseen contingencies. The greater the expected level of expenditures, the greater is the demand for money to hold for precautionary purposes.

The model developed in this text does not make a distinction between the transactions, the precautionary, and the speculative (to be discussed later) motive. All people who demand money do so partly to satisfy all three motives, but as Milton Friedman has argued, "dollars of money are not distinguished according as they are said to be held for one or the other purpose." [4] Every dollar renders a variety of services and is not necessarily used to satisfy one motive for holding money rather than another.

The Relationship Between the Demand for Money and *i*

The relationship between the rate of interest, *i*, and the demand for money, M_d, as we have defined them for the purposes of this analysis, is inverse. Other things being equal, the lower the rate of interest becomes, the greater the amount of money that is demanded. Conversely, the higher the rate of interest becomes, the less money is demanded.

There are a number of reasons why the demand for money increases as interest rates decline.

First, business borrowers demand more funds since the widening spread between the expected return from the use of funds and the cost of getting the funds permits an increase in profitable investment expenditures.

Second, with easier credit, consumers also plan to increase their expenditures and borrowings.

Third, as interest rates decline, lenders become less willing to lend. Interest is regarded by many financial investors as a compensation for the risks of investment. Barring price inflation, there is no possibility of loss if funds are held in the form of money, other than the sacrifice resulting from not getting an interest return on idle funds. Stocks and bonds, however, fluctuate in value. Government bonds and privately issued securities frequently sell beneath par. Thus if bonds are not held to maturity, the holder may sustain a capital loss. Some companies are unable to redeem their bonds. Similarly, in the event of liquidation many stockholders do not receive the book value of their stock holdings. All these risks combine to inhibit lenders from purchasing stocks and bonds. As a consequence, borrowers offer an interest return on bonds and a dividend yield on equities as compensation to the lender for giving up liquidity and a certain com-

---

[3] *Ibid.*
[4] Milton Friedman, "The Quantity Theory of Money: A Restatement," in *Studies in the Quantity Theory of Money,* Milton Friedman, ed. (Chicago: University of Chicago Press, 1956), p. 14.

mand over goods and services. *Therefore, when interest rates decline, the compensation for the risks of financial investment is reduced, and the willingness of lenders to lend falls.*

Fourth, when interest rates have dropped below a certain point, some speculators may wish to hold more of their funds in the form of money because they expect that interest rates will reverse themselves. By getting into money and out of bonds, for example, they may hope to avoid the capital losses incurred by bondholders as interest rates rise.

On the other hand, as interest rates rise, the amount of money demanded decreases. Lenders become more willing to sacrifice the safety afforded by idle money balances for the chances of profit afforded by higher interest rates; their willingness to lend increases. Borrowers, however, prefer to pay off debt rather than incur the higher costs of borrowing. Fewer consumers borrow, for this reason. Businesses find that the cost of funds has increased relative to expected returns from investment, and business borrowing and investment expenditures both decrease as a consequence. Speculators reduce their demand for money and increase their demand for securities so that they may make capital gains if rates subsequently decline as they expect.

The inverse relationship between the demand for money and the rate of interest is frequently ascribed to the speculative motive. By this Keynes meant "the object of securing profit from knowing better than the market what the future will bring forth." [5] This is also called the *asset demand for money.* Basically, the speculative motive arises out of uncertainty. Speculators assume, although no one knows for sure that it will happen, that interest rates will eventually reverse themselves. Thus they tend to demand more money as the interest rate decreases and less money as the interest rate increases. This enables them to move out of and into securities and to make speculative gains. (See the discussion in the preceding two paragraphs.) Actually, ascribing the inverse relationship between the demand for money and the rate of interest to a speculative motive is a weak argument. It would be just as logical for investors to assume that the current trend in interest rates will continue indefinitely. This would mean a positive relationship between the demand for money and interest rates. Most economists now regard the "speculative" explanation of the relationship between the demand for money and the interest rate as weak.

The demand-for-money schedule. The functional relationship between the demand for money and the rate of interest is depicted in Figure 20–5. The rate of interest, i, is measured along the vertical axis, and the demand for money, M_d, along the horizontal axis. Line *LL* represents the amount of money that is desired at varying rates of interest, other things being given. It slopes downward and to the right, showing the inverse relationship between the demand for money and the rate of interest. The position of *LL*,

<hr>

[5] Keynes, *op. cit.*

FIGURE 20–5. The demand-for-money schedule

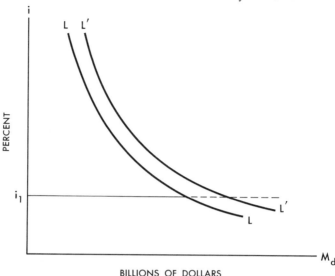

BILLIONS OF DOLLARS

as will be explained in a moment, depends on the value of the other determinants of the demand for money, such as gross national product.

As drawn, line *LL* continues to slope downward and to the right as the rate of interest declines. Frequently, however, this line is shown as becoming parallel to the horizontal axis at some low minimum rate of interest. At this rate, the demand for money becomes perfectly elastic; the yield on securities is so low that it does not pay investors to incur the inconvenience and risk of converting money into securities. The yield may even be so low that it will not cover the broker's fees for the purchase of securities. When such a point is reached, the general expectation will be that interest rates must soon increase. As a consequence, no matter how much money is available in the economy, all of it will be demanded by the public at the low minimum rate of interest. This concept of a perfectly elastic segment of the demand-for-money curve is called the *liquidity trap*. It is depicted in Figure 20–5 as the dotted part of the demand-for-money line starting at i_1. We have drawn the *LL* line downward and to the right beyond i_1 because we are building a general model of income determination. The liquidity trap is in many ways a special case, which some economists argue cannot be verified empirically. (More will be said of this in Chapter 22.)

The Term Structure of Interest Rates

The *interest rate* employed in our analysis is a *weighted average cost of all methods of financing available in the economy*. The cost of each source of funds is weighted according to its relative importance in financing. Thus, for example, if there were only two sources of funds, 4 percent and 6 percent bonds, and the volume of bonds outstanding in each class was $1 million and $5 million respectively, then the average cost of funds would be

$$\frac{\$40,000 + \$300,000 \text{ (annual interest costs)}}{\$1,000,000 + \$5,000,000 \text{ (total value of bonds)}}$$

or $5\frac{2}{3}$ percent.

Actually there are a great many different ways of getting funds in the economy, and each has a cost attached to it. There are the short- and long-term rates of interest on U.S. government securities. There are the interest costs on privately issued industrial, public utility, and railroad bonds. There are the dividend costs to issuers of corporate stocks. In addition, there are the short-term costs of trade credit, of borrowing from commercial banks, of borrowing from consumer finance companies, and of borrowing from sales finance companies. To examine the effects of the interest rate on the demand for money, we should really study the whole spectrum of rates. This would necessitate some extremely complex calculations, however. Thus, to simplify our explanation of this relationship, we use the average cost of all methods of financing on the assumption that there is some stable functional relationship between the yields of all types of financing instruments. Just what the nature of this functional relationship between yields is depends on what theory one accepts concerning the determination of the term structure of interest rates.

There are three widely held theories concerning the term structure of interest rates.

First, there is the *segmented market theory*. According to this view, what happens in the market for one security has little relationship to what happens in the market for other types of securities. It is the demand for and supply of a particular security that determines its yield. Those who are active in the market for long-term securities are not likely to be significantly influenced by yields on short-term securities. Hence securities with different maturities are poor substitutes. This view is popular in the business world but finds little acceptance among economists.

A second theory, one which receives serious consideration by economists, is the *expectations theory*. This theory holds that a long-term rate of interest constitutes an average of expected future short-term rates and that a forward rate is an unbiased estimate of future spot rates. Assume, for example, that people expect interest rates to be higher in the future than they are now. Lenders will demand higher long-term rates of interest. If they do not receive higher rates, they can refrain from lending on a long-term basis and lend instead on a short-term basis. Thus their funds will not be tied up in the future, when interest rates will have increased. The result is an increase in current long-term rates of interest. On the other hand, should people expect interest rates to decline in the future, borrowers will refrain from borrowing on a long-term basis. If long-term lenders are to be able to lend, they must therefore lend at lower rates of interest. Thus the long-term rate declines. It may even become less than current short-term rates.

A third theory, the *liquidity preference theory,* assumes that risks associated with longer-term securities are greater than those for short-term securities. Thus long-term rates tend to be higher than short-term rates. The market demands a premium to hold long-term securities, which are poorer near monies. This theory seems to run counter to the preceding expectations theory. Research on the relative merits of the two theories is as yet inconclusive.[6]

The Relationship Between the Demand for Money and Total Wealth

The relationship between the demand for money and total wealth is positive. The greater the volume of wealth becomes, the more demand there is for money. Wealth increases as income and output increase. Thus the demand for all economic goods, including money, increases as income and output increase. In other words, if wealth rises, the demand for all components of wealth will rise also, provided that they are superior goods.[7] Assuming that individuals seek to maintain some optimum distribution among their different types of wealth holdings, it follows that if the amount of wealth held in one particular form increases, then this optimum distribution of wealth is disturbed. The situation may be corrected by increasing the amounts held in the other forms of wealth, and people usually attempt to do this by converting part of an increase in holdings of one form of wealth into other forms. In this manner, the optimum distribution of wealth can be reestablished. Similarly, the optimum distribution of wealth can be disturbed by a reduction in holdings of a particular wealth form. When this occurs, there is an increase in the demand for that particular wealth form and a decrease in the demand for other forms.

If the argument above is correct, the demand for money will increase when the desired ratio of money to total wealth is disturbed by an increase in total wealth that is unaccompanied by a proportionate increase in the stock of money. Similarly, the demand for money will decrease when the desired ratio of money to total wealth is disturbed by a decrease in total wealth that is unaccompanied by a proportionate decrease in the stock of money.

[6] See Lester Telser, "A Critique of Some Recent Empirical Research on the Explanation of the Term Structure of Interest Rates," *The Journal of Political Economy* (1967 Supplement), pp. 546–60.
[7] A "superior good" in this context may be defined as one for which there is an increase in demand as income and wealth increase. An inferior good is one for which there is a decrease in demand as income and wealth increase. Most goods are superior in this sense of the word. Some low-cost goods such as potatoes and bread will be inferior goods, however.

Thus, if it is the money stock that increases relative to other wealth forms, then the demand for other forms increases and the demand for money decreases, but not by as much as the total of the money stock increase. On the other hand, if there is a decrease in the money stock relative to other wealth forms, then the demand for other forms decreases and the demand for money increases, but not by as much as the initial money stock decrease.

The significance of total wealth as a determinant of the demand for money should not be overemphasized, however. Economists generally regard i and Y as more important determinants of the demand for money since these variables can change quickly, whereas the total volume of wealth in the economy is so large that percentage changes in the total are actually very small and occur only over sizable stretches of time. Thus wealth is regarded as a long-run determinant of the demand for money. Liquid wealth, however, does change comparatively quickly. Since the total of liquid wealth, at least that part of it that is in the form of near monies, is only a fraction of total wealth, percentage changes in liquid wealth are thought to be significant as a determinant of both the demand for money and the demand for consumer goods and services.[8]

The Relationship Between the Demand for Money and Other Variables

X' is a variable that represents all the other forces that can influence the demand for money, such as expectations regarding price and income movements, the desired distribution of the various wealth forms, and the various factors discussed by Irving Fisher and Dennis Robertson (see Table 17–2).

Saying that people expect *prices* to increase is another way of saying that they expect the purchasing power of money to decline. In such a situation, it pays for them to transfer their funds from money to other assets such as consumer durables or equities, which do not normally decrease in price as the price level rises. Thus, with expectations of rising prices, the demand for money decreases. Conversely, expectations of falling *prices* mean that people believe the purchasing power of money will increase. As a consequence they will demand more money, reduce their expenditures, and reduce their holdings of goods that decline in value.

The expectation that future *incomes* will rise simply means that people believe they will be getting more money receipts in the future and thus that their ability to buy goods and services will be enhanced. In anticipation of this, people may decrease their current demand for money and increase current expenditures. The expectation of decreased incomes, however, means that people feel they will need additional money balances to

---

[8] It will be recalled that in Chapter 19 W, liquid wealth, was used as a determinant of consumption demand and personal saving.

cover future outlays. Therefore the current demand for money will increase, and the current rate of expenditures will drop.

If the desired *distribution* of wealth changes, then the demand for individual wealth components will also change. For example, in the United States, the number of alternative liquid-wealth forms has increased in recent years. The comparatively recent development of such liquid-wealth forms as savings and loan association share accounts, pension funds, and credit union share accounts has increased the number of wealth forms competing with money. Similarly, the number of new types of goods and services available each year creates additional uses to which money may be put. The greater the number of goods (liquid and nonliquid) competing with money, the less demand there is for money as an asset.

The various forces mentioned by Irving Fisher and Dennis Robertson also affect the demand for money. For example, the increased use of installment credit lengthens the period of payment on high-priced commodities. This has reduced the need to accumulate money balances. The more credit is used, the less money is needed. Another closely related factor is the system of payments in the community. The more often and the more regularly people are paid, the less money they need to keep on hand. The more regularly disbursements can be made, the easier it becomes to match receipts and disbursements. Hence there is less need to hold money in reserve for unpredictable expenditures. The increasing use of credit, particularly that variety which involves monthly payments, regularizes expenditures. These are all primarily long-term factors, however; institutional changes are only made gradually.

The Demand-for-Money Schedule and Changes in GNP, Total Wealth, and Other Variables

The demand-for-money line in Figure 20–5 shows how the demand for money varies according to the interest rate, other things being equal. Obviously, however, the other determinants of the demand for money, such as Y, W', and X', do not remain unchanged. Suppose Y increases, for example. This causes the demand for money to increase no matter what the rate of interest. Thus LL will shift to the right, to the position represented by $L'L'$. Suppose, on the other hand, that there is a decrease in income and output. This will lead to a decrease in the demand for money and a shift in LL to the left. From this we deduce that there is a whole family of money-demand lines relating demand for money to rate of interest. Each line represents the demand for money at a different level of income. Figure 20–6 describes this relationship. Successive LL lines represent the demand for money at successively higher levels of income, Y_1, Y_2, Y_3, and Y_4. Each higher level of income leads in turn to a successively greater demand for money, and, consequently, an LL

FIGURE 20–6. The relationship between the demand for money, the income level, and the supply of money

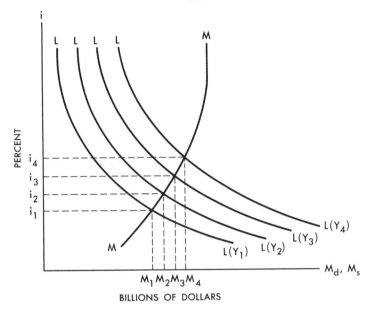

BILLIONS OF DOLLARS

line that is farther to the right. Lower income levels lead to successively lower demands for money and *LL* lines that are farther to the left.

Changes in *W'* also lead to changes in *LL*. Higher wealth levels will raise the demand for money and hence shift *LL* to the right. Lower wealth levels will lower the demand for money and shift *LL* to the left. Similarly, to the extent that the forces included in *X'* operate to increase or decrease the demand for money, *LL* will shift its position also.

Gross national product, the rate of interest, and the demand for money are factors that can change rapidly. Total wealth and the forces represented by *X'*, however, usually change gradually. Thus it is relatively accurate to take the family of money-demand lines as a hypothetical representation of the relationship between *Y*, *i*, and M_d in the short run. In other words, *given W' and X', M_d varies directly with Y and inversely with i.*

THE INTERACTION OF THE DEMAND FOR MONEY
AND THE SUPPLY OF MONEY

In addition to the demand-for-money lines, Figure 20–6 shows the supply-of-money schedule *MM* as developed in this chapter. Assuming that income is fixed at Y_1, there is one money demand line and the money supply line, *MM*. The interaction between these two schedules determines the rate of interest and the actual money stock. Where the two schedules intersect, the demand for money and the supply of money are equal and we have equilibrium in the money market, as at i_1 and M_1. At any other rate of interest there can be no equilibrium since the demand for money and the supply are not equal.

At i_2, for example, given MM and $LL(Y_1)$, there is an *excess supply* of money. The amount of money that can be created exceeds the amount that is demanded. When this occurs, forces are set in motion that tend to reduce the rate of interest. For example, some lenders are willing to accept lower rates of interest, in order to be able to invest their funds. As interest rates decline, the amount of money demanded increases because some borrowers become more willing to borrow. Similarly, some lenders who are unwilling to lend at these lower interest rates reduce their demand for securities and switch their funds to money instead. The banking system also becomes less willing to make loans and create money at this lower rate of interest. Thus we move down and to the right along the demand schedule and down and to the left along the supply schedule until M_d and M_s are equal at an equilibrium rate of interest, i_1.

On the other hand, at i_1, given MM and $LL(Y_2)$, there is an *excess demand* for money; the amount of money available is insufficient to meet the amount demanded. Forces are now set in motion that tend to raise interest rates. Many borrowers may be willing to borrow at interest rates higher than i_1. Thus to ensure that they get the funds they feel they need, they will issue securities bearing yields higher than i_1. This, in turn, will induce some holders of funds to reduce their demand for money and to begin lending instead. Other borrowers, unable to pay the higher rates, will stop borrowing. Thus there will be a tendency for the economy to move up and to the left along the demand curve $LL(Y_2)$. At the same time, the higher rate of interest will induce banks to expand their loans and create additional money. This will cause the economy to move up the MM curve. The increase in the amount of money that banks are willing to create and the decrease in the amount demanded brings the demand and supply of money to equilibrium at i_2 and M_2.

THE RELATIONSHIP BETWEEN Y AND i
(THE LM CURVE)

The preceding discussion assumed a given level of income. The forces that operate to change the rate of interest also work to change the level of income, however. For example, a decline in the rate of interest, as shown in Chapter 19, expands investment and consumption demands, and consequently it expands Y. It is very unlikely, therefore, that Y will remain stable as i changes. There is a different equilibrium rate of interest equating the demand for money with the supply at every different level of income, Y. Figure 20–7 shows this relationship between the level of income and the rate of interest. The left-hand diagram is similar

FIGURE 20–7. The relationship between the rate of interest and the level of income

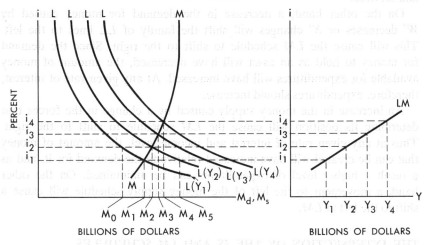

to Figure 20–6. Equilibrium is reached at interest rates i_1, i_2, i_3, and i_4 when income is at the successively higher income levels Y_1, Y_2, Y_3, and Y_4. The right-hand diagram plots the relationship between these alternative income levels and their various equilibrium rates of interest. The relationship is positive, showing that the higher the level of income becomes, the higher the rate of interest that equates the money supply and demand must be. Line *LM* depicts this relationship; at every point on this line, the demand for money is equal to the supply.

At any point to the right of *LM* the demand for money exceeds the supply. For example, if at income level Y_2 the rate of interest is i_1 instead of i_2, then the amount of money demanded is M_5, whereas the amount available is only M_1. This situation should set in motion forces that tend to raise i and reduce Y. Conversely, at any point to the left of *LM* the supply of money exceeds the demand. For example, if at income level Y_1 the rate of interest is i_2 instead of i_1, then the amount of money demanded is M_0, whereas the amount the banking system is willing to create is M_2. Now forces will tend to lower i and increase Y.

The same forces that determine the position of the money demand lines and the money supply schedule determine the position of the *LM* schedule. Should W' increase or the X' forces operate to increase the demand for money, the family of *LL* lines will shift to the right. This will cause the *LM* schedule to shift to the left. A given rate of interest can now equate the demand and supply of money only at a lower level of income and output. At a given rate of interest, assuming the relation between Y and M_d to be unchanged, an increase in the demand for money decreases the amount of money available for expenditures. It will be recalled from our earlier discussion that one of the ways in which money holdings may be increased is by reducing the demand for other goods and services.

On the other hand, a decrease in the demand for money caused by W' decreases or X' changes will shift the family of LL lines to the left. This will cause the LM schedule to shift to the right. Since the demand for money to hold as an asset will have decreased, the amount of money available for expenditures will have increased. At any given rate of interest, therefore, expenditures should increase.

An increase in the money supply caused by a change in the forces that determine its position will cause the LM schedule to shift to the right. Thus at any given rate of interest and income level, the amount of money that can be created will have increased relative to the demand for it, and as a result a higher level of expenditures can be maintained. On the other hand, a movement to the left of the money supply schedule will cause a shift to the left in LM.

THE INTERSECTION OF THE *IS* AND *LM* SCHEDULES

The LM schedule, like the IS schedule, is an important element in our model of income determination. Chapter 19 established that, given the IS line, there is a different possible level of equilibrium income for every different rate of interest. At any level of Y and at any interest rate, planned $I + G + F$ will equal planned $S_p + S_b + T$. The relationship between Y and i under these conditions is inverse. We have established, however, that given the LM line it is possible, at any level of Y, to select an

FIGURE 20–8. The *IS* and *LM* schedules

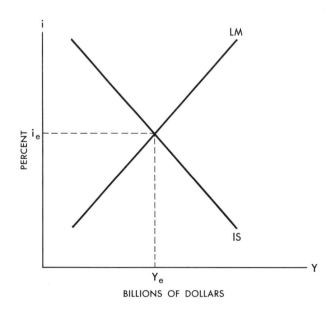

BILLIONS OF DOLLARS

interest rate that will equalize the demand for money and the supply of money. The relationship between Y and i under these money market conditions is positive. Given both the *IS* and *LM* schedules, we are now in a position to determine how the total demand behind gross national product interacts with monetary supply and demand to determine equilibrium output and an equilibrium interest rate.

Figure 20–8 plots the intersection of *IS* and *LM* lines, other things being given. These lines will intersect at only one point (i_e, Y_e), which is the only combination of i and Y capable of producing equilibrium in both the money and commodity markets. Only at point i_e, Y_e will the demand for money equal the supply of money, and *ex ante* $I + G + F$ equal *ex ante* $S_p + S_b + T$. As explained earlier, at any point to the right of the *LM* curve the demand for money exceeds the supply. Conversely, at any point to the left of the *LM* curve the supply of money exceeds the demand. Either of these two situations will set in motion self-corrective forces that will tend to change both Y and i so that the demand for money will equal the supply.

Similarly, any points not lying on the *IS* curve are also points of disequilibrium. At any point to the right of *IS*, $S_p + S_b + T$ exceeds $I + G + F$; at any point to the left of *IS* the sum of I, G, and F exceeds the sum of S_p, S_b, and T.[9] Either of these situations will also set in motion self-corrective forces that will tend to bring $S_p + S_b + T$ into equality with $I + G + F$. In the first case, for example, these forces will tend to contract Y, whereas in the second they will tend to expand it. Chapter 19 examined the forces that cause changes in saving and spending, thereby inducing changes in Y. No mention was made of the monetary sources of change, however. The following chapter will explain some of the important interactions between the money market (*LM*) and the commodity market (*IS*) forces that tend to produce equilibrium in both markets, thereby determining Y_e and i_e.

Supplementary Readings

See end of Chapter 21.

---

[9] From this point on, we shall omit the adjectives *"ex ante,"* "planned," "intended," and so on from $I + G + F$ and $S_p + S_b + T$. When we mean *"ex post,"* we shall state it explicitly.

CHAPTER 21

Applications of the Model
of Income Determination

This chapter shows how our macroeconomic model of income determination can be used to illustrate the interactions between money market and commodity market forces. We assume that the equations of the model developed in Chapters 19 and 20 determine an *IS* and an *LM* line.

THE MODEL IN EQUATION FORM

The equations used in this model are

1.	$M_s = f(H_0, i, Z_0')$	[20–3]
2.	$M_d = f(Y, i, W_0', X_0')$	[20–4]
3.	$S_p = f(Y_d, i, W_0, X_0)$	[19–1]
4.	$T = f(Y, Z_0)$	[19–3]
5.	$S_b = f(Y, U_0)$	[19–4]
6.	$I = f(i, Y, U_0')$	[19–8]
7.	$G = f(Z_0)$	[19–9]
8.	$F = f(J_0)$	[19–10]
9.	$M_d = M_s$	
10.	$I + G + F = S_p + S_b + T$	

The numbers in brackets on the right indicate where each equation was discussed in the text. However, there is one difference between the equations discussed in the text and the ones used here. Here, the subscript $_0$ is used to denote forces that are held constant, for purposes of simplicity. Two additional equations creating conditions necessary for equilibrium are 9 and 10.

Equations 1 and 2 determine the nature of the *LM* line. At any point on *LM*, the condition set up in equation 9 is satisfied. Equations 3 through 8 determine the nature of the *IS* line. At any point on *IS*, the condition set up in equation 10 is satisfied. There are ten variables in this system of equations: M_s, M_d, S_p, T, S_b, I, G, F, i, and Y. Everything else is fixed. Two of the variables, G and F, are known because we have arbitrarily assumed that their determinants, Z and J, are constant. Two other variables, Y and i, are also fixed by the two equilibrium conditions in equations 9 and 10; Y and i are determined by the intersection of LM and IS. Y_d, of course, may be derived from Y, S_b, and T.

SHIFTS IN IS AND LM

Cases Involving a Shift in IS

Effects of an increase in government spending. Let $(LM)_0$ and $(IS)_0$ be the initial LM and IS lines in Figure 21–1. Accordingly, GNP and

FIGURE 21–1. A shift in *IS*

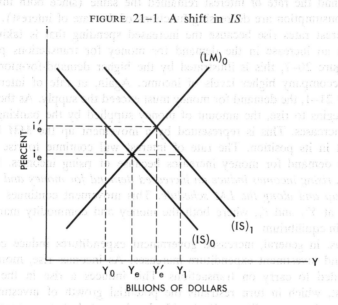

the rate of interest are in equilibrium at Y_e and i_e. Now assume that a change occurs. Suppose that as a result of an anti-poverty program federal expenditures increase, and that they are financed through the sale of securities to the nonbank public. Thus G increases because Z has changed through legislative action. In terms of our diagrammatic analysis, the $I + G + F$ line is raised. As a consequence, the IS line shifts to the right by some multiple of the increase in government spending. This shift is represented in Figure 21–1 by the $(IS)_1$ line.[1]

---

[1] Something else has also occurred to change the position of the LM and IS lines. The method of financing the government expenditure increase has lead to an increase in total liquid wealth and its composition. The nonbank public, after the government has spent the borrowed funds, will have as much money as before, but it will now have more government securities, another wealth form. Thus W', W, and X' have changed. This should shift the IS and the LM lines to the right. These changes are not shown in Figure 21–1 since we have assumed, for short run, that wealth changes cannot affect the economy.

The shift is a multiple of the change in government expenditures because, as we noted in Chapter 19, increased spending in one sector of the economy induces increased incomes, and hence higher levels of spending, in the other sectors. In this case, increased government expenditures should induce increased consumption and investment spending. As a result, the economy will no longer be in equilibrium at i_e and Y_e.

To what extent can the increased government expenditures induce an increase in Y? Were it not for money market forces, these expenditures could cause Y to increase to Y_1. Interest rates rise, however, choking off some investment and consumption expenditures that would have taken place had the rate of interest remained the same (since both investment and consumption are decreasing functions of the rate of interest).

Interest rates rise because the increased spending that is taking place causes an increase in the demand for money for transactions purposes. In Figure 20–7, this is illustrated by the higher demand-for-money lines that accompany higher levels of income. Again, at rate of interest i_e in Figure 21–1, the demand for money must exceed the supply. As the interest rate begins to rise, the amount of money supplied by the banking system also increases. This is represented by a movement up the MM line, not a shift in its position. The rate of interest will continue to rise so long as the demand for money increases because of rising incomes. In other words, *rising incomes induce an increased demand for money and a movement up and along the LM schedule.* This movement continues until we arrive at Y'_e and i'_e, where both the money and commodity markets are again in equilibrium.

Thus, in general, increased government expenditures induce consumption and investment expenditure increases. As incomes rise, more money is needed to carry on transactions. This induces a rise in the rate of interest, which in turn restrains the potential growth of investment and consumption expenditure. It should also be noted that government tax collections and business saving, which are increasing functions of Y, will have increased during this expansionary process.

Effects of a decrease in government expenditures. If, on the other hand, we posit a tax surplus as a result of a decrease in government expenditures and assume that this surplus is being used to retire debt held by the nonbank public, then the process described in the preceding section would be reversed. The IS line would shift to the left, and Y and i would decrease.

Let $(LM)_0$ and $(IS)_1$ be the initial LM and IS lines in Figure 21–1. Accordingly, income and the rate of interest are in equilibrium at Y'_e and i'_e. Suppose that as a result of the end of a conflict, such as the Viet Nam war, federal expenditures decrease. The tax surplus that arises is used to retire debt held by the nonbank public. Initially, there is no change in the stock of money. Subsequently, as interest rates decline, there may be a change in the money stock. In terms of our diagrammatic analysis, the $I + G + F$ line is lowered because of the decrease in G. As a consequence, the *IS* line shifts to the left by some multiple of the decrease in government spending. This shift is represented in Figure 21–1 by the $(IS)_0$ line.

To what extent can the decreased government expenditures induce a decrease in Y? Were it not for money market forces, these expenditures would cause Y to decrease to Y_0. Interest rates decline, however, because the decreased spending taking place causes a decrease in the demand for money for transactions purposes. Lower interest rates in turn induce some investment and consumption expenditures that would not have taken place had the rate of interest remained the same. At rate of interest i'_e in Figure 21–1, the supply of money must exceed the demand. As the interest rate begins to decline, the amount of money supplied by the banking system also declines. The rate of interest will continue to decline so long as the demand for money decreases because of falling incomes. In other words, *falling incomes induce a decreased demand for money that is reflected in a movement down and along the* LM *schedule.* This movement continues until we arrive at Y_e and i_e, where both the money and commodity markets are again in equilibrium.

Effects of an increase in the marginal efficiency of investment. Let $(LM)_0$ and $(IS)_0$ again be the initial *LM* and *IS* lines in Figure 21–1. Now suppose that a change occurs in the investment plans of business. In particular, assume that a technological advance has brought an increase in production with no increase in the overall cost of production. This means an increase in the marginal efficiency of investment, and businesses will desire to increase permanently their rate of expenditures on capital goods. As business carries out its plans to increase investments, the following changes occur in the economy: (a) the output of industry increases; (b) incomes rise because increasing output means increased employment of the various productive resources; (c) with rising incomes people find that personal saving is greater than anticipated—hence there will probably be some increase in both consumption expenditures and personal saving; (d) the induced consumption expenditure increase will cause further rise in output and income; (e) rising income and output will induce additional increments in investment expenditure because investment is an increasing function of the level of income and output; and (f) as a result of all these forces the *IS* line will shift to the right by some multiple of the initial increment in investment expenditures. This shift is represented in Figure 21–1 by the $(IS)_1$ line. It takes into account the initial increment in investment, the induced increase in investment, the induced increase in consumption expenditure, and incidentally, the increases in business saving and government tax collections that, in our model, are positively related to the level of income.

In the absence of changes in money market forces, these increments in expenditures would cause Y to increase to Y_1. However, just as in our earlier discussion of the effects of an increase in government spending, interest rates rise and choke off some investment and consumption expenditures that would have taken place had the rates remained the same. Interest rates again rise because the increased spending taking place causes an increase in the demand for money for transactions purposes. At the old rate of interest i_e, in Figure 21–1, the demand for money must exceed the supply. The rate of interest will continue to rise so long as the demand for money increases because of rising incomes. Again, *rising incomes have induced an increased demand for money and a movement up and along the* LM *schedule*. This movement continues until we arrive at Y'_e and i'_e, where both the money and commodity markets are again in equilibrium.

Other cases leading to shifts in the IS line. We have discussed only three cases involving a shift in the *IS* line. Many other cases are possible. We have used the subscript $_0$ in our model to denote forces that are held constant for purposes of simplicity. If there were changes in any of these forces behind S_p, T, S_b, I, and F, which were assumed constant, then appropriate *IS* shifts would occur. The process would be almost identical with those described, but the initial source of the spending change would differ. Also we have assumed in the preceding cases that money market forces involve movements only along the *LM* curve. Under different assumptions, the *LM* curve might also move.

Cases Involving a Shift in LM

Effects of a change in the money supply schedule. Assuming an economy at equilibrium at Y_e and i_e, suppose there is an open market purchase of U.S. government securities from the nonbank public by the Federal Reserve. This directly increases the money stock holdings of the nonbank public and H, high-powered money. The money supply schedule, MM, must, therefore, shift to the right. As a result, the *LM* curve in Figure 21–2 must shift from $(LM)_0$ to $(LM)_1$. Points i_e and Y_e are now to the left of $(LM)_1$; the supply of money exceeds the demand. Pressures are set in motion that, in the absence of income changes, will drive the rate of interest down to i_1.

Interest rate decreases affect the commodity market, however. Consumption expenditures increase and personal saving decreases. Investment expenditures rise because of the widening spread between the return expected from investment in plant and equipment and the cost of getting funds. As these expenditures increase, income increases, which induces an additional rise in consumption and investment. Business income and government tax collections rise accordingly.

FIGURE 21-2. A shift in *LM*

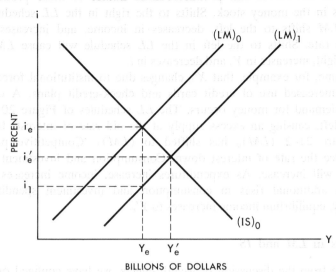

BILLIONS OF DOLLARS

As income goes up due to the expenditure increases described above, the demand for money rises, thereby preventing a fall in the interest rate to i_1. Instead, i falls to some intermediate level such as i'_e. Equilibrium income rises to Y'_e.

Conversely, a sale of government securities to the nonbank public would result in a shift of the *LM* line to the left, with a corresponding decrease in Y and an increase in i. The process described above would operate in reverse.

An additional factor to be considered in a shift of the LM *line is that an increase in* MM *may cause a change in total wealth.* In the case of an open market purchase of securities from the nonbank public by the Fed, there is an increase in the stock of money but no change in total wealth. On the other hand, when the banking system expands money in response to an increase in reserves, the total wealth of the nonbank public rises.[2] This leads to an increase in the demand for consumption goods and shifts the *IS* schedule to the right. However, the resultant increase in the demand for money will restrain forward movement along the *LM* line beyond a certain point. These conclusions concerning the influence of wealth on *IS* and *LM* apply only if we assume that wealth has a short-run influence in addition to its acknowledged long-run influence.

Effects of changes in the money demand schedules. Changes in the

[2] Some economists would contend at this point that the relevant variable is *net worth* rather than total or liquid wealth. Thus when an increase in the money stock occurs as a result of borrowing at commercial banks, the net worth of the nonbank public is unchanged. Both their assets and their liabilities have increased. See Earl Rolph, *The Theory of Fiscal Economics* (Berkeley: University of California Press, 1954).

family of *LL* curves will produce results similar to those produced by changes in the money stock. Shifts to the right in the *LL* schedules will cause *LM* shifts to the left, decreases in income, and increases in the interest rate. Shifts to the left in the *LL* schedule will cause *LM* shifts to the right, increases in *Y*, and decreases in *i*.

Assume, for example, that X'_0 changes due to institutional forces, such as the increased use of credit cards and check-credit plans. A decrease in the demand for money occurs. The *LL* schedules of Figure 20–7 shift to the left, causing an excess supply at the old rate of interest. In terms of Figure 21–2 $(LM)_0$ has shifted to $(LM)_1$. Competitive pressures will force the rate of interest down. Consumption and investment expenditures will increase. As expenditures increase, income increases, which induces additional rises in consumption and investment spending. Ultimately, equilibrium income increases to Y'_e.

Shifts in *LM* and *IS*

Aside from the discussion of wealth effects, we have confined ourselves to cases in which either the *LM* or the *IS* schedule shifts. It is entirely possible, however, that both may change simultaneously.

Consider the case of an increase in government spending. Assume that it is politically inexpedient to raise taxes and that the central bank supports the government bond market. A budget deficit is likely to follow upon the decision to increase expenditures. The Treasury must find some means of paying for the increased expenditure commitments. It may borrow from commercial banks, who in turn sell the securities to the Fed. When the Treasury borrows in this manner, its money balances are increased. As these funds are spent, members of the nonbank public who produce goods and services for the government receive money payments. Thus the money newly created by the central bank and the commercial banking system for the Treasury becomes part of the nonbank public's money holdings. The stock of money increases. As a consequence, *IS* shifts to the right by some multiple of the increase in government spending, and *LM* also shifts to the right. These movements are represented in Figure 21–3 by the movement of *IS* from $(IS)_0$ to $(IS)_1$ and by the shift of *LM* from $(LM)_0$ to $(LM)_1$. The shift to the right in the *LM* curve is smaller than the shift to the right in the *IS* curve. This is because the velocity of money is greater than 1. A \$1 increase in the stock of money will support more than a \$1 increase in the level of expenditures. For example, if the velocity of circulation of money is 4 (which is the same as saying that people want to hold on to \$1 for every \$4 they spend during the course of the year), then an increase of \$10 billion in *Y* can be supported by an increase of only \$2½ billion in the stock of money.

The fact that the increase in government spending was financed by an increase in the stock of money permits the equilibrium level of income and

FIGURE 21–3. Shifts in *LM* and *IS*

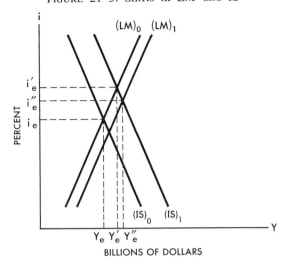

BILLIONS OF DOLLARS

output to rise to Y''_e, rather than to Y'_e. As the level of income and output increase, the amount of money needed for transactions increases. This increase in M_d, in the absence of an increase in the stock of money, would cause interest rates to rise to i'_e. However, with more money available to meet the increased demand for funds, the rate of interest rises only to i''_e, thus helping to maintain consumption and investment expenditures that are related to the rate of interest and permitting Y to increase to Y''_e.

The preceding analysis indicates that the *LM* curve does not shift to the right by as much as the *IS* curve does. Over an extended period of time *LM* could shift to the right more than *IS*, however. If government spending continues at the new high level and if the government also continues to run a deficit, then the stock of money must increase annually. This means that, other things being given, the *LM* curve must continually shift to the right so long as the deficit is financed by the sale of securities to the central bank. Interest rates will continue to fall and income levels to rise. Ultimately, as the economy approaches full employment and the demand for goods begins to exceed the rate of production, price inflation will occur.

The preceding examples of shifts in *LM* and *IS* curves illustrate the many uses to which the model developed in Chapters 19 and 20 may be put. It is important to recognize that the commodity and money markets continually react upon one another. Changes in money market conditions are often related to changes in commodity market conditions and vice versa. The supply of money is particularly important. *Given the demand for money, the model developed shows that the money supply schedule fixes the position of money market equilibrium* (LM) *and, through its influence on the rate of interest, helps determine the direction of change in income and output.* If we relax the assumptions made about short-run influence of wealth, then the supply of money also affects saving and consumption directly, and thereby helps to determine the position of the *IS* line.

THE PRICE LEVEL AND THE PRODUCTIVE CAPACITY OF THE ECONOMY

The Price Level

A trade-off between unemployment and price rise. Up to this point in our analysis, we have made little mention of price change. Implicitly we have usually assumed constant prices, which means that when equilibrium income changes as a result of shifts in *LM* or *IS*, all the change in *Y* is shown as a change in *Q*, real output. The assumption of constant prices is comparatively realistic under conditions of less than full employment. Individual prices may change, but the general price level tends to increase rather slowly as long as the economy has unemployed productive resources available. Once full employment is approached, however, prices are likely to rise sharply.

Figure 21–4 shows a hypothetical relationship between the unemploy-

FIGURE 21–4. The trade-off between unemployment and price level change*

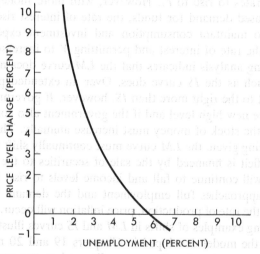

* This diagram is a version of what economists call the "Phillips Curve," which relates unemployment and wage rate change. See A. W. Phillips, "The Relation Between Unemployment and the Rate of Change of Money Wage Rates in the United Kingdom, 1861–1957," *Economica* (November 1958), pp. 283–99.

ment rate and the average price rise. Notice that the price level can be expected to increase slowly as unemployment begins to decline, but as the economy nears full employment, the rate of increase in the price level is much higher. The curve, in other words, shows the trade-off in the economy between unemployment and price change.

Decreases in the unemployment rate will occur as the demand forces we have been discussing expand—as government expenditures increase, as tax rates decrease, as the marginal efficiency of investment increases, as the stock of money increases, and so on. As these demand forces expand, the *LM* and *IS* curves move to the right. Their point of intersection also moves to the right and approaches the maximum amount of goods and services that the economy is capable of producing. This point is represented by Y_f in Figure 21–5. As Y_f is approached, the unemployment rate drops and, as

FIGURE 21–5. The relationship between *LM*, *IS*, the price level, and the productive capacity of the economy

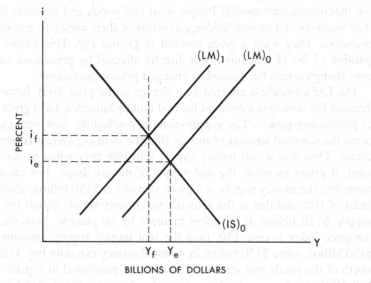

Figure 21–4 demonstrates, the rate of increase of the price level becomes marked. Prices rise so sharply because the remaining unemployed resources are not specialized to the production of the products being demanded. The lack of proper job skills, education, inadequate health standards, and so on almost precludes the hard-core unemployeds' being drawn into the labor market.

One means of making the trade-off between price rise and unemployment loss less marked at high levels of employment is to invest more in the human resource. A human being is, in many respects, comparable to capital in the form of plant and equipment. A man, too, is a productive resource, one which creates a stream of services and output over an extensive period of time. The flow of goods and services produced by the human resource depend on the quantity and quality of the physical plant and equipment with which he works. It also depends upon his own capacities. Thus, given a constant amount of plant and equipment, the human resource will produce more or less according to his innate capacities and the extent to which his abilities have been developed.

By increasing the education, health, and vocational training of the economy's human capital, you increase overall productivity and thus output and income. The improved efficiency of the human resource means that the line shown in Figure 21–4 has shifted to the left and aggregate demand can be more easily satisfied. An expansion of aggregate demand in order to reduce unemployment can now be achieved with a smaller price rise than formerly.[3]

The price level and the **LM** *curve.* How do price fluctuations fit into our macroeconomic model? People want real goods and services; they view their incomes and money holdings in terms of their ability to command real resources. They want a given amount of Q, not PQ. This means that the position of the *IS* schedule is not directly affected by price level variations, even though it may be affected by changed price expectations.

The *LM* schedule is affected by a change in the price level, however. The demand for money is a demand for real money balances, for a given amount of purchasing power. The supply-of-money schedule, however, merely records the nominal amount of money that the banking system is prepared to create. Thus it is a real money supply schedule only when prices are constant; if prices increase, the real supply of money drops. For example, assume that the money supply at a given rate of i is \$150 billion, given a price index of 100, and that at this time the real money supply equals the nominal supply, \$150 billion. If all prices increase by 50 percent, however, so that the price index is now 150, then the real money supply amounts to only \$100 billion, since \$150 billion in nominal money can only buy \$100 billion worth of the goods and services it could have purchased at a price index of 100. With the decrease in the real supply of money, the demand for money exceeds the supply, given the same rate of interest, and pressures are set in motion that tend to raise the rate of interest. As this occurs, consumption and investment demand decrease, thereby leading to income and output drops. Thus we find that for every different price level there is a different *LM* schedule, the schedule for consecutively lower price levels being successively farther to the right. For higher price levels, the *LM* schedules are successively farther to the left. For example, $(LM)_0$ in Figure 21–5 can be used to represent an *LM* curve with a low price level, and $(LM)_1$ can be used to represent an *LM* curve with a higher price level.

[3] The economist will recognize that I ascribed price inflation to *demand pull* rather than *cost push* forces. This does not mean that we cannot have cost push inflation. The period 1955–57 was one in which strong cost push forces may have been at work. I do believe, however, that cost push (wage induced) inflation cannot be sustained for long without the support of strong demand pull forces.

In sum, other things being equal, a rise in the price level is accompanied by a falling real money supply, rising interest rates, and decreased output. On the other hand, a drop in the price level leads to an increase in the real money supply, and thus to a drop in interest rates and a rise in income and output. This may appear paradoxical in light of the fact that in practice output and prices tend to move in the same direction. It must be remembered, however, that we are concerned here with the effects stemming from the price change only. In the real world, prices generally begin rising as product demand increases because of *IS* shifts to the right.

The Productive Capacity of the Economy

Capacity and stable equilibrium. According to our model, the equilibrium Y_e will be the actual Q the economy will tend to produce, so long as we are at less than full employment. Once full employment is reached, however, any intersection of *LM* and *IS* to the right of maximum full-employment output cannot be a position of stable equilibrium. In Figure 21–5, for example, Y_f is the maximum output of the economy. Y_e, therefore, where *IS* and *LM* intersect, cannot be produced. The demand for real goods, Y_e, exceeds the ability of the economy to produce them. Under these circumstances entrepreneurs may raise prices, anticipating greater profits. In an attempt to meet the demand for goods and services, entrepreneurs will also bid labor and other productive resources away from one another. Costs of production will increase. Collectively, however, the most that can happen, since resources are already fully employed, is a redistribution of the composition of output. A greater fraction of total output will be produced by those firms that have successfully lured productive resources away from other firms, but the production of the latter firms will have dropped. The rise in prices, wages, and costs decreases the real stock of money, causing the equilibrium money market schedule, $(LM)_0$, to shift to the left until it reaches $(LM)_1$ and intersects $(IS)_0$ at full employment output, Y_f.

It can also be argued that an intersection of *LM* and *IS* to the left of Y_f is unstable, but only if prices and wages are assumed to be flexible downward. If this situation exists, then the drop in prices caused by entrepreneurs' attempts to induce an increase in the demand for their products will shift *LM* to the right. This will lead to lower interest rates and greater production. Most economists, however, regard the possibility of substantial downward price-wage flexibility in the contemporary American economy as unrealistic.[4] On this basis, an intersection of *LM* and *IS* to the left of Y_f may be regarded as a stable, less-than-full-employment equilibrium point.

The movement toward full employment equilibrium. Technological change, investment expenditures on new plant and equipment, and financial

---

[4] Downward as well as upward price flexibility is important to "theory as logic." This is discussed in Chapter 22.

investment in the human resource all tend to increase the productive capacity of the economy. Our analysis to this point has assumed that full employment equilibrium, Y_f, remains fixed. Actually, with a growing economy it is always moving to the right. For example, in Figure 21–5 the ability of the economy to produce may shift from a maximum of Y_f to, let us say, Y_e. If the economy was originally in equilibrium at i_f and Y_f, with the relevant LM and IS curves $(LM)_1$ and $(IS)_0$, then with the expansion of capacity the economy is still in equilibrium, but it is a *less-than-full-employment* equilibrium. An expansion of demand is needed to bring the economy to a new, and higher, full employment equilibrium. This can be accomplished through an increase in the stock of money, an increase in government expenditures, a decrease in the tax rate, or an increase in investment expenditures. Other possibilities also exist. It is important that the expansion of demand be adequate to raise total demand for goods and services to a level equal to the output that the economy is capable of producing. Nor will the new equilibrium necessarily continue to be a full employment equilibrium. As long as the productive capacity of the economy continues to expand— and it will so long as investment expenditures are positive—Y_f will move rightward. In order to achieve and maintain full employment, the many forces that determine the position of the LM and IS curves must continually change. Only in this way will the intersection of IS and LM move to the right with Y_f. On the other hand, these same forces need to be controlled so that they will not overshoot the mark and intersect to the right of Y_f and cause price inflation. We shall examine economic policies designed to avoid both unemployment and price inflation in Part IV.

Supplementary Readings

THE COMMODITY MARKET

Baumol, William J. *Economic Theory and Operations Research,* 2nd ed. Englewood Cliffs, N.J., Prentice-Hall, 1965, Chapters 18 and 19.

Duesenberry, J. S. *Business Cycles and Economic Growth.* New York, McGraw-Hill, 1958, pp. 49–112.

Eisner, R., and R. H. Strotz. "Determinants of Business Investment." In Commission on Money and Credit, *Impacts of Monetary Policy,* 1963.

Ferber, Robert. "Research on Household Behavior." *American Economic Review* (1962), pp. 19–63.

Friedman, Milton. *A Theory of the Consumption Function.* Princeton, N.J., Princeton University Press, 1957.

Keynes, John M. *The General Theory of Employment, Interest, and Money.* New York, Harcourt, Brace & World, 1936.

Suits, D. B. "The Determinants of Consumer Expenditure." In Commission on Money and Credit, *Impacts of Monetary Policy,* 1963.

THE MONEY MARKET

Brunner, Karl. "A Schema for the Supply Theory of Money." *International Economic Review* (1961), pp. 79–109.

Cagan, Philip. "The Demand for Currency Relative to the Total Money Supply." *The Journal of Political Economy* (1958), pp. 303–28.

Fand, D. I. "Some Implications of Money Supply Analysis." *American Economic Review* (May 1967), pp. 380–400.

Johnson, Harry. "Monetary Theory and Policy." *American Economic Review* (1962), pp. 335–84.

Klein, John J. "Commercial Bank Excess Desired Reserve Positions and Interest Rates." A Report to the Bureau of Business and Economic Research, Georgia State University, 1969.

Meiselman, David P. *The Term Structure of Interest Rates.* Englewood Cliffs, N.J., Prentice-Hall, 1962.

Metzler, Lloyd A. "Wealth, Saving, and the Rate of Interest." *The Journal of Political Economy* (1951), pp. 93–116.

Teigen, Ronald. "Demand and Supply Functions for Money in the United States: Some Structural Estimates." *Econometrica* (1964), pp. 476–509.

Telser, Lester. "A Critique of Some Recent Empirical Research on the Explanation of the Term Structure of Interest Rates." *The Journal of Political Economy* (1967 Supplement), pp. 546–60.

Weintraub, Robert. "The Stock of Money, Interest Rates and the Business Cycle, 1952–64." *Western Economic Journal* (1967), pp. 257–70.

Additional supplementary readings on the demand for money can be found at the end of Chapter 22.

GENERAL EQUILIBRIUM

Hicks, John R. "Mr. Keynes and the Classics: A Suggested Interpretation." Reprinted in American Economic Association, *Readings in the Theory of Income Distribution.* Philadelphia, Blakiston, 1946, pp. 461–76.

Keynes, John M. *The General Theory of Employment, Interest, and Money.* New York, Harcourt, Brace & World, 1936.

Patinkin, Don. *Money, Interest, and Prices,* 2nd ed. New York, Harper & Row, 1965.

CHAPTER 22

Alternative Monetary Theories

Preceding chapters have developed a broad and rigorous model of the macroeconomic determination of income and output. This model was not designed as a comprehensive model of the workings of the American economy, however. It is merely a pedagogical tool intended to depict various economic relationships. Comprehensive models run into many equations, each of which spells out precise functional relationships between the various factors being studied.[1]

This chapter makes a brief survey of various contemporary views of the importance of money in the economy, placing particular emphasis on the policy implications of the Keynesian theory, the "quantity theory," and the "portfolio" theory.[2] In addition, we shall consider some contemporary refinements of the logic of monetary theory, in particular, of Say's law and the relationship between the demand for money and prices.

THE KEYNESIAN POSITION ON MONEY

In brief, the basic Keynesian position is that output is determined by consumption, investment, and government demand for goods and services. Consumption is seen as a function of income, and investment as a function of the rate of interest and the marginal efficiency of investment. In periods of less than full employment, investment demand is relatively interest-inelastic. Government demand is autonomous; that is, it is determined primarily on noneconomic grounds. The rate of interest is determined by monetary supply and demand forces. The supply of money is autonomous, being determined by the monetary authorities. The demand for money is a function of income and the rate of interest, becoming perfectly elastic at some low rate

---

[1] See, for example, Duesenberry, Fromm, Klein, and Kuh, eds., *The Brookings Quarterly Econometric Model of the United States* (Chicago: Rand-McNally, 1965).
[2] The views presented here as representative of the various groups of monetary theorists are the views of the majority of the members of each group, not the entire group. Thus the Keynesian position presented here is that articulated in the works of Alvin Hansen. Similarly, Milton Friedman has been selected as the spokesman for contemporary quantity theories, whereas some twenty years ago Lloyd Mints would have been considered the leading exponent of this position. The "portfolio" school is represented by John Gurley, Edward Shaw, and James Tobin, despite the fact that Shaw's views on many matters are those of a quantity theorist.

of interest. Since consumption is determined by the level of income and output, and since the investment schedule is relatively interest-inelastic, it follows that the economy will not be significantly affected by money stock changes, at least during periods of less than full employment.[3] Consequently, Keynesians feel that fiscal policy should be the principal means of influencing total demand and total output in the economy.

There are three important differences between the Keynesian position and the model presented in Chapters 19 and 20: (1) Keynesians do not agree that interest rate changes are a source of consumption and saving change; (2) they do not believe that investment is responsive to the interest rate, at least during periods of less than full employment; and (3) they are convinced that at low rates of interest there is a liquidity trap. These disagreements result in *IS* and *LM* schedules different from those presented. The Keynesian *IS* line is vertical, or perfectly inelastic, showing that savings and investment do not respond at all to interest rate changes. The Keynesian *LM* line becomes perfectly horizontal at some low rate of interest, showing that all the money stock is demanded. *The position presented in this paragraph may be described as the extreme Keynesian model of* IS *and* LM. The solid *LM* and *IS* lines in Figure 22–1 illustrate these views graphically.

FIGURE 22–1. The Keynesian *IS* and *LM* schedules

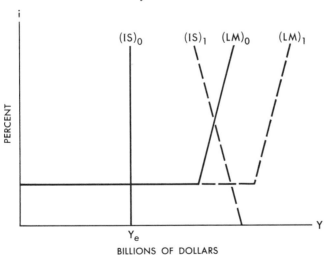

BILLIONS OF DOLLARS

Important policy implications may be drawn from this Keynesian position. First, if the *IS* schedule is interest-inelastic, then money stock changes are unimportant. There is only one possible level of equilibrium income, which is dictated by the position of the *IS* schedule. In Figure 22–1, for example, that income level is at Y_e. Second, fiscal policy—changes in gov-

---

[3] See Alvin H. Hansen, *Monetary Theory and Fiscal Policy* (New York: McGraw-Hill, 1949), Chapters 4 and 5, for a concise statement of this position.

ernment spending and taxation—becomes important. An increase in government spending, for example, will shift the *IS* line to the right by a multiple of the change in government expenditures. The change in income and output will be determined by the shift in the *IS* line.

A more *moderate Keynesian position* would concede that investment demand is responsive to some degree to interest rate changes, particularly as firms approach capacity output. Under these circumstances, moderates believe that the *IS* line slopes downward and to the right, like the broken *IS* line $(IS)_1$, of Figure 22–1. Money supply changes have no effect only so long as the *IS* line intersects *LM* where there is a liquidity trap. The higher the income and the output of the economy become, however, the more likely it is that the *IS* curve will be interest-elastic and thus will not intersect the *LM* curve in the area of the liquidity trap.[4] Under these circumstances, money supply changes can have an economic effect; an increase in the money supply may shift the *LM* line to a new position at $(LM)_1$. Given the $(IS)_1$ line, this will lead to interest rate decreases, investment-expenditure increases, and hence increased consumption spending. A restrictive monetary policy, on the other hand, would shift the *LM* line from $(LM)_1$ to $(LM)_0$. This would lead to increases in the rate of interest and, consequently, decreases in investment and consumption spending.

Under these more moderate Keynesian assumptions, fiscal measures, unaccompanied by money stock changes, would be affected by money market conditions when *IS* intersects the nonhorizontal, or elastic, portion of *LM*. Increased government expenditures would cause some interest rate increases, thereby dampening investment expenditures. However, government spending increases financed by an increase in the stock of money would lead to simultaneous shifts to the right in *IS* and *LM*. Thus, money stock increases would reinforce the effects of the increased government spending on income and output.

THE CONTEMPORARY QUANTITY THEORY POSITION ON MONEY

Contemporary quantity theorists, unlike their neoclassical predecessors, no longer focus on the relationship between money and prices in their analysis. They no longer assume that full employment is the normal state of the economy. Instead, today they stress the relation between money and income. In this respect, their views are comparable to those of Keynesian economists. In many other respects, however, their views differ, and it is these differences that make the money supply, on the whole, a more important variable for the quantity theorist than it is for his Keynesian counterpart.

Many economists today hold the central thesis of quantity to be

[4] See *ibid.*, pp. 79–80.

in the first instance a theory of the *demand* for money. It is not a theory of output, or of money income, or of the price level. Any statement about these variables requires combining the quantity theory with some specifications about the conditions of supply of money and perhaps about other variables as well.[5]

In some ways, this definition is not completely in the quantity theory tradition. Early quantity theorists frequently discussed the relationship between money and prices; other, more recent quantity theorists like Lloyd Mints related money to income. The money supply, to these economists, was the crucial variable because they assumed that the demand for money was stable. The statement just cited, for example, places the emphasis on the demand for money, rather than on the economic policy variable, the money supply. Therefore, a more complete statement might be that *the quantity theory of money argues that there is a predictable relationship between money stock changes and gross national product changes. This follows from the fact that the supply of money is determined independently of the demand for money and that the demand for money is stable relative to its determinants.* Actually, however, no matter which statement of the quantity theory one prefers, the demand for money is an important variable.

According to the quantity theorist, the demand for money and its inverse, velocity, have a stable functional relationship with their determinants. He uses much the same determinants of demand as those discussed earlier—*income, wealth, and rate of interest.* The demand for money is not a constant for the quantity theorist. He merely states that *there is a predictable relationship* between the demand for money and its determinants.

The Keynesian would also agree that the demand for money is a function of income, wealth, and the rate of interest since he believes that the transactions and precautionary components of demand are positively related to the level of income and the speculative demand for money is inversely related to the rate of interest. For those Keynesians who have become "portfolio" theorists, wealth is an important determinant of the demand for money, although money itself is regarded as only one of a whole group of competing financial assets. What then is the difference between the quantity theorist and the Keynesian economist? *First,* the quantity theorist regards the demand for money as more stable relative to expenditures than the marginal propensity to consume $(\Delta C/\Delta Y_d)$. We said in Chapter 19 that the slope of the S_pS_p line is determined by the marginal propensity to save, $\Delta S_p/\Delta Y_d$. The slope of the S_pS_p line, in turn, determines the position of the *IS* line. In essence, therefore, the quantity theorist argues that $\Delta S_p/\Delta Y_d$ and *IS* are comparatively unstable. As a result, he feels that although the income expenditure models are useful for demonstrating economic relationships and for indicating the direction of movements in income, they are not helpful in

---

[5] Milton Friedman, "The Quantity Theory of Money: A Restatement," in *Studies in the Quantity Theory of Money,* Milton Friedman, ed. (Chicago: University of Chicago Press, 1956), p. 4.

making accurate quantitative predictions of gross national product. As an alternative, the quantity theorist proposes that the economist approach the matter by working from money stock changes to changes in gross national product, since velocity exhibits some regularity of behavior. As Figure 22–2

FIGURE 22–2. Gross national product and the money supply in the United States

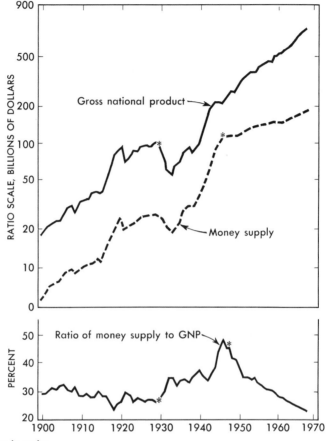

* Change in series.
SOURCE: Board of Governors of the Federal Reserve System, *Historical Chart Book* (1968), p. 66.

indicates, money supply changes and gross national product changes seem to correspond quite closely to each other over time.

In addition some empirical work by quantity theorists tends to support the view that velocity possesses greater stability than the marginal propensity to save.[6] On the other hand, Keynesian economists contend that the tests made of their models have been performed only on the simplest and

[6] Milton Friedman and David Meiselman, "The Relative Stability of Monetary Velocity and the Investment Multiplier in the United States, 1897–1958," in Commission on Money and Credit, *Stabilization Policies* (Englewood Cliffs, N.J.: Prentice-Hall, 1963).

crudest versions, rather than on the more sophisticated econometric models.[7] Still other economists argue that it is incorrect to stress either the marginal propensity to save or the velocity of money to the exclusion of the other variables.[8]

A *second* area of disagreement between quantity and Keynesian economists has to do with the liquidity trap. Whereas Keynesians generally believe that it exists, at least during periods of deep depression and low interest rates, most quantity theorists question its existence. One early study by James Tobin was designed to test the hypothesis that the demand for cash balances is elastic with respect to the rate of interest. The study demonstrated that this thesis appeared to be true for the period 1922–45; it even demonstrated that during the war years the relationship between idle balances and the rate of interest tended to be perfectly elastic.[9] Empirical data for the post-World War II economic world tend to disprove this relationship, however. More recent studies indicate that the amount of money demanded as interest rates decline does not tend to increase relative to the drop in interest rates. In other words, the demand for money does not become interest-elastic.[10]

THE "PORTFOLIO" POSITION ON MONEY

The quantity theorist tends to regard money as a financial asset that is uniquely important for income determination. Portfolio economists, however, regard money as only one of a group of competing financial assets. For these economists, the more types of financial assets there are in the economy in addition to money, the less important money is, and the more difficult the task of the monetary authorities becomes.

Considerable space was devoted to the development of this concept in Chapters 5 and 8. There we argued that nonbank financial institutions create forms of liquid wealth that compete with money for a place in the portfolios of individuals. Thus people are confronted with a choice between these alternative forms. The more successful nonbank financial institutions are in inducing people to maintain their liquid-wealth holdings in the form of savings bank deposits, savings and loan association share accounts, or life insurance policies instead of money, the less control monetary authorities may have over the economy. However, the 1965 and 1966 uses of

---

[7] L. R. Klein, "The Friedman-Becker Illusion," *Journal of Political Economy* (1958), pp. 539–45.
[8] For a professional free-for-all on this issue involving Albert Ando, Franco Modigliani, Michael De Prano, Thomas Mayer, Milton Friedman, and David Meiselman, see *American Economic Review* (September 1965), pp. 693–792.
[9] James Tobin, "Liquidity Preference and Monetary Policy," *Review of Economics and Statistics* (1947), pp. 124–31.
[10] Martin Bronfenbrenner and Thomas Mayer, "Liquidity Functions in the American Economy," *Econometrica* (1960), pp. 810–34; and Karl Brunner and Allan Meltzer, "Liquidity Traps for Money, Bank Credit, and Interest Rates," *Journal of Political Economy* (1968), pp. 1–37.

Regulation Q, and the cooperation of the Federal Reserve and the FHLB, have reduced this lack of monetary control in recent years.

To the portfolio economist, relative interest rates are key variables. When the yield on asset X, for example, rises relative to that on other assets, there will be an increase in the demand for X and a decrease in the demand for other assets. Money is only one form of liquid asset. While it has no measurable yield, it is the safest of all liquid-wealth forms. Hence, as the yield on other assets increases, there will be a decrease in the demand for money and an increase in the demand for other assets, and vice versa. This occurs because money and other assets are substitutes for one another. While other assets do not function as a medium of exchange, they do serve to satisfy the asset demand for money, and hence as their interest yields change, there will be a substitution between them and money.

In terms of the model developed in Chapters 19 and 20, this "portfolio" theory suggests that W' and X' change as a result of the proliferation of financial assets and variations in relative interest yields. Thus it is difficult for anyone to predict the behavior of velocity and harder for the monetary authority to control the position of LM by money stock changes. To be effective, monetary controls must be extended to the liquid-wealth forms created by nonbank financial intermediaries. Thus, whereas the quantity theorist questions the stability of IS, the portfolio theorist questions the stability of LM.

In fact, the chief differences between the position of quantity theorists and that of portfolio theorists boil down, for the most part, to differences in the definition of money. Most economists restrict themselves to the orthodox definition of money developed in this text—currency outside banks and demand deposits. Others, like quantity theorist Milton Friedman, also include time deposits at commercial banks. Still others, like portfolio theorists Edward Shaw and John Gurley, imply (although they do not explicitly say so) that the central bank should define money as consisting of currency outside banks, demand deposits, time deposits at commercial banks, and the liquid-wealth forms created by the aforementioned nonbank financial intermediaries. Interestingly enough, some empirical work seems to indicate that the demand for money is stable for several different definitions of money.[11] Thus it is possible that these differences of opinion may be resolved.

CONTEMPORARY REFINEMENTS OF THE LOGIC OF MONETARY THEORY

Say's Law

The real-balances effect and Say's law. Say's law, as noted in Chapter 19, was an important part of nineteenth- and early twentieth-century mone-

---

[11] Allan H. Meltzer, "The Demand for Money: The Evidence from the Time Series," *Journal of Political Economy* (1963), pp. 219–46.

tary theory. However, the protracted depression of the 1930's and the subsequent development in income-expenditure analysis caused economists to put aside the notion that production creates its own demand. Keynes argued that a situation of satisfied effective demand and full employment production is not normal, but unusual. Nevertheless despite the general abandonment of Say's law, certain theoretical aspects of the principle are still widely discussed in economic literature.

In terms of our income-expenditure model, effective demand and full-employment production are equivalent only when the propensity to save and the inducement to invest are in a particular relationship—when planned $I + G + F$ equals planned $S_p + S_b + T$ at full employment output. Should *IS* intersect *LM* anywhere to the left of full employment output, we would have a less-than-full-employment equilibrium. Figure 22–3 shows a less-

FIGURE 22–3. The relationship between *IS*, *LM*, prices, and output

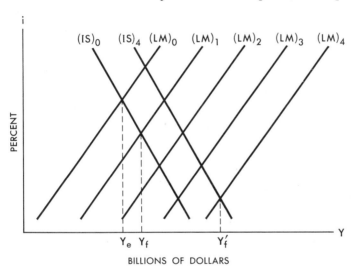

BILLIONS OF DOLLARS

than-full-employment intersection of $(LM)_0$ and $(IS)_0$ at Y_e, which lies to the left of full employment output, Y_f.

Some Keynesian theorists would go even further and declare that less-than-full-employment equilibrium is possible even with downward flexibility of wages and prices. It is on this point that much recent monetary theory has focused. Most economists agree that there are institutional rigidities which prevent downward movements in wages and prices. However, we may, in theory, posit a situation where these institutional rigidities do not exist and, as a result, downward flexibility may be an equilibrator. It is on this theoretical level that the Keynesian argument has been attacked.

We said in Chapter 21 that there is a different *LM* schedule for every different price level. As prices decline, the *LM* schedule shifts to the right. Should the *IS* schedule be sufficiently elastic so that at a positive rate of interest it can intersect *LM* at full employment output, then full employment can be reached via price-level declines. Such an intersection occurs at Y_f in Figure 22–3, when $(IS)_0$ and $(LM)_1$ meet. However, should *IS* not have sufficient elasticity, then it appears that declining prices and less-than-full-employment equilibrium are compatible. This would occur if full employment output were at Y_f' instead of Y_f.

The argument above assumes, however, that the position of *IS* itself cannot be affected by price-level declines. A. C. Pigou and Don Patinkin have demonstrated that, given unlimited wage-price flexibility, full employment output *must* eventually be reached.[12] In their opinion, the *IS* schedule is affected by changes in "real balances" or in real wealth. Thus a drop in the price level increases the real purchasing power of money, and hence total real wealth. Given the desire of individuals to maintain some stable relationship between expenditures, real money balances, and real wealth, there will be an increase in the demand for consumption goods and services. To the extent that businesses are similarly motivated, there will also be an increase in investment expenditures. These changes will cause an upward shift in the $I + G + F$ line and a downward shift in the $S_p + S_b + T$ line. This, in turn, results in a movement to the right in the *IS* line. This process continues so long as prices decline. At some point, therefore, the movement to the right of the *IS* line must lead to an intersection with the *LM* line at a point of full employment output. In Figure 22–3, *LM* and *IS* initially intersect at less-than-full-employment output Y_e. With decreasing prices, both *LM* and *IS* will shift to the right, eventually reaching full employment, when the appropriate schedules are $(IS)_4$ and $(LM)_4$.

This phenomenon is known as the *real-balances effect*. Price-level decreases increase real balances, and hence the demand for goods and services. On the other hand, price-level increases decrease real balances and hence reduce the demand for goods and services. Thus if prices rise, the *IS* schedule shifts to the left, creating the risk of less-than-full-employment equilibrium (assuming that prices do not drop as a result of general overproduction).

Pigou and Patinkin accept the real-world possibility of severe depression and less-than-full-employment equilibrium, but they do not go so far as Keynes did. Given downward wage-price flexibility they believe that full employment must be reached. Given upward wage-price flexibility, less than full employment may also be reached.

How important is the real-balances effect in practice? Although it is important theoretically as a framework of analysis, the real-balances effect is likely to be offset in the real world by the effects of changing price expectations. As prices decline, expectations of continued price decreases tend to decrease spending. The real-balances effect at this point calls for increased spending. Similarly, as prices rise, anticipation of further price

[12] A. C. Pigou, "Economic Progress in a Stable Environment," *Economica* (1947); Don Patinkin, *Money, Interest, and Prices,* 2nd ed.(New York: Harper & Row, 1965).

rises leads to increased spending rather than the decreased spending called for by the changed real balances. Changes in real balances have an important economic effect only when people expect future prices to remain about the same as current prices.

Classical dichotomy. Another part of pre-Keynesian monetary economics, closely related to Say's law, was the *classical dichotomy*. According to this theory, the monetary sector of the economy determines the overall price level, whereas the demand and supply of real goods and services is determined by relative prices only. The price level thus has no effect on the demand for and supply of real goods and services. The real-balances effect denies the existence of this dichotomy, for the change in real balances will affect the demand for and supply of goods and services.

The wealth effect. In terms of our model of income determination, by allowing for the real-balances effect we have now permitted the variable *wealth* to change. As real balances change due to price-level changes, real wealth and the demand for consumption and investment goods and services change. This is an appropriate point at which to mention other forces that also tend to change wealth. The real-balances effect is a price-induced wealth effect. Boris Pesek and Thomas Saving, two contemporary economists, argue that we should also consider an interest-induced wealth effect.[13] They view wealth as simply the present value of the streams of income yielded by wealth discounted at the rate of interest. If the interest rate falls, given the same streams of income, wealth can be expected to increase. As individuals become wealthier, consumption and investment spending will increase. As the interest rate increases, given a constant income stream yielded by wealth, the value of wealth itself decreases, and consequently the demand for consumption and investment goods and services decreases.

The Demand for Money and the Price Level

Another assumption of nineteenth- and early twentieth-century monetary economists was that changes in the price level and the demand for money are proportionate. For example, they believed that an increase of 10 percent in the price level should lead to a 10 percent increase in the demand for money, since people would want to maintain the same command over real goods and services. Similarly, a 10 percent decrease in the price level should lead to a 10 percent drop in the demand for money.

The real-balances effect does not accept this postulate either. Assuming that all goods, including money, are superior goods, it maintains that a rise in the price level decreases real balances. This, of course, decreases total real wealth and real money holdings relative to other wealth forms. If people

[13] Boris Pesek, and Thomas Saving, *Money, Wealth, and Economic Theory* (New York: Macmillan, 1967).

want to maintain a given distribution among wealth forms, the demand for goods and services will decrease and the demand for real balances will increase. This demand is for an amount of real balances less than the volume held prior to the price-level increase, however. Decreasing their demand for goods and services enables people to recoup their real balances, but if these were completely recovered, the distribution among wealth forms would not be the same as before. Real balances would be a larger proportion of total wealth. This means that the demand for "nominal" money balances—real balances demanded, multiplied by the price level—increases, but not by enough to recoup all the real balances lost through price inflation. Thus the demand for money (nominal balance) has increased less than proportionately to the price level, and has less than unitary elasticity.[14]

CONCLUSION

Chapters 16 through 22 have been concerned with monetary theory, the study of the influence of monetary supply and demand forces on the economy. We have seen how economists have changed their views on this topic over the years. Bodin, writing in the sixteenth century, was primarily concerned with the relationship between money and prices. Eighteenth-century theorists saw a connection between money, velocity, and trade. In the nineteenth and early twentieth centuries, most economists assumed a full-employment economy. They concentrated on problems of pricing and resource allocation, accepting Say's law that production creates its own demand. These views were challenged by the economic events of the 1930's, and our contemporary theories were born.

Today, for most economists, monetary theory is an integral part of income-expenditure analysis, which is designed primarily to explain what factors determine income and employment. Thus we developed a contemporary model of income determination, a basic framework that almost any modern economist, whatever his theoretical orientation, can use.

Three different views of the role of money in the economy have been presented in this chapter: the Keynesian view, the quantity theory view, and the portfolio view. All three groups are in agreement as to the logical structure of the appropriate analysis—witness the fact that all can and do use versions of the model developed in this text. Almost all economists today concede that money plays an important role in the economy. The differences of opinion we have discussed are in a sense over detail—how much emphasis should be placed on the role of money. The quantity theorists place somewhat more stress on the importance of money as a causal force in the economy than do the Keynesians. The portfolio theorists stress a broad spectrum of wealth forms, one of which is money.

---

[14] This discussion is comparable to the analysis in Chapter 20 of the relationship between M_d and W'. There, however, we assumed constant prices. A fuller exposition of these views is to be found in Patinkin's *Money, Interest, and Prices*.

Supplementary Readings

Friedman, Milton, ed. *Studies in the Quantity Theory of Money.* Chicago, University of Chicago Press, 1956.

————. "The Demand for Money: Some Theoretical and Empirical Results," *The Journal of Political Economy* (1959), pp. 327–51.

Gurley, J., and E. Shaw. *Money in a Theory of Finance.* Washington, D.C., The Brookings Institution, 1960.

Laumas, Gurcharan S. "The Degree of Moniness of Savings Deposits," *American Economic Review* (1968), pp. 501–3.

Patinkin, Don. *Money, Interest, and Prices,* 2nd ed. New York, Harper & Row, 1965.

Pesek, Boris P., and Thomas R. Saving. *Money, Wealth, and Economic Theory.* New York: Macmillan, 1967.

Ritter, Lawrence S. "The Role of Money in Keynesian Theory." In *Banking and Monetary Studies,* D. Carson, ed. Homewood, Ill., Irwin, 1963, pp. 134–50.

Tobin, James. "Money, Capital, and Other Stores of Value," *American Economic Review* (May 1961), pp. 26–37.

————. "A General Equilibrium Approach to Monetary Theory," *Journal of Money, Credit and Banking* (1969), pp. 15–29.

PART IV

Money and Economic Policy: International and Domestic Policies

CHAPTER 23

The Meaning of Economic Policy

I have become aware that anyone's sense of what is good and beautiful must have a somewhat narrow foundation, namely, his circumstances and his particular brand of human nature; and he should not expect the good or the beautiful after his own heart to be greatly prevalent or long maintained in the world.
—George Santayana, *Dominations and Powers*

POLICY DEFINED

An economic policy is a governmental course of action designed to influence the future behavior of the economy. Basically, there are two types of economic policies: microeconomic and macroeconomic. Those policies that are designed to deal with the problems of specific industrial or regional areas of the economy are called *microeconomic policies*. Farm, labor, business regulation, transportation, "pockets of poverty" policies are all microeconomic. *Macroeconomic policies,* on the other hand, deal with the problems of the economy in the aggregate: unemployment, inflation, and growth. In this final section of the text, we shall confine ourselves to the study of macroeconomic policies.

Macroeconomic policy, or *aggregate economic policy,* as it is frequently called, is *any* government course of action designed to attack national economic problems such as unemployment, inflation, and stalled economic growth. Other matters such as exchange-rate and international-liquidity problems may also enter the arena of macroeconomic policy when they affect the national economy.

Aggregate economic policy has three aspects: First, there is *monetary policy:* any action taken by the Federal Reserve System to affect the economy through its influence on the money stock and member-bank reserve positions. Second, there is *fiscal policy:* any action taken by the Treasury or Congress to affect the economy through the spending, tax, and debt operations of the federal government. Third, there is *international financial policy:* any action taken by the Federal Reserve, the Treasury, Congress, or the executive branch of the federal government to affect the international monetary position of the United States.

Notice that the two words most frequently used in these definitions are *any action.* An *action* is merely a *means* to an *end.* Economic policy is also a *means* to an *end*—the elimination of basic national economic problems such as unemployment, inflation, and poor economic growth. To the extent that our policies help to correct these problems, they are considered effective. To the extent that they inhibit the correction of these deficiencies in the economy, they are deemed to retard economic welfare.

Yet, there are other goals that compete with the elimination of economic want and fear of economic collapse. For example, the freedom of individuals to do as they please so long as they do not harm others physically is usually viewed as a highly desirable political end. Are economic policy actions that restrict individual freedom of action and choice, then, to be regarded as bad, even if they eliminate pressing economic problems? Should economic policy be permitted to enhance the superior power position of the state—which, after all, is merely a collection of individuals—at the expense of the individual members of society?

CHOOSING MEANS AND ENDS

The paragraph above raises a basic question: how are the ultimate goals of society determined, and how are the means to those ends selected?

Economists sometimes contend that it is not their function to deal with such broad social and philosophical questions. It is society's job, they say, to choose ends. It is the economist's job to indicate what means will best achieve the ends selected by society. He uses economic theory as logic and as a set of substantive hypotheses to rank alternative economic policies according to their ability to satisfy the ends decided upon by society. The choice between alternative policies, and ends, however, is left to society.

This position of strict impartiality is illusory. Ethical principles are assumed in making a choice between alternative possibilities. Economics is a social science, dealing with our economic environment and its problems. The economist, like any other scientist, lives in the social and economic environment of his time. He is influenced by the conditions surrounding him. To the extent that his circumstances differ from those of others in society, his thought and behavior patterns will differ. Furthermore, he lives and operates within the context of a given value system. His choice of study, the problems with which he is concerned, the very techniques he employs in scientific investigation, are partially influenced by "his circumstances and his particular brand of human nature." [1] Thus the scientist's so-called impartial statement of alternatives cannot be totally without bias. *The economist, like other scientists, constantly makes normative judgments—hypotheses of what ought to be.* Because of this, it is important that he makes his particular value system explicit.

The economist must also learn to shoulder some social responsibility. He

[1] George Santayana, *Dominations and Powers* (New York: Scribner's, 1951), p. 12.

should be willing to make a specific policy recommendation, once he has made his set of values explicit. As a citizen, it is the scientist's duty to instruct his fellow citizens as well as to learn from them. In short, the economist should attempt to shape both the national ends and the means of achieving them.

How, then, is society to choose the criteria for evaluating economic policy? Several approaches are often used. All usually posit the value judgment that welfare maximization is the ultimate end of policy.

The *first approach* operating on the preceding premise argues that we should *choose that policy which provides more welfare for the members of society than it takes away*. The difficulty with this approach is that it assumes that welfare can be measured. In Part III we said that per capita income is sometimes used as a measure of economic welfare. However, this measure provides us with only a rough idea of how a hypothetical "average" citizen is faring economically. This welfare maximization approach attempts to measure the gains and losses to individuals from particular policy actions, a far more difficult undertaking. Economists and psychologists are agreed that there is no way of measuring exactly human welfare and satisfaction, and consequently no way of measuring gains and losses in individual satisfaction.

If welfare cannot be measured, is there some other way of evaluating alternative policies? Perhaps individuals themselves could rank various combinations of policies according to the amount of satisfaction produced. This technique also runs into difficulty, however. People are reluctant to reveal their preferences. For example, it is frequently argued that taxes should be based on the benefits received from such social goods as education and highways. The individual who receives little benefit would be taxed the least for the social good and those who most value the good would pay the most taxes. Social goods are generally available, however; they would not be removed by nonpayment of taxes. As a result, those who benefit from social goods would attempt to conceal their true preferences. Also, those who need social goods the most are frequently those least able to pay taxes.

A *second approach* argues that in order to maximize welfare we should *choose that policy which produces some gain and no harm*. This approach is, in essence, a policy of inaction. It requires unanimous support for economic policy, and complete unanimity of opinion is, to all intents and purposes, unattainable in this world.

Since society cannot reach a policy decision on the basis of the two previous approaches, it may do so by means of the *voting process*. Ideally, the voting process should reflect the values of the individual voting members of society and thereby permit society to arrive at a rational social consensus on policy. Unfortunately, even this approach has its difficulties. A democratic majority voting process will lead to a rational social decision only if (1) the values of the members of society are relatively homogeneous, and (2) the value systems of the members of society are single-peaked.

The implications of the first condition are obvious. If people have widely disparate views, and if there is no majority that shares the same views, then no consensus can be reached. Whatever decisions are made will be arrived at on the basis of temporary coalitions of competing groups. Thus whenever there is a realignment of groups within coalitions, previous decisions will be changed. Political chaos results. The Weimar government of Germany in the 1920's, the various French governments of the 1940's and 1950's, and the rapidly changing governments of present-day Latin America are all illustrative of the political situation that exists when the members of society have radically different value systems.

The second condition, a single-peaked value system, must also exist before social consensus can be achieved. Assume, for example, that voters are confronted with three policy choices: an extreme left-wing measure, a middle-of-the-road measure, and an extreme right-wing measure. A society that has a relatively homogeneous, single-peaked value system will choose only one of the three alternatives. On the other hand, if the second condition is missing and voters have a double-peaked value system, no consensus is possible. This would occur in the previous example if voters preferred either of the extremes to the more moderate middle-of-the-road measure.

Fortunately, both these conditions have prevailed in the United States. In countries where they do not, policy decisions can be reached by the voting process only on the basis of weak coalitions. If this condition persists, it may so immobilize the government that the only solution may appear to be some form of dictatorship.

SUMMARY AND PREVIEW

Ultimately, our decisions concerning policies and goals must be based on value judgments. In questions of economic and social policy, it is particularly important that we make explicit the *modus operandi* of the value judgment. Within much of Western society, there is a single-peaked value system and relative homogeneity of values. A social consensus may thus be reached by means of the voting process.

When prescribing economic policy, the economist should make his value judgments explicit. To the extent that he can take as given such goals as full employment, stable prices, economic growth, and a favorable balance of payments, he should use the tools of his profession to outline the alternative means available for attaining these goals. In addition, he should take an active part in the decision-making process; he should clearly express his preferences in matters of economic policy.

Succeeding chapters outline alternative monetary, fiscal, and international financial policies. The focus is on the effectiveness of these policies in combating the basic national economic problems of unemployment, inflation, growth, and international financial stability. Where possible, the underlying political bases of the alternative policies are considered.

Supplementary Readings

Arrow, Kenneth J. *Social Choice and Individual Values.* New York, Wiley, 1951.
Dewey, John. *The Quest for Certainty.* New York, G. P. Putnam's Sons, 1960.
Musgrave, Richard A. *The Theory of Public Finance.* New York, McGraw-Hill, 1959, Chapters 4–6.
Rothenberg, Jerome. *The Measurement of Social Welfare.* Englewood Cliffs, N.J., Prentice-Hall, 1961, Chapters 1–2, 12–13.

CHAPTER 24

Exchange Rates and
the Balance-of-Payments Problem

GROSS NATIONAL PRODUCT AND THE
BALANCE OF TRADE

An economy does not function in isolation from the rest of the world; the domestic economic policies of one nation influence economic behavior in other countries, and vice versa. Recession or inflation in one country may have international repercussions.

For example, rising incomes in one nation often lead to increases in the exports of other countries, for as disposable incomes increase, the demand for both domestic *and* foreign goods and services increases. This induces expansion of production abroad. On the other hand, a decline in disposable income at home causes a reduction in the demand for both domestic and foreign goods. This, in turn, can lead to decreased incomes abroad.

The United States is a large nation, and most of its production is designed for the domestic market. Exports usually amount to only about 5 percent of the American gross national product. For this reason, the United States is not likely to be materially affected by economic conditions abroad, except insofar as changes in foreign economic conditions influence American expectations concerning the vigor of the domestic economy.

Imports also represent a small percentage of our gross national product. Their dollar volume, however, is large; total imports for the year 1968 were valued at $48 billion.[1] For many small countries exports to the United States are a major source of their gross national product. Thus the condition of the U.S. economy may well have an important direct effect on the prosperity of these smaller countries.

Goods and services sold abroad are a part of gross national product. They also give rise to a flow of payments into the exporting country. Imports do not contribute directly to gross national product, but they do give rise to a flow of payments out of the importing country. The annual difference in value between a country's imports and exports is termed its *balance of trade.* If exports are greater than imports, the balance of trade

[1] *Federal Reserve Bulletin,* May 1969, p. A–66.

is considered positive. If the value of exports is less than that of imports, the balance of trade is negative. As was shown earlier in Tables 19–1 and 19–3, the balance of trade for the United States has almost always been positive. The payments owed the United States have usually been greater than the payments owed by it to other nations for the purchase of goods and services. Presumably, this should put the United States in a strong position in the international economy.

Generally this is the case, but in the late 1950's and in the 1960's the United States experienced some balance-of-payments difficulties. The balance of trade constitutes only a portion of the balance of payments. Other types of international financial transactions are included in this figure in addition to those involving real goods and services. It is these other transactions that have been the source of balance-of-payments difficulties for the United States.

THE BALANCE OF PAYMENTS

Definition

A nation's balance of payments is a record of the various payments it has made to foreigners and the payments it has received from them over a period of time. The record of the balance of payments is not to be confused with a balance sheet, however. The balance of payments records the *flow* of international payments and receipts; a balance sheet shows a financial position at a moment of time; it is a *stock* concept.

Actually, a country's record of international payments and receipts— its balance of payments—is always in balance over time. This is because the record is an *ex post* concept; it refers to what has already occurred. Actual receipts must always equal actual expenditures. This need not be true *ex ante* (regarding what has not yet occurred), however. Different groups make expenditure decisions at home and abroad. Investors at home decide to make financial investments abroad. Foreign investors do the same. Consumers and businesses at home buy goods and services abroad. Foreigners do likewise. Governments grant loans, make military payments abroad, and so on. Since expenditure plans are made independently by citizens of different countries, there is no reason why the planned foreign expenditures by the citizens of one country need equal the expenditures planned by foreign nationals to be made within the same country. Therefore the balance of payments need not be in equilibrium *ex ante*.

When planned expenditures abroad are greater than expected receipts (planned expenditures by foreigners), then the result is a *balance-of-payments deficit* if the various expenditure plans are carried out. To make up the difference and achieve an *ex post* balance of payments, the debtor country can draw on its previously accumulated balances of foreign monies, borrow foreign monies, or export gold to meet the demands of creditor nations. A country that does not meet its obligations in gold will cover its deficit by transferring to its creditors claims on some internationally accepted money, such as the American dollar.

On the other hand, there is a *balance-of-payments surplus* when expenditure plans are carried out if expected receipts are in excess of planned payments. To make up the difference, foreign countries can follow the same policies: borrow, dip into accumulated balances of foreign monies, or ship gold.

The U.S. dollar stands in a unique position relative to foreign monies in that it serves as international money. Transactions between countries all over the world are settled using dollar deposits. This creates a strong demand for dollars. As a result, when the U.S. balance of payments is in deficit, foreign governments will frequently choose *to accommodate* the United States by accumulating claims to dollars rather than demanding gold.[2] For example, the balance-of-payments deficit of the United States in 1967 was $3.571 billion, yet the actual U.S. loss of gold was only $1.17 billion. Most of the remaining $2.40 billion was made up by the accumulation of $2.80 billion in short-term liabilities against the United States. This build-up of claims against American money enhances the international economic position of the creditor countries.

The U.S. Balance of Payments

Table 24–1 shows the United States balance of payments for 1966, 1967, and 1968. Most of the items listed are self-explanatory. One form of U.S. receipts is the value of its *exports of goods and services,* whereas the value of U.S. *imports of goods and services* is one form of U.S. payments. The difference between the two is our *balance of trade* and was a positive (but apparently declining) item in the U.S. balance of payments in 1968. *Remittances and pensions* consist primarily of emigrant remittances. This is the term used to describe the currency outflow arising when immigrants in the United States send money to friends and relatives abroad. *U.S. government grants and capital flows* include U.S. military and economic grants-in-aid and long-term loans to foreign governments. This item alone was more than equal to the U.S. balance-of-payments deficit of recent years. A large part of these funds find their way back into the United States, however, in the form of merchandise receipts. *U.S. private capital flows* include principally the purchase of plant and equipment facilities abroad by Amer-

---

[2] Even when nations take gold in payment from debtor countries, there is seldom an actual physical transfer of gold from one country to another. For example, many countries have gold "earmarked" for them in the vaults of the Federal Reserve Bank of New York. If the United States owes funds to creditor countries, they may buy gold from the United States Treasury and have it "earmarked" in their name. If others are in debt to the United States, they may sell us some of their "earmarked" gold. In any case, the gold physically remains in the Federal Reserve Bank of New York. This is done because shipping gold from country to country is costly and involves some risk.

TABLE 24–1. U.S. BALANCE OF PAYMENTS, 1966–68

(IN MILLIONS OF DOLLARS)

ITEM	1966	1967	1968
TRANSACTIONS OTHER THAN CHANGES IN FOREIGN LIQUID ASSETS IN U.S. AND IN U.S. MONETARY RESERVE ASSETS			
Exports of goods and services—Total	**43,142**	**45,756**	**50,199**
Merchandise	29,176	30,468	33,376
Military sales	829	1,240	1,423
Transportation	2,608	2,701	2,860
Travel	1,590	1,646	1,762
Investment income receipts, private	5,659	6,234	6,911
Investment income receipts, government	593	624	774
Other services	2,687	2,843	3,094
Imports of goods and services—Total	**−38,063**	**−40,989**	**−48,234**
Merchandise	−25,541	−26,991	−33,273
Military expenditures	−3,735	−4,340	−4,561
Transportation	−2,923	−2,982	−3,162
Travel	−2,657	−3,195	−3,083
Investment income payments	−2,074	−2,293	−2,805
Other services	−1,132	−1,189	−1,350
Balance on goods and services	**5,080**	**4,768**	**1,965**
Remittances and pensions	**−1,015**	**−1,276**	**−1,159**
1. Balance on goods, services, remittances, and pensions	4,065	3,492	806
2. U.S. government grants and capital flow, net	−3,444	−4,210	−3,977
Grants, loans, and net change in foreign currency holdings, and short-term claims	−4,676	−5,191	−5,360
Scheduled repayments on U.S. government loans	803	975	1,115
Nonscheduled repayments and selloffs	429	6	269
3. U.S. private capital flow, net	−4,298	−5,504	−4,860
Direct investments	−3,623	−3,020	−2,743
Foreign securities	−481	−1,266	−1,288
Other long-term claims:			
Reported by banks	337	285	354
Reported by others	−112	−289	−116
Short-term claims:			
Reported by banks	−84	−744	−100
Reported by others	−334	−470	−967
4. Foreign capital flow, net, excluding change in liquid assets in U.S.	2,532	3,185	8,384
Long-term investments	2,156	2,344	5,795
Short-term claims	296	388	666
Nonliquid claims on U.S. government associated with—			
Military contracts	346	64	−86
U.S. government grants and capital	−205	−85	2
Other specific transactions	−12	5	−2
Other nonconvertible, nonmarketable, medium-term U.S. government securities	−49	469	2,010
5. Errors and unrecorded transactions	−210	−532	−199
BALANCES			
Balance on liquidity basis			
Seasonally adjusted (= 1 + 2 + 3 + 4 + 5)	−1,357	−3,571	158
Less: Net seasonal adjustments			
Before seasonal adjustment	−1,357	−3,571	158
TRANSACTIONS BY WHICH BALANCES WERE SETTLED—NOT SEASONALLY ADJUSTED			
To settle balance on liquidity basis	1,357	3,571	−158
Change in U.S. official reserve assets	*568*	*52*	*−880*
Gold	571	1,170	1,173
Convertible currencies	−540	−1,024	−1,183
IMF gold tranche position	537	−94	−870
Change in liquid liabilities to all foreign accounts	*789*	*3,519*	*722*
Foreign central banks and governments:			
Convertible nonmarketable U.S. government securities	−945	455	−10
Marketable U.S. government bonds and notes	−245	48	−390
Deposits, short-term U.S. government securities, etc.	−582	1,537	−2,707
IMF (gold deposits)	177	22	−3
Commercial banks abroad	2,697	1,262	3,382
Other private residents of foreign countries	212	413	368
International and regional organizations other than IMF	−525	−218	82

SOURCE: *Federal Reserve Bulletin*, May 1969, pp. A–70–71.

ican businesses and the purchase of foreign-issued securities. *Foreign capital flows* are the foreign counterpart to U.S. private capital flows—direct foreign long-term investments in the United States and the acquisition of U.S.-issued securities.

These five broad categories resulted in a $3.571 billion deficit in the U.S. balance of payments in 1967. The balancing items were a gold outflow, a *sale* of securities to foreign central banks, and an accumulation of short-term claims against American money by foreign commercial banks. These balancing items added up to more than the deficit in the balance of payments because the United States was making an additional expenditure, the purchase of foreign currencies. On the other hand, there was a small surplus—the first in a decade—in the U.S. balance of payments in 1968. The balancing items were a gold outflow, an accumulation of short-term claims against American money by foreign commercial banks, and a *decrease* in U.S. securities and deposits held by foreign central banks. In years of balance-of-payments deficits most of the balancing items are receipts because they show how foreign governments choose to use the excess of current U.S. payments over receipts. These items are largely self-explanatory. The reason for calling a gold outflow a receipt, however, is not so readily apparent. When U.S. current payments exceed receipts, the creditor countries, as already indicated, may choose to demand gold. The United States must then give up some of its gold holdings in "payment" of its debt. How is this accomplished? Assume, for example, that the deficit of the United States vis-à-vis Country X is $50 million. When Country X demands gold, it does so by using the $50 million in accumulated claims to "buy" gold from the United States. The gold outflow, therefore, is considered an export from the United States, which "receives" $50 million from the sale of gold. In effect, Country X gives us its IOU's on our currency in exchange for gold and we record the receipt of these IOU's as a receipt of that amount in dollars. Gold flows thereby act to balance the flow of payments.

A surplus in the balance of payments, on the other hand, does not mean that the balancing items all become payments. Some move into a payment category, while others remain receipts. For example, in 1968 the principal change in balancing items was the aforementioned decrease in U.S. securities and deposits held by foreign central banks.

Table 24–2 shows that in the early post-World War II period the United States had a balance-of-payments surplus. The productive facilities of European countries had been devastated by the war, and the United States was the only country large enough and sufficiently industrialized to meet the European demands for new plants and equipment. European countries were faced with a "shortage" of dollars, however, because of the lack of U.S. demand for European goods. To solve this problem, the United States helped provide funds for needy countries through unilateral gifts. The Marshall Plan was an early example of such assistance. As Table

TABLE 24–2. SELECTED ITEMS
IN THE U.S. BALANCE OF PAYMENTS, 1947–68
(IN MILLIONS OF DOLLARS)

YEAR	BALANCE ON GOODS AND SERVICES	GOVERNMENT GRANTS AND CAPITAL OUTFLOWS	DIRECT INVESTMENT	LONG-TERM PORTFOLIO	SHORT-TERM PORTFOLIO	OVERALL BALANCE
1947	11,529	−6,121*	−749	−49	−189	4,210
1948	6,440	−4,918	−721	−69	−116	817
1949	6,149	−5,649	−660	−80	187	136
1950	1,779	−3,640	−621	−495	−149	−3,489
1951	3,671	−3,191	−508	−437	−103	−8
1952	2,226	−2,380	−852	−214	−94	−1,206
1953	386	−2,055	−735	185	167	−2,184
1954	1,828	−1,554	−667	−320	−635	−1,541
1955	2,009	−2,211	−823	−241	−191	−1,242
1956	3,967	−2,362	−1,951	−603	−517	−973
1957	5,729	−2,574	−2,442	−859	−276	578
1958	2,206	−2,587	−1,181	−1,444	−311	−3,365
1959	147	−1,986	−1,372	−926	−77	−3,870
1960	4,001	−2,769	−1,674	−856	−1,349	−3,901
1961	5,509	−2,780	−1,599	−1,025	−1,556	−2,370
1962	5,045	−3,013	−1,654	−1,227	−544	−2,203
1963	5,855	−3,581	−1,976	−1,695	−785	−2,671
1964	8,462	−3,560	−2,435	−1,961	−2,146	−2,800
1965	6,944	−3,375	−3,418	−1,078	753	−1,335
1966	5,102	−3,446	−3,543	−257	−413	−1,357
1967	4,768	−4,210	−3,020	−1,270	−1,214	−3,571
1968	1,965	−3,977	−2,743	4,745	−401	158

* Minus numbers are payments.
SOURCE: *Economic Report of the President*, 1968, pp. 306–07; and *Federal Reserve Bulletin*, July 1968, p. A–70; May 1969, p. A–70.

24–2 shows, economic aid played a very important role in reducing foreign balance-of-payments deficits in the early postwar years. In 1947, for example, the American balance of trade was $11.5 billion. In the absence of offsetting forces, this would have led to an $11.5 billion balance-of-payments surplus. The actual surplus for that year amounted to only $4.2 billion, however. Government grants and capital outflows accounted for $6.1 billion, almost the entire difference between the balance-of-trade surplus and the balance-of-payments surplus. This government aid enabled other countries to buy goods and services in the United States.

As the rest of the world gradually recovered from the after-effects of World War II, the dollar shortage gradually diminished. Foreign economies, aided by U.S. economic assistance, were able to resume the production of an ever wider variety of goods and services. As a consequence, people in the United States began to purchase more goods abroad. This occurred to such a degree that our imports grew more rapidly than our exports, cutting down the size of our balance-of-trade surplus. At the same time, U.S. government grants, which had dropped by two-thirds through the year 1954, began to increase; both economic aid and military expenditures abroad rose. Most of these expenditures were directed toward less developed nations, as part of our cold war strategy. Britain, Germany, France, and other developed nations of the West that we assisted immediately after World War II no longer need economic aid. The United States continues to make military expenditures in many countries, however, because we have deemed it necessary to maintain a large military establishment overseas. These grants and military expenditures, combined with a decreased trade surplus, contributed to balance-of-payments deficits in the late 1950's and 1960's.

An additional factor contributing to the deficit was the sharp increase in private capital outflows starting in 1956. Private direct investment and long-term security purchases abroad increased to more than four times their pre-1956 levels in the 1960's. Expanded foreign markets and greater political stability abroad tended to expand these long-term financial outlays. Higher interest rates abroad on long-term securities also stimulated overseas investment. From time to time higher foreign short-term interest rates also increased the outflow of short-term funds.

The small balance-of-payments surplus of 1968 was caused by high interest rates in the United States. Full employment, a strong demand for funds, and a war economy combined to raise U.S. interest rates to postwar highs, thereby inducing American banks and corporations to borrow Eurodollars (see Chapter 7). At the same time, Europeans invested extensively in American securities. These trends continued into 1969. Most economists believe the reversal of the payments deficit in 1968 will turn out to be temporary, because rising U.S. prices have contributed to a reduced trade surplus.

Balance-of-Payments Equilibrium

A country's balance of payments is said to be in equilibrium when *ex ante* receipts and payments are equal. This means that when the expenditure plans are carried out, there will be no surplus or deficit, and the payments and receipts will continue to equal each other over time without the country having to resort to any of the accommodations previously cited (selling gold, borrowing foreign monies, dipping into previously accumulated balances of foreign money, and so on).

A country that continually has a balance-of-payments surplus or deficit clearly does not have a balance-of-payments equilibrium and so must make adjustments to correct the situation. When a country has a continuing surplus, it means that other countries are short of funds with which to buy goods and services in the surplus country. Therefore, the surplus country must make adjustments to provide foreigners with additional funds, or the deficit countries will be forced to cut down on their expenditures in the surplus country. Thus, when the United States had a balance-of-payments surplus after World War II, it provided other nations with funds in the form of grants-in-aid. More recently, other countries with surpluses, such as Germany, have found different solutions to the problem. Germany, for example, revalued its currency upward. Deficit nations, on the other hand, must either cut back on payments or stimulate surplus nations to increase their expenditures. One common solution for the deficit nation is currency devaluation; Britain did this in 1949 and 1967, and France did this in 1969. In other cases, a change in the interest rate structure can also help to achieve a balance-of-payments equilibrium.

Thus, in general, continual surpluses dictate the need for a permanent increase in payments or decrease in receipts; continual deficits require a permanent decrease in payments or increase in receipts. If the measures taken to achieve these goals are successful, a balance-of-payments equilibrium will be achieved and there will be only a minimal fluctuation in the balancing items of gold flows and short-term claims.

The following chapter examines specific solutions to international balance-of-payments difficulties. We will begin this discussion by explaining the connection between the balance of payments and the exchange rate. To this point no mention has been made of the fact that different countries employ different monetary units of account. This, as we shall see, creates important balance-of-payments problems.

THE EXCHANGE RATE

Introduction

Each country has its own monetary unit of account. Thus prices and money in the United States are added up in terms of the dollar. The unit of account in France is the franc; in Japan, the yen; and in Germany, the Deutsche mark. Within the boundaries of each nation, each currency circulates freely. In international trade, however, it does not, for there is no single international unit of account. Although dollars are often used to settle international transactions, importers and exporters usually need specific currencies to carry on their transactions. For example, United States exporters receive claims against foreign money in payment for their goods, but they need American currency to meet their internal obligations. Conversely, importers need foreign monies to buy goods abroad. Consequently these merchants make use of the foreign exchange market, where different types of currencies may be obtained. This market consists of the banks, brokers, and agents who deal in the purchase and sale of foreign exchange (foreign currency).

The principal suppliers of foreign currency in this market are exporters and those who sell securities abroad; the principal demanders of foreign currency are importers and buyers of foreign securities. *The exchange rate tells us the number of units of domestic currency that is necessary to pur-*

chase foreign currency. In other words, the exchange rate is the price of domestic currency in terms of foreign currency. It records how much of one country's currency is needed in exchange for a given amount of another country's currency. For example, the exchange rate between the American dollar and the German Deutsche mark during recent years has been approximately 1 Deutsche mark = $.25. From the American point of view, this means that one dollar equals four Deutsche marks.[3]

The Relationship Between the Exchange Rate and the Balance of Payments

We have said that the demand for a country's currency depends on the total value of its exports, the inflow of remittances and pensions, the inflow of foreign government capital, and the inflow of private foreign capital funds. On the other hand, the supply of a nation's currency depends on the total value of its imports, the outflow of remittances and pensions, the outflow of government funds, and the outflow of private capital funds.

Thus, at a given rate of exchange, should the demand for a nation's currency exceed its supply, there is a balance-of-payments surplus. On the other hand, at a given exchange rate, should the supply exceed the demand, there is a balance-of-payments deficit. Should the exchange rate change, however, the amounts of a nation's currency demanded and supplied will also change, and so will the balance of payments. Not only does the exchange rate give us the price of one country's currency relative to foreign currency, it also tells us how much foreign goods and services cost in terms of one's own currency (assuming prices in the foreign country remain unchanged).

For example, if a German product costs 12 Deutsche marks, then, with an exchange rate of $1 = 4 Deutsche marks, the cost in dollars of the German product is $3. Should the exchange rate change to $1 = 5 Deutsche marks, the dollar price of the German good is reduced to $2.40. This should lead to an increase in the U.S. demand for the commodity. In addition, it should cause an increase in the total amount of American money supplied as foreign exchange. This assumes, however, that the American demand for the German good is *price-elastic*—that the amount of the German product demanded expands more than proportionately to the decrease in the price of the product to Americans. For example, if at a price of $1 ten units of product are demanded, then at a price of $.50 per unit the amount demanded would expand to more than twenty units, leading to expenditures in excess of $10.

---

[3] We use the term "exchange rate" here as if there were only one rate of exchange between two different national currencies. Actually, there are a number of different rates. For example, there is the *cable rate,* the *thirty-day rate,* and the *sixty-day rate.* Generally, the rate will be higher the sooner one wants foreign monies. If a government has established a fixed ratio between its currency and that of other countries, then these various exchange rates will be very close to the official rate. As of October 24, 1969, the mark was revalued to 1 Deutsche mark = $.27.

A drop in the exchange rate also works in the opposite direction. If the exchange rate falls to $1 = 3 Deutsche marks, the price of the goods to Americans is increased.[4] This will cause a decrease in the amount demanded. If the American demand for the product is price-elastic, total expenditures on the product will decrease and the amount of American currency supplied in the foreign exchange market will also decrease. Hence, *the quantity of a country's currency supplied in the foreign exchange market will tend to increase with increases in the exchange rate.* This statement, however, assumes (1) that the demand for foreign goods is elastic and (2) that other things remain equal, that there is, for example, no change in capital flows or in the foreign prices of goods and services. This situation is illustrated in Figure 24–1 by the part of the *SS* curve that slopes upward and to the right.

FIGURE 24–1. A hypothetical supply and demand for dollars in the foreign exchange market

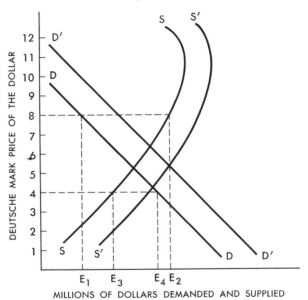

MILLIONS OF DOLLARS DEMANDED AND SUPPLIED

Conversely, should the demand for foreign goods and services be price-inelastic, then, as the exchange rate rises, the total volume of currency supplied decreases. When the demand for a product is price-inelastic, the amount of the product demanded expands less than proportionately to a decrease in the price of that product. Hence there would be an increase in the number of units sold but a decrease in total expenditures. In the foreign

[4] By a fall in the exchange rate we mean a decrease in the amount of a foreign currency that a unit of another given currency can command. For the other country, however, this situation is viewed as a rise in the exchange rate because its currency can now command more units of the depreciated foreign currency.

exchange market, expenditures on imports are part of the supply of a nation's currency. When an import is price-inelastic, therefore, the supply of currency slopes upward and to the left as a result of decreased expenditures on foreign goods and services. This decreased supply of currency is shown in the backward-bending part of the *SS* curve in Figure 24–1.

The demand schedule for a country's currency slopes downward and to the right, as is shown by line *DD* in Figure 24–1. The demand for a country's currency is equal to the total payments other countries are willing to make. *Thus, other things being equal, the lower the exchange rate, the lower the price of a country's exports and the greater the amount of its currency demanded will be.* Assume, for example, that an American product costs $1. When the exchange rate is $1 = 4 Deutsche marks, the cost of the American product to a German buyer is 4 Deutsche marks. Should the exchange rate fall to $1 = 3 Deutsche marks, then the price of the good to a German falls to 3 Deutsche marks. This lower price will probably induce Germans to purchase more of the American product. In order to purchase more of this product, however, additional American money is needed since the dollar price of the product remains unchanged. The change in the exchange rate simply reflects a change in the Deutsche mark price. For this reason, other things being equal, the demand for a country's currency will almost always slope downward and to the right in terms of the demand curve in Figure 24–1.[5]

Figure 24–1 shows hypothetical demand and supply schedules for American dollars. For the sake of simplicity we have assumed a two-country universe, consisting of Germany and the United States, in which Germany represents the rest of the world with which the United States trades. On the vertical axis we can measure the Deutsche mark price of the dollar. The number of dollars demanded and supplied at varying exchange rates is measured on the horizontal axis.

The balance-of-payments surplus or deficit is really the difference between the demand and supply schedules, *DD* and *SS*. For example, in terms of our hypothetical supply and demand schedule, if the exchange rate is $1 = 8 Deutsche marks, we know that the supply of American dollars exceeds the demand for American dollars in the foreign exchange market. American payments exceed receipts, causing a balance-of-payments deficit equal to $E_2 - E_1$ million dollars. This deficit can be sustained by accommodation only when the debtor country is able to borrow foreign currency, export gold, draw on previously accumulated balances of foreign monies,

---

[5] If the German demand for American goods in this illustration had been price-inelastic, the demand curve for American dollars would still have sloped downward and to the right. For price-inelastic goods, Germans would be giving up less of their own currency to get American dollars if the value of the mark were raised. The total number of dollars demanded would still increase with a decrease in the exchange rate. This is so because the dollar price of the American goods would be unchanged by the revaluation of the mark. Therefore, as they seek to purchase more American goods, Germans would need more American dollars.

or persuade the foreign countries to permit a build-up of their claims against the currency of the debtor country.

On the other hand, when the exchange rate is $1 = 4 Deutsche marks, the demand for American dollars exceeds the supply. American receipts exceed payments and there is a balance-of-trade surplus equal to $E_4 - E_3$ million. For there to be no balance-of-payments deficit or surplus, the exchange rate must be $1 = 5+ Deutsche marks. This rate will bring equilibrium to the balance of payments, since it is at this point that the demand and supply schedules intersect.

The Position of the Foreign Exchange Demand and Supply Schedules

The position of the *DD* and *SS* curves in Figure 24–1 depends on a series of given factors. *First* is the *level of domestic income.* As incomes increase, the demand for home-produced *and* foreign goods and services increases also. Therefore, if income in the United States should increase, the demand for foreign goods would increase, and the supply of American dollars in the foreign exchange market would grow accordingly. In terms of Figure 24–1, the *SS* line would shift to the right, to *S'S'*. At any given exchange rate, this would mean that the supply of currency has increased relative to the demand. Thus any deficit existing prior to the income increase has widened, and any surplus existing prior to income increase has narrowed. At the same time, the demand for American currency has decreased, possibly from *D'D'* to *DD*. American industry produces to meet both foreign and domestic demands. When domestic demand expands, there will be a shift of production to meet the increased domestic demand. Hence there will be fewer American goods available to foreigners, fewer American exports, and a decreased demand for American currency at any given exchange rate. The decreased demand for American currency will further aggravate any balance-of-payment deficit.[6]

Conversely, a decrease in domestic income reduces the demand for foreign goods and services. The supply of the currency decreases, deficits narrow, and surpluses widen. In addition, the production of goods for foreign markets expands relative to that for domestic markets, and the demand for American currency expands, possibly from *DD* to *D'D'*. This helps to narrow a balance-of-payments deficit or to widen a surplus.

Second, incomes abroad affect the position of the demand for and supply of currency. Increased incomes abroad mean that other nations demand both more domestically produced goods and more foreign goods. For example, an increase in German gross national product induces an increase in the demand for American goods. To get more American goods, however, the Germans need more American dollars. Thus the *DD* line

[6] My colleague, Miltiades Chacholiades, is to be thanked for pointing out this possibility.

shifts to the right, becoming $D'D'$. If, prior to the German income change, there had been a deficit U.S. balance of payments, this deficit would now have narrowed. At the same time, German producers increase domestic production at the expense of exports; this should shift the supply of U.S. currency to the left, possibly from $S'S'$ to SS.

Third, prices at home relative to those abroad affect both the demand for and the supply of currency in the foreign exchange market. Suppose that prices in the United States decline relative to those in Germany. This makes the American products more attractive than the comparable German products. Both Americans and Germans demand more American goods and fewer German goods. The result is a decrease in the supply of American currency entering the foreign exchange market (a shift to the left in SS) and an increase in the demand for American currency by Germans (a shift to the right in DD). This improves the American balance-of-payments situation, unless the elasticities are unfavorable. On the other hand, a rise in prices in the United States relative to those in Germany will increase the supply of American dollars in the foreign exchange market and decrease the demand for American dollars. More German products and fewer American products will be demanded; the American balance-of-payments situation will worsen.

Fourth, interest rates at home relative to those abroad influence the demand for and supply of currency in the foreign exchange market. Should interest rates decline in the United States relative to those in Germany, the demand for dollars will decline and the supply will increase. The decline in U.S. interest rates makes German securities more attractive as a financial investment. As a consequence, Germans demand fewer American securities, and hence less U.S. money. Americans also purchase fewer of their own securities and increase their purchases of German securities, thereby further increasing the supply of American dollars on the foreign exchange market. Conversely, a rise in U.S. interest rates relative to those abroad will increase the demand for American dollars and decrease the supply.

And fifth, expectations are an important determinant of both the demand for and the supply of currency. Suppose that the domestic political stability of a country becomes threatened. As a rule, this situation will cause a capital flight to take place. The inhabitants of this country will try to transfer their currency holdings into the currency of a nation with greater stability. At the same time, foreign demands for the goods, services, and securities of the troubled nation will diminish. This will cause DD to shift to the left and SS to the right. The balance-of-payments situation will worsen.

Expectations concerning future exchange rates are also important. If, for example, it looks as though the exchange rate will increase, then it pays to postpone purchases abroad until one's own currency is actually able to command more foreign money. Such a delay causes a shift to the left in the SS curve. At the same time, foreign nations try to get into the currency that is soon to be appreciated; they prefer to buy goods, services, and securities prior to the change in the exchange rate. This causes a shift to the right in the *DD* curve. Reverse movements will occur when a drop in the exchange rate is expected.

SUMMARY

This chapter has examined some of the monetary effects of a nation's international balance of payments. It has explained the relationship between the balance of payments and the exchange rate. A nation's balance of payments is in deficit when, at a given exchange rate, the demand for its currency is less than the supply in the foreign exchange market. Conversely, there is a balance-of-payments surplus when the demand for a country's currency is greater than its supply in the foreign exchange market. A major part of the following chapter is devoted to various solutions to balance-of-payments difficulties.

Supplementary Readings

Haberler, Gottfried. *A Survey of International Trade Theory*. Princeton, N.J., Princeton University Special Papers in International Economics, 1961.
Holmes, Alan R. *The New York Foreign Exchange Market*. New York, The Federal Reserve Bank of New York, 1959.

Alternative International Economic Policies

Chapter 24 examined the relationship between the balance of payments and the exchange rates. Chapter 25 considers some alternative solutions to balance-of-payments problems. In addition, it briefly examines the problem of international liquidity and international monetary organizations.

POLICIES FOR THE BALANCE-OF-PAYMENTS PROBLEM

Adjustments Under Flexible Exchange Rates

One way to establish a balance-of-payments equilibrium is by means of a *freely flexible exchange rate*. When the exchange rate is above the equilibrium level, the supply of currency exceeds the demand, and there is a balance-of-payments deficit. If the government permits its exchange rate to fluctuate freely in response to market forces, however, the exchange rate will decline in response to this deficit. The price of domestic goods will then drop relative to foreign goods and purchases of domestic goods and services will increase accordingly. Foreigners will increase their purchases of goods and services in the country experiencing the exchange rate decrease. This will cause the amount of currency demanded to increase. At the same time, imports will fall and the amount of currency supplied will decrease. Hence the balance-of-payments deficit will decrease.

On the other hand, should the exchange rate be below the equilibrium level, the demand for money exceeds the supply in the foreign exchange market and there is a balance-of-payments surplus. The currency that is in relatively short supply can be expected to increase in value relative to other currencies. This will increase the price of domestic goods relative to foreign goods. Citizens of the surplus country, induced by the increased value of their currency abroad, will step up their foreign purchases and decrease their domestic purchases. Conversely, citizens of other countries will decrease their purchases abroad and increase their domestic purchases. Thus the amount of the surplus country's currency demanded will decrease and the amount of its currency supplied will increase. In this fashion the balance-of-payments surplus will decrease.[1]

If a country allows its exchange rates to fluctuate freely, payments equilibrium will be quickly established and chronic balance-of-payments deficits and surpluses will be eliminated. Proponents of an international policy of this sort believe that it would permit a nation to design its monetary and fiscal policies with purely internal problems in mind. No longer need there be a conflict between policies for internal and external economic stability. For example, interest rates are often decreased by the monetary authorities as a means of stimulating the economy during a recession. This domestic policy often endangers balance-of-payments stability, however. As Chapter 24 showed, a decline in domestic rates relative to those abroad will tend to expand a balance-of-payments deficit. Thus the monetary authority is forced to choose between continuing to keep interest rates low to stimulate economic recovery or raising them to eliminate the balance-of-payments deficit.

Fiscal stabilization policies face the same dilemma. Anti-recessionary fiscal policies could well involve both a decrease in taxes and an increase in government spending. This would lead to much-needed increases in income and output, but it would also conflict with balance-of-payments stability. Rising incomes lead to increased purchase of goods and services abroad, and, as previously noted, the supply of currency widens relative to the demand for it in the foreign exchange market. Thus the balance-of-payments deficit is increased.

Permitting exchange rates to fluctuate freely can eliminate this conflict between internal and external objectives. No surplus or deficit in the balance of payments can long continue because changes in the exchange rate induce changes in the amounts of currency demanded and supplied in the foreign exchange market. Thus the demand for currency and the supply tend to balance each other.

In spite of these advantages, there is strong opposition to the use of flexible exchange rates as an international monetary system. In fact, monetary authorities themselves are usually opposed to such an arrangement. Most countries prefer to fix the value of their currency in relation to the currencies of other nations because they fear that flexible exchange rates would leave the determination of the exchange rate to speculators rather than to free-market demand and supply forces.

With freely fluctuating exchange rates, if speculators expect the rates to decline, for example, they can force the decline by switching to a more

---

[1] Professional economists will recognize that the preceding analysis assumes the Marshall-Lerner condition to be satisfied. According to this condition, a decrease in the exchange rate will improve the balance of payments of a country and an increase in the exchange rate will worsen it if the sum of the elasticities of demand for a country's exports and of its demand for imports is greater than one.

valuable currency. Since a decline in the exchange rate decreases the ability of a currency to command other currencies in exchange, it pays the speculator to sell a currency before it depreciates. He simultaneously purchases other currencies. This action increases the supply relative to the demand for the depreciating currency, however, thereby providing the force needed to drive the exchange rate down.

When will the actions of the speculator actually tend to be destabilizing? Precisely when the internal conditions of a country warrant a continuing depreciation in the exchange rate. This is most likely to occur if domestic monetary and fiscal policies are causing continuing price rises relative to price levels abroad. Thus it is chiefly domestic price inflation that triggers currency speculation that is destabilizing in terms of exchange-rate determination, rather than the flexible exchange rates themselves.

In sharp contrast, when exchange-rate movements appear to be temporary, the actions of the speculator may actually have a stabilizing influence. If the exchange rate has temporarily declined and speculators expect it to return to old levels, they will buy more of the depreciated currency because they expect to make a profit by selling the currency after it has returned to higher levels. This added demand for currency when it is depreciated will push exchange rates up.

Most countries are anxious to guard against the possibly destabilizing effects of speculative currency manipulation nonetheless, and consequently they keep firm control of the value of their currency in the foreign exchange market. This effectively prevents flexible exchange rates from becoming a feasible international economic policy. Fixed exchange rates, on the other hand, are no guarantee that speculative currency manipulation will not take place. Speculation that the United States would devalue the dollar led to significant gold-reserve losses in the spring of 1968. Likewise, speculation that France would devalue the franc in late 1968 led to a halving of French gold reserves in late 1968. France finally did devalue the franc, but not until August 1969.

Adjustments Under the Gold Standard

Many countries describe the value of their currencies in terms of gold. The dollar, for example, is defined by an act of Congress as being equal to 1/35 ounce of gold. This presumably puts the United States on the gold standard; that is, the U.S. Treasury presumably stands ready to buy and sell gold at $35 an ounce. Not everyone, however, is able to buy and sell gold from the U.S. Treasury. Domestically, American citizens are prohibited from owning gold except as jewelry, in coin collections, or for industrial purposes. Internationally, the United States buys and sells gold only in its transactions with other governments. Prior to March 1968, foreigners who were private citizens could also buy and sell gold in dealings with the U.S. Treasury. This change in policy was triggered by speculation regarding an increase in the dollar price of gold.

The following discussion describes how balance-of-payments adjustments *should* take place under the gold standard. They do *not* take place in this manner in the real world because countries are unwilling to accept the internal consequences of the gold standard.

Under the gold standard, each country defines its money in terms of gold; governments should be prepared to exchange gold for currency and vice versa on demand. In addition, variations in the supply of gold should be permitted to affect the stock of money. The relationship of each unit of account to gold establishes the exchange rates between the different units of account. For example, if the dollar is worth 1/35 ounce of gold and the Deutsche mark 1/140 ounce of gold, then the exchange rate between the two currencies is $1 = 4 Deutsche marks; the dollar is worth four times as much gold as the Deutsche mark.

How would a balance-of-payments adjustment take place under such a gold standard? For simplicity, let us assume that there are only two currencies to deal with, the dollar and the Deutsche mark, which represents the unit of account for the rest of the world. Let us further assume that initially there is a balance-of-payments equilibrium. Now imagine that the American preferences for foreign goods and services increase. This leads to an increase in the demand for foreign goods and an increase in the supply of dollars in the foreign exchange market. The United States now has a balance-of-payments *deficit*. Since the U.S. government is unwilling to decrease the gold content of the dollar, it cannot permit the exchange rate to decrease. Therefore, the U.S. must *lose gold* to the rest of the world. To protect itself against a loss of gold, the central bank in the United States is expected to *raise interest rates*. Other countries, in turn, decrease their interest rates in response to the gold inflow. As we noted in Chapter 24, this change in interest rates would tend to improve the balance-of-payments position of the deficit country.

This loss of gold reduces commercial bank reserves in the United States and causes some contraction in deposit money. Deflationary forces are activated in the U.S. economy. At the same time, in other countries the gold inflow increases reserves, and banks with the additional lending capacity expand loans. The lower interest rates abroad encourage foreigners to borrow more at home. In the United States, however, borrowing has become more expensive. Businesses must put a stop to capital expansion in plant and equipment because the margin between expected returns from investment and the cost of funds has narrowed. As a result, employment decreases in the United States.

If prices and wages are flexible in the United States, there also will be *downward pressure on the price level*. At the level of prices prior to the gold outflow, the demand for goods is now less than the supply. With prices and wages flexible downward, however, some of the loss of employment in the United States will be temporary. In time, declining prices will *stimulate demand for home-produced goods* by both Americans and foreigners. Americans will also purchase fewer goods and services abroad. Thus the real demand for goods relative to the supply will tend to be maintained.

Abroad, however, the situation is reversed. Lower interest rates have encouraged increased borrowing, expenditures on capital goods have risen, and income and output have increased. Since the rest of the world may be close to full employment, very little of the increased demand can be satisfied. As a consequence, there is upward pressure on prices and wages abroad. Thus the price level in the United States has decreased relative to prices abroad. This, in turn, leads to an *increase in the demand for American currency and a decrease in its supply.* Conversely, the demand for the Deutsche mark (the unit of account we have posited for the rest of the world) decreases and its supply increases. In this fashion, the *balance-of-payments deficit* for the United States is *wiped out.*

This process makes the important assumption that there is downward price flexibility, which assures full employment. Our theoretical analysis in Part III showed that this typical nineteenth- and early twentieth-century economic assumption has proven unrealistic in the twentieth-century world. We now know that it is possible to have less-than-full-employment equilibrium. The flaw in the gold-standard mechanism for adjusting balance-of-payments differences is that it ignores this possibility.

Assume that prices and wages are not flexible downward. This assumption means that changes must be made in income, output, or employment to achieve a balance-of-payments equilibrium. If prices do not decline in the United States as gold flows out, the money stock declines and interest rates rise. As a consequence, income, output, and employment must fall. Decreases in income reduce the demand for foreign goods and this, in turn, means that the supply of American dollars in the foreign exchange market decreases. So long as the deficit remains, however, gold will continue to flow out and domestic income and output will continue to drop. Once income has dropped sufficiently, the supply of American currency will again equal the demand and the balance-of-payments deficit ends. Internal stability has been sacrificed for external stability.

Adherence to the gold standard prevents national monetary authorities from exercising sufficient control over the domestic level of employment and prices. With wage and price rigidity, deficits tend to lead to unemployment; surpluses, during periods of full employment, tend to lead to inflation. Thus internal price and employment stability are often sacrificed for balance-of-payments stability.

This was roughly the state of affairs prior to World War I for those countries on the gold standard. Monetary authorities at the time were chiefly concerned with protecting their reserves. As gold flowed out, they increased interest rates; as gold flowed in, they decreased interest rates. Following World War I, however, central banks gradually became more and more interested in maintaining domestic equilibrium. Countries went off the rigid type of gold standard described here to improve domestic stability. Hence, although most economies of the Western world still maintain some fiction of a gold standard externally, most currencies are not convertible into gold internally. Even those countries that do not define their money in terms of gold frequently attempt to maintain a stable rate of exchange between their currency and the American dollar or the British pound sterling, which are still based on gold.

This adherence to the semblance of a gold standard in international trade creates difficulties in the contemporary economic world. We do not permit exchange rates to fluctuate freely so as to correct balance-of-payment difficulties. We do not permit an automatically functioning gold standard to correct for balance-of-payments difficulties, either. How, then, do contemporary economies make adjustments in their balance of payments?

Adjustments Under Fixed Exchange Rates

The gold standard is one type of system that depends on fixed exchange rates. No nation follows the rules of the gold standard, however. As a result, monetary authorities must make many *ad hoc* adjustments to maintain stable exchange rates and a balance-of-payments equilibrium. The United States is used as an example because its economic policies have such strong international repercussions.

The relation between gold and the U.S. economy. Internally gold has little significance for the U.S. economy. The average citizen has not been able to redeem his coin, currency, and deposit money for the money metal gold since 1933. Today gold is important to the United States chiefly as a source of international reserves. By defining the dollar as equal to 1/35 ounce of gold, the United States has obligated itself to turn over 1/35 ounce of gold to foreign monetary authorities in exchange for every U.S. dollar they have accumulated. Since the volume of dollar claims to gold increases with a balance-of-payments deficit and decreases with a balance-of-payments surplus, gold flows are likely to increase with deficits in the U.S. balance of payments and decrease with surpluses.

Table 25–1 lists the balance of payments and the net gold flows for the United States from 1956 to 1968. Notice that the years of largest deficits were also the years of the heaviest gold outflows. Only one of the two years of balance-of-payments surplus had a net gold inflow.

Because of continuing balance-of-payments deficits in the 1960's, the United States had continual gold outflows. The net effect was to reduce the gold stock of the United States from $21.8 billion at the end of 1955

TABLE 25–1. THE BALANCE OF PAYMENTS
AND NET GOLD PURCHASES OR SALES
BY THE UNITED STATES, 1956–68
(IN MILLIONS OF DOLLARS)

YEAR	BALANCE OF PAYMENTS	NET GOLD PURCHASES OR SALES
1956	− 973	280
1957	578	772
1958	−3,365	−2,294
1959	−3,870	−1,041
1960	−3,901	−1,669
1961	−2,370	− 820
1962	−2,203	− 833
1963	−2,671	− 392
1964	−2,800	− 36
1965	−1,335	−1,547
1966	−1,357	− 431
1967	−3,571	−1,009
1968	158	−1,121

SOURCE: Balance of payments: see Table 24–2; net gold purchases or sales: see *Federal Reserve Bulletin*, May 1964, p. 648; July 1968, p. A–72; May 1969, p. A–72.

to $10.9 billion at the end of 1968. The United States still had 26 percent of the noncommunist world's gold in 1968, but this was significantly less than the 58 percent it held at the end of 1955.[2]

U.S. adjustments to balance-of-payments deficits. There are a number of ways in which a country can reduce a balance-of-payments deficit. Most of them involve stimulating the demand for its currency and discouraging increases in the supply in the foreign exchange market. Among the most commonly used techniques are (1) depressing domestic income levels, (2) reducing the internal price level, (3) lowering the exchange rate (devaluation), (4) permitting the loss of gold reserves and other international reserves to continue, (5) raising internal interest rates, (6) reducing government expenditures abroad, (7) imposing trade and exchange controls, (8) inducing one's citizens to buy fewer goods and securities abroad, (9) inducing foreign nations to purchase more goods and securities, and (10) setting up special arrangements with the central banks of other countries. Most of these policies can be used in reverse when there is a balance-of-payments surplus.

The first four of these remedies have not been palatable to the United States. *Depressing domestic income and price levels* would mean sacrificing internal stability. The best that can be done on this score is to prevent price inflation. A *reduction in the exchange rate* is not politically feasible; both Democrats and Republicans are firmly committed to keeping the dollar freely interchangeable with gold at $35 an ounce. This commitment was

[2] *Federal Reserve Bulletin*, May 1961, p. 624; May 1969, p. A–86. Following April 1968, the U.S. gold stock remained almost constant through 1969.

made to reduce speculation on the dollar and to permit the dollar to continue to serve as an international medium of exchange. Other countries have not been so reluctant to change their exchange rates, however. Britain underwent a substantial devaluation of the pound in 1949 and again in 1967. Germany, which in recent years has had a balance-of-payments surplus, revalued her currency upward in 1961. This was done in part to relieve the United States of some of its balance-of-payments difficulties. It should be pointed out that if the United States devalued the dollar (lowered the exchange rate), other countries could retaliate by also reducing their exchange rates. This latter action could cancel out any beneficial effects of U.S. devaluation. The fourth remedy, to *permit the continued loss of international reserves,* would not serve to correct an excess of supply over demand for American currency in the foreign exchange market. It would merely permit a deficit to continue, and eventually the loss of gold would require more remedial action in the absence of a change in the exchange rate.

The other approaches listed above have been more feasible, and varieties of these policies have been followed by the United States. *Monetary policy has been directed toward discouraging capital outflows.* The Federal Reserve abandoned its "bills only" policy in 1961 in an effort to *keep long-term interest rates low and short-term rates relatively high.* By buying long-term securities, the Federal Reserve provided funds needed to stimulate an economy operating at less than full employment. By selling short-term securities, it tried to keep short-term rates high, thereby inducing individuals and businesses with temporarily idle funds to purchase short-term securities in the United States rather than abroad. This policy fell into disuse in 1965, when the higher short-term rates that accompanied the Viet Nam war financing efforts made such operations no longer necessary.

The Federal Reserve also used the discount rate to help relieve balance-of-payments deficits. For example, the Federal Reserve increased the discount rate in July 1963 in an effort to relieve the balance-of-payments deficit. It was hoped that this action would not depress the economy internally. The discount rate was increased again in November 1964. The aim then was to counter a rise in the British short-term rate from 5 to 7 percent. Britain had increased its rate in order to reduce pressure on the pound resulting from an adverse balance of trade and payments. The American action was designed principally to prevent an increased flow of U.S. dollars to Britain pursuant to a widened spread of interest rates in Britain's favor. Finally, the discount rate increases in March and April of 1968 were in part designed to offset speculation on the dollar and thereby help reduce outflows of U.S. gold reserves.

The Federal Reserve also attempted to relieve balance-of-payments deficits in the United States by issuing restrictive guidelines on foreign lending by American banks and nonbank financial institutions. This type of policy tends to shift the supply curve of American currency to the left, thereby reducing a balance-of-payments deficit. Figure 25–1 shows how such

FIGURE 25–1. Exchange-rate determination

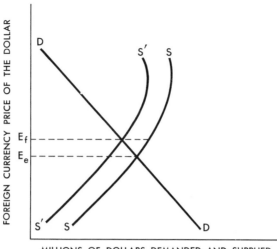

measures operate. At the fixed exchange rate E_f there is a deficit in the balance of payments. By shifting the supply curve to the left through such measures as restraining the amount of foreign lending by American banks, the deficit can presumably be eliminated. This is illustrated in Figure 25–1 by a movement of the supply curve SS to $S'S'$. Whether such an elimination of the balance-of-payments deficit can be permanent depends on the underlying economic and psychological variables that help to determine the demand for supply of currency: relative interest rates, relative price levels, relative rates of growth in income, and confidence in the dollar relative to confidence in foreign currencies. Measures that restrict lending are merely temporary accommodations. When such restrictions are removed, the balance-of-payments deficit will recur unless internal inflation is controlled and interest rates have increased relative to those abroad.

Another means of reducing a balance-of-payments deficit has been the *direct entry of the U.S. Treasury and the Federal Reserve into the foreign exchange market as buyers and sellers.* All purchases of foreign currency are carried on by the special manager for foreign currency of the Federal Reserve Bank of New York. By using its sizable foreign exchange holdings, the Federal Reserve can buy back dollars that are held by foreigners, thereby reducing the chance of a gold outflow.

The federal government can also take *fiscal action* to correct the balance-of-payments deficit. The *rate of military expenditures* abroad was reduced in the early 1960's, for example. Some American military installations in other countries were closed and regulations permitting military dependents to live abroad were tightened. Our allies were encouraged to increase their armament purchases from the United States. Military expenditures, of course, increased with the intensification of the Viet Nam war in 1965. In addition, since 1961 the Department of Defense has paid premiums of up to 50 percent in order to purchase goods in the United States for use abroad, rather than purchasing them on the world market.

Trade and exchange controls can also be used to decrease the balance-of-payments deficit. Tariffs and import restrictions are trade controls. An increase in tariffs raises the price of foreign goods and services to importers. This decreases the demand for foreign goods and services, reduces the supply of the importing country's currency on the foreign exchange market, and reduces its balance-of-payments deficit. Import quotas also restrict the supply of a country's currency. Under import quotas, only a given amount of foreign goods can be imported, regardless of the demand for the product. Exchange controls work somewhat differently. They restrict the use that nationals and foreigners may make of funds acquired in trade. For example, a foreign nation may be required to spend a given portion of its exchange receipts in the importing country, or the exporters of the country with the controls may be forced to sell their receipts of foreign currency at an official rate to their government in exchange for domestic currency.

The United States government does not endorse such trade and exchange controls as a means of adjusting the balance-of-payments deficit. It is officially and ideologically committed to the removal of trade barriers. It favors a free flow of goods, services, and funds throughout the world. To Americans, the economic common sense of such a policy is obvious; if other countries can be persuaded to reduce their barriers, then foreign demand for American goods, services, and securities will expand, thereby increasing the demand for American currency and decreasing the national balance-of-payments deficit.

The position of the United States on this matter, however, is somewhat ambivalent. On the one hand, it has *taken the lead in reducing barriers* to encourage the free flow of goods and funds among nations. On the other hand, it has also *adopted restraints* that amount to barriers. In 1961, for example, the United States reduced the duty-free exemption for returning tourists to $100 per person. In effect, this raised the price of foreign goods to American tourists and caused the demand for foreign goods and the supply of American dollars going abroad to decrease. In 1964 the United States enacted a restrictive measure called an *interest-equalization tax*. The tax applies to all Americans who purchase new or outstanding foreign securities (Canadian securities are exempted) maturing in more than three years. It was extended to cover long-term bank loans in 1965. The tax is designed to reduce the interest differential between American and foreign securities so as to decrease the supply of American currency in the foreign exchange market. In spite of these apparent contradictions, United States policy is still primarily to encourage international trade by eliminating trade and exchange controls.

Aside from the previously mentioned interest rate changes, tourist import restrictions, interest-equalization tax, and lending guidelines, little was done directly through 1968 to curb the domestic demand for foreign goods, services, and securities, or to stimulate the foreign demand for domestic production and securities. Some effort was made to require recipients of American foreign aid to spend these funds in the United States. Dollars provided other nations by the Agency for International Development must be spent in the United States, even if the price of goods is cheaper abroad. Overall, there was a lack of direct government controls designed to manipulate the position of demand for supply of currency schedules. This is in keeping with the American commitment to maintaining free markets.

In any case, the *main line of defense* against deficits has been *monetary*. The actions taken have been primarily in two areas: (1) efforts have been made to *maintain high interest rates,* and (2) *special arrangements have been set up with the central banks of other countries.* Under the latter policy, foreign governments were persuaded to make prepayments on U.S. loans and military purchases in the United States. This gave only temporary relief to the balance-of-payments deficit, however. A more important feature of our financial arrangements with other countries has been the lessening of speculation on the dollar by the use of devices such as *swap arrangements* and, until 1968, the *Gold Pool.*

In general, a *swap,* in this sense of the word, is an arrangement whereby a central bank agrees to exchange its currency for another currency for a limited period of time, usually not in excess of six months. This enables a country that is experiencing a temporary balance-of-payments deficit to use the foreign currency it acquires in a swap to buy back its own currency in the foreign exchange market and thus reduce the possibility that expanding foreign claims will result in a gold outflow. When we buy up our own currency in this fashion, the demand for dollars expands and the supply of other currencies in the foreign exchange market increases. Speculators who had counted on a deterioration in the price of the dollar relative to other currencies are thus disappointed.

The Federal Reserve presently has arrangements with the Austrian National Bank, the National Bank of Belgium, the Bank of Canada, the Bank of Denmark, the Bank of England, the Bank of France, the German Federal Bank, the Bank of Italy, the Bank of Japan, the Bank of Mexico, the Netherlands Bank, the Bank of Norway, the Bank of Sweden, the Swiss National Bank, and the Bank for International Settlements. Swap arrangements have been particularly helpful in relieving the pressure on the U.S. balance of payments caused by short-term capital flows. These arrangements also help other countries. For example, the Bank of England borrowed $1.35 billion under its swap line from the Federal Reserve at the time of British devaluation of the pound in 1967.

The fact that the Federal Reserve and the Treasury may purchase foreign exchange directly stabilizes expectations concerning the rate of exchange. When President Kennedy was assassinated in November 1963, for example, the Federal Reserve Bank of New York immediately offered to exchange foreign currency for dollars. This demonstrated that the Federal Reserve System was willing to support the dollar in the foreign exchange market, that there would be a continuation of current U.S. economic policies. It helped prevent widespread panic sales of dollars in the foreign exchange market.

The *Gold Pool* was an arrangement whereby various central banks operated in the London gold market to stabilize the price of gold. In the absence of efforts to stabilize the price of gold, speculation had caused serious fluctuations in the gold market. In the fall of 1960, for example, when the continuing U.S. balance-of-payments deficit led to an expectation of a decrease in the gold content of the dollar, many speculators rushed to get out of dollars and into gold. As a consequence, the dollar price of gold in the London market began to hover around $40 an ounce instead of close to $35 an ounce. By selling and buying gold defensively, the Gold Pool helped to stabilize the world price of gold and to minimize the effects of private speculation from 1961 to 1968. The Gold Pool was unable to halt speculative buying of gold in March of 1968, however. As previously noted, the United States was willing to buy and sell gold to everyone except American citizens. In the spring of 1968, when foreigners speculated that the American dollar would be devalued, they rushed to purchase gold at $35 an ounce. The U.S. Treasury supplied gold to private markets at this price through the London Gold Pool. However, the increased supply of American gold going into the gold market was unable to keep the private market price of gold from rising to almost $45 an ounce. The effect was to end the London Gold Pool, and the United States began to initiate new policies regarding the purchase and sale of gold.

The United States will still sell gold to foreign governments in exchange for dollars at the fixed price of $35 an ounce. However, the United States will not normally do this for any country that wants the gold "to replace the gold sold in private markets." [3] In addition, the U.S. Treasury no longer buys gold from domestic mines or sells it to domestic industrial users. These individuals now have to deal exclusively in the private market for gold.

Evaluation of techniques designed to eliminate the balance-of-payments deficit. It is difficult to determine the overall effectiveness of these techniques in eliminating the U.S. balance-of-payments deficit. Certainly the deficit decreased through 1966 from its high of $3.9 billion in 1960. But in 1967 the overall deficit again increased markedly. As can be seen from Table 24–2, the balance on goods and services began to deteriorate in 1965. There was a rise in imports attributable in part to increased inflationary pressures within the United States. As we noted earlier, when prices at home rise relative to prices abroad there will be an increase in the demand for foreign goods and services. This causes a corresponding decrease

[3] *Federal Reserve Bulletin,* March 1968, p. 254.

in the demand for domestic currency and increase in the supply of domestic currency. The balance-of-payments deficit thus tends to widen. The increase in military spending abroad following 1965 also tended to worsen the balance-of-payments deficit. However, aside from direct investments, U.S. private capital flows leveled off and declined somewhat following the imposition of the interest-equalization tax. Thus it appears that the international economic policies followed by the United States had some effect in reducing the supply of American currency relative to the demand for American currency in foreign exchange markets. However, rising domestic price levels associated with increased defense expenditures tended to worsen the U.S. balance-of-payments deficit in 1967. The improvement in 1968 was caused by the increase in domestic interest rates relative to interest rates abroad.

With fixed exchange rates, there is no automatic force that can continually adjust for persistent balance-of-payments deficits or surpluses. Governments are forced to manipulate the position of the demand for and supply of currency schedules in foreign exchange markets. The international goal of all governments appears to be an end to balance-of-payments deficits and the achievement of a permanent balance-of-payments surplus. This is a self-contradictory goal, since surpluses must always be matched by deficits. One way to correct for chronic deficits and/or surpluses is to provide for some form of flexible international exchange-rate determination. As can be seen from Figure 25–1, with exchange-rate flexibility the exchange rate could move down to E_e. This would effectively eliminate the need to artificially manipulate the position of demand and supply schedules so as to maintain the exchange rate at the arbitrarily fixed rate of E_f. The argument that a country needs fixed exchange rates in order to guard against the destabilizing effects of currency speculation is no longer acceptable. The 1967 and 1968 speculation on the stability of the British pound, the American dollar, and the French franc led to significant gold outflows.

THE PROBLEM OF INTERNATIONAL LIQUIDITY

The term "international liquidity" refers to the distribution and quantity of the gold reserves and foreign exchange holdings of all the countries of the world. Just as in our domestic economy commercial banks need more reserves in order to create the additional money needed for a growing economy, so in the world as a whole more gold reserves and foreign exchange are needed to carry on the increase of international trade. International liquidity is provided principally through gold production or deficits in the U.S. balance of payments. American deficits mean foreign surpluses and hence more international liquidity with which to carry on international trade and financial transactions.

As we noted in the preceding discussion, American deficits cannot always be expected. Should the U.S. again achieve comparative price stability and maintain high interest levels, we may again have a substantial surplus, as we did after World War II. Should this occur, the problem may become one of reducing a European balance-of-payments deficit and an American balance-of-payments surplus. A continuing American surplus would mean a continual contraction of international liquidity. Even in the 1960's, with American deficits, world trade expanded more rapidly than the total supply of gold and dollars. *To many economists this meant that there was a shortage of international liquidity.* The shortage would have been even worse without the deficit in the American balance of payments.

There would, of course, be no problem of international liquidity were exchange rates allowed to fluctuate freely. With flexible exchange rates, the currency of every country could be used to buy goods and services internationally. As we noted earlier, however, most countries fear currency speculation and therefore prefer to keep firm control over their currency in the foreign exchange market—hence the almost universal desire for a fixed exchange rate. Unfortunately the gold drains on France, England, and the United States during 1967 and 1968 demonstrated that speculation and a loss of gold reserves can occur even with fixed exchange rates. This forces a country to accumulate extra reserves in order to meet speculative drains and thereby aggravates any shortage of international liquidity.

How is additional international liquidity to be provided in a world of fixed exchange rates? Most proposals concentrate on improving international monetary cooperation by strengthening the International Monetary Fund and by means of devices such as the previously discussed swap arrangements and the now defunct Gold Pool.

The *International Monetary Fund (IMF)* is one international financial institution that is designed to help provide international liquidity. The Fund, established after World War II by the principal Western powers, seeks to promote free trade, to stabilize exchange rates at equilibrium levels, and to sell foreign currencies to countries experiencing deficits in their balance of payments. There were 113 members of the International Monetary Fund in 1969. Each member nation is assigned a quota of gold and currency that it must contribute to the Fund on request. The quota also indicates how much foreign currency a member nation may buy from the Fund when it has a balance-of-payments deficit.

The Fund acts to assist members when they experience temporary difficulties in their balance of payments. For example, when a country has a balance-of-payments deficit, it can draw (buy) foreign exchange from the IMF to the extent of its quota. This helps to reduce pressure on the deficit country to lower its exchange rate. The drawing must be repaid to the Fund within five years. Presumably the deficit country will undertake measures in the meantime to correct its balance-of-payments deficit. It cannot be forced to do so, however, and this weakens the power of the IMF.

Drawing rates are limited by a country's quota. Because of this limitation and the general belief in the shortage of international liquidity, a *Group of Ten* countries (Belgium, Canada, France, West Germany, Italy, Japan, the

Netherlands, Sweden, the United Kingdom, and the United States), which had met for several years to discuss international monetary problems, in 1967 agreed on a proposal to provide for *supplementary international reserves* through the IMF. These supplementary reserves are to be in the form of special drawing rights (SDR) in the IMF. Special drawing rights for IMF members are to be in proportion to their IMF quotas. When used, they need be repaid only in part. Countries with deficits are to draw on both their quotas and their SDR's to acquire the foreign currencies needed. In effect, the proposal is a means of expanding a country's international liquidity without requiring the borrower to make an additional contribution of gold to the IMF.

Under present (1969) regulations, members of the IMF must contribute an amount of gold to the Fund equal to 25 percent of their quota or 10 percent of their holdings of gold in U.S. dollars, whichever is smaller. Expanded industrial and private demands for gold and a slow annual rate of production in the 1950's and 1960's has led to a slow rate of growth in world gold stocks relative to the demand. The proposal of the Group of Ten would add to international liquidity without simultaneously increasing the demand for gold. The Board of Governors of the IMF approved these proposals in 1967, but the plan will not go into effect until a sufficiently large number of countries have ratified it. This is expected to occur in early 1970.

The Triffin plan. Some economists feel that swap arrangements and proposed improvements of the International Monetary Fund are still inadequate for meeting liquidity needs over the long run. Various alternative proposals that seem radical, at least to international bankers, have been made. Robert Triffin, for example, a well-known American economist, argued as early as the 1950's that the International Monetary Fund needed to be strengthened so that it would be comparable to a central world bank. The proposed arrangement for SDR's bears some relationship to Triffin's ideas. According to Triffin's plan, all nations would turn over their holdings of national currencies to a reorganized Fund in exchange for new reserves—deposits with the Fund. International reserves would then consist only of gold and deposits with the Fund. Reserves would expand as the Fund made loans to member nations and thus enhance the ability of member nations to trade in an expanding world economy. Actually, the reorganized Fund would operate in much the same way that the Federal Reserve System does when it expands Federal Reserve credit, which expands member bank reserves and thus increases their lending ability. Triffin does not propose an unlimited expansion of international liquidity, of course; he would limit expansion to 3 or 4 percent a year, just enough to cover the need for additional international money as trade expands.

The principal objection to plans of this nature is political. Nations would have to comply with the international financial policies of the Fund. It seems most unlikely that countries still accustomed to thinking in terms of "the defense of the national interest" will comply, as a group, to a supranational Fund.

As long as proposals such as the Triffin plan or some forms of flexible exchange rates are politically unpalatable, then it seems likely that we must continue to limp from one international financial crisis to another.

Supplementary Readings

Aliber, Robert Z. "The Adequacy of International Liquidity." In Commission on Money and Credit, *Monetary Management*. Englewood Cliffs, N.J., Prentice-Hall, 1963.

American Economic Association, "International Liquidity." *American Economic Review, Papers and Proceedings* (May 1968), pp. 586–651.

Harris, Seymour E., ed. *The Dollar in Crisis*. New York, Harcourt, Brace & World, 1961.

Kindleberger, Charles P. "Flexible Exchange Rates." In Commission on Money and Credit, *Monetary Management*. Englewood Cliffs, N.J., Prentice-Hall, 1963.

Lutz, Friedrich A. *The Problem of International Liquidity and the Multiple Currency Standard*. Essays in International Finance, No. 41. Princeton, N.J., Princeton University Press, 1963.

Meade, J. E. "The International Monetary Mechanism." *The Three Banks Review*, No. 63 (1964), pp. 3–25.

Triffin, Robert. *Gold and the Dollar Crisis*. New Haven, Yale University Press, 1960.

Alternative Fiscal Policies

Fiscal policy posits the same goals as monetary policy: full employment, price stabilization, economic growth, and a balance in the flow of international payments. Fiscal policy is both discretionary and automatic, however, whereas monetary policy today is wholly discretionary. The instruments of fiscal policy are the tax, government expenditure, and the debt management practices of the Congress and the Administration.

Chapter 26 considers the tax and spending instruments of fiscal policy as they are used to help stabilize the economy. Some mention is also made of the relationship between fiscal policy and economic growth. Debt management practices, already discussed in Chapter 14, are not examined here, because debt management and Federal Reserve policy instruments are fairly well coordinated. This is important, of course. Discretionary management of the debt by the Treasury can have a powerful influence on commercial bank reserve positions. Hence the need for coordination between Federal Reserve and Treasury policies with regard to debt management.

FISCAL POLICY AND ECONOMIC STABILITY

Fiscal Policy in Recession

Variation in government expenditures is one way in which fiscal policy can be used to cure a recession. Let us assume that there is an increase in government expenditures. Let us further assume that federal tax collections are constant and that there has been a balanced budget prior to the present situation. Under circumstances such as these, increased government expenditures will directly raise the level of spending in the economy. To the extent that consumption and investment expenditure increases are induced by a rise in income resulting from new government spending, the total rise in the level of income will be some multiple of the government expenditure increase. If the increase in government spending is not accompanied by an increase in the stock of money, however, there will be some rise in interest rates and some dampening of the potential rise in income and output. Interest rates increase because increased spending means increased demand for money relative to the supply. In our income-expenditure model this assumes that the *IS* schedule intersects the rising portion of the *LM* schedule (see diagrams in Chapter 21).

If the recession were severe, it would probably be best to finance the additional government expenditures by increasing the money stock. This would shift both *IS* and *LM* to the right, with monetary forces reinforcing the increase in government expenditures.

On the other hand, in a mild recession, when unemployment is not particularly high, there is a danger that an increase in government spending may result in price inflation. A shifted *IS* may intersect *LM* to the right of full employment output. For this reason, money stock increases should not be permitted to reinforce government spending increases during mild recessions. A decision to correct a minor downward cyclical disturbance by increasing government expenditures can be self-defeating unless financed through the least inflationary channel, borrowing from the nonbank public. Full employment and stable prices are not necessarily compatible goals.

Fiscal policy can also combat a recession by *decreasing government tax collections.* In an economy with a balanced budget, a decrease in government personal-tax collections will lead to an increase in disposable income, and in consumption spending. If business taxes are also lowered, the resultant increase in business saving should stimulate business investment expenditures. These additional consumption and investment expenditures will lead to a rise in income and output that is a multiple of the decrease in government tax collections. Thus decreased tax collections, like increased government expenditures, can lead to increased income and output.

Decreased government tax collections may also have money market effects. The way a deficit (whether expenditure- or tax-induced) is financed will lead to changes in the stock of money if securities are sold to either the central bank or the commercial banks.

There is at least one important *difference between decreased tax collections and increased government spending* as tools for promoting economic recovery. Increased government expenditures directly cause increased spending, whereas tax decreases cause increased spending indirectly. Assume, for example, that the marginal propensity to consume is .80. An increase of $1 billion in government spending directly increases gross national product by that amount. Subsequently, the marginal propensity to consume comes into play, and, barring money market effects, there will be $800 million, $640 million, etc., increases in the level of income. A decrease of $1 billion in government tax collections, however, will not directly affect spending in this manner. Instead, disposable income is increased by the amount of the tax decrease, $1 billion. This then induces $800 million, $640 million, etc., increases in the level of income. The difference in the effects of these two policies is in the initial effect of the $1 billion of government spending increase on the gross national product. A billion-dollar rise in spending has a greater overall effect on the economy than a billion-dollar decrease in tax collections. Thus *government spending changes are more potent than tax changes as a contracyclical policy instrument.* Government spending increases are also more likely to cause price inflation than tax decreases of comparable dollar amounts. As a curative for a mild recession, therefore, a decrease in taxes seems preferable to an increase in government spending.

The Revenue Act of 1964 and the Excise Tax Reduction Act of 1965 are examples of tax decreases that occurred during periods of continuing economic expansion. This is not to say that these actions were entirely inappropriate, since the unemployment rate in 1964 was still in excess of 5 percent while in 1965 it averaged $4\frac{1}{2}$ percent. The Revenue Act of 1964 provided for a permanent cut in income tax rates for all individual and corporate taxpayers. The maximum marginal personal income tax rate was cut from 91 to 70 percent, and for most corporations the tax rate fell from 52 to 48 percent. The Excise Tax Reduction Act of 1965 repealed federal excise taxes on various appliances, radios, television sets, jewelry, furs, and luggage and reduced rates on automobiles and telephone services. The action of 1964 was somewhat belated since there had already been discussions in the Kennedy Administration concerning possible tax decreases in early 1961. Nevertheless it is generally felt that the Revenue Act of 1964 helped maintain the economy on a path of expansion with relatively little price change. The Excise Tax Reduction Act of 1965, however, did not become effective until July 1965, and it coincided with an increase in Viet Nam war expenditures. While unemployment was still in excess of 4 percent, the excise tax reduction, overall, does not seem to have been appropriate.

Fiscal Policy for Inflation

During periods of full employment and rising prices, the instruments of fiscal policy may be used in the opposite way to offset inflation. *Government expenditures may be reduced or government tax collections increased.* If this occurs, then at a given level of income planned $I + G + F$ becomes less than planned $S_p + S_b + T$. The *IS* line shifts to the left. This will lead to a reduction of income and output amounting to some multiple of the reduction in government spending or the increase in tax collections. If the decrease in government spending or the rise in tax collections occurs without any change in the money supply, interest rates will also decline (unless, of course, price rises continue through the period of declining income).

Government spending decreases directly reduce income and thereby induce consumption and investment expenditure decreases. Raising taxes reduces disposable income and thereby induces consumption and investment expenditure decreases also. The government spending decrease exerts a more powerful downward influence on income, however, than a comparable dollar increase in tax collections.

The degree of inflation present in the economy should dictate which antiinflationary fiscal measure would be appropriate. For a runaway inflation, the reduction in government spending might be more desirable because of its swifter and greater impact. For a mild inflation, on the other hand, the less depressive effects of a tax increase seem preferable. In either case, aggregate demand should not be allowed to fall so sharply as to cause less than full employment equilibrium.

Anti-inflationary fiscal measures can also have an important effect on the money supply. A drop in government spending or an increase in taxes may lead to a Treasury surplus, for example. If these funds are held idle or are used to retire government securities held by the central banks, the money supply is decreased. This, in turn, sets up forces that keep interest rates high (*LM* shifts to the left), reinforcing the effects of the increasing government surplus on income. (Chapter 14 treated the mechanics of tax surpluses in some detail.)

In recent years there have been two tax increases designed to offset inflationary pressures during periods of full employment. The Tax Adjustment Act of 1966 restored excise tax rates on automobiles and telephone services to the pre-1965 level. This action was taken rather quickly by Congress. In June of 1968 Congress passed a surcharge on individual and corporate income taxes. This surcharge was 10 percent on income taxes paid by individuals and by corporations. Economists had discussed the need for an income tax rate increase as early as 1966, but the President did not recommend the surcharges until January 1967. Congress was obviously very slow in responding to the President's recommendation.

The 1968 surcharge on individual and corporate income taxes provides one example, however, of the coordination between fiscal and monetary action. Following the enactment of the surcharge in June 1968, the Federal Reserve moved to a policy of monetary ease. It is evident that the Federal Reserve believed the tax rate increase would significantly reduce demand in the economy, thereby giving rise to a less than full employment situation. One infers that the Federal Reserve thought the tax increase too large. To offset possible unemployment in the economy, the Federal Reserve returned to a policy of monetary ease in the summer of 1968.

Effects of Changes in Tax Rates

The relationship between discretionary spending policy and a stabilizing tax structure. In the preceding analysis we assumed that government tax changes were accomplished without reference to the tax structure of the nation. Our approach assumed that the government could deliberately vary the *amount* of its tax collections to help stabilize the economy. No mention was made as to *how* the tax collections would be varied, however. In point of fact, the *amount* of tax collections, as indicated in earlier chapters, varies automatically with the level of income. As gross national product increases, the amount of government tax collections increases; as gross national product decreases, tax collections decrease.

Assume, for example, that there is a proportional income tax of 20 percent. For simplicity, imagine this tax rate to be geared to gross national product. Under these circumstances, for every $1 billion dollar change in gross national product, there will be a $200 million change in tax collections. Thus *the nature of the tax structure itself tends to dampen whatever phase of the cycle is current.* For this reason our federal tax system is frequently called an *automatic stabilizer.* Changes in government tax collections occur automatically, without the need for discretionary action by Congress or the President.

The income-expenditure model developed in Chapters 18–21 assumed a tax structure that was geared to the level of income. Under this model, the federal actions affecting equilibrium income are changes in government spending and changes in the "tax rate." The *IS* line does not necessarily shift with changes in the amount of tax collections, as was assumed earlier in this chapter. Only when the amount of tax collections changes as a result of changes in the tax rate will the *IS* curve shift.

How much of a change in government expenditures is needed to change aggregate economic activity by a given amount when tax collections are not fixed but are geared to the level of income? More than with the fixed tax collections! Assume, for example, that the government wants to increase disposable income by $1 billion directly. Ignoring the effects on business income and the induced effects on consumption and investment, we find that only a $1 billion increase in spending is needed. If taxes are stated in fixed amounts, a $1 billion increase in government spending will induce an equivalent increase in disposable income throughout the economy. If taxes are stated in proportion to personal income, however, at a uniform rate of 20 percent, then a $1 billion increase in government spending will cause disposable income to rise by only $800 million; $200 million will come back to the government in the form of taxes. Thus with a proportional personal income tax government spending will have to be increased by $1.25 billion in order to produce a $1 billion increase in disposable income. Similarly, in reverse, a reduction of $1.25 billion in government spending is needed to cause a $1 billion decrease in disposable income.[1]

A change in the tax rate. What happens when tax rates are changed? In terms of the analysis discussed in Chapter 19, an increase in the tax rate will move the $S_p + S_b + T$ line up and to the left, leading to a movement of the *IS* line down and to the left. This shift is from $(IS)_0$ to $(IS)_1$ in Figure 26–1. Notice that the *IS* lines intersect the upward sloping part of *LM*. We assume that there has been no change in the stock of money resulting from a tax surplus. The result of an increase in the tax rate is thus a decrease in disposable income, which induces reductions in consumption and invest-

---

[1] *If* $\Delta Y_d = \Delta G - .2\Delta G$, *then* $\Delta G = \dfrac{\Delta Y_d}{.8}$ and $\Delta G = \dfrac{\$1 \text{ billion}}{.8} = \$1.25$ billion.

FIGURE 26–1. Effects of a change in the tax rate

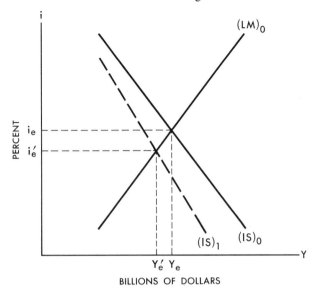

BILLIONS OF DOLLARS

ment expenditure. Equilibrium income is reduced from Y_e to Y_e', with a drop in the interest rate from i_e to i_e'. If, prior to the tax rate change, there was full employment and rising prices, the increase in the tax rate would reverse the increase in prices, halting the shifts in *LM* to the left that were probably taking place. If the tax increase is timed properly, the resultant equilibrium income, Y_e', should also be full employment income and output.

Lowering the tax rate should have reverse effects. If no money stock changes result from a deficit, and if Y_e is full-employment output and the initial *IS* line is $(IS)_1$, then a decrease in the tax rate will push the line from $(IS)_1$ to $(IS)_0$. This leads to increased disposable income and induces increases in consumption and investment spending. Equilibrium moves up from Y_e' to Y_e, and the rate of interest rises from i_e' to i_e.

Like government spending changes, tax-rate changes must be carefully planned. Many offsets are possible. For example, a tax cut designed to stabilize the economy could lead people to believe that the government anticipated a severe recession. As a result, expectations for the economic future would worsen. In anticipation of declining incomes, personal saving would increase and business investment plans would be postponed or scaled down. Clearly these events could more than offset the desirable effects of a tax cut. On the other hand, a tax cut or increased government spending may lead people to believe that the government is willing to do almost anything to offset a possible recession. As a result, they may come to assume that severe recession is impossible; the government will take care of everything. Spending plans, instead of being revised downward, will thus be revised upward. In the aggregate, this increase in demand may overshoot the full employment point and cause price inflation.

Another reason for careful government planning of contracyclical fiscal policy is that it can have a serious impact on the money market. As previously noted, the stock of money can fluctuate with surpluses and deficits. Therefore, debt management should attempt to complement tax and spending changes.

FISCAL POLICY AND ECONOMIC GROWTH

Poorly planned fiscal policy can also inhibit economic growth. For example, during periods of inflation appropriate contracyclical fiscal policy calls for an increase in tax rates. If the tax increase is imposed on business, the expected after-tax rate of return from investment projects is thereby reduced. In the absence of offsetting reductions in the cost of funds (interest rate), investment expenditures will decline. A decrease in investment expenditures may lead to real plant and equipment production decreases as well. Thus economic growth is retarded, for to raise the productive capacity of the economy, there must be an expansion of real investment, technological change, and an improved work force.

With this in mind, some have argued that during inflation and full employment the appropriate contracyclical fiscal policy would be to increase taxes on consumers rather than to raise taxes on business. This, it is suggested, would restrain consumption demand and possibly cause a redistribution of output from consumer to producer goods. Thus we could simultaneously help stem inflation and increase the productive capacity of the economy. A complementary monetary policy would be to keep interest rates high for consumers by means of selective credit controls, and to maintain low interest rates on long-term credit to encourage business expansion.

During a recession, on the other hand, there is normally no conflict between stabilization and growth policies. Increased government expenditures and decreased tax rates promote expansion in both demand and growth.

Fiscal action was taken several times in the early 1960's to stimulate economic growth. In October of 1962 Congress passed an Investment Tax Credit Bill which provided an incentive for new investment for depreciable equipment. And in July 1962 the Treasury established new depreciation guidelines. This action permitted businesses to write off the cost of new plant and equipment over a shorter period of time. Since depreciation expenses are regarded as a cost of production for tax purposes, the shortened depreciation period increased businesses' recorded costs of production and thereby reduced the amount of taxes they had to pay. These actions resulted in a greater volume of funds becoming available to business enterprises for investment in new plant and equipment.

FISCAL POLICY AND THE BALANCE OF PAYMENTS

As we noted in Chapter 25, government expenditure and tax policies can influence the balance of payments. For example, government lending and spending abroad by the United States contributes to the supply of American dollars in the foreign exchange market. On the other hand, the interest-equalization tax, lending guidelines, and tourist import restrictions represent attempts to restrict the flow of dollars out of the United States.

In addition, the contracyclical timing of government spending and taxing may also influence the balance of payments. For example, a period of less than full employment calls for increased government spending and/or a decrease in government tax collections. This action will stimulate demand in the economy. *IS* schedules will shift to the right. Unfortunately, expanded demand means an increase in the demand for both domestically produced and foreign goods and services. Hence, it is possible that the supply of a country's currency in foreign exchange markets can expand relative to the demand.

This expansion in the supply of currency is somewhat offset by the fact that expanding the demand for goods and services means an increase in the amount of money demanded for transactions purposes. Interest rates therefore increase. That is, so long as the new *IS* schedule intersects an upward-rising *LM* schedule, interest rates will rise. This can be seen in Figure 26–1 if we consider $(IS)_1$ as the original *IS*, and $(IS)_0$ as the new *IS* line. Here the interest rate rises from i_e' to i_e. Should the rise in domestic interest rates not be sufficient to prevent a balance-of-payments deficit, restrictive monetary action may be necessary. This would shift the *LM* curve to the left, but hopefully not enough to choke off the beneficial effects on employment that are expected to stem from the expansive fiscal policy. *We therefore see that a fiscal policy designed to increase income and employment may contribute to a balance-of-payments deficit.*

On the other hand, the fiscal policy of raising taxes and/or reducing government spending to fight inflationary pressures during a period of full employment is consistent with a policy of reducing a balance-of-payments deficit. However, should the restrictive policy take place in a nation that is experiencing continual balance-of-payments surpluses, then the country's restrictive fiscal policy is inconsistent with what should be its international economic policy—a reduction in a continuing balance-of-payments surplus.

PROBLEMS OF DISCRETIONARY FISCAL POLICY

Our analysis points toward discretionary decreases in government spending and increases in tax rates during periods of full employment and rising prices and the reverse of these policies during recession. These policies are not easy to implement, however. Many of the problems that plague monetary policy in this regard also affect fiscal policy. We have already pointed out the dangers of overshooting the full employment mark when using anti-recessionary fiscal policy. There are also problems of allocation and lag.

The Allocation Problem

When the government spends funds, it can alter the structure of national production by creating a demand for specific goods and services. Business responds by producing those goods and services. On the other hand, tax measures affect the disposable income of consumers and businesses; a change in disposable income leads to changed investment and consumption demands for specific goods and services. In this way tax and spending policies are comparable in their impact on production. There is this difference, however. Tax measures permit the private sector of the economy to determine what goods are to be produced. If one values an economy in which individual free choice determines the allocation of resources, then a contracyclical tax policy is to be preferred to a contracyclical spending policy. Of course, the government must undertake those projects (e.g., defense, public education, highways, and social security) that have been approved by a social consensus. The doctrine of individual choice simply suggests that there should be a minimum of interference with the allocation of resources chosen by the free market for privately produced goods *and* by social consensus for social goods.

The Lag Problem

The problem of lags can also affect fiscal policy. There are three main lags in economic policy: (1) the lag between the time when economic action becomes necessary and the time this need is recognized, (2) the lag between the recognition of the need and the remedial action, and (3) the lag between the action and the time when the effects of the action are felt in the economy.

The first lag is as long for discretionary monetary policy as for fiscal policy. The second lag, however, is much longer for fiscal policy than for monetary policy. Monetary action can quickly be taken by the Board of Governors, but discretionary fiscal action usually involves an Act of Congress, and the legislative wheels grind slowly. As we noted earlier, the most recent personal income tax increase was first proposed in January of 1967 and not passed until July of 1968.

In some matters, discretionary response to need can be swift. The Administration, so long as it operates within the confines of the budget passed by Congress, can speed up or decrease the rate of government expenditures simply by issuing an order. The increase in the rate of defense expenditures ordered in the latter part of 1957 and early 1958, for example, helped to overcome the 1957–58 recession. An overall change in government spending or tax rates, however, requires an Act of Congress.

The third lag, the lag between the action and the time when the effects of the action are felt in the economy, lasts either six to nine months or twelve to sixteen months for monetary policy. The lag is considerably shorter in tax matters. The effects of tax action are usually felt within the first six months.[2] Changes in government expenditures, however—public works projects, for example—take time to plan. If expenditures are already planned, contracts introduce a delay. "The steps in appropriation, allocation of funds, bidding, contract award, and construction are of such length that only a small fraction of construction can be expected within a year from the initiation of a program." [3] Even the previously mentioned changes in the rate of defense spending "take a considerable period before they register themselves in output . . . . Aircraft contracts, for example, change output by only 20 percent of the contract by the end of six months, 55 percent by the end of three quarters, and are nearly fully reflected in output change by the end of a year." [4]

The length of these government spending lags is of such a nature as to suggest that changes in government spending are not really a suitable means of economic stabilization, at least for mild recessions and short-lived inflations. For such problems discretionary taxes or monetary policy actions appear to be more appropriate. However, as we noted above, the lag between recognition of the need and the action is usually very long for tax measures. In addition, while tax cuts are always politically palatable, peacetime tax increases are almost impossible to get through Congress. This means that, in practice, tax changes can seldom be used to correct peacetime inflation.

FISCAL POLICY AS AN AUTOMATIC STABILIZER

Automatic fiscal action is at least a partial solution to this dilemma; it helps stabilize the economy without direct action by government authorities, thus eliminating the first two lags. The third lag is of comparatively short duration. In this regard, automatic fiscal policy appears to be superior to both discretionary fiscal and discretionary monetary policy. There is no automatic monetary policy.

There are two principal automatic fiscal stabilizers at work in the U.S. economy: (1) the federal income tax system and (2) the social security program.

[2] Albert Ando, E. Cary Brown, Robert M. Solow, and John Kareken, "Lags in Fiscal and Monetary Policy," in Commission on Money and Credit, *Stabilization Policies* (Englewood Cliffs, N. J.: Prentice-Hall, 1963), p. 2.
[3] *Ibid.,* p. 11.
[4] *Ibid.,* p. 11.

The Federal Income Tax System

We have already mentioned that as incomes increase, government tax collections rise, thereby restricting the growth in disposable personal and business income. Actually, our personal income tax is progressively scaled. As incomes rise, the tax collections increase more than proportionately to the growth in income. Thus disposable income becomes an increasingly smaller percentage of gross national product as the latter rises. This helps restrain inflationary forces in the economy. On the other hand, as incomes fall, government tax collections decrease more than proportionately to the decline in income. People move into lower tax brackets, and disposable income becomes a greater fraction of gross national product. This helps reduce the severity of an economic downturn.

The Social Security Program

Our second automatic fiscal stabilizer is the social security program. As income and employment drop, employee contributions to social security decline and increasing amounts of unemployment compensation are paid to the unemployed. This tends to maintain disposable income and thereby lessens the impact of recession. As economic recovery gets under way, unemployment drops, unemployment compensation decreases, and social security tax collections increase. This in turn helps to prevent a recovery from becoming a boom.

Automatic Stabilizers and Less Than Full Employment Equilibrium

To the extent that automatic stabilizers dampen upward and downward movements in the economy, they seem to be an effective means of combating both inflation and deflation. There is also a possibility that they may dampen recovery, however. Gross national product and full employment output expand over time. With a progressive income tax structure, people move into higher income-tax brackets as gross national product increases. Thus the average income tax rate increases. This means that at higher levels of income and output more of an effort is needed to keep the economy at full employment output. For example, a $1 billion increase in government expenditure directly increases disposable income by $1 billion when taxes are unchanged, by $800 million when the average income tax rate is 20 percent, and by only $700 million when the average income tax rate drifts up with economic growth to 30 percent. Thus, larger injections of government spending are needed to keep the economy at full employment as the average tax rate climbs.

It is possible that occasional downward revisions of the tax-rate structure might solve this problem. This was one of the arguments behind the 1964 tax reduction. There is one drawback, however. *Lowering the tax-rate structure makes the economy more subject to volatile upward and down-ward movements in economic activity.* Government control of the economy is weakened. As consumption and investment expenditures increase because of a favorable business outlook, the accompanying increase in government tax collections at the new lower tax rate may not be enough to thwart inflation. Similarly, in a recession the accompanying decrease in government tax collections will be less than the decrease under higher tax rates. Thus a lower tax-rate structure may not be able to cushion decreases in disposable income either.

SUMMARY AND EVALUATION OF FISCAL POLICY

Discretionary fiscal policy is subject to long lags arising from the slowness inherent in the legislative and administrative decision-making process. Discretionary monetary policy works much faster in this respect. Once tax changes have been made, however, discretionary tax policy operates more rapidly than monetary policy. Automatic fiscal policy can be very helpful in stabilizing the economy, but possibly at the expense of high employment levels. Periodic downward adjustments in tax rates may be the solution.

Conclusions concerning the potential effectiveness of fiscal policy are mixed. In a deep depression there is no problem in deciding policy; the obvious course is to raise government expenditures and cut taxes. In a runaway inflation, the need to lower government expenditures and increase taxes is equally obvious. Of course, if a wise economic policy were followed in the first place, we would not get into deep depressions or runaway inflations. Policy problems arise when mild inflations or recessions occur, however. Particular care must be taken, for example, in the discretionary use of both monetary and fiscal policy measures when the economy is close to full employment. Because of lags we are in danger of aggravating ensuing phases of economic fluctuations.

In practice, there has been little use of discretionary fiscal policy by Congress since the end of World War II. Congress and the President have seldom deliberately changed government expenditures for purposes of economic stabilization. Government expenditure changes are usually prompted by changing national defense commitments and pressing community needs. Tax cuts have not usually been thought of as anti-recessionary legislation either. There have been three principal tax cuts in the last two decades. The tax cuts of 1949 and 1954 were fortunately executed in the midst of recessions, but were not planned as a means of pulling the economy out of a slump. The 1964 tax cut, however, was officially justified as a means of increasing spending and reducing unemployment during the then current economic expansion. The 1968 tax increase was clearly planned as a means of reducing the rate of increase in spending and stemming inflationary pressures in the economy.

Supplementary Readings

Ando, Albert, E. Cary Brown, Robert M. Solow, and John Kareken. "Lags in Fiscal and Monetary Policy." In Commission on Money and Credit, *Stabilization Policies.* Englewood Cliffs N.J., Prentice-Hall, 1963, pp. 1–163.

"Federal Fiscal Policy in the 1960's." *Federal Reserve Bulletin,* September 1968, pp. 701–18.

CHAPTER 27

Alternative Monetary Policies

Monetary policy in the United States is administered and executed by the Federal Reserve System. As you will recall, the capstone to the decision to set up a system of central banking in the United States was the financial panic of 1907. This demonstrated conclusively the inherent defects of the national banking system: the lack of an elastic currency system, the pyramiding of reserves, the inadequate check-clearing facilities, and the overly rigid reserve requirements. The Federal Reserve System had as its original purpose the rectification of these shortcomings. By correcting the inadequacies of the national banking system, it was thought that we could eliminate financial panic forever.

The depression of the 1930's proved otherwise, of course. As a result, various additional monetary reforms were instituted. Federal Deposit Insurance was inaugurated. The Federal Reserve System was given the power to change reserve requirements. Open market operations became recognized as an important tool of contracyclical economic policy, and currency was no longer redeemable in gold. Because of these reforms of the 1930's and the present viable, adaptive character of the Federal Reserve System, many economists now believe that the economy is depression-proof. Others, however, point to nonbank financial institutions as potential sources of economic difficulty. The dangers of discretionary policies as compared with automatic policies have also been stressed. Debates on how to improve policy, the banking system, and the economy in general are countless. These debates take place in Congress, within the administration, in academic circles, among the lay public, and within the Federal Reserve System itself.

In this chapter we will deal with some of the proposals that have been advanced on how to effect these improvements by changing the goals and strategy of monetary policy.

ECONOMIC GOALS AND FEDERAL RESERVE POLICY

Present monetary policy, as administered by the Federal Reserve System, recognizes four main goals: (1) full employment, (2) stable prices, (3) economic growth, and (4) a balance in the flow of payments to and from foreign countries. To accomplish these ends the Federal Reserve System relies on general monetary control techniques.

Monetary Controls in Recession

The logic of the control techniques is quite simple, as we pointed out in Chapters 12 and 13. *To eliminate unemployment and the accompanying sluggishness in economic growth, the Federal Reserve has available the power to lower discount rates, reduce reserve requirements, and purchase U.S. government securities.* The use of some combination of these policies should result in an increase in the stock of money. In terms of our income-expenditure model and Figure 27–1, the *LM* schedule shifts to the right,

FIGURE 27–1. Shifts in the *IS* and *LM* schedules caused by monetary and fiscal policy changes

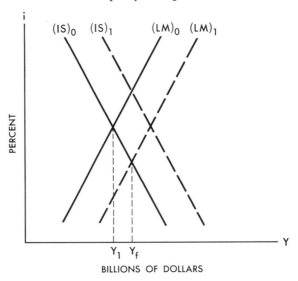

BILLIONS OF DOLLARS

from LM_0 to LM_1, with an increase in the stock of money. Theoretically, interest rates will then decline, and consumption and investment expenditures will rise. Income and output increase from Y_1 to Y_f. Economic growth is restored through rising investment expenditures; the productive capacity of the economy expands. Unemployment drops as businesses respond to increased demands for goods and services. Recession ends.

Although this appears to be a perfectly logical chain of analysis, it contains several hidden assumptions. If these policies are to work in the prescribed manner, the *IS* schedule must be sufficiently responsive to interest rate changes to intersect an *LM* schedule somewhere close to full employment output, Y_f. If the economy is deeply depressed, however, these conditions are not likely to be met. As a result, many economists recommend stronger policy measures. They suggest fiscal policy measures that will directly increase spending, thereby shifting the *IS* schedule to the right, from IS_0 to IS_1. This type of policy does not rely on indirect influences on consumption and investment spending via interest-rate changes.

Will the suggested monetary techniques for correcting slow growth and recession also promote the other two goals of monetary policy: stable prices and a balanced flow of payments on the international market? To the extent that spending is generated by these money stock increases and directed toward the goods and services produced by depressed industries, little price-level change is to be expected. However, should spending increases occur in industries that are already operating close to capacity, then the increase in the money stock will result in some price inflation. As a result, the real stock of money will decline. Thus, the shift to the right in the *LM* schedule resulting from money stock increases will be offset by a shift to the left in the *LM* schedule arising out of the price-level increase. Interest rate increases may also occur. Thus, an easy-money policy may not be compatible with both price stability and the elimination of unemployment.

Balance in the flow of payments may also be adversely affected by these monetary techniques. A decrease in interest rates, by expanding the supply of currency relative to the demand for it in foreign exchange markets, tends to increase any existent balance-of-payments deficit. For this reason it might be advisable to use fiscal measures to increase spending directly and to simultaneously use restrictive monetary measures to keep interest rates relatively high. There is some evidence that the Federal Reserve followed such a policy during the early and mid-1960's. We pointed out in Chapter 25 that the Federal Reserve increased the discount rate several times in 1963, 1964, and 1968. These actions were designed principally to prevent increased outflows of U.S. dollars. In addition, the Federal Reserve abandoned its "bills only" policy in favor of "operation twist." Under the new policy, the Federal Reserve sold some short-term U.S. government securities so as to raise the yields and thus eliminate short-term capital outflows. Simultaneously the Federal Reserve began to purchase long-term government securities in order to depress long-term interest rates and thereby induce investment demand increases domestically that could help sustain employment levels.

Monetary Controls in Inflation

The logic of inflation control techniques is rather straightforward. Sell U.S. government securities, raise discount rates, and increase reserve requirements and the result should be a decrease in the stock of money. This would shift the *LM* schedule to the left. Inflation usually occurs during periods of full employment, and investment and consumption expenditures, other things being equal, are likely to be interest-responsive in such periods. As a result, the *LM* shift should induce interest-rate increases and investment and consumption expenditure decreases. The fall in the demand for goods and services, relative to a stable rate of output, should then stop the increase in prices.

The assumption "other things being equal," however, tends to conceal offsetting forces. Expectations for continued growth in income and prices, for example, may lead to continual increases in demand (shifts to the right in the *IS* schedule). As a result, the Federal Reserve might have to resort to repeated use of its control techniques. Should not fiscal techniques be used to reduce directly the rising demand for goods and services? A reduction in government expenditures or a rise in taxes would shift the *IS* line back to the left and possibly eliminate price inflation as well.

The use of monetary techniques to stem inflation calls for considerable care. Should monetary restrictions be too severe, the result could be a deficiency of demand relative to the productive capacity of the economy. In terms of our income-expenditure model, if the *LM* is shifted to an intersection with the *IS* at some point to the left of full employment output, less-than-full-employment equilibrium may result. Thus, anti-inflationary techniques are not always compatible with the full employment goal of economic policy.

If a monetary policy is too restrictive it may also discourage needed investment expenditure in new plant and equipment. By decreasing this investment, a restrictive monetary policy can also impede economic growth.

How effective are these policy techniques in controlling inflation if the source of inflation is an increase in costs rather than an increase in the demand for goods and services? Assume, for example, that unions have been successful in securing wage increases. Firms will pass some of the increased costs on to consumers in the form of higher prices. This is a factor that may lead to recession. Higher prices mean reduced real purchasing power of money balances (*LM* shifts to the left), and induced rises in interest rates. Consumption and investment expenditures may fall off as a result, and these reduced expenditures will mean less employment and output. Clearly, under such circumstances a restrictive monetary policy would be disastrous. Reductions in the money stock would shift the *LM* schedule further to the left. Thus, it is extremely important for the Federal Reserve to determine carefully whether the cause of inflation is demand or cost increases.

An anti-inflationary monetary policy will help to eliminate an unfavorable balance of payments. As previously noted, a restrictive monetary policy will raise interest rates and thereby tend to reduce a balance-of-payments deficit. It should be recognized that a restrictive monetary policy is inappropriate for a country with a balance-of-payments surplus, however. A rise in interest rates simply tends to widen an existing favorable balance of payments. This is an acceptable situation only when the surplus in the balance of payments is merely a temporary phenomenon. A surplus country needs to take measures to restore equilibrium in the balance of payments. Germany, for example, undertook in 1968 to make it more difficult for foreigners to purchase goods and services in West Germany. The United States government, on the other hand, in its period of surplus, made extensive grants to foreign governments.

SPECIFIC POLICY PROPOSALS

The preceding analysis has emphasized the difficulties inherent in policy implementation. The evidence suggests, however, that by careful use of our present monetary techniques the Federal Reserve can (1) reverse mild recessions and help induce economic recovery and (2) check a rise in prices.

Many modern critics of monetary policy, however, feel that this is not enough, that under the present system of controls we may well find ourselves unable to cope with future depressions and inflations. Other critics argue that the discretionary use of power by the Federal Reserve is a principal source of economic instability. These economists urge that appropriate automatic guidelines be set up for the implementation of monetary policy techniques. For the rest of this chapter we will study the two proposals for monetary reform that have created the most controversy in recent years.

Financial Intermediary Control

According to the "portfolio" economists discussed in Chapter 22, money is only one of a group of competing financial assets. The liquid assets that are created by nonbank financial intermediaries have steadily increased in dollar volume relative to the stock of money. Aside from the recent uses of Regulation Q, the economic control techniques of the Federal Reserve directly affect only commercial banks, however. Nonbank financial institutions are regulated, but by agencies whose principal function is to safeguard the claims of the depositors and account holders. In recognition of these changes in our financial system, proposals have been made to expand economic control techniques to include the financial activities of the nonbank financial intermediaries. These controls, it is reasoned, may be either an extension of existing Federal Reserve controls or an entirely new system.

These proposals are all primarily concerned with offsetting the velocity effects of nonbank financial intermediary operations. As you will recall, these institutions create liquid wealth when they tap the idle funds of savers. The funds come to the financial institutions in the form of demand deposits. These deposits are then loaned to borrowers and the borrowers spend these funds for goods and services. Thus velocity, the turnover of the money supply, is increased.

As in commercial banks, the ratio of cash assets to liabilities and capital accounts created by nonbank financial institutions is fractional. There are required reserve ratios for nonbank financial institutions, but they are usually quite low, and, unlike commercial banks, often include such assets as U.S. government securities. These reserve requirements are not normally adjusted in a contracyclical manner; they remain fixed. Thus in periods of restrictive monetary policy nonbank financial intermediaries may continue to expand their lending activity and enhance their competitive position vis-à-vis commercial banks. This occurs, of course, only if the nonbank institutions are successful in their efforts to induce people to change the composition of their liquid-wealth holdings. A switch from demand and time deposits at commercial banks to savings and loan association share accounts, time deposits at mutual savings banks, or life insurance policies must take place. As discussed extensively in earlier chapters, the use of Regulation Q from 1964 through 1968 served to bring the growth rate of commercial banks more into line with growth rates of nonbank financial institutions.

One specific proposal sometimes advocated is to *extend the legal reserve requirement to nonbank financial intermediaries.* Table 27–1 shows that

TABLE 27–1. THE AVERAGE RESERVE REQUIREMENT FOR MEMBER BANKS AND THE ACTUAL RATIO OF CASH ASSETS TO SELECTED LIABILITIES AND CAPITAL ACCOUNTS FOR VARIOUS NONBANK FINANCIAL INTERMEDIARIES,* 1954–68

YEAR	RESERVE REQUIREMENT FOR MEMBER BANKS†	SAVINGS AND LOAN ASSOCIATIONS	MUTUAL SAVINGS BANKS	PRIVATE LIFE INSURANCE COMPANIES
1954	13.7	7.3	3.8	1.8
1955	13.1	6.2	3.5	1.7
1956	13.0	5.7	3.3	1.7
1957	12.7	5.0	2.8	1.6
1958	12.0	5.4	2.6	1.5
1959	11.5	4.0	2.3	1.4
1960	11.4	4.3	2.5	1.4
1961	11.2	4.7	2.3	1.4
1962	10.9	4.9	2.4	1.4
1963	10.2	4.4	2.0	1.3
1964	9.2	3.7	1.7	1.2
1965	8.9	3.5	2.0	1.2
1966	8.7	3.0	1.8	1.1
1967	8.1	3.3	2.0	1.1
1968	9.1	2.3	1.5	0.9

* Calculated as the ratio of cash assets to savings accounts, time deposits, and 80 percent of total assets for savings and loan associations, mutual savings banks, and private life insurance companies, respectively.

† The average reserve requirement was calculated in the following manner: Σ (country bank demand deposits) (country bank reserve requirement) + (central reserve city demand deposits) (central reserve city reserve requirement) + (reserve city demand deposits) (reserve city reserve requirement) + (all time deposits at commercial member banks) (time deposits reserve requirement) ÷ Σ (all member bank demand deposits) + (all member bank time deposits).

SOURCE: Computed from various issues of the *Federal Reserve Bulletin,* 1955–69; *Survey of Current Business,* 1962–67; and Institute of Life Insurance, *Life Insurance Fact Book,* 1955–68. All data as of June 30 of the various years.

nonbank financial intermediaries operate with actual reserves far below those required for commercial banks. Considerable adjustments would be called for if nonbank financial intermediaries were to have exactly the same reserve requirements as commercial banks, however. Nonbank financial intermediaries would be forced to liquidate large volumes of earning assets, and this could have deflationary repercussions. One alternative to this proposal might be to reduce commercial bank reserve requirements to the level of the actual reserve ratios of the nonbank financial intermediaries. This would expand commercial bank lending capacity; it would also call for the sale of government securities by the Federal Reserve to mop up excess reserves. *On the other hand, it can be argued that Regulation Q gives the Federal Reserve all the power that it needs over nonbank financial intermediaries.* We learned in 1966 that Regulation Q is potentially a powerful instrument of economic policy.

Assuming that Regulation Q and/or the extension of the legal reserve requirement to nonbank financial intermediaries can become part of our kit of economic control measures, will the new controls eliminate undesired changes in velocity as a source of economic instability? Not entirely, because commercial banks are able, to some extent, to reshuffle the asset composition of their portfolios from U.S. government securities to loans. Some nonbank financial intermediaries have this same ability. This could affect velocity within the context of a given Federal Reserve policy. This technique, however, has definite limits. Should financial institutions divest themselves of too many U.S. government securities, the safety and solvency of their assets becomes threatened, since, unlike loans, government securities are almost riskless if held to maturity.

Automatic Monetary Policy

Our present use of monetary controls is discretionary. Deliberate decisions are made by the monetary authorities to use their powers in a particular way to offset economic disturbances. The proposal to expand monetary controls to cover nonbank financial intermediaries would expand discretionary monetary policy. The presumption of discretionary policy advocates is that the authorities, in a free society, can be counted on to act skillfully in their use of powers, without usurping individual freedom.

Other economists are not so optimistic. They oppose discretionary policy on two levels, that of political philosophy and that of empirical economics.

Discretionary monetary policy and political philosophy. Those who quarrel with discretionary monetary policy on *political* grounds are opposed to all types of discretionary government policies. Their political position is typically that of the nineteenth-century liberal, who wanted freedom from government interference. Individuals should be free to go their own way, he felt, so long as they did not interfere with the rights of others to do likewise. Present-day critics view extensive regulation of the economy by the government as a hindrance to individual free choice and initiative. The American productive process is based largely on free product and resource markets. Interfere too much with these processes, and you restrict individual freedom of action and set up authorities who coerce rather than act in response to the social consensus. Even the implementation of a social consensus decision must be carefully watched, lest there be a tyranny of the majority. The advocates of this position, however, do not mean that free enterprise and individual freedom of action should be left entirely unrestricted. They are not saying that political anarchy is a superior form of government. Instead, they seek a rule of law to implement the liberal philosophy, rules that authorities cannot change at their discretion.

Stability in the value of money and the lessening of economic fluctuations are important policy goals to all economists. They guarantee the individual an opportunity to have control over his own economic decisions. He is not free to do so when inflation reduces the purchasing power of money or when inadequate demand leads to lack of employment. Some type of regulation is needed. But what type will best preserve political liberty and economic freedom of action? Authorities or rules? The "liberal" economists suggest the latter.

Rules have the merit of being simple and easily understandable. The realities of our economic and political world may make such simple rules impractical, however. We have a plurality of goals that occasionally conflict with one another. As we demonstated earlier, price stability and full employment are not always compatible. A "rule" to impose price stability on the economy may lead to unemployment. A "rule" to maintain full employment may lead to rising prices. A discretionary authority may solve this dilemma. If the goals are not in conflict, there may be conflict among several means of arriving at the goals. Discretionary decisions have to be made concerning what the correct "package" of means is and when it should be implemented. As one economist has argued, "The nature of economic progress, the plurality of goals, the plurality of authorities, the plurality of tools, all of these operate to make impracticable the conduct of monetary management in conformity with a 'rule.' " [1]

Rules and economic empiricism. Those who advocate "rules" instead of "authorities" do so on the basis of *economic empiricism,* too. The principal economic basis for advocating rules instead of authorities is that, in the past, monetary authorities have often made the wrong policy decisions. This was particularly true during the 1930's and 1940's. Recently, the record has been better. To some economists, however, the present

[1] Jacob Viner, "The Necessary and the Desirable Range of Discretion To Be Allowed to a Monetary Authority," in Leland B. Yeager, *In Search of a Monetary Constitution* (Cambridge, Mass.: Harvard University Press, 1962), p. 273.

improved performance record does not alter the picture. They remember how the wrong policy decisions of the past intensified monetary instability; in their view, discretionary policy remains a continuing source of economic instability. As a solution, they propose automatic monetary policies and various other banking reforms.

100 percent reserve banking. One such reform that is frequently proposed is the elimination of fractional reserve banking and the creation of *100 percent reserve banking.* Commercial banks would be required to maintain reserves equal in value to 100 percent of their demand deposit liabilities. Thus they could no longer be lenders of funds, unless they were themselves permitted to issue stocks and bonds on a large scale. In effect, this proposal would eliminate commercial banking as we know it today.[2]

Our experiences during the early 1930's gave rise to this proposal for 100 percent reserves. Bank reserves were (and are today) only a fraction of deposit liabilities. Banks were unable to redeem their deposit liabilities. There were widespread bank failures. Perverse decreases in the stock of money occurred. A 100 percent reserve system would remove a major source of economic instability; people would know that their deposits could be immediately converted into currency at any time.

Deposit insurance produces almost the same degree of confidence as would 100 percent reserves, however, and with far less revamping of our financial institutions. For this reason, most economists have considered the 100 percent reserve proposal impractical. The Federal Deposit Insurance Corporation, established in 1935, assures the safety of bank deposit liabilities. In addition, it is generally felt that the 100 percent money proposal is not politically feasible. Such a proposal would encounter widespread opposition from both professional bankers and borrowers.

The 100 percent money proposal is frequently an assumption behind rules suggested for an automatic monetary policy. It is not, however, an indispensable ingredient of an automatic policy.

The rule of stabilization of the price level. In past decades, the most widely acclaimed rule for automatic monetary action has been what is known as the *stabilization of the price level.* Henry Simons and Lloyd Mints were the architects of this rule. They suggested that the rule instruct the central bank to buy government securities whenever the price index fell beneath some particular level. The resultant increase in the stock of money would decrease the deflationary forces at work in the economy. Mints and Simons hoped "that the announced policy, when implemented by annual additions to the stock of money, would result in an autonomous

---

[2] For a discussion of how to institute this policy change, see George Tolley, "100 Per Cent Reserve Banking," in Yeager, *ibid.,* pp. 275–304.

maintenance of a high average level of output and an absence of serious movements in the price index." [3] On the other hand, during periods of rising prices they suggested that the central bank be instructed to sell government securities once the price level rose above some particular level. The decrease in the stock of money was expected to put downward pressures on the price level. Mints and Simons recognized the limitations of their system, however: "If price-level stabilization is a poor system, it is still, from a liberal viewpoint, infinitely better than no system at all." [4]

The promised advantages of this policy lie in the fact that it corresponds to the most understandable meaning of the concept of monetary stability, and it affords the opportunity for prompt and ample action to offset disturbances. However, from this latter fact also arises a possible drawback. Of necessity, discretionary control over the extent of open market operations would be given to the monetary agency, and the lag in effect might conceivably cause an unwanted magnification of autonomous developments.[5]

One of the chief economic advantages of a monetary policy involving a rule such as that recommended by Mints and Simons is its automatism. Hence, it is called an "automatic" monetary policy. Once the specified conditions for action are met, the monetary authority must take appropriate corrective measures. Thus, there is no delay resulting from the deliberations and hesitations of a discretionary monetary authority. Some discretionary lag would remain, of course, but action should still be prompter with the rule than without it.

In addition to the stable prices rule, Mints and Simons also considered "increasing the stock of money at a rate roughly equivalent to the rate of increase in the volume of transactions." [6] By stabilizing the money supply, they thought that perverse variations in money would be eliminated as a source of economic instability. Velocity changes could still cause instability, of course. Thus they felt that the stable price-level rule was superior on this score: "A price-index rule . . . defines . . . appropriate measures for dealing with velocity changes." [7]

Stable money growth rules. More recently, however, various *stable money growth* rules have been reexamined by Milton Friedman, Clark Warburton, Edward Shaw, James Angell, and others. Of the proposed variants of this rule, that of Milton Friedman has received the most attention among professional economists.

---

[3] Lloyd W. Mints, *Monetary Policy for a Competitive Society* (New York: McGraw-Hill, 1951), p. 225.
[4] Henry Simons, *Economic Policy for a Free Society* (Chicago: University of Chicago Press, 1948), p. 174.
[5] Mints, *op. cit.*, pp. 224–25.
[6] *Ibid.*, p. 123.
[7] Henry Simons, "Rules Versus Authorities in Monetary Policy," reprinted in American Economic Association, *Readings in Monetary Theory* (Homewood, Ill.: Irwin, 1951), p. 355.

The stable money growth rule recommended by Friedman states:

Instruct the System to use its open market powers to produce a 4 percent per year rate of growth in the total of currency held by the public and adjusted deposits in commercial banks. The System should be instructed to keep the rate of growth as steady as it can week by week and month by month and to introduce no seasonal movement in the money stock.[8]

The proposed policy changes would remove from the Federal Reserve System the burden of determining discretionary contracyclical monetary policy. For Friedman and other quantity theorists there is a close relationship between changes in the money supply and changes in economic activity. Empirically:

The rate of change of the money supply shows well-marked cycles that match closely those in economic activity in general and precede the latter by a long interval. On the average, the rate of change of the money supply has reached its peak nearly sixteen months before the peak in general business and has reached its trough over the twelve months before the trough in general business.[9]

If this relationship is so steady, then possibly the Federal Reserve, instead of stabilizing the growth of the money supply, should change the rate of growth of the money supply so as to attain a predetermined rate of economic activity. This might be an equally acceptable rule for stable monetary growth were it not for the qualification "on the average" in Friedman's empirical work:

This is highly consistent behavior as such observations go and sufficient to pin down the *average* lead within a rather narrow range. But it is highly variable behavior for the individual episode with which policy must be concerned . . . monetary changes have their effect only after a considerable lag and over a long period and . . . the lag is rather variable.[10]

It is the *variable lag*, for Friedman, that makes discretionary monetary policy impractical and rules out the advisability of the Federal Reserve's manipulating variations in the rate of growth of the money stock. Why? Because we cannot predict precisely when a change in the rate of growth in the money stock will have its economic effects. It is entirely possible that the first effects of stepping up the rate of growth of the money supply during a recession would be felt during a subsequent boom. Similarly, the first effects of a decrease in the rate of growth of money during an inflation may be felt in the subsequent recession, thereby aggravating the current crisis. Thus changes in the money stock remain a source of economic instability.

[8] Milton Friedman, *A Program for Monetary Stability* (New York: Fordham University Press, 1960), p. 100.
[9] Milton Friedman, "The Supply of Money and Changes in Prices and Output," in Joint Economic Committee, *The Relationship of Prices to Economic Stability and Growth: Compendium*, Document No. 23734 (Washington, D.C.: 1958), pp. 249–50.
[10] Milton Friedman, *A Program for Monetary Stability*, pp. 87–88.

It should be noted, however, that the policy recommendation is not for a stable money supply, but rather for stable *growth* in the money supply. The reason for providing for a steady increase in the money supply is simple. As income and output expand with economic growth, more money is needed to carry on the increasing volume of transactions. If the money supply is not permitted to expand, price deflation can occur unless there is a velocity offset. This could lead to general unemployment.

Economists' reactions to the variable lag. Many contemporary economists disagree with Friedman's policy recommendations and empirical results. They contend that the lag in monetary policy (and fiscal policy as well) is short enough for a change in policy to have a stabilizing influence on income and output. J. M. Culbertson, for example, states:

The broad record of experience seems to me to support the view that anticyclical monetary, debt-management, and fiscal adjustments can be counted on to have their predominant direct effects within three to six months, soon enough that if they are undertaken moderately early in a cyclical phase they will not be destabilizing.[11]

Robert Solow and John Kareken, in an empirical study, also reach conclusions different from Friedman's:

Our conclusion is that it [monetary policy] works neither so slowly as Friedman thinks, nor as quickly and surely as the Federal Reserve itself seems to believe. We find that the effect of monetary policy on the flow of expenditures is far from overwhelming, though it exists and is of a magnitude worth exploiting in the interests of economic stability. We also find that though the *full* results of policy changes on the flow of expenditures may be a long time coming, nevertheless the chain of effects is spread out over a fairly wide interval. This means that *some* effect comes reasonably quickly and that the effects build up over time so that some substantial stabilizing power results after a lapse of time of the order of six or nine months.[12]

Finally, one economist, after reviewing the empirical literature, has concluded:

There is overwhelming evidence of a substantial lag in the effect of monetary policy, but there is no convincing evidence that the variance of the lag is great. Whether or not the lag is long and variable enough to make discretionary policy [as currently conducted] less desirable than a fixed rule depends in good part upon which of the several studies of the lag turns out to be correct.[13]

These disparate results should not be taken as the basis for despair

[11] J. M. Culbertson, "Friedman on the Lag in Effect of Monetary Policy," *The Journal of Political Economy* (1960), p. 621.
[12] Albert Ando, E. Cary Brown, Robert M. Solow, and John Kareken, "Lags in Fiscal and Monetary Policy," in Commission on Money and Credit, *Stabilization Policies* (Englewood Cliffs, N.J.: Prentice-Hall, 1963), p. 2.
[13] Thomas Mayer, "The Lag in the Effect of Monetary Policy: Some Criticisms," *Western Economic Journal* (September 1967), p. 342.

regarding the likelihood of arriving at wise policy choices among discretionary and automatic monetary policy proposals. Rather, the controversies mentioned here, and in the chapter on alternative monetary theories, are the outward manifestations of a healthy scientific discipline. The process of setting up alternative hypotheses and policy prescriptions is all part of seeking to understand more fully the nature of the world. In many respects, the more that we learn about the world and about economics, the more we recognize the complexity of apparently simple phenomena. Frequently, when we investigate problems, instead of solving them we find new questions to be answered.

MONEY AND THE ECONOMY

There seems general agreement today that monetary policy influences income and employment through interest rate and wealth (portfolio) effects. Variations in the stock of money influence interest rates and accordingly investment demand, the demand for consumer durables, and the balance of payments. In addition, variations in the stock of money disturb the given distribution among wealth forms. Accordingly, an increase in the nominal stock of money, given the price level, will increase the level of one form of wealth—real cash balances. If businesses and consumers desire to maintain a given distribution among wealth forms, there will be an increase in the demand for goods and services.

This brief description of the process by which money stock changes affect the economy is consistent with the Keynesian, portfolio, and quantity theory approaches to monetary theory and policy. Keynesians stress interest-rate effects on investment demand. Portfolio economists stress substitution effects among wealth forms that occur as a result of changing interest-rate differentials. Quantity theorists stress wealth effects that occur as a result of changes in the level of real cash balances. Overall, no matter what their theoretical position is, economists believe that money is important for the economy. Through any of the mechanisms described, variations in the stock of money will affect income and spending. A decline in the quantity of money will reduce the level of employment, output, and prices, and an increase in the quantity of money will raise them. The closer we are to full employment, the more money stock variations are likely to affect the price level; the closer we are to having a significant amount of unemployment, the more money stock variations are likely to affect real output and employment.

Supplementary Readings

Fand, David I. "Keynesian Monetary Theories, Stabilization Policy, and the Recent Inflation." A paper presented to the Conference of University Professors, Oxfordshire, England, September 13, 1968.

Friedman, Milton. *A Program for Monetary Stability*. New York, Fordham University Press, 1960.

Gurley, J. G., and Edward Shaw. "Financial Intermediaries and the Saving-Investment Process." *Journal of Finance* (1956), pp. 257–76.

Mann, Maurice. "How Does Monetary Policy Affect the Economy?" *Federal Reserve Bulletin* (1968), pp. 803–9.

Mayer, Thomas. "The Lag in the Effective Monetary Policy: Some Criticisms." *Western Economic Journal* (1967), pp. 324–42.

Mints, Lloyd W. *Monetary Policy for a Competitive Society*. New York, McGraw-Hill, 1950.

Shaw, Edward. "Money Supply and Stable Economic Growth." In American Assembly, *United States Monetary Policy*. New York, Columbia University Press, 1958, pp. 49–71.

Simons, Henry. *Economic Policy for a Free Society*. Chicago, University of Chicago Press, 1948.

Index

Page numbers in italics refer to tables and figures.

System Open Market Account, 155

T account. *See* Balance sheet
T regulation, 242, 243 fn.
Tax. *See also* Federal income tax
 corporation, 453
 effect of decrease of, 452
 effect of rate changes in, 453–54, *455*
 interest-equalization, 443
 symbol for receipt of, 331
Tax Adjustment Act of 1966, 453
Tax and Loan Accounts, 56–57
Telser, Lester, 378 fn.
Temin, Peter, 137 fn.
Thornton, Henry, 300–01
Time deposits, 12–14, 50, 55, 57–58
 demand for, 88–89
 interest on, 235, *237*
 open-account, 58
 reserve requirements for, 102–03
Tobin, James, 400 fn., 405 fn.
Tolley, George, 471 fn.
Trade, *308*
Trade controls, 443
Transactions motive, 373
Treasury, 16, 56–57, 260–68
 cash holdings of, 280
 currency issued by, 22, 141, 175, 261, 280
 debt management by, 263–68
 and deficits, 260–61, 265–66
 economic policy of, 415
 gold holdings of, 173, 261

gold regulation by, 132, 133
location of funds of, 262–63
use of surpluses by, 253, 264–65
Treasury-Federal Reserve Accord of 1951, 227, 229, 233, 255
Triffin, Robert, 448
Triffin plan, 448–49
Truman, Harry S, 227
"Truth in lending" bill, 241

U regulation, 242, 243 fn.
Unemployment, 228, 229, 252, 253, *394*
Unit banking, 33, 40–41, 42–43
United States notes, 22, 130
Units of account, 3, 20, 127, 427

Variable lag, 473, 474
Vault cash, 14
Veterans Administration (VA), 69, 269, 271, 273
Vickers, Douglas, 297 fn.
Viner, Jacob, 470 fn.

Walras, Leon, 295, 313 fn.
Warburton, Clark, 258 fn., 472
Wealth, 9–10, 378–79, 391, 409. *See also* Liquid wealth; Real wealth
Welfare, 417
Wicksell, Knut, 295
Wiggins, Suzanne, 352 fn.
Work force, 253 fn.

Yeager, Leland B., 470 fn., 471 fn.